THE HANDBOOK OF INTERNATIONAL CONNECTIVITY STANDARDS

THE HANDBOOK OF INTERNATIONAL CONNECTIVITY STANDARDS

Edited by
Gary R. McClain, Ph.D.

 VAN NOSTRAND REINHOLD
New York

Van Nostrand Reinhold
115 Fifth Avenue
New York, New York 10003

Chapman and Hall
2–6 Boundary Row
London SE1 8HN, England

Thomas Nelson Australia
102 Dodds Street
South Melbourne, Victoria 3205, Australia

Nelson Canada
1120 Birchmount Road
Scarborough, Ontario M1K 5G4, Canada

16 15 14 13 12 11 10 9 8 7 6 5 4 3 2 1

CONTENTS

6   OPEN SYSTEMS INTERCONNECTION (OSI)   111

Kenneth M. Zemrowski   111

7   X.400   151

David Eng   151

8   X.500 DIRECTORY SERVICES   157

Judy Cross   157

9   THE BASICS OF HIGH-LEVEL DATA LINK CONTROl171

Dale Gulick   171

10   A SURVEY OF U.S. GOSIP VERSIONS 1 AND 2   195

Bob D. Tausworthe   195

xii THE HANDBOOK OF INTERNATIONAL CONNECTIVITY STANDARDS

FOREWORD

Computer networks are affecting all facets of our daily lives. We find them at the workplace, in schools, and in our communities. Our present day cable television links may one day become our home link to the world's networks. To achieve this kind of interoperative communications and use of network services will require open systems architectures and networks. To this end, standards for computer interaction at all levels are required.

Open systems are the wave of the future. The concept has been embraced by governments throughout the world, as well as by businesses and academics. The problem at present is that open systems cannot be achieved without well described and accepted standards for all elements of a system. Open systems require interoperability of a variety of hardware and software from disjointed vendors. For example, a processor from Apple must be able to be connected to a processor from Sun, or DEC, or IBM, without complex translation hardware or software. The only way to achieve this is through open systems and standards so that processors can communicate with each other and perform useful work.

Standards in all aspects of computer systems are required if future systems and applications are to be truly interoperable. Standards for interfacing peripherals such as disks, printers, database back end servers, tape drives, plotters, and many others must be developed, as well as software standards for operating systems, for database systems, for applications interaction with the systems, and for communications.

A key to a future of interoperable systems working together is the communications system. Communications must be standardized so that systems can communicate openly. Enterprises are keenly aware of the need for unimpeded communications. The lifeline of today's organizations is their corporate information. Organizations want to interconnect all of their information sources together and have their most important asset available for their use, with a seamless connection, and without impact on present applications. Standards are required to achieve this.

Communications standards have led the way towards open systems. Standards at the hardware and software levels have been embraced by industry, and new products are emerging every day that are based on the use of these standards. If a company is to compete in the future, it must provide products that adhere to standards.

Standards for networks have been evolving since the beginning of the network with ARPAnet in the 1960s. Once networks became accepted by users, the need for standards emerged as users and developers complained that the company proprietary systems and communications schemes were limiting the ability of enterprises to perform needed tasks. These problems and issues led to the development of international standards organizations such as the International Standards Organizations Open Systems Interconnect Standards Group. This group ultimately developed the OSI interconnection standards, an effort that marked a milestone in communications standards. From the original specifications of the OSI have come more concrete standards such as those for local area networks. Examples are the 802 standards for contention- and token-based systems. These were followed by other standards for file transfers and for wide area network interconnects, examples being the FTP protocols and X.25 protocols.

Even the government and, in particular, the military have begun to see the advantages of standards. In the past, military systems were developed as needed to meet a requirement, with no concern for interoperability with anything else. With today's shrinking defense dollar, and with longer lifetimes expected for systems, the defense department has embarked on efforts to standardize military computing equipment, and to develop or embrace standards for future military systems. The SAFENET II standard has fixed on the ISO 802 FDDI standard as one example.

The Handbook of International Connectivity Standards encompasses a wide range of topics on network connectivity and standards. This book should attract a wide audience, which will include students, educators, designers, practitioners, hardware and software developers, and systems managers who use or wish to use computer networks. The book addresses concepts in open systems to define what is needed and what can be gained by this technology and discusses major enterprise-wide communications standards such as DECnet and SNA. The OSI model is described, along with standards derived from it.

The book goes on to address one of the fastest growing areas of communications: local area networks and standards activities and products in this area. The book then concludes with discussions of wide area networks and data exchange standards. *The Handbook of International Connectivity Standards* is a compilation of writings from a variety of practitioners in the computer communications field. Their combined contributions will make this a must read for anyone involved in computer communications use and development.

—Paul J. Fortier

PREFACE

The Handbook of International Connectivity Standards is a comprehensive guide to major connectivity standards being used in North America and throughout the world. The content of this book was compiled with the objective of providing readers with a solid overview of the structure and design of the standards, and with examples of how they are implemented and used.

I owe a special debt of gratitude to those who contributed chapters. The authors are all experts in their own right who took time out from their active schedules to create chapters that would serve as a valuable reference for technology professionals. *The Handbook of International Connectivity Standards* is a result of their generous participation.

The individuals who contributed chapters are also affiliated with leading companies and other organizations that are dedicated to providing standards-based solutions to their customers. This dedication is reflected throughout the book.

—*Gary R. McClain, Ph.D.*

I

THE EMERGENCE OF
WORLDWIDE STANDARDS

1

OPEN DISTRIBUTED COMPUTING

Mikael Edholm

INTRODUCTION

The objective of computer networks is to provide a mechanism for access and manipulation of information. In most organizations this information is dispersed across multiple locations. Data is stored in various formats and in different databases. Applications reside on a multitude of computer systems made by a variety of computer vendors. While one computer system may provide one organizational unit with desired information, the same information may not be accessible by another unit. The sharing of information on an enterprise-wide scale has become almost impossible in many organizations.

In order to efficiently operate a business, each individual within the enterprise should have the ability to access all the information necessary, wherever it is located and whenever it is needed. Information for design, purchasing, manufacturing, sales, and accounting purposes, to name just a few, need to be accessed by the individuals concerned. Common resources, such as computing power and printing facilities, must be shareable, scalable, and widely accessible by all users as well as by all interdependent applications. Only a truly open distributed computing system can provide this transparent access to information, in the manner required. Only a seamlessly integrated network will enable users and applications to share the available resources.

BENEFITS OF OPEN DISTRIBUTED COMPUTING

There are five key benefits provided by an open distributed computing system. They are described here.

An open distributed computing system provides **flexibility,** i.e., the capability to optimize the use of available resources. Shared resources that are transparently accessible reduce the overall cost of a system by limiting the use of duplicated, and often idle, resources. The basic technology enabling this flexibility is a client/server architecture. Shared resources are located in servers; dedicated resources act as clients of the servers. The network provides the infrastructure.

Moves, adds, and changes to the system are handled by scalable resources. Moving an application to a larger or smaller system, from a different vendor, implies easy **portability** of application software. This is enabled by the use of standardized Application Programming Interfaces (API). APIs provide software developers with common environments for application integration, allowing applications to be moved from one system to another with minimum effort.

Interoperability between clients and servers is guaranteed by adherence to standards. Common networking protocols enable transparent communications when the networked systems are provided by multiple computer vendors. Depending on the complexity of the network, these protocols should be able to address communication services ranging from simple terminal access to interprocess communications.

Centralized and distributed management capabilities must be an integral part of any open distributed computing system. Shared information and resources are beneficial to a business only if reliably available. A networked system needs careful management to enhance productivity. Each component of the system, whether a computer, a peripheral, a bridge, or a router, must become a manageable object. An integrated management system can then provide network systems and applications management capabilities, maximizing network uptime.

While open distributed computing undoubtedly offers great benefits over existing environments, there is still a large number of existing systems installed. Legacy systems need to become integrated with the new applications environments to **protect investments** already made. Again, adoption of and adherence to standards will facilitate this move.

OPEN DISTRIBUTED COMPUTING ENVIRONMENTS

Based on organizational needs, an enterprise may typically contain one or more of four distinct computing environments (see Figure 1.1). Two of these environments provide access to information. They are typically transaction-oriented administrative applications environments. Common applications include ordering, invoicing, and funds transfers. These environments can be described as **host access** and **global access** environments, respectively.

The other two computing environments support the activities of "knowledge workers." Typical applications include project management, design, and development. These environments can be described as **resource sharing** and **cooperating applications** environments, respectively.

As the information technology needs evolve over time, so do the associated computing environments. Most enterprises have host access and resource-sharing environments implemented today. Many organizations are already seeing the evolution from host to global access. Likewise, many organizations are beginning to distribute the resource-sharing capabilities from their local area networks into global environments. In doing so, they are often adding network services that enable applications to interact and cooperate. In effect, they are implementing the basic fundamentals of the cooperating applications environment.

To fully understand the implications of the environments previously described, it is necessary to examine them in a little more detail.

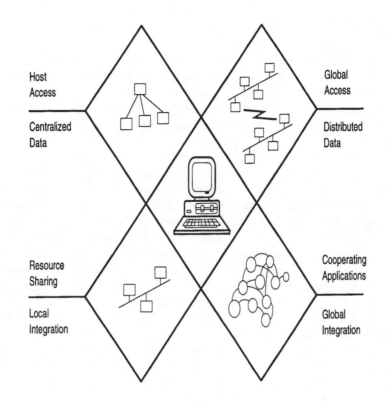

Figure 1.1   Open distributed computing environments.

Host Access

With host access the processing power of local and remote hosts is the key. Terminals are attached to local servers through terminal controllers. Remote hosts are linked via modems. Desktop computers, such as personal computers (PCs) and workstations, access hosts through terminal emulation, in effect becoming terminals of the hosts. Peripheral resources are mainly centralized or attached to the hosts. Access is allowed on a time-sharing basis, controlled by the host.

Local processing power exists at the desktop level, but no sharing of data occurs. To a limited extent, desktop users with frequent need of peripherals may be provided with individual resources. A printer may, for example, be added to a technical writer's PC.

A typical application example would be an electronic mail system, storing and forwarding messages between employees. The mail application resides on a local or remote host, but is accessible from terminals and desktops. To the end user, application access is possible, but cumbersome. It is necessary to know the location of data and applications, as well as the means of accessing it. Elaborate log on procedures predominate, and productivity is highly dependent on the management of the centralized resources.

Global Access

Although common today, the centralized host access environment is rapidly being replaced by a distributed system, a global access environment. Each island of information, each individual local area network, is becoming part of a greater whole.

In a global access environment, data can be interactively manipulated without geographical constraints. It can also be stored and forwarded at a later, more convenient time, if multiple time zones or similar concerns are of importance. As more resources become available to the end users and their applications, the total power of the networked system is greatly increased.

The move from host access to global access environments is taken in steps. First is the communications infrastructure, consisting of bridges, routers, modems, and associated remote access points. Based on the choice of infrastructure, a limited number of transport mechanisms must be put in place. The choices made regarding the deployment of transport mechanisms will influence the network services required, as will the applications development. Standardized application programming interfaces are used to ensure easy portability of applications to alternative systems. A geographical and resource view of the network is made possible by centralizing the network management functions to a single point on the extended local area network (LAN). Network management applications can then correctly balance the utilization of resources in this dynamic environment.

Moves, additions, and changes to the networked system will frequently occur. A high degree of computing platform scalability is imperative. Adopting a client/server architecture will help in minimizing the growing pains of the network, as will a strict adherence to defined standards.

The end user perspective of a typical global access environment can be described using a sales statistics application as an example. The objective of the application is to produce a monthly sales report, based on multiple sources of statistical data.

In a simple computing environment, the end user may handle manual transfer of data, from local storage to spreadsheet application, to the mail system. A typical user would download his Lotus 1-2-3 spreadsheet and enter data that has been stored on a local disk. Processing the data locally will produce an updated spreadsheet, perhaps with some graphic illustrations of current trends. The spreadsheet is then added to a memo, in a word processing application. Finally, the report is sent through the electronic mail application.

In a more developed environment, user agents handle such tasks on a predetermined basis, requiring minimal end user interaction. Agents can be instructed to gather data from specific databases on certain dates, to process the information, and to produce and mail reports on other given dates. Still, the environment is subject to certain restrictions. Commonality of data representation is necessary. Location of information needs to be determined beforehand.

Resource Sharing

Physically, resources in an LAN environment are distributed over a limited geographical area. A workgroup with individual PCs can share output through nearby printers and plotters. Mini- or mainframe servers provide centralized storage of large volumes of data. Complex application programs require external communications facilities. The network topology determines the use of enablers such as media, access methods, and physical network components. Transparent access is facilitated by the introduction of common user interfaces.

The common user interface will typically provide the capability of displaying multiple applications simultaneously. A server may provide access to an electronic mail application, storing and forwarding messages that are displayed in one window on a client, i.e., a PC or a terminal screen. Another window may display a spreadsheet application, downloaded from a server seen as a networked drive. A third window may display locally available data, such as sales statistics or production numbers stored on a local disk drive.

Through the use of a network operating system, time sharing of resources is possible. Printouts can be queued to handle multiple users; files can be shared by several users and applications. A design team, for example, can simultaneously work on different aspects of the same design, entering and deleting data in a common database, and print or plot the results on resources attached to a central server.

This type of environment is an improvement over the mere data access made possible by the virtual terminal and messaging facilities provided by the previously described environments. Multiple applications can run concurrently. Expensive resources can be shared, reducing idle time, and improving productivity. However, the resource sharing described is still subject to certain restrictions. Data needs to have a common representation. End users or application developers still need to know the location of the available data. There is also a minimal amount of integrated applications, requiring end users to manually switch between applications and combine the data into meaningful information.

Cooperating Applications

The fourth environment takes the client/server model one step further, by combining key elements of the previous stage with new capabilities. Task brokering, network computing systems, enhanced file manipulation support, and concurrent commit and recovery functionality split and distribute applications across the networked system.

To the end user, the network is completely transparent. There is no longer a need to know where data is stored, how it is stored, or how to access the data. Even manipulation of data is highly automated, especially in the case of routine tasks.

The windowing environment remains. User agents handle most of the application work. Distributed databases are seamlessly integrated through equally distributed directory services. Remote procedure calls, transaction processing monitors, and protocols handle the application logic in real time, independent of specific end user commands.

A cooperating applications environment is now possible. Consider a travel reservation system as an example. A booking agent may want to arrange a trip from San Francisco to New York for a corporate employee. The employee already has an individual preference profile entered into a local database. Another database may contain corporate travel guidelines, providing spending limits, and corporate agreements with various travel-related organizations. The travel reservation system also has access to car rental reservation databases, airline reservation databases, and hotel reservation databases.

The booking agent will see a windows-based entry system on the terminal screen. By entering the employee name, destination, and time, the booking application will automatically query the airline reservation system and choose the appropriate flight. The booking application then queries the hotel reservation database and reserves a room for the given period. If the hotel is further from the intended destination than would have been preferred, the booking application also queries a car rental reservation system for the availability of a car, the size of which is determined by the corporate guidelines in yet another database.

Having made all the necessary reservations, a report is generated, with a complete itinerary. The report is then automatically dispatched through the electronic mail network to the employee. Simultaneously, tickets are being printed at the booking agent's counter.

A truly open distributed computing system is at work in this example. Several applications cooperate, share information, and synchronize activities to perform a complex sequence of tasks. The end user never needs to know how and where data was accessed. The on-line transaction capabilities of the system, combined with the distributed applications and logic, takes care of business, without human involvement after the initial request is entered.

OPEN DISTRIBUTED COMPUTING ARCHITECTURE

The creation of an open distributed computing environment has to be based on a conceptual framework, or architecture (see Figure 1.2). From an organizational perspective, business applications are the key components, the centers of activities. Applications that perform critical tasks do so in interaction with their immediate environment. An application may "talk" to a user at a desktop, "ask"

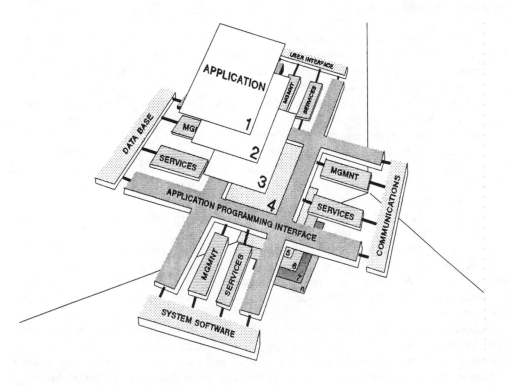

Figure 1.2   Open distributed computing architecture.

a database for information, "tell" a processor to compute a formula, or "request" access to other applications via a communications link. When operational, applications have "dialogues" with users, databases, systems, or other applications.

In a traditional computing environment, applications dialogues were conducted through the use of detailed, system-specific calls. Each computer system required a different type of dialogue. Applications were custom made, efficient but hard to modify, and difficult to adapt to changing surroundings.

In an open distributed computing environment, applications have generic dialogues. The way a service is requested is defined by a standard API. APIs provide sets of common macro commands that translate generic application service requests into system-specific commands. Applications developed for use with standard APIs become highly portable, from one system to another, from one user interface to another, from one database to another, etc.

As described, there are four major classes of APIs: user interface, database, operating system, and network. The first three enable the "open" in open distributed computing. The fourth is the key to extending the open into a distributed environment.

Beyond the APIs lie the services. A service is what a resource can provide to an application. A user interface service can, for example, provide windows for a graphical user environment. A database service can be a facility for definition and manipulation of data in a relational database. Operating systems services can provide language-independent system calls. Again, these services provide the "open" environment. The distributed functionality lies within the network service domain.

To better understand how applications are distributed and conduct dialogues, it is necessary to take a closer look at a subset of the application integration architecture, the network architecture.

NETWORK ARCHITECTURE

The enabling technology behind a distributed computing environment is best described within a modular network architecture (see Figure 1.3). Five building blocks make up this model.

At the base, the **communications infrastructure** block defines the available media, access methods, data link protocols, and the corresponding routing algorithms. Above the infrastructure, **transport mechanisms** handle tasks such as end-to-end reliability, session establishment and termination, syntax encoding, and basic application integration services. The **services** block defines what functionality the network can provide the applications. Virtual terminal services, messaging, and file services provide base level capabilities. Directory services and interprocess communication protocols handle the more advanced capabilities. The **management** block interacts with the previous three blocks, to provide fault detection, isolation, and correction, as well as operations support mechanisms.

Surrounding these four blocks, and shielding the applications from the underlying functionality, is the **application programming interface** block. The common APIs enable standardized access to each high-level service, as well as each underlying level of a layered protocol architecture.

Communications Infrastructure

Going back to the first block, the communications infrastructure, it can easily be seen that a communications infrastructure needs to handle several tasks. Applications typically require support

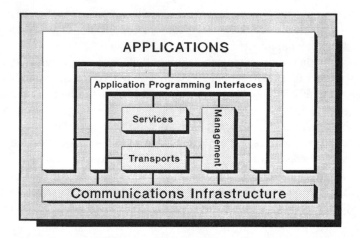

Figure 1.3   Network architecture.

for local area networks, LANs, wide area networks (WANs), and combinations thereof. They may also require a wide range of speeds, access methods, and media. Basic infrastructure technologies can be defined by the possible throughput of data and by the latency of data. Throughput is typically measured in megabytes per second (MBytes/s). Latency, the time between request and reply, is measured in milliseconds (ms).

Current networking technology provides WAN capabilities with sufficient throughput for store-and-forward applications, such as electronic mail and electronic data interchange (EDI). On a typical WAN, approximately one-tenth of a MByte/s throughput can be achieved. The latency is typically above one second.

Existing local area networks provide better throughput and better latency. Throughput can be up to one MByte/s and the latency might come down to 1 ms. This is adequate for most types of file transfer operations, the dominating application environment on an LAN.

In the future, these networking environments must be enhanced. The requirements of emerging applications for imaging, animation, and remote database access are far beyond today's limitations. WANs will need to handle throughput speeds up to 100 MBytes/s, with a latency of less than a second. LANs need approximately the same throughput speeds, but with a latency coming down towards 0.1 ms, if an application or an end user is to have a satisfactory dialogue over the networked system (see Figure 1.4).

Transport Mechanisms   The reliability of the communication dialogue is handled by the second block of the network architecture, which is the transport mechanism. Two types of standard networking transport protocols exist. **De jure** standards are based on adherence to internationally agreed-upon committee developments. **De facto** standards are based upon individual developments submitted to the public domain or on market presence by dominant vendors.

Personal computer networks typically use de facto standards, for lack of equivalent de jure standards. De facto standards are mainly SPX/IP, used by Novell NetWare systems, Xerox Network

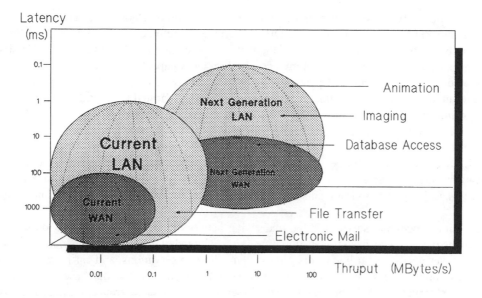

Figure 1.4 Network evolution.

System (XNS), which exists primarily in engineering applications environments, and TCP/IP, primarily existing in mixed PC and LAN environments.

LANs typically use TCP/IP, or to some extent XNS, as the dominant multivendor of de facto standards. For IBM environments, Systems Network Architecture (SNA) is obviously dominant. The de jure protocols are all based on Open Systems Interconnection (OSI), a rapidly emerging consensus solution to network transport mechanisms.

In the wide area environment, TCP/IP and SNA make up the bulk of de facto standards, again with an emerging presence of de jure standards based on OSI.

Network Services   The network service block can be defined along similar lines, de jure and de facto. An additional dimension will classify their complexity. As computing environments grow in complexity, the services required will change. Thus, host access environments depend on virtual terminal services while global access environments add store-and-forward messaging services to the basic terminal connectivity. The resource-sharing environments are heavily dependent on file manipulation services. The cooperating applications environment incorporates all of the former services while adding powerful interprocess communication services.

Starting with the basic services, virtual terminal capabilities can be implemented in several ways, based on the choice of underlying transport mechanisms. If TCP/IP is used, Telnet is the service of choice. If OSI is used, VTP is the corresponding service. For IBM environments, 3270 protocols are frequently used. Messaging and file services are divided along the same lines, store-and-forward protocols such as OSI's X.400 are frequently used in the wide area environment while de facto standards tend to dominate in local area networks.

Standardized messaging services are provided by the X.400 store-and-forward protocol. Enhanced addressing functionality is provided by the X.500 distributed directory services protocol. On top of the X.400 standard, two information structures are added: Electronic Data Interchange (EDI), based on the de jure EDIFACT definitions, and Office Document Architecture and Interchange Format (ODA/ODIF). EDI is the standardized method of computer-to-computer exchange of business documents such as purchase orders and invoices. EDI replaces paper transactions and considerably shortens the ordering, billing, and payment cycles in a variety of corporate environments. ODA provides standardized compound document transfer, such as integrated text and graphics, and, at a later stage, images. The integration of these services and information structures, combined with access capabilities to LAN-based electronic mail systems enable the design and deployment of large-scale messaging backbones.

The LAN environment will be enhanced by the implementation of the distributed computing environment (DCE), where file services, directory services, and security enablers are the key components. Engineering environments in particular will benefit from the integrated technologies of DCE.

Transaction processing services is the underlying networking technology for a wide range of service industries. Standardized transaction processing is intended for use with applications such as automatic teller machines, airline reservation systems, hotel reservations, and car rentals, to name just a few examples. The key protocol is the OSI TP, supplemented by remote database access (RDA), remote procedure calls (RPC), and synchronization services such as concurrent commit and recovery (CCR).

In summary, the emergence of distributed applications is pushing network service technologies towards integration and enhancement of existing services, as well as towards development of certain new areas of functionality. These changes are primarily driven by the needs of three key application areas: messaging, transaction processing, and the distributed computing environment.

Management   The management block interacts with all three previously mentioned blocks. Open distributed computing management can be structured into three levels, depending on the view of the network. In its simplest form, management consists only of interconnection management, providing a geographical view of the network. The second step adds the possibility of managing resources on the network. At the top, an applications view adds management of the interaction between applications across the network.

There are five areas of management functionality at each of the three levels.

- **Performance management** deals with the measurement of network throughput and system uptime.
- **Fault management** deals with the identification, isolation, and correction of network errors.
- **Configuration management** deals with the structure and dynamics of the network.
- **Accounting and billing management** deals with the financial aspects of the provided network services.
- **Security management** deals with the access privileges and data integrity across the networked system.

Throughout the network system, events occur. These events are monitored by the management system, providing a base of network statistics. These statistics are analyzed within the five functionality areas. Corrective action is then taken by management applications that will issue commands to the managed objects of the network system. These objects can be clients or servers, in the form of computers, instruments, peripherals, or network components such as bridges, routers, and the like.

For example, imagine a manufacturing facility with three sequential production lines. Goods are moved from line A, to line B, to line C. At each step, bills of material must be printed, and the goods forwarded just-in-time, to ensure a smooth production flow. Any disturbance will cause a pile of goods in progress to build up between the lines, and a shortage of material will occur at following lines.

Now, a network printer at the first line fails to print a bill of material, due to a failure in the modem connection. Interconnect management detects the fault and sets off an alarm. Information about the fault is passed on to the systems management level. Here, the fault is isolated, and the output is spooled, i.e., rerouted, to a nearby printer. The applications management meanwhile informs the manufacturing application of the delay in data delivery. Production is slowed down in anticipation of new data, thus avoiding inventory build-up at an intermediary processing stage.

Each management level in this model builds on the previous, until applications finally interact to achieve the desired fault correction, and restore normality to the network.

Application Programming Interfaces

Application programming interfaces are key to the portability of applications. APIs surround the infrastructure, transport mechanisms, services, and management blocks, providing a common mechanism for accessing the underlying network functionality. By adhering to common standards, such as the portability guides (XPG) published by the X/Open Company Ltd., applications may achieve a high degree of portability. In other words, applications can be developed on small, dedicated development engines, and later ported onto production systems from various vendors.

Currently, a range of APIs address the various levels of a network protocol stack. There is an API for each and every service at the application layer, as well as APIs for each and every level below. An application developer thus needs to learn and use multiple APIs. To minimize the difficulties of applications development, work is in progress to define unified APIs. These APIs will sit at the top of a hierarchy of programming interfaces, addressing functionality requests to the appropriate level of the network protocol stack. Ultimately, a single high level should emerge from these efforts.

NETWORK PROTOCOL CHOICES

Which set of network protocols should an applications developer choose? The answer depends on two key factors: the functionality requirements and the need for interoperability with other computer systems.

Imagine a diagram where the X-axis shows the degree of functionality, on a scale from low to high, and the Y-axis shows the degree of interoperability, again on a scale from low to high. Within this diagram, various networking protocols can be positioned according to their values of the two criteria.

Proprietary protocols, residing on a multitude of legacy systems, typically provide a high degree of functionality. A large number of services are provided, and the transport mechanisms are usually optimized for the particular systems providers' equipment. Unfortunately, this is achieved at the expense of interoperability with other systems providers' equipment. Proprietary protocols will thus be positioned in the upper left corner of the diagram, representing high functionality with minimal interoperability.

At the opposite end of the scale, the lower right hand corner, de facto standard protocol suites reside. These protocols are often part of the public domain, freely adopted by any system manufacturer, and widely implemented throughout the computer industry. Today, de facto standard protocols suites, such as TCP/IP, are often bundled with computer systems from most major manufacturers and enjoy a significant market presence. Their widespread acceptance is largely due to their ease of implementation, something that has been achieved at the expense of functionality. While they provide most basic network services, none has been optimized for any given manufacturer's equipment. Thanks to the rapid increase in computing power, this is no longer a major concern. More serious is the lack of new developments. For a protocol set to be considered a de facto standard, and to become widely deployed, it needs to be perceived as stable. New developments can thus take considerable time to reach significant market presence levels. Also, any given modification to an existing protocol may seriously impair its usefulness for interoperability with other systems.

Today, only one protocol suite can claim to bring the best of both worlds, which is high functionality in combination with a high degree of interoperability. This is the open systems interconnection (OSI) suite of protocols. OSI today encompasses more than eighty different standards, providing the five basic classes of network services, a choice of transport mechanisms, and a choice of underlying infrastructure components. The rich and varied functionality of OSI has now been combined into profiles. A profile is a vertical slice through the OSI protocol stack, limiting the number of implementation options, while still addressing specific needs of an industry or an application environment.

Thanks to the use of profiles, OSI is rapidly becoming the most popular multivendor protocol, surpassing de facto standards such as TCP/IP or NetBIOS in functionality and versatility (see Figure 1.5). Other de facto standards, such as DECnet and SNA offer additional functionality, but are considerably less multivendor than OSI. The multivendor aspect of DECnet, as well as that of SNA, is now being addressed through the gradual incorporation of OSI services into the two proprietary architectures.

OSI is rapidly moving in two directions: towards increased functionality and towards increased multivendor connectivity. More and more companies endorse and adopt OSI standards as the basis for their communication architectures. More and more protocols are added to already existing OSI standards, extending their usefulness to an ever-increasing range of application environments.

OSI DEPLOYMENT

User acceptance of OSI varies around the world. In Europe, one company in three is now implementing OSI. Close to another one in three is committed to implementing OSI in the near future. An additional one in four is seriously interested in OSI. In the United States, only one company in ten is currently implementing OSI. Twice that amount is committed to OSI, and one company in three declares an interest in OSI. Adding the implementing, committed, and interested segments together, approximately 60 percent of U.S. respondents in a recent Yankee Group survey would fall into this new segment. The situation is similar in Europe, although the trend towards implementation is more pronounced.

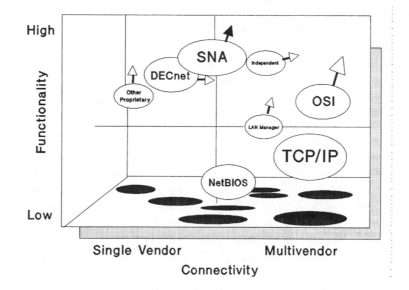

Figure 1.5   Technology trends.

The U.S. market is lagging the European market in the adoption of OSI standards. Currently, this time lag is in the range of one to two years. The time lag can largely be explained by looking at the introduction dates of mandatory government OSI profiles. In the United Kingdom, OSI networking protocols became a mandatory requirement for government information technology purchases as early as January 1989. Sweden followed suit in April 1989. Other Nordic countries made the same decision later the same year.

In the United States, a Government OSI Profile (GOSIP) is in force as of August 1990, a year and a half behind the United Kingdom. Based on current maturity of OSI protocol standards and the availability of OSI-based products, the United States can be expected to close this gap in the near future. OSI is now poised for growth, on both sides of the Atlantic.

It is also worth noting that GOSIPs typically include more than just a subset of OSI standards. A typical GOSIP is divided into four subprofiles: transmit (T), application (A), formats (F), and characters (C).

The T subprofile specifies OSI protocols to be used for media access, internet routing and transport. The A subprofile specifies the upper layers of the protocol stack, from the session layer to the application layer. The F subprofile extends the specification outside of the basic OSI protocols, into the area of data exchange. Here, the Electronic Data Interchange (EDI) format is specified, as is the Office Document Architecture (ODA). The C subprofile deals with regional character subsets, to correspond to the various languages that have to be supported by implementations of OSI.

The inclusion of format standards have considerably added to the momentum of OSI deployment. OSI-based EDI implementations are currently experiencing triple-digit growth in most industrialized nations.

OSI will not become the multivendor standard overnight. A long period of transition from de facto standards currently used, to the de jure OSI standards, can be expected. There are three basic phases of this transition: pilot implementations, subnetworks based on OSI, and a long coexistence phase before the ultimate dominance of OSI comes about.

In the pilot phase, the typical user will require a simple platform onto which he can port a distributed application. The user will install OSI in a controlled environment, isolated from the operational backbone of his organization. The pilot will serve as a knowledge build-up basis for the application developer.

In the second phase, applications based on OSI emerge. The former pilots become integrated with the corporate backbone, but handle specific tasks. The tasks chosen are typically based on which unique OSI functionality has driven the pilot to success. To preserve the existing de facto standards-based backbone, dual or parallel protocol stacks need to be part of the target applications platform.

During the long coexistence phase, it is expected that OSI will gradually overtake the deployment and use of de facto standards. New applications will use OSI network protocols. Older applications are likely to stay with de facto standards. Their peaceful coexistence is assured by the fact that output messages, from the dual stack machines, can be transferred over a common link. When application integration becomes necessary between heterogeneous networking environments, application layer gateways can be used. At a lower level, multiprotocol routers enable OSI and de facto standards to share a common media.

Standards exist for the transport and application approaches. Products have been entering the marketplace since early 1990.

If distributed applications need to share a common link and media, but in a single vendor environment, tunneling may be a temporary solution. Tunneling provides the possibility to encapsulate messages based on one networking standard, into frames sent by another networking standard. As no standards for this approach exist, the multivendor connectivity benefit of OSI will be lost when proprietary tunneling techniques are used. Again, it can be clearly demonstrated that only strict adherence to internationally agreed-upon standards can guarantee the desired multivendor functionality that is required of the network.

Conformance and Interoperability

To be truly multivendor, applications using OSI products must be sure that the services, transport mechanisms, and links conform to the existing standards. Conformance to a given profile, or part thereof, can be tested at designated test centers throughout the world. Non-profit organizations such as the Corporation for Open Systems (COS), in the United States, or the Standards Promotion Agency (SPAG), in Europe, are recognized test centers for their respective markets. For the Japanese market, INTAP provides a similar service.

In addition, a few vendors of OSI products have become accredited by such test centers, and have in-house testing capabilities to aid in their development efforts. At the time of writing, Bull HN Information Systems Inc. and Hewlett-Packard Corporation are the only COS accredited test centers in the United States.

Conforming to a standard does not guarantee interoperability, however. There are various ways an OSI protocol can be implemented, and numerous options to the basic services may or may not be included in an OSI product. Interoperability is the key to the distributed applications environment and should be demonstrated by an OSI vendor upon request.

Many vendors have long had interoperability testing programs in place. By linking systems via OSInet, EurOSInet, OSIcom, and related organizations' networks, vendors can easily test their respective product offerings for interoperability. In addition, major trade shows often feature OSI LAN and WAN interoperability as a key topic of the demonstrations provided.

OSI Today

What does OSI offer its users today? Consider the following example.

Five organizations interact in a global marketplace. They are a manufacturer of finished goods, a distribution center, a sales outlet, a supplier of raw materials, and a financial institution. The manufacturing company has recently developed a new product, XYZ, and is now actively seeking customers around the world. One of the manufacturer's sales outlets receives a request for product information from a customer. Some of the desired information is immediately available, but the new pricing structure is lacking. A request for pricing information is sent off to the manufacturing entity, asking for an update.

The manufacturing company stores product information in a central database. It is a huge file with new prices, options, and quantity discounts. In response to the request from the sales office, a sales support application dispatches the information over the corporate OSI network, using the OSI File Transfer, Access, and Management protocol (FTAM). At the manufacturing company, a cooperating manufacturing management application decides to make sure sufficient quantities of product XYZ can be made available to the sales office to meet the expected demand. It sends a query off to the local distribution center, asking how much of product XYZ, option ABC, is available. The distribution center database automatically responds.

For this simple exchange, no file transfers need occur. A basic store-and-forward mechanism for data exchange is usually sufficient. The applicable OSI service would then be based on the CCITT X.400 set of protocols. If the exchange needs to take place in real time, as is frequently the case, OSI can still handle the request. The OSI remote database access (RDA) protocol would then be used in place of X.400.

Assuming the distribution center application does not find sufficient quantities of the product in stock, it reports this finding to a just-in-time (JIT) manufacturing application back at the factory. If JIT decides to make additional quantities to meet the expected demand, raw materials need to be ordered from a supplier and shipped to a production center. Orders have to be generated, bills of material need filling out, and invoices must be paid. Ordering and invoicing are considerably more complex tasks than file transfer or electronic messaging. Basic OSI services need to be supplemented by additional functionality to handle business applications of this kind.

This additional functionality is provided by a translation service called Electronic Data Interchange (EDI). An EDI translator uses X.400 as its transport mechanism. There is now a United Nations standard called Electronic Data Interchange For Administration, Commerce, and Trade (EDIFACT), which is rapidly being deployed around the world. EDIFACT does not only format data. It also includes facilities for copying messages to multiple locations. This is typically used for providing banks with the transaction data necessary to complete the financial portion of a deal. When a bank receives EDI information, it will extract the applicable data and transfer the correct funds from one account to another. Returning to the previous example, EDI based on X.400 is used to order, document, and invoice the necessary raw materials for the new production run. Copies of the transactions are then sent to the banks in question. Funds transfer applications at two locations are notified of the activity, and use OSI TP to execute the transfer between the relevant accounts in real time.

OSI services are useful not only between remote locations, over WANs but are also highly applicable within the manufacturing entity. Expanding the example to include intracompany communications within the production center, the following scenario evolves.

When the JIT application receives notice that a production run should start, using the material ordered through the EDI application, job data is immediately transferred to a production line cell controller. As this would typically be in the form of a set of instructions, arranged in a file, FTAM would be the applicable OSI protocol. The cell controller downloads instructions to the factory floor equipment. These instructions are real-time commands, such as start, stop, open, and close.

OSI provides a generic set of semantics for communications between intelligent factory floor devices. More than eighty specific commands are included in the OSI Manufacturing Messaging Specification (MMS), used for shop floor control applications. MMS commands also enable upload of data, from programmable logic controllers (PLCs) or numerical controllers (NCs) on either a continuous basis or in response to alarm triggers. In certain cases, such as large production cell, a large number of intelligent devices are interconnected. For the cell controller to find the correct device, a directory service may be a necessary addition. OSI provides this functionality through the use of the OSI Directory Services protocol, X.500.

Once the production run is finished, a bill of material is sent to the scheduling application, residing in an area manager computer. Since the amount of data to be transferred is likely to be large, the OSI file transfer protocol, FTAM, will again be the most applicable service to use. If an insufficient quantity has been produced or additional demand has materialized, the area manager may decide to initiate a new production run. For this purpose, more raw material will be needed, and an EDIFACT message will be sent to the supplier, commencing a new production cycle.

Meanwhile, the area manager will inform the distribution center of the availability of the recently produced goods, and arrange for their transportation to the geographical location desired.

CONCLUSION

The creation of a cooperating applications environment is already a possibility today. Using a sound application architecture, the combination of open systems elements such as standardized user interfaces, open databases, scalable processing power, and extensive network communications facilities can result in considerable productivity gains.

If the underlying network architecture is based on the Open Systems Interconnection suite of protocols, an application developer can be assured of investment protection, as well as continued functionality improvement over the long term.

If the dialogues between these elements are supported by standardized applications programming interfaces, a high degree of applications portability will add significantly lower cost of ownership to the benefits already achieved by the functionality gains.

Open distributed computing provides four key benefits, based on the same number of underlying technology enablers.

- Flexibility is achieved through the implementation of a client/server architecture.
- Portability of applications is achieved through adherence to common application programming interface specifications.
- Interoperability between different vendors' equipment is achieved through the adherence to internationally agreed-upon networking standards.
- Productivity is enhanced through deployment of fully distributed network, systems, and applications management applications.

II

MAJOR ENTERPRISE-WIDE COMMUNICATIONS STANDARDS

2

SNA—THE NEXT GENERATION AND PEER-TO-PEER SNA

Anura Gurugé

INTRODUCTION

Systems Network Architecture (SNA) is a comprehensive specification of an integrated set of logical functions, conventions, procedures, protocols, message unit formats, and utility services. This specification, which can be thought of as being an architectural framework (or even a blueprint) deals with all the key issues associated with realizing, operating, and managing reliable, populous, sophisticated, and far-flung data communications environments. Contemporary SNA also includes the definition of a standard application programming interface (API) through which application programs can freely interact with each other across SNA environments.

SNA, despite its near universal support by computer and communications vendors, is nonetheless a proprietary networking scheme introduced by IBM in 1974. It thus predates PCs by seven full years, and Token-Ring LANs by eleven years. This vintage has in no way affected SNA effectiveness or popularity.

SNA today has an awesome iron grip over the worldwide commercial data communications arena, particularly in the larger, multinational, Fortune 1000 ilk companies, 80 percent of whom have an SNA network of some sort. In total there are in excess of 40,000 registered SNA networks in production use today, with some serving as many as 60,000 users. SNA is still considered to be the most popular and heavily used networking scheme within commercial organizations, and was recently cited as the most important communications standard considered when selecting new equipment in a worldwide survey of 870 IBM installations. All in all, this is an impressive performance in a climate that is increasingly favoring non-proprietary, open systems solutions.

THIS IS NOT YOUR FATHER'S SNA

SNA, however, has not been resting on its laurels. It bounded into the 1990s—its third decade of existence—brimming with competence and bristling with vigor that belied its age. The neo-SNA of the 1990s bears little, if any, resemblance to the seminal, landmark networking scheme that so revolutionized the scope, as well as the efficacy of data communications in the late 1970s. The demeanor, the personality, and the basic fabric of SNA have been dramatically and extensively overhauled and updated over the last five years. The much maligned, but nonetheless hugely successful, S/370 host-centric, hierarchical, "master-slave" architecture, with its marked preference for the static configurations that dominated the computer industry for nearly fifteen years, is rapidly becoming but a legend.

The neo-SNA that has supplanted it is very much a dynamic, peer-oriented, cooperative processing-biased, robustly resilient, and comprehensively manageable networking scheme, second to none for wide area networking (WAN). The transformation has been so dramatic that IBM could be excused if they decided to remarket it, if it was ever deemed to be necessary, with a campaign that revolved around the slogan: "This is Not Your Father's SNA!"

SNA's metamorphosis has occurred over eight distinct intermediary transformations spread over its seventeen-year life span. (See Figure 2.1.) From its unprepossessing, inauspicious, and faltering debut as the SNA that was only capable of catering to the most rudimentary, leased-line, star-networks radiating from a single S/370 host, SNA has blossomed to be the blueprint for some of the largest and most complex commercial networks—interconnecting multiple hosts and mini-computers, and serving tens of thousands of end users via intricate webs of LAN and WAN connections. Figure 2.2 summarizes the key architectural and implementational enhancements that were instrumental in effecting this transformation.

Phase	Period	Salient Characteristics
SNA 0	1974	One Host, One Local Communications Controller, Leased Lines
SNA 1	1975	One Host, Two Communications Controllers: One Local, One Remote
SNA 2	1975	One Host, Multiple Communications Controllers, Switched Links
SNA 3	1977	Multiple Hosts: "Cross-Domain" Interactions
SNA 4	1978	Fully Interconnected "Mesh" Networks
APPC	1982–1983	Emphasis on Inter-Program Communications (LU 6.2) and Peer (T2.1) Nodes
SNI	1984	Free Interactions Across Autonomous SNA Networks
Peer	1987–1989	T2.1 Node Integration, Alternate Sessions (XRF), and Casual Connections
APPN	1991 →	Dynamic, Peer-Oriented Next Generation SNA

Terms Used
APPC —Advanced Program-to-Program Communications
APPN —Advanced Peer-to-Peer Networking
T2.1 —Type 2.1 (peripheral) Nodes
SNI   —SNA Network Interconnection
XRF   —Extended Recovery Facility

Figure 2.1   The nine distinct phases of the SNA metamorphosis.

1991   APPN/SNA, IBM'S multiprotocol, SNA–capable Router
1990   APPC/MVS
1989   SNA/FS, SNA/MSII, SNADSII, Casual Connections
1988   31-Bit Subarea Addressing, New 72.1 Node, AS/400 APPN
1987   Type 2.1 Node Integration, APPCCMD, XRF, SAA
1986   SNA/MS, Token-Ring, NetView, XI, S/36 APPN
1985   23-Bit ENA
1984   SNI, Native VM Support
1983   Type 2.1 Nodes, SNADS, NSI
1982   APPC, DIA, DCA, CTCA, Switched Subarea (X.25)
1980   X.21
1979   Network Management, Parallel Sessions, NTO
1978   Parallel Links, Interconnected Meshes
1977   Multi-Host, X.25
1975   Remote Communications Controllers, Channel Attached Controllers
1974   SNA 0, SDLC

Figure 2.2   SNA—an impressive timeline.

The crawling larva that was derided by most is now a captivating and compelling Blue Monarch that gracefully glides across the global networking arena with impunity, scorning the lunges of would-be predators with their "open" nets.

NEO-SNA: THE BROAD THEMES

There are two overriding and fundamental themes that characterize and set the tone of today's neo-SNA: its emphasis on program-to-program communications, and its marked preference for peer-to-peer–oriented control and interaction mechanisms.

Two landmark architectural extensions to SNA in the early 1980s, referred to as LU Type 6.2 and Type 2.1 nodes, supplied the framework by which to realize this. LU Type 6.2 specifies a repertoire of protocols and services in conjunction with a generic but all-encompassing API for interprogram communications. In parallel, Type 2.1 nodes provide the physical and logical connectivity, as well as local control functions, to enable LU 6.2 interactions to be conducted on a symmetrical, peer-oriented basis across a non-hierarchically structured and controlled network.

SNA LOGICAL UNITS

SNA end users, such as terminal operators, application programs, and I/O devices, interact with an SNA data communications environment, and via this environment with other end users through SNA Logical Units (LUs). Thus, LUs are the ports (or the interfaces) through which end users gain access to an SNA environment so that they may use the resources provided by it, as well as to communicate with other end users. LUs, in effect, provide the functions necessary to enable end users to interact with an SNA environment and to use the resources and the control mechanism of that environment to conduct orderly interactions with other end users.

An end user can only communicate with another end user via an SNA environment when both parties have accessed the environment through LUs. End user-to-end user communication is then realized by means of SNA-defined transactions between the LUs. Given that all such communications occur through the exchange of message units across the SNA path control network, LUs can, in such instances, be regarded as providing a gateway function between end users and the path control network. However, two end users do not necessarily have to be attached to the SNA environment at the same time to be able to communicate with each other. SNA now provides store-and-forward capabilities that allow an end user to send data to other end users who may not be attached to the SNA environment at the time the data transfer operation is initiated. (SNA supports asynchronous or non-real-time communications between end users, for example SNADS.)

LUs perform the necessary data path establishment, data transformation, data flow management, error recovery, and data transfer functions that are needed to initiate and support end user-to-end user communications. Thus, an LU should be viewed as a collection of customizable functions that are tailored to meet the specific requirements of and end user, and are then used by that end user to communicate with the SNA environment and through it with other end users. In this context, an LU can be thought of as a communications subsystem for SNA end users that provides them with some of the communications services they require, in much the same way that an applications programming subsystem (for example, IBM's CICS/VS) provides high-level storage, database and communication access mechanism to its client application programs.

LU Type 6.2, in this context, is just another type of LU that may be used in an SNA environment. An LU Type 6.2, however, is a specialized and highly evolved LU expressly designed and optimized to support peer-to-peer transaction processing and biased interactions between application program end users via a standard API. The exclusive support of application program end users, and the standard, formally documented API to its communications services are, in the end, the two quintessential and differentiating characteristics of the LU Type 6.2.

In addition to peer-to-peer networking, and direct, program-to-program communications geared towards cooperative processing applications, the other salient characteristics of today's SNA can be summarized as follows:

- On-the-fly dynamic reconfiguration, high-availability, fault-tolerant features to facilitate non-stop, months-at-a-time, long-duration network operation.
- A growing repertoire of value-added, application level, integrated utility services for data distribution, data access, and data filing, such as: SNA Distribution Services (SNADS), Distributed Data Management (DDM), SNA File Services (SNA/FS), and Document Interchange Architecture (DIA).
- Comprehensive management facilities embracing fault management, response time monitoring, automatic inventory (i.e., asset) tracking, and configuration-change control.

LU TYPE 6.2: THE PANACEA FOR COMMUNICATIONS

LU Type 6.2, in addition to being a strategic solution for program-to-program communications (or Advanced Program-to-Program Communications [APPC] as IBM prefers to refer to it), was also an attempt to rectify in one fell swoop all the problems hitherto associated with the crucial end user-to-SNA interface. Prior to LU Type 6.2 (or simply LU 6.2) SNA surprisingly, but excusably given its ground-breaking role, did not specify a standard interface (or boundary) between it and the users wishing to use it. Consequently, every SNA product, whether from IBM or another vendor, implemented its own customized interface for end user access.

Identifying a standard, generic, all-encompassing API for SNA-based interprogram interactions was one of the (some would even say the) most notable achievements of LU 6.2. The LU 6.2 API, often referred to in SNA parlance as the LU 6.2 Protocol Boundary, has now established a consistent, clearly demarcated, and easily comprehensible access mechanism into SNA, albeit just for application programs. This, however, is not as limiting as it would appear at first sight.

The other two end user classes are terminal users and I/O devices. With the ubiquitous deployment of micro-processors, most (if not all) terminals (which are invariably PC-type workstations these days) as well as I/O devices now contain control software to govern the functioning of the actual hardware. It is this control software (which in the context of LU 6.2 can be viewed as an application program) rather than the hardware, which now interacts with SNA. Thus, contemporary terminal equipment and other I/O devices, such as printers of disk drives, can now be thought of as all being front-ended by application programs.

The application front end view of computing permits one to treat all the interactions that need to be supported by SNA in the future as being between application programs (i.e., software entities). Given that interprogram interactions is what LU 6.2 is all about, it alone will be able to support all the future communications requirements demanded of SNA, thus becoming the single strategic vehicle for all future SNA-based interactions. This universal facilitator role is the other major contribution of LU 6.2.

In the past, SNA supported a multitude of disparate, end-to-end, interaction transport mechanism types, known in SNA as LU-LU Session types, that were based primarily on the end user pairings being served, with some tempering to cater to the data transmission characteristics the end users wished to use. Thus, interactions between a 3270 terminal user and an application program in an S/370 host (TSO, for example) were supported across an LU-LU Session Type 2, while a print-out requested by that user, which was directed to a 3270 printer, would require a session Type 3 (or possibly Type 1) depending on the printer data-stream preferred by the application. All in all, there were seven distinct session types (0, 1, 2, 3, 4, 5, 6, and 7) where LU-LU Session Type 6 always dealt with interprogram communications. There never was, and most likely never will be, a session Type 5. LU 6.2 is, in essence, the third major refinement to this category of interprogram sessions, hence the .2 notation.

Now that SNA can at last see itself being able to handle all future requirements just using 6.2, it will in time be able to relinquish support for the other session types gradually, and just standardize and concentrate on LU 6.2. SNA, however, will not be able to abandon the other session types for a long time yet. The bulk (i.e., 80–90 percent) of traffic on today's SNA networks flows over session types 2, 3, and 1, with the first, which supports the 3270 terminal traffic, being the most pervasive. Applications based on LU 6.2 are only now beginning to make their presence felt. However, IBM's SAA Phase 1 objectives of cooperative processing and distributed data are based entirely upon a foundation of LU 6.2, on the very good premise that these computing techniques are entirely reliant on interprogram interactions. Thus, the next generation of major applications for the strategic IBM platforms, including those exploiting the transparent database-sharing "data warehouse," concept jointly developed by IBM and Information Builders, will be developed around constructs dependent on LU 6.2.

THE ANATOMY OF AN LU TYPE 6.2

LU 6.2s facilitate distributed processing in its broadest context by acting as intelligent, value-added interfaces between application programs and the SNA Path Control Network. The Path Control Network serves as the transport mechanism for all the interprogram interactions conducted by these application programs.

An LU 6.2 in its entirety can be viewed as consisting of three distinct components. (See Figure 2.3.) These three components are: a set of quintessential LU characteristics; the famed LU 6.2 Protocol Boundary (i.e., generic API); and a set of LU 6.2 standard, value-added, cross-application utility services known in LU 6.2 parlance as Service Transaction Programs (STPs).

The key characteristics of an LU 6.2 can be summarized as follows.

Support of Multiple End Users

Prior to LU 6.2, SNA never wholeheartedly tackled the thorny, but seminal, issue of end user-to-LU correspondence. Whether an LU should support only one end user or multiple end users was left as an implementation-specific decision. Traditionally most IBM implementations opted for the conceptually convenient one-for-one mappings.

From the outset, LU 6.2 advocated the possibility of a single LU 6.2 concurrently serving multiple local applications as shown in Figure 2.3. All the communications facilities provided by LU 6.2 are explicitly geared towards the support of multiple end users.

Session Multiplicity

An LU being able to support multiple LU-LU sessions concurrently has been a basic concept of SNA from the very start. Most S/370 host ACF/VTAM application program LUs relied on this, with one host LU serving a network of LUs front-ending terminal users via a series of LU-LU sessions. Multiple LU-LU sessions were, however, never exploited by peripheral node implementations (e.g., 3274 control unit).

Just as with the support of multiple end users, LU 6.2 dispelled any potential ambiguity about the viability of it supporting multiple, as well as parallel, sessions by explicitly addressing its capability to do so from the very start. There is also a link between supporting multiple end users and the desirability of being able to participate in multiple and parallel sessions. Each application program-to-application program dialogue requires the dedicated use of an underlying session for the duration of that dialogue. To provide adequate communications bandwidth for a series of concurrently active dialogues, an LU 6.2 would have to support multiple sessions (and even parallel sessions) if two or more of the dialogues were between the same end points.

LU 6.2 Conversations

SNA sessions, whether between LU 6.2s or other LUs, provide an end-to-end relationship and transport mechanism between session partner LUs. Given that LUs are by definition at the interface between SNA and end users, sessions do not extend beyond the boundaries of an SNA environment. However, it would be convenient and useful to have similar end-to-end relationships between end users, particularly application programs. LU 6.2 caters to this with the concept of conversations.

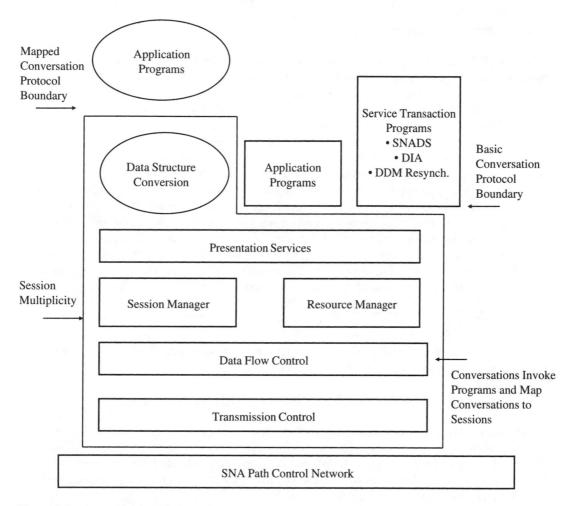

Figure 2.3   Anatomy of an LU Type 6.2.

Whereas sessions are pipes between LUs, LU 6.2 conversations are pipes between application programs. Each conversation must be mapped onto an underlying session, and requires exclusive use of that session for the entire duration that it is active. However, when a conversation is terminated, another conversation may be mapped on to the underlying session relinquished by the previous session.

Peer-to-Peer Operation

LU 6.2 always assumes that both LU-LU sessions and application program-to-application program conversations will be established and conducted on a strictly peer-to-peer basis. Most functional responsibility, but in particular error recovery, is always symmetrically apportioned between LU 6.2 session partners.

Synch Point Resynchronization

LU 6.2 includes an integral resource checkpointing mechanism for ensuring that the integrity of protected resources, such as databases, can be maintained during transactions affecting those resources (e.g., database update) by an end-to-end cooperative process. Thanks to this process, LUs could either commit to the success of a transaction and hence the continued integrity of a target protected resource, or request a roll-back operation in the event of an unsuccessful transaction.

LU 6.2s offer two levels of resource synchronization monitoring support. There is a mandatory, basic level, known as CONFIRM support, which allows partner application programs to confirm the successful completion of a specified unit of work. In the event of an unsuccessful transaction, the application programs, as opposed to the LUs serving them, have the onus of performing any necessary error recovery. This level of synchronization, though adequate for some transaction processing applications, is only effective when being used between just two application programs. It is usually inadequate to satisfactorily handle distributed transactions involving multiple and, possibly, cascaded application programs cooperatively interacting with each other. To cater to such applications, LU 6.2 provides an optional, two-phase commit process, which ensures that the changes called upon by a given transaction are only applied (ie., committed to) once all the application programs have confirmed that they can perform their piece of the transaction. SAA's Distributed Data techniques are contingent on this LU 6.2 two-phase commit processing capability.

The generic STPs currently provided by IBM include DIA, SNADS, and DDM, as well as some LU 6.2 housekeeping utilities related to backward-compatibility (with LU 6.1) resource resynchronization and session-multiplicity control.

MOVE TOWARDS PEER-TO-PEER NETWORKING

Slowly but surely, IBM is now torqueing SNA (both in terms of architecture and implementation) towards eventually becoming a bona fide peer-oriented networking scheme. To achieve this successfully, the hitherto imperative umbilical cord between every SNA node and a Systems Service Control Point (SSCP) in a central S/370 host had to be severed. It was the need for SSCP-centric clustering that led to the traditional, hierarchical SNA networks.

This SSCP dominance resulted from SNA's original network address-based session establishment and message routing technique. All SNA resources in a particular network, such as LUs, PUs (Physical Units), SSCPs, and links, were assigned one or more unique network addresses relative to that network. To ensure initial configuration and subsequent reconfiguration flexibility, these network addresses are not preassigned or permanently associated with a resource. Network addresses are assigned each time a network is (re)started (i.e., activated).

In the case of ACF/VTAM-based networks, network addresses are sequentially assigned to the resources appearing in the ACF/VTAM definition statements and relevant ACF/NCP "gens" each time VTAM (and the SSCP it contains) is started. Other addresses will be added when necessary to deal with dynamically configured resources. A given resource, particularly an LU, could therefore have a different network address each time the network is started, depending on when its definition was encountered relative to other resources.

This transient address assignment precludes end users and the LUs serving them from being able to use network addresses as a consistent means of identifying other end users. Instead, users and LUs use network-unique names to identify other users and their LUs. Unfortunately, SNA networks, even today, can only route messages using destination network addresses. Names have to be converted to the appropriate network addresses before message units can be exchanged through the SNA network. Only the SSCP that assigned the current network address to a given resource has the up-to-date translation table to perform this name-to-address conversion. In essence, SSCPs are centralized Directory Servers. In the 1970s, the disk storage, memory, and processing power required to perform this directory services function for a reasonably sized network could only easily be found on S/370 hosts. This reliance on hosts for centralized directory services is what prevented SNA from being able to readily offer an alternative to its much maligned hierarchical, host-rooted networks.

THE PIVOTAL TYPE 2.1 NODES

The Type 2.1 node architecture unveiled in 1983 introduced the very first SNA node that could function without any SSCP intervention. Type 2.1 (T2.1) nodes contain a Control Point (CP) component that performs many of the functions normally associated with SSCPs, specifically those of configuration management, directory services, and operator liaison, but on a strictly local basis. Configuration management functions handled by the CP also include physical resource, such as link, activation, deactivation, and monitoring functions handled in other SNA nodes by the PU component of the node. Thus, T2.1 nodes are also the only SNA nodes that do not contain a PU. It is this lack of a PU that has resulted in such nodes being increasingly referred to as nodes, as opposed to the PU Type designation endemic when referring to other node types.

A T2.1 node CP maintains a manually created directory of the names of all resources (LU 6.2s in this case) in its node, as well as those in other logically adjacent nodes with which LUs in its node might want to establish sessions. In the case of a remote LU the directory entry will also contain the link over which the node containing that node can be contacted.

In marked contrast to SSCP-centered networks (now referred to as subarea networks), T2.1 node CPs do not assign network, or for that matter even local, addresses to LUs. Instead, T2.1 nodes use an LU name-based session establishment scheme. Sessions are identified by a dynamically assigned session index value, known as the Local-Form Session Identifier (LFSID). The LFSID is placed in the Transmission Header (TH) fields occupied by the destination and origin address in the case of traditional SNA nodes.

The session establishment request (i.e., an SNA BIND) sent from one LU to an LU in another node will identify the target LU by its name within the body of the BIND request. This name-based session establishment does not, however, mean that T2.1 LUs can arbitrarily fire off BINDs without CP involvement. Before a T2.1 LU can issue a BIND, it has to deal with its coresident local CP to obtain three distinct pieces of information. These are the link (address) across which the target LU can be contacted, a unique LFSID for the proposed session, as well as another identifier, known as a Fully-Qualified Procedure Correlation Identifier (FQPCID), which is used during session initiation to group the interactions related to a particular session.

The process by which an LU obtains this information is analogous to the session initiation procedure used between LUs and SSCPs across SSCP-LU sessions in subarea networks. The key difference is that all the T2.1 node session initiation interactions occur within the confines of the node. The first message unit that flows out of a T2.1 node relative to the establishment of a proposed session is the actual BIND request. There are never any CP-to-CP interactions. CPs are node-specific entities with no external visibility of relevance. Apart from link-level XID exchanges during link activation, the only sessions or meaningful interactions that occur between T2.1 nodes are those between LUs.

APPN—THE NEXT GENERATION SNA

This local autonomy, and SSCP- and thus S/370-independence, make T2.1 nodes an attractive means for realizing peer-oriented networks among small computers. Thus, T2.1 nodes can be found on most, if not all, IBM and non-IBM mini-computers and workstations. APPN, being T2.1 node- and LU 6.2-based, automatically supports any LU 6.2 (i.e., APPC) applications. In addition, it currently supports the following IBM mid-range applications and services: Display Station Pass-Through (DSPT), File Transfer Support, SNADS, DDM, Network Management Alert Forwarding, and AS/400 Electronic Customer Support.

The current T2.1 architecture, nonetheless, has significant defects, the most serious being that it does not support intermediate node routing. T2.1 nodes can only deal with point-to-point interactions between logically adjacent nodes. (See Figure 2.4.) End-to-end interactions between non-adjacent nodes, which need to pass through multiple intermediate nodes, can only be realized if each of the intermediate nodes provides a non-architected application level relay function. Obviously, in today's far-flung data processing environments, a networking scheme is of little use if it can only support communications between adjacent nodes. Also, T2.1 nodes only support a single link between any two pairs of adjacent nodes. For protection against individual data link failures, as well as to gain additional bandwidth, it is now quite common for installations to use multiple links between key nodes. T2.1 nodes would have been regressive in such instances.

IBM overcame the limitations of T2.1 nodes with APPN, which was prototyped on S/36s and AS/400s as product-specific, implementation-oriented extensions to the T2.1 architecture in the late 1980s. In March of 1992, APPN was at last elevated to being a fully endorsed SNA and SAA architecture, and is now poised to become the basis for the Next Generation SNA.

APPN is technically innovative, very contemporary, easy to implement, and a dynamically configurable, totally peer-oriented networking scheme.

PEER-TO-PEER SNA

Systems Network Architecture's (SNA's) LU Type 6.2 and Type 2.1 (T2.1) node architectural extensions form much of the basis for the new 1990s SNA, which focuses on program-to-program communications and cooperative processing applications based on program interactions. This new SNA is also highly dynamic, resilient, comprehensively manageable, and peer-to-peer oriented.

LU 6.2 addresses the requirements for interprogram communications and provides a generic but powerful Application Program Interface (API) through which to realize such interactions. T2.1 nodes support these LU 6.2 interactions by offering the physical and logical connectivity and the local control functions necessary to enable these interactions to be conducted on a symmetrical, peer-oriented basis across a non-hierarchically structured and controlled network.

Classic Point-to-Point Configuration

Scope of T2.1 Node Architecture

T2.1 Point-to-Point "Meshes"

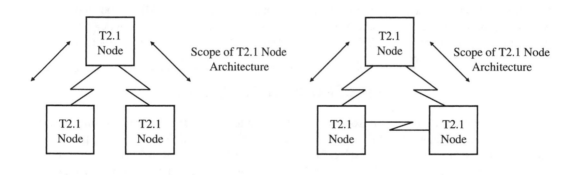

T2.1 Multipoint

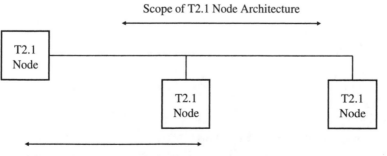

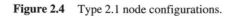

Figure 2.4   Type 2.1 node configurations.

T2.1 nodes are now widely implemented by IBM, most mini-computer vendors, and some third-party PC applications. (See Figure 2.5.) Despite this endorsement, T2.1 nodes have limited applicability and appeal, even in today's strictly peer-to-peer, T2.1 node-only networks. To start, their inability to perform intermediate routing, and their disinclination to support multiple parallel links between the same pair of nodes, limit the scope of the type of network that can be realized with T2.1 nodes in practice; the only exceptions are certain PC-to-PC applications on PC LANs. Also, most production SNA environments are still based along the lines of the traditional, quintessential SNA mold of the late 1970s. (They are S/370 host-centered and also hierarchically controlled.)

To make a true impact and facilitate the gradual move towards the peer-oriented, new SNA of the 1990s, T2.1 nodes have to be able to participate freely within the traditional, hierarchical SNA environments. Recognizing this, IBM had to make another architectural extension to SNA, this time to the actual bedrock, hierarchical SNA (Phase 4) architecture that had held sway since 1978. This landmark extension is referred to as Type 2.1 node integration.

On the other hand, the Casual Connections facility, which will be discussed in more detail later in this chapter, is a non-strategic, implementational (as opposed to architectural) byproduct of the T2.1 node integration extension. This extension is mainly of interest for short-term, tactical applications until APPN support becomes available on all major IBM platforms, including S/370 hosts and 37xx communications controllers.

TYPE 2.1 NODE INTEGRATION

From the beginning, T2.1 nodes, despite their peer orientation, could freely participate in traditional, SSCP-ruled subarea networks. However, the initial architectural and implementation support for such participation was severely limited and lackluster. In essence, T2.1 nodes were defined, appeared, and acted as if they were just plain Type 2 nodes, just as the SNA node in a 3274 or 3700 control unit. T2.1 node LUs required SSCP intervention across SSCP-LU sessions to establish sessions with LUs

- AS/400
- S/36
- S/38
- RS/6000
- ACF/VTAM for S/370 hosts
- ACF/VTAM for 37xx Communications Controllers
- System/88
- PC and PS/2
- Series/1
- 3820
- Transaction Processing Facility (TPF) for S/370 hosts
- Displaywriter
- Scanmaster
- 5520

Figure 2.5   IBM's key Type 2.1 node implementations.

in the subarea network, and it was not possible to establish sessions between T2.1 nodes across the subarea network.

In mid-1987, the basic subarea network architecture (i.e., SNA-4), and the T2.1 node addressing scheme, were enhanced to facilitate the seamless integration of T2.1 nodes into traditional subarea networks. These changes were incorporated into ACF/VTAM Version 3 Release 2, and ACF/NCP Version 4 Release 2. T2.1 node-resident LU 6.2s could now freely participate in subarea networks without in any way having to deviate from their native, SSCP-independent mode of operation.

T2.1 node-resident LU 6.2s were now permitted to establish sessions with host-resident ACF/VTAM application program LUs, or with LUs in other T2.1 nodes accessed via the subarea network, without having to issue or accept SNA Session Services requests over SSCP-LU sessions. They could now have multiple sessions, including parallel sessions, even with ACF/VTAM application program LUs. When establishing and participating in inter-T2.1 sessions, the entire subarea network, regardless of its configuration, complexity, and geographic diversity, appears to these T2.1 node LUs as if it were just a simple, point-to-point link between physically adjacent nodes.

This new breed of emancipated T2.1 node LUs is referred to as independent LUs, in deference to their SSCP-free, autonomous status. At present, only LU 6.2s resident in T2.1 nodes are capable of being independent LUs. LUs in all other node types, which still require an active SSCP-LU session to be able to participate in an SNA environment, are now known as dependent LUs to highlight their inherent reliance on SSCP intervention. Figure 2.6 summarizes the differences between independent and dependent LUs.

Independent LUs can reside in T2.1 nodes, which, although attached to subarea nodes, do not explicitly include an SNA Physical Unit (PU) component. They also do not require an SSCP-PU session to be deemed active. In T2.1 nodes, whether peer-attached or subarea network-attached, the functions normally associated with being performed by a PU in other SNA node types (particularly those related to physical configuration management) are handled by the configuration services subcomponent of the T2.1 node's control point (CP).

In addition to being able to house independent LUs, the ability to function without an SSCP-PU session now clearly differentiate T2.1 nodes from all other SNA node types. T2.1 nodes that wish to exploit their new found prowess can no longer masquerade in subarea networks as SSCP-PU session-reliant Type 2 nodes containing dependent LUs.

ACF/VTAM Version 3 Release 2, ACF/NCP Version 4 Release 2, and subsequent releases, support a new ACF/VTAM operand called Exchange Identification (XID) on PU definition NCP macros and VTAM statements. T2.1 nodes are now defined to ACF/VTAM and ACF/NCP by stating PUTYPE=2, XID=YES. XID=YES causes a link-level XID with an SNA-defined, format Type-3 information field (XID3) to be sent to the node. If the node rejects the XID3 (i.e., either time-outs or responds with an XID that does not contain a format Type-3 information field), it is assumed to be a Type 2.0 node. A successful XID exchange identifies a node as a true T2.1 node.

The desirability of the optional SSCP-PU session for alert forwarding is negotiated during this exchange. Requesting an SSCP-PU session in this manner does not affect the T2.1 node designation of a node and its ability to continue to house independent LUs. A T2.1 node's CP will act as a surrogate PU and support an SSCP-PU session established following an XID-based solicitation.

Within T2.1 nodes, independent LUs are defined by assigning an SNA local address of zero to each (LOCADOR=0). Multiple independent LUs, up to a theoretical maximum of around 64,700 per link, can be defined in this manner. In addition to independent LUs, T2.1 nodes, in the interest of

Dependent LUs—Generic	Independent LUs
Require an SSCP-LU session.	Do not require an SSCP-LU session.
Capable of supporting any LU-LU session type (i.e., 0, 1, 2, 3, 4, 6, 6.1, 6.2, and 7).	Can only be LU Type 6.2.
Can reside in any of the five SNA node types (i.e., 5, 4, 2.1, 2, and 1).	May only reside in Type 2.1 nodes.
Node containing LU must have an SSCP-PU session.	SSCP-PU session with the Type 2.1 node containing LU is optional, and only required for forwarding SNA alerts to an SSCP focal point.
Can typically initiate third-party establishment of an LU-LU session between two other LUs, as well as being able to request the third-part termination of an existing LU-LU session between two other LUs (i.e., can issue SNA INIT-OTHER & TERM OTHER requests).	LU Type 6.2s do not support third-party session initiation or termination (i.e., they do not support INIT-OTHER and TERM-OTHER). A third-party dependent Lu may, however, initiate or terminate an LU-LU session involving an LU Type 6.2.
Dependent LUs in Type 2, 2.1, or 1 Peripheral Nodes	
Can only establish sessions with S/370 host (Type 5 node) resident application program (LUs).	Can establish peer-to-peer sessions with host-resident LUs and with other LUs in Type 2.1 nodes.
Can only act as the secondary (slave) LU in any LU-LU session.	Can be either a PLU or an SLU of a session. In the case of multiple, concurrent sessions with the same partner LU. Parallel sessions can be the PLU of some of these sessions and the SLU in the others.
Can only support one active LU-LU session at any one time (restriction imposed by implementations rather than by the architecture).	Can support multiple LU-LU sessions.
Lack of multiple sessions automatically precludes parallel sessions.	Can support parallel sessions.

Figure 2.6 Dependent vs. independent LUs.

backward compatibility, can also contain up to 255 dependent LUs. These dependent LUs are defined, following the definition of the independent LUs, with non-zero local addresses within the range of 1 to 255.

Most SNA installations are only just beginning to explore the exciting possibilities of T2.1 node integration, particularly for interconnecting dispersed S/36s, S/38s, and AS/400s on a peer-to-peer basis through existing hierarchical backbones. The emerging support for T2.1 node passthrough, via a 3174 for token-ring-attached PCs, will greatly accelerate the deployment of this capability. Just as in the case of APPN, new applications that explicitly exploit independent LUs have yet to hit the market. Many are being developed under the SAA banner, since independent LUs are the bread-and-butter LUs of SAA.

THE MECHANICS OF TYPE 2.1 NODE INTEGRATION

There were two significant disparities that had to be resolved before T2.1 node LUs could interact freely with subarea networks in their native SSCP-independent mode. T2.1 node LUs rely on LU name-identified session establishment requests (BINDs), and the message units that they use are prefixed by an arbitrary, dynamically assigned session index value known as the Local-Form Session Identifier (LFSID). In marked contrast, subarea networks always require network address-identified BINDs, and destination and origin address-prefixed message units. To incorporate T2.1 nodes seamlessly within subarea networks, the subarea network had to provide a conversion facility that could accommodate these two distinct modes of operation across the T2.1 node-to-subarea network boundary.

SNA devised a convenient approach to deal with this conversion. It would front-end the independent LUs in the T2.1 nodes with surrogate, SSCP-dependent subarea network LUs. These surrogates would represent the independent LUs within the subarea network as if they were bona fide, SSCP-subservient, dependent LUs. These surrogate LUs would perform the necessary conversion functions and act as a relay for message units across the subarea network boundary.

When an independent LU attempted to establish a session by issuing an unsolicited, LU name-identified BIND, the surrogate LU front-ending that LU would intercept it and perform a session initiation process, modeled exactly along the lines of that used by a standard dependent LU. The network address of the target LU would be obtained, as well as one that is dynamically allocated for the origin-independent LU.

The physical attachment of a T2.1 node to a subarea node is always directly supported by the boundary function (BF) component of that subarea node, just as in the case of the attachment of any other peripheral, such as a Type 2.0 or 1 node. All message units to or from a peripheral node always have to go through a BF, which is also responsible for performing the conversion between the pan-network, network addresses, and the node-relative local addresses used by peripheral nodes. Given that the BF was already performing some address conversions, it was the obvious candidate for providing the surrogate LU support for independent LUs.

A BF with an attached T2.1 node now appears to that T2.1 node as if it were just another adjacent T2.1 node. All the remote LUs within the subarea network, or accessed through that network, are defined within the T2.1 node's CP directory as if they were all located within the BF node. Thus, an independent LU wishing to establish a session with any of those remote LUs directly issues an LU name-identified BIND to the BF. This BIND cannot go beyond the BF at that juncture as it does not contain any valid addresses. The BF then uses a set of new T2.1 node integration-specific SNA requests, to solicit the relevant addresses from the SSCP.

CASUAL CONNECTIONS

Casual Connections, introduced with ACF/VTAM Version 3 Release 3 in November 1979, is an intriguing and somewhat innovative facility that further confirms IBM's commitment to a peer-oriented SNA, and demonstrates the company's sense of urgency to reach this goal. Casual Connections permits S/370 hosts, along with any necessary channel-attached 37xx communications controllers, to be defined to and to connect with each other as if they were merely T2.1 nodes. Thus, traditional Type 5 (and 4) subarea nodes can now masquerade as dynamic, unfettered T2.1 nodes. Casual

Connections is a clever exploitation of the subarea network enhancements to accommodate T2.1 integration.

The prime attraction of the Casual Connections facility is that it permits intersubarea node connections to be defined relatively easily and succinctly compared to those required to specify traditional subarea-to-subarea routes. Cross-domain resources can now be defined without Cross-Domain Resource Manager (CDRM), Cross-Domain Resources (CDRSCs), Adjacent SSCP (ADJSSCP), and PATH statements. A measure of the giant strides made by SNA to facilitate dynamic definitions is that even without the use of Casual Connections, cross-domain LUs can now be dynamically located using default SSCP selection and dynamic ADJSSCP tables without the need for CDRSCs and ADJSSCP definitions. Installations now have a choice as to how to minimize their SNA definitions. (Default SSCP Selection and dynamic ADJSSCP were initially offered on ACF/VTAM Version 2 Release 2, and ACF/VTAM Version 3 Release 3, respectively.)

Obviously, there are some drawbacks associated with using Casual Connections; if there were none, all intersubarea connections could potentially be replaced overnight. The two main drawbacks are: the lack of support for transmission groups (parallel link), and the inability for potential LUs to initiate sessions, such as with the terminal operator-entered LOGON <application name>. Casual Connections, true to its T2.1 node roots (as opposed to APPN), does not support the dynamic location of remote LUs via selective broadcast searches, so all remote LUs have to be defined at the source Type 5 nodes. Therefore, in some instances, the amount of definitions required between Casual Connections, as opposed to standard ACF/VTAM Version 3 Release 3 paths, becomes an interesting and sometimes difficult trade-off. Nonetheless, the Casual Connections facility is ideally suited for either back-up or short-duration low-traffic connections, especially if switched connections are to be used.

The Casual Connections configurations that are possible today are shown in Figure 2.7.

Bolstering the usefulness and applicability of Casual Connections was a major, hidden-agenda goal of ACF/VTAM Version 3 Release 4. This release permits direct channel-to-channel casual connections to be established between hosts, without any intermediary ACF/NCP intervention. This could be accomplished via traditional channel-to-channel adapters (CTCAs), ESCON CTCAs, and even 3172-based remote CTCs. When used in conjunction with ACF/NCP Version 5 Release 4, multiple but non-parallel links (multitail T2.1 support) can also be used where necessary with switched 56 Kbps or T-1 links. In the case of switched connections they can also benefit from ACF/VTAM Version 3 Release 4's dynamic network access features that appear to relax further the need to predefine switched nodes.

Casual Connections, at least at present, is an expeditious if not truly elegant solution. Nonetheless, this facility provides a basic infrastructure and the motivation to start moving subarea nodes away from their traditional, hierarchical connection scheme. The inevitable availability of subarea node

VTAM 3.3 (+)	<-> VTAM 3.3 (+)	VM Systems with Integrated Comms. Adapters (ICA)
VTAM 3.4	<-> VTAM 3.4	MVS CTCA, or 3172 Remote CTC
VTAM&NCP	<-> VTAM&NCP	VTAM 3.2+PTF, or VTAM 3.3 (+)
VTAM&NCP	<-> VTAM 3.3 (+)	VTAM 3.2+PTF, or VTAM 3.3 (+) <-> VM ICA

Figure 2.7   Casual Connections configurations.

support for APPN, most likely within the next twelve months, will be the next logical step in this progression.

ADVANCED PEER-TO-PEER NETWORKING

Advanced Peer-to-Peer Networking (APPN) is S/370 host-independent, intrinsically peer-oriented, biased towards program-to-program cooperative processing applications, and designed from ground up to favor highly dynamic route selection, resource definition, and network configuration. With APPN, IBM can safely say that: "This Is Not Your Father's SNA!"

In addition to being strictly peer-to-peer based, and devoid of any dependence on a central controlling host, the other key, quintessential feature of APPN that truly differentiates it from the traditional SNA can be summarized as:

1. Automatic registration of end node resources,
2. Automatic, on-the-fly location of undefined remote resources via network-wide, broadcast searches, and
3. Automatic, continuous monitoring and updating of network topology and path configurations.

With APPN, the LU 6.2s resident in a peripheral end node do not have to be defined to the network node within the APPN backbone network to which the end node is to be attached, as is the norm in comparable traditional SNA scenarios. The network node will automatically query the end node for the LUs resident in that node, and dynamically register the LUs in its directory when a connection is first established between an end node and a network node. The only definition required in the network node is that for the communications port through which the data link connection to the end node would be established. In this respect, APPN provides a compelling plug-and-play networking environment, where network administrators of possibly even users could just plug an end node (such as a workstation or a mini-computer) into a port in an operational APPN network without the need for any predefinition, in much the same way that workstations can now be hooked up to LANs.

This ability to connect end nodes freely to an APPN network, without the burden of the time-consuming and tiresome task of having to define all the LUs in the end nodes, is obviously a great boon for network administrators. This is also good for users who will have gained more or less on-demand access to the network without having to wait until the next "re-gen" to have their LU included. The bulk of the definitions required in traditional SNA networks are for the LUs in peripheral end nodes such as those found in 3x74 control units, PCs, S/36s, S/38s, and AS/400s. If this APPN capability were available today with ACF/VTAM and ACF/NCP, it would be possible to support all such end nodes without a single PU or LU definition statement (or macro), thus reducing the length of typical network definition files, if not the actual network definition effort, by nearly 80 percent.

Network nodes use an APPN-specific protocol to request the names of the LUs resident in an end node, once a successful link level connection is established between the end node and the network node. The LU registration interactions occur between a CP component in the network node and a corresponding CP in the end node, across two LU Type 6.2-based CP-to-CP sessions.

APPN complements its automatic end node LU registration facility with an automatic broadcast search capability for locating remote LUs, which obviates the need to define potential target destination LUs anywhere other than at their logical, home network node. When an APPN network node receives an LU-LU session activation request from an LU that is either resident within that network node itself or in an end node attached to that network node, it searches its dynamically updatable remote LU location directory to determine if the location of the destination LU has been found previously and entered in the directory. If the subject destination LU's location is not found in the directory, the network node will construct and forward a broadcast LU search request to all its adjacent network nodes with which it has active CP-to-CP sessions. These adjacent nodes will in turn continue to forward the search request to their adjacent network nodes. When the search request eventually reaches the home network node at which the LU in question is defined, either as residing in the network node itself or in an end node attached to the network node, it will return a response to the network node that initiated the search, identifying itself with a node name.

Once a source network node has located the remote destination LU that is to be the target of an LU-LU session, it sets about calculating the optimum route through the APPN network for that session. Each network node contains an APPN topology database that records dynamically updated information about the characteristics of the links and network nodes found within the APPN network; this information includes link speed, connect time cost, transmission cost, propagation delay, and level of security.

An LU issuing a session activation request (such as SNA BIND) will implicitly specify the class-of-service (COS) required by that session through a node name associated with the session. The COS permits an underlying route for a given session to be selected based on a stated set of criteria, such as fastest link speed and least expensive transmission cost.

Using the COS criteria specified for a particular session, a source network node will calculate the optimum route for that session. The session activation BIND request will then be forwarded to the target destination LU along that route. The BIND request will have a route selection control vector (RSCV) appended to it, which will identify the overall end-to-end route that will be used by the session. Intermediate network nodes routing the BIND will use this information in the RSCV to create the relevant routing table entries for that session, referred to in APPN as session connectors. Once the session is established, all the message units exchanged relative to that session will always flow along the same route as that initially traversed by the BIND.

The CPs in adjacent network nodes regularly interact with each other across CP-to-CP sessions to convey the up-to-date status and topological configuration of the overall APPN network. Each time a new link or network node is activated, an operational link or network node fails, or a previously failed link or network is reactivated, a status change notification is propagated to all the network nodes in the network from one adjacent network to another. Network nodes dynamically update their topology databases to reflect the latest topological configuration status that they have received. Thus, optimum path calculations for new sessions that are to be established are always based on the latest network configuration data.

APPN, just like traditional SNA, does not yet support dynamic alternate routing. Thus, link failure will result in all the sessions routed over that link failing, just as in SNA today. However, a notice of the link failure will be quickly propagated across the network so that paths that used to traverse that link can be tagged as inoperative. Just as in SNA, LUs can attempt to activate a new session when an unexpected session failure is encountered. The network node receiving the new session activation request will attempt to find a new route that satisfies its requested COS, based on the latest topological configuration.

Type 2.1 Node Architecture	Advanced Peer-to-Peer Networking
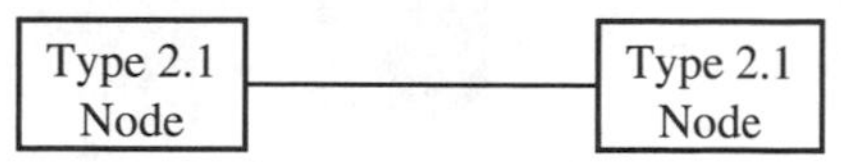	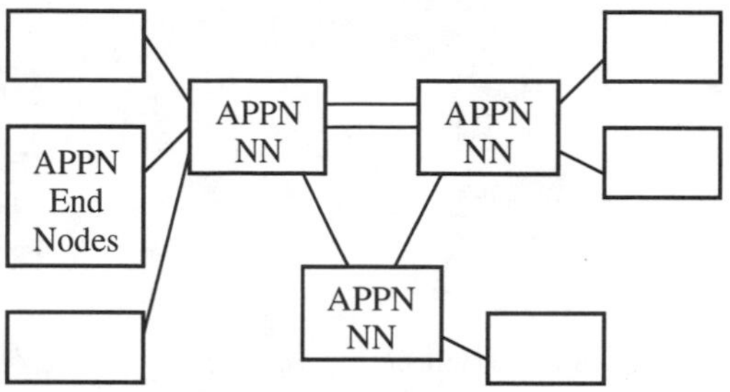
Formally published extension to the basic SNA-4 architecture. Non-IBM implementations available.	Originally an S/36 and AS/400, product-specific extension to the Type 2.1 node architecture. No published specification as yet for APPN network nodes. At present, IBM network nodes are proprietary.
Local point-to-point interface between logically adjacent Type 2.1 nodes. No architected capability for intermediate node routing.	Comprehensive intermediate node routing.
Single link between a pair of adjacent nodes. Multiple and multipoint links if one node has connections to multiple, logically adjacent nodes.	Multiple links between adjacent networking nodes. However, no single-pipe parallel link (i.e., SNA Transmission Group) capability, as yet.
Static, manual definition of remote LUs.	Automatic, dynamic remote LU location via broadcast search and cache directory. Automatic registration of end node LUs (AS/400 networking and end nodes only). Dynamic network reconfiguration based on changes in status of route and LU availability.
Only supports interend user LU-LU sessions between nodes. A node's Control Point (CP) does not have any external visibility, relevance, or interactions.	LU-LU sessions as per Type 2.1 nodes. CP-CP control sessions between networking nodes, as well as AS/400 networking and end nodes.

Figure 2.8   Type 2.1 nodes vis-à-vis APPN.

THE COMPOSITION OF APPN

APPN is modeled on top of the SNA Type 2.1 node architecture. Figure 2.8 summarizes and highlights the differences between the Type 2.1 node architecture and APPN.

APPN as a tangible networking scheme first saw the light of day in 1986 when it was introduced on the S/36. However, it only came to being in its current form (with automatic registration of end

APPN End Nodes	APPN Network Nodes	LEN End Nodes
 Apple Macintosh	 AS/400	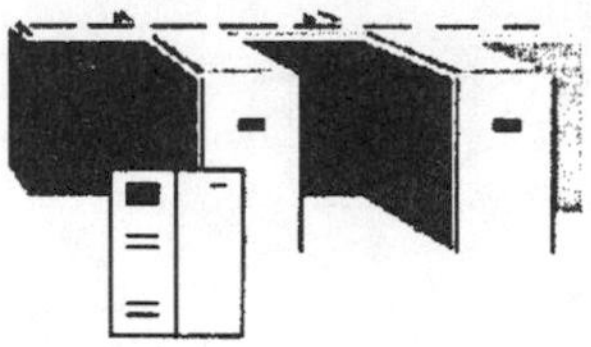 ACF/VTAM &ACF/NCP
• Dynamic Resource Registration	• Intermediate Node Routing	• Same as a Straight Type 2.1 Node
• Multiple Links to a Network Node	• Multiple Links	• Single Link
• No Intermediate Node Routing	• CP-CP Sessions with other Network Nodes	• Manual LU Definition
• CP-CP Session with Network Node	• Supports APPN End Nodes and LEN End Nodes	• No CP-CP Sessions
• Partially published architecture	• No published architecture as yet	• Published architecture

Found in:
  AS/400
  NS/2 with OS/2
  Apple Macintosh
  Siemens/Nixdorf
  Novell, etc.
	Found in:
	  AS/400
	  3174
	  NS/2 with OS/2
	  S/36
		Found in:
		  ACF/NCP and ACF/VTAM
		  APPC/PC
		  OS/2
		  S/38
		  AS/400, etc.

Figure 2.9   APPN node types.

node LUs and parallel links) when the AS/400 was unveiled in June 1988. In March 1991, coinciding with the elevation of APPN from being a totally unpublished, IBM-propripetary prototype architecture to that of a quasi-published, SAA-cum-SNA architecture, APPN support was also included in OS/2 (via SAA Networking Services/2 [SAA NS/2]) and IBM 3174 Establishment Controllers (via a new level of microcode). At the same time, IBM revealed that Apple Computers, Novell, Siemens/Nixdorf, and System Strategies Inc. had all indicated that they would be implementing APPN end node support.

An APPN network consists of one or more APPN network nodes (NNs), each of which can optionally support a set of one or more link-attached end nodes (ENs). When multiple APPN NNs are present, they can be interconnected in any appropriate mesh-type topology that ensures that any particular NN that needs to interact with another NN can do so either via a direct connection, or via a path traversing one or more intermediary NNs. The interconnected NNs provide the SNA path control network for a given APPN environment, which is capable of intermediate node routing, on-the-fly remote LU location, automatic end node LU registration, optimum session path calculation, and automatic monitoring of network topology status.

At present, the only systems that act as APPN NNs are AS/400s, S/36s, 3174s, or OS/2 workstations with NS/2. APPN now subdivides end nodes into two distinct categories: APPN end nodes and low-entry networking nodes (LENNODEs). Automatic end node LU registration and multiple links to an adjacent network node are only possible with APPN end nodes. In effect, APPN end nodes, initially introduced with the AS/400 in 1988, are now the preferred end nodes for APPN networks. An APPN end node has a CP-to-CP session with the network node to which it is attached, across which APPN-specific functions, such as automatic LU registration, are performed. Figure 2.9 summarizes the characteristics of APPN NNs, APPN end nodes, and LENNODEs.

The nodes in an APPN environment can be interconnected via either dedicated or switched SDLE point-to-point links, dedicated SDLC multipoint links, X.25-based packet switching networks, token-ring LANs, or S/370 host channels.

GLOSSARY

ACF/NCP. Network control program that executes in a local of remote communications controller.

ACF/VTAM. An S/370 host-resident SNA-oriented teleprocessing access method that provides the host-based control functions needed to realize an SNA environment in an S/370-centered system.

Boundary Function. A component of SNA subarea nodes, such as Type 5 (for example, ACF/VTAM in an S/370 host) or Type 4 (ACF/NCP in a 37xx Communications Controller) nodes. They provide message unit interchange support for peripheral (i.e., Type 2, 2.1, or 1 nodes) attached to that subarea node.

DDM. Distributed Data Management. A scheme for file transfer and transparent record-level access to remote data files.

DIA. Document Interchange Architecture. A synchronous (real time) document distribution and filing scheme.

Node. The SNA-specific software, the pertinent hardware, and the interfaces to that hardware, which together implement all the functions of SNA on a particular piece of equipment, whether it be an S/370 host, a 3745 Communications Controller, a 3174 Control Unit, an AS/400, or a PC. SNA functional components, such as LUs, SSCPs, and PUs, reside within SNA nodes. It is the SNA node rather than the PU within that node that fully characterizes the implementation of SNA on a given product.

PU. An SNA-specific piece of software found in an SNA node, which invokes and performs the functions needed to control, operate, and monitor physical entities (such as data links) and their configuration, relative to a set of SNA resources. Contrary to expectation, an SNA Physical Unit (PU) is not a physically intact or tangible component, such as a host, a communications controller, or a 3174 control unit.

SNADS. SNA Distribution Services. A generalized, asynchronous (i.e., non-real time) scheme for document or message distribution using store-and-forward techniques.

SNA/FS. SNA File Services. A scheme for file transfer and filing, as well as for enterprise-wide file naming.

SSCP. System Services Control Point (SSCP) is a directory service, configuration management, network management, and system operator liaison focal point. Every traditional SNA network has to have at least one SSCP. SSCPs can only reside in SNA Type 5 nodes. Type 5 nodes are typically only implemented by IBM on relatively large, general-purpose computers, such as S/370s, S/38s, AS/400s, and S/88s. On S/370s, ACF/VTAM provides the Type 5 node and hence the SSCP function.

Subarea Network. An SNA network based around Type 5 and Type 4 nodes; this is a traditional, S/370 host-based SNA network.

REFERENCES

Gurugé, A. May 1991. "SAA—A Bold New Outlook." *FOCUS Systems Journal* 4, no. 3.

———September 1991. "SAA—The Anatomy," *FOCUS Systems Journal* 4, no. 5.

———November 1991. "SAA—A Bold New Outlook," *FOCUS Systems Journal* 4, no. 6.

3

DIGITAL'S NETWORKING STANDARDS STRATEGY— DECnet, OSI, AND TCP/IP

Robyn Mosher

INTRODUCTION

Purpose of Standards

Standards are not a new concept. For thousands of years, standards arose as solutions to problems in manufacturing, transportation, communication, commerce, and science. Examples of standards defined in the last hundred years include the width of railroad tracks (so railways could connect isolated cities across the country), electrical standards, the metric system, the telephone network, environmental/pollution standards in automobiles, and air traffic control standards. Along with the advent of computer and information technology came a need for standards to regulate hardware, software, networks, and virtually every aspect of this industry.

There are many technical and business reasons for standardizing computer networks. In the 1990s, companies purchase equipment that will perform essential business functions, with the best performance and least cost. This results in complex networks that are multivendor and multiprotocol. These businesses also restructure organizations and work assignments, to increase productivity and/or respond to economic declines. Standards help organize such businesses' networks, by providing guidelines by which the various vendors' products can interoperate, thus allowing networks to be easily expanded and modified. Standards aid in the design of added-value applications, and foster a user-oriented development environment. Simply put, without networking standards, products would not interoperate, networks would be a management nightmare, critical business problems would not be solved, and communications technology would grind to a halt.

Standards have become central to the information technology industry. Over 250 subcommittees of official standards organizations are working on information technology standards. More than 1,000 standards are either adopted or in development by these organizations. Standards are defined for all architectures and levels of networking: TCP/IP, OSI, DECnet, SNA, and many others.

In conjunction with the introductions to TCP/IP, OSI, and DECnet provided in this book and in other references, this chapter presents the standards used in each of the three network architectures. It shows a case study of a TCP/IP, DECnet, and OSI network and reviews technical issues and proposed solutions. Because the scope of this topic is too broad to be covered by a single chapter, publications for further reading are provided in the References section.

To preface an in-depth discussion of the TCP/IP, OSI, and DECnet standards, a brief review of standards classifications is necessary.

Open Standards and Open Systems

Open systems refers to heterogeneous software, hardware, or networks that support multiple vendors' products. TCP/IP and OSI are open systems because they are based on "open" standards; that is, they were designed to provide communications between multiple vendors' equipment and were designed without a particular vendor in mind. The Digital Network Architecture is seen as a "proprietary" standard, meaning it was originally designed for a homogeneous environment containing only DECnet systems. (IBM's SNA is the other prevalent example of a proprietary system.) Digital, however, recently made DECnet more open by licensing it to other vendors, enabling them to modify DECnet to run on their own hardware systems.

A **de facto** standard refers to an unstandardized product design that becomes popular and widely used, without having gone through a formal standards process or being governed by an official standards body. As one example of a de facto standard, most U.S. car radio manufacturers place the on/off button to the left side of the radio console, to be easily reachable by the driver.

A **de jure** standard is one that is first officially developed and mandated by an official standards authority, often on an international level and, subsequently, products are developed to follow the standard. An example of a de jure standard is the U.S. electrical standard of 120V, for wiring houses and using household appliances. Electrical standards have unfortunately not yet been standardized worldwide, which poses a problem for business travelers, but promotes business for manufacturers of electrical adapters.

De facto and de jure standards are all around us, in everyday products as well as computer networks. In the networks world, OSI is an international de jure standard, mandated and architected by the ISO. DECnet is considered a company de facto standard, since its specifications and implementations were developed simultaneously. It became a popular Digital standard, which resulted in its current licensing to other vendors. TCP/IP is generally referred to as a de facto standard, because it was developed, became popular, and was widely used before becoming officially standardized.

Digital's networking began seventeen years ago when two PDP-11s were linked together. This original "network" of two nodes was expanded into a family of networking products known as DECnet. In the 1980s, Digital added TCP/IP and OSI support to the Digital Networking Architecture. In 1991, Digital formally introduced ADVANTAGE–NETWORKS, its strategy to support open network standards, including OSI, TCP/IP, and DECnet, as the cornerstone of Digital's networking.

In summary, Digital's ADVANTAGE–NETWORKS architecture currently supports DECnet (a de facto, proprietary standard), OSI (a de jure, open standard), and TCP/IP (a de facto, open standard). These three network suites and their governing standards bodies are described in full in the following sections.

HISTORY AND EVOLUTION

The Digital Network Architecture (DNA) was originally developed in the early 1970s, when networking was not widespread in the computer industry. DECnet is the product family based on the DNA architecture. Digital published its formal DNA specification at approximately the same time as IBM announced its Systems Network Architecture (SNA). In the seventeen years since DNA was introduced, the architecture has evolved through five phases. The fifth and current phase, known as ADVANTAGE–NETWORKS, integrates OSI and DECnet protocols and allows them to coexist and interoperate with TCP/IP.

DECnet Features and Advantages

Besides its maturity and large installed base, DECnet has some technical features and applications that complement those of OSI and TCP/IP. DECnet can be configured flexibly to support many nodes in local- or wide-area configurations. Videotex (VTX) and VAX Notes are two powerful applications available to DECnet users. A benefit to DECnet programmers is that DECnet is "feature-rich"— DECnet has standard services that the programmer can use without having to build them from the bottom up. There are gateways from DECnet to IBM/SNA, to TCP/IP networks, and connections to X.25 are, as mentioned previously, in a mature stage of development.

DECnet now has over one million licenses in use. Digital's worldwide business network, known as the EASYnet, is the world's largest private computer network. It spans over 70,000 DECnet nodes worldwide, along with 18,000 TCP/IP hosts. Digital's 17 years of DECnet development have given Digital expertise in networking that facilitated its incorporation of TCP/IP and OSI products into its current networking architecture and strategy.

DNA Phase I

Phase I of the Digital Network Architecture was announced in 1974. The DECnet products built under Phase I supported only PDP-11 mini-computers running the RSX-11 operating system. Standards were defined for point-to-point network communications between pairs of processors. Although rudimentary by today's standards, the DNA Phase I architecture was revolutionary at a time when batch processing and terminal-to-host, timesharing computing were the norm. The concepts of sending electronic mail to remote systems or institutions, or LAN distributed computing, were unheard of to the average computer user or vendor at that time.

DNA Phase II

Phase II of the Digital Network Architecture was introduced in 1976. Phase II DECnet products supported many Digital operating systems that were available at the time, including RSX-11M, RSX-11D, IAS, RSTS, and RT. Phase II still only supported point-to-point communications between pairs of processors; it did not yet include intermediate node routing capabilities. One enhancement in Phase II was the guarantee of backward compatibility. One enhancement in Phase II was the guarantee of backward compatibility, that is, engineers would not make incompatible changes from one phase of the architecture to the next. Also, the Phase II standard was defined precisely, which enabled many different DECnet implementations to interoperate. This was a first step towards solving the interoperability problems that would become paramount as networks grew more complex.

DNA Phase III

Digital's Network Architecture, Phase III, was introduced in 1980. Phase III DECnet products supported Digital's major operating systems: RSX-11M, RSX-11M+, RSX-11D, IAS, RSTS, RT, VMS, Tops 10, and Tops 20. There were many enhancements in Phase III. Network size was expanded to allow users to connect up to 255 processors, in any configuration. With these larger networks came a need for reliable routing. Phase III introduced an adaptive routing capability that allowed each node to determine the locations of all other nodes and to route messages across the network, often through several intermediate nodes. Also, since larger networks were more complex to monitor and manage, Phase III introduced an architecture for network management. Finally, in Phase III Digital introduced gateways from DECnet to other networks such as those based on IBM's SNA, and wide-area X.25 standard networks. The Phase III architecture, with its new routing, management, and gateway features, was maturing rapidly in response to the developing networking market. Digital became known as a leading network integrater in this time frame.

DNA Phase IV

The Digital Network Architecture, Phase IV, was introduced in 1982. Phase IV supported the following operating systems: VMS, ULTRIX, RSX-11M, RSX-11M+, RSX-11D, IAS, VAXELN, DOS, OS/2, and P/OS. Phase IV defined a new standard for 16-bit addressing, which allowed users to construct networks of up to 64,000 nodes. Phase IV added support for the Ethernet standard (developed jointly by Digital, Intel, and Xerox), which provided high-speed communications and the ability to connect many devices to the local area network. Once again, the increased addressing and larger network size required a more sophisticated routing capability. Phase IV expanded the Phase III adaptive routing standard to include support for hierarchical routing. Hierarchical routing is a method that allows efficient adaptive routing to be done in large networks, by dividing the network into subdivisions known as "areas." Thus, the DECnet model of segmenting network addresses and network topology into "areas and nodes" originated in Phase IV.

DNA Phase IV is a layered architecture that is similar to the ISO model, particularly on the lower layers. In fact, the ISO network layer is very similar to the DECnet network layer. However, the ISO standards were not final at the time DECnet Phase IV was introduced. (In fact, they are still evolving.) So, there are some differences between the ISO model and DECnet Phase IV.

Digital's Network Architecture, Fifth Generation: ADVANTAGE–NETWORKS

The fifth generation of Digital's Network Architecture was announced in 1987, under the name "DNA Phase V." The main goal of this phase was to incorporate support for ISO standards into the Digital architecture. Inherent goals of Phase V were backward compatibility with, and increased performance over, Phase IV DECnet networks. Other important improvements in Phase V were link state routing, which added more efficiency for very large networks, and improved network management based on the Enterprise Management Architecture (EMA). The product, now known as DECnet/OSI, is available on both VMS and ULTRIX operating systems.

Clarifying ADVANTAGE–NETWORKS

The development of DECnet/OSI products went on from 1987–1991 and the name "Phase V" became synonymous with DECnet and OSI. However, Digital is also a leading supplier of TCP/IP products and is committed to equal support for all three protocol families. Hence, the name "ADVANTAGE–NETWORKS" was defined as an umbrella term to encompass DECnet Phase IV, DECnet/OSI (dual DECnet and OSI stacks available on both VMS and ULTRIX platforms), and the TCP/IP products, which Digital has shipped for many years prior to the formal ADVANTAGE–NETWORKS announcement.

To avoid confusion, a second point about ADVANTAGE–NETWORKS should be clarified. At this time, not all three stacks (DECnet, OSI, and TCP/IP) are sold together. DECnet and OSI are sold together on both VMS and ULTRIX platforms. TCP/IP is also offered on both platforms, but separately from DECnet/OSI. Digital is considering selling all three stacks together in the future, as well as the possibility of letting users separately purchase each component "à la carte."

TODAY'S STANDARDS: DECnet, OSI, AND TCP/IP

History and Popularity of OSI and TCP/IP

DECnet, OSI, and TCP/IP, the foundation of Digital's ADVANTAGE–NETWORKS, evolved via separate paths. Some background on the history and popularity of OSI and TCP/IP, and the standards bodies that govern them, follows.

OSI

OSI (Open Systems Interconnection) is a networking architecture based on international standards for communications between open systems, as defined by the International Standards Organization (ISO). OSI is mandated by many worldwide governments, with many computer vendors now developing and delivering OSI products. ISO's OSI reference model, shown in Figure 3.1, defines a seven-layer architecture, with each layer performing a different function. Any vendor wishing to be OSI-compliant must follow the design specifications of the seven-layer model. The ISO model was designed in layers to facilitate modular software development and to define a set of protocols and services at each layer upon which all vendors would standardize. The goal of the OSI standard is to create a computer network analogous to today's telephone network. One can buy a phone from any vendor, plug it into a phone socket, and connect to another telephone in any part of the world.

The market penetration of OSI is still in the early stages. Some factors that will move OSI products into existing networks are: Government OSI Profile (GOSIP) mandates (worldwide government procurement requirements that mandate OSI implementation by vendors); virtually unlimited network addressing for larger/international businesses; and OSI applications, such as X.400 mail, X.500

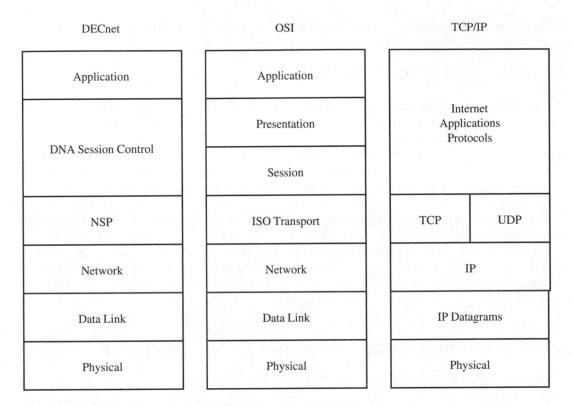

Figure 3.1   Digital network architectures: DECnet, OSI, and TCP/IP.

directory services, and Electronic Data Interchange (EDI). EDI provides communication between a business, its customers, and its suppliers. Since the potential OSI customer base is extensive, vendors designing OSI-compliant systems and applications can expect a large market for their products.

All OSI standards are generated by the International Standards Organization (ISO), the International Consultative Committee for Telephony and Telegraphy (CCITT), and the Institute for Electrical and Electronics Engineers (IEEE) among others. The ISO also coordinates the efforts of such national standards bodies as the American National Standards Institute (ANSI) and the British Standards Institution (BSI). A decade of work by the ISO's OSI standards subgroup has resulted in several hundred international OSI standards (such as bit-specifying protocols, transfer syntax, and layer-service definitions) in the seven-layer model. Despite the large number of standards, OSI standards will never be a "complete" set, since new applications and technologies will always arise, requiring new standards to govern them.

TCP/IP

TCP/IP (Transmission Control Protocol/Internet Protocol), formally known as the Internet protocol suite, is a mature de facto standard with a large installed base and existing applications. In the 1970s and 1980s, TCP/IP emerged as the predominant network protocol standard for open systems. The TCP/IP protocol architecture is defined by a four-layer model that maps roughly to the ISO stack (see Figure 3.1). Each layer has separate standards for protocol communications within that layer and interfaces to the layers above and below it. The TCP/IP architecture is defined in a set of documents known as Request For Comments (RFCs). TCP/IP standards development is governed by the Internet Activities Board (IAB) and Internet Engineering Task Force (IETF).

Reasons for TCP/IP's popularity include its capacity to link multiple vendors' operating systems (including UNIX, VM, MVS, MS-DOS, and many others), its inclusion free-of-charge with UNIX, its maturity and large installed base, the huge number of applications that run over TCP/IP, and the TCP/IP-based Internet network. The Internet links university, research, and business institutions worldwide. Its growth was slow and steady from 1980 through 1988, when growth became geometric. The size of the Internet went from under 100,000 hosts (in 1988) to over 500,000 (in 1991) to its current estimated size of 1.2 million hosts.

TCP/IP standards are administered by the Internet Activities Board (IAB) and the Internet Engineering Task Force (IETF). The IAB coordinates evolution of the Internet protocols, and the majority of the standardization and protocol development activities take place in the working groups of the IETF, a subsidiary of the IAB. The IETF began in January 1986 as a forum for technical coordination by contractors for the U.S. Defense Advanced Projects Agency (DARPA), working on the ARPAnet, U.S. Defense Data Network (DDN), and the Internet core gateway system. Since that time, the IETF has grown into a large international community of network designers, operators, vendors, and researchers concerned with the evolution of the Internet protocol architecture and the smooth operation of the Internet.

Protocols that become standards in the Internet go through a series of steps or "states" (proposed standard, draft standard, and standard), which involve increasing amounts of scrutiny and experimental testing. It is a general IAB practice that no proposed standard can be promoted to draft standard without at least two independent implementations. Promotion from draft standard to standard generally requires operational experience and demonstrated interoperability of two or more implementations.

The IAB may require that a protocol be implemented by all systems on the Internet. For example, this rule is true for the Internet Protocol. Few protocols are required on all systems, however, since there is such a variety of possible systems. Therefore, a protocol's status is designated as either recommended, elective, or "limited use" if it is not intended to be implemented widely. The IAB also recommends that all TCP/IP implementations be network-manageable. Current IAB standards, their status, and RFC number are listed at the end of the chapter.

DECnet Standards Governance, in Contrast to OSI and TCP/IP

The Digital Network Architecture (DNA) is the architecture standard for the design of DECnet communication products. DNA consists of an architectural overview document, a set of specifications for each layer, and descriptions of how the protocols and interfaces at each layer interrelate. The components of DNA are controlled by Digital and copyrighted, but are available to the public and other vendors who wish to design DECnet-compatible hardware and software products. DECnet standards development is governed by Digital Equipment Corporation.

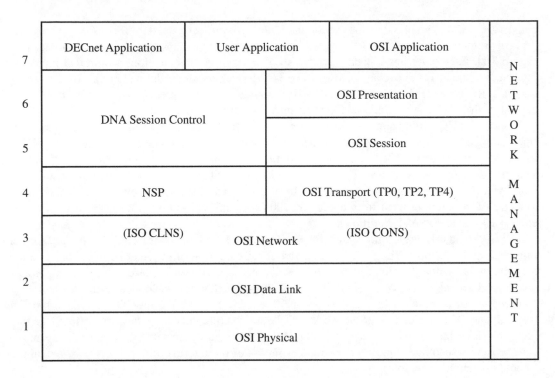

Figure 3.2 DECnet/OSI integrated stack.

SPECIFIC PROTOCOL STANDARDS FOR DECnet, OSI AND TCP/IP

DECnet Protocol Standards

DECnet defines standards for communications between systems, based on a layered application that maps to the ISO model shown in Figure 3.1. The DNA seven-layer model is very similar to the ISO model because the two evolved from common roots. Digital's fifth generation networking integrates the DECnet and OSI protocol stacks in the model shown in Figure 3.2. A brief description of a few main DECnet protocols at different layers follows.

DNA Lower Layer Protocols DNA Network Services Protocol (NSP) is a transport protocol defined in the DNA Phase IV End Communication layer. This protocol was enhanced and refined by ISO to specify the class 4 (TP4) protocol. There are many similarities between NSP and TP4. NSP establishes connections with a peer NSP entity and sends data, control, and acknowledgment messages.

At the datalink layer, DECnet Phase IV supports the Digital Data Communications Message Protocol (DDCMP), the X.25 protocol (based on the CCITT X.25 recommendation for public data network interfaces), and the Ethernet protocol.

Application Layer Services

File Transfer—Data Access Protocol (DAP) is used for file transfer in DECnet, via the VMS $COPY command, ULTRIX #dcopy command, or the programming READ and WRITE statements.

Remote Login—Command Terminal Protocol (CTERM). Provides terminal emulation for local and remote DECnet terminals.

Electronic Mail—Mail-11 is the mail protocol in DECnet, upon which VMSmail is based. (All-IN-1 mail, another mail application that Digital produces, is not part of the DECnet protocols but rather is a layered application.)

Directory Service—Directory services are provided by a node database in DECnet Phase IV and by DECdns in DECnet Phase V.

VAXNotes—This is a powerful DECnet application; an "electronic bulletin board" that allows DECnet users worldwide to participate in roundtable discussions using their terminals or workstations.

Videotex—This application is an on-line information database with an almost infinite array of subjects, accessible to any DECnet user. The information provided (for example: course listings or product updates) can be configured for customized applications to include any sort of information that users want.

OSI Protocol Standards

Although there are hundreds of existing OSI standards, this section addresses a few key, formal, and emerging OSI network standards that are of high interest in the industry today. A more complete listing of OSI standards is given at the end of the chapter. While it is unlikely that any vendor or user would implement all the OSI standards provided (GOSIP profiles typically define a subset of OSI standards for vendors to conform to), the OSI standard contains them all to encompass the wide range of vendor and customer computing needs.

The lowest layers of the ISO model specify standards for network datalinks—typically, Ethernet, Token Ring, or FDDI. The highest level specifies standards for user applications such as file transfer (FTAM), mail (X.400), terminal emulation (VTP), and directory services (X.500). OSI standards at the application service level do not include application program interfaces (APIs). Projects are underway in the IEEE, X/Open, and elsewhere to develop APIs for these services.

To preface the discussion of OSI protocols, a definition of the terms "connectionless" and "connection-oriented" protocols and network services is given here.

Connection-oriented and Connectionless Protocols   *Connection oriented* assumes that, within a given layer of a protocol suite, there are mechanisms that ensure reliable communications with the same peer layer at another node running the same protocol suite. Connectionless assumes that no reliability is provided by the services at a particular layer. All data is usually sent in datagrams and reliability is not maintained for delivery or receipt to the other node at that peer protocol layer. (If errors occur in packet sequencing, rather than resequencing, the packet is usually just retransmitted.

Connectionless protocols are often "faster" to use since they lack the added functionality necessary to ensure reliable communications; thus, they are used in applications where speed is necessary and sequencing less critical.

TP4 and TCP provide connection-oriented transports for OSI and TCP/IP respectively. If packets are determined to be delivered out of sequence, then these transport protocols will correct the problem in both OSI and TCP/IP.

CLNS and IP, in contrast, are connectionless Network Layer 3 protocols for OSI and TCP/IP respectively. There is no guarantee of delivery, flow control, or boundary alignment for these protocols. They rely on TP4 and TCP to resolve those issues of protocol order.

UDP (an alternate TCP/IP transport besides TCP) is a connectionless transport protocol, used by the Internet protocol suite to send simple messages where packet resequencing is not important. For instance, one-packet ICMP messages use UDP, since sequencing is irrelevant if only one packet is sent. UDP is faster than TCP since it has less error checking overhead. It is also used to improve performance in Network File Systems (NFS) applications.

A brief description of some main OSI protocols follows.

Transport Layer protocols   OSI specifies five classes of transport protocols termed TP0–TP4. Digital supports TP0, TP2, and TP4. (TP1 and TP3 are not widely implemented in the industry, nor are they mandated by any GOSIP profile.) Classes 0–3 run over the CONS; class 4 can run over the CONS or CLNS Network Service. A brief description of TP0, TP2, and TP4 follows.

TP0—The simplest transport protocol, TP0 assumes that most requirements for supplying a reliable transport connection are handled by the network layer. TP0 belongs to OSI transport class 0: simple class.

TP2—TP2 is an enhancement of TP0 and supports creation of multiple transport connections using a single network connection. TP2 belongs to OSI transport class 2: multiplexing class.

TP4—TP4 performs all required protocol functions to provide a reliable transport connection running on top of either the CLNS or the CONS. TP4 belongs to OSI transport class 4, the error detection and recovery class. TP4 is the recommended transport protocol and is expected to be the most widely used in DECnet/OSI networks.

Application Layer Protocols   The major OSI applications are File Transfer and Access Method (FTAM), Mail (X.400), Directory Services (X.500), and Virtual Terminal Protocol (VTP).

FTAM—FTAM defines the functions required to support access to and transport of a remote file system in the OSI environment.

X.400—X.400 is a store-and-forward OSI message handling standard. X.400 defines a number of standard message handling services for electronic mail systems.

VTP—Virtual Terminal Protocol is OSI's remote login/terminal interconnect protocol.

X.500—X.500 Directory Services is a powerful name/information service standard for OSI. X.500 allows information about all objects in the network to be consistently stored, retrieved, and managed.

TCP/IP Protocol Standards

TCP/IP protocols are grouped in layers that roughly map to layers in the OSI model. There are four well-defined layers in the TCP/IP model (corresponding to layers 2–4 and 7 of the ISO model) with some UNIX-TCP/IP functionality mapping to layers 5 and 6. The four layers used are the Physical/Datalink, the Network Layer, the Transport Layer, and the Applications Layer. Generally, a TCP/IP application will use the four layers as follows.

- An application protocol such as file transfer;
- A transport-layer protocol, such as TCP, which provides services for the FTP application;
- An internetwork-layer protocol, such as IP, which routes the datagram to its destination; and
- The network access layer protocols, which manage the physical medium, such as FDDI, Ethernet, etc.

Some of the major TCP/IP protocol and application standards are summarized next. For a full listing, see the References section.

Internet Lower Layer Protocols   Transmission Control Protocol (TCP) is a connection-oriented transport protocol, responsible for ensuring that data and commands are sent reliably to the destination. Functions of TCP include breaking data into packets, sequencing packets, retransmitting if errors, checksum for error correction, keeping track of port-to-port connection, and flow control/windowing. TCP is similar to NSP in DECnet or TP4 in OSI.

User Datagram Protocol (UDP) is a connectionless datagram service, used in place of TCP in applications that send small amounts of data or that do not require high reliability. (For example, name server requests are one-packet messages and don't need data packeting or sequencing. They use UDP for faster performance.) UDP is also used by Network File Services (NFS) for high-performance remote file access. UDP has no equivalent DECnet protocol, but is similar to CLTS in OSI.

Internet Protocol (IP) is responsible for routing of packets and ensuring that data reaches its destination. IP handles addressing, routing, packet fragmentation, and has its own checksum in addition to the TCP checksum.

Application Layer Services

File Transfer Protocol (FTP) allows a user on any computer to move files to or from another computer (which runs FTP) on the network. Security is handled by requiring the FTP user to key in a username and password on the target computer.

Remote Login (TELNET)—allows a user to remotely connect to any other computer on the network.

Electronic Mail (Simple Mail Transfer Protocol, or SMTP)—allows a user to send messages to users on other computers.

Berkeley Internet Name Domain (BIND)—the TCP/IP standard naming service that binds network names to network addresses.

RPC—Remote Procedure Call. A standard that allows a central application to execute subroutines on remote hosts, which may be currently underutilized. This speeds up program execution and maximizes network efficiency. RPC is often used for transaction processing. There are two RPC standards in use, Sun's RPC and the Apollo/NCS RPC which was accepted by the Open Software Foundation (OSF) as its Distributed Computing Environment (DCE) Remote Procedure Call standard.

NFS—Network File Systems. A de facto UNIX standard that allows transparent access to files on remote systems from a local system. Files appear as virtual local files and can be edited, typed, or mounted as if they were part of the local file system.

STANDARDS CONFORMANCE TESTING
FOR OSI, TCP/IP, and DECnet

General Conformance Testing

The goal of conformance testing is to increase the likelihood that separately developed protocol implementations will interoperate. This is done by ensuring that each implementation meets or conforms to the relevant protocol standards in terms of the feature implemented and the way the protocol is used. Governments, user groups, large corporations, and standards agencies define or adopt profiles that specify which specific standards (or elements within standards) a product must implement for it to be adopted for a particular use. Examples of these are the U.S. and U.K. Government OSI Profiles, or GOSIPs as they are known. Conformance testing is the method that is used to demonstrate adherence to these profiles.

When a system is tested for conformance, a formal System Conformance Test Report (SCTR) is produced by the testing laboratory. When the SCTR indicates conformance, a verification brand or mark is sometimes issued. The conformant product may also be placed on a register of conformant products (such as the U.S. Government's register of products which are conformant to U.S. GOSIP).

Digital's Conformance Testing

Digital is committed to developing open systems products that are reliable, standards-based, and conformant. As a result, Digital tests its products rigorously for quality, interoperability and standards conformance. As one example of its commitment, Digital has invested millions of dollars to implement, maintain, and staff the test centers in Littleton, Massachusetts (U.S.A.), Reading, England, and Brisbane, Australia.

In 1991, Digital's Network Performance and Conformance Engineering (NPACE) testing centers in Littleton, Massachusetts, received accreditation by the United States Government's National Institute of Standards and Technology (NIST) to test for OSI compliance to GOSIP and for TCP/IP compliance to the United States Defense Communications Agency (DCA). Additionally, the Corporation for Open Systems (COS) granted Digital's OSI testing center with accreditation as a First Part Test Center for COS conformance testing.

TCP/IP Conformance Testing

TCP/IP conformance testing is done by independent labs and vendors. Digital's Network Performance and Conformance Engineering (NPACE) laboratory is one approved site for TCP/IP Conformance testing. Digital's TCP/IP Conformance and Performance Test Facility has been accredited by NIST's National Voluntary Laboratory Accreditation Program (NVLAP) to test implementations of TCP/IP protocols using the U.S. Defense Communications Agency (DCA) test system. The DCA test system requires that any host TCP/IP implementation be certified as conformant by an accredited test facility, before allowing that implementation to be purchased for use by the Department of Defense. Digital was only the third company in the world to gain this difficult accreditation.

In most cases, the DCA requires this testing to be performed by an independent (third party) test facility. However, Digital's accreditation allows the testing environment and test engineers from other accredited test centers to perform the testing for Digital's TCP/IP products at its own test facility.

OSI Conformance Testing

Verification of OSI conformance is performed according to ISO standards 9646, parts 1 through 5. These standards define the strict rules by which tests are developed and test labs are operated to determine the conformance of OSI protocol implementations.

ISO, as well as test tool vendors working in cooperation with various testing consortia, have defined tests for key OSI standards and profiles. These tests are then used by accredited testing laboratories, such as the facilities operated by Digital, the Corporation for Open Systems (COS), or the U.K.'s National Computing Centre (NCC), to certify OSI conformance.

Other OSI testing initiative centers include OSIone, the worldwide interoperability testing consortium, which provides ongoing demonstrations of the practical applications of OSI networking standards.

Digital's NPACE Laboratories are approved by NIST and COS to do first-party testing of OSI products. Digital's OSI-based products are developed in various locations around the world. These labs serve as a focal point for worldwide OSI testing for U.S. GOSIP compliance and COS Mark testing.

Digital's U.S. GOSIP Version 1.0 Validation

Digital's OSI Conformance and Interoperability Testing Center has been accredited by NIST/NVLAP to test for OSI conformance and to validate OSI products for U.S. GOSIP Version 1.0. (This accreditation process involved rigorous proficiency and quality tests that NIST assessors performed to ensure NVLAP that Digital's engineering staff was proficient to run OSI testers.) Digital has been certified to test FTAM, MHS, TRANSPORT, X.25, and CLNP Internet for U.S. GOSIP Version 1.0.

Current plans call for both maintaining Digital's accreditation for U.S. GOSIP Version 1.0 and enhancing the laboratory's capabilities in line with future versions of U.S. GOSIP testing requirements.

Digital's COS Accreditation for COS Mark Program

The Corporation For Open Systems International (COS) is a not-for-profit, research-and-development consortium of more than sixty of the world's leading computer and communications vendors and users dedicated to accelerating the introduction of communications products based on OSI, ISDN, and related international standards.

In 1991, COS accredited Digital's OSI Conformance and Interoperability Test Center as a First Party Test Center under the COS Mark Program. The COS Mark Program, a testing and licensing process under which COS awards a COS Mark to computer and communications products that meet COS requirements, is a strong statement of OSI conformance in the marketplace. To become accredited as a COS Mark First Party Test Center, an applicant facility must undergo a two-stage process: a review of the test center's overall qualifications, followed by a comprehensive validation of testing capabilities against specific COS profile specifications.

As a result of Digital's accreditation, Digital is now able to conduct conformance tests for CLNP Internet, Transport (classes 0 and 4), MHS, and FTAM. Testing for these protocols is accomplished by using COS test systems, which are recognized by NIST as Means of Testing for compliance to GOSIP.

DECnet Conformance Testing

Digital recognized the need for rigorous testing to ensure the interoperability of its networking products early in the history of DECnet. Since the DECnet protocols were implemented by Digital on a large number of heterogenous operating systems, interoperability testing of all versions of every product on each operating system were deemed impractical. As a result, Digital established one of the world's first data communications conformance testing laboratories in 1979 prior to the introduction of DNA Phase III. This lab, which was operated independently from the product development organizations, developed test processes, tools, and suites that were used to ensure that the separately implemented versions of DECnet interoperated successfully. Since DECnet Phase III, the Digital Network Architecture has formally required proof of conformance as a requirement for a product to ship.

Digital has recently expanded the use of its DECnet conformance testing tools. Now that other vendors license and build DECnet protocols for their own systems, Digital requires conformance to be demonstrated by these implementations. Digital requires the use of its test tools for this process, and reviews the results of each test campaign in detail, before any product may use the DECnet name.

A COMPARISON OF DECnet, OSI, AND TCP/IP PROTOCOLS

All three protocol suites employ a layered architecture. The lower layers of Phase IV DECnet are very similar to the OSI lower layers. TCP/IP also maps roughly to the ISO model. All three employ a layered architecture to facilitate product development, by allowing engineers to design modular standardized hardware (at the lower layers) and software (at the upper layers). The layered approach also makes the network easier to manage, though not necessarily less complex.

At the upper (application) layer, all three networking protocol suites provide the same services: file transfer, mail, remote login capability, name servers, etc. At this level, a "a network is a network," and while the protocols and commands for an application such as mail may be different between OSI, TCP/IP, and DECnet, each one of them "gets the job done," and enables users of that protocol to communicate with each other. Users may run two such applications simultaneously. For instance, they may perform terminal emulation using both the DECnet Sethost command and the TCP/IP TELNET command, interchangeably on one system. Alternately, users may gateway between applications. For instance, one group running DECnet's VMSmail may gateway to others running SMTP on the Internet. The common roots that exist between the layered network suites make such gateways possible and also make possible such technologies as integrated IS-IS routing, which is discussed in the following section.

The implementation of DECnet, OSI, and TCP/IP protocols differs technically in such areas as placement of information in a packet, address sizes, individual field sizes, etc. A detailed comparison of differences at the "bit" level is outside the scope of this chapter.

The objective of this chapter is to describe the three network protocol standards, as they are supported by Digital, and to describe strategies for making them coexist in a network. For instance, many businesses based their original networks on one protocol, often TCP/IP or DECnet, and now wish to incorporate OSI because of GOSIP mandates or features such as OSI's extended addressing. A customer scenario is provided in the following section of this chapter as a proposed way of integrating the three protocol suites in a painless fashion.

A Comparison with Other Network Architectures

In all three architectures—OSI, TCP/IP, and DECnet—nodes have a peer relationship to each other. Any node can communicate with any other without consulting a central controlling node. This reduces communication overhead and increases network performance. Traditional SNA, in contrast, requires a central controlling node. SNA was developed to network a host-centric style of computing—one large machine with many terminal connections. Digital chose to base DECnet on the peer-to-peer style for several reasons: so its networks could be distributed; to increase performance; to eliminate the single point of failure that one central controlling node would cause; and also because the single workstation/mini-computers that are popular today were not designed to hold the quantity of information that a centralized model would require.

CASE STUDY OF BUILDING A NETWORK THAT SUPPORTS COEXISTENCE OF TCP/IP, OSI, AND DECnet

Today's business networks contain multiple vendors' applications and network protocols. These mixed networks challenge the network manager who must design the network, maintain it, and decide on equipment purchases as the network grows. To make networks manageable, vendors' products must not only be standardized, they must coexist, interoperate, and integrate with other vendors' products and technologies at many levels.

It is important to work from a common definition of the previous terms. **Coexistence** means that products will work on the same system and/or same network, simultaneously, but not "together." **Interoperability** means products are able to exchange data with each other. Integration means products exist on the same framework, share services, and present a seamless interface to the user.

As OSI protocols become widely implemented and used, the IETF recognizes that there will be an increasing need to support interoperability of OSI and TCP/IP protocols. The IETF is now formulating strategies for interoperability, and portions of the Internet now support both TCP/IP and OSI protocols. One example is that OSI applications can use the Internet. X.500 is being run over the Internet in a pilot project with 500 universities/businesses using 500,000 names. As OSI grows in usage, many OSI applications will continue to run over TCP/IP, to combine OSI's robust services (such as X.400), with existing TCP/IP resources such as large backbones including the Internet. One key technology for running OSI applications over TCP/IP, known by its TCP/IP specification as "RFC 1006," has become popular. Other coexistence technologies include: dual protocol stacks (running two protocols, such as TCP/IP and OSI, on the same machine); application gateways (that map TCP/IP applications to OSI and vice versa); and multiprotocol network routers, terminal servers, PC products, and network management stations.

Since the current technology favors coexistence of networking protocols, more than true integration, the following case scenario is largely based on the **dual stack** method. Both TCP/IP and OSI run on most machines but have autonomous addresses, applications, services, etc. This results in an issue common to dual stack networks: to communicate network users must essentially be "bilingual." They must "speak" the syntax of both protocols, by remembering both TCP/IP and OSI commands and interfaces. There is little or no transparency. Also, for all systems to communicate, every system on the network must either run both TCP/IP and OSI, or employ "interpreters" (gateways) to translate OSI protocols for TCP/IP machines and vice versa.

In future networks, some part of the hardware or software will be assigned to store information about what protocols each system employs, to offload this task from the user and to create network application transparency. Then, users could issue generic network commands to send mail, transfer files, or access a name server, without having distinct commands for TCP/IP and OSI. Today, they still have to know the difference between FTP and FTAM, between the SMTP mail and X.400 mail commands, and between the BIND and X.500 name servers. Removing this limitation, by creating new standards to facilitate network transparency, will be a main challenge of this decade.

CASE SCENARIO

For a network manager, the challenge is to build a standard-conformant network, using some or all of the aforementioned technologies, that meets the company's business needs and budget.

A brief case study of the steps one company took to upgrade a network is outlined here (the company name has been changed). Many implementations will involve OSI, TCP/IP, and DECnet. But for simplicity, this case study shows a TCP/IP network where the customer wanted to add OSI. An explanation of how they would further expand their network to include DECnet is given after the scenario.

Preparing a TCP/IP LAN for OSI

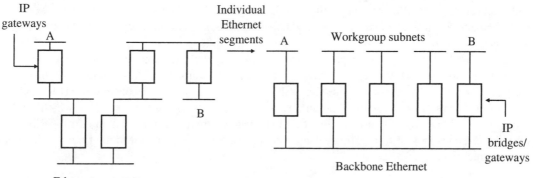

Before modification to accommodate OSI, the network shown here is a TCP/IP-only engineering network with many Ethernet segments daisy-chained via IP gateways. To get from Ethernet segment A to Ethernet segment B, a packet must make multiple "hops" through four gateways. After topology modification to accommodate OSI, the network uses a central backbone as a multiprotocol LAN. Each Ethernet segment connects to the LAN via a bridge or gateway or combination bridge/gateway. Getting from any segment A to any segment B requires two hops. This topology maximizes routing efficiency, cleans up network management, and improves performance.

Figure 3.3   Network configuration upgrade example.

Speed Daemons, Inc. (SDI), a UNIX engineering company, had a TCP/IP network with TCP/IP-specific topology (subnetworks) and many TCP/IP-only products, such as IP routers. As part of its strategic initiative toward open networks, Speed Daemons decided to expand their network to include OSI. Technical and business management worked closely to evaluate the company's needs and determine what technical applications would be required to support its existing and future business. The team agreed on a two-step, two- to three-year upgrade process, which include planning and implementation stages.

The planning stage included SDI's evaluation of the current network, research of OSI technology and products, and changes to network topology (where necessary) to support multiple protocols and provide a foundation for OSI. Since SDI's original TCP/IP network was based on autonomous subnetworks (typical in IP configurations), it was desirable to restructure the topology to better fit a central corporate network. (See Figure 3.3.) The infrastructure to support OSI was built into the network even before OSI products were there, which saved time, money and user downtime.

Once the network topology was changed, the technical staff evaluated SDI's equipment and software, and implemented changes in the following order to ensure the network supported both protocol standards. The implementation stage also included the actual system installation and user training.

Naming and Addressing Conventions

Since most systems on the new network would need to run both TCP/IP and OSI, it was necessary to ensure that each system had both an IP and OSI address. The network administrator obtained unique address prefixes from allocation authorities for IP and OSI. (The end user need not remember either IP or OSI addresses since name servers handle address lookups and routers move packets from one address to another.)

TCP/IP and OSI each had separate autonomous name/information lookup services on this company's network. SDI chose the Berkeley Internet Name Domain (BIND) name server standard for TCP/IP and X.500 directory services for OSI. Both naming services were installed and functioning without error across the network, enabling users to access either. Users must know which one to access and understand the interface to both, if they want to obtain information on both TCP/IP and OSI objects. This lack of transparency is an issue that needs to be resolved in the future with some form of integrated naming service.

Routing Infrastructure

The routing infrastructure was modified to support TCP/IP and OSI across the network, with some sections supporting other protocols such as SNA, DECnet, AppleTalk, etc. The TCP/IP-only routers from the original TCP/IP network were not capable of transmitting OSI packets; therefore, SDI had the choice to either replace them and lose their investment, or to place them in IP-only "islands" of the new network. Since the company had one engineering department that wanted to retain a TCP/IP-only network, the TCP/IP routers were placed there.

SDI's multiprotocol routing design allows packets to be delivered efficiently and reliably from the source to the destination, regardless of the packet's format and with minimum network and management overhead. Traditional multiprotocol routers make use of separate routing algorithms for TCP/IP and OSI, which require independent configuration and management (a method known as Ships in the Night [or SIN]). SDI chose a newer routing system, Integrated Routing, which uses the OSI IS-IS routing protocol with TCP/IP extensions to route both TCP/IP and OSI packets. IS-IS was designed for robust operation, simplicity of configuration and network management, and efficient operation over a wide range of network sizes.

With IS-IS there is only one routing protocol to configure and manage, and a single protocol to respond, automatically, if a link or other resource should fail. In contrast, with SIN, failure of network resources causes multiple routing protocols to respond at the same time in an uncoordinated fashion. Integrated routing also requires fewer network resources, including router CPU and memory, and network bandwidth.

Terminal Servers

Terminal servers and other network servers/clients that supported TELNET and had current or future capability to support VTP. Any servers or hosts that supported only one protocol, such as LAT, were connected to the new TCP/IP-OSI network via individual gateways. In cases where no such gateways existed, the particular equipment was isolated to "islands of computing."

Network Management

SDI considered all the routers, devices, hosts, and applications on the network—existing and planned—and chose one network management system to manage both TCP/IP's Simple Network Management Protocol (SNMP) and OSI's Common Management Interface Protocol (CMIP). Two methods for SNMP and CMIP coexistence are RFC 1006 (running CMIP Over a TCP transport via the TCP/IP standard known as RFC 1006) and Common Agents (a feature built into network management systems that enables protocol-transparent exchange of network management parameters).

Common Agents and RFC 1006

Network management stations interact with agents (i.e., systems to be managed) to request and receive status information on the current state of the network. This status could include routing information, number of packets sent, TCP information, system power ON/OFF, etc. This can all be defined as Management Information Base (MIB) variables.

In the **Common Agent scenario**, when the management station requests MIB status from the agent, the agent has a "protocol engine" that dispatches the status request and converts data into a common format understood by all protocols. This provides a level of protocol transparency between TCP/IP and OSI, since the organization could deploy the common agent to each of its end systems and access them using either SNMP or CMIP. Also, network management stations can use access modules to provide extensibility to network management. For example, such access modules could support information regarding newly defined MIB variables such as swap space, excessive paging, mail queues full, and others.

RFC 1006 is a TCP/IP standard that provides a means to execute OSI applications on top of the TCP transport service. As an example of how RFC 1006 provides coexistence (and partial integration), an OSI FTAM file copy could be executed from a TCP/IP end system to another TCP/IP end system using RFC 1006. If RFC 1006 is used in conjunction with a transport service bridge, then the OSI FTAM file copy could be executed from the OSI end system, through the transport service bridge, to a TCP/IP end system or vice versa.

Both the Common Agent and RFC 1006 strategies gave SDI's network manager tools to manage a multivendor/multiprotocol environment and an infrastructure to support both the Internet and ISO standards evolution for network management. SDI chose a management station that supports both SNMP and CMIP in a user-transparent fashion, and employs both common agents and RFC 1006 for coexistence.

Software Applications

When adding OSI to the network, some software and hardware needed to be modified slightly. SDI's network manager, along with programmers, tested the new OSI applications over the dual TCP/IP OSI network, based on its multiprotocol routers, terminal servers, and management equipment. They made some minor configuration changes and modified drivers where necessary to fully tune the new network.

Expanding the Coexistence Beyond TCP/IP and OSI

The preceding scenario shows one example of how an actual company modified their TCP/IP network to support TCP/IP and OSI. Only TCP/IP and OSI protocols were employed by SDI. However, the case can easily be expanded to add DECnet or other protocols.

For instance, Digital supported coexistence early on by designing a widely used DECnet-to-TCP/IP gateway (which maps SMTP to Mail-11, FTP to DAP, and TELNET to CTERM, all bidirectionally) and shipping it with every DECnet-ULTRIX license. Digital's DECnet/OSI provides integration of DECnet and OSI on both VMS and ULTRIX platforms. Digital also provides application layer gateways between TCP/IP and OSI (FTAM-FTP, VTP-TELNET, X.400-SMTP) and between DECnet and OSI (FTAM-DAP, VTP-LAT). Digital's SNA interconnect and PC interconnect products continue to be supported and enhanced.

Digital supports RFC 1006, a TCP/IP standard that allows OSI applications to run over a TCP/IP transport. Also, Digital terminal servers support TELNET and LAT. Digital's PC interconnect software supports TCP/IP and DECnet transports (with OSI planned). Digital routers support Integrated IS-IS routing OSI CLNP, TCP/IP, and DECnet (phases IV and V). Digital's DECmcc management station manages SNMP, DECnet, and CMIP, among others.

CONCLUSION

In today's marketplace, network users have limited vendor allegiance and are building or expanding networks that are multivendor, multiprotocol and multitechnology. Companies purchase applications that suit their business needs. They should not have to be concerned with (or even aware of) the underlying network infrastructure. TCP/IP, OSI, and DECnet provide a standardized networking foundation that lets users accomplish their business goals efficiently, and with the best investment protection.

Digital has been committed to networking standards since its announcement of the first DECnet products in 1975. Digital's strategy is to support multiple networking protocols, de jure and de facto standards, open and proprietary architectures, and to design products to eventually integrate OSI, DECnet, and TCP/IP in a seamless manner.

ACKNOWLEDGMENTS

Special thanks to Jim Bound, Dave Farmer, Peter Viscarola, Judy Cross, Rich Rosenbaum, Bill Duane, Audrey Augun, Faye Allen, and Joyce Radnor for providing assistance and editorial help on this chapter.

REFERENCES

Internal Digital Publications

Commitment to Standards: An OSI Guide to Management. Digital, 1988.

DECnet/DNA Phase IV General Description. Digital, 1982.

DECnet/DNA Phase V General Description. Digital, 1987.

DECnet/OSI: The Foundation for Open Networking. Digital, 1990.

DECnet/OSI Transition: Planning for Open Networking. Digital, 1992.

Digital's Networks: An Architecture with a Future. Digital, 1986.

Introduction to DECnet Phase IV. Digital, 1983.

Open Systems Handbook: A Guide to Building Open Systems. Digital, 1991.

External Publications

Cargill, Carl. *Information Technology Standardization*. Maynard, MA: Digital Press, 1989.

Comer, Douglas. *Internetworking with TCP/IP: Principles, Protocols, and Architecture*. Englewood Cliffs, NJ: Prentice Hall, 1988.

Gross, Phill. 1991. "IETF Report to the ISOC Newsletter." IETF Chair.

Martin and Leben. *DECnet Phase V: An OSI Implementation*. Maynard, MA: Digital Press, 1992.

Mosher, Robyn. August 1991. "A Peaceful Coexistence for TCP/IP and OSI." *Networking Management Magazine*.

Rose, Marshall. *The Open Book: A Practical Perspective on OSI*. Englewood Cliffs, NJ: Prentice Hall, 1990.

IMPORTANT TCP/IP STANDARDS (FROM RFC 1200)

All Internet standards are published as RFCs. However, not all RFCs specify standards. (Some of them are notes with general information.) RFCs can be copied via the pointer below. Some general RFCs are mentioned here, followed by the specific networking standard RFCs.

How to Get Copies of RFCs

RFCs can be obtained via FTP from NIC.DDN.MIL, with the pathname RFC:RFCnnnn.TXT where "nnnn" refers to the number of the RFC. A list of all RFCs may be obtained by copying the file RFC:RFC-INDEX.TXT. Log in with FTP username ANONYMOUS and password GUEST.

The NIC also provides an automatic mail service for those sites that cannot use FTP. Address the request to SERVICE@NIC.DDN.MIL and in the subject field of the message indicate the file name, as in "Subject: SEND RFC:RFCnnnn.TXT."

Some RFCs are now available in PostScript. These may be obtained from the NIC in a similar fashion by substituting ".PS" for ".TXT."

Important "General Information" RFCs

The RFC 1200: "IAB Official Protocol Standards" memo is a global listing of all IAB official protocol standards. It describes the state of standardization of protocols used in the Internet as determined by the IAB. Very good information is contained here; it is highly recommended reading. (To obtain the most recent edition of the "IAB Official Protocol Standards" memo [RFC 1200], the file RFC:IAB-STANDARDS.TXT may be copied via FTP from the NIC.DDN.MIL computer following the same procedures used to obtain RFCs.)

RFC 1122/23 and RFC 1009 are two documents that summarize the requirements for host and gateways in the Internet, "Host Requirements" (RFC-1122 and RFC-1123) and "Gateway Requirements" (RFC-1009).

TCP/IP Standards by Layer

Physical/Datalink Layers (Layers 1,2)
Ethernet, X.25

Network Layer (Layer 3)
Internet Protocol (IP)—RFC 791, RFC 963, RFC 950
Internet Control Message Protocol (ICMP)—RFC 792
Address Resolution Protocol (ARP)—RFC

Transport Layer (Layer 4)
Transmission Control Protocol (TCP)—RFC 793
User Datagram Protocol (UDP)—RFC 768

Session Layer (Layer 5)   Not really defined for IP, though some RPC functionality maps to this layer; used by NFS.

Presentation Layer (Layer 6)   Not really defined for IP, though XDR functionality maps to this layer; used by NFS.

Application Layer (Layer 7)
FTP—RFC 959
TELNET—RFC 854 and 855
SMTP—RFC's 821 and 822
SNMP

IMPORTANT OSI STANDARDS

An ISO standards document is prefixed by the letters ISO, followed by a code number indicating its origin (ISO xxxx). The CCITT standards relating to data network services are prefixed by "X" (X.25, etc). The date following the number, e.g., X.25 (1984) refers to the edition of the recommendation or update.

ISO 7498—Overall ISO Seven-layer OSI Basic Reference Model Definitions

Physical (Layer 1)
   CCITT X.21: 15-pin physical connection for circuit-switched networks
   CCITT X.21 BIS: 25-pin connection similar to EIA RS 232-C

Datalink (Layer 2)
   ISO 4335/7809: High-level Data Link Control (HDLC) Specifications
   ISO 8802.2 (IEEE 802.2): Local Area Logical Link Control (LLC) Specifications
   ISO 8802.3 (IEEE 802.3): Ethernet Standard
   ISO 8802.4 (IEEE 802.4): Token Bus Standard
   ISO 8802.5 (IEEE 802.5): Token Ring Standard
   ISO 8886: Data Link Service Definition
   ISO 3309: HDLC Frame Structure
   ISO 4335: HDLC Control Elements of Procedures
   ISO 7776: HDLC Procedures—X.25 LAPB DTE
   ISO 8885: HDLC XID Frames
   ISO 9314.1: Fiber Distributed Data Interface (FDDI), Physical Labor Protocol (PHY)
   ISO 9314.2: FDDI Media Access Control
   ISO 9314.3: FDDI Physical Layer Medium Dependent (PMD)
   ISO 10038: LAN MAC Sublayer Interconnection (MAC bridging)
   EIA RS-232C: Hardware Devices
   EIA RS-422: Hardware Devices
   EIA RS-423: Hardware Devices
   ANS X3.T9.5/84-49: FDDI Station Management (SMT)

Network (Layer 3)
   ISO 8473: Network Layer protocol and addressing specification for connectionless network service
   ISO 8208: Network Layer protocol specification for connection-oriented service based on CCITT X.25 specifications
   CCITT X.25: Specifications for connecting data terminal equipment to packet-switched networks
   CCITT X.21: Specifications for accessing circuit-switched networks
   ISO 8348: Network Service Definition
   ISO 8648: Internal Organization of the Network Layer
   ISO 8878: Use of X.25 to provide the OSI connection-mode network service
   ISO 8880.1: Protocol combinations to provide and support the OSI network service—general principles

ISO 8880.2: Protocol combinations to provide and support the OSI network service—provision and support of the connection-mode network service

ISO 8880.3: Protocol combinations to provide and support the OSI network service—provision and support of the connectionless-mode network service

ISO 8881: Use of X.25 over local area networks to provide the OSI connection-mode network service

ISO 9542: End system to intermediate system routing exchange protocol for use with the protocol for defining the connectionless-mode network service

ISO 10589: Intermediate system to intermediate system intradomain routing exchange protocol for use in conjunction with the protocol for providing the connectionless-mode network service (ISO 8473)

TR 9575: OSI Routing Framework

TR 9577: Protocol Identification in the Network Layer

Transport (Layer 4)

ISO 8072: OSI Transport Layer service definitions

ISO 8073: OSI Transport Layer protocol specifications

ISO 8602: Protocol for providing the connectionless-mode transport service

Session (Layer 5)

ISO 8326: OSI Session Layer service definitions, including transport classes 0, 1, 2, 3, and 4 (TP0–TP4)

ISO 8327: OSI Session Layer protocol specification

Presentation (Layer 6)

ISO 8822/23/24: Presentation Layer specifications

ISO 8649/8650: Common Application and Service Elements (CASE) specifications and protocols

OSI Lower Layers:

Task To Task: OSI Session and OSI Transport

Applications (Layer 7)

X.400: OSI specification for electronic message handling (electronic mail)

FTAM: OSI specification for File Transfer and Access Method

VTP: OSI specification for Virtual Terminal Protocol, specifying common characteristics for terminals

JTM: OSI specification for Job Transfer and Manipulation standard (similar to a Remote Job Entry [RJE] function)

ISO 8571: File transfer, access, and management (FTAM)

ISO 8640: Service definition—Association Control Service Element (ACSE)

ISO 8650: Protocol Specification—Association Control Service Element (ACSE)

ISO 9040: Virtual Terminal Service: Basic Class

ISO 9545: Application Layer Structure

IMPORTANT DECNET STANDARDS

For more details on the following protocols, see the DECnet Phase IV General Description.

Physical Layer (Layer 1)

Physical media includes thinwire and thickwire coaxial cable, twisted pair cable, RS-232, and other electrical/wiring standards, and numerous device controllers.

Datalink Layer (Layer 2)

Digital Data Communications Message Protocol (DDCMP)—ensures integrity and correct sequencing of messages between adjacent nodes.

Ethernet Protocol—allows communication between adjacent nodes connected by an Ethernet Local Area Network.

X.25 Protocol—implements the X.25 packet level (3) and X.25 frame level (2) of the CCITT X.25 recommendation for public data interfaces.

Routing Layer (Layer 3)

DNA Routing Protocol—handles routing and congestion control.

End Communication Layer (Layer 4)

Network Services Protocol (NSP)—handles all the system-independent aspects of managing logical links.

Session Control Layer (Layer 5)

DNA Session Control Protocol—used for functions such as sending and receiving logical link data, and disconnecting and aborting logical links.

Network Application Layer (Layer 6)

Data Access Protocol (DAP)—used for remote file access and transfer.

Network Virtual Terminal Protocol—a family of protocols used for terminal access throughout the network.

X.25 Gateway Access Protocol—allows a node which is not connected directly to a public data network to access the facilities of that network through and intermediary gateway node.

SNA Gateway Access Protocol—allows a node which is not connected directly to an IBM SNA network to access the facilities of the SNA network for terminal access and remote job entry.

The Loopback Mirror Protocol—used for network management logical link loopback tests.

Network Management Layer (Layer 7)

Network Information and Control Exchange (NICE) Protocol—used to trigger down-line loading, up-line dumping, testing, reading parameters and counters, setting parameters, and zeroing counters.

Event Logger Protocol—used to record significant occurrences in lower layers. An event could result from a line coming up, a counter reaching a threshold, a node becoming unreachable, etc.

Maintenance Operation Protocol (MOP)—performs data link level loopback tests, remote control of unattended systems, and down-line loading/up-line dumping of computer systems without mass storage.

DNA PHASE V ARCHITECTURAL SPECIFICATIONS

Bridge and Extended LAN Archietecture

Common Management Information Protocol (CMIP) Specification

CSMA/CD Data Link Functional Specification

CSMA/CD (Ethernet) Local Area Network Specification

Data Access Protocol (DAP) Functional Specification

DDCMP Functional Specification

DDCMP Network Management Specification

Distributed Authentication Security Service (DASS)

Distributed System Management Entity Model

Distributed System Security Architecture Preliminary Design

DNA Naming Service Functional Specification

DNA Phase V General Description

Engineering Requirements for the DEC RPC Architecture

Enterprise Management Architecture—General Description

Event Logging Functional Specification

Foundation Services Specification

HDLC Specification
Local Area Transport Architecture

Maintenance Operations Functional Specification

Making the Transition from Phase IV

Modem Connect Functional Specification

Network Control Language (NCL) Specification

Network Interconnect (NI) Node Product Architecture Specification

Network Management Architecture

Network Routing Layer Functional Specification

NI Node Product Architecture Specification

NSP Functional Specification

OSI Transport Protocol Functional
Specification

OSI Upper Layer (OSUL) Architecture

Representation of Time for Information
Interchange

Session Control Layer Functional Specification

Terminal Software Architecture Foundation
Services Specification

Terminal Software Arcitecture Network
Command Terminal Specification

Time Service Functional Specification

Unique Identifier Functional Specification

X.21 Functional Specification

X.25 Access Specification

4

TCP/IP

Michael Smith

INTRODUCTION

TCP/IP has become a far-reaching and pervasive subject—more than can be covered in one chapter. TCP/IP now runs on almost every computer system. This chapter focuses on understanding what TCP/IP does, why it has become so successful, TCP/IP roots, the systems that made it successful, and where that success may lead.

The network and transport protocols that are the backbone of the UNIX, University, government research, and some commercial computing networks today are discussed. This chapter examines IP as a network protocol and TCP as a transmission service. A view of the protocol that reveals its architectural scope and inherent limitations is provided.

WHAT IS TCP/IP?

TCP/IP is a term for a data communications architecture based on layered protocols, designed to minimize the effects of heterogeneous transmission systems, allowing processes in hosts to communicate over networks without regard to underlying topologies. In other words, TCP/IP is a common way for computers to communicate.

TCP/IP grew out of an effort by the Department of Defense (DoD) to architect a common data communication standard. Today, TCP/IP-based products are the fastest growing segment of the networking business.

TCP/IP has not always been so popular. In the late 1970s and early 1980s, many considered TCP/IP "inferior" technology to Xerox Network Systems (XNS) protocols. Many believe that Xerox could have pre-empted TCP/IP by putting all of XNS (including upper layers such as Clearinghouse, Courier, and Virtual Terminal) into the public domain. TCP/IP's limited addressing capabilities, difficulty supporting things like bit synchronous communications, and weaknesses in the "upper layers" make TCP/IP a target of DNA, SNA, and OSI proponents.

In spite of these limitations, TCP/IP is very successful. TCP/IP has been successful for several reasons. The three factors contributing most heavily to TCP/IP's success are

- DoD funding
- free ARPAnet
- Berkeley (almost free) UNIX

Other factors include the following.

- Its "open" nature, due to the fact that no commercial vendor controls the specifications.
- Its simple model provides error-free data communication across a wide variety of heterogeneous transmission systems.
- Its maturity. Both IP and TCP have been a stable specification for years and have been implemented many times.
- Its following. More than 20,000 college students have been involved with the development and support of the Internet. 20,000 devoted college students (working mostly for free) could make almost anything successful.

TCP/IP success will be limited for several reasons.

- IP's limited address structure is already a problem. RFC 1827 describes these limits in detail.
- Its lack of upper-layer support (e.g., APPN or ACSE equivalents) makes more work for network application developers and causes more interoperability issues.
- It's a U.S. standard. Foreign countries are forced to follow something that is essentially beyond their control.
- The main test-bed of TCP/IP, the Internet, has evolved into a production network. Innovation has been made more difficult. This drives many college students to development systems (e.g., OSI IS-IS).
- While every computer systems vendor is offering TCP/IP products, all have announced OSI as their choice of future systems architecture.

TCP/IP MODEL

TCP/IP's architectural model is similar to the classic OSI seven layers only at the network and transport layers (see Figure 4.1). Even at these layers, TCP/IP deviates. For example, the Internet Control Message Protocol (ICMP) is both a part of IP and a client as well. IP's network interface does not map to a data link. Rather, IP ties to any transmission system at almost any layer.

TCP and IP can be distinguished by their distinctly different roles.

- IP deals with the network.
- TCP deals with the end-system processes that use the network.

ISO's OSI   FNC's TCP/IP

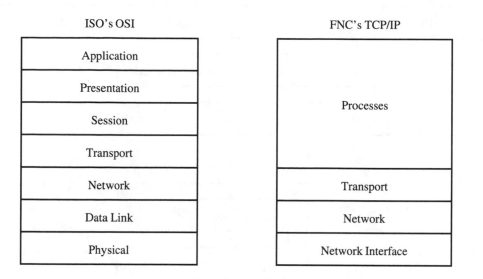

Figure 4.1 The Federal Network Council's TCP/IP model as compared to the International Standards Organization's Open System Interconnect.

Processes in TCP/IP are monolithic (see Figure 4.2).

- telnet for terminal emulation
- ftp for file transfer
- smtp for electronic mail

They provide their own session support, data representation and interpretation, association control, and other process services. Since there are no standard protocols within TCP/IP for these higher levels, there are no common elements to speed implementation or enhance interoperability (see Figure 4.3).

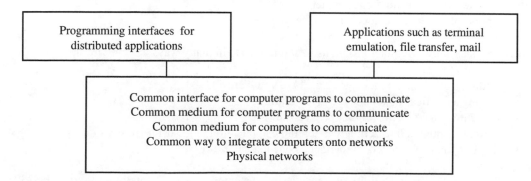

Figure 4.2 TCP/IP processes.

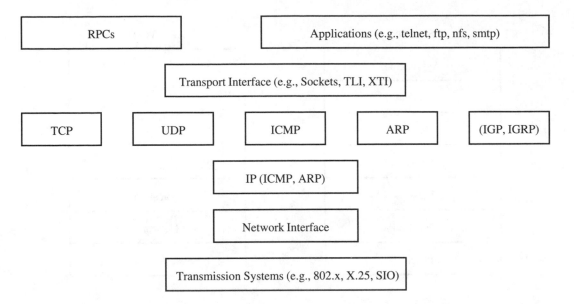

Figure 4.3 Protocol hierarchy.

TCP/IP defines a standard model to homogenize various networks for passing streams of data between processing running on different machines. (In this context, network means anything from a transmission system, e.g., Ethernet, to a complete network infrastructure such as X.25. These streams of data are multiplexed across networks by packet switching.

TCP/IP provides computer systems

- datagram service (connectionless and unreliable)
- basic broadcast datagram services
- address resolution
- connectionless, reliable datagram service
- connection-oriented data stream service
- facilities for routing and management
- support of widely used network applications

These services allow computer programs to communicate in many ways, ranging from

- sending a brief, single message (e.g., "Are you there?")
- sending a notification to many (e.g., an alarm)
- transmitting a collection of data (e.g., a file)
- facilitating human interaction with a remote application (e.g., airline reservation system)
- coupling many computers to interact as one logical processor

TCP/IP does this over a variety of transmission systems (e.g., X.25, satellite, Ethernet, RS232), dealing with errors, dynamic changes in communication paths, translating different physical addresses to a common network address, providing security, and allowing for management.

THE IP NETWORK

ARPAnet

When the DoD needed a test-bed for their new communication architecture in 1968, it commissioned (through the Defense Communications Agency) building of several data communication networks as part of the Defense Advanced Research Projects Agency (DARPA) Internet Project. (See Postel, Jon.) ARPAnet, a research/academic network, is one of these data communication networks.

ARPAnet began in 1969, connecting the University of California at Los Angeles, Stanford Research Institute, the University of California at Santa Barbara, and the University of Utah. This original network tied a Scientific Data Systems (SDS, later bought by Xerox) Sigma 7, IBM 360/50, DEC PDP-10, and SDS 940 together.

ARPAnet was not originally TCP/IP based. The original four nodes were connected via Interface Message Processors (IMP, based on Honeywell 316 minis) over telephone lines, using a packet switch protocol called the Network Control Program (NCP). This supported two applications—telnet and ftp. TCP/IP was introduced in 1975. A very good summary of ARPAnet can be found in the October 1989 issue of *ConneXions*. The 1979 Bolt Beranek Newman (BBN) ARPAnet "Completion Report" describes the full details.

INTERNET PROTOCOL (IP)

Definition

The Internet Protocol describes an unreliable, connectionless, packet-oriented data communication mechanism. This mechanism allows machines to send/receive electronic data in a basic way over many different media without considering these differences. IP does for data what the post office did for letters. When you send a letter, you do not need to know where or how or by what means it travels. You just need to know where you want it to go (by addressing it). You really do not even need to know that address's physical location.

IP is described in RFC 791 and other RFCs, including 760, 1154, 1025, 815, 781, and 1071. Detailed descriptions are also available in Comer and Stallings.

Network Interface Layer

The network interface is an abstraction of the underlying transmission system that allows IP to work with a variety of different systems in the same way. This abstraction is achieved by two conditions

First, IP must compromise by using least common denominator functionality across transmission systems. For example, even though X.25 provides virtual circuit capabilities, IP cannot pass this reliable service up to its clients (e.g., TCP).

Second, IP must have a broad and robust set of common denominators to prevent it from becoming a bottleneck—abilities to use a wide range of packet sizes, data rates, and address resolutions.

VERSION	HEADER LENGTH	SERVICE TYPE	PACKET LENGTH
IDENTIFICATION	FLAGS	FRAGMENT OFFSET	
TIME TO LIVE	PROTOCOL	HEADER CHECKSUM	
SOURCE IP ADDRESS			
DESTINATION IP ADDRESS			
IP OPTIONS	PADDING		

Figure 4.4   The IP header fields.

Examples of Network Interface Layers

4.3BSD and XINU are publicly available examples of TCP/IP implementations, including network interfaces. MS-DOS and IBM PC-DOS use a Network Device Interface Specification (NDIS) that is available to the public. Other operating systems vendors publish their own interfaces.

IP Header

The IP header is 20–24 octets long and contains 12–14 fields. Some of these fields break down into subfields not described here (see Figure 4.4). Some of these fields have obvious meaning (e.g., source IP address). VERSION is the version number of the Internet Protocol. This is needed as changes are made so that each end can rationalize back to a version that both understand. SERVICE TYPE describes the importance, throughput, reliability, and delay. IDENTIFICATION, FLAGS, and FRAGMENT OFFSET are used to break down and reassemble the packet through networks that cannot handle large packets. TIME TO LIVE specifies how long (not precisely) the packet can be sent through the Internet without being delivered. PROTOCOL specifies which higher layer protocol (e.g., TCP, ARP) created the datagram. IP OPTIONS field is typically used for testing and debugging.

Internet Control Message Protocol (ICMP)

The ICMP describes a mechanism for messages needed to manage the Internet. Management includes control, error reporting, and discovery. ICMP is not a higher layer protocol such as TCP, but rather a part of IP. This does not model well, but ICMP's functionality is critical to the function of IP.

The ICMP header contains a TYPE FIELD (one octet) and various data fields. The TYPE FIELDS are

- 0   Echo Reply
- 3   Destination Unreachable
- 4   Source Quench
- 5   Redirect (reroute)

- 8   Echo Request
- 11   Time Exceeded for a Datagram
- 12   Parameter Problem
- 13   Timestamp Request
- 14   Timestamp Reply
- 15   Information Request
- 16   Information Reply
- 17   Address Mask Request
- 18   Address Mask Reply

RFC 792 describes ICMP in detail.

Address Resolution Protocol (ARP)

ARP is a way to map and translate physical addresses (e.g., the Ethernet address of a UNIX host, the Token-Ring address of a PC, the X.25 address of a mainframe) into an IP address (e.g., 128.213.34.82) and vise versa. This is needed to allow machines to address each other in a common way.

Address resolution is achieved through a series of broadcasts and/or direct messages. If a source wishes to know a destination's address, it might send a broadcast (ARP request) asking for an IP's physical address. It might also send a request to a specific device. This device would have been designated as a proxy for remote devices. Since most broadcasts do not go beyond a router (an IP gateway), routers often act as proxies, using their own physical addresses.

A converse protocol exists for the purpose of allowing machines to discover their own IP address—Reverse Address Resolution Protocol (RARP). This is used by machines that must share a small pool of IP addresses or machines that boot from the network.

RFC 826 describes ARP in detail. RARP is described in RFC 903.

Routing Protocols

IP does not describe the protocols used to route datagrams through the Internet. Today, there is no single definitive routing protocol. The most widely used protocol today is Routing Information Protocol (RIP), taken from XNS. Another widely used routing protocol, IGRP, is proprietary. Other routing protocols include OSPF, IS-IS, and Hello.

Routing is an involved subject. Routing protocol subdivisions follow.

Internal vs. External   Routers (or IP gateways) define the boundaries between a network and the Internet (or that which is not the network). This is usually viewed in terms of what can be controlled locally and what cannot be. An analogy might be phone systems.

If your company has a phone system, the people who run it can decide your phone's number, what services your phone set provides (e.g., second line, voice mail), and who you can and cannot call. Less obviously, these people manage how calls are connected within the company (e.g., over microwave, fiber, satellites). Rules established to manage this could be called **interior protocols.** When someone in the company wants to call another country, the company usually accedes control to an outside phone company, which has its own rules. These rules could be called **exterior protocols.** (Phone people do not actually call their rules interior/exterior protocols, but people who route data over Internetworks do distinguish these.)

Distance vs. Link State Algorithms   There are two common ways to decide which route to send a datagram—the short way or the fast way. Some routing protocols (e.g., RIP) measure the distance (actually, the number of routers) between source and destination to decide which route to send a packet. Others (e.g., OSPF) just look down their links (roads) to see the clear/fast way. The algorithms that distinguish these alternatives are very involved and quite different.

In short, distance-based routing protocols are simpler but scale poorly (because every router needs to know about every other router to judge distance). Link state (or vector) algorithms scale better but are more complex.

Dynamic vs. Static   There is a somewhat archaic distinction between static routing protocols (used in very old or very small Internets) and dynamic routing protocols (most used today). With static routing, tables are loaded into routers or end systems and generally not changed. This is simple but does not manage contingencies. For example, when a link fails, there is no automatic way to reconfigure the routes. Dynamic routing handles contingencies well but is more complex.

IP ADDRESSING

Purpose of Network Addressing

Network addressing must facilitate network routing. The first premise of addressing is **global uniqueness.** Every point on the network must be uniquely and lastingly identified. This means that the address space must be at least as large as the number of nodes on the network. Also, the address of a node should not require changing if it physically moves or the topology changes. However, this may partly be in conflict with another "rule" of addressing that says the lower-layer service point (e.g., MAC address) should be derived easily from the network address. This association can expedite end routing (e.g., just extract the MAC address from inside the network address and insert it into the MAC header).

Next, the network addresses must have **uniform scheme** or **dynamic handling.** Addresses must be consistent enough in format to allow dynamic handling. This means that even though the address is not fixed in size for other characteristics (e.g., ASCII, binary), it must be of uniform design to allow the network to route. In theory, this rule could allow an infinite number of schema. In practice, there are two limitations.

1. The address scheme cannot be too simple.
2. The address scheme cannot be too complex.

If the address is too simple (e.g., a random number), it may not facilitate intelligent routing. This would then mean that either the source must supply the routing information, the intermediate nodes must have unique information about every needed destination on the network, or the data goes to many places other than its destination. If the addressing scheme is too complex, the routing service may not be able to figure out how to forward it quickly enough. (This is one reason why MAC-level bridges outperform routers.)

Optional Uses of Network Addressing   Network addressing allows for more than routing of data. By providing a unique identity to every point on the network, the entire system can be directly controlled. For example, it can facilitate administration (accounting, service, and support) and provide security.

Network/Host Address   The IP address is a single, fixed-length value that represents a host within a network. Networks are logically delineated by network numbers and physically partitioned by network routers (known as Internet gateways). The network number and the host address share the address space. See the next section for the syntax of IP addressing.

IP networks tie heterogeneous topologies together into a catenet. IP addressing facilitates the routing of data over this catenet, masking the differences of the underlying topologies. The two-part address facilitates this routing in a simple way. However, its simplicity is also its weakness. By defining only one profile of delineation, there are no provisions for different topologies. Regarding all networks (Ethernet, Token Ring, X.25, ISDN, etc.) the same way ignores the characteristic advantages of each, making other network functions, such as administration, more difficult.

The IP Address Format

The IP Internet address is 32 bits broken into four groups. It is typically represented by twelve decimals separated into decimal triads by decimal points; for example, "221.008.100.012." This is known as **dotted decimal notation.** Each triad represents one octet and, therefore, has a range of values between 0 and 255. The values 0 and 255 are exceptional cases.[1] An IP address such as 345.987.555.256 would not be valid, for each triad's value is greater than 2^8. The value of the first triad defines the class of the Internet address. This class determines which triads are treated as the network portion and the host portion of the address. This is broken down in Table 4.1. 001.001.001.001 through 127.254.254.254 are Class A addresses. 128.001.001.001 through 191.254.254.254 are Class B addresses. And 192.001.001.001 through 223.254.254.254 are Class C addresses. 009.001.001.001 through 009.254.254.254 would be all the nodes on a Class A network with a network number of 009. And, 203.100.231.001 through 203.100.231.254 would be all the nodes on a Class C network with a network number of 203.100.231. In addition, IP multicasts use the 254.000.000.000 through 255.255.255.255 range. IP multicast traffic is typically contained within each subnet.

---

1   In certain contexts, certain fixed addresses have specific functional significance. For example, the address 0 is to be interpreted as meaning "this," as in "this network." The address of all 1s means "all," as in "all hosts." For example, the address "144.016.255.255" can be interpreted as all the hosts on network 144.016. Or, the address "000.000.000.037" can be interpreted as meaning host 37 on "this network."

Table 4.1 The IP Address Format

Address Class	Decimal Range	HEX Range	Binary Representation	IP Address Format n = network, h = host
A	0 to 127	00-7F	00000000-011111111	*nnn*.hhh.hhh.hhh
B	128 to 191	80-8B	10000000-101111111	*nnn*.nnn.hhh.hhh
C	192 to 223	C0-DF	11000000-110111111	*nnn*.nnn.nnn.hhh

The first three bits in the IP address indicate whether you have a big network, Class A with up to 16,516,350 (255^2*254) "host" nodes; a medium network, Class B with up to 64,770 (255^2*254) "host" nodes; or a small network, Class C with 254 "host" nodes. It also means there are 127 possible Class A networks, 16,002 (63*254) possible Class B networks, and 1,999,996 (31*254^2) possible Class C networks. All totaled, that is about 2 billion unique addresses, or slightly less than half the 2^{32} possible with four octets.

Two billion might still sound like a lot, until the Network Information Center (NIC[2]), which is the authority responsible for assigning network numbers, assigns to you a Class C address and you realize there are 1,000 nodes on your network, each with 32 points to cover. This means you have 254 host addresses for 32,000 addressable points to cover.

IP Subnets

An obvious limitation to IP addressing is the potentially small number of addresses available. The problem is compounded by the fact that every addressable network port on every node must have a separate IP address. In many cases, Class C addresses are assigned to those who have several "small" segments and have Internet gateways (routers) linking them together. The reasoning behind this is the limited number of Class A and Class B addresses. The NIC asks, "Why give out a Class B network address when a few Class C addresses might do?"

Subnet Masking   Subnet masking is a convention for partitioning the host portion of the IP address into subnetwork and host parts. Subnet masking does not extend the IP address. It somewhat makes a Class B address into a bunch of Class C addresses or a Class A address into a bunch of Class B addresses. So, instead of being assigned a few Class C addresses, you can argue to get a Class B address and do your own subnet masking. This gives you the latitude to have more than 254 host addresses on a segment and still have your Internet gateways do their job.

Specifying a Subnet Mask   The IP address is either "nnn.hhh.hhh.hhh," "nnn.nnn.hhh.hhh," or "nnn.nnn.nnn.hhh." When an Internet gateway gets a packet with one of these addresses to forward, it masks out the Internet (nnn) portion of the address. Depending on the address class, the mask varies

---

2 At Stanford Research Institute (SRI) International, Menlo Park, California.

Table 4.2   Possible Subnetwork Addresses

078.000.000.000	078.016.000.000	078.032.000.000	078.048.000.000
078.064.000.000	078.080.000.000	078.096.000.000	078.112.000.000
078.128.000.000	078.144.000.000	078.160.000.000	078.176.000.000
078.192.000.000	078.208.000.000	078.224.000.000	078.240.000.000

from eight to twenty-four bits. With subnet masking, you effectively make the first part of the host portion (hhh) of the address into a part of the Internet (subnetwork) address.

Example 1: Class A Internet Address

This example is a large company that has been assigned one Class A address. They have sixteen large local area networks (LANs) spread over seven cities, tied together by Internet gateways on leased (e.g., T1, 56Kbps) phone lines. Each LAN has thousands of nodes. The following mask is assigned:

255.240.000.000

This creates a subnet mask of:

(11111111) (11110000) (00000000) (00000000)

Possible subnetwork addresses are displayed in Table 4.2.

So, if a plain IP address looked like "nnn.hhh.hhh.hhh" then a subnet IP would be "nnn.ssh.hhh.hhh." In this case, "ss" represents the subnet. Wonder why the first and last addresses are crossed out? Subnet values 000 and 240 have the same functional significance as network and host addresses of 000 and 255. This means a subnet value of 240 would indicate "all subnets" and 000 would indicate "this subnet." Admittedly, using decimal notation for the octets obscures the meaning. Table 4.3 shows the translation to binary.

Any IP address having a value with a binary interpretation that overlays the masked bits will be interpreted as being on that subnet. Four masked bits means you have 2^4 combinations. When you

Table 4.3   Subnetwork Address in Binary

078.000.000.000	=	01001110.00000000.00000000.00000000
(11111111) (11110000)	=	01001110.**1111**0000.00000000.00000000
nnn.ssh.hhh.hhh	=	nnnnnnnn.**ssss**hhhh.hhhhhhhh.hhhhhhhh

Table 4.4   Subnetwork Address Options

078.071.012.134	=	01001110.01001011.00001100.10000110
(11111111) (11110000)	=	11111111.11110000.00000000.00000000
078.064.000.000	=	01001110.01000000.00000000.00000000

set this up on your network, the high four bits of the host address will be masked off. That will designate which subnetwork you are on. Address 078.071.012.134 would be on subnet 078.064.000.000. (See Table 4.4.) This is done by ANDing the IP address to the mask and digging out the subnet number. Remember, nothing happens to the IP address, the identity of the source or destination, or connection service. It just gives the routers more of a network number to play with.

Example 2: Class B Internet Address

This example is a college campus that has been assigned one Class B address. They have eight local area networks (LANs) in three buildings, tied together by routers on leased (T1) phone and PBX lines. Each LAN has hundreds of nodes. The following mask is assigned:

255.255.224.000

This creates a subnet mask of:

(11111111) (11111111) (11100000) (00000000)

Possible subnetwork addresses are displayed in Table 4.5. The router would only know this is a Class B address and that the subnet mask was (11100000) because it is specified. Once again, the first and last addresses are crossed out because they are special cases. (See the previous explanation.) To the rest of the world, 128.042.097.012 just specifies a network node on Internet address 128.042. Subnet masking has no effect on Internet Routing Tables.

THE TCP "COMPUTER OPERATING SYSTEM"

In the early 1980s, the DARPA funded development of TCP/IP protocols on a version of UNIX. Most of this work was done in 1981 by the University of California at Berkeley and BBN. This release was known as 4.1cBSD (Berkeley Software Distribution). This version of UNIX, originally designed to run on DEC VAX, became the operating system for a new class of computers—workstations (see

Table 4.5   Possible Subnetwork Addresses

128.042.000.000	128.042.032.000	128.042.064.000	128.042.096.000
128.042.128.000	128.042.160.000	128.042.192.000	128.042.224.000

Berkeley Services	Telnet	FTP	SMTP	DNS	SMTP	NSF
						XDR
						RPC
BSD TCP Sockets						
TCP UDP						
IP						
Network Interface Layer						
802.3	802.4	802.5	X.25		FDDI	SIO

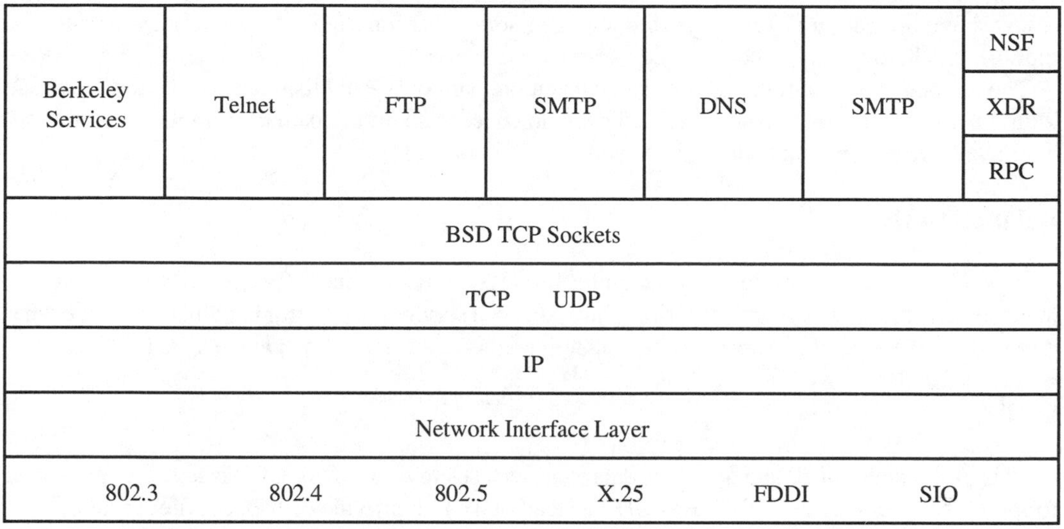

Figure 4.5   BSD version 4.x.

Figure 4.5). Commercial versions of UNIX for workstations (e.g., SUN OS) adopted most of Berkeley's TCP/IP functionality. You can get a copy of the Berkeley UNIX, including TCP/IP, by contacting the Computer Systems Research Group in the Computer Science Division of the University of California at Berkeley. The current release is 4.3rBSD, which includes OSI protocols.

TCP/IP, as an extension of the UNIX, is bound into the **kernel** (along with the device drivers tying IP to the Network Interface) when the UNIX kernel is built. This procedure varies with the implementation of UNIX.

IP and TCP run as background processes (system daemons). System daemons begin when the operating system is booted, are always available, spend most of the time waiting to send/receive data, and often create other processes (often transient) to handle requests. These services are made available as process groups (like the control process group for terminals) via interfaces such as sockets. (Stevens explains this in detail; see References.)

TRANSPORT CONTROL PROTOCOL (TCP)

While IP circulates datagrams between machines, TCP handles the traffic of programs (tasks, processes, etc.) that run on these machines. IP relates to machines—hardware with physical addresses. TCP relates to information agents that send and receive files, messages, transactions—streams of data.

Definition

TCP defines the mechanisms for providing a reliable stream between processes that send/receive electronic data. If the post office is a way to describe IP, the phone may be a metaphor for TCP. With letters, communication is very asynchronous and somewhat unreliable (especially as it relates to timing). It is hard to carry a conversation over the mail.

The phone acts as a circuit to carry a conversation. You only establish that connection once, use it until the conversation is completed and have no concern about the path of the call (e.g., satellite, microwave, fiber) or what happens once you are disconnected.

Relation to IP

TCP is a client of IP and uses IP's datagram services to move data. TCP provides virtual circuit management, reliable delivery, buffering, and associated services (e.g., error handling). Imagine what it would be like to manage a post office that delivered one word at a time, at the speed of light.

UDP

UDP is also a client of IP and uses IP's datagram services to move data. UDP is a datagram service for processes. For example, NFS uses UDP instead of TCP to provide distributed file services.

UDP provides unreliable datagram services to processes that do not want to deal with the overhead of TCP. Simple messages, semaphores, acknowledgments, and alerts are more quickly sent using UDP.

As a client of IP, UDP uses datagram services to move data. UDP provides the ability to distinguish multiple destinations (e.g., programs) at a given machine. But processes must deal with an unreliable mechanism and with errors, data loss or corruption, duplication, delays, etc.

UNIX Processes and TCP/UDP

TCP/UDP is accessed via ioclt (input/output control) system calls and signals (asynchronous notifications or software interrupts). The metaphor for this is called **sockets** (establishing connections) or **streams** (a continuous flow of octets). This allows processes to communicate within a machine or across an Internet. (This is also explained at length by Comer and Stevens; see References.)

Transport Layer Interfaces   In order to use the services of TCP, mechanisms must exist for applications to access these services. Early network applications used proprietary mechanisms, often creating monolithic modules. 4.2BSD provided a standard **application programming interface** (API) for accessing these services in UNIX, called sockets. TLI and XTI, newer APIs built on this model, are transport independent.

Sockets   The metaphor of sockets is very appropriate in describing the nature of this service interface. The socket interface was first implemented in 4.1cBSD UNIX and has since been ported to SUN OS, UNIX V, XENIX, OS/2, and even DOS.[3]

---

3   The sockets metaphor is closely tied to the UNIX conventions for file I/O (pipes, streams, etc.). These conventions do not always apply to other operating systems. Sockets for DOS has numerous differences from UNIX.

When a process requests the network services of the system, it calls for a socket (system connection) with a particular protocol:

socket_descriptor = socket (family, type, protocol);

This returns an identifier, not unlike a file descriptor, that identifies a socket through which passes communication of the kind specified in the socket request. This is like a guest calling the hotel operator for an outside line (the guest may want local or long distance, international, operator assist, etc.). The parameters of this call follow.

Family: UNIX internal protocols, IP, XNS, CLNP, IMP
Type: stream, datagram, raw, sequenced packet, message
Protocol: UDP, TCP, ICMP, raw

Once this socket has been identified, a program can use it for communication irrespective of the types of networks, distances, etc. Services include

bind(socket_descriptor, socket_address, len) to identify
connect(socket_descriptor, remote_address, len) to contact
accept(socket_descriptor, caller_address, len) to answer
send(socket_descriptor, buffer, len, flags) to transmit
recv(socket_descriptor, buffer, len, flag, caller_address, len)
close(socket_descriptor) to "hang up"

These calls form the basis for TCP/IP communication.

Transport Layer Interface (TLI)   TLI (and its sister, the X-Open Transport Interface—XTI) is another transport level interface similar to sockets. In fact, TLI/XTI supports most socket primitives. These interfaces differ from sockets in the context of the STREAMS architecture (developed by AT&T). However, the services are very similar to sockets.

Other Interfaces   Within the UNIX environment, sockets, TLI, and XTI are the predominant APIs for accessing TCP. There are also higher level APIs that access the transport, either directly or through sockets/TLI/XTI. For other operating systems, de facto APIs have been ported over TCP/IP.

Remote Procedure Calls (RPCs)

RPCs, developed by SUN Microsystems,[4] are a part of the STREAMS architecture developed by AT&T and advocated by others (e.g., NetWise, SUN). STREAMS architecture includes TLI, too. Remote Procedure Calls are a much higher abstraction of an API that manages differences in

---

4 RFC 1050, June 1988.

machines, process identification, and even data representation. Originally designed for UNIX, NetWise has ported this interface to a wide variety of other operating systems.

NetBIOS

The NETwork Basic Input/Output System (NetBIOS) developed by Intel/Sytek/IBM/Microsoft, is the prevalent LAN API for PCs. Most often associated with a "redirector" that directs file I/O to the network, NetBIOS uses a control block protocol to provide five basic services.

- General Services (e.g., reset, status)
- Name Support
- Datagram Service
- Session Control
- Session Data Transfer

NetBIOS is documented in several texts.[5]

APPLICATIONS

Many applications use TCP. Three of the original applications are terminal emulation, file transfer, and electronic mail.

TELNET

TELNET terminal emulation actually predates TCP. Before networks, terminals were attached to hosts via serial lines. Telnet was a transparent means for doing the same thing over a network. TELNET is basic character mode. Today, X-Windows is becoming the dominant graphics-mode terminal emulation. However, TELNET is still by far the most widely used. Screen control is managed through escape sequences (common to the particular ASCII terminal) and several control functions. They are:

- Interrupt Process
- Abort Output
- Ping
- Erase Character/Line
- Synchronize
- Break

---

5   A good article on the NetBIOS interface is in *3TECH*. (See References—Kouri and Nolde, and Smith.)

FTP

FTP is a basic file transfer protocol. It is generally an interactive process (like TELNET) that allows copying of files from one system to another. There are a large number of commands to establish connections (including access control), view file systems, check status, provide translation, and even a help facility.

SMTP

SMTP is Simple Mail Transfer. It allows for messages to be sent/received asynchronously, including aliases, groups, and forwarding. SMTP also has provisions for attachments, including binary files.

SNMP

The Simple Network Management Protocol (SNMP) is not really an application, but is often manifested as one. SNMP agents reside in systems running TCP/IP and are managed by SNMP systems (e.g., SUN Net Manager, Hewlett-Packard OpenView, Synoptics Lattisnet). SNMP provides discovery, configuration management, diagnosis, and control.

CONCLUSION

TCP/IP is a robust, mature networking technology with widespread support and many implementations. TCP/IP is based on network support and transmission services. It provides a basic framework for building large complex network infrastructures.

REFERENCES

Black, U. B. *OSI—A Model for Computer Communication Standards*. Englewood Cliffs, NJ: Prentice Hall, 1991.

Comer, D. E. *Internetworking with TCP/IP*. Vol I. Englewood Cliffs, NJ: Prentice Hall, 1990.

Comer, D. E. and Stevens, D. L. *Internetworking with TCP/IP*. Vol. II. Englewood Cliffs, NJ: Prentice Hall, 1990.

Kouri, M. and Nolde, W. 1991. "The NetBIOS Application Interface," *3TECH* 1, no. 3.

Postel, Jon. 1981. *Computer Network*, no. 5.

Smith, M. 1991. "TCP and OSI Addressing," *3TECH* 1, no. 3.

Stallings, W. *Handbook of Computer-Communication Standards*. New York: Macmillan, 1987.

Stevens, W. R. *UNIX Network Programming*. Englewood Cliffs, NJ: Prentice Hall, 1990.

5

XNS

John Stidd

INTRODUCTION

Xerox Network Systems (XNS) was the earliest internetworking protocol suite. It is still one of the most commonly used protocol suites in distributed networks composed of multiple local area networks (LANs). XNS is used by Xerox's office systems products, but most XNS networks are not from Xerox. Many LAN providers, including Ungermann-Bass and 3Com, have supported XNS as one of the methods of internetworking. Other network providers, such as Novell (NetWare) and Banyan (Vines) have used XNS as a base for the development of their own network architectures. (See References—Miller.) (It is really only the XNS Internet Transport Protocols, described in this chapter, that have been used by providers other than Xerox. The XNS upper layers, Courier and the Application Layer protocols, have largely been used only by Xerox products.)

In recent years, the importance of XNS has lessened, as the information technology industry has embraced non-proprietary network architectures, such as TCP/IP. It is likely that this trend will continue, with the ultimate adoption of the Open Systems Interconnection (OSI) protocol suite modeled in ISO 7498 and detailed in many ISO standards. However, it is still appropriate to include XNS in a handbook of this type, both for historical reasons and because of the still significant XNS install base.

It is not possible here to provide a complete treatment of all aspects of XNS. There is literature that does this, but it occupies a few feet of bookshelf space. Here, we are hovering over the subject in order to understand how it all fits together and how additional details can be obtained on the parts of interest. In addition to the references, a complete bibliography of XNS standards and instructions on how to order them are provided at the end of the chapter.

In the late 1970s and early 1980s a group of people working at Xerox Corporation's Palo Alto Research Center (PARC) and Office Systems Division (OSD) developed a distributed network architecture for data communications and computer services called Xerox Network Systems (XNS). This same group also developed Ethernet, covered elsewhere in this book, and the Star Workstation, which introduced the graphical user interface entities like windows and icons that are so familiar today on personal computer systems and UNIX workstations. The Star and XNS were born and grew up together. The two efforts were synergistic, and the products of a vision of an office systems technology that would revolutionize the workplace. The Star has been covered in many places, and is outside the scope of this book. In this chapter, we will focus on XNS, and attempt to provide an overview of it and the many documents that define it.

XNS is a network architecture that supports distributed computing. By distributed computing we mean a network of computer resources, some of which are owned and controlled by single users (workstations), and others that are shared resources, such as file services. A user of a distributed system has a local computer system with the capability to manipulate local data, and a connection to an extended network offering shared information and functions, such as large databases, high-speed printing, and electronic mail. XNS enables the construction of distributed computing networks that literally cover the earth.

Xerox Corporation's research and development facilities are completely interconnected by XNS. Sitting at my desk in California, I can

- Send and receive electronic mail, including compound documents, to and from New York, Dallas, every country in Europe, Japan, and other Asian countries.
- Retrieve a document from a file service in Tokyo (or, more typically, from a local file service).
- Print a document on either of two printers that are within 50 feet of my office, or on any other printer on the network, except that I would not normally use a printer that I could not walk to.
- Interconnect with and use other networks, such as the ARPA/NSFnet, through gateway facilities.

THE ARCHITECTURE OF XNS

XNS supports a distributed system that is a group of interconnected Ethernet LANs, as shown in Figure 5.1. Each of the LANs connects some number of user workstation systems and shared server systems. LANs are interconnected through Internetwork Routing Services (IRS). Figure 5.1 is intended to show a small typical configuration, rather than to display all of the possibilities.

XNS is a suite of communications protocols that provides both connectivity and application functionality throughout an extended network of Ethernets interconnected by point-to-point communications vehicles such as leased lines. The term used in the XNS standards to concisely indicate such extended networks is **internet.** The citizens of an internet can be any of several different types of user workstations or personal computers, and can also be shared resources called **services** of various types. The services provided on an XNS network can include filing, printing, mail, and several different types of gateways to other types of networks and systems. There is no master entity, such as a mainframe computer, that controls an XNS network. In this regard, XNS networks are similar to OSI and TCP/IP networks, and unlike, for example, IBM's early System Network Architecture (SNA) networks.

Today it is traditional to support a discussion of network architecture with an illustration showing the relationship of the subject to the seven-layer OSI Reference Model. Figure 5.2 is such an illustration. The rest of this section assumes familiarity on the part of the reader with OSI. Readers unfamiliar with OSI may wish to skip directly to the section on Internet Transport Protocols.

At Layers 1 and 2 (Physical and Data Link), three separate protocol suites are presently supported. Most of the citizens of an XNS internetwork will be connected to an Ethernet. Ethernet is one of the

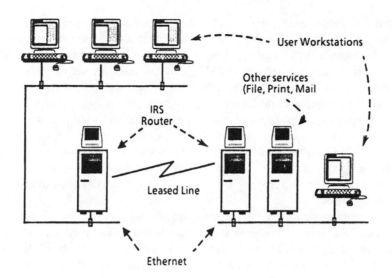

Figure 5.1   Small XNS internetwork.

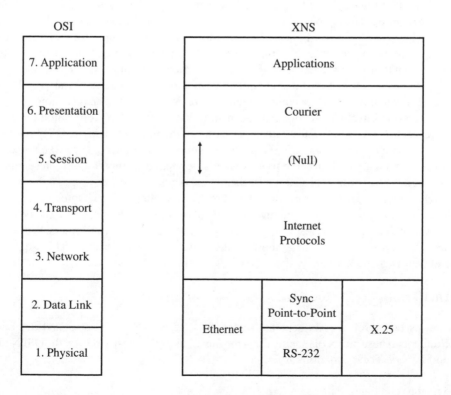

Figure 5.2   XNS and OSI.

earliest and still one of the most widely used LAN technologies. Ethernet is covered in detail elsewhere in this volume. Here it will be sufficient to state that Ethernet is a bus-type LAN with a transfer rate of 10 megabits per second operating over a maximum distance of 1,500 meters.

Two point-to-point wide area network (WAN) protocol suites are also supported, primarily to enable IRS routers to communicate with each other over longer distances. The Synchronous Point-to-Point protocol at the Data Link Layer runs over the telephone system using dedicated (usually leased) lines. Switched (dial-up) lines are not supported, for the reason that IRS routers must frequently communicate with each other, whether or not there is any Application Layer traffic between them. The XNS Synchronous Point-to-Point protocol is documented in the standard of that name. (See Bibliography.) Briefly, this protocol uses a bit-synchronous framing format and a computed frame check sequence for error detection, as in High-Level Data Link Control (HDLC). (See References—ISO 3309.)

Routers can also communicate through packet-switched data networks by using the X.25 protocol suite. (X.25 is actually a Network Layer protocol. The illustration is not quite correct in this regard. The XNS protocols use X.25 in much the same manner that the Internet Protocol (IP) uses X.25 over the ARPA/NSFnet, i.e., a point-to-point connection over which the internetwork Network Layer entities communicate.)

The six Internet Transport Protocols collectively accomplish the same functions as the OSI Network and Transport Layers, including data exchange, routing, and end-to-end error detection and recovery, where required. The equivalents of both connection-oriented and connectionless Transport are provided by the XNS Sequenced Packet Protocol and Packet Exchange Protocol, respectively. The Internet Datagram Protocol provides most of the OSI Network Layer functionality, with the Routing Information Protocol used to enable IRS routers to know of the next router to which a packet must be sent in order to move a step further toward its destination. Other Internet Transport Protocols have no exact OSI counterparts. More complete information is given in the next section.

XNS has no Session Layer. All session management is done at the XNS Application Layer.

Courier, the Remote Procedure Call Protocol, is shown in the illustration at the OSI Presentation Layer. Courier is the XNS equivalent of ISO Abstract Syntax Notation One. (See References—International Standard 8824.) Both of these protocols provide a standard method of representing data exchanged by higher-level protocols. Courier further defines standard message types to be employed in client-server dialogues. There is more information on Courier later in this chapter.

At the Application Layer, XNS has a number of protocols to support the various Network Services offered by Xerox, including Mail, File, Print, Clearinghouse, Authentication, and others. In the section on the XNS Application Layer, a table showing the correspondence between XNS Application protocols and their OSI counterparts will be given.

The Internet Transport Protocols

As mentioned earlier, there are six separate protocols. Collectively they are called the Internet Transport Protocols. These protocols supply the same functions as those provided by the OSI Network and Transport Layers. These functions are

- Routing and relaying of data
- End-to-end connection (virtual circuit) establishment, where required

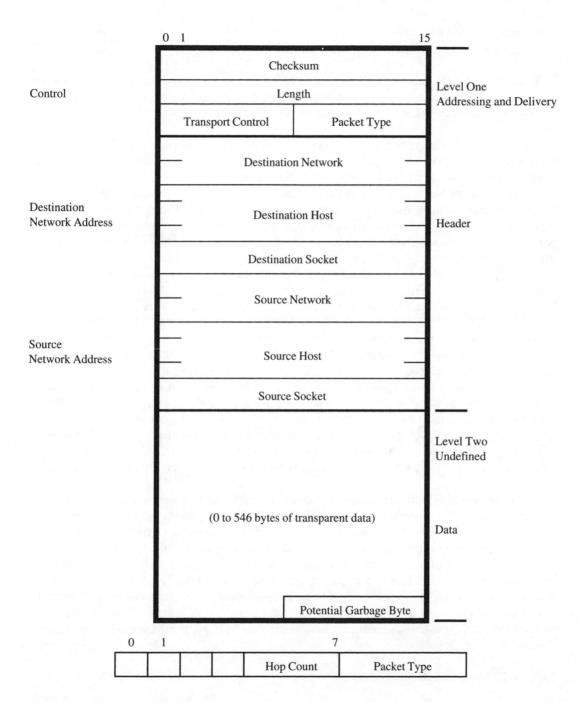

Figure 5.3 The internet packet.

- Error detection and recovery
- Maintenance of internetwork topology information to enable routing

XNS subdivides the Internet Transport Protocols into two levels. Level One includes the Internet Datagram Protocol, which is used to route packets through the internetwork. **Packets** are up to 546 bytes of data representing the Level Two protocols. Figure 5.3 shows the format of an internet datagram.

An internet datagram contains four control fields, source and destination addresses for the datagram, and data. It will be helpful to discuss the addressing first. Each address consists of three fields: a Network Number, a Host Number, and a Socket Number.

A **Network Number** uniquely identifies the Ethernet on which the addressee resides. Network Numbers must be unambiguous over an internetwork, and can and should be globally unique, in order to support the connection of previously unconnected internetworks. A registration authority exists to provide globally unique Network Numbers. The Network Number is used by a router to identify the Ethernet to which a packet should be sent.

A **Host Number** uniquely identifies the addressee. The Host Number is also an Ethernet protocol entity and is assigned by a registration authority operated by the Institute of Electrical and Electronics Engineers (IEEE). The Host Number is used by the destination Ethernet to transfer the packet from the router to the destination system (host). There is some redundancy in this scheme. Theoretically, the Host Number is all that is required in order to identify the source and destination systems; but in practice, the use of Network Numbers greatly simplifies the routing problem. With Network Numbers, routers are not required to know where every host in an internetwork is located.

A **Socket Number** is the logical identifier of a process within a host system. A process in the source might use Socket Number 2 to communicate with a destination process through Socket Number 7. The association of Socket Numbers with specific processes is done above Level One. The Internet Datagram Protocol only moves packets between the addresses that are supplied by its user. Some Socket Numbers are "well-known," i.e., associated with specific functions and types of processes. For example, routing information is exchanged between routers through Socket Number 1 on all routers.

In OSI parlance, this protocol is **connectionless,** meaning that each packet has complete addressing information in it and is transferred independently of all other packets on the internetwork. A connection-oriented protocol, by contrast, would support the notion of a **virtual circuit** and would number the packets in sequence. The routers would need to keep track of the source and destination addresses associated with each virtual circuit and be careful to deliver the packets to their customers in the correct sequence. There is a connection-oriented Internet Transport Protocol in XNS (the Sequenced Packet Protocol) at Level Two. Since Ethernet itself is inherently connectionless (at the Data Link and Physical Layers), it is easiest and cleanest to use a connectionless Network Layer protocol, like IDP, above it. A virtual circuit connection can be implemented at the Transport Layer, if necessary. XNS does this.

Control Fields of an Internet Datagram

Checksum.   The optional checksum is the one's complement add-and-left-cycle (rotate) of all of the 16-bit words of the packet excluding the checksum itself. The checksum may be checked by each of the intermediate routers, as well as the destination host; if found to be in error, it is permitted that the packet can simply be discarded. In other words, all error recovery goes on above Level One.

Length.   This is the length of the packet in bytes, including the checksum.

Transport Control Field.   This field is used only by routers and should be initialized to zero by the source host. It contains the **hop count,** which is incremented by each router through which the packet passes. (The router must modify the checksum when it increments the count.) The hop count is never allowed to exceed a maximum value of 16. When the maximum value is reached, the packet is discarded. This prevents the possibility of a packet being routed in an endless loop. Later on, there will be a discussion of the use of the Level Two Error Protocol to notify the source of a packet that this type of problem has occurred.

Packet Type.   This is a number that identifies which of the five Level Two protocols is being used in the data field.

A packet may be simply discarded at any time for a variety of reasons, including the reasons previously mentioned and congestion in the queues managed by the routers. The entity that discards the packet may use the Level Two Error Protocol to inform the source of the packet that this has happened, but this is not required. The reader should not be concerned about this. Higher-level services are able to detect any error that has occurred and resend the lost packets, or, in some cases, to detect that nothing has happened as a result of the transmission of a single packet and to respond to this appropriately. The approach taken by IDP and other connectionless Network Layer protocols, including that defined for OSI, works quite well on a statistical basis, and is much simpler to implement than a more complicated protocol that did error recovery between routers and maintained state information for each packet. (See References—Boggs and Schoch, and Metcalfe.)

Level Two Protocols

Routing Information Protocol (RIP).   Each IRS router in an internetwork has a routing table that identifies intermediate routers that can be used to get a packet to its final destination. The information in this table is created and maintained from data in the RIP packets exchanged between routers.

Error Protocol.   Any entity in the internetwork can use the Error Protocol to report that an error has been detected and a packet discarded. The Error Protocol packet is always sent to the source of the discarded packet. The Error protocol is a useful diagnostic tool. Its use is optional.

Echo Protocol.   The Echo Protocol is used to verify the existence and correct operation of an internet citizen. Any citizen can send any other citizen an Echo Request packet, to which the correct response is an Echo Reply packet.

Sequenced Packet Protocol (SPP).   SPP provides reliable transmission of a sequence of packets. The order of the packets is maintained, and positive confirmation of packet delivery is provided. SPP is the XNS counterpart of the OSI connection-oriented Transport Protocol. (See References—ISO 8073.)

Packet Exchange Protocol (PEP).   PEP provides the Level Two protocol for the transmission of a single packet. In addition to the data being sent, PEP packets also have a Client Type field that contains a registered value identifying the client of the protocol. This enables the destination socket to determine which of several possible process types would be interested in the packet. PEP is the counterpart of the OSI connectionless Transport Protocol. (See References—ISO DIS 8602.)

We have tried to carefully avoid giving the impression that Level Two Internet Transport Protocols correspond to OSI Transport. The reason is that some of them are performing Network Layer management functions as defined in the OSI Reference Model, Part 4: Management Framework (OSI4), in particular the Routing Information Protocol. It is better to look at the Internet Transport Protocols as performing the combined functions of the Network and Transport Layers.

Complete information on the Internet Transport Protocols can be found in the standards document of that name published by Xerox Systems Institute. (See Bibliography.)

Courier

Most XNS applications use Courier, the Remote Procedure Call Protocol to implement client-server communication. Courier protocol data units are transferred using one of the XNS Transport protocols, PEP or SPP, previously described. Courier has two primary functions:

1. To provide a standard method of representing primitive data types, such as integers, strings, and Boolean constants, and a method of specifying constructed data types such as Records and Sequences.
2. To use the above to provide a standard method of encoding remote procedure calls, returns, and abort/reject responses to calls.

A remote procedure call message is sent by a client to a service as shown in Figure 5.4. The service either returns results or reports the failure of the remote operation. From the client's point of view, a remote procedure call is like a local procedure call—the call is made and results are returned by the procedure. The remote procedure performs its execution in a remote system, but this is not particularly obvious to the client process. Instead of just staying on the stack until used by a local procedure, the parameters to the remote procedure and the value returned from the procedure are exchanged over a communications link using the lower-level XNS protocols. This is why standard methods of representing data types must be employed on both sides of the exchange. Also accessible to both sides must be the information contained in a Courier **remote program,** which defines both the sequence and types of the parameters to be exchanged by the call and return or abort/reject.

In addition to the Remote Procedure Call machinery, the Courier standard also defines the XNS Bulk Data Transfer protocol. **Bulk data** is an arbitrarily long sequence of bytes that is too large to be modeled as an argument or result of a remote procedure. A file is a good example of the type of thing that would be transferred with the Bulk Data Transfer protocol. The transfer of bulk data involves three parties: the initiator, the sender, and the receiver. The initiator requests the transfer of data from the sender to the receiver. Often, the initiator is the same entity as either the sender or receiver. A workstation client might initiate a file transfer from a file service to itself. In the more general three-party case, a workstation might initiate a transfer from one file service to another.

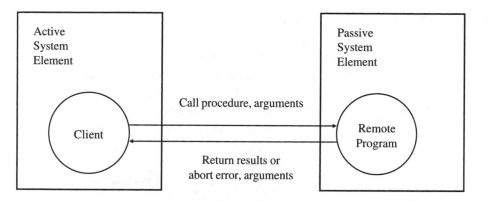

Figure 5.4   Sending a remote procedure call message.

Courier is one of the ancestors of the ISO Abstract Syntax Notation One. (See References—International Standard 8824.)

The XNS Application Layer

XNS supports a number of standard Application Layer protocols for the functions provided by distributed systems. Included are Mailing, Filing, and Printing protocols. There is also a Virtual Circuit Terminal Protocol (VTCP) that is used primarily by workstations emulating terminals communicating to remote hosts via the XNS network. Directory service in an XNS network is provided by the Clearinghouse Service and its corresponding protocol. The Authentication Service and Protocol enables processes to prove to other processes that they are who they say they are. It also provides the backbone for XNS security. The Time Protocol is used to maintain current time and date throughout the network. Table 5.1 shows the correspondence of these XNS protocols with their ISO/OSI counterparts, if such exist.

Authentication   Clients must authenticate themselves to services. They must prove that they are who they say they are. A **password** is a string of characters that is known only to the user and to the computer system that validates the user's identity. If the user enters the password correctly, he is permitted to log on to the system. In XNS parlance, this is called Simple Authentication.

The XNS Authentication Protocol supports the exchange of information between a client and an authentication service necessary to validate the client. A valid client receives a **credential** (a distinguishing piece of information), which can be presented to other services as proof that the client is authentic. In order to get access to a file service, for example, a client would first obtain a credential from an authentication service, and then attempt to log on to the file service with his own identity and the credential. The file service would check the credential for validity and verify that the specific client had the right to access the file service by checking an access control list. If both the credential and the client's identity are legitimate, access is permitted.

There is a severe problem with the security of this scheme, as it has been described so far. The physical link between the client and service can be "tapped" and the password or credential read by

Table 5.1   XNS Protocols and Their OSI Counterparts

XNS Protocol	OSI Counterpart
Mail	CCITT X.400 series/ISO 10021 Message Handling Systems
Virtual Terminal Circuit Protocol	ISO 9041 Virtual Terminal Protocol
Filing	ISO 10166 Document Filing and Retrieval
Printing	ISO 10175 Document Printing Application (going to DIS)
Clearinghouse	CCITT X.500/ISO 9594 The Directory
Authentication	no exact counterpart
Time	no current counterpart

a third party. The third party can then impersonate the legitimate client and gain access to network resources that would otherwise be unavailable to the imposter.

Remember that both client and server are likely to be on the same Ethernet. Every entity on the Ethernet can see all of the traffic on the cable connecting the entities. Ethernet citizens normally ignore all of the packets not intended for them, but nothing prevents an entity from spying, if it has been designed to do this. Even if the client and the service are on different Ethernets, a spy located on one or the other networks or on the telephone connection between them could intercept the password and other information. It must be emphasized that it is generally impractical to guarantee the physical security of the connection between two network entities.

The XNS solution to this security problem is called Strong Authentication. With Strong Authentication, every citizen of the network has a strong key used for encryption of selected data elements. This key is known to both the client and the Authentication Service. The Authentication Service itself is assumed to be secure from tampering. (This is reasonable. It is possible to provide both physical security and secure password protection for individual computer systems.)

A Strong Authentication sequence proceeds in four steps, as detailed here and shown in Figure 5.5:

1. Client A sends a request for credentials to the Authentication Service. The request includes the client's name, A, the name of the service that the client wishes to use, B, and a random number called the **nonce,** generated by the client.
2. The authentication service knows A's key and uses it to encrypt four pieces of information to be returned to A: the credential that A will send to B as proof of identity, the nonce, B's name ("B"), and a conversation key for use between A and B. The client should verify that the nonce and B's name are the same as those sent in step 1. This is to foil a bogus authentication service from replaying an earlier real response. Since this information is encrypted with A's key, a bogus client A would not be able to read it. The credential contains A's name, an expiration time, and the conversation key. Also, it is encrypted with B's key.

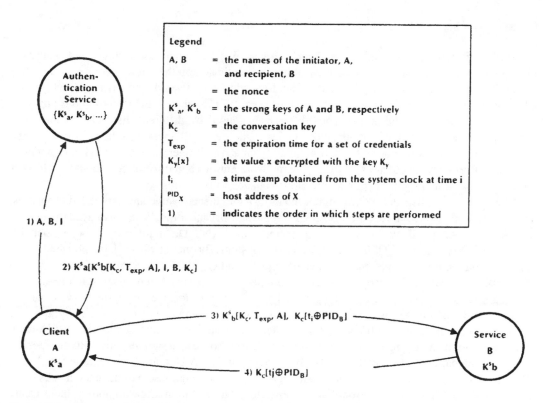

Figure 5.5   Strong Authentication.

3. A sends a log on request to B that includes the credential and a timestamp encrypted with the conversation key. This log on request normally belongs to some other Application Layer protocol and includes the authentication information along with other information required by the other protocol. B decrypts the credential and extracts the conversation key, the expiration time, and A's name. B knows that the credential was originally produced by the authentication service because it was encrypted with B's key. Therefore, it knows that the client A is legitimate. In order to use the credential, A had to decrypt it using A's key. The expiration time provides a limited life to the credential. B knows that it was recently produced. The conversation key enables B to decrypt the timestamp. If all of the information is correct and consistent, A is permitted to log on to B, assuming A has the right to do this. There is no way for any entity to pose as A without knowing A's strong key.

4. B returns a message to A containing another timestamp exclusive or'ed with B's processor ID and encrypted with the conversation key. A can decrypt this to determine that it is actually B that responded.

The encryption technique used in Strong Authentication is the algorithm defined in FIPS 46, Data Encryption Standard (DES). (See References—Federal Information Processing Standard 46.)

Clearinghouse

XNS has a directory service called the **Clearinghouse.** The Clearinghouse is a distributed service, meaning that, from a client's point of view, it may be replicated on the internetwork. Any instance of the Clearinghouse Service may be used to find the attributes associated with any name or any other Clearinghouse operation. From a client's point of view, all instances of the Clearinghouse provide the same services, ignoring performance differences caused by different distances on the internetwork. A client will typically use the closest Clearinghouse for all operations. Each instance of the Clearinghouse does not replicate the entire directory database. Rather, each Clearinghouse contains directory information about a subset of the internetwork entities and information about which other Clearinghouses contain information about entities outside its own subset.

Each entry in the distributed Clearinghouse has a Distinguished Name and associated properties. The name is composed of three parts: Object, Domain, and Organization. When displayed to humans, the parts are separated by colons (:). For example, my XNS Distinguished Name is John M. Stidd:OSBU North:Xerox. (OSBU stands for Office Systems Business Unit.) A Distinguished Name can have aliases. For example, mail addressed to just Stidd:OSBU North:Xerox will reach me. All of the citizens of an XNS network have names, not just the users. The printer nearest to my office is Wintergreen:OSBU North:Xerox. My personal file drawer is located on a file service named DeAnza:OSBU North:Xerox. The Domain and Organization names usually have geographic or organizational significance to humans, but the Clearinghouse doesn't care about this. The Domain and Organization names are used by the distributed Clearinghouse to assign responsibility for specific subsets of the name space to particular Clearinghouse entities. A Domain Clearinghouse will have all of the names belonging to its domain. An Organization Clearinghouse will have the names of all of the Domain Clearinghouses for that Organization. Organization Clearinghouses have easily constructed names, so that the Clearinghouse entity that initiates a search for a name can address the Organization Clearinghouse. (See References—Oppen and Dalal.)

Each Distinguished Name in the distributed Clearinghouse is associated with Properties, which are attributes of the named object. One of the Properties possessed by many of the objects in the Clearinghouse is the object's Network Address, consisting of a Network, a Host, and a Socket, as discussed previously in the section on Internet Transport Protocols. Objects that want to access services have a Strong Key Property. This is retrieved from the Clearinghouse by the Authentication Service during the creation of a credential for the client object, as previously described. (This is an example of a service, in this case Authentication, being the client of another service, Clearinghouse. In fact, virtually all of the XNS services are clients of Clearinghouse.) There are dozens of other properties, many of them specific to particular types of objects. More complete information can be found in the standards documents for Clearinghouse listed in the Bibliography.

Even an apparently simple interaction between a client and service requires a number of other interactions with the Authentication and Clearinghouse services. This is not a problem for human users, since client software on the workstation handles all of these interactions automatically, in a manner that hides them from the user.

Mailing

The XNS Mail Service is a network service that supports multiple clients. From the view of a client, XNS Mail provides an internetwork-wide–store-and-retrieve service for messages to other clients. The most common occurrence of this type of process is, of course, the software in a user's workstation that interchanges mail with other users by communicating with the Mail Service. There are also automatic processes that use the Mail Service. In particular, the Clearinghouse Service uses the Mail Service to update the distributed Clearinghouse database. (See References—McClain.)

Filing

XNS Filing Protocol supports networked file services that can be accessed by clients in order to store and retrieve files. The XNS File Service supports directories and subdirectories to any level of nesting. A file has a number of attributes, including a type assigned by its owner, and several timestamps and user names indicating when it was last accessed, for what purpose, and by whom. The Filing Protocol uses the Courier Bulk Data Transfer protocol to accomplish actual file transfers and provides additional machinery for the storage and retrieval of file attributes.

XNS Filing is functionally similar to the ISO 10166 Document Filing and Retrieval (DFR) standard.

Printing

XNS provides a Printing Protocol that enables clients (usually workstations) to send documents to networked print services with instructions on the paper size to be used, the number of copies to be printed, and other properties of the print job that are not included in the document itself. A high-end networked printer might offer such capabilities as two-sided printing, stapling, and other forms of document finishing. These options can be invoked through the XNS Printing Protocol, in conjunction with a Print Service (computer process) that can directly control the operation of the printer.

Much of the philosophy and capability of the XNS Print Protocol is being embodied in an international standard under development, "Document Printing Application (DPA)," which is planned to become ISO 10175. It is expected that DPA will be needed by OSI and other networks that support printers with complex page composition and document-finishing capabilities.

Virtual Terminal Circuit Protocol (VTCP)

VTCP is used between a client that needs access to resources outside the XNS internetwork and a service that provides a gateway to these resources. The VTCP client is often terminal emulator software that provides an asynchronous terminal or IBM 3270 window on the user's workstation. The service controls the telephone connection and simply passes data between the client and the outside resource once the connection is established.

Time

XNS maintains a time standard across the internetwork. A client can request the time from any Time Service on the internetwork. The distributed Time Service provides the time and date to clients, in the form of a 32-bit number of seconds elapsed between 12:00 A.M. on January 1, 1968, and the present. The Time Service response packet also includes information about the time zone of the service responding, so that the client can format the time appropriately for a user. The Time Protocol is just the Packet Exchange Protocol previously discussed, with a Client Type of TimeService (1). The Time Services communicate among themselves in order to maintain a common time. (See References—Marzullo.)

CONCLUSION

This has been a brief and high-level overview of the pieces of XNS and how they interact in a distributed internetwork. The best sources of detail on XNS protocols are the standards documents themselves, listed in the Bibliography. The Xerox XNS General Information Manual contains more overview material on XNS and discusses XNS in the context of the Xerox product line. All of the standard references are available from the standards organizations and from third-party suppliers of standards documents. Many of the other references are available from the Xerox Palo Alto Research Center and the National Technical Information Service (NTIS).

REFERENCES

Boggs, David R., Schoch, John F., Taft, Edward A., and Metcalfe, Robert M. July 1979. "Pup: An Internetwork Architecture." Xerox Palo Alto Research Center.

Federal Information Processing Standard 46. Data Encryption Standard (DES). U. S. Department of Commerce.

International Standard 7498—Information Processing Systems—Open Systems Interconnection. Basic Reference Model, Geneva: ISO.

International Standard 7498-4—Open Systems Interconnection—Basic Reference Model—Part 4: Management Framework. Geneva: ISO Secretariat. April 24, 1989.

International Standard 8824—Information Processing Systems—Open Systems Interconnection. Specification of Abstract Syntax Notation One (ASN.1). Geneva, ISO.

ISO 3309, Data Communications—High-Level Data Link Control Procedures—Frame Structure. 1979.

ISO 8073, Information Processing Systems—Open Systems Interconnection. Connection oriented transport protocol specification. July 1986.

ISO DIS 8602, Information Processing Systems—Open Systems Interconnection. Protocol for providing the connectionless-mode transport service. August 1985.

Marzullo, Keith A. "Maintaining the Time in a Distributed System." Ph.D. diss. published by Xerox Office Systems Division in OSD-T8401. Stanford University, 1984.

McClain, Gary R., ed. *Open Systems Interconnection Handbook*. New York: McGraw-Hill (Chapter 9, X.400 and Xerox Network Systems Mail by John Stidd), 1991.

Metcalfe, Robert M. "Packet Communication." Ph.D. thesis, Harvard University M.I.T. Project MAC TR-114, December 1973.

Miller, Mark A. *Internetworking, A Guide to Network Communications*. Redwood City, CA: M&T Books (pages 286–288 have a discussion of the Novell, Banyan, and 3Com XNS implementations), 1991.

Oppen, Derek C. and Dalal, Yogen K. 1981. "The Clearinghouse: A Decentralized Agent for Locating Named Objects in a Distributed Environment." OPD-T8103. Xerox Corporation.

BIBLIOGRAPHY

This is a complete bibliography of all of the XNS standards documents published by Xerox. All are available to be ordered from the Xerox Systems Institute (XSI), located at 3400 Hillview Avenue, Palo Alto, California, 94304. Please contact XSI for pricing and ordering information.

XNS Protocol	Document Number	Description (Taken from the XSI Catalog)
Authentication Protocol	XNSS 098605	Defines the Authentication Protocol used in Xerox Network Systems starting with Office System Software Release 5. This document also serves as a guide for using the Authentication Service.
Bulk Data Transfer (Appendix F to Courier)	XNSS 098605	Describes a standard that facilitates the construction of distributed systems by providing a single bulk data transfer discipline for an open-ended set of higher-level application protocols.
Character Code Standard	XNSS 059003	This standard specifies the character codes to be used for exchange of text information among Xerox Network System elements and the forms in which sequences of numerical codes can be represented. The primary purpose of this document is to provide an accurate specification of character codes and the encoding of a string of these codes.

XNS Protocol	Document Number	Description (Taken from the XSI Catalog)
Clearinghouse Entry Formats	XSIS 168404	Defines Clearinghouse property types and the structure of their entries in terms of Courier data types.
Clearinghouse Protocol	XNSS 078404	Defines the Clearinghouse directory service protocol used in Xerox Network Systems. This document also serves as a guide for using a Clearinghouse Service.
Courier: The Remote Procedure Call Protocol	XNSS 038112	Describes Courier, the Remote Procedure Call Protocol—the request/reply discipline used by many application protocols in Xerox Network Systems.
The Ethernet, A Local Area Network: Data Link Layer and Physical Layer Specifications	XNSS 018211	Contains the specification of the Ethernet, a local area network developed jointly by Digital Equipment Corporation, Intel Corporation, and Xerox Corporation. The Ethernet specification is the result of an extensive collaborative effort by the three corporations, and several years of work at Xerox on an earlier prototype Ethernet. It is intended as a design reference document, rather than an introduction or tutorial.
Filing Protocol	XNSS 018211	Describes a protocol for interaction between clients and file services. It is both a guide for using a File Service, and a specification for the implementation of such a service.
Font Interchange Standard	XNSS 239007	Defines a digital representation for interchange of fonts and font metrics.
Internet Transport Protocols	XNSS 029101	Describes the family of internetwork packet transport protocols used uniformly across the variety of communications media, digital processors, and office applications in Xerox Network Systems. This document is not a rigorous specification in the formal sense, but describes the protocols and provides the rationale behind many of their features. It also provides the necessary information for designing an implementation.
Interpress Electronic Printing Standard, Version 3.0	XNSS 049011	Defines a digital representation for interchange of material to be printed or otherwise imaged.
Magnetic Tape Format Standard	XNSS 248810	Provides a magnetic tape format that is used to communicate data between computer systems. It enables users to access remote services via magnetic tape in a manner consistent with uni-directional communications facilities (refer to Simplified Transport Protocol).

XNS Protocol	Document Number	Description (Taken from the XSI Catalog)
Mailing Protocols	XNSS 148812	Defines the protocols used to support the exchange of electronic mail on Xerox Network Systems. Included are the client-to-service protocols and the message formats. This document is intended as essential reference information for implementors of Mail Service client software (e.g., workstation mail tools) rather than as a usage guide or tutorial.
Miscellaneous Printing Standards	XNSS 329009	Defines a number of miscellaneous printing standards. This version defines alternate encodings for the Interpress Electronic Printing Language, along with standard transformations of fonts and characters into the Xerox printing architecture from other schemes.
Printing Protocol	XNSS 119005	Defines the protocol used in sending an Interpress file to an XNS printer, or to inquire about the status of the printer or the status of a print request.
Raster Encoding Standard	XNSS 178905	Defines a digital representation for interchange of all raster images.
Secondary Credentials Formats	XNSS 258605	Defines the types and formats of certain secondary credentials. Secondary credentials are arbitrary authentication data required by certain recipients, such as foreign operating systems.
Sequenced Packet Protocol Connection Parameter Negotiation	XNSS 339011	Provides a way for SPP to negotiate a set of stream parameters at connection establishment time. The parameters that can be manipulated with SPP Negotiation include parameters of the SPP Stream itself and of the lower-layer services used by SPP.
Simplified Transport Protocol	XNSS 278810	Defines a transport protocol that provides an efficient means of transferring data to XNS services via uni-directional communication facilities, such as magnetic tape.
Sixel Protocol	XNSS 298811	This data link layer protocol provides a mechanism for encoding binary data for transmission across byte-oriented restricted communication facilities.
Synchronous Point-to-Point Protocol	XNSS 158412	Describes the protocol for the interconnection of individual communicating entities or data terminal equipment over a data link.
Time Protocol	XNSS 088404	Defines the Time Protocol and time standard used in Xerox Network Systems.

XNS Protocol	Document Number	Description (Taken from the XSI Catalog)
Virtual Terminal Circuit Protocol	XNSS 349105	Defines the vehicle by which foreign protocols and formats are exchanged in support of the terminal-to-host model. The protocol provides at least for reliable transportation across the communication medium connecting the foreign system to the system element providing the transport service. Additional functions may be provided depending on the foreign system. In particular, VTCP is used by terminal emulator clients to communicate with services connected to remote hosts.
XNS General Information Manual	XNSG 068504	Provides a general overview of XNS services and Xerox products supporting XNS. 182 pp.

III

OPEN SYSTEMS INTERCONNECTION AND RELATED STANDARDS

6

OPEN SYSTEMS INTERCONNECTION (OSI)

Kenneth M. Zemrowski

INTRODUCTION

The OSI standards were developed to allow computer systems built by different vendors to exchange data. Even though these computer systems have different operating systems and vary in how data is processed internally, as long as the information that passes between the processors conforms to the OSI international standards, information can be interpreted upon receipt and communication is possible. Openness, in this context, does not necessarily imply that the network is public.

With the growing importance of computer interconnection, there was a need for increasingly sophisticated and powerful communications standards, as well as improved planning to support future growth and produce well-coordinated, timely standards. By the early 1980s, proprietary solutions were causing difficulty in establishing networks. (Unfortunately, the process of gaining industry-wide consensus can often be time-consuming.)

By developing a Reference Model of OSI, ISO expected to provide a common basis for the coordination of standards development for the purpose of systems interconnection, while allowing the existing standards to be placed into perspective within the overall reference model.

Open Systems Interconnection (OSI) involves the exchange of information between open systems, but not the internal functioning of each individual system. (Open systems environments would be concerned with the openness of individual systems, and the portability of the applications. OSI is primarily concerned with interoperability.) This exchange of information is facilitated by the mutual use of applicable standards.

The OSI Reference Model does not provide a protocol (or even selection of protocols). Rather, it provides a conceptual and functional framework that allows international teams of experts to work productively and independently on the development of standards for each layer of OSI. Another consideration was the ability to accommodate existing protocols in the framework. The OSI model has sufficient flexibility to accommodate advances in technology and expansion in user demands.

This flexibility is also intended to allow the phased transition from existing implementations to OSI standards. Besides flexibility to accommodate change, the framework helps support planning.

OSI addresses both the network interconnections and the interworking of applications. Applications may be user-developed, or include standard applications such as message handling or file transfer.

The important principles are that (1) each layer performs a unique, generic, well-defined function, and (2) layer boundaries are designed so that the amount of information flowing between any two adjacent layers is minimized. A particular layer has to provide a sufficient number of services to the layer immediately above for that layer immediately above to properly perform its functions.

The functions of each of the protocol layers will be explained later in this section. The protocols can be connection-oriented or connectionless. In connection-oriented protocols, a user must set up a virtual connection, which is valid for the life of the communications activity, and disappears when the communications activity disappears. The converse of this is connectionless activity, whereby the user does not set up a virtual connection but communicates by transmitting individual "pieces" of information. An example of the former is a telephone conversation; an example of the latter is message delivery by the postal service.

OSI standards have been developed under the aegis of the International Organization for Standardization (ISO), with many of the standards developed collaboratively with the International Telephone and Telegraph Consultative Committee (CCITT).

BASIC PRINCIPLES OF LAYERING

The first step in OSI standards development was the creation of an OSI Reference Model. This model, developed by the International Standards Organization (ISO), is divided into seven layers; each layer provides a well-defined set of functions necessary for the effective transmission of data. Each of these layers provides a service to the layer above by carrying on a conversation with the same layer on another processor. The rules and conventions of that conversation are called a **protocol.** The information that is passed between a layer on one processor and the corresponding layer (or peer entity) on another processor is called a **protocol data unit (PDU).**

The OSI framework imposes a seven-layer model to define the communications processes that occur between systems. (See Figure 6.1.) The Reference Model (ISO 7498-1:1984) describes seven layers, as well as the relationships between a layer and the layer below it. The reference model, and other standards, define the services necessary to perform the functions. Other standards specify the protocols for how the information is actually communicated. Only protocols are actually implemented; the service definitions describe the structures and functions that are performed—while the protocols describe the detailed formats and dialogues.

Service primitives are special messages that define the services that a layer provides. The details of how the services are implemented are transparent to the service user, which is usually the next upper layer. Communication between layers is via a service access point (SAP), which is a special location through which service primitives pass. Service request and service response information pass between adjacent layers at the service access point. Service definitions are defined primarily for the purpose of developing protocol specifications.

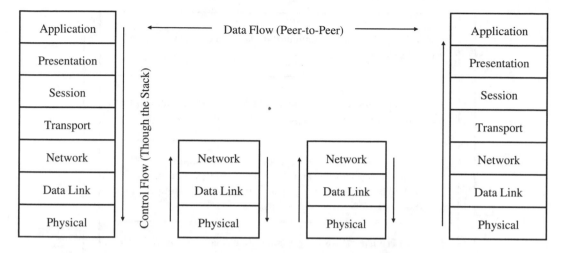

Figure 6.1   Data flow and control flow from end system through intermediate nodes to end system.

For any layer (N+1), the reference models describe services provided by the immediately lower layer (N). For example, the Application Layer (Layer 7) uses services provided by the Presentation Layer (Layer 6).

Layers 1 to 6, together with the physical media for OSI, provide a step-by-step enhancement of communication services. The boundary between two layers identifies a stage in this enhancement of services at which an OSI service standard is defined while the functioning of the layers is governed by OSI protocol standards. In several cases, there are several standards defining services and protocols for a particular layer, especially at the Application Layer.

According to ISO/IEC 7498-1, several principles are used in determining the seven layers in the Reference Model and will also guide future decisions.

1.   Do not create so many layers as to make the system engineering task of describing and integrating the layers more difficult than necessary.
2.   Create a boundary at a point where the description of services can be small and the number of interactions across the boundary are minimized.
3.   Create separate layers to handle functions that are manifestly different in the process performed or the technology involved.
4.   Collect similar functions into the same layer.
5.   Select boundaries at a point that past experience has demonstrated to be successful.
6.   Create a layer of easily localized functions so that the layer could be totally redesigned and its protocols changed in a major way to take advantage of new advances in architectural, hardware, or software technology without changing the services expected from and provided to the adjacent layers.
7.   Create a boundary where it may be useful at some point in time to have the corresponding interface standardized.

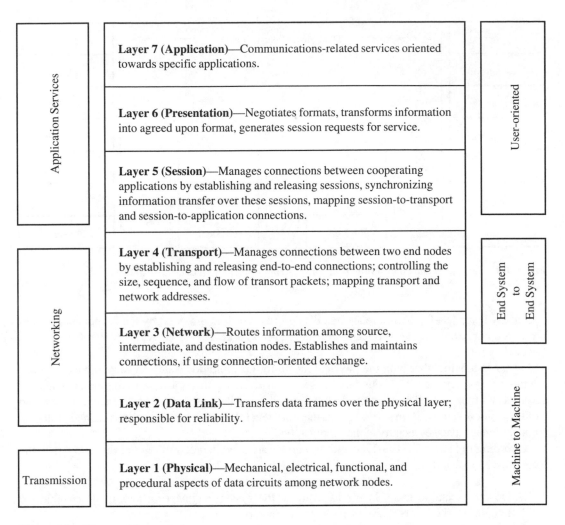

Figure 6.2 The seven-layer stack.

Within the abstract model, an open system is logically composed of an ordered set of subsystems. Adjacent subsystems communicate through their common boundary. Entities in the same layer are termed peer entities.

It is important to note the distinction between the abstract model expressed in ISO 7498-1 and the real model, which is embodied in implementations. The real model does not require discrete separations between the layers, which may reduce the protocol overhead. However, a "glued together" stack might make it more difficult to perform conformance tests, which usually rely on an exposed stack at various layers.

Use of a layered model can help understanding as well as giving a framework for developing standards (see Figure 6.2). The framework gives an organization to the functions that would need to be performed anyway. Consider an analogy with the telephone system, which will be used to introduce the names of the lower layers of the protocol stack.

Layer 1 (Physical)

Mechanical, electrical, functional, and procedural aspects of data circuits among network nodes.

Analogy   To connect to the telephone network, we must have the actual wires and connectors, and electrical signaling protocols. There are various types of connectors, definitions of voltage levels and signaling rates, and assigned functions to each wire in a cable.

Layer 2 (Data Link)

Transfers data frames over the physical layer; responsible for reliability.

Analogy   A data link is signaled (to our ears or to a fax or modem) by presence of a dial tone. Hanging up terminates a data link.

Layer 3 (Network)

Routes information among source, intermediate, and destination nodes. Establishes and maintains connection, if using connection-oriented exchange.

Analogy   In a telephone system, this activity is similar to dialing the phone number, and being processed through the various intermediate exchanges and long-distance networks.

Layer 4 (Transport)

Manages connections between two end nodes by establishing and releasing end-to-end connections; controlling the size, sequence, and flow of transport packets; mapping transport and network addresses.

Analogy   This is similar to the ringing and busy signals.

Layer 5 (Session)

Manages connections between two cooperating applications, by establishing and releasing sessions, synchronizing information transfer over the session, and mapping session-to-transport and session-to-application connections.

Analogy   Establishment and release are similar to the "Hello" and "Good-bye" of a telephone conversation (including the protocol of asking for the desired party); the conversation forms the remainder of the session. This could also be compared to the handshake between two facsimile machines through the completion of the transmission.

Layer 6 (Presentation)

Negotiates formats (if not prenegotiated) and transforms information into the appropriate format.

Analogy   Determining screen size or color capabilities when using a terminal. Choosing a common language for a human conversation.

Layer 7 (Application)

Responsible for providing services to the actual applications to accomplish information transfer, involving not only the exchanges of data but also security checks, negotiating the exchange mechanisms, and requesting specific application services.

Analogy   The purchase of a theater ticket using a telephone reservation service involves several exchanges of data.

- Examples of stacks
  - Short stacks and full stacks
- End-systems and intermediate systems (ES-IS)

In actual practice, many implementations do not include a full seven-layer stack. In some cases, a "short stack" of the lower three layers (or sometimes up to transport) are used; although this is often done for interoperability with existing systems, it is sometimes used to avoid the cost of implementing and using the upper layers. However, new techniques are being developed that minimize the overhead of using the upper three layers while preserving the OSI architecture.

In some of these approaches, the protocol data for a layer (e.g., Presentation) is minimized, but the Presentation layer is still present. Some experiments are using a single octet. Other implementations minimize turnaround times by gambling that operations will be successful; if they are, then you gain some time, although if recovery is needed, this will take a little longer. These implementations opt to trade capability for overhead.

Besides the "short stack," some implementors have begun to use a "skinny stack." Full capabilities are preserved for data transfer, but special mechanisms are used to set up and tear down an association (which is potentially very time consuming). OSI has matured to the point where there is a better understanding of the legal shortcuts.

There are instances in which even a full OSI implementation will require fewer than seven layers. OSI only uses seven layers for end systems (ES). For intermediate systems (e.g., routers), only the lower three layers are involved. In many networks, a node may serve as an intermediate system (IS) but will also be an ES for some applications.

Addressing occurs at many layers. In this discussion, it will be introduced with the Transport Layer.

The way an interface will be implemented depends to a certain extent on the way the adjacent protocol layers are implemented, and to a great extent on the operating system environment. Basically, there are two categories: an open or accessible interface and an embedded interface. An embedded interface is "invisible" to program users. The protocols are enmeshed and entangled so that there is no clear boundary between them. In an open interface, there appears to be a clear, well-defined boundary separating two distinct pieces of code.

PROTOCOLS AND SERVICES

Each layer defines data units that are used within the communication between layers. Ultimately, it includes the application data, which is augmented by overhead data to perform the necessary functions for OSI.

For any given layer, the data transferred between entities on behalf of the adjacent upper layer is considered user data. Data of the application layer is considered user data to the Presentation Layer. The principle continues downward through the OSI stack; that is, for example, the data needed by the Session Layer is considered user data to the Transport Layer (even if the Session Layer data only includes protocol control information needed for coordinating their joint operation). As shown in Figure 6.3, protocol-control-information is added to each successive data unit as the data passes down the stack; the protocol-control-information is used by the corresponding layer at the other end system. The information transferred between entities at adjacent layers to coordinate their joint operation is considered interface-control-information.

A protocol data unit (PDU) is a unit of data specified in the protocol for a layer, consisting of protocol-control-information and possibly user data of the adjacent upper layer. Protocol standards will sometimes use abbreviations such as TPDU (Transport PDU), SPDU (Session PDU), etc.

The OSI architecture does not limit the size of data units; however, protocol standards for individual layers may impose limitations. In order that efficiency or other considerations do not pose a limit to the PDU size for upper layers, blocking can be used to map several service-data units (SDU) in a single PDU. On the other hand, concatenation can be used to map multiple PDUs into a single SDU.

Separate standards are developed for protocols and services. Protocol specifications are written in terms of the data that is exchanged between layers, while service definitions describe the types of services provided by the lower of two adjacent layers on behalf of the upper layer. Because it is possible to "see" the PDUs, compliance is specified through the protocols. However, this does not weaken the determination of conformance, because if the services do not work correctly, the protocols, which are actually specified in terms of services, will not work correctly either.

The protocol is used to transfer the service request. The services are actually provided at service access points (SAPs), which have several important properties:

- When an entity requests a service from the lower layer, it is done via a service-access-point, which permits the upper layer entity to interact with the service provider.
- The entities from adjacent layers that are attached to a specific SAP are in the same system.
- The relationship between entities at adjacent layers is not one-to-one with respect to SAPs. An entity can be concurrently attached to more than one SAP at the lower layer, which could be the same or different entities; similarly, the lower layer entity can be attached through more than one upper layer entity through SAPs. However, any single SAP can only be connected to one entity at the lower and upper layers.

Service access points also become important for programming interfaces. There are efforts underway to standardize application program interfaces (APIs) so that access to the services can be portable at the source code level.

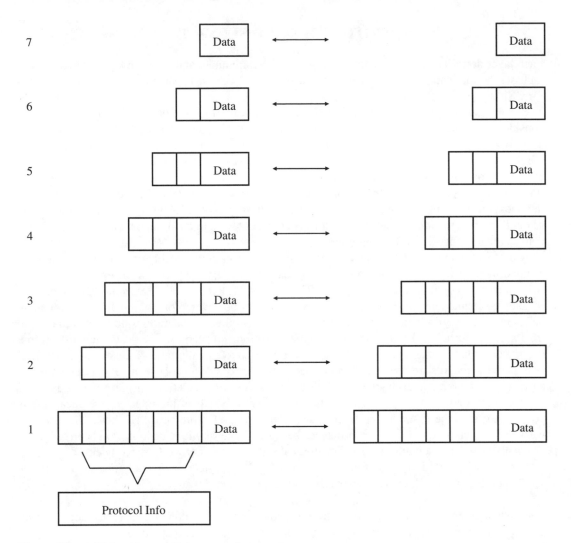

Figure 6.3   Addition of protocol data to perform services.

	Control	Data	Combined
Peer entities	Protocol-control-information	User data	Protocol-Data-Unit (PDU)
Adjacent layers	Interface-control-information	Interface data	Interface-data-unit

Figure 6.4   The passing of data between layers.

HOW AN ASSOCIATION IS ESTABLISHED

When an application entity needs to communicate with another, an association must be established between the source and destination entities. Any given application process is represented to its peer by one or more application entities (AE). The aspects of an application process that need to be taken into account for the purpose of OSI are represented by one or more AEs. An AE represents one and only one application process in the OSI environment.

For purposes of OSI, an application process is defined as "an element within a real open system which performs the information processing for a particular application."

Application entities are associated with each other at the top layer, with the associations carrying down through the stack between corresponding layers. AP titles and AE titles may be used so the AEs can be independent of their Presentation Layer addressing. An AE attaches to one or more Presentation Service Access Points (PSAPs), in order to make it addressable.

Application entities are joined through "associations," which permit them to exchange information. For information to be exchanged within two or more entities at a specific layer, i.e., (N+1), an association is established between them in the immediately lower layer (N) using an N-layer protocol; for example, to exchange information between peer entities at the Presentation Layer, an association is established at the Session Layer using the Session Layer protocol.

Regardless of the method used, establishment of an association requires some knowledge of the lower layers, which comprises:

1. knowledge of the addresses of the peer entities involved (e.g., corresponding entities in the network-to-network layers for each side of the interface)
2. knowledge of a protocol agreed by the peer entities for use at least to initiate communication
3. knowledge of the availability for communication of the peer entities
4. knowledge of the quality of service (QOS) available from the lower layer

At the lower layers, there are also protocols involved with connection establishment. For example, this could include an exchange of version information to ensure that both sides are using the same version of the protocol. A calling entity sends information of all supported versions to a called entity. The called entity examines whether there are any supported versions common to the calling and called entities. If there is more than one common version, the highest common version is selected. If there is no common version, the connection establishment request is refused.

At several layers, especially Network and Transport, QOS can be negotiated at the beginning of an association. For connectionless, there is no negotiation—take it or leave it. If there are minimum standards for establishing a connection (e.g., the connection is not worthwhile unless the QOS criteria can be satisfied), the connection may be rejected.

Quality of service (QOS) is the collective name given to a set of parameters associated with data transmission between (N) service access points. Different parameters can be defined for each layer. Quality-of-service parameters may be optionally selectable. The Data Link layer establishes and maintains a selected quality of service for the duration of the data link connection. The quality-of-service parameters include mean time between detected but unrecoverable errors, residual error rate (where errors may arise from alteration, loss, duplication, disordering, misdelivery of data-link-SDU, and other causes), service availability, transit delay, and throughput.

For connection-oriented service, possible parameters include:

- Expected transmission delay
- Probability of corruption
- Probability of loss or duplication
- Probability of wrong delivery
- Cost
- Protection from unauthorized access
- Priority

APPLICATION LAYER

All OSI services needed by the application process are provided by the Application Layer. The generalized interface at the Application Layer is supplied by ACSE. Specialized services, such as FTAM and MHS, also provide commonly needed general functions.

The highest level of abstraction is the Application Process (AP). All other features of the Application Layer serve to support the AP. All other layers serve to support the communication between two application entities. An AP represents a set of resources, including processing resources, within a real open system that may be used to perform a particular information processing activity. An AP may organize its interactions with other APs in whatever way is necessary to achieve a particular information processing goal. An AP is an abstract representation of those elements of a real open system that perform information processing for a particular application. It represents a set of resources, including processing resources, within a real open system that may be used to perform a particular information processing activity.

Any given application process is represented to its peer by one or more application entities, so there can be more than one connection. An application entity is an active element within an application process, embodying a set of capabilities pertinent to OSI and corresponding to a specific application-entity type. The aspects of an application process that need to be taken into account for the purpose of OSI are represented by one or more AEs. An AE represents one and only one application process in the OSI environment, but an AP may be represented by a set of AEs: Each AE in this set is of a different AE type. Different application processes may be represented by AEs of the same AE type. An AE type is a class of application entities in terms of a set of capabilities defined for the application layer.

The activity of a given AP is represented by one of more AP invocations; cooperation between APs takes place via relationships established among AP invocations. At a particular time, an AP may be represented by none, one, or more AP invocations. An AP invocation is responsible for coordinating its interactions with other AP invocations. An AP invocation is a specific utilization of part or all of the capabilities of a given application process in support of a specific occasion of information processing.

ACSEs provide common association or connection control services that are needed by a number of applications; it is more efficient to incorporate these services into a common protocol than to reproduce them, perhaps differently, in every application. The ACSE protocol performs essential services for the application, such as connection establishment, connection release, and error notification. An ACSE is an ASE that provides the exclusive means for establishing and terminating all application associations. An AE always includes an ACSE.

The Application Layer contains all functions that imply communication between open systems and not already performed by the lower layers. These include functions performed by programs as well as functions performed by human beings. The lower layers provide the services through which the application entities cooperate.

The AE contains a set of one or more application-service elements (ASEs) (always including one consistent means to establish all associations and related control functions that coordinate the various ASEs). An ASE is a set of application functions that provides a capability for the interworking of AE invocations for a specific purpose. ASEs may call upon each other and/or upon presentation services to perform their function. The only means by which application processes in different systems may communicate is through the exchange of application-protocol-data units. These APDUs are generated by ASEs. An ASE contains all the functions and corresponding APDUs that are required for a protocol machine which is logically complete and consistent in itself. The capabilities of an individual ASE are defined by the specification of a set of APDUs. This constitutes the application protocol between two ASEs of the same kind.

A service definition conveys the understanding of the function carried out by the ASE. These service definitions for ASEs are conceptual, so do not imply conformance. Service definitions may be used in defining specialized standards at the application layer.

Users may have reasons to request that the vendor provide an accessible interface to one or more layers in their implementations. An accessible Transport Layer interface allows a user to write software which uses the services of OSI Layers 1–4 to reliably transfer data between different end systems. An accessible interface to the Association Control Service Element (ACSE) allows different applications to access the ACSE to perform common application layer services. An accessible interface to the MHS Message Transfer Agent allows users to write their own User Agents, which use the services of the Message Transfer System to transfer information to each other.

The Application Layer differs from the other layers of OSI in several important respects. The internal structure of an AE is recursive; an AE is made up of one or more application service objects (ASOs), each of which is made up of a collection of application-service elements and/or application service objects and a control function. These ASEs, ASOs, and control functions are combined in various ways to form various types of ASOs and AEs. The Application Layer, as the highest layer of OSI, does not provide connections within the Application Layer. As a result, relationships formed by the transfer of information between AE invocations in the Application Layer have particular significance.

The File Transfer, Access and Management (FTAM) Protocol provides a means of communicating about groups of related information, i.e., files. A user can move files, interrogate the properties of files, and manipulate files on a variety of different systems, without knowledge of the characteristics of any particular file system. This is accomplished by means of a common communications model and language, as described in the standard.

The Message Handling Systems (MHS) application is based on the CCITT X.400 Series of Recommendations. These recommendations specify a store-and-forward Message Transfer System consisting of individual Message Transfer Agents, which cooperate to deliver a message from Interpersonal User Agents serving an originator to Interpersonal User Agents serving one or more recipients.

The Transaction Processing (TP) application supports the provision of the ACID properties (Atomicity [the total work is performed or nothing is done], Consistency [work is performed accurately and correctly], Isolation [while the work is being performed inconsistent data is not available to other transactions], and Durability [the work is fault-tolerant]) including the necessary commitment, concurrency, and recovery to support transaction processing.

The Remote Operations Services (ROS, sometimes referred to as ROS Element or ROSE) was designed originally to support coordination with processes on remote systems, particularly in an office processing environment. ROS is used by MHS and is sometimes used by applications in which the implementors want to avoid some of the details of implementation.

PRESENTATION LAYER

The Presentation Layer provides the mechanisms for achieving a machine independent representation of application data that AEs communicate. This process is related to representation and manipulation of structured data for the benefit of application programs. When networks involve end systems with differing architectures (or possibly unknown architectures), the internal representation of data may differ. Similarly, a new system may require revised structures in order to take advantage of new system capabilities.

The Presentation Layer provides for common representation to be used of the data transferred between AEs. This relieves AEs of any concern with the problem of "common" representation of information; that is, it provides them system independence. The syntactic independence is provided in the following way.

The AEs can use any syntax and the Presentation Layer provides the transformation between these syntaxes (via an encode/decode capability) and the syntax needed for communication between AEs. This transformation is performed inside the open systems. It is not seen by other open systems and, therefore, has no impact on the standardization of presentation protocols.

The abstract syntax, which is expressed in a language Abstract Syntax Notation One (ASN.1) is typically compiled off-line into a machine-readable form for the encoder/decoder to interpret while processing a particular PDU. A porting of an application dialogue defined using an abstract syntax notation is referred to as an abstract syntax.

ASN.1 is described by ISO 8824. The syntax notation is strongly typed like Pascal or Ada. This allows the Presentation Service to achieve interoperability with a very large base of OSI applications. Strong typing is also useful for detection of programming or unsignaled communication errors.

It is necessary that each side of the transfer understand the content and meaning of what is being transferred. Accordingly, the Presentation Layer will take information from the applications and convert this information into a form and structure that can be recognized and interpreted by the destination OSI end system.

The Presentation Layer covers two complementary aspects of this representation of information:

- The representation of data to be transferred between AEs
- The representation of the data structure that AEs refer to in their communication, along with the representations of the set of actions that may be performed on this data structure

Because the Presentation Layer knows the abstract syntaxes that are to be employed by the AEs, the Presentation Layer is responsible for selecting mutually acceptable transfer syntaxes.

The concrete syntax includes those aspects of the rules used in the formal specification of data which embody a specific representation of that data. The transfer syntax signifies the concrete syntax used in the transfer of data between open systems. Presentation context is an association of an abstract syntax with a transfer of syntax.

The Presentation Layer provides the following facilities:

- Identification of a set of transfer syntaxes
- Selection of transfer syntax
- Access to session services

One of the potential Presentation Layer services is special-purpose transformations, such as data compression, which can be useful in reducing the cost or time of data transmission. Presentation layer services can also be used for code conversion.

AEs agree on the abstract syntaxes that will be used for their communication. It is necessary that these abstract syntaxes are represented in appropriate transfer syntaxes for communication to take place. The structure of the APDUs of an ASE is specified by at least one named abstract syntax. To transfer these APDUs between AE invocations using the Presentation service, it is necessary to establish one or more presentation contexts for each abstract syntax. During an association, occurrences of these APDUs are linked to presentation contexts. Each presentation context specifies a pairing of a particular abstract syntax with a transfer syntax.

There is not a single predetermined transfer syntax for all of OSI. In connection mode, the transfer syntax to be used on a presentation connection is negotiated between the correspondent presentation entities. Thus, a presentation entity must know the syntax of its application entity and the agreed transfer syntax. Only the transfer syntax need be referred to in the Presentation Layer protocols.

In OSI, the syntaxes used by AEs that wish to communicate may be very similar or quite dissimilar. When they are similar, the transformation functions may not be needed at all; however, when they are dissimilar, the Presentation Layer service provides the means to converse and decide where needed transformations will take place.

Negotiation (or selection) of transfer syntax takes place between two presentation entities when an AE provides the name of an abstract syntax for which a transfer syntax is required. In connection-less-mode, the transfer syntax is selected, but cannot be negotiated. Syntaxes can be registered. At the highest level, these syntaxes may be registered through standards bodies. They may also be registered by an industry group (e.g., air traffic control) or by a single organization.

Each combination of abstract syntax and transfer syntax is called a **presentation context.** From the viewpoint of the AE, a presentation context represents a specific distinct use of an abstract syntax.

Presentation Layer Services and Organization

The services of the Presentation Layer are specified in IS 8822. The Presentation Layer deals with generic functions that are needed by many different kinds of applications; specifically, a common means is provided of representing a data structure in transit from one end system to another.

The Presentation layer is organized in terms of functional units. The kernel functional unit provides: (1) data representation functions (as described), and (2) connection-oriented functions. Representation deals with the way the actual data is coded or represented during data transfer. Connection functions deal with establishing, preserving, and managing the connection between two applications.

The Presentation Layer has sometimes been criticized for the overhead involved in processing ASN.1. Some applications may wish to forego the benefits of the Presentation Layer, while still retaining compatibility with it. To fully avoid the use of abstract syntax, Unstructured Data Transfer (UDT) can be used so that a prenegotiated format (e.g., a "record layout") can be used. Thus, the Presentation Layer will perform no services, but the cost of performing those services will be eliminated.

In recognition of the sometimes undesirable cost of using the Basic Encoding Rules (BER), Lightweight Encoding Rules (LWER) have been devised. Lightweight encoding rules are useful in applications in which some flexibility is needed, but it is possible for the formats to be prenegotiated (for example, in a well-defined interface) or other limitations are acceptable.

SESSION LAYER

The purpose of the Session Layer is to provide the means necessary for cooperating presentation entities to organize and to synchronize their dialogue and to manage their data exchange. To do this, the Session Layer provides services to establish a session connection between two presentation entities and to support orderly data exchange interactions, and to release the connection in an orderly manner. The only purpose of the Session Layer for connectionless-mode communication is to provide a mapping of transport addresses to session addresses.

The Session Layer provides user-oriented services to aid in the orderly and reliable flow of information between users in two different end systems. These services provide for increased efficiency in managing the dialogue between applications. The Session Layer protects applications and users from irregularities and problems in the underlying network. Token management is a facility of the session service, which allows correspondent presentation entities to control explicitly whose right it is to exercise certain control functions.

A presentation entity can access another presentation entity by initiating or accepting a session connection. A presentation entity may be associated with several session connections simultaneously in relation to one or more presentation entities.

The initiating presentation entity designates the destination presentation entity by a session address. In general, there is a many-to-one correspondence between the session addresses and transport addresses. This implies that at session connection establishment time, more than one presentation entity is a potential target of a session connection establishment request arriving on a given transport connection.

The session connection establishment service allows the presentation entities cooperatively to determine the unique values of session connection parameters at the time the session connection is established. The token management service allows the presentation entities to control explicitly whose turn it is to exercise certain control functions.

There are two types of dialogue control. Either end can send data at any time (duplex) or each end can take turns sending data (half duplex). In the latter case, tokens are used to control the direction of data transfer and which process is authorized to send data. Data may also be expedited, which means that it has a higher transmission priority. Data may be typed, which allows it to be sent even if the sender does not possess the token.

The synchronization services allow the connection to reset to a defined point and agree on a resynchronization point. Loss of data is possible. The Session Layer provides a synchronization facility that allows presentation entities to define and identify synchronization points and to reset a session connection to a predefined state and to agree on a resynchronization point.

The activity concept allows session service users to distinguish logical pieces of work called **activities.** Each activity consists of one or more dialogue units. Only one activity is allowed on a session connection at a time, but there may be several consecutive activities during a session connection. An activity may also span more than one session connection.

There is a one-to-one mapping between a session connection and a transport connection at any given instant. However, the lifetime of a transport connection and that of a related session connection can be distinguished so that a transport connection supports several consecutive session connections.

When providing the connectionless-mode, the Session Layer provides a one-to-one mapping of Session-connectionless mode transmission onto transport-connectionless-mode transmissions.

The Session Layer protocol is organized in terms of functional units; examples of these functional units are kernel (basic connection and data transfer) and duplex. Also included are half-duplex, expedited data, minor synchronize, major synchronize, typed data, activity management, resynchronize, and exceptions.

TRANSPORT LAYER

The transport service provides transparent transfer of data between session entities and relieves them from any concern with the detailed way in which reliable and cost-effective transfer of data is achieved.

Control of data transportation from source end open system to destination end open system (which is not performed in intermediate nodes) is the last function to be performed in order to provide the totality of the transport service. Thus, the upper layer in the transport service part of the architecture is the Transport Layer. The Transport Layer relieves higher-layer entities from any concern with the transportation of data between them. Correspondingly, the Transport Layer is relieved of any concern with routing and relaying since the network service provides network connections from any transport entity to any other, including the case of tandem subnetworks.

All protocols defined in the Transport Layer have end-to-end significance, where the ends are defined as correspondent transport entities. Therefore, the Transport Layer is OSI end system oriented and transport protocols operate only between OSI end systems. The Network Layer protocol is the highest protocol at an Intermediate System—performing services on behalf of the Transport Layer.

When providing the connectionless mode, the Transport Layer provides a connectionless-mode service that maps a request for transmission of transport-service-data unit onto a request to the connectionless-mode-network service. In connection mode, the transport service provides the means to establish, maintain, and release transport connections. Transport connections provide duplex transmission between a pair of transport addresses.

More than one transport connection can be established between the same pair of transport addresses. A session entity uses transport-connection-end point identifiers provided by the Transport Layer to distinguish between transport-connection end points.

The Transport Layer has five classes of services defined. These service classes are characterized by combinations of selected values of parameters such as throughput, transit delay, and connection set-up delay and by guaranteed values of parameters such as residual error rate and service availability. These classes are:

Class 0:   Simple class, with basic Teletex capabilities. (TP-0)

Class 1:   Basic error-recovery class, designed for X.25. Provides minimal error recovery for errors signaled by network and includes sequence numbers so TPDUs can be resequenced. (TP-1)

Class 2:   Multiplexing, which enhances Class 0 but assumes a highly reliable network without a need for error recovery. Supports multiplexing of multiple transport connections onto a single network connection. (TP-2)

Class 3:   Provides multiplexing and basic error recovery (TP-3 = TP-1 $\cup$ TP-2).

Class 4:   Error detection and recovery, providing the ability to recovery from lost or out-of-sequence TPDUs. Provides retransmission, duplicate detection, flow control, connection establishment and termination, and recovery from crashes.

The basic distinction is between connection oriented (CO) and connectionless (CL). Connection-mode transmission is appropriate in applications that call for relatively long-lived, stream-oriented interactions between entities in stable configurations. For example, Virtual Terminal, FTAM, or Job Transfer. Connectionless forms of data transmission might be associated with particular forms of data transmission such as LANs or digital radio, and particular types of applications, such as remote sensing and banking.

It is a basic characteristic of connectionless-mode service that no negotiation of parameters for a transmission takes place at the time the service is accessed and no dynamic association is set up between the parties involved. However, considerable freedom of choice can be preserved by allowing most parameter values and options (such as transfer rate, acceptable error rate, etc.) to be specified at the time the service is accessed. In a given implementation, if the local (N)-subsystem determines immediately that the requested transmission cannot be performed under the conditions specified, it may abort the transmission, returning an implementation specific error message. If the same determination is made later, after the service access has been completed, the transmission is abandoned, since the servicing layer is assumed not to have the information necessary to take any other action.

A connection is established by referencing, either explicitly or implicitly, a transport address for the source session entity and an address for each of one or more destination entities.

Multi-end point connections are connections that have three or more connection end points. Two types of multi-end point connection are currently defined: centralized and decentralized. In the

centralized mode, data sent by the entity associated with the central-connection end point is received by the entities associated with all other connection end points. The data sent by an entity associated with any other connection-end point is received by the entity associated with the central connection end point. A connection requires establishment and release procedures. Some protocols provide for the combining of connection establishment and connection release protocol exchanges.

The establishment of a connection by peer entities of a layer requires:

- The availability of a connection immediately between the supporting entities; and
- Both entities be in a state in which they can execute the connection establishment protocol exchange.

The process continues downward through the layers until an available connection is found or the physical medium for OSI is encountered. The release of a connection is normally initiated by one of the entities associated in it. Release can also occur as the result of an exception condition in the layer or layers lower than it.

Connection-oriented Transport Protocol

The basic function of connection-oriented Transport is to provide the difference between the quality of service desired by the Transport Layer user and that which is provided by the Network Layer. Messages can be broken into individual packets; the Connection-oriented Transport Protocol at the other end system reassembles the packets into a message. The protocol provides reliable, orderly end-to-end data transfer. This means that data packets are received uncorrupted and in the correct order by the Transport Layer user.

There are many parameters that are negotiated between two communicating Transport entities. These provide for proper flow control, proper sequencing, and proper error detection and retransmission of lost data. The international standard (ISO/IEC 8073:1988) contains provisions for five classes of Transport service (Class 0 through Class 4). Class 4 assumes the least about Network Layer services and provides the most capability.

Connectionless Transport Protocol (CLTP)

The Connectionless Transport Protocol (CLTP) is used to provide the Connectionless Transport Service (CLTS). The CLTP is to be used only as an option among participants with a similar capability. Although there currently are no detailed implementation agreements for connectionless protocols at OSI layers above the Transport Layer, the Connectionless Transport Protocol is included so that non-OSI applications can take advantage of its services or for future applications.

Functions used in modes of communication include those listed in Figure 6.5. Error notification may or may not lead to the release of the network connection, according to the specification of a particular network service.

The **expedited network** SDU transfer is optional and provides an additional means of information exchange on a network connection. The transfer of an expedited network SDU is subject to a different set of network service characteristics and to separate flow control.

Function	Connection Oriented	Connectionless
Connection establishment and release	X	
Suspend	X	
Resume	X	
Multiplexing and splitting	X	X
Normal data transfer	X	X
During establishment	X	
Expedited	X	
Flow Control	X	X
Segmenting	X	X
Blocking	X	
Concatenation	X	X
Sequencing	X	X
Acknowledgment	X	X

Figure 6.5   Functions used in modes of communication.

A transport entity that is receiving at one end of network connection can cause the network service to stop transferring network SDUs across the service-access point. This **flow control** condition may or may not be propagated at the other end of the network connection and thus be reflected to the transmitting transport entity, according to the specification of a particular network service. Each network entity can dynamically control (up to the agreed maximum) the rate at which it receives data-link SDUs from a data-link connection. This control may be reflected in the rate at which the Data Link Layer accepts data-link SDUs at the correspondent data-link-connection end point.

The Network Layer may provide sequenced delivery network SDUs over a given network connection when requested by the transport entities. This function preserves the order of SDUs that were submitted to the layer.

In order to limit protocol complexity, segmentation and reassembly are not provided in layers above the Network Layer. As a consequence, the size of SDUs in layers above the Network Layer is limited by the size of the PDU used in the layer below and by the size of its own protocol-control information.

Connectionless

Connectionless-mode transmission is the transmission of a single unit of data from a source SAP to one or more destination SAPs without establishing a connection. (This approach is sometimes called **datagrams.**) A connectionless-mode service allows an entity to initiate such a transmission through a single-service access. A connectionless-mode service does not have a clearly distinguishable lifetime.

The basic connectionless-mode service is not required to exhibit any minimum values of the quality of service measures and is not required to exhibit peer flow control.

Since the basic connectionless service is not required to maintain the sequence of service data units, there are no requirements to provide sequencing functions. Thus, an entity at a particular layer does not provide the servicing layer any information about the logical relationships between datagrams, other than the source and destination addresses.

Connectionless does not provide any negotiation, although there is QOS or version checking on a take-it-or-leave-it basis.

Despite the lack of a requirement to maintain sequencing, the characteristics of the particular medium or subnetwork may provide a high probability of in-sequence delivery. A stack may contain combinations of layers using connection-oriented services and other layers using connectionless services. For example, the lower layers may be connectionless, but the upper layers may use connection-oriented services. In order to provide these capabilities, OSI uses **relay functions.** When the Transport Layer is unable to provide the agreed quality of service and all possible recovery attempts have failed, the transport connection is terminated and the session entities are notified.

ADDRESSING

Note: Addressing traverses layers, but this is an appropriate place to discuss.

In the OSI Reference Model, reliable data communications occur between two end systems, usually via one or more intermediate systems. End systems are terminus systems, where data transfers originate or terminate. Intermediate systems are "transit systems," through which information passes from one end system (source) to the other end system (destination). In many cases the Intermediate System must perform routing to determine the path.

The terms **end system** and **intermediate system** refer to roles in transmittal of data and not to any special configurations. An individual system may be an end system or an intermediate system at different times or with respect to different data streams. Intermediate systems are used to interconnect subnetworks in OSI communications.

Intermediate systems are used to link together subnetworks to provide paths connecting end systems. An end system may be connected to more than one subnetwork; similarly, a subnetwork may have multiple end systems connected to it (see Figure 6.6). The actual physical connections are labeled as subnetwork points of attachment (SNPAs).

A service-access point is identified by a unique Network Service Access Point (NSAP) address.

An NSAP is an identifier that uniquely distinguishes one end system from another in a network of systems. An intermediate system will "read" the NSAP address and determine where to send the packet (a similar function to that of a post office in reading an address for an envelope). Each NSAP is unique globally in the context of OSI; an NSAP value must be known to all other systems communicating with this system. The NSAPs themselves only have meaning to the communicating entities, such as OSI Network Layer service entities.

The NSAP also identifies a point at which network service is provided to the Transport Layer, which is responsible for the end-to-end transfer of data in the OSI model. There may be any number of NSAPs for an end system. These NSAP values must be known to the "end-to-end" communications software that runs in end systems. NSAPs are encoded as unique strings of characters (or numbers) that may be interpreted reading from left to right using the hierarchical model described previously. Each NSAP value in an end system specifies a different user of the Network Layer service.

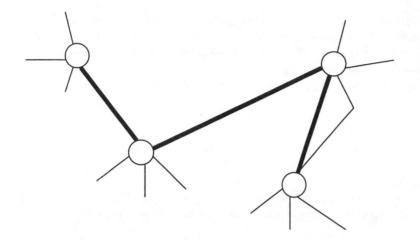

Figure 6.6 An ES may be on two or more subnetworks; subnetworks may be chosen for their differing technology.

Intermediate systems route information based upon selected components of NSAPs received in transit. If the NSAP "matches" the system address, that system is in fact the destination system. If not, then a routing table is used to find the next system along the route to the destination.

The NSAP is the only address in OSI that identifies end systems uniquely; all other OSI addresses identify intermediate systems or end-system processes. Globally unique NSAP addresses are important because increased communication across different subnetworks in a distributed global environment is anticipated. If every end system in all organizations is assigned a unique address, then every end system can potentially communicate with every other end system. NSAPs are the first category of objects which must have registration authorities established to assure assignment of unique addresses for all.

In sum, an OSI network is composed of end systems on different subnetworks interconnected by intermediate systems. NSAPs identify the end points of network communications, or the service access points of the Network Layer. The NSAP selector allows different users of the Network Layer service to be distinguished.

Routing is accomplished by a function within a layer that translates the title of an entity or the service-access-point address to which the entity is attached into a path by which the entity can be reached. This sometimes uses a directory (i.e., X.500), which translates global titles of peer entities into the NSAP addresses through which they cooperate. Use of the directory allows an application to dynamically associate with a process to perform a required function, by knowing only the name of the other application—or possibly by using a "yellow pages" feature to find the desired service.

Within a given layer, a hierarchical structure of addresses simplifies address-mapping functions because of the permanent nature of the mapping it presupposes. The model does not impose the hierarchy in all layers in order to allow more flexibility in address mappings and to cover the case where an entity attached to more than one subordinate layer service-access point supports only one service-access point. The structure of an address is known by the same layer entity that is attached to the identified service-access point; however, the superior layer entity does not know this structure.

The connection-end point identifier consists of two parts:

- The address of the service-access point, which will be used in conjunction with the connection
- A connection-end point suffix, which is unique within the scope of the NSAP

For example, at the Transport Layer, when a session entity requests the Transport Layer to establish a transport connection with another session entity identified by its transport address, the Transport Layer determines the network address identifying the transport entity, which serves the correspondent session entity.

Because transport entities support services on an end-to-end basis, no intermediate transport entity is involved as a relay between the end transport entities. Therefore, the Transport Layer maps transport addresses to the network addresses which identify the end transport entities.

A routing function within a layer enables communication to be relayed by a chain of peer entities. The fact that communication is being routed by intermediate peer entities is known by neither the lower layers nor by the higher layers. Any entity that participates in a routing function may have a routing table.

An entity can be accessed either by its address or by the entity title. In order to establish uniquely identified entities, registration authorities have been established by ISO (and subsequently by ANSI, the U.S. government, etc.) to register unique names within hierarchies. As an analogy, consider postal addressing schemes: The postal service determines zip codes, cities (or other local governments) decide basis address structure, and housing developments might actually name the streets. While 123 Elm Street in Springfield is hardly unique, when used in a hierarchy (below either zip code or state name) the identifier becomes unique. Similar principles apply in OSI. One of the more prominent responsibilities of ISO registration authorities is to register organization names, so organizations are uniquely identified.

OSI names and addresses consist of attribute-value pairs that are hierarchical in nature and combine to uniquely identify or locate an OSI object. Since the relationship between the components of a name or address is hierarchical, it follows that the registration authority for names and addresses should also be hierarchical. A governing organization does not always have sufficient knowledge of organizations lower in the hierarchy to wisely assign values within those organizations. Thus, an approach frequently taken is to delegate registration authority to the lower organizations in the name or address hierarchy.

No one element in the sequence is necessarily unique, but all the elements considered together in the proper order are unique as a group. Also, each element with the same immediate parent is unique at its level. The term **sequence** implies a definite ordering of elements. To create a unique sequence, an ADP system may "pick off" elements in a path down the tree, and append each selected element to the end of the list of previously selected elements. To decode or **parse** a unique sequence, an ADP system will read the elements of the sequence in the order encountered from the beginning of the sequence, and construct a "path" in the hierarchical identification tree.

Registration authorities are created to register names of objects and, in some cases, to advertise these names. For example, the telephone companies assign numbers to subscribers and publish some of the numbers in a telephone directory. In the OSI world, some names are included and registered in the standard.

IDP	DSP (Domain Specific Part)

IDP = Initial Domain Part

AFI	IDI	DFI	AAI	RS	RD	AR	ESID	NSEL

AFI = Authority and Format Identifier
IDI = Initial Domain Identifier (allowing different addressing domains
DFI = DSP Format Identier
AAI = Administrative Authority Identifier
RS = Reserved
RD = Routing Domain
AR = Area (to allow unique routing areas)
ESID = End System Identifier, which identifies a unique open system
NSEL = NSAP Selector (identifying a service access point)

Figure 6.7   The NSAP addressing structure.

If applications want to exchange objects not included in the standard, such objects must be registered somewhere, so that no one else will use the same number for a different body part or a different number for the same body part. In the future, when a standard is approved that will require further registration of names, the procedure for registration and the registration authority will be approved at the same time.

The NSAP addressing structure incorporates various numbering schemes or types of addresses to deal with the diverse users of packet data. The NSAP address consists of two major parts, the Initial Domain Part (IDP) and the Domain Specific Part (DSP). The IDP is subdivided into two parts that are specified by ISO 8348/Addendum 2.

The first part, Authority and Format Identifier (AFI), identifies the type of address being used and gives the syntax of the DSP. The second part, Initial Domain Identifier (IDI) specifies the domain to which the address belongs.

The format of the DSP is not defined by ISO 8348/Addendum 2, but must be established by the registration authority for the 0005 domain. A typical format used is illustrated in Figure 6–7.

An administrative domain is defined by ISO as a collection of end systems, intermediate systems, and subnetworks operated by a single organization or administrative authority. These domains may or may not be synonymous with organizational entities.

Within an administrative domain there may be zero, one, or more routing domains. A routing domain is a set of end systems and intermediate systems that operate according to the same routing procedures and are wholly contained within a single administrative domain. Systems within a routing domain possess the following properties: (1) a high degree of trust in exchanging routing information with other such systems, and (2) use of the same routing protocols as other such systems. These properties may not be present in systems outside this routing domain. A routing domain is divided (usually partitioned) into subdomains called **areas.** A minimal amount of routing information needs to be transferred between adjacent areas in order to determine the most appropriate path to a system within a particular area.

The system ID field identifies a unique system within an area. Once the end system is found, the directional routing stops; now all that remains is to find the appropriate user of the network layer service within that end system. This is done by examining the value of the NSAP selector field. The NSAP selector field identifies the user of the Network Layer service, usually a Transport entity.

A TSAP selector identifies a point within a computer system where information is passed in both directions between the Transport Layer and the Session Layer. The TSAP selector does not have to be unique globally, but must be unique within an end system; it is appended to the NSAP address (forming a TSAP address) to identify a user of the Transport service. There may be more than one TSAP selector per end system; each identifies a separate user of the Transport service.

The TSAP selector has meaning only within an end system. If a particular TSAP selector of one end system must be known to another end system, that value could be conveyed *a priori* or by a common directory service.

The Session Service Access Point (SSAP) Selector identifies a point in the system through which information passes in both directions between the Session Layer implementation and the Presentation Layer implementation. The SSAP selector identifies a user of the Session service. There may be more than one SSAP selector per end system; each would identify a different user of the Session service.

Any value may be inserted for the SSAP selector as long as it is the correct type and format, and is correctly interpretable at the other end system. In transmitting information the SSAP selector is appended to the end of the TSAP address (forming an SSAP address). If it is necessary for one end system to know the SSAP selector for another end system, then that information could be conveyed *a priori* or via a common directory service.

The Presentation Service Access Point (PSAP) Selector identifies a user of the Presentation service in an end system. The PSAP selector does not have to be globally unique. PSAP selectors are encoded in Abstract Syntax Notation (ASN.1) type OCTETSTRING. There may be more than one PSAP selector per end system; each value identifies a different user of the Presentation service.

Any value may be inserted for the PSAP selector as long as it is the correct type and format and is correctly interpretable at the other end system. If it is necessary to identify a PSAP selector on one end system to another end system, a common directory service could be used, as well as an *a priori* method. A PSAP address consists of the PSAP selector appended to the SSAP address, and is intended to globally identify an application.

NETWORK LAYER

In OSI, some open systems will act as the final destination of data. Some other open systems may act only as intermediate nodes, forwarding data to other systems. This leads to identification of a Network Layer on top of the Data Link Layer. Network-oriented protocols, such as routing, are grouped in this layer. Thus, the Network Layer provides a communication path (network connection) between a pair of transport entities, including the case where intermediate nodes are involved.

The Network Layer provides the functional and procedural means for connectionless- or connection-mode transmission among transport entities and, therefore, provides to the transport entities independence of routing and relay considerations associated with connectionless- or connection-mode transmission.

Network Layer services provide for the transparent transfer of data between transport entities. This service allows the structure and detailed content of submitted data to be determined exclusively by layers above the Network Layer. The Network Layer contains functions necessary to provide the Transport Layer with a firm Network/Transport Layer boundary, which is independent of the underlying communications media in all things other than quality of service. Thus, the Network Layer is able to mask the differences in the characteristics of different transmission and subnetwork technologies into a consistent network service.

The Network Layer provides independence from routing and relay consideration associated with the establishment and operation of a given network connection. This includes the case where several subnetworks are used in tandem or in parallel. The transport entities can ignore underlying resources such as data-link connections used to provide the network connections. This is important in systems formed by two or more subnetworks, for example, when several LANs are involved.

Any relay functions and hop-by-hop service enhancement protocols used to support the network service between the OSI end systems are operating below the Transport Layer, i.e., within the Network Layer.

According to ISO/IEC 7498-1, a **real subnetwork** is a collection of equipment and physical media that forms an autonomous whole and that can be used to interconnect real systems for purposes of data transfer. A subnetwork is a representation of a real network such as a carrier network, a private network, or an LAN. A subnetwork may itself be an open system, but this is not essential to achieve openness at a system level.

The service provided at each end of a network connection is the same even when a network connection spans several subnetworks, each offering dissimilar services. The need to offer different services is one reason for using different subnetworks. Subnetworks may also be needed when different media are involved, such as satellite communications, radio, or LANs.

The quality of service (QOS) is negotiated between the transport entities and the network-service at the time of establishment of a network connection. While this quality of service may vary from one network connection to another, it will be agreed for a given network connection and be the same at both network-connection end points. QOS at the Network Layer includes security, priority, congestion experienced, and cost.

The Network Layer uniquely identifies each of the end open systems (represented by transport entities) by their network addresses. This may be independent of the addressing needed by the underlying layers.

Network connections are point-to-point; however, more than one network connection may exist between the same pair of network addresses.

Network connections are provided by network entities in end open systems but may involve intermediate open systems which provide relaying. These intermediate open systems may interconnect subnetwork connections, data-link connections, and data circuits. Routing functions determine an appropriate route between network addresses.

As in the Transport Layer, there are two types of service available from the Network Layer—Connection Oriented and Connectionless. The function of the Network Layer is to relay and route network service user packets to the correct destination, while at the same time masking the differences in the underlying subnetwork technologies (e.g., X.25 and CSMA/CD). The source and destination network service users may be on the same subnetwork or different, interconnected subnetworks.

Connectionless Network Service (CLNS)

The Connectionless Network Service (CLNS) is provided by the Connectionless Network Protocol (CLNP), which allows different subnetwork technologies to be interconnected. The CLNP masks the differences between these subnetwork technologies and allows these differences to be transparent to the OSI Network Layer user.

The services of the existing subnetwork technologies such as LANs must be augmented to provide the OSI Network Layer service; this enhancement is also provided in the CLNP. Since the protocol to provide this service is connectionless, each protocol data unit is routed separately and the header of each protocol data unit contains addressing information as well as information relating to optional services provided by the protocol (e.g., priority and security).

The End System (ES)–Intermediate System (IS) Protocol is a dynamic routing protocol that operates in the network to support CLNP. It operates over either point-to-point links or broadcast subnetworks. Functionally ES-IS:

1. enables ISs to dynamically find ESs that are attached to the same subnetwork,
2. enables ESs to dynamically find ISs that are attached to the same subnetwork,
3. enables ESs to locate each other on a single subnetwork,
4. when two or more ISs are attached to the same subnetwork, enables ISs to redirect ESs to the IS representing the most efficient route to a given destination, and
5. allows ESs to automatically configure their OSI addresses.

Connection-oriented Network Service

Use of the CONS can improve efficiency when operating over a single logical connection-oriented subnetwork (e.g., a single X.25 subnetwork or an ISDN). Use of this service can, under certain circumstances, avoid the overhead associated with the CLNP and may permit interoperability with end systems that do not implement CLNP.

Subnetwork Technologies

Different subnetwork technologies provide for transfer of data packets between adjacent nodes of a network. This corresponds to the lower portion of the Network Layer, the Data Link Layer, and the Physical Layer. The nodes of a wide area network are separated by long distances, whereas local area networks are usually contained within a small geographic area. This difference is responsible for the different technology used in the two types of networks. The functionality required to transfer data packets between "adjacent" nodes of a subnetwork is provided by the Physical Layer and the Data Link Layer.

Because Network Layer functions provide for a wide variety of configurations supporting network connections ranging from point-to-point configurations to network connections supported by complex combinations of subnetworks with different characteristics, it is common to structure network functions into sublayers. This is not generally done when the access protocol to the subnetwork supports the complete functionality of the OSI network service, but may be useful in other cases.

With Connection-oriented Network Layer, the three sublayers are (top to bottom):

- Subnetwork Independent Convergence Protocol (SICP)
- Subnetwork Dependent Convergence Protocol (SDCP)
- Subnetwork Access Protocol

In a Connectionless network, the Network Layer comprises two sublayers:

- Internetwork Protocol (IP)
- Subnetwork Specific Protocol (SSP)

DATA LINK LAYER

The control of interconnection of data circuits in the Physical Layer from the Network Layer requires interaction between a network entity and a physical entity in the same open system. Since the Reference Model permits direct interaction only between adjacent layers, the network entity cannot interact directly with the physical entity. This interaction is thus described through the Data Link Layer, which intervenes transparently to convey the interaction between the Network Layer and the Physical Layer.

Some physical media (for example, a telephone line) require specific techniques to be used in order to transmit data between systems despite a relatively high error rate (i.e., an error rate not acceptable for the great majority of applications). These specific techniques are used in data-link procedures that have been studied and standardized for a number of years. Newer physical communication media (for example, fiber optics) require different data-link control procedures. These procedures are included in the Data Link Layer.

The Data Link Layer takes the raw transmission facility provided by the Physical Layer and transforms it into a link that appears substantially free of transmission errors to the network layer. It performs this function by taking bits and forming them into data frames; these data frames are then transmitted sequentially. The Data Link Layer provides error detection and, optionally, correction (involving two computers directly connected) across a line between nodes of a subnetwork.

The Data Link Layer provides functional and procedural means for connectionless-mode transmission among network entities and to establish, maintain, and release data-link connections among network-entities and to transfer data-link SDUs. A data link is built upon one or several physical connections. If needed, the Data Link Layer provides data-link-end point identifiers that can be used by a network entity to identify a correspondent network entity.

The Data Link Layer conveys to network entities the capability of controlling the interconnection of data circuits within the Physical Layer. This function is particularly used when a physical connection is established/released across a circuit-switched subnetwork by relaying within an intermediate system between data circuits, which are elements of the end-to-end path under control of a network entity which makes the appropriate routing decisions as a function of the path requirements derived from the network signaling protocols.

The Data Link Layer checks the number and position of bits received, and performs various calculations to determine if there is an error, e.g., if a "1" bit is accidentally received as a "0."

Synchronization of sender and receiver is important in this layer. The Data Link Layer emphasizes **box-to-box communications,** that is, management of bits between directly connected computers.

The Data Link Layer provides delimiting and synchronization, sometimes called framing, which provide recognition of a sequence of physical SDUs (i.e., bits) transmitted over the physical connection, as a data-link PDU.

The portion of the subnetwork technology that resides in the Network Layer is responsible for routing and relaying within the subnetwork, if necessary. For instance, in an X.25 subnetwork, the X.25 Packet Layer Protocol provides for the internal routing (i.e., from switch to switch) of X.25 packets from one X.25 subscriber to another. Alternatively, in "8802" subnetworks (IEEE 802), the Network Layer component is logically empty, since the method of transfer is broadcast and there is no explicit subnetwork routing performed.

The X.25 protocol establishes a virtual circuit between two machines; this is a definite path connecting the two machines through intermediate machines. This path is valid for the lifetime of the connection. Source and destination addresses, as well as other information, are put on a call setup packet; data packets follow.

The X.25 packet layer (Layer 3) protocol is concerned with data format and meaning in a frame, as well as subnetwork routing and virtual circuit management. When one system wants to connect to another system, a logical circuit is set up between them; there are a number of parameters that specify various kinds of information. Some functions are: reset and clearing a circuit (when a call request cannot be completed).

PHYSICAL LAYER

It is essential that an open architecture permits usage of a realistic variety of physical media for interconnection with different control procedures. This led to the creation of physical layer as the lowest layer.

The Physical Layer provides mechanical, electrical, functional, and procedural means to activate, maintain, and deactivate physical connections for a bit transmission between data-link entities. A physical connection may involve intermediate open systems, each relaying bit transmission within the Physical Layer. Physical Layer entities are interconnected by means of a physical medium.

The Physical Layer allows for the correct pin settings and signaling techniques of interfaces to lines so that bits of data may be transmitted from one machine to another machine. Issues here involve the nature of the physical medium, and ensuring that proper synchronization is applied for the transfer. There are a large number of Physical Layer specifications, depending on the physical medium employed. The mechanical, electromagnetic, and other media dependent characteristics of physical media connections are defined at the boundary between the Physical Layer and the physical media.

SOME OTHER TOPICS

The initial OSI model addressed only the basic framework. As OSI matured, the framework has been expanded to include security (ISO 7498-2) and naming and addressing (7498-3); in addition, the OSI family of standards now includes many additional areas, such as network management (ISO/IEC 7498-4).

OSI Security

The basic framework for OSI security is described in ISO 7498-2. The basic security framework has been divided into an Upper Layers Security Model and Lower Layers Security Model—partly to divide the work among the committees involved in OSI, but also because the security mechanisms for the upper and lower layers are different. (The responsibilities are different, so the vulnerabilities are different.)

The Upper Layers Security Model (fourth working draft, SC21 N5447, 1990-10-30) describes a basic model:

"The generation and processing of security information are performed by *generic security functions* (GSFs), whose specifications fall outside the scope of OSI but which can be invoked by OSI entities to provide the required security service(s). GSFs generate and process security information exchanged using OSI protocols in the Application and Presentation layers. The logical structure of exchanged security information can be standardized in OSI so it can be represented in OSI protocol exchanges.

"The exchanged security information, generated and processed by GSFs, can be either generic in nature or application-specific. As far as possible, generic security elements should be factored out to carry security information in support of the requirements of a wide range of applications. This is facilitated by the concept of security exchanges and an associated notational framework which can allow security implements specifications to be referenced by any application standard."

The security model defines GSFs including *security transformation functions* to support confidentiality and *security check–value functions* to support integrity. Within the upper layers, these functions can be invoked from within the Application Layer or Presentation Layer. When some mechanisms, such as encryption, are involved, it may be necessary to perform the function at the Presentation Layer, so the encryption is applied to the transfer syntax. Otherwise, both sender and receiver would be required to use the same presentation syntax, which limits the value of the Presentation Layer.

Although the Upper Layers model defers to the Lower Layers model for completion of the description of provision of security services, it briefly discusses the use of lower layer services to show how the two models relate.

"Lower Layers security services may be used to provide additional protection beyond that provided in the Upper Layers. In particular, Lower Layers security services may be used to protect protocol-control information of the higher layers and provide a higher degree of traffic flow confidentiality."

Regardless of the layer at which lower layer services are provided, the Transport Layer is involved because it provides the Quality-of-Service parameter, which is the only means by which an application can influence the selection of Lower Layer security services for a particular instance of communication. This is critical for many applications since the protection requirements vary according to type of message, etc.

The Integrity Framework addresses integrity protected data, which can be provided through encryption or error detecting/correcting codes. The WD also discusses the relationship of integrity to party-to-party authentication and access control.

The mappings of services to layers in ISO 7498-2 should only be considered a framework and not a dependable guide to where the services will be defined within other OSI standards or where they should be implemented. Thus, it seems that the Application Layer is generally responsible for mechanisms involving the identity of the sender or receiver and the lower layers are merely responsible for ensuring that all data—including security mechanisms—are transmitted with confidentiality and integrity intact. The Transport Layer seems to be the best candidate, although some services may also be desirable in the lower three layers.

The security services that may be provided by the protocol which performs the subnetwork access functions associated with the provision of the OSI network service are as follows:

1. peer entity authentication
2. data origin authentication
3. access control service
4. connection confidentiality
5. connectionless confidentiality
6. traffic flow confidentiality
7. connection integrity without recovery
8. connectionless integrity

Peer entity authentication (as defined in ISO 7498-2:1988) is a special case of party-to-party authentication, which is defined in CD 10181-2. Note that the "… Upper Layers do not provide for authentication of any entities below the Application Layer."

"Party-to-party authentication only provides assurance to an identity at an instant of time. To maintain this assurance throughout the duration of an association, connection integrity is required. In some cases it may be necessary to obtain further assurance of the identify of an entity after a period of time through additional authentication exchanges."

Like peer-entity authentication, "Data origin authentication is provided by protocol and identification of the data being authenticated in the Application Layer."

The OSI Systems Management standard also contains parts addressing security. The Security Alarm Reporting Function (DIS 10164-7) may soon be approved by JTC1. The security audit trail function (ISO/IEC 10164-8) and "objects and attributes for access control" (CD 10164-9) received many comments during the latest ballot period, but are making significant progress.

System Management

System management includes functions in the Application Layer related to the management of various OSI resources and their status across all layers of the OSI architecture.

Within the OSI architecture, there is a need to recognize the special problems of initiating, terminating, and monitoring activities and assisting in their harmonious operations, as well as handling abnormal conditions.

The management activities of concern are those that imply actual exchanges of information between open systems. Only those management activities which imply actual exchanges of information between remote management entities are pertinent to the OSI architecture. Other management activities local to particular open systems are outside its scope. Similarly, not all resources are pertinent to OSI.

Application management relates to the management of OSI application processes. The following is a list of typical activities that fall into this category (but it is not exhaustive):

1. Initialization of parameters representing application processes
2. Initiation, maintenance, and termination of application processes
3. Allocation and deallocation of OSI resources to application processes
4. Detection and prevention of OSI resource interference and deadlock
5. Integrity and commitment control
6. Security control
7. Checkpointing and recovery control

Systems management relates to the management of OSI resources and their status across all layers of the OSI architecture. The following list is typical of activities that fall into this category:

1. Activation/deactivation management includes:
   • activation, maintenance, and termination of OSI resources distributed in open systems, including physical media for OSI
   • some program loading functions
   • establishment/maintenance/release of connections between management entities
   • open systems parameter initialization/modification
2. Monitoring includes:
   • reporting status or status changes
   • reporting statistics
3. Error control includes:
   • error detection and some of the diagnostic functions
   • reconfiguration and restart

Layer management includes two aspects. One of these is concerned with layer activities such as activation and error control. This part is implemented by the layer protocol to which it applies.

The other aspect of layer management is a subset of systems management. The protocols for these activities reside within the Application Layer and are handled by systems-management-application entities.

The OSI reference model and architecture do not dictate any particular fashion of degree of centralization of management functions. This principle calls for a structure in which each open system is allowed to include any collection of systems-management functions and each subsystem is similarly permitted to include any layer-management functions. If necessary, connections between management entities are established when an open system that has been operating in isolation from other open systems becomes part of the OSI environment.

"Systems management provides mechanisms for the monitoring, control, and coordination of resources within the OSI environment and OSI protocol standards for communicating information pertinent to those resources. In order to describe management operations on resources in the OSI environment, the resources are viewed as managed objects with defined properties. Information required for systems management purposes in any open system may be provided through local input, may result from input from other open systems through systems management (application layer) communication or may be a result of lower layer protocol exchanges.

"Systems management is applicable to a wide range of distributed processing and communications environments. These environments range from local area networks interconnecting small systems, to interconnected corporate and national networks on a global scale. Small-scale environments may be managed by appropriate small-scale management systems, consisting of a single manager capable of controlling and coordinating the open communication environment through a number of agents. The standards and concepts are also applicable to large-scale environments supporting multiple managers.

"There are three main groupings within the set of systems management standards. They are:

1. A set of standards specifying systems management functions;
2. A set of standards related to the specification of managed objects.
3. A set of application layer service and protocol standards for communicating information relating to management functions."

The overview describes models for these groupings. It also describes the conformance requirements.
    ISO/IEC 10164-8, IT—OSI—Systems Management—Part 8: Security audit trail function, defines the security audit trail function, which is a systems management function which may be used by an application process in a centralized or decentralized management environment to exchange information and commands for the purpose of systems management, as defined by CCITT Rec X.700 or the equivalent ISO 7498-4.
    ISO/IEC 10164-8 defines:

• a set of notifications for security-related events that are to be sent to a security audit trail log. The contents of the security audit trail log may be used in a security audit.
• a set of service primitives that constitute the security audit trail function
• the parameters that are passed in each service primitive
• any necessary information for the semantic description of each service primitive
• the conformance requirements to be met by implementations of this specification

Conformance Testing   For several years, all projects for development of OSI protocol specifications have also proposed parts dealing with Protocol Implementation Conformance Statements (PICS) pro formas and abstract test suites. These abstract test suites form the basis for conformance tests that can be run against any implementation claiming conformance to OSI.
    The standards community—including the many major users and producers—have been very active to increase the likelihood that OSI-compliant systems will interoperate. Standards have been pub-

lished for the seven-layer stack (ISO/IEC 7498-1) as well as for each of the layers—to define the requirements and interfaces for all the layers. However, merely publishing a specification is not enough. How can we demonstrate conformance? ISO/IEC Joint Technical Committee 1 (JTC1) Subcommittee 21, "Information Retrieval, Transfer, and Management for OSI," which is responsible for the upper layers, has mandated that all OSI standards be accompanied by standards for an "Abstract Test Suite," a conformance test suite based on the abstract test suite, and a Protocol Implementation Conformance Statement (PICS), which summarizes the options and results, providing a uniform report.

With these documents, not only are we provided a definition, but we also receive details on how to test that an implementation conforms to the specification. Unlike an acceptance test that a typical user might generate, these tests have been designed—and reviewed—by top international experts in OSI; these are very costly resources which have been provided on a voluntary basis.

Obviously, having a test suite is not enough; who will run the tests? Do you trust your potential vendor? Or would you prefer a third party? Several organizations worldwide have been gearing up to provide conformance testing services and issue recognized certificates that a particular implementation conforms to a given version of a standard. Many of these organizations have already been accredited to issue certificates. It is worth noting that the European community is very strong about certification and mutual recognition of certificates, which is likely to have a very strong influence on vendors interested in selling products worldwide.

With certification, an implementation is tested with a rigorously controlled test suite with official witnesses of the testing organization. Generally, an entire stack (through the seven layers) is tested with testing proceeding from the bottom of the stack upwards through the layers. A conformance test report (in a standard format) is written and a certificate will be issued if the test is successful. Users should accept these certificates as proof of conformance.

Conformance testing verifies that a protocol implementation performs as the standard specifies. Most conformance test scenarios concentrate on single layer testing. A single layer of the OSI protocol stack is tested using the services of the lower layers that have been tested previously and are, therefore, presumed to work correctly.

Conformance testing alone will not ensure that an OSI protocol suite will work correctly. No conformance test system can ensure that all errors in a protocol implementation will be detected. In addition, single layer conformance testing is not always possible, because some vendors merge the functionality of two or more layers in a protocol implementation. However, conformance testing will increase significantly the probability that a product interoperates with other products.

While conformance testing increases the probability of interoperability, it is not a guarantee. Interoperation testing will still be needed. This could actually include some of the user's own messages to begin testing more than the vendor-supplied software. First, though, additional conformance testing (and specification work) can improve the odds.

Interoperability testing simulates the "real-life" conditions under which the vendor's product will be seen. Since vendors of OSI products are building implementations to operate with implementations developed by other vendors, it is in both the customer's and vendor's interest to duplicate as closely as possible the environment in which the product will be used before product acceptance is completed. In general, interoperability testing detects configuration options that are set in an incompatible manner. Such errors are relatively easy to overcome. Interoperability tests are getting much more attention.

Care should be taken to ensure that non-standard enhancements do not compromise basic interoperability.

Many international standardized profiles (ISPs) are being developed to actually select various options through all the layers of the stack. Although the Government Open System Interconnection Profile (GOSIP) is one of the more famous profiles (actually it is a collection of profiles), there are many more being developed.

Industry profiles are also being developed; these are harmonized within a particular industry (e.g., aeronautics) but can also be processed as international standardized profiles. Thus, even if a network's requirements are not satisfied by GOSIP, there might be another profile that fits. As with the base protocol, each ISP can be conformance tested; this is not done with new test suites but by using tailoring of the basic test suite. Even without use of the test suite, the form of the ISP is a useful discipline to documenting how the systems of a network will actually use GOSIP. This can greatly help in publishing interface specifications, especially when different groups within an organization have responsibility for various components. One of the great values of the ISP formats is that they are rigorous, well-understood, and required if there is expectation of approval as an ISP.

COEXISTENCE AND TRANSITION

Most OSI implementations will need to fit into existing networks, which may use industry-wide protocols such as TCP/IP or vendor-unique protocols.

Vendors will make suggestions as to how to provide a smooth transition to OSI while preserving capabilities inherent in their particular user interface during the OSI transition process. The vendor whose architecture differs radically from OSI is likely to emphasize the private architecture approach while offering gateways to OSI products. On the other hand, the vendor whose private architecture is close to that of OSI is more likely to effect a smooth transition to a total OSI solution; in this case, private architecture solutions will have a limited life.

Gateways are possibly the most effective approach. However, a network must consider whether to convert when the new protocols are introduced, wait until major changes are needed for the application, or schedule the conversions on a time-available basis. Availability of special features in vendors' implementations is also a major consideration—if you need the features and cannot wait for the standards. At present, it still may not be possible to cut over to a fully compliant implementation because of the need for special features.

Several examples are apparent, in the form of directory service enhancements and network management solutions. In either case, vendors may offer interim solutions as enhancements to OSI products, in the absence of standards supporting these capabilities. Interim specifications may be proposed as a short-term solution. Users may wish to accept these options, and require that the vendor propose a transition path to the standard OSI solutions when they become available in products.

Another example is that of security enhancements to OSI products. Many users have security needs that must be added as options to existing OSI products. Comprehensive security standards are not available currently. Users may accept interim security solutions, if needs exist. These solutions should be moved to OSI solutions in the future, and it is recommended that vendors provide a plan or specific commitment for such a transition.

Vendors may upgrade their products to align with evolving base standards or functional profiles, or they may provide additional functionality beyond that specified in the standard or profiles. In these instances, care should be taken that use of the extensions will not compromise future interoperability, or that there are adequate plans for migrating to the standard once the desired features are standardized.

The transition to open systems is concerned with both implementing OSI and providing interim interoperability with existing protocols until OSI implementation is complete. Interoperability provides a capability for the older protocols on existing networks to interoperate with the open systems protocols being produced. It is necessary to support the existing protocols for the expected life of the systems using them.

Extremely large, diverse networks may choose to use a multifaceted approach to transition, which might include: (1) developing a full stack of OSI protocols in a portable operating system environment (e.g., ISODE and POSIX), (2) having both protocols coexist on a particular host (dual-protocol host), (3) converting from one Application Layer protocol to another (Application Layer gateway), and (4) supporting both IP (Internetwork Protocol) and CLNP at the Network Layer (multiprotocol routers).

Multiprotocol Routers

In order for coexistence to occur, it is necessary to provide OSI hosts, on a local area or wide area network, the ability to communicate with other OSI hosts on another non-OSI local area or wide area network. The availability of multiprotocol routers reduces the number of components, and therefore presumably reduces the cost and complexity for LANs that are composed of a mixture of various protocol hosts, allowing the use of older protocols in areas in which OSI protocols are not yet mature (e.g., internetwork routing and network management).

The Internet Protocol (IP) or CLNP performs the routing functions required to connect nodes on the same network or different networks. A multiprotocol router is a device that will be able to distinguish between the OSI and non-OSI internetwork protocol data units. When a packet arrives at an intermediate system, a network layer protocol identification field is checked and then the packet is passed to the appropriate module (either IP or OSI CLNP).

Dual-protocol Hosts

It is also possible to support multiple protocols on a single host. A dual-protocol host has the complete OSI and other protocol suites available as part of its networking capabilities.

A dual-protocol host can be used directly by applications to communicate to any destination on the network—for both OSI and non-OSI protocols. It can also be used as a staging point for manual interoperation between a host that has only non-OSI protocols and a host that has only OSI protocols by using a dual-protocol host as an intermediary. New applications may use OSI—or applications may support both interfaces until the older interface is phased out. Another approach is to use file transfers to move data from one protocol host to another, but this approach is likely to be unsatisfactory for most applications.

Application Layer Gateways

An Application Layer gateway is a dual-protocol host which contains a conversion module residing at the Application Layer of each protocol stack. This module performs the semantic, syntax, and service transformation required for the protocol conversion. Gateways could be in use for a period of several years as existing systems are upgraded or replaced. These do have impacts of cost, delays, physical space, etc.

Other concerns for interoperability involve: (1) the sharing of hardware resources such as terminals and communication links, (2) support for interoperation of a basic set of application functions, (3) addressing across multiple subnetworks which might use different formats and mappings for addressing schemes. In addition, there is the need for application-to-application interoperation. Important components of study include identifying functional layer incompatibilities.

The most comprehensive and simplest interoperability is achieved by implementation of equipment conforming to a single full-function networking architecture. For environments involving multiple vendor architectures, a compromise may exist between the level of interoperability achieved and the number of vendor environments to be supported.

Terminal protocol converters or emulators provide an inexpensive and effective interoperability capability for single architecture networking environments. Gateways may be optimized for performance but are difficult to extend to support additional protocols if a network involves many vendors' environments.

Vendors whose architectures do not map conveniently to the OSI architecture may decide to provide gateways or protocol converters as a long-term solution, while (1) providing for a gradual transition to OSI, or (2) allowing both OSI and the existing native architecture to coexist permanently. It is possible that special user services which exist in the native architecture will be preserved by the vendor; OSI will be available via special hosts or processors. As another approach OSI could be used to permanently interconnect two native architectures.

Interoperability with "Short Stack" OSI Systems

Many systems are based on OSI's lower layer protocols, but have not implemented the OSI protocols for Session Layer and above; this approach is sometimes called a "short stack." Necessary functions of the upper layers are provided by non-standard software; for example, the application using the short stack will still provide selected functions normally done by the upper layers. This might be done to optimize the application, or to minimize the conversion to use an existing application in conjunction with an OSI network. Use of a short stack has no effect on Intermediate systems (which has only the Lower Layers), but a short stack might not work correctly with an OSI end system despite being able to coexist. This may be acceptable if the application using the short stack does not need to interface with all other applications.

In contrast to the some other approaches, the Application Layer gateway is architecturally correct and is particularly useful in the relaying of messages between Message Transfer Agents which use Transport Class 0 and the CONS, and those which use Transport Class 4 and the CLNP. In addition, implementations of the Application Layer gateway for this purpose are expected to be widespread. The Application Layer gateway can also be used to implement security services at the Application Layer.

The best means of assuring interoperability across CLNP, CONS, and the most common range of Transport classes is the use of end systems capable of supporting all the required services. Many vendors offer Transport Classes 0, 2, and 4 and also offer both CLNP and CONS. This solution will work well when an end system is connected directly to a wide area network supporting CONS. When end systems are attached to a local area network, where CONS is usually not supported, products containing only Transport Class 4 and CLNP are appropriate.

OSI permits flexibility in addressing schemes. While this allows for greater flexibility in tailoring for a particular network's unique requirements, it also complicates interoperability among networks. Profiles, such as GOSIP, generally standardize the addressing formats. It is necessary for ISs to route to destinations in routing domains that use other addressing formats, such as those specified by ANSI or ECMA (European Computer Manufacturers Association). Such interconnectivity will take place via interdomain routing (e.g., routing domains using GOSIP addressing and routing procedures should not be expected to contain non-GOSIP ESs), as described in ISO/IEC 10737.

For interdomain routing, it is necessary for ISs to be capable of routing PDUs to other domains, based on variable length administration/routing domain identifiers, specified as address prefixes. Similarly, it is necessary that end systems be able to deal with NSAP addresses for remote ESs as variable length octet strings, up to twenty octets in length, whose internal structure, beyond the initial domain identifier (IDI), is not interpreted directly.

FUTURE OF OSI

High-speed networks supporting time-critical applications will require a reexamination of the protocols used to bridge the transmission fabric and the applications. Existing process control applications and sensor data distribution applications require different transport layer techniques based on low latency with little processing overhead and multicast transfer. This has led to the development of non-standard solutions, but standards committees are now adding these issues to their strategic plans, and will ultimately lead to standard solutions.

To some extent, the hardware technology will also drive the OSI solutions. With increases in bandwidth, applications will be able to use larger transfers at higher rates. Increases in processor power will help overcome some of the processing overhead of OSI, but there is also an effort to reduce the overhead. Latency is the time delay between the transmission of data and the reception by the peer entity. It is related to transit delay across networks, but includes associated processing delays. Latency is also related to the speed of the medium. For many real-time and near real-time systems, latency is more critical than the actual throughput figures. Systems will probably need to be able to control the amount of latency through use of QOS.

Transport protocol must be able to support high throughput applications.

Multicast capabilities are needed above the Data Link Layer. Since many network technologies support multicast and group addressing, it is necessary to extend the use to the upper layers. In addition, some applications are likely to require more reliable multicast, which would ensure that all active group members receive a transmission. Besides being useful for applications involving broadcast to multiple recipients, multicast is also useful for fault-tolerant systems, in which transactions are sent to backup processors.

Efficient transactions relate to the ability to provide the Transport Service user with a means of quickly exchanging a moderate amount of critical information. This may involve RPCs or request/response protocols. It is characterized by the ability to exchange information with a minimum time delay. This implies that either the mechanism uses a minimum of overhead exchanges, or performs them very quickly.

Considerable progress has been made in specifying protocols and environments for Open Distributed Processing, which coordinates the standards activities in database as well as OSI to develop standards that specify distributed processing protocols and services. These projects require extensive liaison.

The OSI protocols provide for coexistence of multiple protocol versions (hence also transition to new protocols). During association, the protocol-version identifier is conveyed to ensure that both entities use the same (and newest common) protocol version. The definition of a new protocol-version identifier presumes a minimal common knowledge with the protocol identified by the preceding protocol-version identifier. When such a minimal common knowledge cannot be achieved, the protocols are considered to be independent and different.

Changes made in a protocol will not always imply the need for a new protocol version (or for a new protocol). A new protocol version (or new protocol) becomes necessary when these changes lead to a significant functional modification which cannot be compatibly negotiated using the existing protocol specifications so that a real open system utilizing the newly specified protocol functions would not be able to communicate with a real open system utilizing the old specifications.

BENEFITS OF OSI

Open systems benefit users because they need not be tied to a single vendor and vendors will eventually benefit through access to a larger market. Properly applied data communication protocol standards can:

- reduce system or network development time
- ease procurement problems with commonly available equipment that conforms to standards. TCP/IP already provides these benefits, so this is not really a major factor in choosing OSI.
- enhance the marketability of products and standards that meet recognized interface standards
- shorten system checkout, debugging, and installation time by providing a defined performance base
- enhance maintainability by providing compatible test devices

OSI also permits considerable flexibility with respect to the physical interface. For example, connections to X.25 networks may support RS-232, EIA-530, or V.35 depending on speed and distance requirements. As a second example, IS 8802-3 interfaces may be provided using fiber optics techniques.

The important point is that OSI has been deliberately designed to provide a generic set of functionality which may be used in almost any system. Furthermore, it gives a great deal of flexibility to users. Standard networks may be joined to create a large GOSIP-compliant internetwork.

For example, OSI, in Layers 1–4, provides a service which allows end systems on one subnetwork to reliably transfer data to end systems on other subnetworks. This reliable transfer service is a foundation upon which a user can develop protocols which do not conform to an international standard but do meet a specific user need. The reliable transfer service, in turn, can use a Connectionless Network Service which masks the differences between various network technologies and allows the transfer of data among different subnetworks, or, optionally, use a Connection-oriented Network

Service to transfer data more efficiently when all end systems are attached to X.25 or ISDN subnetworks.

Other building blocks are available. At the Application Layer, the Association Control Service Element (ACSE) is designed to provide common Application Layer services which currently include the management of connections. The ACSE performs all required interactions with the Presentation Layer.

TP-4 is message oriented, unlike some earlier protocols that were bit or byte oriented. This allows end systems to intelligently coalesce incoming data rather than being interrupted to handle unnecessary task wake-ups.

- Development—eliminate development (and life cycle costs) of custom interfaces
- Procurement—portable software and lower layer interface boards available as COTS
- OSI more robust for large networks, particularly in terms of management

When TCP/IP was devised, its addressing structure allowed for expansion well beyond most futurist's projections. It is now beginning to encounter address limitations (partly as a result of its great success). OSI's naming services and addressing structure accommodate many more addressees and provide vastly greater flexibility—and should be able to handle great increases in technology.

Because of the many existing networks, there has been substantial work on interfacing OSI with the existing networks. This will help provide a smoother transition path, as well as removing some of the objections to OSI, and providing larger networks with which OSI implementations can interface.

It is quite likely that OSI will benefit from more modernization efforts than existing protocols. For example, multicast protocols are likely to lead to better support for fault-tolerant distributed systems.

CONCLUSIONS

OSI has been somewhat slow in gaining acceptance. Standards have taken years to reach full maturity, and many areas still require extensive work. Many users have made large investments in older technologies and continue to generate a high demand for compatible and familiar technology. One of the significant drawbacks is the low availability of commercial products for OSI. OSI requires new—and expensive—development work, which vendors are reluctant to undertake until they are convinced that the demand—and pricing structures—will provide adequate returns.

Many existing non-OSI systems have substantial investments in hardware that cannot adequately support the more powerful OSI implementations.

Federal procurement requirements for the use of GOSIP are likely to encourage more vendors to produce OSI implementations, which will make more implementations available to industry users.

Early implementors of OSI have found that the vast number of possible options at each layer presents many opportunities for incompatibility. The concept of profiles can help overcome this problem (as well as allowing industry groups to tailor OSI to their own needs) but profiles are not a panacea.

Many of the standards are complicated and hence are sometimes more difficult to implement; greater investments are needed in software development before products are ready to generate revenue. Arguably, the software development techniques need to be more advanced. In addition, customers often compared first implementations of OSI against second or third generations of older protocols. While this certainly is valid from the customer's perspective, who must meet certain performance requirements, it does not provide a valid assessment of the OSI design—only the current state of the art in implementing the design. Is it the implementation or the architecture that is the bottleneck.

Similarly, until recently, many of the OSI standards have only been at the Draft International Standard (DIS) level, so there has been uncertainty about maturity. As more people have produced implementation, defect reports—and subsequent corrigenda—have resulted, so the standards have improved. With some earlier protocols, the protocols were first developed and then described, while in ISO, the standardized protocols were described and then implemented (although some test implementations were developed by people involved in the standards process).

Some detractors assert that the need to go through all seven layers results in poor performance. First, it is not necessary to have discrete separations between each of the layers, although it may be helpful to have such a separation to enable that the protocol is handled correctly at each layer. Other detractors criticize the functions performed by each of the layers; however, with the possible exception of BER, these functions need to be performed anyway. OSI formalizes the relationship and structure of the functions.

7

X.400

David Eng

INTRODUCTION

Gateways between mail systems are nothing new. They have been in existence since the second electronic mail system was deployed. The X.400 protocols arc important because of the widespread acceptance of X.400. All important industry segments have embraced X.400—public electronic (e-mail) network vendors, host mail vendors, computer companies, end users, and international government agencies. No other messaging gateway technique has such universal backing.

HOW X.400 CAME ABOUT

In 1981 a number of office equipment vendors, computer manufacturers, and value-added telecommunications service providers began work on what they initially intended to be a comprehensive set of technical specifications for interconnecting e-mail systems. They pursued their goal under the auspices of the Consultative Committee for International Telegraphy and Telephony (CCITT), the standards-making body of the world's Postal, Telegraph, and Telephone administrations (the PTTs). In 1984, the CCITT approved the results of this collaborative effort as a series of eight documents called the X.400-series Recommendations for Message Handling Systems (X.400 for short). Thus was brought into being a set of internationally recognized data communications standards for e-mail.

In the course of meeting its e-mail objectives, the CCITT addressed and solved two other important data communications problems in a way that has shaped today's data communication technology. First, the CCITT recognized the need to develop standards broader than those required for e-mail alone, e-mail being the exchange of interpersonal electronic memoranda. It viewed this as just one application of a more generic facility that has come to be known as **messaging**. Messaging is the reliable, store-and-forward conveyance of digitally encoded information of all kinds, from a single source to one or more recipients, perhaps widely distributed. Distinguishing e-mail from messaging enabled the CCITT to create both an architecture and a family of data communication protocols for interconnecting messaging systems such that one can easily define and integrate a variety of messaging applications. Among them are e-mail (the original focus of the standardization effort), electronic data interchange (EDI), and store-and-forward facsimile.

Recognizing the need for a protocol specification tool, CCITT developed a notation for precisely describing the information to be exchanged between X.400 components, along with a set of rules for encoding such information as binary data so that it can be communicated via a network. CCITT's second contribution of a fundamental nature was to recognize the utility of making the notation and encoding rules general enough to support any Open Systems Interconnection (OSI) application, not just messaging. Known as **Abstract Notation One (ASN.1)**, the notation and encoding rules have since been adopted by all OSI standardization organizations as the means for specifying application protocols and the data structures they encompass.

In 1985 CCITT began three years of follow-on work resulting in important extensions to X.400. The extensions enable, among other things, secure messaging (using cryptographic techniques), full internetworking with the international postal system, and the use of electronic directories for authentication, user-friendly naming, and distribution lists. The expanded Message Handling recommendations ratified in 1988, referred to as X.400 (1988), are the result of a collaborative effort between CCITT and the International Organization for Standardization (ISO). Thus, there are now ISO International Standards that are editorially and technically aligned with X.400.

Since its issuance in 1984, X.400 has achieved widespread acceptance throughout the messaging industry. Nearly every office equipment vendor, computer manufacturer, and value-added service provider now offers, or is committed to offering, X.400 interconnect capability. The earliest contributors to the X.400 standardization effort envisioned a multivendor messaging network comparable in scale and eventual utility to the international telephone network and postal system. Following major initiatives in 1988–1989, the majority of PTT-provided e-mail services and the commercially provided public services in almost all countries of the world are actively pursuing the interconnection of their respective services. The construction of a global messaging network is now clearly underway, with X.400 as its blueprint.

WHAT X.400 STANDARDIZES

In X.400 terminology, a computer (or computer process) responsible for message transfer is called a **message transfer agent (MTA)**, a computer responsible for message storage is called a **message store (MS)**, and a computer that submits and takes delivery of, or retrieves, messages on behalf of a user is called **user agent (UA)**. Taken together, the MTAs are called the **message transfer system (MTS)**. The UAs, the MSs, and MTS, taken together, are called the **message handling system (MHS)**.

X.400 also provides for the relaying of messages to and from communication systems and devices of other kinds, for example, the telex network, the postal system, and facsimile terminals. A computer (or computer process) responsible for such relaying is called an **access unit (AU)**. The MTS is considered to encompass AUs.

As illustrated in Figure 7.1, X.400 standardizes four major protocols for interconnecting MHS components:

- **P1**: specifies how two computers responsible for message transfer (that is, two MTAs) relay message from one to the other.

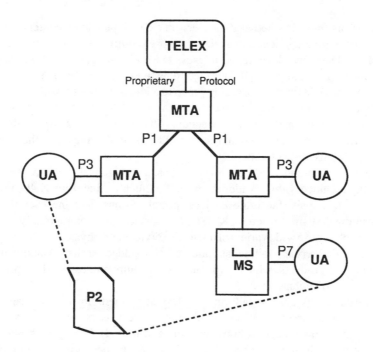

Figure 7.1   X.400 components and protocols.

- **P3:** specifies how one computer (a UA) submits and takes delivery of messages via another computer responsible for message transfer (an MTA).
- **P7:** specifies how one computer (a UA) submits and interactively retrieves messages via another computer responsible for message storage (an MS).
- **P2:** more a format specification than a protocol, P2 specifies how the contents of messages representing ordinary office memoranda (e-mail) are structured for purposes of message transfer, submission, and delivery of the MTS.

Additionally, X.400 identifies a family of format specifications, of which P2 is an example, whose members govern user-to-user (more precisely, UA-to-UA) communications by means of the MTS in particular applications, such as e-mail.

THE TECHNICAL MERITS OF X.400

A number of technical characteristics make X.400 suitable for e-mail system interconnection on a worldwide scale. These same characteristics make X.400-based messaging systems a suitable basis, or platform, for a wide variety of information exchange applications. In considering the technical merits of X.400, messaging vendors and users are likely to identify the following characteristics as most important.

X.400 carefully distinguishes between the electronic envelope and its contents, thereby enabling a wide range of messaging applications, including those requiring the store-and-forward exchange of office memoranda, office documents, telexes, facsimile images, voice messages, structured business transactions (for example, EDI), and electronic funds transfer (EFT) instructions. Recognizing this, the CCITT in 1988 formed a working group to address the use of X.400 as the basis for EDI, and recently initiated additional projects to consider the use of X.400 in other areas. Data communication users, manufacturers, and industry associations have identified X.400 as the technical basis for industry-specific file transfer, store-and-forward facsimile offerings, and the interconnection of voice messaging systems, respectively.

X.400 employs an open-ended address format. Thus, a wide range of non-X.400 communication systems are readily included within its address space. Technically, therefore, X.400 users can address, for example, telex terminals, facsimile devices, postal patrons, and the users of essentially all pre-X.400 messaging systems. Presently, X.400-based services and commercially available products provide interconnections to a wide variety of telematic services and physical delivery systems. Service providers offer these delivery capabilities as optional, value-added services. Manufacturers offer them as optional features of products, which corporate users acquire and establish as privately operated, organizational communication systems.

X.400 also provides options for tailoring the format or medium of a message to a particular recipient, thereby enabling meaningful communication between users with widely varying equipment and for securing the communication between users end-to-end, thereby making X.400 useful in sensitive commercial applications such as EDI and EFT. Secure messaging relies upon cryptographic techniques.

WHY X.400 HAS BEEN ACCEPTED

The acceptance of X.400 by users and suppliers alike is due to several factors. First, OSI standards in general are increasingly accepted as the desired technical basis for multivendor office systems, which corporations in increasing numbers demand. Vendors, in particular, have been quick to incorporate X.400 in their product plans, in part because of the "open" nature of its definition. X.400 defines a technologically new and therefore commercially neutral messaging architecture; it does not embrace one of the major proprietary architectures, which would have given competitive advantage to one particular manufacturer. For those companies that do promote a proprietary messaging architecture, X.400 represents a single, uniform, high-function definition of the interface to other vendors' mail and messaging products, or as the basis on which private systems using the proprietary architecture can interconnect with public services.

The applicability of X.400 to a variety of communication platforms, and its extensibility with respect to applications and "value-added features," also make X.400 more attractive. X.400's application layer protocols can govern communication over a wide variety of transport media, including public and private wide area (for example, X.25) data networks, dial-up and leased telephone lines, and local area networks (LANs). Additionally, X.400 makes no attempt to standardize the user interfaces or other purely local features of messaging systems or applications (for example, message creation, display, printing, and logging), thereby permitting product differentiation.

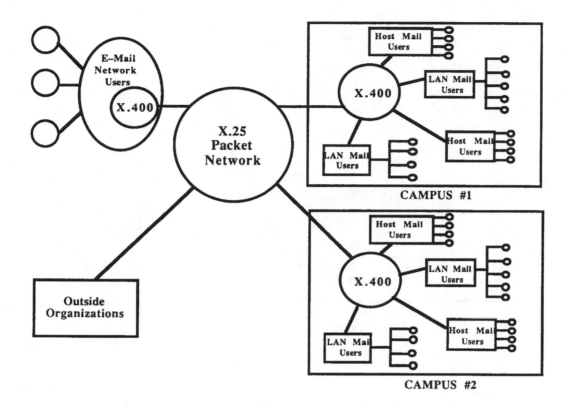

Figure 7.2   Large end users can connect their entire organization using X.400 as the backbone.

Figure 7.2 shows an X.400-based messaging system for a large user organization. As shown in the figure, inside of each large end user site is an X.400 message center. This facility, located across several computer platforms, performs the activity of converting a message, routing the message, and administering the interdepartmental messaging function.

The acceptance of X.400 by service providers is easy to understand. Because it is the CCITT standard for message handling, X.400 without question is the way in which the PTTs will interconnect—indeed, are interconnecting—national messaging systems. Such systems are destined to form the "backbone" of a global messaging network.

X.400 has sufficient technical strength to sustain the creation of a worldwide value-added communication network integrating both public and private (that is, corporate) systems, and supporting a wide variety of applications. This is largely due to X.400's identification and definition of a set of generic message transfer functions, and its clear separation of those functions from other message-processing functions that depend upon the end-to-end significance to messaging applications of the information they exchange by means of messages. The MTS of X.400 provides the technical basis for building an infrastructure for integrated messaging and invites users and vendors to identify and implement a wide range of messaging applications.

8

X.500 DIRECTORY SERVICES

Judy Cross

PURPOSE OF DIRECTORY SERVICES

Computer network technology offers unlimited opportunities for increasing individual and work-group productivity through the distribution of work across an unconstrained number of systems. Today's electronic desktop user has access to a variety of network functions including file transfer, remote login, and distributed applications, which allow the user to capitalize on resources and data located anywhere in the network. Yet, industry experts generally agree that despite great leaps forward in network functionality, the promised increased productivity goals have yet to be fully realized.

This opportunity includes a base requirement, namely, that the location of resources and data is known so that they can be accessed. Each type of network in operation today has some scheme whereby this information can be made available: TCP/IP users rely on the Domain Name System (DNS)/Berkeley Internet Name Daemon (BIND) and DECnet/OSI offers the Digital Distributed Name Service (DECdns). Each electronic mail service provides a subscriber database. While each service is adequate for its own application, in today's environment of multivendor, multiprotocol networks, it is an administrative nightmare to coordinate all of these services in a single network.

It has become common to have a single entity registered in several different services, each subject to its own rules for data definition and access. Additionally, many of these services rely on file structures and access techniques that will not scale enough to accommodate large enterprises and global networks. (For example, a given service may require that all information is stored in a single file on a single system. This requirement places a limit on how much information can be maintained.) It is apparent that a single directory service that can accommodate networks of all sizes will reduce both the administrative and technical obstacles to providing true open networking.

The evolving X.500 Directory Service standard is viewed as the key enabling technology for meeting this requirement. Among all of the potential benefits X.500 offers, the most critical is the ability to locate networked information and resources without having to first know their physical address. Through a single operation anywhere in the network, information such as the address of an electronic mail subscriber can be made immediately and transparently available via a query using a name that has meaning to the end user.

For the past several years, CCITT and ISO have been working on Recommendations and International Standards for an Open System Interconnection Directory Service. The X.500 series of recommendations have been published as the ISO 9594 standard. (See References for a list of all components of ISO 9594.) ISO and CCITT define the models and protocols for Directory Services that enable different software vendors to build products that can work together to create a single networked Directory Service that can scale to any size. As a result of the publication of these standards, computer users are increasingly demanding that their directory requirements be met by products conforming to these standards.

The X.500 Directory Service is closely associated with the X.400 Messaging Standards. X.400 is an application that clearly requires a directory service due to the complexity of subscriber (O/R or Originator/Recipient) addressing and the sheer size of the subscriber database. X.400 mail users require a facility that allows them to locate the addresses of those individuals they wish to send mail to, similar to the services provided today by the telephone companies with their publication of subscriber directories.

X.500 is also useful in contexts other than electronic mail. Distributed file and print services, transaction processing, and distributed applications of all types can take advantage of a network-wide directory service. The scope of X.500, therefore, extends beyond maintaining mail subscriber information to encompass information about any network object of interest to the users of the network.

The purpose of the Directory Service standards is to define the structure and protocols required for the storage and retrieval of information about network objects, be they people, files, applications, or data elements. This information includes such things as network addresses, routing information, security features, telephone numbers, and so forth. Such information can be used, for example, by a messaging application that could store routing information that enables it to route messages across a network to the recipients.

The use of X.500 has been mandated by the United Kingdom Government OSI Profile (GOSIP). It is scheduled to be included in United States GOSIP Version 3, due to be published in the spring of 1992, becoming effective in October 1993. X.500 has also been adopted by the Open Software Foundation (OSF) as part of its Distributed Computing Environment (DCE). Within the DCE, X.500 is to be used as a global service with Cell Directory Service (CDS) acting as a local naming service.

This article describes the basic components of the X.500 standards. To set the context, directory services are defined. Digital Equipment Corporation's X.500 offering is described as a sample implementation.

DEFINITION OF DIRECTORY SERVICES

A Directory Service provides information about a given object, typically structured in such a way that the information can be accessed by a key identifier. As an example, the telephone directory provides addresses and telephone numbers of individuals and businesses using a key identifier of the individual's surname or the business name. The directory allows for a search even when the exact key is not fully known, although the search is much quicker when the exact spelling of an individual's last name is known.

Certain rules are required for any directory service to be useful.

- Access to information is consistent
- Key identifiers have meaning to the end user
- Information that is retrieved is accurate—changes propagate within a reasonable period of time
- Identifiers are independent of their physical location—the object's physical location in the network can be changed without affecting the way the object information is accessed

THE X.500 DIRECTORY SERVICE STANDARD

The X.500 Directory is a collection of cooperating OSI application processes (typically in different open systems), which together hold a single logical database containing information about a set of real world objects. People and programs can read and modify the stored information, subject to the application of security policies. Accessors of the directory are represented by Directory User Agents (DUA). The distributed directory is held in multiple Directory System Agents (DSA). The relationship between these components is shown in Figure 8.1.

The logical database of object information is known as the Directory Information Base (DIB). The structure of the DIB is known as the Directory Information Tree (DIT). The following sections describe the details of these components, first describing how information is structured and then how the information is accessed.

Information Structure

The purpose of the directory is to store information about any objects of interest and to allow access to the information for query, modification, and management. In order to provide these services, the entries must be organized in a consistent, well-known manner. As an example, libraries store and retrieve information based on a model of information.

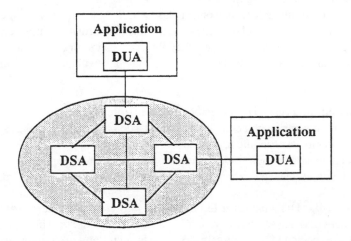

Figure 8.1   X.500 Directory services.

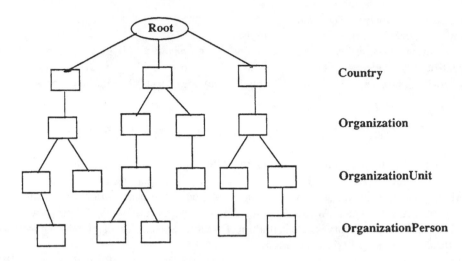

Figure 8.2 X.500 Directory information tree.

The model defines categories of information (such as computer science) with subcategories as required (such as networks, database, and application programming languages). Subcategories are defined to whatever depth is required to identify all information areas. The X.500 Directory Service also provides such a model.

Objects of interest to the network community are represented in the database as entries. Entries are defined as sets of attributes, which in turn have values.

Directory Information Base   All information to which the Directory Service provides access is called the Directory Information Base (DIB). The DIB includes information about all objects of interest and their relationships within the directory.

Objects are classified into at least one object class where they share common characteristics with other objects in that class. Object classes are used to control the relationships between objects in the DIB. An object class may be a subclass of another object class (its superior or superclass) from which it inherits certain characteristics. Subclasses, in turn, may have subclasses of their own, down to an arbitrary level.

Directory Information Tree   The Directory Service stores information as directory entries, in which each entry represents an object in the real world, such as a person, a place, an organization, or a computer. The directory entries are organized into a Directory Information Tree (DIT), a hierarchically structured database in which some entries are subordinate to others.

Figure 8.2 illustrates the DIT structure and shows the superior and subordinate relationships between entries.

The structure of the DIT enables it to be divided into coherent pieces that can be distributed throughout the network. These pieces are known as naming contexts. The number of entries in an X.500 directory is expected to be extremely large, too large for any one computer system to hold. By

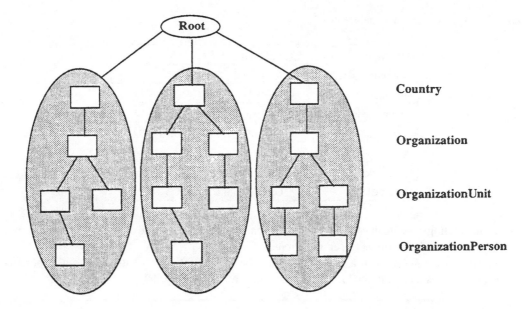

Figure 8.3   Naming contexts.

dividing the DIT into appropriate naming contexts, the directory can be distributed across a large number of computer systems. The shaded areas in Figure 8.3 show how a DIT can be divided.

As each naming context is a known part of the whole DIT, the entire directory can be managed as a single logical entity. This allows the cost of managing the DIT to be shared by several systems. This ability also means that there is really no limit to the size of the DIT. (In fact, the goal of X.500 is to have a single directory for all systems and users in the world. Each network domain will be represented as a part of the single DIT with access being subject to the security procedures of that domain.) As the DIT grows in size, more X.500 Directory Service components (DSAs and DUAs) can be added to manage the added entries.

Whenever an entry is created or modified, the directory service ensures that the entries conform to the rules appropriate to their class and attributes. This checking is provided based on a set of rules, known as the **schema.** It is possible for different parts of the DIT to be constructed according to different sets of rules. Each DSA has a copy of the schema that applies to all entries that it holds.

Classes   Every entry is classified according to the characteristics of the real world object that it represents. When an entry is created, a class must be specified. The X.500 standard defines several default classes. It is also possible to define other classes.

Each class definition specifies certain rules about entries for objects belonging to that class. These rules include:

- mandatory attributes—attributes for which at least one value must be specified
- optional attributes—attributes for which values may be specified

Table 8.1   Directory Entry Components

Attribute	Value(s)
Common Name	Joan Smith
Surname	Smith
Telephone Number	(222)555–1212
Postal Address	"142 Main St, Hometown, USA"
Postal Code	12345
Description	Project Supervisor
Object Class	Organizational Person

- name bindings—state that the attribute-value pair that forms the name of an entry must be chosen from a particular attribute or set of attributes
- structure rules—state that a given entry must be subordinate to an entry of another specified class (defines a level in the hierarchy where the entry must appear)

Directory Entries

Within the Directory Service, real world objects are represented as directory entries. Each entry is composed of a set of attributes, each of which has one or more values. The attributes represent all of the information that needs to be stored about that object. Table 8.1 shows a sample entry. Note that the Object Class to which the entry belongs is identified as one of the entry's attributes. Figure 8.4 shows the structure of a given directory entry. Each directory entry must be uniquely (or unambiguously) identifiable in order to be accessed correctly. This will be discussed later in this section.

Attributes   An **attribute** is a description of a characteristic of the entry. As an example, a person (object class) has a name (attribute) and a job title (attribute). The person's actual name and job title are the values of the attributes.

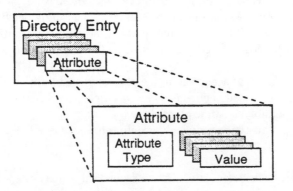

Figure 8.4   Directory entry components.

Each attribute type is associated with an **attribute syntax**, which defines the format of its value and whether the attribute is allowed to have more than one value. For example, the telephonenumber attribute class uses the telephonenumbersyntax, which defines the attribute as having more than one value and that each value must be a printable string.

Each attribute syntax also defines a matching rule. The matching rule specifies how the Directory Service will compare attribute values with each other for certain user requests. For example, for many attributes, the attribute syntax is insensitive to case, so the Directory Service would consider that the attribute values commonname="JoAN SmitH" and commonname="joaN smITH" match. Other syntaxes are numeric, and have matching rules that allow the Directory Service to tell whether a value is more or less than a suggested value. Matching rules allow for queries on groups of entries, such as locating all employees with home addresses within a given postal code.

Entry Names   The hierarchical structure of the DIT is the basis of each entry's unique, unambiguous name.

A typical entry may have several attribute values that represent names by which the real world object is known, such as surnames and common names. One or more of these attribute-value pairs is known as the relative distinguished name (RDN). Each entry has a relative distinguished name. However, the RDN by itself cannot uniquely identify a given entry; surname=Smith could identify hundreds of different individuals. In order to provide a unique identifier, each entry also has a distinguished name (DN). A distinguished name identifies an individual entry in terms of that entry's position in the hierarchy of the DIT.

A distinguished name consists of all RDNs in the path from the root (top) of the DIT to the actual entry. Each RDN contains an attribute type and value chosen from the attributes of the entry that it represents. No two entries that have the same immediately superior entry can have the same RDN. (In some cases, an RDN can contain more than one attribute type and value.) Thus, each RDN is unique among the subordinates of a given entry. Using this process, it is now possible to distinguish between the Smith who works in the finance department of Company X and the Smith who works in personnel. Figure 8.5 shows how relative distinguished names are combined to generate unambiguous distinguished names.

In the example, the entry representing Joan Smith (at the bottom left) has a distinguished name made up of four RDNs. The first three RDNs represent the three entries that form a path from the root of the DIT to Joan's entry. (Note that, by convention, the root of the DIT is at the top of the picture.) The fourth RDN is that of Joan's entry itself. Since each RDN is unique relative to its superior entry, the distinguished name is also guaranteed to be unique.

Alias Entries   Although an entry has only one distinguished name, it is possible to create separate alias entries for an entry. An alias entry serves as a pointer to the "real" entry, thereby allowing alternate paths to the object information. For example, if Joan Smith has recently married, she may still be known by her unmarried name, Joan Meredith. An alias entry may be created that has the RDN commonname="Joan Meredith" as a subordinate of the entry with the RDN organizationalunitname=Sales. In this case, the alias entry's distinguished name is identical to that of Joan's real entry, except for the last RDN. The alias entry has an attribute that contains the distinguished name of the entry that really represents Joan Smith. If Joan's unmarried name is used as the key to her entry, the Directory Service will automatically display the new entry.

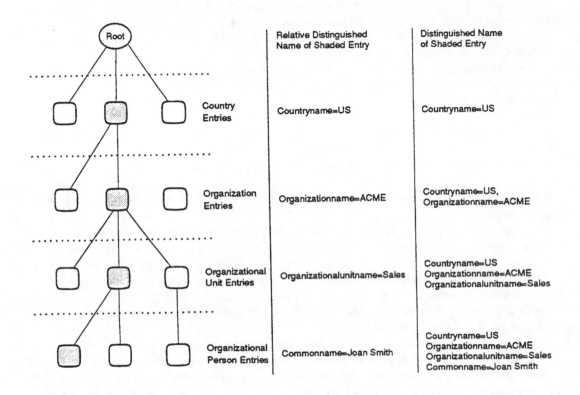

Figure 8.5   Generation of distinguished names.

Another reason to create an alias entry is when someone moves from one part of an organization to another. A new entry can be created in the appropriate part of the DIT to represent the person's new position in the organization. The original entry can be replaced with an alias entry that refers to the new entry. Anyone trying to access the person with the old organizational information will automatically be given the new entry.

Operation of the Directory

Information is useless unless it can be accessed. The X.500 standard defines two components, the Directory User Agent and the Directory Service Agent, to provide access to the information stored in the DIB. The Directory User Agent (DUA) is the interface between the requester of the information (end user) and the holder of the information, the Directory Service Agent (DSA).

Directory User Agent   The Directory User Agent (DUA) is the end user's interface to the X.500 directory. The DUA allows users to form requests for directory information, such as a request to view or create an entry. The DUA ensures that each request is formatted correctly, and then uses a standard protocol to pass requests to a DSA. The DUA uses the same protocol to receive answers back from the DSA. Upon receipt of the answer, the DUA presents the information to the user. A single DUA may access one or more DSAs.

A given DUA may be configured to allow query only or query and modify. This helps to prevent unauthorized changes to the contents of the directory.

Directory Service Agent   The Directory Service Agent (DSA) is a server. It is responsible for storing directory entries and for providing access to them. A DSA is also responsible for redirecting requests for information that it does not store.

The amount of directory information a DSA can hold depends on the resources available on the DSA's node. To enable the DIT to expand beyond the capacity of a single DSA, the X.500 standard allows data to be distributed among several DSAs.

Each DSA may hold one or more naming contexts. The ability to distribute directory information across many DSAs means that there is no limit to the amount of information that can be stored in total, as new DSAs can be added at any time.

Even though each DSA only manages part of the DIT, it does not mean that a user needs to know which DSA to query for a particular piece of information. Each DSA maintains a set of knowledge information that helps it redirect a request to a more relevant DSA. Using these references, DSAs are able to cooperate to handle a user request.

The DSA and directory applications cooperate to provide two main types of access to directory information:

- Interrogations of the directory information
- Modifications of the directory information

The interrogation services provide different ways of looking at the information in the directory, such as inspecting particular attributes of an entry, or searching for entries that have a specified set of attributes. The modification services allow directory administrators to create new entries, remove entries, and modify the attributes of entries.

Access   When it is necessary to access an object, either for query or modification, the DUA serves as the interface to the end user. The DUA will establish a connection to a DSA, typically one defined as the default for that DUA.

The standard mode of obtaining information is to have the DSAs communicate with each other to obtain the requested data. This is known as chaining. Where the first DSA does not hold the entry, it will connect to other DSAs directly. When the data is found, the original DSA will return it to the DUA. Figure 8.6 shows this process.

Alternatively, the DSA could respond to the DUA with a referral. In this case, the DSA does not have the requested information but believes it knows which DSA does. The DUA then connects to the referred DSA to obtain the information. This process will continue until the information is obtained. Figure 8.7 depicts this process.

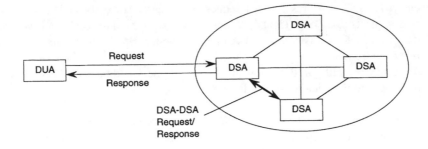

Figure 8.6   Chaining.

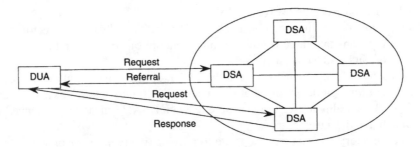

Figure 8.7   Referral.

BENEFITS AND LIMITATIONS OF X.500

X.500 standards activities are providing a blueprint for internationally agreed upon interfaces, structures, and protocols for a global Directory Service. Its structures allow directories to be built and maintained for networks of all sizes.

The limitations of X.500 are mainly due to the fact that the standard is relatively new and not yet fully defined. The 1988 recommendations published by CCITT do not support access controls (security features), replication, or shadowing of data. These areas are being addressed in the 1992 CCITT publications.

In the interim, enough of the standards are defined for implementation efforts to begin. Many network vendors have announced products and/or programs to comply with X.500.

A critical milestone for full acceptance of X.500 is the adoption of a naming scheme that will provide a common schema for the upper layers of an international DIT. In the United States, the North American Directory Forum (NADF) has been formed to deal with this issue. The NADF is a consortium of network vendors and customers.

IMPLEMENTATION OF X.500: DIGITAL EQUIPMENT CORPORATION

Digital's X.500 Directory Service is an implementation of the ISO and CCITT series of standards and recommendations for Directory Services. The Directory Service also conforms to Digital's Enterprise Management Architecture, which will allow the management of the X.500 Directory Service components to be consistent with the management of other applications, systems, and databases within the network. As Digital's DSA and DUA implementations use standard protocols, they can interwork with other vendor's X.500 conformant DSAs and directory applications.

The X.500 Directory Service contains the following components:

- The Directory Server
- Directory Administration Tools
- A Search Utility
- Callable interfaces to X.500 (XDS and XOM) (available as part of an OSI Application Developer's Toolkit)

Digital's X.500 Directory Service provides the standard DUA and DSA components and implements the standard protocols for communication between them. Digital also provides client applications to "front-end" the DUA. One such application is a lookup facility where the application provides a "user friendly" interface that allows the user to enter search parameters. The lookup facility will then format the parameters in accordance with the standards defined for the DUA.

The Directory Service includes a default schema that can be used as is or modified to suit the needs of a given network. The X.500 directory applications refer to the schema to find out how to display entries. The schema includes instructions on what order to display attributes in, and what language to use for the display. If information is accessed that conforms to a schema that the directory application does not recognize, the application will attempt to display the information as sensibly as possible.

An added value of Digital's X.500 Directory Service product is its ability to replicate data. The X.500 standard defines procedures for distribution of data but does not specifically support replication in the 1988 recommendations. The recommendations do recognize the usefulness of replication and provide some rules for its use, for example, the ability to define whether a response to a request is from an "original" entry or a replica.

Replication allows copies of a given naming context to be located in more than one place. This provides a backup of the information as well as the ability to respond to inquiries faster. Digital's current name/directory services, DECdns and the Distributed Directory Service (DDS) for electronic mail, already support replication. Replication in the X.500 product is being provided in advance of CCITT's 1992 publications. The ability to replicate information makes Digital's Directory Service product suitable for large organizations who want all of their users and applications in several locations to have efficient access to a large amount of directory information.

MIGRATION TO X.500

Although the X.500 Directory Service Standards have been published, few implementations are currently in place. One reason for this is that most networks today already have some form (or forms) of Directory Service. While most network planners want to consolidate their multiple directory services into one, they are faced with a massive migration task.

Challenges

Migration to X.500 requires change. This change is most evident in the fact that network managers must now organize information across the entire enterprise. Typically, directory information has been defined only in the context of a given application and only for the users of that application (as an example, electronic mail subscribers). The definition of an X.500 schema appears to be a daunting task.

A second obstacle to migration is the existence of a multitude of directory services, each having its own rules for organization and access. The information in each of these services must be somehow redefined and reorganized to fit the structures defined by X.500. In many cases, there is no clean path.

Solutions

A solution to the migration concerns involves the definition of a coherent, evolutionary path from today's proliferation of services to a single service. Such a path of necessity must include interim services that can understand several different directory services and be able to reconcile requests in (for example) DNS syntax into a format that can be used by a DUA. Conversely, DUAs must have an associated service that enables them to access a BIND or DECdns name space in order to fulfill a user's request.

Many vendors, including Digital, are working on such an interim solution. Service gateways that can resolve different syntaxes and access rules allow end users to have the full benefit of what appears to be a single directory while at the same time allowing for the gradual migration of information into a single structure.

The efforts of the NADF are designed to ease the problem of defining a corporate name space by creating a standard for the upper layers of the DIT. Lower layers of the DIT can then follow existing conventions in use by corporations, such as organization units or locations, employee names, and ID numbers and system names.

CONCLUSION

In an age of multivendor networks, standards are critical. With standards, hardware and software from different vendors can coexist and interoperate within a single network. The beneficiaries are the end users, who can perform the tasks necessary to their work without concern for the underlying structures and protocols in their network. Administrators and managers can also benefit by having a consistent management interface regardless of the entities being managed.

Using an X.500 directory, all components of the network can be located. Application processes can cooperate and people can communicate. The X.500 Directory Services provide the key link between these elements.

REFERENCES

X.500 and Related Standards

ISO 9594-2 (X.501) Information Processing Systems—Open Systems Interconnection—the Directory—Models.

ISO 9594-3 (X.511) Information Processing Systems—Open Systems Interconnection—the Directory—Abstract Service Definition.

ISO 9594-4 (X.518) Information Processing Systems—Open Systems Interconnection—the Directory—Procedures for Distributed Operation.

ISO 9594-5 (X.519) Information Processing Systems—Open Systems Interconnection—the Directory—Protocol Specification.

ISO 9594-6 (X.520) Information Processing Systems—Open Systems Interconnection—the Directory—Selected Attribute Types.

ISO 9594-7 (X.521) Information Processing Systems—Open Systems Interconnection—the Directory—Selected Object Classes.

ISO 9594-8 (X.521) Information Processing Systems—Open Systems Interconnection—the Directory—Authentication Framework.

ISO 10021-3 (X.407) Information Processing Systems—Text Communication—Abstract Service Definition Conventions.

ISO 8825 (X.409) Information Processing Systems—Open Systems Interconnection—Basic Encoding Rules for Abstract Syntax Notation One (ASN.1).

BIBLIOGRAPHY

Black, Uyless. *The X Series Recommendations.* New York: McGraw-Hill, 1991.

———*OSI: A Model for Computer Communications Standards.* Englewood Cliffs, NJ: Prentice Hall, 1991.

Plattner, B., Lanz, C., Lubich, H., Muller, M., and Walter, T. *X.400 Message Handling: Standards, Interworking, Applications.* Reading, MA: Addison-Wesley, 1991.

Rose, Marshall T. *The Little Black Book.* Englewood Cliffs, NJ: Prentice-Hall, 1992.

9

THE BASICS OF HIGH-LEVEL DATA LINK CONTROL

Dale Gulick

INTRODUCTION

High-level Data Link Control (HDLC) procedure is an International Standards Organization (ISO) standard. The details of the standard are spelled out in two separate documents. ISO 3309 specifies the lower-level frame structure, while ISO 4335 specifies the "elements of procedures" that govern the flow of data across some communication channel. We will discuss these two parts of the standard individually, but first a bit of history.

HDLC is a generalization of the original Synchronous Data Link Control (SDLC) developed by IBM in the early 1970s. The early details were described in 1972 in a paper by James P. Gray (IBM) (*Proceedings of the IEEE*, Vol. 60, no. 11). IBM formalized SDLC in 1974 in a General Information Manual and started shipping SDLC-equipped 3767 and 3770 terminals as well as optional adaptors for the 3271, 3275, and 3704/5 products. In 1976 the ISO issued the first version of the 3309 and 4335 standards, revising and expanding them in 1979 and 1984.

It should be noted that nobody uses HDLC per se. Rather, HDLC is the basis for a class of specific standards such as Link Access Protocol (LAP), Link Access Protocol Balanced (LAPB) and Link Access Protocol D channel—ISDN (LAPD).

HDLC resides at layer 2 of the ISO Open Systems Interconnect (ISO-OSI) 7-layer model. Layer 2 is the Data Link Layer. It is responsible for transmitting data provided by layer 3 (Network Layer) using the facilities of layer 1 (Physical Layer). As such, HDLC is independent of the details of both layers 1 and 3. Layer 2 guarantees to layer 3 that the data has been received without error. Since errors are inevitable, HDLC provides for the detection of errors and the retransmission of the data. In both the standards documents and practical implementation, the protocol is split into two parts, layer 2 minus (L2–) and layer 2 plus (L2+). L2– handles the real-time functions such as packet delimiting, address inspection, and error detection. L2+ establishes the layer 2 point-to-point connection, acknowledges the receipt of packets, checks sequence numbers, and otherwise maintains the orderly flow of data. In the great majority of applications, L2– is handled in hardware and L2+ is handled in software.

L2–

In HDLC, data is transmitted in chunks called **packets.** These packets are delimited by unique eight-bit characters called **flags.** They contain an address, control information, user data (optional), and an error detection code. The address identifies the sender or the receiver of the data. The control information is used by higher levels of the protocol to manage the flow of data. The user data is contained in the information field. Packets that are used for protocol control often omit the information field; this is the only optional field. The error detection code is a Cyclical Redundancy Check (CRC), which resides in the Frame Check Sequence (FCS) field of the packet. In addition to addresses, control, data, and error checking, HDLC employs such mechanisms as flags, zero insertion/deletion, and abort characters.

Aside from the utilization of packets, the quintessential characteristic of HDLC is its use of a zero insertion/deletion technique to create unique data-independent control characters. It works like this: The data to be transmitted is inspected as each bit is sent. If five consecutive ones appear in the data stream, a zero is inserted. This insures that no matter what data the user is transmitting, the receiver will never see more than five consecutive ones, unless a control character containing at least six consecutive ones is intentionally transmitted (without inserting a zero). On the receive side, every time five consecutive ones are received, the next bit is tested. If it is a zero, it is deleted. If it is a one, then the receiver has detected a control character. As a result, unique **control characters** can be created that have six or more consecutive ones. (The term control character is not strictly formal, and should not be confused with the control field, which we will discuss later. It is used here to refer to opening and closing flags and aborts.)

The following section is a glossary of HDLC L2– terms and functions. After covering these basics, we will summarize layer 2– by examining the flow of packets between a transmitter and a receiver.

General Terminology

Frame In the HDLC environment, data is transmitted in frames. All of the HDLC derivatives such as SDLC, LAPB (X.25), and LAPD share the same basic frame format. (See Table 9.1.)

Flag (General) The eight-bit flag character is identical for all of these protocols. It is exactly 01111110. Its bit pattern is unique within a frame because the zero-bit insertion technique used does not allow six contiguous ones to be present in the packet portion of a frame. The flag character can perform three functions: opening flag, closing flag, and interpacket fill character.

Opening Flag The opening flag is defined as the last, perhaps only, flag prior to a non-flag, non-abort character. (The abort character is defined later.) All valid packets must begin with a flag. The opening flag indicates the beginning of a packet. When flags are being used as interframe fill characters, a non-flag, non-abort character must be received before the preceding flag can be identified as an opening flag.

Table 9.1   Frame Format

OPENING FLAG 01111110	ADDRESS (1 to bytes)	CONTROL (1 or 2 bytes)	INFO (OPTIONAL)	FRAME CHECK SEQUENCE (16 or 32 bits)	CLOSING FLAG 01111110

Address   The principal difference between the lower levels of the various HDLC protocols is the address field. All addresses are of an integer number of bytes in length. In general, an address can be one, two, or N bytes long.

The length of an N byte long address is determined by the value of the least significant bit in each byte of the address (see Table 9.2). This bit, called the Extended Address (EA) bit, identifies the last byte of the address. All of the bytes of an N byte long address will have the EA bit cleared to a zero except the last byte of the address. The presence of an EA bit set to a one indicates that byte is the last byte of the address. The length of the address field affects the detection of a short frame. (Refer to short frame definition.)

In some protocols the second bit (bit 1) of the first byte of the address is used to indicate whether the frame is a command or a response. (We will talk a great deal about commands and responses in the L2+ section.) This bit, called the Command/Response bit (C/R), can be either a one or a zero without invalidating the address.

Table 9.2   C/R, EA Bit Positions

7	6	5	4	3	2	1	0	
						C/R* 0/1	EA * 0	BYTE 1
							0 EA * 0	BYTE 2
							0 EA * 1	BYTE N

*C/R, EA bits are not used in all variants of HDLC (SDLC for example). These bit positions are treated as normal address bits for these protocols.

Control Field   The control field immediately follows the address field and, among other things, identifies the type of packet. Other functions include sequence numbers and a poll/final bit. The control field can be either one or two bytes long. The length of the control field has an impact on the detection of a short frame.

Information Field   When present, the information field follows the control field and precedes the frame check sequence. The information field contains the data that is being transmitted between users.

Frame Check Sequence   The Frame Check Sequence (FCS) is a 16-bit word that is produced by the CRC generator and checked by the CRC checker. Mathematically, it is the ones complement of the sum [modulo 2] of the remainder of:

$$X^K [X^{15} + X^{14} + X^{13} + \ldots + X^2 + X + 1]$$

divided [modulo 2] by the generator polynomial $X^{16} + X^{12} + X^5 + 1$, where K is the number of bits in the frame existing between, but not including, the final bit of the opening flag and the first bit of the FCS, excluding bits inserted for transparency. Furthermore, it is the remainder after multiplication by X^{16} and then division [modulo 2] by the generator polynomial $X^{16} + X^{12} + X^5 + 1$, of the content of the frame, between, but not including, the last bit of the opening flag and the first bit of the FCS, excluding bits inserted for transparency.

Closing Flag   The closing flag is the last field in the frame. It indicates the end of the frame and signals that the FCS should be checked.

Packet   A packet is a frame minus the opening and closing flags.

Mark Idle   When frames are not being transmitted over the link, the link is said to be idle. When the link is idle, the transmitter can be programmed to send an all ones pattern. This is referred to as a Mark Idle (MI) condition. Specifically, an MI is defined as at least fifteen contiguous ones.

Flag Idle   Prior to and between frames, back-to-back flags can be transmitted over the link. This is referred to as a Flag Idle (FI) condition and is selected by program control.

Abort Character   Any pattern of at least seven contiguous one bits is said to be an abort character. An abort character is a physical entity, not to be confused with the abort condition, which is an action. It is important to note that there is a subtle difference between an abort character and a mark idle condition. Back to back, abort characters do not necessarily constitute a mark idle condition. A repeating pattern of seven ones followed by a zero (01111111011111110111111...) is a series of abort characters, but not a mark idle.

Abort   The abort condition is an action that takes place in response to the detection of an abort character while the HDLC receiver is in-frame (after the opening flag, but before the closing flag has been received). An abort causes the termination and discarding of the packet being received. Aborts are asynchronous events in that they can be detected on bit boundaries as well as byte boundaries.

Transparency (Zero-bit Insertion/Deletion) Zero-bit insertion/deletion, often referred to as bit stuffing, is a technique used to provide data transparency. By this we mean a method by which packet data patterns are prevented from appearing as flags, aborts, or mark idles when they appear in the received data stream. Flags, aborts, and the mark idle condition all consist of six or more contiguous one bits. The bit-stuffing technique examines the contents of a packet to be transmitted, on a bit-by-bit basis, from the first bit after the opening flag to the last bit of the FCS, and inserts a zero in the bit stream after any pattern of five contiguous ones, thus ensuring that six or more ones do not appear in the data stream. The receiver, in turn, examines the data stream and removes the inserted zeros that follow five contiguous one bits.

Short Frame The minimum length of a valid packet is protocol specific. This is usually four, five, or six bytes. Any frame that is received with fewer than this legal minimum number of bytes in its packet is called a short frame and is considered an error that should be discarded.

Long Frame On a theoretical basis, a frame can be any length greater than the specified minimum. As a practical matter, however, a maximum packet length must be set to prevent buffer overrun. This length is dynamic and can vary on a data call-by-data call basis. Any received frame with a packet that exceeds this maximum length is referred to as a long frame and is considered an error. Note that the detection of a long frame error must take place as soon as the maximum legal number of bytes has been exceeded, not when the entire frame has been received.

Non-integer Number of Bytes Received If a closing flag is detected and a non-integer number of bytes has been received, that is to say that the character preceding the flag contained fewer than eight bits, a non-integer number of bytes condition exists. Some protocols allow this condition as a normal mode of operation. It is referred to as bit residue. Other protocols consider this condition an error.

Order of Bit Transmission The bytes are transmitted in ascending numerical order; inside a byte, the least significant bit (bit 0) is transmitted first. (Note: The FCS is numbered and transmitted in reverse to this convention.)

L2– Packet Transmission and Reception

Transmission First, let us assume that the L2+ function has some packets to transmit. L2– does not care about the purpose or type of packet—to L2–, packets are packets. To start with, the link is idle, and the transmitter is sending either mark idle or flag idle depending on the flavor of protocol being used. When the command to transmit a packet arrives from L2+, an opening flag is transmitted (if mark idling a flag is transmitted, if flag idling the flag character currently being sent is considered the opening flag). After sending the opening flag, the zero insertion and CRC calculation mechanisms are turned on and the packet portion of the frame (exclusive of the FCS) is transmitted. Note that L2– sees the bits between the end of the opening flag and the start of the FCS as just some data to be sent. The meaning of the data is the province of L2+. When the last bit of the data provided by L2+ has been sent, the FCS bits are transmitted. At this point the closing flag is sent and the transmitter returns to sending idle. At any point during the transmission, the transmitter could decide that the transmission of this packet should be stopped. To do this, an abort is transmitted and the transmitter returns to sending idle. The request to abort the packet can come directly from layer 2–, due to some problem such as not receiving data fast enough from L2+, or the request can come from L2+ or some other higher-layer function.

Reception   At the receive side, the receiver starts off idling, looking at the incoming bit stream on a bit-by-bit basis for the presence of a flag. Note that when a flag is detected, it may not be the opening flag of a packet since the transmitter may be flag idling. Once a flag is detected, the receiver looks at the next character to see if it is a non-flag, non-abort character. If one is found, zero deletion and CRC checking are enabled and the reception of data begins. If the character following the flag is another flag, the receiver begins looking for a non-flag, non-abort character again. If the character following the flag is an abort, the receiver starts looking for a new flag.

While the data is being received, the receiver inspects the data stream on a bit-by-bit basis for a closing flag. When one is detected, several events occur. First, the FCS is checked to determine if the data is error free. Second, the number of characters received is checked to make sure the packet is of the minimum length. Third, in some protocols the length of the last character received before the closing flag is checked to verify that it contained eight bits. If not, the packet contains a non-integer number of bytes and is rejected. (Alternately, if the protocol allows data to be sent on other than 8-bit boundaries, the number of bits in the last character is important to the hardware, but does not constitute an error.) Finally, the receiver starts looking for another packet. During the reception of the packet, two other tasks are performed. One task is to look at the data on a bit-by-bit basis to see if an abort character has been sent. If an abort is detected, the receiver stops receiving data and starts looking for a new packet. The other task is to count the number of characters received to detect if the packet is overly long. If a long packet is detected, the reception is terminated and the receiver starts looking for a new packet.

L2+

The HDLC Elements of Procedures are defined in the ISO 4335 standard. Before diving into the details, it is useful to recognize the evolution of the protocol. The original version of the elements of procedures, written in 1976, defined a system in which one terminal assumed the role of master (or **primary**) and the other terminal(s) were slaves (or **secondaries**). The primary terminal was responsible for organizing the data flow and for link-level error recovery. In this arrangement, primaries send command frames while secondaries send response frames. This master/slave relationship is referred to as an **unbalanced protocol.** In 1978 the ISO issued an addendum to the original standard that further defined the support for multiple secondaries connected to the primary. Some of the new features include the capability for a secondary to logically disconnect from the link, for the primary to cause the secondary to reinitialize its link control program, for the primary to command a secondary to initiate station-specific procedures, etc. In 1980, a second addendum was released that established a balanced mode of operation. In effect, a single terminal could now operate as both a primary and a secondary. This balanced operation constitutes a fundamental change to the original master/slave relationship, allowing all terminals to operate as equals. The unbalanced system reflected the mainframe → non-intelligent terminal view of the computing world, while the balanced system is more aligned with the network of peer computers environment that exists today.

Table 9.3   Packet Types and Fields

Frame Type	Control Field							
	1	2	3	4	5	6	7	8
Information	0	N(S)			P/F	N(R)		
Supervisory	1	0	S	S	P/F	N(R)		
Unnumbered	1	1	M	M	P/F	M	M	M

With that brief bit of history behind us we turn our attention to the L2+ details. First, we will look at the basic packet types and the data fields they contain, followed by the flow of these various packet types during a data call. Since the standard evolved from unbalanced to balanced operation and, as we shall see later, the balanced mode is implemented by combining the functions of the primary and the secondary into each terminal, the discussion is based on the unbalanced procedures, with the balanced mode being treated as an extension. While this tact is beneficial in fostering understanding of the protocol, the reader should be cautioned not to place too much importance on the unbalanced mode. The majority of actual HDLC-based systems operate in balanced mode.

Packet Types and Fields

There are three basic packet types: Information (I frame), Supervisory (S frame), and Unnumbered (U frame). The control field portion of the packet is used differently for each of these three packet types. See Table 9.3.

I Frame   In general, the I frame is the only type of packet allowed to contain an information field; thus, its primary use is to carry user data.

S Frame   The S frame performs supervisory control functions including acknowledgment of I frame reception and performing flow control by requesting a temporary suspension of I frame transmission.

U Frame   The U frame provides additional link control capabilities. Since the U frame does not have sequence numbers, five bits are available for specifying new functions. The 5-bit M, or modifier, field allows 32 command and 32 response functions to be defined.

The various subfields that make up the control field of each of the three packet types hold the key to understanding the HDLC Elements and Procedures. For the reader wishing to gain a thorough understanding of the information in the remainder of this chapter, it is recommended that some time be spent studying the Sequence Numbers and Poll/Final Bit sections that follow, as these concepts are central to following the discussion of the L2+ protocol. It is also helpful to keep in mind that the terms command and response are significant only in that they indicate whether a primary or a secondary sent the packet. (To further confuse things, in balanced operation, both sides send both commands and responses.)

SEQUENCE NUMBERS

The transmitting send sequence number, $N(S)$, and transmitting receive sequence number, $N(R)$, are used to establish an order and identity for I frames transmitted and received. (I frames have both $N(S)$ and $N(R)$ numbers, while S frames only have $N(R)$ numbers.) The maximum sequence number plus one is referred to as the modulus, and equals 8 for protocols using a single byte control field, and 128 for protocols using an extended control field. The maximum number of sequentially numbered I frames that can be outstanding (not acknowledged) cannot be greater than the modulus minus 1. This restriction prevents the ambiguity of having two outstanding packets with the same number. It is common practice to further restrict the number of outstanding packets based on the buffer size of the terminals, but the minimum should be specified to be greater than the round trip transmission delay in the network.

The $N(S)$ number in an I frame is the next number in sequence. (That is, the $N(S)$ of an I frame equals the number of the I frame transmitted just prior, plus one [modulus]). The $N(R)$ number in an I or S frame equals the expected $N(S)$ number of the next I frame it expects to receive. To keep track of the $N(S)$ number, each terminal maintains a variable called the Send State Variable $V(S)$, which is the sequence number of the next I frame to be sent (modulus). When an I frame is transmitted in sequence, the transmitter uses the value of $V(S)$ as the $N(S)$ field for that packet, and increments $V(S)$. (Note: Only I frames have $N(S)$ fields). Like the $V(S)$ variable, there is a corresponding $V(R)$ variable that denotes the next I frame to be received in sequence. When an error-free I frame is received with its $N(S)$ field in sequence, $V(R)$ is incremented, i.e., $N(S) = V(R)$. All I and S frames contain an $N(R)$ field, which indicates the expected sequence number of the next received I frame. Whenever an I or S frame is transmitted, its $N(R)$ field is set equal to $V(R)$. This indicates to the receiver of the I or S frame that the transmitting terminal has correctly received all I frames numbered up to $N(R)-1$, thus acknowledging those frames.

POLL/FINAL BIT

The P/F bit functions as the poll (P) bit in command frames (primary to secondary) and the final (F) bit in response frames (secondary to primary). The operation of the P/F bit is further dependent on the mode of operation of the network. In non-balanced operation, two modes are allowed. One, called Normal Response Mode (NRM) restricts the secondary to initiating transmission only in response to explicit permission from the primary. The other mode is called Asynchronous Response Mode (ARM) and allows the secondary to initiate transmission without first receiving explicit permission from the primary. In balanced mode, each terminal is both a primary and a secondary. This is referred to as a **combined station.** Balanced mode is similar to ARM in that both sides of a link can initiate transmission, but unlike ARM, both terminals can issue commands or responses. In this mode, the use of a command or a response is situational instead of positional. (In NRM and ARM one terminal is always the primary; in balanced mode, since each terminal is both a primary and a secondary, a command or a response frame is used based on the situation.)

The poll P/F bit is sent by the primary to solicit, or poll, a response or sequence of responses from secondaries. On any link only one frame may be outstanding with the P bit set to a 1. Before the primary can send another frame with the P bit set to 1, a response must be received from the secondary with the F bit set to a 1. If this does not take place before some time-out occurs, the primary retransmits the command with the P bit set to 1.

In NRM, the poll bit is set to a 1 to request response frames from the secondary, and the secondary cannot transmit until it receives a command frame with the poll bit set to a 1, or an Unnumbered Poll (UP) command. The primary can solicit I frames from the secondary by setting the poll bit in either an I or S frame. One way that the primary can restrict the secondary from sending I frames is to send a Receiver Not Ready (RNR) S frame with the poll bit set.

In ARM, the secondary can send I frames without explicit permission from the primary. The poll bit in ARM is used by the primary to request acknowledgment of the receipt of a command. If, for example, the primary wishes to receive acknowledgment of a command sent to a secondary, it sets the poll bit in that command. At the earliest opportunity the secondary will respond with its final bit set.

The function of the final P/F bit also depends on the mode of operation of the network. In NRM the final bit indicates the last frame transmitted as a result of a previous poll command. After sending a packet with the final bit set, the secondary must wait for another poll command before transmitting again.

In ARM, the final bit indicates the response frame transmitted as a result of the poll command. The transmission of a frame from the secondary to the primary with the final bit set does not indicate that the frame is the last frame that the secondary plans to send. It is only an indication that the secondary received a frame from the primary with the poll bit set.

The receive sequence number, $N(R)$, in frames having the poll or final bit set is of particular importance. Since frames with the P/F bit set are always sent in pairs (one F for each P), the $N(R)$ in these frames can be used to check for sequence number errors. This is referred to as **checkpointing.** In both NRM and ARM, the $N(R)$ of any frame with its P/F bit set must acknowledge at least all I frames transmitted previous to and concurrent with the last frame transmitted with its P or F bit set or error recovery should be initiated. In NRM, the $N(R)$ of correctly received I or S frames that have their P/F bit set confirms previously transmitted I frames through $N(R)-1$. In ARM, the secondary will resend a transmission (one or more response frames) if the transmission is not acknowledged within a system specified time-out. The standard requires that, in the case of two-way alternate communication, the time-out interval used by the secondary must be greater than that used by the primary to ensure that any contention is resolved in favor of the primary.

In balanced mode, the use of the P/F bit is the same as in ARM except in the areas of checkpoint retransmission and the clearing of busy conditions. In balanced mode, checkpointing is initiated only if an I, Receiver Ready (RR) or Receiver Not Ready (RNR) packet with the F bit is set to 1, not if the P bit is set to 1 (in ARM, checkpointing would be initiated in both cases). Concerning the busy condition, the receipt of an I frame with the P bit set to 1 does not clear an outstanding busy condition in balanced mode. (The busy condition is discussed in more detail later in the Exception Condition Handling section.)

Table 9.4 summarizes the P/F functions.

COMMAND AND RESPONSE FRAMES

As we saw earlier, there are six basic packet types. They are: Information (I), Supervisory (S), and Unnumbered (U) frames in both the command and response directions. The type of packet defines how the bits in the control field are used.

Table 9.4   P/F Functions

Mode	NRM				ARM				ABM	
SIMULTANEOUS OR ALTERNATE	A		S		A		S		S	
P/F	P	F	P	F	P	F	P	F	P	F
SOLICIT INFORMATION	X		X							
LAST FRAME	X	X		X						
SOLICIT S OR U RESPONSE	X		X		X		X		X	
CHECKPOINTING	X	X	X	X	X	X	X	X	X	X

Information Transfer Commands and Responses

I frames are used to transfer data across the link. The data is carried in the I field of the packet, and each packet is sequentially numbered. The control field is divided into separate bit fields as shown in Table 9.5. (Note: This table shows a single byte control field. We will discuss the extended control field later.)

The control field contains fields for the send sequence number, $N(S)$, and the receive sequence number, $N(R)$. The $N(S)$ field indicates the sequence number of that frame. The $N(R)$ sequence number is used to acknowledge the correct receipt of frames. This is done by sending an $N(R)$ equal to the $N(S)$ of the next packet the sending unit expects to receive, i.e., $N(R)$ equals the $N(S)$ of the last correctly received packet, plus 1.

Supervisory Command and Response Frames

Supervisory frames are numbered, and are used to perform functions such as packet acknowledgment, polling, flow control (by temporarily suspending transmission), and error recovery. S frames do not carry user data and thus do not have an I field. Since no I field is present, the sequence numbers at both the transmitter and receiver are not incremented as a result of sending or receiving S frames.

Table 9.5   I Frame Control Field Bit Usage

Bit	Function
1	0 = Information Frame
2–4	N(S)—Send Sequence Number 0–7
5	P/F P = Poll (Command), F = Final (Response)
6–8	N(R)—Receive Sequence Number 0–7

Table 9.6   S Frame Control Field Bit Usage

Bit	Function		
1–2	10 = Supervisory Frame		
3–4	Command/Response Type		
	00	RR Receive Ready	
	01	REJ Reject	
	10	RNR Receive Not Ready	
	11	SREJ Selective Reject	
5	P/F P = Poll (Command), F = Final (Response)		
6–8	N(R)—Receive Sequence Number 0–7		

The control field format is shown in Table 9.6. (Note: This table shows a single byte control field. We will discuss the extended control field later.)

S frames contain an $N(R)$ sequence number that is used to acknowledge previously received (correct) packets. As with I frames, the value of $N(R)$ indicates that frames up to, but not including, $N(R)$ have been received without error.

The supervisory commands and responses follow.

Commands:

RR—Receive Ready
RNR—Receive Not Ready
REJ—Reject
SREJ—Selective Reject

Responses:

RR—Receive Ready
RNR—Receive Not Ready
REJ—Reject
SREJ—Selective Reject

Receiver Ready (RR)   This command or response is used to indicate that the unit is ready to receive I frames, acknowledge previously received I frames, and to clear a busy condition that was indicated by an RNR. Additionally, the primary can use the RR to solicit a response from a secondary by setting the poll bit to 1.

Receiver Not Ready (RNR)   Receiver not ready indicates that the primary or secondary is temporarily unable to receive additional I frames. The $N(R)$ field acknowledges correctly received frames up to $N(R)-1$. Subsequently, received I frames are ignored. The busy condition is cleared when an

RR, REJ, SREJ, SARM, SNRM, SARME, SNRME, or UA frame is received, or if an I frame is received with its P/F bit set.

Reject (REJ)   Reject is used to indicate that all frames having a sequence number of N(R) and greater should be retransmitted. Also, all frames having a sequence number of N(R)–1 are positively acknowledged. The reject is used by both primary and secondaries. Only one reject (or SREJ) can be outstanding in a given direction at a time. The reject exception condition is cleared when the station that sent the REJ receives an I frame with N(S) equal to the N(R) of the original REJ.

Selective Reject (SREJ)   The selective reject is used to request retransmission of a single packet. The N(R) field indicates the sequence number of the packet to be retransmitted. A selective reject also acknowledges all packets up to and including N(R)–1. The SREJ condition is removed when the desired packet is received. While an SREJ is outstanding, the sender of the SREJ cannot send an REJ or another SREJ. If packets have been transmitted that have sequence numbers greater than the N(R) indicated in the SREJ command/response, these packets are not retransmitted. Just the one requested is retransmitted.

Unnumbered Command and Response Frames

The U frame commands and responses are used to increase the number of link control functions. U frames do not increment the sequence number counters at either transmit or receiving ends. Unlike the I and S frame command/response pairs, there are separate U frame commands and U frame responses, i.e., all of the I and S link control functions can be sent by either the primary or the secondary, while the U frames are direction dependent.

The control field format is shown in Table 9.7. (Note: This table shows a single byte control field. We will discuss the extended control field later.)

COMMANDS

The commands, which are sent from primary to secondary, are used to set the mode of the link. When the primary sends one of the command types, the secondary must acknowledge acceptance by sending an unnumbered acknowledgment frame (UA). The UA takes precedence over any I and S frames pending at the secondary. The secondary can ignore all frames received until it sends the UA. In two-way alternate communications, the receipt of a command restricts the secondary to sending only a single UA response frame. In two-way simultaneous communication, the secondary can wait until the first available **respond opportunity** before sending the UA. If appropriate, the secondary can continue transmission after sending the UA.

Set Normal Response Mode (SNRM)

This command is used to set Normal Response Mode. The primary sends this command to the addressed secondary, causing the secondary to respond at the first response opportunity with a UA frame that has its F bit set to a 1. Once the secondary accepts the SNRM command, it sets its send

Table 9.7   Control Field Format

Command	\multicolumn{4}{c}{Control Field}			
	1 2	3 4	5	6 7 8
	1 1	M M	P	M M M
SARM	1 1	1 1	P	0 0 0
SNRM	1 1	0 0	P	0 0 1
DISC	1 1	0 0	P	0 1 0
SARME	1 1	1 1	P	0 1 0
SNRME	1 1	1 1	P	0 1 1
SIM	1 1	1 0	P	0 0 0
UP	1 1	0 0	P	1 0 0
UI	1 1	0 0	P	0 0 0
XID	1 1	1 1	P	1 0 1
RESPONSE	1 2	3 4	5	6 7 8
	1 1	M M	F	M M M
UA	1 1	0 0	F	1 1 0
CMDR	1 1	1 0	F	0 0 1
DM	1 1	1 1	F	0 0 0
RD	1 1	0 0	F	0 1 0
RIM	1 1	1 0	F	0 0 0
UI	1 1	0 0	F	0 0 0
XID	1 1	1 1	F	1 0 1

and receive variables to zero. Any previously transmitted I frame that has not been acknowledged is left unacknowledged. Retransmission of any unacknowledged frame is a decision left at a higher layer of the software.

Set Normal Response Mode Extended (SNRME)

This command is used to set the extended form of the Normal Response Mode. In NRME, the control field is extended to two bytes instead of one. As with the SNRM, the primary sends this command to the addressed secondary, causing the secondary to respond at the first response opportunity with a UA frame that has its F bit set to a 1. Once the secondary accepts the SNRME command, it sets its send and receive variables to zero. Any previously transmitted I frame that has not been acknowledged is left unacknowledged. Retransmission of any unacknowledged frame is a decision left at a higher layer of the software.

Set Asynchronous Response Mode (SARM)

The SARM command directs the addressed secondary to enter asynchronous response mode. The secondary responds with a UA at the first response opportunity. Upon acceptance, the secondary sets its send and receive variables to zero. Any previously transmitted I frame that has not been acknowledged is left unacknowledged. Retransmission of any unacknowledged frame is a decision left at a higher layer of the software.

Set Asynchronous Response Mode Extended (SARME)

The SARME command directs the addressed secondary to enter the extended form of the asynchronous response mode. In ARME, the control field is extended to two bytes instead of one. The secondary responds with a UA at the first response opportunity. Upon acceptance, the secondary sets its send and receive variables to zero. Any previously transmitted I frame that has not been acknowledged is left unacknowledged. Retransmission of any unacknowledged frame is a decision left at a higher layer of the software.

Disconnect (DISC)

The disconnect command is used to terminate an operational mode set by a previous command. It informs the addressed secondary that the primary is suspending operation and the secondaries should assume a logically disconnected mode. In a switched network, the logical disconnect may cause the physical layer (layer 1) to go "on-hook." Prior to taking any action on the command, the secondary responds with a UA. Any previously transmitted I frame that has not been acknowledged is left unacknowledged. Retransmission of any unacknowledged frame is a decision left at a higher layer of the software. For obvious reasons, there is no extended form of this command.

Set Initialization Mode (SIM)

The SIM command causes the secondary to enter Initialization Mode (IM) and initialize its link level functions. The secondary acknowledges its acceptance of the SIM with a UA. Upon acceptance, the secondary resets its send and receive state variable to zero, and does not acknowledge any previously received and as yet unacknowledged I frames. The SIM command can be used by the primary to cause a secondary to reinitialize if the secondary is operating abnormally, or if the primary wishes to upgrade the secondary's control program. The secondary may request an SIM by sending a Request Initialization Mode (RIM) response.

Unnumbered Poll (UP)

This command, also known as the **group poll,** is used to solicit responses from a group of secondaries. (This group can contain only a single secondary, making it an individual poll.) The UP command cannot be used to acknowledge outstanding packets. As one would expect, UP packets must use a group address instead of an individual address.

The secondaries, which receive the UP, respond in the same manner as they would when being polled individually (individual address). That is to say that they respond with a frame containing their address, plus the N(S) and N(R) required by the particular response frame being sent. UP packets having the P bit set to 1 cause each individual secondary to respond with at least one frame (the last one having the F bit set to 1). UP packets with the P bit cleared to 0 cause the secondary(ies) to respond if it has:

1. An I/UI frame(s) to send
2. An I frame to retransmit due to it not having been acknowledged
3. Received but not yet acknowledged one or more I frames
4. An exception condition or status change that needs to be reported
5. A status that must be reported again (DM or CMDR , for example)

The primary knows that the secondary has completed transmission if a link idle (15 ones) is detected following the transmission of a packet. Also, if a time-out occurs, the primary assumes that the secondary(ies) does not intend to transmit anything.

Unnumbered Information (UI)

The UI allows a primary to send an I frame to one or more secondaries without impacting the N(S) or N(R) status. UI commands are not acknowledged by the secondaries. This is useful for such functions as a broadcast real-time clock (say, once per second) and does not incur the cost penalty of requiring an acknowledgment.

Exchange Identification (XID)

The primary uses the XID command to request the addressed secondary to identify itself. An optional I field can be included in the XID packet that provides the primary's identification and/or characteristics. The secondary responds unless it has a UA pending for some set mode command, or a CMDR condition exists. If the I field of the XID packet exceeds the maximum buffer size allowed by the secondary, a CMDR condition may be established.

Set Asynchronous Balanced Mode (SABM)

This command places the addressed station in Asynchronous Balanced Mode (ABM). As with the other mode-setting commands, upon acceptance, the secondary sets its send and receive variables to zero. Any previously transmitted I frame that has not been acknowledged is left unacknowledged. Retransmission of any unacknowledged frame is a decision left at a higher layer of the software. Additionally, sending an SABM can be used to report the end of a busy condition.

Set Asynchronous Balanced Mode Extended (SABME)

Like the SABM, this command places the addressed station in Asynchronous Balanced Mode (ABM); however, in this case the extended control field is used. As with the other mode-setting commands, upon acceptance, the secondary sets its send and receive variables to zero. Any previously transmitted I frame that has not been acknowledged is left unacknowledged. Retransmission of any unacknowledged frame is a decision left at a higher layer of the software.

Reset (RSET)

This command is used only in asynchronous balanced mode. When received, a combined station will reset its receive state variable to zero and acknowledge with a UA response. Upon receipt of this acknowledgment, the original sending station will reset its send state variable to zero. Retransmission of any unacknowledged frame is a decision left to a higher layer of the software. The RSET command will reset all frame rejection conditions except an invalid N(R) at the addressed combined station that has been reported by a frame reject (FRMR). Note that the station detecting an invalid N(R) can clear the condition by sending an RSET (in place of an FRMR).

RESPONSES

There are seven unnumbered responses.

Unnumbered Acknowledge (UA)

The UA is used by the secondary to inform the primary that it accepts and acknowledges an unnumbered command. The secondary does not take any action on the command until after it sends the UA frame.

Command Reject (CMDR)

The command reject is used in unbalanced mode (ARM or NRM) by a secondary to respond to one of the following conditions:

1. receipt of a command that is not valid or not implemented,
2. the receipt of an Information (I), Unnumbered Information (UI), or eXchange IDentification (XID) frame that is too big for the secondary's buffer,
3. the receipt of a packet with an invalid N(R).

The invalid N(R) is defined as one that points to a previously acknowledged frame or to a frame that has not been transmitted and is not the next one in sequence to be transmitted.

The command reject is an example of a packet that has an information field, but is not an I frame. In the case of the CMDR, the information field is used to provide the primary with the reason for the command reject. The information field is used as shown in Table 9.8.

Rejected Command Control Field

This is the control field of the command frame that is being rejected.

N(S)—The current send sequence variable at the secondary (bit 10 is the LSB).

Bit 13—In ISO 4335, this bit is 0. In LAPB this bit is a 1 if the rejected frame was a response, and a 0 if it was a command.

Table 9.8   Information Field for a CMDR

1 2 3 4 5 6 7 8	9	10 11 12	13	14 15 16	17	18	19	20
Control Field From Rejected Command	0	N(S)	0	N(R)	W	X	Y	Z

N(R)—The current receive sequence variable at the secondary (bit 14 is the LSB).

W—This bit is set to 1 to indicate that the control field of the command frame that is being rejected was invalid and the command is not being implemented.

X—This bit is set to 1 to indicate that the control field of the command that is being rejected is considered by the secondary to be invalid because the command packet also contained an information field, which is not allowed with the command. Note that bit W must also be set if bit X is set.

Y—This bit is set to 1 to indicate that the information field in the received packet was too long for the secondary's receive buffer.

Z—This bit is set to indicate that the control field of the received packet contained an invalid N(R).

Additionally, the W, X, Y, and Z bits may all be 0, indicating an unspecified rejection of the packet for one of the specified reasons.

Note that the information field is 20 bits long. It is normal practice to pad the field with zeros on the end to satisfy the integer number of bytes requirement (i.e., four zeros are added to the end so that the total number of bits in the packet is evenly divisible by eight).

In cases where the extended control field is being used, the information field is as shown in Table 9.9.

Table 9.9   Information Field for the Extended Control Field

1–16	17	18–24	25*	26–30	33	34	35	36
Extended Control Field From Rejected Command	0	N(S)	0	N(R)	W	X	Y	Z

*Note that bit 25 is equivalent to bit 13 in the non-extended form. In LAPB and LAPD it represents whether the rejected frame was a command or response.

Frame Reject (FRMR)

The frame reject is used only in asynchronous balanced mode and is similar to the command reject (CMDR). The control field of an FRMR is the same as that of the CMDR. The information field differs only in one bit, that being bit 13 for non-extended operation or 25 for extended operation. This bit, which was always a 0 in non-balanced operation, is used as follows: If the bit is a 0, the rejected frame was a command. If the bit is a 1, the rejected frame was a response. When a combined station receives an FRMR, it responds by reinitializing the link in either one or both directions via an RSET or an SABM(E) command. If the combined station is incapable of reinitializing one or both directions of the link, it responds with an FRMR of its own. After sending an FRMR, the combined station will either stop sending I frames if the reject condition was cause by an invalid N(R) or continue to send I frames if the reject is caused by the receipt of an illegally large packet or the receipt of an invalid command or response.

Disconnect Mode (DM)

There are two disconnect modes, Normal Disconnect Mode (NDM) and Asynchronous Disconnect Mode (ADM). These modes correspond to the two connect modes, Normal Response Mode (NRM) and Asynchronous Response Mode (ARM). The DM response is used to report to the primary that the secondary is either in NDM or ADM depending on the operating mode of the system (NRM or ARM). In NDM or ADM, the secondary is logically disconnected from the network and is only capable of the following:

1. Accepting a mode-setting command (SNRM, SARM, SNRME, SARME, SIM, or DISC)
2. Accepting an XID command
3. Transmitting a DM, XID, RIM, or RD

As a minimum, a disconnected secondary must respond with a DM having the F bit set to 1 whenever a command frame is received with the P bit set to 1. Disabled secondaries cannot establish a CMDR condition, and must respond to a DISC command with a DM. If a secondary is active (ARM, NRM, IM) when a DISC command is received, a UA response is returned if the secondary can enter ADM or NDM.

Request Disconnect (RD)

The RD response is used by the secondary to inform the primary that it wishes to be placed in disconnect mode. In a switched network, the RD may be viewed as a request to go **on-hook.** If a secondary sends an RD and then receives a command frame other than a DISC, it will honor the command frames (if it can). If the secondary still wishes to be disconnected, it reissues the RD.

Request Initialization Mode (RIM)

The RIM response is used by the secondary to inform the primary that it needs initialization. Once an RIM is sent, the secondary will only respond to an SIM, DISC, or XID command.

Unnumbered Information (UI)

The UI response allows a secondary to send an I frame to the primary without impacting the N(S) or N(R) status. The UI is not acknowledged by the primary.

Exchange Identification (XID)

The XID response is sent as a reply to an XID command from the primary. An optional I field can be included in the XID response packet that provides the secondary's identification and/or characteristics. The secondary responds to an XID command unless it has a UA pending for some set mode command, or a CMDR condition exists.

EXTENDED CONTROL FIELD

The 8-bit control field format imposes a restriction on the number of outstanding packets at any one time. This number (eight) is equal to the modulus number. This can be a severe restriction on networks with long delays such as satellite links or on high-speed networks that can receive a large number of frames quickly before the higher layers of software can get around to processing them. The obvious solution is to increase the modulus. This requires a larger control field, thus the extended mode, which sets the modulus to 128. If the primary does not know the mode of the secondaries connected to it, it must send each secondary an SARME or SNRME (the "E" being the operative part of the command) using the non-extended control field format. If the secondary (or secondaries) acknowledge the command to switch to extended mode, then the primary and secondaries start using the 16-bit control field format. The extended format control field for the I, S, and U frame types is shown in Table 9.10. Note: The X parameter is reserved and these bits are set to 0, and the U bit is not specified. Also, bits 2 and 10 are the LSBs of the sequence numbers.

EXCEPTION CONDITION HANDLING

Problems occur in real world data communication links. Therefore, a means is required to recover from exceptions as gracefully as possible. HDLC provides mechanisms for handling exceptions arising from transmission errors, malfunctions, and the like.

Table 9.10   Extended Format Control Field

Frame Type	Control Field			
	1	2 3 4 5 6 7 8	9	10 11 12 13 14 15 16
Information	0	N(S)	P/F	N(R)
Supervisory	1 0	S S X X X X	P/F	N(R)
Unnumbered—ISO 4335	1 1	M M U M M M	P/F	X X X X X X X
Unnumbered—LAPB, LAPD	1 1	M M P/F M M M	Second Octet Not Used	

Busy

If a station is temporarily unable to receive (or continue to receive) I frames, a Receiver Not Ready (RNR) frame can be transmitted. This causes the transmitter of the I frames to stop transmitting until the RNR condition is cleared. Note: The station that sends the RNR can still transmit I frames even after sending out the RNR.

N(S) Sequence Errors and Recovery

An N(S) sequence error occurs when an I frame is received without errors (FCS valid) but with the N(S) value not equalling the receivers receive state variable. (The receive state variable is equal to the N(S) value of the next expected packet in sequence.) The receiver discards and does not acknowledge the I frame or any subsequently received I frames until an I frame is received with the correct N(S). (The receiver does not increment its receive state variable until the correct N(S) is received.) The N(R) and P/F fields of I frames received with an N(S) sequence error are still considered valid, assuming that the packet does not have an FCS error. In the event of an N(S) sequence error, the following remedies are available.

Poll/Final Bit Recovery (Checkpoint Retransmission)   When a station that has been sending I frames receives a frame with the P/F bit set to 1, it sequentially retransmits any unacknowledged I frames that have sequence numbers less than or equal to the N(S) sequence number of the last P/F frame transmitted, starting with the lowest numbered I frame that has not been acknowledged. There are four conditions in which checkpoint retransmission is not allowed, these being:

1.   If an REJ has been received with the P/F bit equal to 0, and it has been acted upon, checkpoint retransmission is inhibited on the next P/F frame received.

   In balanced mode, if an REJ command is received with the P bit set to either 0 or 1, or an REJ response is received with the F bit set to 1 and it is acted upon while a P bit set to 1 is unanswered, then retransmission is inhibited on the next packet since it would cause a duplicate I frame to be retransmitted.
2.   If an SREJ has been received with the P/F bit equal to 0, and it has been acted upon, checkpoint retransmission is inhibited on the next frame with the P/F bit equal to 1, if this frame is an SREJ and its N(R) value is equal to the N(R) of the first SREJ.

   In balanced mode, if an SREJ command is received with the P bit set to either 0 or 1, or an SREJ response is received with the F bit set to 1 and it is acted upon while a P bit set to 1 is unanswered, then retransmission is inhibited on the next packet.
3.   If an unnumbered format frame is received with its P/F bit set to 1.
4.   If an SREJ is received with its P/F bit set to 1. In this event, the SREJ retransmission takes precedence over the checkpoint retransmission.

REJ Recovery   The REJ command/response can be used to initiate retransmission due to a sequence error earlier than the checkpointing technique (poll/final bit recovery), since there is no requirement to wait for a frame with the P/F bit set to 1. Only one "sent REJ" exception condition can be present from one station to another at any one time. The sent REJ exception is cleared when the requested I frame is received, when the command/response time-out occurs, or if a checkpoint retransmission cycle was initiated concurrent to or following the REJ completes. An REJ may be repeated if the station determines (by time-out or checkpointing) that the requested I frame will not be received. This can occur if the original REJ gets lost or is received in error, or if the requested I frame is simply not retransmitted, or if an error occurs in its retransmission. Only one REJ command/response is allowed within a checkpoint cycle. The retransmission of I frames starts with the I frame indicated by the N(R) field of the REJ frame. Retransmission initiated by an REJ is inhibited if retransmission of a particular frame occurs due to checkpointing and an REJ is received that would also start retransmission beginning with the same frame (indicated by the N(R) in the REJ frame).

SREJ Recovery   In most cases the SREJ is a more efficient mechanism for recovering from a sequence error. The SREJ command/response causes the retransmission of only the rejected frame, and not frames transmitted subsequent to that frame. This is very useful in cases where the software examines an entire multipacket transmission only after the last packet has been received. If one of the packets in the group has a sequence error, the SREJ requests retransmission of only that packet.

Due to the details of the protocol, some restrictions apply to the use of SREJ. If a station sends an SREJ with the P/F bit cleared to 0, and this "sent SREJ" condition is not cleared by the time the station is ready to send a packet with the P/F bit set to 1, the station must send an SREJ with the P/F bit set to 1 and the N(R) field equal to that of the original SREJ. (In balanced mode, the SREJ is a response, and its F bit is set to 1.) If a station receives and acts on an SREJ with the P/F bit cleared to 0, and subsequently receives one with the same N(R) and the P/F bit set to 1, it will ignore this new SREJ. In balanced mode, if the combined station receives a command with the P bit set to 1, the transmission of a response with the F bit set to 1 takes precedence over the transmission of all commands except mode-setting commands.

Sending a packet with the P/F bit set to 1 can cause a problem since it can cause checkpoint retransmission. For this reason, a station should not send an SREJ with the same N(R) as that of the previously sent frame having the P/F bit set to 1.

Any given station can have only one outstanding SREJ at a time (an SREJ that has been sent, but has not been cleared). The SREJ condition is cleared when the I frame in question is received correctly, when the command/response time-out expires, or when a checkpoint cycle is initiated concurrent to or following the transmission of the SREJ. When the SREJ condition is cleared by a time-out or checkpointing, the requested I frame will not be received. (This can be caused by an error in the SREJ or the SREJ being lost.) In this event, the SREJ can be repeated.

Time-out Recovery   When a single packet or the last packet in a group is lost or received and rejected because of an FCS error, a sequence error will not be detected and an SREJ or REJ will not be issued. For this reason, a time-out is used by the station that sent the unacknowledged I frame(s). In the event of a time-out, the sender must determine where to begin retransmission, and resend the packet(s).

FCS Errors

Any packet received with an invalid FCS will be discarded, and no action will be taken. The receiving station cannot take any action because, since the packet contains errors, it cannot even know with certainty that it was the intended recipient of the packet. Recovery will be initiated as a result of a sequence error or a time-out.

Command Rejection

If a packet is received without error and it contains an invalid command/response, an invalid frame format, an invalid N(R), or if its length exceeds the buffer receiver's capacity, a command rejection condition exists. If this takes place at the primary, recovery must take place at a higher layer. At the secondary, a command reject (CMDR) response is sent to the primary, after which no new I frames are accepted until the condition is cleared (except for the examination of the P bit and the N(R) field). The CMDR is repeated at each respond opportunity until the primary responds. A mode set command or a disconnect command will reset the CMDR condition.

FRAME RELAY

Having covered the split between layer 2– and 2+, a few words about frame relay are in order. In most large networks, transmission between two end points may be routed via one or more intermediate nodes, i.e., a telephone call from Miami to Houston may be routed through Orlando and Dallas. In standard HDLC-based data networks, such as X.25, layers 1, 2, and 3 of the protocol stack are employed at each hop in the connection. This was originally required because of the relatively high error rates on analog phone lines. With the advent of the digital telephone network, the error rates have improved significantly. As a result, the overhead of running the layer 2+ and layer 3 protocols at each hop in the link is not justified. Frame relay takes advantage of this by only using the layer 2+ and layer 3 protocols between end points of the link, and running the layer 2– protocol on the intermediate hops. In essence, the intermediate nodes handle the address field and check the FCS of each packet, but do not deal with acknowledgment of correctly received packets. Bad packets are simply dropped from the network, leaving the protocol at the end points to recover. In a network with a low error rate, this is much more economical.

The most common form of frame relay is based on LAPD and is a subset of CCITT recommendation Q.922. The standards are, however, still evolving.

CONCLUSION

In this chapter we have covered the basics of HDLC protocols. We have examined the split between the hardware related layer 2– and software related layer 2+ functions. We have looked at the details of both of these sublayers following the generic ISO 3309 and 4335 standards, with a few of the LAPB and LAPD specific variants thrown in for good measure. What we have not covered are the layer 1/2 interface or the layer 2/3 primitives. The L2 to L3 boundary is of particular interest since all of the details covered in this chapter exist to satisfy the needs of layer 3.

ACKNOWLEDGMENT

The author thanks Charles Crowe of Telesoft International, Inc., for his review of this chapter and his many helpful suggestions. (Any errors are, of course, the responsibility of the author.)

10

A SURVEY OF U.S. GOSIP
VERSIONS 1 AND 2

Bob D. Tausworthe

INTRODUCTION

The United States Government Open Systems Interconnect Profiles (GOSIP) version 1 was created in order to facilitate the use of the International Standards Organization (ISO) OSI protocols by government agencies. But it was only the initial step. U.S. GOSIP 2 starts where version 1 left off. It provides additional protocols and services that allow even greater functionality than the original specification. Simply put, it fills the holes present in GOSIP 1, thus making the U.S. GOSIP a viable profile for government and commercial vendors.

The reason for GOSIPs is simple: Government agencies do not, under normal circumstances, have the ability to contract with specific vendors to solve their procurement needs. Instead, procurement of computer systems must be done on a bid-by-bid basis. The government procurement process mandates that agencies make decisions based solely upon requirements and cost. This policy has left the government with (arguably) the world's largest multivendor networks, often without the ability for agencies' systems to communicate with one another. Since the purpose of the OSI protocols is to allow for interoperating of computer networks in an open systems environment, it is natural for the United States government to satisfy their multivendor networking needs by moving towards this set of protocols.

Commercial companies are also finding themselves with similar multivendor networking problems. There are several reasons for this. In the past, many companies did not have a unified purchasing strategy for networking products. Entities within a company would often purchase computer systems without regard for other entities within the company. This resulted in companies having incompatible computer systems and, thus, incompatible networks. Still, some companies merged with, or bought, other companies, and, along with them, their existing computer and networking infrastructure. More often than not, these new systems were incompatible with the parent companies' own systems.

Even companies that provided strategies for purchasing computer systems found themselves with a need to solve the multivendor networking problem. They wanted a "mix and match" approach when purchasing systems. They wanted to take advantage of each vendor's strengths while not locking themselves into a single vendor's product line. Some companies moved away from the centralized mainframe approach, desiring instead to embrace client-server technologies, equipping their staff with workstations and server systems often made by different vendors. An approach such as this could only be successful if multivendor networking is a reality.

Although commercial companies have arrived at their networking problem from a different road than the United States government, the desired solution is the same: an open networking environment that allows for effortless interoperating of dissimilar computer systems. Wouldn't it be great for customers and vendors alike if the solution which the United States government is pursuing would work for the commercial industry as well? This chapter intends to show that this is indeed the case. The guidelines specified in the U.S. GOSIP can be used by businesses as a base to solve their open system networking problems. Version 2 fills out the profile so as to make the U.S. GOSIP offering a viable solution to everybody's open systems needs.

CREATION OF THE OSI PROTOCOLS

Every major vendor has products that provide, to one degree or another, data communications between its computer systems. Many have created proprietary network architectures that allow communication only between systems sold by that vendor. Other vendors who want their computer systems supported on networks of this type must implement the proprietary solutions as well as maintain their own network development. IBM's Systems Network Architecture (SNA), and DEC's Decnet Phase IV are examples of solutions of this type. Many vendors, such as SUN and Hewlett Packard, provide products that allow their computers to communicate on these networks, but at a large development cost to the vendors, and with only limited benefit for their customers.

To satisfy the open systems networking needs of federal agencies as well as companies, vendors' systems must be capable of communicating with each other in a normal and predictable manner. In 1976 the International Standards Organization (ISO) began work on a communication architecture that would allow any vendor's systems to communicate in this way. This effort resulted in the definition of the "OSI Reference Model." The model is defined in ISO International Standard 7498, Information Processing Systems—Opens Systems Interconnection—Basic Reference Model, and in Recommendation X.200, Reference Model of Opens Systems Interconnection for CCITT Applications, which is published by the International Telegraph and Telephone Consultative Committee (CCITT). The reference model was defined in such a way as to be independent of hardware and software requirements; it can be implemented on any vendor's systems.

The OSI reference model provides a framework by which systems may communicate. It does not define the protocols necessary for actual communication to be accomplished. The definition of these protocols is an ongoing process. Many have already been adopted by ISO and more are currently under development.

USER PROFILES

The protocols alone, however, are not sufficient for effective interoperation in an open systems environment. Many of the protocols are incompletely specified, leaving the definition of field values or functionality as "local matters," or "for further study." Some protocols have several equivalent modes of operation and do not specify which one to use. Also, a protocol is sometimes found to have errors after it has been adopted.

Because of these problems, it became necessary for groups requiring interoperable systems to produce guidelines called **Operational Profiles** or, simply, **profiles**. The purpose of a profile is to specify a set of protocols to be used for data communication and define any ambiguities that the protocol specifications may have. When vendors implement a set of protocols using a profile as the guideline, the chance that their implementations will interoperate with each other is greatly increased. Examples of groups that have defined profiles are: the National Institute of Standards and Technology Implementor's Workshop (NIST Implementor's Agreements), the Manufacturing Automation Protocol and Technical Office Protocol (MAP/TOP Profiles), and the ENV profiles created by the European standards bodies CEN/CENELEC. The U.S. GOSIP and the U.K. GOSIP are also profiles. They are the profiles that the respective government agencies must specify conformance to in their procurement requests that include OSI protocols.

CREATION OF THE U.S. GOSIP

Version 1 of the U.S. GOSIP was published as "Federal Information Processing Standard 146" (FIPS 146) in August 1988 by the National Bureau of Standards (which later became the National Institute of Standards and Technology [NIST]). On August 15, 1990, use of FIPS 146 became mandatory for all government procurements that specify computer networking compatible with the functionality specified by the U.S. GOSIP. Version 2 was published as FIPS 146-1 on April 3, 1991. It was intended to supersede FIPS 146 in its entirety. Version 2 is mandatory for all procurements issued after October 3, 1992.

Three separate groups of sources are used to create the U.S. GOSIP. FIPS 146 classifies these as Primary, Secondary, and Tertiary. The sole primary source was the "Stable Implementation Agreements for Open Systems Interconnection Protocols" created and maintained by the NIST Workshop for Implementation Agreements for Open Systems Interconnection Protocols. This document is commonly called the "NIST Implementor's Agreements." Except for the few differences listed in FIPS 146, and its revision in FIPS 146-1, U.S. GOSIP conforms to the NIST Implementor's Agreements profile.

Secondary sources are used to create a complete set of functionality when the NIST Implementor's Agreements did not suffice. Secondary sources for the U.S. GOSIP include: International Standards and Recommendations, Draft and Proposed Draft International Standards, and working papers within the international standards bodies. The key phrase is "international standards." The U.S. GOSIP is not to be based upon any standard, however mature, which is not part of the international standards process. Tertiary sources, however, are used to supply functionality not derived from the international standards process. They are interim solutions allowed because of necessity when international standards do not provide necessary functionality. All functionality derived from tertiary sources will be replaced with suitable primary or secondary substitutes when they become available.

THE NIST IMPLEMENTOR'S AGREEMENTS

Because the NIST Implementor's Agreements is the primary source for functionality in the U.S. GOSIP, this document deserves a closer look. The NIST Implementor's Agreements was created by a consortium of vendors, users, and national and international standards bodies with the intent of producing a profile that provides functionality meeting the requirements of most OSI users. Virtually every group that has produced, or is in the process of producing, a profile has used the Implementor's Workshop as a forum to discuss the OSI protocols and their uses. MAP/TOP, ANSI, and CEN/CEN-ELEC have all participated in the Workshop. Because of this, most of the profiles they have generated are, for the most part, compatible with the Implementor's Agreements.

Work in the Implementor's Workshop is an ongoing process. The Workshop meets several times a year to discuss the evolutions of OSI technology. It produces "Ongoing Agreements" at these meetings. These are distributed for review. Once these Agreements have been deemed stable, they are used to amend the Stable Implementor's Agreements. Therefore, as the OSI protocols evolve, so does the Implementor's Agreements.

THE U.S. GOSIP PROFILE VERSION 1

Version 1 specifies compliance requirements or recommendations for all layers of the OSI Reference Model. This is done by specifying amendments to the NIST Implementor's Agreements profile. The complete suite of protocols supported by the U.S. GOSIP version 1, and the functionality defined, is shown in Figure 10.1.

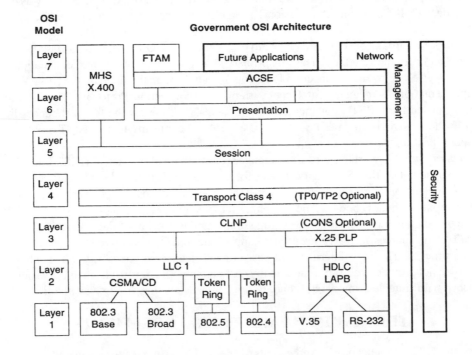

Figure 10.1   Government OSI architecture.

Physical Layer

Version 1 does not require any specific physical layer standards. It allows vendors to use any non-proprietary interfaces that best suit the transmission medium line speed, modem type, and transmission distance. It does, however, recommend the use of EIA RS-232-C for line speeds up to 19.2 kilobits/second, and CCITT V.35 for line speeds above 19.2 kbit/second when using X.25 as the data link protocol, or for point-to-point links.

Data Link Layer

The data link protocols that may be used in conjunction with X.25 are: High-Level Data Link Control (HDLC) and Link Access Procedure B (LAP B). The data link protocols that may be used in conjunction with ISO 8802/2 (IEEE 802.2) are: ISO 8802/3 (IEEE 802.3), ISO 8802/4 (IEEE 802.4), and ISO 8802/5 (IEEE 802.5).

No one data link protocol is required by the U.S. GOSIP. Instead, it specifies a set of standards that vendors may implement, any one being sufficient to claim compliance with the U.S. GOSIP. So, for instance, a vendor that creates a product that operates using IEEE 802.3 is just as compliant as a vendor that creates a product that operates over X.25/LAP-B. It is up to the purchasing requisition to specify which standards are required. Whatever data links are chosen must conform to the guidelines specified in the Workshop Agreements.

Network Layer

The Network Layer for all U.S. GOSIP implementations must be ISO 8348/AD1, the Connectionless Mode Network Service (CLNS), and ISO 8473, the Connectionless Mode Network Protocol (CLNP). Specific additions to the NIST Implementor's Agreements for this protocol profile are:

- End systems must be able to control the value of the lifetime parameter for PDUs that they originate.
- Checksums must be supported and the end system must have the capability of enabling/disabling its use.
- The use of the priority option must be supported with highest priority PDUs being processed first.

These additions complement the Implementor's Agreements Profile. They do not make the two incompatible.

In addition to CLNP, ISO 8348, The Connection-Oriented Network Service (CONS), operating over X.25 as per ISO 8878 may also be used in conjunction with X.400 MHS when it's operating over public data networks. However, every U.S. GOSIP–compliant implementation must support CLNP over at least one data link protocol.

ISO 9542, The End System to Intermediate System Routing Exchange Protocol (ES-IS), is not part of version 1 of the U.S. GOSIP. However, since it is part of the NIST Implementor's Agreements, most vendors' GOSIP–compliant products also include it in their network layer implementations. The ES-IS protocol has been added to U.S. GOSIP version 2.

Transport Layer

The Transport Layer must be ISO 8073, The Connection-Oriented Transport Protocol, class 4 operation. The recommended length for the transport selector is 2 octets, although selector lengths up to 32 octets should be supported.

Transport class 0 operation may also be used in conjunction with CONS for the purposes of operating X.400 MHS over public data networks.

There is no specific requirement for an Application Programmatic Interface to the Transport Layer. The U.S. GOSIP leaves this requirement to the purchaser to determine.

Session Layer

ISO 8327, Basic Connection-Oriented Session Protocol, must be used as the Session Layer. Both session version 1 and session version 2 are allowed. Session version 2 is limited to 10,240 octets of user data. The recommended length for session selectors is 2 octets, although selector lengths of up to 16 octets should be supported.

The following session functional units are allowed: Kernel, Duplex, Expedited Data, Resynchronize, Exceptions, Activity Management, Half-duplex, Minor Synchronize, Major Synchronize, and Typed Data. The specific set of functional units required is dependent on the applications layer services supported and the Session Application Programmatic Interface requirements defined by the purchaser.

There is no specific requirement for an Application Programmatic Interface to the Session Layer. The U.S. GOSIP leaves this requirement to the purchaser to determine.

Presentation Layer

ISO 8823, Connection-Oriented Presentation Protocol, will be used as the Presentation Layer. The recommended length for presentation selectors is 2 octets, although selector lengths of up to 4 octets should be supported.

Application Layer

ISO 8650, Protocol for the Association Control Service Element, must be supported for all applications except X.400.

Version 1 of the U.S. GOSIP specifies two application layer protocols: FTAM and X.400 MHS. The support of the File Transfer, Access, and Management (FTAM) protocol has been divided into two categories: full-purpose systems and limited-purpose systems. A full-purpose implementation provides positional file transfer, simple file access, and management. This means it can transfer simple text, binary, record-oriented, and indexed sequential files. These file types may also be accessed remotely without the entire file being transferred.

A limited-purpose implementation of FTAM provides simple file transfer and management. This means it must support at least the transfer of simple text and binary file types. A limited-purpose FTAM must be able to interoperate with a full-purpose FTAM where the two implementations have common capabilities.

A version 1–compliant implementation of the X.400 Message Handling Service (MHS) will have the Message Transfer Service and the Interpersonal Messaging Services as they are specified in the NIST Implementor's Agreements. In version 1.0, X.400 is the only application that may operate over Transport Class 0 and CONS. To be truly compliant with the U.S. GOSIP, this is only allowed when the communication between two Message Transfer Agents occurs when at least one of the Agents resides entirely and exclusively inside a public message domain under the administration of a public data network. All Agents residing in private management domains must operate over Transport Class 4 and, therefore, CLNP. If a system is connected to both a public and a private domain, it must adhere to the guidelines.

An agent in such a configuration is often used as an "application gateway" for forwarding messages from a private to a public domain. An Application Gateway is the only supported method for relaying between CONS and CLNS networks in version 1. Interworking Units such as Transport relays and MSDSG Gateways are not supported.

Companies not under government acquisition control are not limited by the restrictions for operating X.400 MHS. A company can choose to use Transport Class 0 and CONS when performing message transfer within private domains. Many vendors allow their FTAM service as well as their X.400 to be used over Transport Class 0 and CONS.

ADDITIONS AND CHANGES FOR VERSION 2

U.S. GOSIP version 2 has updated the original GOSIP to add functionality that will make the profile more usable, as well as adding protocols that were not yet mature at the time version 1 was created (see Figure 10.2).

Physical Layer

EIA RS-530 has been added as a recommended interface for use when transfer rates exceed 20 kilobits/second. ISDN has also been added as a recommended link. Specific functional requirements for the use of ISDN will be discussed in a later section.

Data Link Layer

The only change to this layer is the addition of ISDN service. See the special section on ISDN use for specific functional requirements.

Network Layer

ISO 8348/AD1, the Connectionless Mode Network Service, is still the mandated network service. Additions to this service are as follows:

- An end system must now be able to control the lifetime parameter for PDUs that they originate via configuration management functions.
- The security parameter is now supported as an optional parameter. It is up to the Acquisition Authority to decide on a per-procurement basis whether or not it is required.

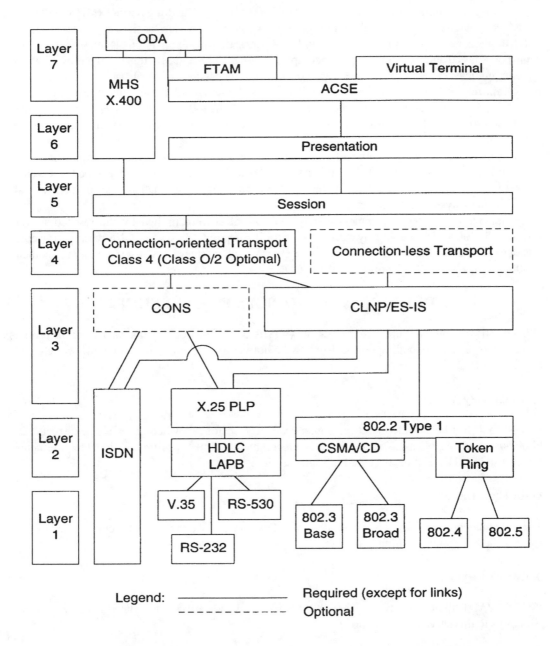

Figure 10.2   U.S. GOSIP Version 2.

- The processing of PDUs by order of priority has been removed as a requirement.
- CLNS may now be supported over ISO 9574, ISDN. It is up to the Acquisition Authority to decide on a per-procurement basis whether or not it is required. Specific functional requirements for the use of ISDN will be discussed in a later section.

In addition, version 2 specifies the use of ISO 9542, the End-System-to-Intermediate-System routing protocol for end systems interconnected by LAN or point-to-point CLNS networks. Use of the ES-IS protocol is not required for end systems interconnected by WANs (e.g., Public Data X.25 networks).

The Connection-Oriented Network Service (CONS) may now also be supported over ISDN networks.

Integrated Services Digital Networks

Version 2 of the U.S. GOSIP has added support for ISO 9574, Integrated Services Digital Networks (ISDN), for both CLNS and CONS networks. Each has its own requirements on how it is to be used. However, below the Network Layer, a common set of operating characteristics are defined.

Physical Layer   Version 2 allows for the Basic Rate Interface (BRI) as well as the Primary Rate Interface (PRI). The BRI should provide 16 kilobits/second on the D-channel and up to two 64 kilobits/second B-channels. The PRI should provide 64 kilobits/second on the D-channel and up to twenty-three 64 kilobits/second B-channels. It is up to the Acquisition Authority to decide on a per-procurement basis whether BRI or PRI is required.

Data Link Layer   When operating over ISDN, CCITT recommendation Q.921 should be used over the D-channel and ISO 7776 (LAP-B) should be used over the B-channels.

Network Layer: CLNS   CLNS will operate directly over an ISDN service in accordance with the NIST Implementor's Agreements. X.25 will not be used.

Network Layer: CONS   CONS will operate directly over an ISDN network's B- and D-channels as per the provisions in ISO 9574 and the NIST Implementor's Agreements. X.25 will not be used.

Transport Layer

Version 2 adds a few recommendations to the use of a Connection-Oriented Transport Service as follows.

- It is recommended that user data not be sent during connection establishment or disconnect. However, any user data received will be sent to the Transport Service user.
- The support of Transport Expedited Data is an optional feature. It is up to the Acquisition Authority on a per-procurement basis to determine whether it is required.

Version 2 allows for the use of ISO 8642, the Connectionless Transport Service (CLTS), as optional functionality. It is up the Acquisition Authority to decide whether it is required in a particular procurement. CLTS is only specified to operate over CLNS; version 2 does not make any provisions for CLTS over CONS.

Session Layer

No additions or changes are specified.

Presentation Layer

No additions or changes are specified.

Application Layer

U.S. GOSIP version 2 adds two more application layer services to their profile specification: Basic Class Virtual Terminal Service (VT) and the Office Document Architecture (ODA) information exchange format.

Version 2 defines two categories of Virtual Terminal service systems: simple systems and forms capable systems. A simple system provides basic TTY services, meaning a service that is a line or character at a time exchange. Simple systems use the ASCII control character set for functions such as "carriage return" and "form feed," and should conform to the Implementor's Agreements TELNET profile for Virtual Terminal service.

A forms capable system is for forms-based applications that allow for local entry of information and validation of the data by the terminal system. It supports more advanced control functions such a cursor movement, and erase screen, as well as forms field protection. It should conform to the Implementor's Agreements forms profile specification.

Virtual Terminal service shall conform to ISO standard 9040, and the Virtual Terminal protocol shall conform to ISO standard 9041. Specific considerations for conformance to U.S. GOSIP version 2 are as follows:

- Any system supporting the Multiple Interaction Negotiation option, must support the Switch Profile and No Negotiation options as well.
- Any system supporting the Switch Profile Negotiation option must also support the No Negotiation option.
- In addition to ASCII, seven-bit USASCII and the International Reference version of ISO-646 graphic repertoires must also be supported for both simple and forms capable systems.

The ISO standards for Office Document Architecture (ODA) defines rules for the interchange of complex documents by allowing for the description of its layout as well as rules that describe the character, raster, and geometric content of the document. The documents may be defined in formatted form, which is the form most suitable for printing and displaying, or in the formatted processable form, which is the form used when further processing of the information is desired.

U.S. GOSIP version 2 allows the use of either X.400 or FTAM services for transferring ODA documents. In the case of FTAM, ODA documents should be transferred using FTAM-3 document type.

CONFORMANCE AND INTEROPERABILITY TESTING

NIST has been given the responsibility of providing a conformance testing program for version 1 and version 2 of the U.S. GOSIP. NIST has contracted with the Corporation for Open Systems (COS) to provide the test program for verifying vendors' compliance. COS operates the U.S. GOSIP testing program in much the same way it manages its own conformance accreditation program. Independent sites are allowed to go through a certification program and become COS accredited test sites. These sites have the ability to run the tests on a vendor's OSI product and determine conformance to the U.S. GOSIP protocols suite. Vendors themselves have the ability to become accredited test sites. Hewlett-Packard, for example, has become an accredited test site and has the right to verify conformance for its products as well as the products of other vendors who contract with HP to perform the testing.

Once the test site has passed a vendor's implementation, the vendor may then apply to the National Computer Systems Laboratory for a Certificate of Conformance Testing. Once conformance testing has been passed, the vendor's product may undergo interoperability testing.

Presently, NIST does not have an interoperability test suite. Instead, NIST has created the OSINET network. OSINET is a network available to vendors to facilitate the performing of interoperability testing. A vendor who wishes to perform this testing subscribes to the OSINET network. They contact the vendors they wish to test against and access their implementations over OSINET. Although informal, the OSINET testing process does provide a common network over which many vendors' products can be accessed. By subscribing to OSINET, a vendor can test against many implementations instead of having to negotiate with each vendor separately or buy the vendor's product and test in house. Vendors can also test their U.S. GOSIP–conformant products with other vendors' products, which may conform to OSI profiles other than the U.S. GOSIP.

The U.S. GOSIP requires conformance products for federal agency procurement. Companies, however, are not under this restriction. It is important for companies to know the conformance status of a vendor's product, or the strategy for achieving conformance. However, it is more important for a company to know how well a vendor's implementation interoperates with other vendors' products. Companies should be sure to verify that the products they wish to purchase interoperate with each other.

COMPARISON OF THE U.S. GOSIP TO OTHER PROFILES

Table 10.1 is a comparison of the U.S. GOSIP profile to four other major profile families: U.K. GOSIP version 3.0, the MAP/TOP family of profiles version 3.0, the NIST Implementor's Workshop Agreements version 3.0, and the CEN/CENELEC ENV profiles. These families of profiles were chosen because they cover the major OSI user groups in both the United States and Europe.

The purpose of this table is simply to give the reader some idea of the functional breadth of the various profiles and to show how U.S. GOSIP fits into the profile scheme. It should give companies a relative measure of how well the U.S. GOSIP profile interoperates with other user profiles.

Table 10.1   U.S. GOSIP Compared to Other Profiles

Layer	USG	NIST	UKG	MAP	TOP	ENV
Physical/Link						
802.3	X	X	X		X	X
802.4	X	X		X	X	
802.5	X	X	X		X	X
X.21	X	X	X		X	X
X.21 bis	X	X	X		X	X
HDLC	X	X	X		X	X
LAP B	X	X	X		X	X
Network						
CLNP/X.25	X[1]	X			X	
CLNP/802.2	X	X	X	X	X	X
CONS/X.25	X[1,2]	X	X			X
CONS/802.2		X[3]	X[4]			X
ES-IS	X	X	X	X	X	X
Transport						
TP4/CLNP	X	X	X	X	X	X
TP4/CONS		X	X			
TP0/CONS	X[1]	X	X			X
TP0,2/CONS		X	X			X
Session						
Version 1	X	X	X	X	X	X
Version 2	X	X	X	X	X	X
Pres/Application						
ACSE	X	X	X	X	X	X
FTAM File Transfer						
Simple	X	X	X	X	X	X
Positional	X	X	X	X	X	X
Hierarchical	X	X	X	X	X	X
FTAM File Access						
Positional	X	X	X	X	X	X
Full	X	X	X	X	X	X
FTAM Management	X	X	X	X	X	X

Notes:
1. Only 1984 X.25 is allowed.
2. To be used only by X.400 MHS over public data networks.
3. 802.2 Type I service shall be used.
4. 802.2 Type II service shall be used.

The table is only a qualitative comparison since some of these profile families include up to seven separate profiles (e.g., CEN/CENELEC). Also, the profiles have their own way of defining each layer's requirements. For instance, the U.K. GOSIP and CEN/CENELEC profiles define layers 1 through 4 in **transport profiles** and include layers 5 through 7 in each individual **application profile**.

All of these profile families specify X.400 MHS 1984 operation. They allow communication between user agents and message transfer agents and between adjacent message transfer agents.

WHAT THE U.S. GOSIP DOESN'T PROVIDE

Although the U.S. GOSIP provides a stable base for performing intervendor networking, it does not provide some functionality that many companies deem necessary for systems to do real work. Also, the U.S. GOSIP imposes certain restrictions on the functionality it does define, therefore making it less attractive to non-government companies. This section discusses these shortcomings and attempts to provide solutions for these deficiencies.

Probably the largest deficiency in version 1 of the U.S. GOSIP is its omission of the ES-IS protocol. This is rectified in version 2 of the U.S. GOSIP, but it does make systems that implement only version 1 limited in their effectiveness on Local Area Networks. However, most vendors understand this. They also understand that version 1 U.S. GOSIP is the only profile that does not require its use. MAP/TOP, NIST Implementor's Agreements, and the U.K. GOSIP all require the use of ES-IS protocol over LANs. Therefore, vendors usually add support of the ES-IS protocol to their OSI implementations. HP, DEC, SUN, and AT&T all provide ES-IS in their OSI products.

The U.S. GOSIP does not define specific application programmatic interfaces (APIs), which should be used to access the various layer services. It says only that APIs should be provided and it is up to the purchaser to specify which services are required. All vendors provide APIs to some layers in the protocol suite, but there is little standardization among them. Few profiles specify APIs. Except for MAP 3.0, which specifies an API for FTAM, API definitions are non-existent. Various user's groups are now trying to tackle this problem, but it will be several years before all vendors offer consistent interfaces. AT&T, along with DEC, IBM, HP, and other vendors, is working on creating consistent APIs for use with ACSE/Presentation, Transport, and CONS. The Network Management forum is doing the same thing for X.400. Other groups, such as POSIX and X/OPEN, are also working along similar lines. Companies should be sure to ask vendors to specify what APIs they support and at what layers.

Similarly, the U.S. GOSIP does not specify interactive interfaces for its FTAM and X.400 services. This is not unusual. Most other profiles do not specify these either. However, it is important to know how these services are to be used. This is especially true for X.400. Of particular importance is whether the vendor's MHS implementation acts only as a gateway (Message Transfer Agent), or can be used in a user agent configuration as well. If the latter is true, the interactive interface to the user agent is very important.

The U.S. GOSIP is somewhat different than other profiles in that it has specific requirements concerning the use of addresses at all layers in its protocol profile. It defines a family of NSAP addresses, which federal agencies must use, and defines default selector values for the FTAM and X.400 MHS services. Companies cannot use these NSAPs, as they are reserved for the government (although, currently, the government is allowing companies to share their NSAP space in order to promote the use of NSAPs), and the selectors defined may not fit into a company's addressing strategy.

The U.S. GOSIP does, however, allow communication with non-government networks and, therefore, requires that U.S. GOSIP–compliant implementations support any valid NSAP address format. Valid format means the NSAP conforms to ISO 8348/AD2, Addendum to the Network Service Definition Covering Addressing. So even though the U.S. GOSIP defines a specific NSAP address space, companies can use their own NSAP address structures in U.S. GOSIP–compliant products.

The selector value specifications are only guidelines. The U.S. GOSIP requires compliant implementations to accept any valid selector value within the constraints listed previously. Since the constraints listed in the protocol section are in line with all other major profiles (except MAP/TOP 3.0, which allows presentation selector values of up to 16 octets; U.S. GOSIP/NIST only allow up to 4 octets for a presentation selector), virtually any profile-compliant address can be used with the U.S. GOSIP.

U.S. GOSIP does not have any Directory Service specifications. This is because X.500, the CCITT Directory Service Standard, was not stable when the U.S. GOSIP was written. Instead, the U.S. GOSIP suggests the use of well-known addresses or the registration of addresses with a central authority, namely NIST. Almost all vendors supply some form of Directory Service product, whether it is X.500 or a proprietary solution. Companies wishing to use Directory Services will need to evaluate an individual vendor's solution to see if it meets their Directory Service needs. Companies should also verify the vendor's plans for transitioning their Directory Service product to an X.500-based solution.

The U.S. GOSIP allows interworking between CONS and CLNP networks only at the Application Layer by way of application gateways. This is insufficient for many companies, especially those who operate both in the United States and in Europe. Companies who need this functionality should be sure to query the vendor on their strategies to solve this problem.

The U.S. GOSIP only supports Transport class 4 over CLNP (TP4/CLNP). Although it does allow limited use of Transport class 0 over CONS (TP0/CONS), there are other Transport class/Network Layer combinations that customers may want to use. The most important one is Transport class 2 over CONS (TP2/CONS). Transport class 2 has many advantages over Transport class 0. It allows the use of expedited data and the ability to multiplex several transport connections over a single X.25 virtual circuit. Another possibility is Transport class 4 over CONS (TP4/CONS). This is less popular, but it does have advantages when interworking between CONS and CLNP networks.

The U.S. GOSIP does not support the use of CONS and X.25 over 802.2 networks. This profile is gaining popularity mainly in Europe where most networks are X.25 based. U.K. GOSIP, and CEN/CENELEC support this profile. The NIST Implementor's Agreements support this as well, but in a slightly different way. As there are very few vendors who actually offer this profile in a product today, companies who need this functionality should evaluate vendors' products very carefully.

FUTURE VERSIONS OF U.S. GOSIP

The U.S. GOSIP is an evolving profile. New versions of the U.S. GOSIP are being created by NIST to address the limitations of the current version. New versions become the mandated profile eighteen months after publication. Figure 10.3 shows the evolution from current to future versions of the U.S. GOSIP.

These services and the versions listed for release are not final. NIST should be contacted to obtain revised schedules and dates for release.

GOSIP 1
Pub Feb 89 / Req'd Aug 90

FTAM NBS 2 subset
— Positional File Transfer (T2)
— Management (M1)
— [Simple File Access (A1)]

MHS/X.400'84

Transport Classes 0 and 4

TP0 only for X.400
public messaging domains

Connectionless Network Service
(CLNS)

X.25, 802.3, 802.4, 802.5

GOSIP 2
Est. Pub Oct 90 / Req'd June 92

FTAM NBS 2 subset
— Telnet Profile
— Forms Profile

ODA/ODIF

ES-IS Routing Protocol
• Connectionless Transport
  Protocol (CLTP)
• Connection-Oriented
  Network Service (CONS)

ISDN

GOSIP 3
Est. Pub Oct 91 / Req'd June 93

FTAM NBS 3 subset

MHS/X.400'88/EDI

VTP
— X3, page, and scroll profiles

X.500 Directory Services

MMS Manuf. Message Spec.

CGM/SGML

Network Management
• Security Enhancements

IS-IS Routing (Intra-domain)
• TP2

FDDI

GOSIP 4
(Date undetermined)

DTP (Distributed Transaction
Processing)

RDA (Remote Database Access)

IS-IS Routing (Inter-domain)
• Additional Security Enhancements
• Additional Network Management
  Functions

Source: NIST

Figure 10.3   The evolution of U.S. GOSIP.

QUESTIONS TO ASK VENDORS

Here is a list of questions companies should ask vendors about their U.S. GOSIP–compliant implementations. The answers to these questions will give companies a good idea about how well a vendor's product will suit their needs. It will also tell the company how robust the product is and how committed to OSI the vendor is.

- What Link Layer standards does the product support?
- What versions of X.25 does the product support—1980, 1984, or 1988?
- What layers have supported Application Programmatic Interfaces? What are the interfaces? What is the vendor's strategy for moving towards standardized interfaces?
- What is the vendor's strategy for obtaining U.S. GOSIP conformance marks? Is the vendor an accredited test center?
- Has the vendor performed interoperability testing? What vendors can the product interoperate with?
- What versions of U.S. GOSIP does the product support?
- What is the vendor's strategy for moving its product from version 1 to version 2?
- If the product supports only version 1, does the product support the ES–IS protocol?
- Can the product support any valid NSAP address format?
- Can the product support TP0/CONS over private X.25 networks?
- Can FTAM operate over TP0/CONS?
- Is TP2,0/CONS supported? Is TP4/CONS supported?
- What is the vendor's strategy for providing Directory Services?
- Can the X.400 MHS act as an Application Gateway between TP4/CLNP and TP0/CONS networks?
- Does the vendor support Interworking Units such as MSDSG or Transport Relays?
- What functionality does the FTAM have—full-purpose or limited-purpose? Does the vendor have an interactive interface? What other user profiles does the product support?

CONCLUSION

Companies are looking at the OSI protocols as the solution to their intervendor networking problems. However, the protocols themselves do not guarantee interoperability between vendors' implementations. Consortiums of users and vendors have been created to write profiles of the protocols to help ensure interoperability between OSI implementations. Choosing which profile, or profiles, to use may be one of the most important decisions a company will make in the next few years. The U.S. GOSIP is a profile that companies should evaluate.

The U.S. GOSIP is a profile that has many benefits for companies. Since it is based upon the work of the NIST OSI Implementor's Workshop, companies are assured that the U.S. GOSIP complies with the most popular user profiles. Also, since the U.S. GOSIP is an evolving profile, a company's OSI network may evolve with it, thereby ensuring a smooth transition towards full OSI.

Copies of the U.S. GOSIP and additional information about the U.S. GOSIP program may be obtained at the following address:

Order Number: FIPS PUB 146 (version 1) or FIPS PUB 146-1 (version 2)
U.S. Department of Commerce
National Technical Information Service
Springfield, VA 22161

The NIST Implementor's Agreements may be obtained from the following address:

National Institute of Standards and Technology
NIST Workshop for Implementors of OSI
Building 225, Room B-217
Gaithersburg, MD 20899

11

802.3/ETHERNET

Ian Crayford

INTRODUCTION

Market Perspective

In terms of installed base, Ethernet is the most popular LAN technology currently deployed. Depending on the estimates used, Ethernet currently accounts for some 40–45 percent of the installed base, as of 1991. Figure 11.1 refers specifically to the personal computer (PC) industry, which is the largest market segment for LAN interconnectivity.

Figure 11.2 shows the anticipated growth rate for Ethernet connectivity, on a worldwide basis, throughout the early 1990s.

Figure 11.3 shows the breakdown of PC adapter cards for the primary LAN technologies currently in use. As can be seen, Ethernet outstrips all other technologies, with the vast majority of the LAN adapter marketplace moving to Ethernet and Token Ring, with proprietary implementations such as Arcnet and LocalTalk losing market share.

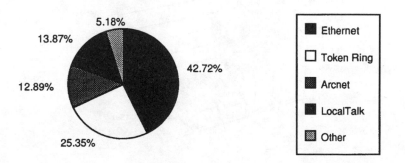

Figure 11.1 Worldwide PC adapter card installed base by LAN technology. *(Source: IDC [1991].)*

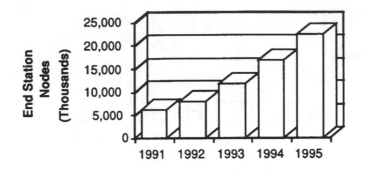

Figure 11.2 Estimated worldwide Ethernet end station shipments.

While many analysts have predicted that Token Ring would equal and surpass Ethernet shipments early in the 1990s, this has proved incorrect—primarily due to the effect that Twisted Pair Ethernet (10BASE-T) has had in fueling the Ethernet marketplace at the expense of Token Ring. It is currently uncertain whether Token Ring will ever reach parity with the Ethernet market (in terms of units shipped, not necessarily in revenue), due to the inherently lower cost of implementing an Ethernet node.

The technical reasons behind the widespread acceptance of Ethernet in general and the 10BASE-T version in particular will be discussed later in this chapter.

Historical Perspective

The invention of Ethernet is credited to Bob Metcalfe and David Boggs, then of Xerox,[1] in 1973. Bob Metcalfe went on to found 3Com and promote the use of Ethernet as a local computer network standard.[2] The initial Ethernet standard was developed by the DEC, Intel, and Xerox (DIX) consor-

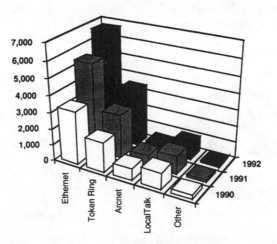

Figure 11.3 PC adapter card breakdown by LAN technology. *(Source: IDC [1991 actual, 1992/3 estimates].)*

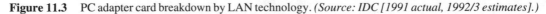

tium, formed in 1979, with the first Ethernet[3] *Blue Book* published in 1980. At that time, the Ethernet standard was submitted to a newly formed IEEE group (later to be defined as IEEE Project 802). In 1982, after much wrangling due to potentially competing standards from IBM (Token Ring) and General Motors (Token Bus), Project 802 split into three committees: 802.3 for Ethernet, 802.4 for Token Bus, and 802.5 for Token Ring. Late in 1982, the DIX and IEEE versions became one and the same (with only minor changes from the original Ethernet), and so was born the 802.3 (Ethernet) standard.

802.3 has been adopted by numerous national and international standards bodies including the National Bureau of Standards (NBS), the European Computer Manufacturers Association (ECMA), the American National Standards Institute (ANSI), and finally, in February 1990, by the International Standardization Organization (ISO), under which it is known as 8802-3.

Adding further to this chronology, the IEEE has created specifications for several versions of 802.3 to support different kinds of media, allowing the use of thick coaxial cable (the original Ethernet), thin coaxial cable (Cheapernet), Unshielded Twisted Pair (UTP), fiber optic, and even a broadband coaxial version. The recent trend for heterogeneous network management has not passed unnoticed by the standards-making body, and draft documents for management (defined in more detail later) have recently been added and are in the final stages of the balloting process.

The following section will provide a broad overview of 802.3/Ethernet–based networks. This will include an overview of the Ethernet protocol, a view of the typical implementation technologies used, tradeoffs between various media choices and topologies, rules for configuration, future standards developments, and a look at new trends in implementation.

ISO/OSI—SEVEN-LAYER MODEL

As shown in Figure 11.4, 802.3/Ethernet resides within Layer 1 (Physical) and Layer 2 (Data Link) of the ISO/OSI seven-layer reference model. 802.3 is just one of the Layer 1/2 standards that are administered by the IEEE 802. Others include 802.4 (Token Bus), 802.5 (Token Ring), 802.6 (Metropolitan Area Network), and 802.11 (Wireless Networks) (see Figure 11.5).

Figure 11.6 shows the relationship between the ISO reference model and the actual implementation within an Ethernet node.

Ethernet is a packet-based Local Area Network (LAN), built on the Carrier Sense Multiple Access with Collision Detect (CSMA/CD) access protocol. This is the basis by which any Ethernet node determines if it is permitted to transmit over the shared medium (regardless of medium type). The Media Access Control (MAC) layer is responsible for the enforcement of the CSMA/CD protocol.

In this architecture, devices are connected to a shared medium and have equal priority access to it. All devices are permitted to "listen" (receive), but only one device at any time is permitted to "talk" (transmit). Any device wishing to transmit must first sense if the medium is currently active. This is effectively the "Carrier Sense" part of the algorithm. If the medium is already active, the node must wait until the activity stops, and a predetermined period of silence passes. If the node detects that the channel is free, it may initiate a transmission attempt. If, after starting its transmission, its data collides with that of another station attempting to transmit at the same time, the transmitting station(s) will continue to transmit for a short additional period to ensure that the collision propagates throughout the network, and then "backoff" for a random period of time before attempting the transmission again. This access protocol will be discussed in more detail in subsequent sections.

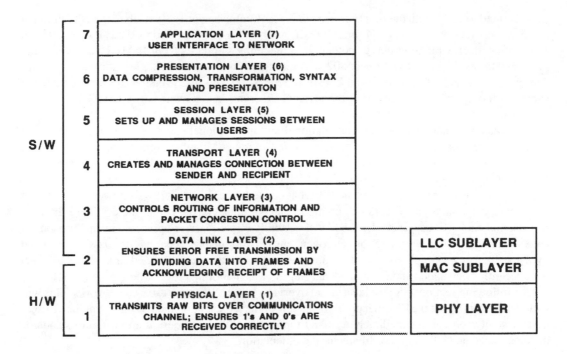

Figure 11.4 OSI (Open Systems Interconnection) reference model.

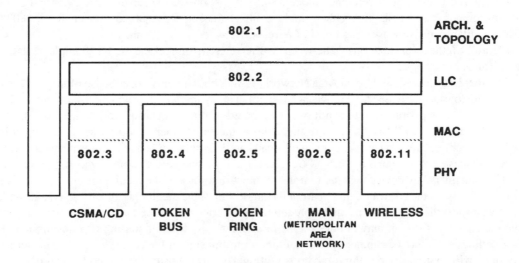

Figure 11.5 Relationship of ANSI/IEEE standards.

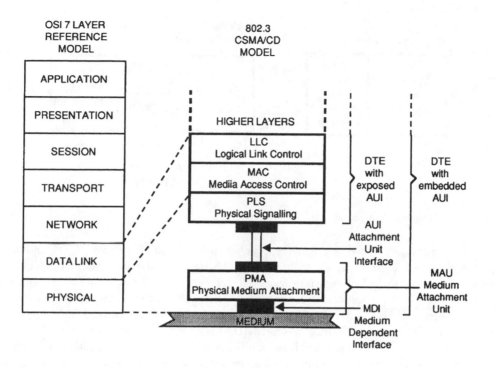

Figure 11.6 Relationship of OSI and IEEE reference models.

The Physical Signaling (PLS) and Attachment Unit Interface (AUI) subsystems support the signaling scheme between the MAC layer and the Medium Attachment Unit (MAU). The MAU is responsible for the actual physical and electrical interface to/from the particular type of medium.

Since Ethernet is a mature technology, functionality has been integrated into VLSI circuitry, which has permitted continued reduction in size, cost, power consumption, and complexity of interfacing to an 802.3/Ethernet network.

The Media Access Control (MAC) sublayer and the Physical (PHY) layer are primarily supported directly in silicon, with implementations available from several semi-conductor companies. The Logical Link Control (LLC) sublayer, which, with the MAC, forms the Data Link Layer (DLL), is normally implemented in software, as are the layers above. Early silicon solutions were typically partitioned into three functional integrated circuits (ICs), as shown in Figure 11.7. Advanced silicon implementations, which integrate all of the functionality of the MAC and PHY layers, are now being produced with hardware support for the LLC functions. These will be discussed in more detail later.

MEDIA ACCESS CONTROL FRAME FORMAT

Ethernet supports a 10 Mbps data rate (hence, the "bit time" or time taken to transfer a single bit of information is 100 ns), although 802.3 actually encompasses data rates between 1 and 20 Mbps.

Figures 11.8 and 11.9 show the format of the 802.3 and Ethernet frames, respectively.

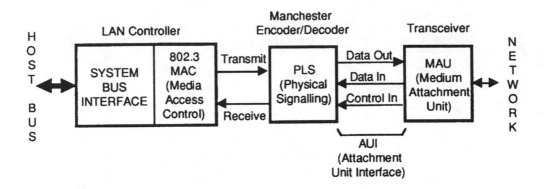

Figure 11.7   Typical node hardware.

The frame commences with a preamble sequence, which is an alternating "1, 0" pattern. The preamble provides a single frequency on the network (5 MHz) at the start of each frame, which allows the receiver to "lock" to the incoming bit stream. This is followed by a "start of packet" marker, which indicates that the data portion of the message will follow. Either the "Start Frame Delimiter" or "Synch" sequence will be used (see below for additional details on the specific differences).

The next two fields are the Destination Address (DA) and Source Address (SA) for the frame. Both are 48-bit values which are transmitted least significant bit (LSB) first. The Destination Address is used by the receiving MAC to determine if this incoming packet is addressed to this particular node. If the receiving node detects a match between its own unique node address and the address within the DA field, it will attempt to receive the packet. Other nodes, not detecting a match, will ignore the remainder of the packet.

Three types of destination addressing are supported:

1. Individual (Physical)—The DA field contains an individual and unique address assigned to one node on the network.
2. Multicast (Logical)—If the first bit (LSB) of the DA field is set, this denotes that a Group Address is being used. The "group" of nodes that will be addressed is determined by a higher-layer function, but in general the intent is to transmit a message to a logically similar subset of the nodes on the network—for instance, to all printing devices.

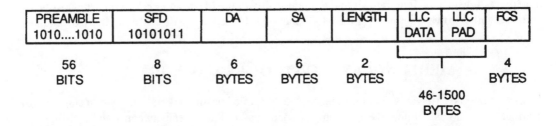

Figure 11.8   802.3 frame format.

PREAMBLE 1010....1010	SYNCH 11	DA	SA	TYPE	DATA	FCS
62 BITS	2 BITS	6 BYTES	6 BYTES	2 BYTES	46-1500 BYTES	4 BYTES

Figure 11.9 Ethernet frame format.

3. Broadcast—The broadcast is a special form of multicast address, where the DA field is set to all 1s. This address is reserved, and all nodes on the network must be capable of receiving a broadcast message.

The Source Address (SA) field is supplied by the transmitting MAC, which inserts its own unique address into this field as the frame is transmitted, indicating it was the originating station. The receiving MAC is not required to take action based on the SA field.

Administration of network (node) addresses can be managed either locally or globally. If the second bit in the DA field is set, the address is locally administered. Hence, address assignments will typically be managed by the local network manager. If the second bit in the DA field is clear, the address is globally administered by a registration authority such as the ISO or IEEE. Most LAN adapters are shipped with globally administered addresses, which the hardware supplier programs during the manufacturing process. Global administration minimizes any potential conflicts as networks grow in size and are interconnected to other previously isolated LANs. Details of how to obtain globally administered addresses should be directed to the appropriate authority.[4]

The two-byte Length or Type field follows the SA field. The choice of length or type is dependent on whether the frame is 802.3 or Ethernet compatible, respectively (see below for additional details on the specific differences). The high-order byte of the Length/Type field is transmitted first, with the LSB of each byte transmitted first.

The Data field contains the actual packet data that is being transferred and is 46–1,500 bytes in length. The LLC function is responsible for fragmenting data into block sizes suitable for transmission over the network. Data bytes are transmitted sequentially with the LSB of each byte transmitted first.

Finally, the Frame Check Sequence (FCS) is a four-byte field that contains the cyclic redundancy check (CRC) for the entire frame. The CRC is computed by the transmitting station on the Destination Address, Source Address, Length/Type, and Data fields, and appended as the last four bytes of the frame. The same CRC algorithm is used by the receiving station to compute the CRC value for the frame as it is received. The value computed at the receiver is compared with that appended by the transmit station, providing an error detection mechanism in case of corrupted data. The CRC bits within the FCS are transmitted in the order MSB to LSB.

For additional details on these definitions, consult the current 802.3[5] and/or Ethernet[6] specifications.

The primary differences between the 802.3 and Ethernet frames are:

1. The "Start Frame Delimiter" (SFD) of 802.3 is defined as a byte with the "1, 0, 1, 0, 1, 0, 1, 1" pattern, whereas the "Synch" bits of Ethernet are a "1, 1" sequence. However, in both cases, the preamble plus start of frame indication is 64 bits long.

2. 802.3 and Ethernet both specify that a packet must be in the range of 64–1,518 bytes. However, the actual data field in 802.3 is permitted to be smaller than the 46-byte value that is necessary to ensure this minimum size. 802.3 handles this by requiring the Media Access Control (MAC) layer to append "pad" characters to the LLC Data field before sending the data over the network. Ethernet assumes that the upper layer(s) ensure that the minimum data field is 46 bytes before passing the data to the MAC, and the existence of pad characters (although they may have effectively been inserted by the upper layer software) is unknown to the MAC.

3. 802.3 uses a "Length" field which indicates the number of data bytes (excluding pad characters) that are in the data field only (excluding the FCS field). Ethernet, on the other hand, uses a "Type" field in the same two bytes to identify the message protocol type. Since valid Ethernet Type fields are always assigned to be above the maximum 802.3 packet size, Ethernet and 802.3 packets can coexist on the same network.

Note that the packet size of 64–1,518 bytes refers to the number of bytes after the start of frame, up to and including the Frame Check Sequence. The preamble is used only by the Manchester Encoder/Decoder (the clock/data recovery circuit within the PLS function) to "lock on" to the incoming receive bit stream and allow data decoding. Preamble is not passed through the MAC to the host system.

OVERVIEW OF 802.3 IMPLEMENTATION MODEL

Media Access Control (MAC) Sublayer

The MAC sublayer is responsible for the enforcement of the CSMA/CD protocol. The primary requirements of the MAC are:

1. Transmit and receive message data encapsulation
   a. Framing (frame boundary delimitation, frame synchronization)
   b. Addressing (source and destination address handling)
   c. Error detection (physical medium transmission errors)
2. Media access management
   a. Medium allocation (collision avoidance)
   b. Contention resolution (collision handling)

Transmit and Receive Message Data Encapsulation   The MAC layer is responsible for the formatting of the transmit frames. This requires that the relevant fields of the frame are transmitted in the correct order (as defined in the "Media Access Control Frame Format" section), starting with the correct preamble/SFD sequence, followed by the actual frame contents (including DA, SA, Length/Type, and Data), and finally the calculated CRC is appended as the FCS field. The MAC effectively converts the byte-oriented data passed to it from the host (computer) side and serializes this into a bit stream that can be transmitted over the network medium.

   When receiving, the MAC must deserialize the incoming bit stream, to reassemble the frame into bytes. The preamble is ignored, but once the SFD is detected, the MAC must delineate the DA field from the receive frame and compare this with the appropriate stored address (dependent on the type of destination addressing being used). If no match exists, the MAC discards the receive frame and waits for the medium to become inactive. If a match exists, the MAC will receive the incoming frame, compute its own independent CRC, and compare this with the CRC obtained from the FCS field (the last four bytes) of the received frame. If the values computed at the transmitter and receiver do not match, the MAC must report an error. If the frame contained an exact number of bytes, a "CRC Error" is reported.

If a partial byte is received, the MAC must report an "Alignment Error" instead of the CRC Error. Since the CRC at the receiver is computed on the number of complete bytes received, the Alignment Error is intended to show that some bits may have been lost (or added) due to an error in decoding the received data.

Note that a phenomenon referred to as "dribbling bits" may cause some additional bits to be detected at the receiver. This occurs in normal network operation and is due to the tolerancing allowed in the various transmitters and receivers in the signal path. Dribbling bits will have no effect (they will be discarded by the MAC) unless eight bits are added, in which case a full byte will be detected, causing the CRC to fail (since the last byte will consist of dribbling bits, not a true FCS byte). Normally configured or operating networks will not add eight dribbling bits.

Other errors can be monitored and/or reported by the MAC, although these are more connection related and are therefore discussed within the PLS/AUI and PHY subsystem definitions.

Media Access Management   All devices on an Ethernet network must timeshare the common communications medium. All nodes on the network have equal priority access to the medium. Multiple nodes may simultaneously receive data from the medium, but only one node at any time is permitted to transmit. A station wishing to transmit must first sense if the medium is currently active. The PLS function detects and passes the state of "Carrier Sense" to the MAC. If the network is currently busy, carrier sense will be active, and the station will defer its transmission until the activity ceases, and a predetermined period of silence passes. This period of inactivity is known as the Inter Packet Gap (IPG) interval. The IPG delineates each packet (with a 9.6 μs interval) and allows all stations to detect carrier sense as inactive.

Once the IPG has expired, a station is permitted access to the medium and may start to transmit. If two (or more) stations have been waiting for access to the medium, then they may start to transmit at essentially the same time. Since the medium is shared, their transmissions will interfere and become garbled, causing a "collision." All stations must have a "Collision Detect" capability. The stations that are transmitting will detect the collision and commence a "jam" sequence, which means they will continue to transmit for a predetermined time after the collision has been detected. This time guarantees that stations at the extremes of the network will be able to detect the collision condition. Once the jam sequence has completed, the station will cease transmission, and the network will become inactive again once the last station ceases. The stations that were transmitting will perform a "backoff" algorithm, which causes them to reschedule their transmissions at a later point. The backoff period is computed individually in each station using a pseudo-random sequence generator. This is intended to cause the colliding stations to reschedule their next transmission attempt at different intervals to avoid a subsequent collision.

The time taken to guarantee that a station can detect a collision is determined by the round trip delay of the network. Assume that a station starts to transmit a message, and the message propagates through the network to another remote station, which starts to transmit just at the point that the first station's message begins to arrive. The remote station will detect a collision almost immediately (dependent on the actual implementation). However, the originating station will not be aware of the collision until the event propagates back through the network. So the round trip delay, called the "slot time," determines how long it takes to detect a collision. The slot time imposes a maximum network length, in order to ensure that collisions are detected within a predetermined period of time. The slot time is 51.2 μs (512 bit times) for 802.3/Ethernet.

In very busy networks, with high traffic rates, collisions are experienced as a normal part of the medium access protocol. Up to sixteen attempts are permitted to transmit the Ethernet packet (or frame). The Ethernet LAN controller (implemented in silicon) is responsible for the handling of retransmissions. The controller will compute the interval before the retransmission is allowed based on a "truncated binary exponential backoff" algorithm, which provides a controlled pseudo-random mechanism to enforce the collision backoff interval before retransmission is attempted.

As stated in ANSI/IEEE Standard 802.3, 1990 Edition, 4.2.3.2.5:

"At the end of enforcing a collision (jamming), the CSMA/CD sublayer delays before attempting to retransmit the frame. The delay is an integer multiple of slot time. The number of slot times to delay before the nth retransmission attempt is chosen as a uniformly distributed random integer r in the range:

$$0 \leq r \leq 2^k$$

where

$$k = \min(n, 10)."$$

Notice that according to this algorithm, as the number of retransmission attempts increase (as "n" gets larger), the number of choices for the retry interval ("r," the randomly chosen integer) becomes larger. Hence, the randomness allows the dispersion of retries when the network is heavily utilized and several stations are involved in the collision, in an attempt to alleviate congestion.

If the transmission is unsuccessful after all sixteen attempts, the MAC will abandon the frame transmission and inform the upper layer software, which is responsible for taking appropriate action.

Physical Signaling (PLS) Specification

Although part of the Physical (PHY) Layer, the PLS function resides in the DTE and is responsible for four principal functions. These allow transmit Data Output, receive Data Input, Carrier Sense, and Error Sense. A fifth optional function is provided for in the 802.3 Standard (Monitor Mode[7]) but this is so seldomly implemented in practice that it is not discussed here.

The PLS provides the interface between the MAC layer and the AUI. The MAC transmits serial data which is output in "Non Return to Zero" (NRZ) format. The MAC typically operates at standard logic levels (i.e., 5V TTL or CMOS compatible). The data is "Manchester encoded" by the PLS and transmitted over the AUI to the MAU, using a differential signaling technique. Manchester encoding allows both clock and data information to be combined into a single "bit-symbol." Each bit-symbol consists of two halves, with the first half being the logical inverse of the data bit to be encoded, and the second half of the symbol always being the logical value of the data bit itself (or the inverse of

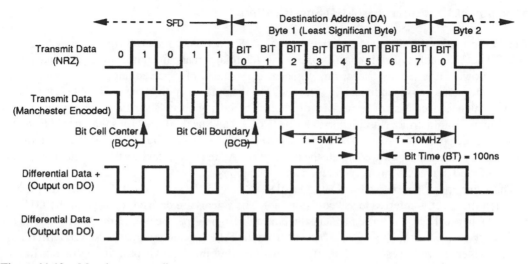

Figure 11.10   Manchester encoding.

the first half). This guarantees that there is always a signal transition in the center of each bit-symbol (or Bit Cell Center, BCC). Figure 11.10 shows the relationship of clock, NRZ, and Manchester encoded data. Note that a sequence where each successive data bit differs from the previous bit (such as preamble) exhibits a 5 MHz frequency, whereas a sequence containing identical data (all 0s or all 1s) exhibits a 10 MHz frequency.

The conversion from single-ended logic levels from the MAC to the two-wire differential signaling required by the AUI specification allows the AUI signals to pass through the transformer isolation barrier in the AUI path. This is designed to provide DC isolation between the DTE (host computer) and the network medium, in the event of network fault condition.

The three input functions provided to the MAC by the PLS allow the MAC to perform the CSMA/CD protocol.

The Data Input function takes the Manchester encoded bit stream received from the MAU, via the AUI, and decodes it to provide the receive data function for the MAC. The receive decoder uses the fact that the preamble sequence of the frame will exhibit a 5 MHz frequency. This allows a device such as a phase-locked-loop to lock to the incoming wave form, effectively providing a clock reference to allow decoding of the remainder of the frame.

The Carrier Sense function allows the MAC to determine if there is network activity. The PLS will return the state of Carrier Sense as active when there is transmit activity from the node or receive or collision activity detected on the network.

The Error Sense function allows the node to detect if the MAU and the associated AUI are operational and connected. After each transmit packet from the MAC, the MAU is required to send back a signal to indicate that its collision logic has been tested and is operational. This signal is referred to as "Signal Quality Error Test" or SQE Test. If the indication is not passed back, the MAC will report that the MAU is either malfunctioning or not correctly connected.

In addition, the PLS and MAC can also use the fact that if no Carrier Sense is detected during an actual transmission, then the MAU or the AUI is malfunctioning.

Attachment Unit Interface (AUI) Specification

The AUI provides the signaling path between the PLS function of the DTE (or a repeater) and the MAU. The AUI cable typically consists of three differential signal pairs (although an optional fourth pair is allowed, it is virtually never implemented in practice), plus power and ground connections. Each of the signal pairs is individually screened. The maximum length of the AUI cable is limited to 50 m, which can consist of a number of cables joined together. The "Physical Signaling and Attachment Unit Interface Specification" of the IEEE 802.3 Standard[8] specifies that the DTE should have a female connector and the MAU should have a male connector; hence, the AUI cable requires opposite mating connectors to complete the connection. All the connectors are the familiar fifteen-pin D-Type found in many computer interconnect applications.

The signal pairs are defined as Data Out (DO), Data In (DI), and Control In (CI, frequently, although incorrectly, referred to as "collision in"). The signals are defined in terms of the DTE (or repeater); hence, DO is the transmit data path. Note that from the perspective of the MAU, the signals appear reversed, so although DO is an output from the DTE it is an input to the MAU. Differential signaling is employed on each of the interface signals to allow the signals to pass through a transformer isolation barrier, which provides the DTE (typically an expensive computer system) protection from severe network medium faults.

Data is output from the DTE on the DO pair (in Manchester encoded form) during transmission and is also returned (looped back) by the MAU to the DTE using the DI pair. In this way, the MAC/PLS functions are able to observe the complete operational status of the AUI and MAU.

During reception, Manchester encoded receive data passes to the DTE via the DI pair.

If a collision is detected, a 10 MHz pulse train is sent by the MAU over the CI pair to inform the DTE. In addition, the SQE Test burst is also returned to the DTE a short period after each frame transmission has completed. The SQE Test burst must commence within a window of 0.6–1.6 µs, and should last 5–15 bit times.

Medium Attachment Unit (MAU) Specification

The MAU provides the functional, electrical, and mechanical interface between the DTE and the particular network medium in use. It is Important to note that the MAC, PLS, and AUI functions are preserved regardless of medium; only the MAU is required to change.

The MAU has six primary functions to perform. These are Transmit Data, Receive Data, Loopback, Collision Detection, SQE Test, and Jabber Protection. In addition, in some MAUs a seventh function, Link Integrity, is performed.

Transmit Data   The DTE will present Manchester encoded data for transmission over the network on the DO pair of the AUI. The MAU is responsible for receiving the data on DO and forwarding this over the network. The MAU provides the necessary drive capability to transmit the data over the network and does not modify the content of the data in any way.

Receive Data   The MAU is responsible for ensuring that the valid Manchester data received from the network is passed to the DTE using the DI circuit of the AUI. The MAU performs signal amplitude and pulse width detection on the received signal to ensure its quality, before forwarding the unmodified data to the DTE.

Loopback   Manchester data output from the DTE to the MAU on the DO pair must be returned to the DTE using the DI pair. This loopback mechanism is used by the MAC to indicate that valid network transmission and reception paths exist.

Collision Detection   The MAU is responsible for the detection of collisions on the network. If the MAU detects a collision, it reports this back to the DTE by sending a 10 MHz wave form on the CI pair of the AUI. The actual mechanism of collision detection is dependent on the particular medium and will be discussed under the headings "Topology Issues" and "The Increasing Dominance of 10BASE-T." During the collision condition, the MAU continues to return data back to the DTE using the DI pair. When the node is no longer involved in the collision but the network is still active, the MAU returns data from the network over the DI pair. If the node is the last device to continue to transmit after the collision condition has ceased, the MAU returns the data received on the DO pair (from the DTE) to the DI pair.

SQE Test   After the transmission from the DTE completes, the MAU is responsible for sending a Signal Quality Error (SQE) Test message over the CI pair of the AUI. This requires the MAU to attempt to test as much of its collision detection logic as possible and, if functional, indicate this by transmitting a short 10 MHz burst on the CI pair. The SQE Test burst must commence within 0.6–1.6 µs of the transmission ending and should last 5–15 bit times. Note that if the transmission attempt resulted in a collision and the CI pair was activated, the test is considered to have been performed and does not have to be repeated at the end of the transmission.

The SQE Test function is normally provided with an enable/disable feature. The function should be enabled when the MAU is connected to a DTE. The DTE provides a "blinding period" during which it looks for the SQE Test burst after each transmission and does not interpret this as a collision indication. The SQE Test feature must be disabled if the MAU is connected to a repeater, since the repeater does not provide any blinding period and will detect the SQE Test burst as a collision.

Jabber Protection   The Jabber mechanism is provided to prevent a single node, which continues to transmit for excessively long periods, from completely utilizing the network. If a DTE transmits on DO for an abnormally long period (20–150 ms), the MAU will interrupt the transmission of data on the network, disable the loopback path to DI, and indicate a collision using the CI pair. The MAU remains in this state until the the data output from the DTE ceases (DO becomes silent), and an "unjab" time expires (0.5 s–0.25 s).

Link Integrity   Some MAUs provide a mechanism which detects if a valid communications path exists over the network. This mechanism is primarily used in MAUs that use separate transmit and receive signaling paths, such as twisted pair and fiber. This facility is important in ensuring correct network operation is these systems, since a break in the receive signal path will render the Carrier Sense facility inoperable. This is discussed more fully in the section on "The Increasing Dominance of 10BASE-T."

ANATOMY OF AN ETHERNET NODE

Figures 11.11, 11.12, and 11.13 explain, in simple overview terms, the functional capabilities of each part of an Ethernet node, the data flow for packets transmitted by the host over the network, and the reception of packets from the network and passed to the host. The example shown is for a 10BASE2 coaxial implementation, although the functionality is equally valid for other media.

TOPOLOGY ISSUES

Each of the topologies defined within the 802.3 specifications is defined using a specific nomenclature. For instance, Ethernet (thick coaxial cable) is defined as 10BASE5 (pronounced "ten-base-five"). This actually defines some of the key aspects of the network. The "10" is the network data rate (10 Mbps). The "BASE" refers to the fact that baseband signaling is employed. The "5" is the maximum segment length in 100 m units and rounded off (so, 500 m for thick Ethernet). Cheapernet, which is defined as 10BASE2 (thin coaxial cable), is 10 Mbps, baseband, 200 m (the distance is actually limited to 185 m, but is rounded up).

Two recent additions to the 802.3 suite of standards from a topology point of view allow the use of Unshielded Twisted Pair (UTP) and fiber optic media. Both of these break the previous nomenclature rules and cause some confusion.

The UTP standard is defined as 10BASE-T and is 10 Mbps, baseband, using twisted pair cable. The target cable length defined by the 10BASE-T standard is 100 m, although distances that exceed

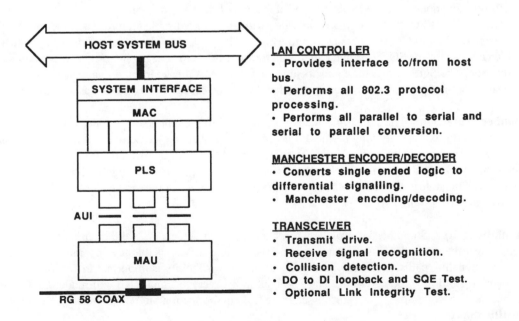

Figure 11.11   Ethernet node—hardware functional overview.

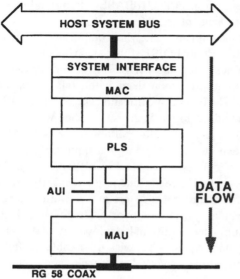

TRANSMIT OPERATION

1. Data moved from host memory to temporary controller store (FIFO).
2. Wait for Carrier Sense inactive and IPG time to elapse.
3. Parallel to serial conversion. Send Preamble/SFD, DA, SA, Length and Data; compute/send CRC.
4. If Collision Detect then "Backoff" and re-try after random interval.

5. Manchester encode transmit bit stream.

6. Receive on DO,Tranmit onto medium, Loopback DO to DI.
7. Watch for transmit Jabber (faulty controller).
8. Perform SQE Test at end of transmission.

Figure 11.12 Ethernet node—transmit data flow.

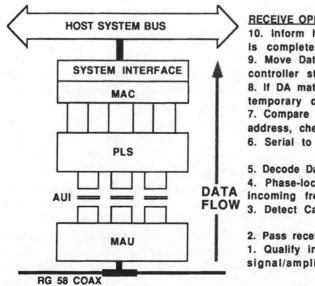

RECEIVE OPERATION

10. Inform host that receive packet is complete.
9. Move Data from temporary controller store to host memory.
8. If DA match, place receive Data in temporary controller store (FIFO).
7. Compare DA with internal address, check received CRC.
6. Serial to parallel conversion.

5. Decode Data and Clock.
4. Phase-lock-loop "locks" to incoming frequency.
3. Detect Carrier Sense.

2. Pass receive data to DTE over DI.
1. Qualify incoming waveform signal/amplitude.

Figure 11.13 Ethernet node—receive data flow.

this are permitted if the cable is of higher quality than specified. 10BASE-T is currently the newest of the 802.3 standards, receiving final approval in September 1990.

The specifications for the use of a fiber optic medium are somewhat complicated by the fact that there are actually four categories that are defined. These are FOIRL (Fiber Optic Inter Repeater Link), 10BASE-FL (FiberLink), 10BASE-FB (Fiber Backbone), and 10BASE-FP (Fiber Passive). Since there are various lengths for these, they will be discussed in more detail within this section under the headings "Fiber Optic" and "Mixed Topologies." The FOIRL specification was defined in 1987. The 10BASE-FB/FL/FP specifications are recent additions to the 802.3 suite. They were in the final balloting stages at the time of writing. Until completion of this balloting process, they are not considered an official IEEE standard. They are expected to receive formal approval late in 1992.

Other standards of note are StarLAN (1BASE5[9]) and broadband (10BROAD36[10]). StarLAN provides a 1 Mbps data rate and employs UTP cable. However, due to the relatively high cost of connecting this into existing Ethernet networks (requiring a "store-and-forward" device), this particular implementation has gained minimal popularity in large networks. The advent of 10BASE-T (discussed later in detail) has essentially eliminated additional deployment of this network. 10BROAD36 allows the use of CATV (Community Antenna Television) or cable TV–type inter-connectivity components to provide an 802.3 compatible network. Due to their very small comparative market share, neither of these derivatives of 802.3 will be discussed further.

Coaxial

Traditional Ethernet (802.3, 10BASE5[11]) and Cheapernet (802.3, 10BASE2[12]) are coaxial-wired systems. The coaxial cable provides the linear bus to which all nodes are connected. Signaling is accomplished using a current sink technique with the center conductor used for signal, and the shield used as a ground reference.

10BASE5 (Ethernet)

10BASE5 was the original architecture defined by the DIX group and adopted by the IEEE 802.3 committee. The topology is far from friendly from a cost, installation, and maintenance point of view. The cable is thick (approximately 10 mm or 3/8″) and does not easily bend. It is generally installed in the above-ceiling or below-floor space, with the actual connection to the node (DTE) taking place via an Attachment Unit Interface (AUI) cable. The AUI cable is a multipair cable that provides the required signal and power connections between the network node (DTE) and the Medium Attachment Unit (MAU), which is located on the coaxial cable (see Figure 11.14). The AUI cable can be a maximum of 50 m long and is connected at each end with fifteen-pin D-Type connectors, used in most computer applications. The MAU converts the digital signals from the DTE to the current drive required to signal over the coaxial bus. The 10BASE5 MAU is typically clamped to the coax cable, and integral probes pierce the cable to make connection to the inner center conductor and surrounding (but insulated) shield. This mechanism is often referred to as an extrusive or "vampire" tap connector (see Figure 11.23). An alternate intrusive tap mechanism requires the coaxial bus to be cut and connectorized; then, two coaxial connectors provided on the intrusive MAU are used to rejoin the cable and connect into it.

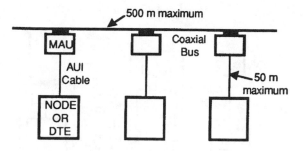

Figure 11.14 10BASE5 coaxial bus topology.

10BASE5 specifies a maximum cable length of 500 m and a maximum number of nodes of 100. The length and node count can be increased by the use of repeaters (explained in more detail later), which allow multiple cable segments to be connected together.

In today's modern office environment, this topology is difficult to work with. Even simple changes may require access to the cable, movement of the MAU, and rerouting of the AUI cable. The AUI cable is itself almost as thick as the coaxial cable. With an intrusive tap, the entire network will have to be broken and reconnected, clearly not a preferable situation. The vampire tap is a complex connector mechanism and is therefore relatively difficult to install and requires trained installation staff. However, despite these limitations, a substantial installed base of Ethernet configurations exists. These are primarily in backbone applications, where the 500 m distance is an advantage, and relatively few devices are directly connected—or in installations where large concentrations of Engineering Work Station (EWS) systems are deployed, since these were the first to integrate the Ethernet function onto the motherboard.

10BASE2 (Cheapernet)

In order to alleviate many of the cost and installation difficulties associated with thick coax, the 10BASE2 standard was defined to allow the use of thin coax, frequently referred to as Cheapernet.

In 10BASE2, the fundamental difference is that the cable is brought to the DTE, and the MAU is (typically) integrated into the network node, eliminating the need for the AUI connectors and cables (see Figure 11.15). The thin coax cable is much more flexible due to its smaller diameter (approximately 5 mm) and can, therefore, be brought directly to the desktop system (either dropped down from the ceiling or picked up from the floor). The MAU connection to the coaxial bus is also simpler, requiring the use of a simple "T" or "BNC" connector (see Figure 11.24).

However, use of the cheaper cable does have some drawbacks, since some of the key electrical properties are degraded over those exhibited by thick coax. As a direct result, the 10BASE2 standard specifies a maximum cable length of 185 m and a maximum number of nodes of 30. Similar to 10BASE5, the length and node count can be increased by the use of repeaters.

The distance limitation is still adequate for most office-size installations and has led to the widespread deployment of Cheapernet-based networks, especially in the desktop personal computer (PC) connectivity arena. This is largely due to the fact that the connectors (BNC type), cable (RG58

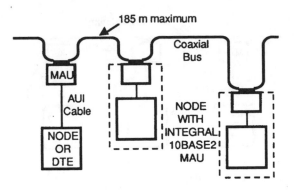

Figure 11.15   10BASE2 coaxial bus topology

A/U or RG58 C/U), and PC-compatible Ethernet adapter cards are all widely available and fairly simple to install with minimal training.

A special cautionary note is worth adding in the case of 10BASE2—the specification requires that no more than 30 mating pairs are present. This may permit 30 nodes to be connected if no other breaks (requiring additional connectors) have been made in the cable.

Despite the fact that the AUI is not externally needed, many 10BASE2 products are offered with the option of bypassing the integrated 10BASE2 MAU. They provide an AUI connector to allow access to a remotely located MAU (such as a 10BASE5 version) via a standard AUI cable. Note, however, that while not prohibited, the AUI is rarely used in 10BASE2 installations.

Twisted Pair (10BASE-T)

Twisted pair Ethernet (802.3 10BASE-T[13]) is able to use standard voice grade telephone cable (22–26 gauge), employing separate transmit and receive pairs (four wires). The system uses a star topology, with a "repeater" at the center of the star (see Figure 11.16). The repeater (or hub) performs signal amplitude and timing restoration (the repeater is described more exactly in the "Repeater Definition" section). It takes the incoming bit stream and repeats it to all other ports connected to it (but not back to the originating port). In this sense, the repeater acts as "logical coax," so that any node connected to the network will see another's transmission. Differential signaling is employed with one pair acting as the transmit path and the other as receive. Further introductory material on the 10BASE-T standard, and its primary differences to the earlier 10BASE2 and 10BASE5 coaxial topologies, is available in various publications.[14,15]

Since separate transmit and receive signal paths are employed in the UTP cable, the 10BASE-T MAU at each end of the link (at the DTE and the repeater) employs a Link Integrity test to monitor for end-to-end continuity. This is performed by each MAU transmitting a "link test" pulse when the DTE has no packet data to transmit. The receiver in each MAU must detect packet data or link test pulses to remain in the "Link Pass" state. If the MAU detects neither, it will enter the "Link Fail" state and effectively prevent the DTE from transmitting on the network. A "Link Status" indication is mandated, which provides a useful external indicator to the user that the node is connected and operational. This is discussed in more detail in the section "The Increasing Dominance of 10BASE-T."

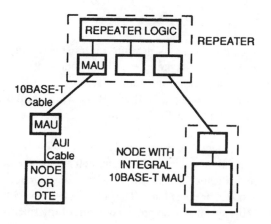

Figure 11.16 10BASE-T twisted pair star topology.

A network based on the 10BASE-T standard directly addresses some of the inherent disadvantages that are present in coaxial-wired systems. The point-to-point nature of the topology eases the tasks of network management, cable administration, and reconfiguration due to moves, additions/deletions, or changes.

The cable is inexpensive and commonly available telephone grade (Type 3), 100Ω Unshielded Twisted Pair (UTP). Simple, inexpensive RJ45 type telephone jack connectors are used to connect the MAU to the medium. In North America, suitable UTP cable is widely deployed in existing building telephone installations. Since, in many cases, existing unused telephone cables can be used, installation can be minimal. In many countries where other cables types are commonly used, investigation is underway to adapt 10BASE-T to run on other unshielded or shielded cable grades (120Ω and 150Ω, for instance). Even if cable is not already available, it is simple to cable all of the work areas within an office building and make individual connections at any time on an "as-needed" basis, using a patch panel typically located in a wiring closet. Unlike a coax LAN, detailed planning of the cable routing to attempt to provide coverage for existing and potential new users is not required at installation time.

Although the cable distance is targeted at 100 m (distance varies according to cable quality), this covers the vast majority of wiring closet/desktop requirements. Since this actually defines a spherical coverage area with a 100 m radius from the repeater, the distance capabilities are often better than for 10BASE2 (as an example), where the overhead associated with cabling to and from each desktop system can significantly erode the overall end-to-end distance capability.

10BASE-T MAUs can be connected via an AUI, or both the MAU and AUI can be embedded within the DTE or repeater. This is also an important issue, in that the provision of an explicit AUI incurs a significant cost penalty. 10BASE-T allows this to be eliminated where appropriate and permits greater integration than is possible in a 10BASE2 architecture. The specifics of these changes, why they are important, and how they are affecting the future deployment of Ethernet/10BASE-T LANs are detailed under the heading "The Increasing Dominance of 10BASE-T."

Fiber Optic

Using fiber optic cable as a communications medium offers several key advantages over typical copper-based media. The primary benefits are its very high bandwidth and low attenuation characteristics. In addition, since it is an optical medium, it is neither affected by, nor does it emit, high-frequency electrical noise (i.e., external EMI and RFI). This, combined with the difficulty in "tapping" into the fiber without physically breaking the connection, makes it secure against eavesdropping or intrusion.

Fiber also has some disadvantages. It is generally more expensive than copper media. This differential is reducing as it gains popularity and manufacturing processes improve. In addition, cheaper grades of fiber, such as Plastic Optical Fiber (POF), although not directly supported at this time by any 802.3 specification, can be considered. The optical-electrical components, used to convert the electrical domain of the host system to the optical domain of the fiber communications channel, add significantly to the cost of the network interface at the node and repeater. In addition, the connectors are more expensive, and connectorization is more difficult to deal with, requiring skilled (costly) installation personnel.

In a strictly 802.3/Ethernet network environment, the bandwidth capability is essentially unused, since the baseband signaling rate occupies only a small fraction of the available bandwidth. For these reasons, the fiber versions of Ethernet are primarily used where the long distance, noise immunity, and/or security benefits are paramount, and cost is secondary.

All the fiber MAU specifications are common in that they require two separate fibers to provide a transmit and receive signaling path. In all cases, the use of 62.5/125 μm nominal diameter fiber is specified, although other types are not precluded.

The Fiber Optic Inter Repeater Link (FOIRL) was the first of the fiber standards to be defined. When originally developed, it was restricted to be a repeater-to-repeater only link and was intended to provide a long-distance connection (up to 1 km) between remotely located repeaters. Although technically excluded from being permitted as a repeater-to-DTE link, the FOIRL signaling scheme was commonly adopted for this purpose where fiber was required at the desktop. The FOIRL specification has subsequently been relaxed to permit repeater-to-DTE connections during the development/balloting of the 10BASE-FL draft. In either case, FOIRL (like 10BASE-T) requires the use of repeaters to act as a central point of concentration for a group of nodes. See Figures 11.17 through 11.21 for examples of the use of FOIRL in a system topology.

Since separate transmit and receive signaling paths are employed (similar to the 10BASE-T MAU), the FOIRL MAUs at either end of the link monitor to ensure that continuity exists. The FOIRL standard specifies that an "active idle" signal of 1 MHz is transmitted by each MAU and used for link integrity. If the receiving MAU fails to detect this activity (defined as a "low-light" condition), it enters the "Link Fail" state and prevents the DTE from transmitting onto the network.

FOIRL requires an F-SMA plug (fiber optic cable) and socket (MAU) connector arrangement.

The 10BASE-FL,[16] 10BASE-FB,[17] and 10BASE-FP[18] draft documents have been developed to address different market requirements.

The 10BASE-FL is specified to supersede the original FOIRL specification, allowing both repeater-to-repeater and repeater-to-DTE links. It is compatible in all functions, including the 1 MHz active idle and the fact that the idle signal and packet data are asynchronous to each other. However, it does provide some improvements over the original FOIRL:

1. The maximum distance between MAUs is extended to 2 km.
2. The cheaper ST™ plug (fiber optic cable) and socket (MAU) connectors are specified.
3. Relaxed rise/fall time signaling specifications enable reduced drive power requirements (important for embedded MAU applications).
4. As an interesting side note, the MAU state machines were adopted directly from the 10BASE-T MAU standard.

See Figures 11.17 through 11.21 for examples of the use of 10BASE-FL in a system topology.

10BASE-FB is designed to provide an optimized interface for interrepeater links. The 10BASE-FB MAU is essentially defined as embedded within a repeater, with no exposed AUI. A 2.5 MHz active idle signaling technique is used to indicate that the transmit path is idle. In addition, the transmit data from the repeater is synchronized to this idle signal, enabling the receiving MAU to remain locked to the active idle/packet data transitions. In this way, the response time of the receiver is increased, since a PLL or similar function within the MAU receiver can remain locked to the incoming signal (a PLL in a DTE or repeater would normally be locked to a local clock until preamble commenced, at which point it would take several bit times to acquire lock to the incoming, but phase unrelated, clock). In addition, the 10BASE-FB specification supports:

1. A maximum distance between MAUs (repeaters) of 2 km.
2. The use of the cheaper ST™ plug (fiber optic cable) and socket (MAU) connectors.
3. A "remote fault" signaling scheme, allowing the MAU to indicate jabber, low light, or loss of synchronization to the MAU located at the other end of the link.

Since 10BASE-FB is essentially a backbone technology and is still in its formulative stages, there is currently a very small installation base. See Figures 11.17 through 11.21 for examples of the use of 10BASE-FB in a system topology.

10BASE-FP uses passive "Optical Star." The star and fiber optic cabling effectively provide the overall medium. The star has no active components and is not a repeater. Signals entering any port on the star are output on all other ports, including the originating port. Hence, if multiple receive signals occur simultaneously at the star, the signals interfere, causing a collision.

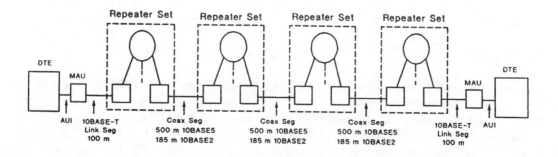

Figure 11.17 Maximum transmission path with three coax segments and two link segments.

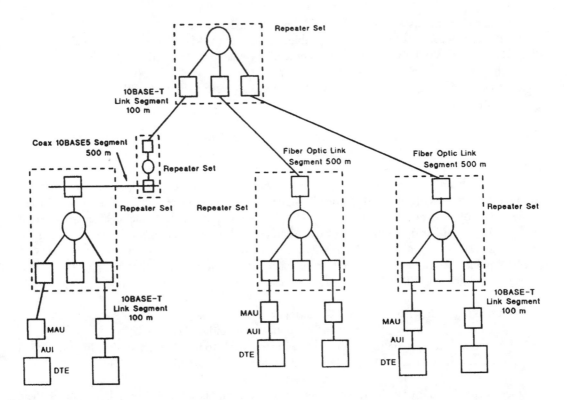

Figure 11.18   Example of maximum transmission path using coax segments, 10BASE-T link segments, and fiber optic link segments.

The use of 10BASE-FP falls into niche applications, where power is not available, or in hazardous areas when electrical signaling/power is impractical.

To ensure that collisions can guarantee to be detected, the fiber optic passive MAU has several major differences from other types of 802.3 MAU. This means 10BASE-FP MAUs are more complicated, not widely supported by LAN equipment vendors, and hence not deployed in main-stream office environments. For this reason, 10BASE-FP is not discussed further in this chapter, although Figures 11.20 and 11.21 show examples of the use of 10BASE-FP in a system topology.

Mixed Topologies

Networks can be constructed that mix the various 802.3 media technologies, making use of the most advantageous attributes of each. Since only the Physical Layer interface changes in each case (the type of MAU), the various implementations are fully interoperable at the DTE (MAC, PLS, and AUI). A few basic rules need to be obeyed to guarantee that the network does not become oversized, which causes problems if the detection of collisions cannot be guaranteed within the slot time. These rules are outlined below, with some simple examples of mixed media networks. Note that these rules guarantee that the network will not become oversized, so they are relatively conservative. For

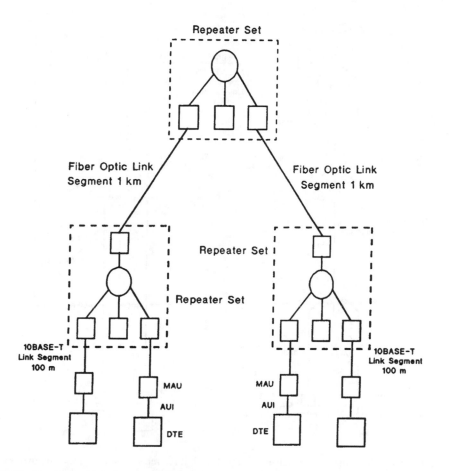

Figure 11.19 Example of maximum transmission path with three repeater sets and four link segments (two are 100 m 10BASE-T and two are 1 km fiber).

networks that need to go outside these rules, to increase the distance and/or coverage of the LAN in a particular installation, detailed rules are specified in the "Systems Considerations for Multi-Segment Networks" of the IEEE 802.3 standard[19] (note that amendments have been made to this section to incorporate topologies for 10BASE-FL/FB/FP and are part of the balloting process for these draft documents). The detailed topology rules require that a precise model of the LAN installation can be produced.

In the case of coax (10BASE2 and 10BASE5) and passive fiber (10BASE-FP) segments, the medium is referred to as a "mixing segment," since signals share the same transmission path and "mix" when a collision is generated. Essentially, any medium where more than two MAUs can be interconnected is classified as a mixing segment. Twisted pair (10BASE-T) and active fiber segments (FOIRL, 10BASE-FL, and 10BASE-FB) are referred to as "link segments," since they form point-to-point links where only two MAUs are directly connected, and collision is detected logically by the presence of activity on both the transmit and receive links.

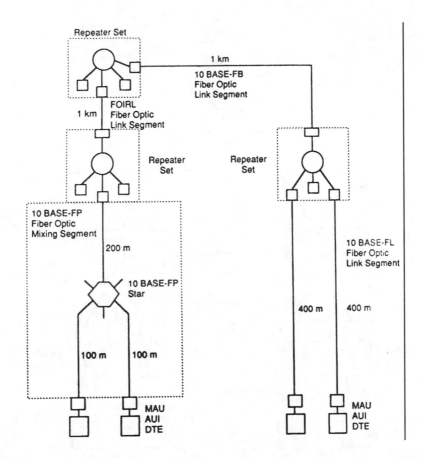

Figure 11.20   Example of maximum transmission path with three repeater sets and four segments (one 1 km 10BASE-FB, one 1 km FOIRL link segment, one 400 m 10BASE-FL, and one 300 m 10BASE-FP).

Generalized topology rules:

1. Repeater sets are required to interconnect segments.
2. MAUs that are part of repeater sets count towards the maximum number of MAUs on a segment.
3. The maximum transmission path between any two DTEs can consist of up to five segments, four repeater sets (including AUIs if provided), two MAUs, and two AUI cables.
4. AUI cables for 10BASE-FL and 10BASE-FP must not exceed 25 m (since an MAU is required at each end of the segment, the total AUI cable length will be 50 m per segment for these two implementations). All other AUI cables are permitted to be 50 m each.
5. When a transmission path consists of four repeater sets and five segments, up to three may be mixing segments, and the remaining two must be link segments (see Figure 11.17). When five segments are present, each fiber optic link segment (FOIRL, 10BASE-FL, or 10BASE-FB) cannot exceed 500 m (see Figures 11.17 and 11.18), and each 10BASE-FP segment cannot exceed 300 m (see Figures 11.20 and 11.21).

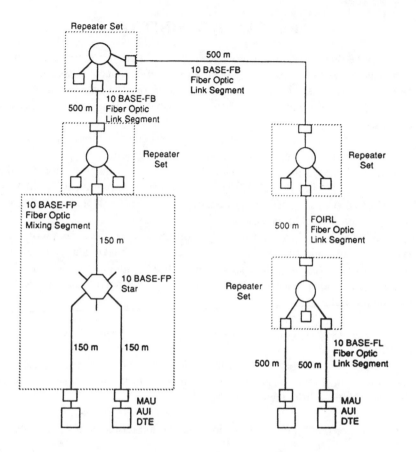

Figure 11.21 Example of maximum transmission path with four repeater sets and five segments (two 500 km 10BASE-FB, one 500 m FOIRL, one 500 m 10BASE-FL, and one 300 m 10BASE-FP).

6. When a transmission path consists of three repeater sets and four segments, the following additional rules apply:
   a. The maximum length of any interrepeater segment must not exceed 1,000 m for FOIRL, 10BASE-FL, or 10BASE-FB segments, and must not exceed 700 m for a 10BASE-FP segment.
   b. The maximum length of any repeater to DTE segment must not exceed 400 m for a 10BASE-FL segment (see Figure 11.20), 400 m for any segment terminated using a 10BASE-FL MAU (such as an FOIRL link connected to a DTE), and 300 m for a 10BASE-FP segment (see Figures 11.20 and 11.21).
   c. The number of mixing segments is not restricted.

Figures 11.17 through 11.21 show some examples of maximally configured networks for various types of mixed media.

REPEATER DEFINITION

A repeater is a device that allows extension of the physical network topology beyond the normal restrictions imposed using a single cable segment in terms of distance and node count.

There are several exact definitions that relate to the definition of a repeater under the 802.3 standards, and a number of generalized industry terms that are also used and occasionally cause conflict and confusion.

A "repeater unit" is defined within 802.3 to be the basic repeater function, which obeys the detailed requirements for restoration and repeating of data between segments.

A "repeater set" is defined within 802.3 to include the "repeater unit" function plus the associated MAUs and AUIs (if explicitly provided). Since a repeater set may have the MAUs physically embedded, no external AUI may be present and, depending on the implementation, no actual AUI circuits may be present internal to the design.

The generic term "hub" is frequently used in industry to describe an interconnectivity device normally based on a star topology. The term "repeater" is more technically correct in the case of Ethernet/802.3 networks. Recently, the terms "Smart Hub," "Intelligent Hub," and/or "Enterprise Hub" have been used (among others) to describe a class of internetworking devices which has the following general properties:

1. Multiple network protocols supported (i.e., 802.3/Ethernet, 802.5/Token Ring, ANSI X3T9.5/FDDI).
2. Multiple media types supported (i.e., fiber optic, coaxial, and twisted pair cables).
3. Manageable from a remote network management entity, which routinely interrogates and receives notifications from the intelligent hub.

Throughout this chapter (and in the industry in general), the terms "hub" and "repeater" are used synonymously.

In its most generic form, the repeater is an "n" port device. Data received on one port is repeated to all ports except the active receiver, with signal amplitude and timing restored on the retransmitted (repeated) wave forms. If the repeater detects receive activity from two (or more) ports, this constitutes a collision and the repeater will send a jam pattern on all ports, including the active receive ports. In this way, a transmitting node connected to a repeater port will observe two or more devices actively transmitting (itself and the repeater), detect a collision, and backoff. See Figure 11.22.

The reception and retransmission of the signals, and the associated delays through the repeater, are closely specified in the section "Repeater Unit for 10 Mbps Baseband Networks" of the IEEE 802.3 Standard.[20] The intent of the repeater is to restore the signal and remove the effects of amplitude distortion (caused by signal attenuation) and timing distortion (caused by jitter, defined as the amount that transitions of the bit-symbol vary from the ideal), which the signal experiences as it propagates through each network segment.

Because of the active regeneration in the repeater, all ports are isolated from each other and do not rely on the operation of neighboring devices for their own operation. Cumulative jitter effects cannot occur (unlike Token Ring), and the performance of each individual port can be monitored.

The repeater can optionally isolate a port detected as experiencing either an excessive duration of collision or an excessive number of consecutive collisions. In this way, the repeater can be used to

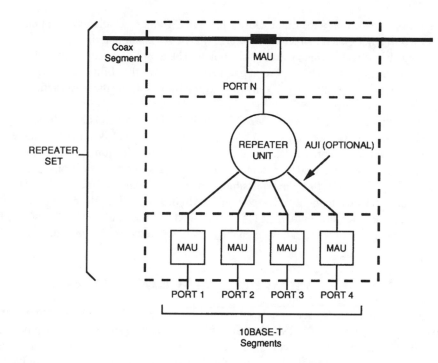

Figure 11.22   Generalized repeater definition.

isolate faulty segments from the remainder of the network automatically. This is referred to as "partitioning" the port.

Since the repeater is centrally located, and since all traffic received from any segment connected to it is repeated to all other segments, the repeater is an excellent place to monitor traffic conditions and locate network management tasks.

Note that when an MAU is connected to a repeater, the SQE Test function must be disabled. The repeater does not permit any "blinding time" during which the SQE Test function is allowed over the AUI's CI pair. All activity detected on the CI pair will be detected as a collision, so the SQE Test function will cause extreme network degradation due to collision activity. Refer to the section "Medium Attachment Unit (MAU) Specification" for more details.

BRIDGE DEFINITION

Bridges are devices that operate at the MAC sublayer level, above the PHY layer in which a repeater operates. The bridge may connect identical MAC technologies (such as Ethernet-to-Ethernet) or dissimilar ones (such as Ethernet-to-Token Ring) together.

Simple bridges are typically two port devices. In the case of an Ethernet-to-Ethernet bridge, the device not only allows extension of the physical network topology but also isolates the "subnetworks" on either side into separate "collision domains." This means that a collision that occurs on one side of the bridge is not transferred to the other. Only valid MAC frames, which appear on one network, and are addressed to a node on the other subnetwork, will be retransmitted onto it.

The various mechanisms by which packets are known to be addressed to a remote subnetwork are outside the scope of this chapter. The important point is to recognize the ability of the bridge to isolate local traffic within a particular subnetwork, only forwarding frames where the MAC address is located on a remote subnetwork.

If the device is a "local bridge," both the MAC functions will typically reside in the same physical enclosure and be internally connected by a high-speed bus/processor subsystem. A "remote bridge" effectively converts the MAC protocol to another type of communications protocol to allow two remote bridge devices to be connected together using a long-distance communications system capable of achieving far greater distances than those possible with conventional LAN technology. The devices are typically connected by a telephone or leased line link. In this case, since the communications link will almost certainly be much slower than the LAN (i.e., 64 Kbps), the true benefit of only transferring those packets which are destined for a device on the remote subnetwork can be seen.

THE INCREASING DOMINANCE OF 10BASE-T

The IEEE 10BASE-T standard has reemphasized the predominance and acceptance of Ethernet-based networks in office environments.10BASE-T redefines some of the key attributes of the physical layer interfaces for 802.3/Ethernet–type networks. These changes have directly allowed enhancements to be made in the ability to add network management and reduce the initial installation and long-term cost of ownership of LANs.

The following section will focus on the key technology differences between thick coax (10BASE5), thin coax (10BASE2), and twisted pair (10BASE-T), which are the three most popular implementations of 802.3/Ethernet. It will also describe how these differences have led to the widespread adoption of 10BASE-T as the office network of choice.

Collision Detection

All 802.3-based networks rely on the fact that all devices are permitted to listen to the channel, but only one may transmit at any given time. If two or more devices transmit simultaneously, a "collision" is sensed, and the nodes involved are forced to reschedule their transmissions after a random interval.

The Medium Attachment Unit (MAU) is responsible for the detection of collisions. Current MAU implementations consist largely of a transceiver integrated circuit, with additional passive components, power supply, and connectors, etc. Serial data originating from the LAN controller in the Data Terminal Equipment (DTE) is passed to the MAU using the Attachment Unit Interface (AUI). If the MAU detects a collision, it reports this back to the controller using the AUI. See Figure 11.23.

With a coaxial topology, all nodes are connected to the center conductor of the cable. The transceiver can detect two or more devices transmitting on the network, since the voltage seen on the center conductor will exceed a "collision threshold" (–1.6V nominally). In order to drive the coax cable, the transceiver requires a relatively high negative supply voltage (typically –9V), making it an unsuitable candidate for most of the mainstream CMOS semi-conductor processes currently available.

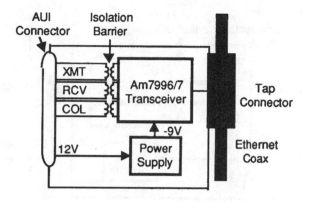

Figure 11.23 10BASE5 MAU.

Since 10BASE-T uses separate transmit and receive signal paths, "logical" collision detection is implemented. While data is transmitted from the node to the repeater on the transmit wire pair, the receive pair should remain idle. If both the transmit and receive pairs become active simultaneously, the 10BASE-T transceiver detects a collision. The voltage levels employed in 10BASE-T (5.0V ± 0.6V peak to peak) can be met using standard 5V CMOS logic levels.

Isolation

An isolation barrier is required in all long-distance network topologies to protect the DTE from potentially hazardous voltages, which may be present during fault conditions on the medium.

In a coax-based network, this DC isolation is located in the AUI path, since the coax transceiver must be DC coupled to the center conductor to permit collision detection.

With 10BASE-T, the logical collision detection scheme eliminates the need for a DC path to the medium (see Figures 11.24 and 11.25). The isolation barrier can be relocated to the medium side of the 10BASE-T transceiver. Removal of the requirement for isolation in the AUI path allows the 10BASE-T transceiver to be integrated with the remainder of the 802.3 node components (MAC and PLS) as a single piece of silicon (see Figure 11.26).

Link Integrity

In a coax system, when the node transmits, the MAU simultaneously receives the transmission (since both the transmitter and receiver are connected to the coax center tap), and returns this to the controller as an indication of transmit to receive path integrity.

The separation of the transmit and receive paths in 10BASE-T has two potential drawbacks. The first is that the DTE cannot sense its own transmission; the second is related to this, in that it cannot detect a failed link.

In a 10BASE-T system, separation of the transmit and receive cable pairs, combined with logical collision detection, means that when driving the transmit twisted pair, the transceiver will not see

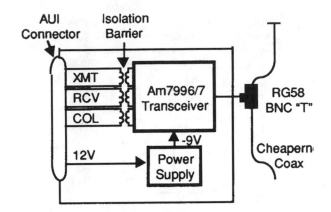

Figure 11.24 10BASE2 MAU.

activity on the receive pair (unless a collision occurs). Since the transceiver can no longer observe its own signal transmission (unlike the coax system), the loopback path to the controller is implemented internally to the MAU. The controller is made to believe that the transmit to receive integrity is present, and no difference is detected between a coax or a twisted pair medium. However, a mechanism is necessary to ensure that a failure in the transmit or receive path can be detected.

In the case of a broken transmit path, the node would be unable to send data over the network—an important point. However, a broken receiver (or receive cable) has far more serious implications. The node loses its ability to monitor the network for activity or collisions. A node with data to transmit would do so regardless of current network activity and may cause a collision with an existing message.

Since recovery from a collision is a fundamental of the 802.3 Media Access Control (MAC) function, it would appear that this is not a serious problem. However, in a correctly configured and operating network, collisions are guaranteed to occur within a defined window after transmission

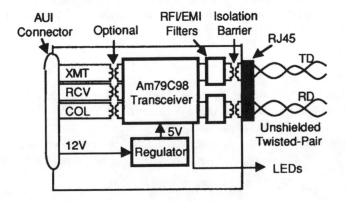

Figure 11.25 10BASE-T MAU.

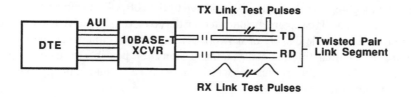

Figure 11.26   Link test transmission/reception.

commences, defined as the "slot time." A transmission experiencing a collision within the slot time will be automatically retried by the sending node. Up to fifteen retries (sixteen attempts total) are permitted before the node aborts the transmission. A collision after the slot time (512 bits or 51.2 μs), on the other hand, will result in a "late collision," and the node will abandon the transmission immediately. Most 802.3 LAN controllers incorporate a late collision indication to advise the host processor of this condition. Upper layer software then has the responsibility to recognize this and reschedule the transmission.

A feature defined as "link test" is used to ensure network integrity. A simple heartbeat pulse is sent by the transmitter of the 10BASE-T MAU (at the repeater or DTE) in the absence of network traffic. The link test pulse is a uni-polar pulse (positive only), unlike the normal 10BASE-T differential signaling used for packet data. If the receiver of an MAU does not see either packet data or a link test pulse within a defined time window (16 ms ± 8 ms), it will enter a "link fail" condition, which disables the data transmit, data receive, and loopback functions. Disabling the transmit function prevents the disturbance of existing network traffic. Disabling the loopback path warns the DTE that there is a failure, since the transmit (DO) to receive (DI) loopback path is interrupted. Therefore, if the receive pair is disconnected, the MAU will enter the link fail state, and further transmission will be disabled. During link fail, the transmission and reception of link test pulses continues. To reestablish the link, at least two consecutive link test pulses or a single receive packet must be received. See Figure 11.27.

Status Indicators

Most 10BASE-T transceivers incorporate additional status features to allow simple diagnosis of the network or node state.

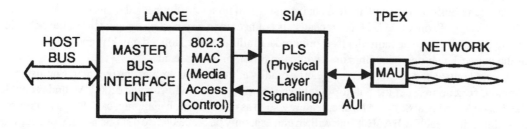

Figure 11.27   Ethernet node chip set.

The external indication of the link status is mandated by the 10BASE-T standard. Transmit, receive, and collision activity can all be separately indicated (in the coax MAU, receive is always active during transmit), to provide a simple display of network activity. In addition, since the link test pulse is uni-polar, unlike the normal differential data transmissions, it is possible to detect the polarity of the receive signal path. This is a useful feature which can be used to automatically detect and correct simple wiring installation errors.

THE USER COMMUNITY

For the user community, 10BASE-T brings several key advantages.

Reduced Installation Cost

The cost of LAN cable installation far outweighs the cost of the cable itself. If existing unused telephone cabling can be used, savings are significant. Even if new cabling has to be installed, costs are generally lower since identical connection technology is widely used in telecommunication applications; therefore, it is inexpensive and familiar to installation personnel.

Long-term "Cost of Ownership" (COO) Benefits

During the lifetime of an LAN, the long-term COO may far outweigh the original equipment cost. Addition or movement of users is more difficult in coax-based Ethernet. Connection to the coax cable requires specialized tools, and the coax bus may not be physically accessible. 10BASE-T is literally "plug and play." Reconfiguration is as simple as adding a new connection or plugging into a prewired connection from the repeater. When the user is moved (or switches off its system), link test pulses stop being transmitted, and the repeater port effectively shuts down.

Ease of Fault Isolation, Management, and Security

In large corporate networks, the ability to manage and maintain the network is vital. Many businesses depend on their communications facilities. The LAN is required to be a utility—much like the telephone system. When a person picks up the telephone, he or she expects to hear a dial tone. In the same way, when a user accesses a networked service, it is expected to be available.

On a coax bus, faults are difficult to analyze, since all nodes are connected to the cable at all times. With 10BASE-T, only one DTE (or repeater) is connected to any port on a repeater. So the behavior of any connection can be individually monitored. A failure can be isolated quickly, and the remainder of the network can operate unimpaired while the problem is corrected.

Access control and network security can be readily administered through the repeater. For instance, the manager can instruct the hub to shut down a particular link on Friday at 5:00 P.M. and reenable the link on Monday at 8:00 A.M. Other features, such as configuration mapping, can also be monitored at the hub, since each 10BASE-T link will, in general, only be connected to a single node. Connections to repeaters (and coax segments) do not obey this rule since they appear connected to a group of nodes, but this fact also allows these links to be identified.

Even in small or low-cost installations, where a "network manager" job function is not warranted, the single point of concentration, point-to-point connectivity, and the addition of rudimentary status indicators, make diagnosing a problem on a 10BASE-T network a less daunting task than checking the entire coax for a potential connection problem.

Volume Manufacturing Benefits

The 10BASE-T topology enables cost-effective silicon integration. This will ultimately drive down the 10BASE-T system cost in two ways. First, the high demand for integrated circuits and board-level products will generate fierce competition for market share, from both semi-conductor and systems companies. Second, the sheer size of the market opportunity will necessitate high-volume manufacturing.

Interoperability and Standardization

The overwhelming demand from the user community is for interoperability based on open standards.

10BASE-T, in itself a standard, is also driving the creation and adoption of additional standardization. The lack of a centrally located point for monitoring and/or management has long been a criticism leveled at coax-based 802.3/Ethernet. The 10BASE-T hub-based star architecture removes this as an obstacle.

Due to the widespread adoption of hub-based topologies supporting Ethernet, Token Ring, and FDDI, the standardization of network management information and its exchange is also under way. Currently, Simple Network Management Protocol (SNMP) is the de facto standard employed in Ethernet networks for the management of infrastructure components (i.e., bridges, routers). Several standards organizations and network vendors are actively working on the definition of standards to allow the management of repeaters, and particularly 10BASE-T repeaters. This is described in more detail under the heading "Integration at the Repeater."

INTEGRATION AT THE NODE

Silicon vendors began the integration process at the transceiver. The huge installed base of AUI-compatible machines made this the natural choice and allowed the technology to be proven in a small device. The AMD Am79C98 TPEX™ (Twisted Pair Ethernet Transceiver™) is a fully compliant AUI-based 10BASE-T transceiver. The device incorporates the 10BASE-T drivers and receivers and provides for status LEDs, as well as the ability to auto detect and correct the receive signal polarity. The device was jointly developed by AMD and SynOptics Communications Inc., an acknowledged leader in the 10BASE-T marketplace.

Clearly, the volume consumption for 10BASE-T node connections will be in the desktop computer market, including IBM™ and Macintosh™ personal computers, Engineering Workstations (EWS), X-Windows™ terminals, etc. In addition, there is significant opportunity for network growth in the mobile computer (laptops and palmtops) market segment.

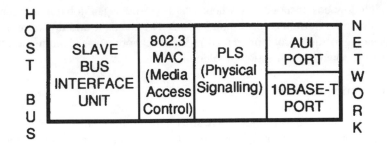

Figure 11.28   MACE™ block diagram.

Non-PC–based Applications

There are several significant market segments, which require networking as a standard or optional feature, outside the PC area. These include applications such as the Engineering Workstation (EWS), X-Windows™ terminal, and Laser Beam Printer (LBP).

The concept of LAN connectivity on the motherboard is not new. Virtually all Engineering Workstation (EWS) systems are shipped with Ethernet on the motherboard, although an AUI is usually the network connector of choice, requiring an external transceiver. The Am7990 LANCE™ (Local Area Network Controller for Ethernet™), a first-generation Ethernet controller, is widely used in this area.

Most medium- to high-performance LBPs offer networking as an optional feature. Some incorporate the entire "print server" hardware and software capabilities. In almost all cases, the LAN connection is offered as an add-in card, due to the inability to predict the end user's preferred LAN technology. However, the prevalence of 10BASE-T will cause some vendors to integrate the chip set onto the LBP motherboard as a standard feature, making 10BASE-T the cheaper and preferred technology, with other LAN options being offered as retrofit.

AMD's Am79C900 ILACC™ (Integrated Local Area Communication Controller™) has already taken the first step in the integration process, incorporating the controller (DMA controller and MAC function) and the Manchester encoder/decoder (the PLS function of the Serial Interface Adapter, or SIA) in a single CMOS device (see Figure 11.28). The device is a 32-bit version of the popular LANCE™ and offers software compatibility. Derivatives of the LANCE™/ILACC™ family already incorporate the 10BASE-T transceiver.

Both the LANCE™ and ILACC™ are bus master devices, suitable in many systems. However, in some applications, a slave-based Ethernet controller would be preferable, due to the synergy with other slave peripherals in the system.

The Am79C940 MACE™ (Media Access Controller for Ethernet™) provides a simple slave interface and offers a high level of integration. The device integrates the MAC, PLS, and 10BASE-T functions, also providing an AUI port to support an external transceiver for an alternate medium. 10BASE-T status LEDs and sophisticated power savings and networking features are also supported.

Personal Computers (PCs)

The commodity PC-compatible market has continued to offer LAN connectivity as an add-in card, due to the cost and space associated with network chips and the lack of a predominant standard for office networking in the PC arena. This is by far the largest market segment for Ethernet chip sets. A typical add-in card consists of the LAN components (supporting thick, thin, or twisted pair Ethernet) and the "glue" logic to interface to the appropriate bus, of which the PC/AT™, EISA, MCA™, and various Macintosh™ buses are the most prevalent.

Two distinct add-in card architectures are predominant—bus master or bus slave. Both types are generally non-intelligent. The use of node processors on the card, popular when bus and processor speeds were lower, is now rare in Ethernet applications, except in specialized areas where some form of protocol processing is required (i.e., bridges and routers).

Bus mastership allows DMA directly between the LAN controller and system memory, so no on-board shared memory is required. A good example of a bus master design is the Novell NE2100 and NE1500T, or EXOS™ 105, products. This network card is ideally suited for client applications, due to its high performance and low cost (no on-board memory).

Numerous papers have been written comparing these two competing approaches, and numerous tests have been performed to try to prove that one approach is universally better than the other. Basically, there is no clear winner for all applications.

Bus mastership allows DMA directly into the system memory, so no on-board shared memory is required. However, if the Network Operating System (NOS) cannot react fast enough to a receive message request and allocate a buffer for the receive frame, then the receive packet has to be placed in an intermediate memory area and copied to the final location once the NOS provides the address. This wastes time performing the double copy.

A shared-memory approach allows additional latency for the NOS to prepare a receive packet location, but requires an on-board memory to buffer the packet locally, plus logic to arbitrate access to the memory between the LAN controller and the host.

In a client-server architecture, the receipt of client information (packet data) is governed by the speed of response of the server. There is minimal client-to-client traffic, although the server receives requests for data from all clients. Therefore, the server requires fast disk and LAN subsystems, but since there is generally one server to several nodes, this is not a major problem. The clients, on the other hand, do not usually have multiple sessions in progress, although they may talk to more than one server in some cases. Since there are many client machines, the essential requirement is good performance at reasonable cost.

With the submicron-level geometries that are available to mainstream silicon vendors, and the fact that the 10BASE-T transceiver can be implemented in this technology, it is now possible to integrate virtually the entire add-in card into a single chip. Only those components requiring custom programming (i.e., remote boot PROM and IEEE address PROM) need remain external to the integrated Ethernet node silicon. Note that it is already possible to integrate the MAC, PLS (the Manchester encoder/decoder implemented by the SIA) and 10BASE-T transceiver functions. However, this still does not provide the most cost-effective system solution. The incorporation of the bus interface logic, to provide a single chip, bus-specific LAN controller, offers the optimal level of integration. This has now been performed in the PCnet-ISA™ chip from AMD. Figure 11.29 shows the level of integration accomplished using this approach (note that the filers/magnetics common in all approaches have been omitted for clarity).

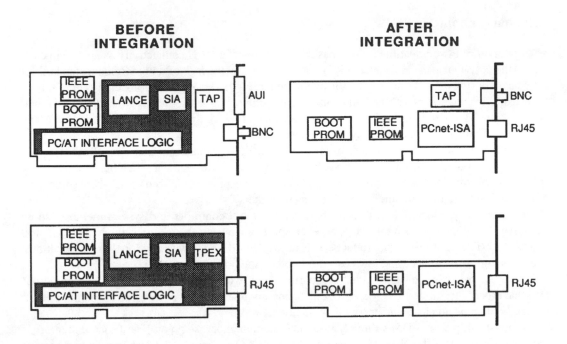

Figure 11.29   NE2100 (top) and NE1500T (lower) equivalent architectures.

This approach clearly reduces the component count, complexity, and form factor for the Ethernet add-in card market. In addition, the RJ45 "phone jack" connector used for 10BASE-T incurs a minimal space overhead in terms of board area and computer backpanel space. The increased integration, reduction in component cost, and reduction in form factor that 10BASE-T brings, are the attributes that will allow Ethernet to become a standard feature on the PC motherboard.

Currently, laptop and palmtop PCs are most frequently networked using an external adapter, which provides an Ethernet connection using the computer's parallel printer port. Here, battery life is the important factor. To address this, Ethernet node chips must incorporate sleep capabilities for low-power applications (as do the PCnet-ISA and MACE devices), allowing the incorporation of 10BASE-T onto the mobile computer motherboard.

INTEGRATION AT THE REPEATER

Several key influences are at work in the evolution of silicon for the repeater market.

Market Demand

Prior to 10BASE-T, repeaters were relatively low-volume devices. For this reason, merchant semi-conductor suppliers had not attempted to "siliconize" the repeater function (although several network system vendors produced implementations using gate arrays or similar). In the 10BASE-T star topology, "the repeater is the network." This reliance, coupled with market demand, has provided the catalyst to encourage semi-conductor vendor participation. This will have immediate system cost benefits in the 10BASE-T market. Longer-term benefits will be realized as silicon vendors amortize the 10BASE-T development effort and migrate the repeater technology to coaxial and fiber media. This will result in an overall lowering of repeater technology cost, an increase in offerings, and a more stable baseline of standard features. These factors will, in turn, increase user acceptance and broaden demand.

Hub Architecture

Manageability of the network service has become a key issue. The acceptance of the star architecture as the preferred scheme for cabling and management in most office environments fits perfectly with 10BASE-T.

Nodes can be selectively enabled or disabled, or the link status can be examined. The type of network traffic on any port can be monitored to allow statistics on network activity or collision frequency to be accumulated for any specific time period.

Standardization

The 10BASE-T standard enforces a mandatory feature set on repeaters to ensure interoperability and minimize network disruption. The IEEE Repeater Standard[20] allows the "partitioning" algorithm to be optionally implemented. In 10BASE-T, the partitioning algorithm is mandated on all repeater ports with a 10BASE-T MAU. The purpose of partitioning is to monitor the port for either an excessive number or an excessive duration of collisions. In either occurrence, the repeater port is "partitioned," disabling its transmit function, although the receive function remains active to permit automatic healing once the fault condition is relieved.

In a 10BASE-T configuration, a simple wiring error or physical short circuit, which directly connects the transmit and receive circuits together, is an example of how partitioning protects the network integrity. Each time the repeater receives data on a correctly configured port, it will repeat the data to all other ports. The 10BASE-T MAU with transmit and receive shorted together will always generate a collision indication, since both transmit and receive functions will become active simultaneously. Hence, a collision will be generated for every packet. In this case, the partitioning state machine for the port will isolate the transmit function of the miswired port after a predefined maximum number of consecutive collisions have been detected (>30).

The importance of multivendor interoperability at the hub is generating a high degree of activity in the standardization of management information and its transaction, as can be seen by several developments.

IEEE Repeater Management Draft   The IEEE is working to create a "Layer Management for 10 Mbps Baseband Repeaters" standard (frequently referred to as the Hub or Repeater Management Draft[21]), which will define the Management Information Base (MIB) variables that can be monitored and controlled by a managing process.

The name is confusing in itself. The Repeater Management Draft does not describe *how* to manage a repeater, only *what* can be managed. Whether the management is performed locally or remotely, using either the LAN itself (in-band management) or an alternative communication channel (out-of-band management), is independent of the variables to be managed and is not addressed by the draft document.

The Repeater Management Draft defines the "managed objects" for the repeater. The classes of objects fall into three basic types:

- *Attributes*—Provide status information about the operational state of the repeater and/or the network, such as repeater health, number of collisions, total bytes received, total frames received, etc.
- *Actions*—Allow the management process to alter the state or value of an object, such as reset the repeater, switch on or off a port, etc.
- *Notifications*—Unsolicited messages which originate from the repeater itself. These are deliberately kept to a minimum to avoid excessive network overhead; therefore, only significant events such as loss and return of power are reported.

As a further distinction, the objects relate either to the entire repeater, or to a specific individual port. Since one of the principal advantages of a star-based network architecture is the ability to monitor and diagnose traffic to the port level, most of the statistics covered are per port.

The various attributes, actions, and notifications are grouped into three "capabilities." These are defined as:

- *Basic Control (Mandatory)*—Provides simple indication of repeater state and allows port enable/disable functions.
- *Performance Monitor (Optional)*—Provides detailed counting of network traffic activity and error conditions on a per port basis.
- *Address Tracking (Optional)*—Provides node address detection and monitoring on a per port basis.

For a repeater to be considered compliant to any of the capabilities, it must implement all of the managed objects within the capability.

IETF 802.3 Repeater MIB   The Internet Engineering Task Force (IETF) has adopted the IEEE Repeater Management Draft and is working in parallel with the IEEE to speed its incorporation into a published specification within the Internet community. This will ensure that migration to this feature will be rapid and widespread.

Novell HMI Specification   In October 1991, Novell announced the Hub Management Interface for 10BASE-T Repeaters,[22] an extension to the existing Open Data-link Interface (ODI) specification for device drivers for the Novell 3.X operating system environment. This specification, again using the IEEE Repeater Management Draft as the original template, defines the attributes that can be managed in a repeater attached to, or integrated within, a Novell file server.

In addition to the Repeater Management features, some additional extensions, which specifically address 10BASE-T ports, have been added.

Novell currently has an installed base of some 55 percent (IDC estimate for 1991[23]) in the PC LAN Network Operating System (NOS) marketplace. HMI has been widely endorsed by numerous LAN hardware and software vendors. The incorporation of HMI functionality and the ability to monitor a server resident hub using SNMP are important steps in the merging of the corporate MIS and PC LAN worlds.

SNMP and CMIP Specifications Currently, Simple Network Management Protocol (SNMP) is the de-facto standard employed in 802.3/Ethernet networks for the management of infrastructure components (i.e., bridges, routers). However, other network management protocols are being developed, such as the Common Management Information Protocol (CMIP), which is used in OSI-based protocol stacks.

In addition to the HMI announcement, Novell also announced the future availability of an SNMP agent as a NetWare Loadable Module (an applications software program). This allows the HMI devices present within a file server to be managed from a remote Network Operations Center (NOC), using the SNMP protocol.

High Reliability

The star architecture has one distinct drawback—the repeater is itself a potential single-point failure. Since the repeater is responsible for the regeneration of all network traffic, failure could isolate all attached nodes. Silicon integration of the repeater brings with it a reduction in the number of interchip connections, a major contributor to mechanically related failures. From the system perspective, the integration can and should allow for "hot swappable" modularity and redundancy at the medium level, if required.

Silicon Availability

AMD's Am79C980 Integrated Multiport Repeater™ (IMR™) integrates all functions of an 802.3-compliant repeater on a single chip, including the Manchester encoder/decoder, FIFO, repeater state machines, and eight complete 10BASE-T MAUs. In addition, the device supports a single AUI port (see Figure 11.30), a management port, and an expansion port. AMD worked jointly with Hewlett-Packard to implement the functionality of H.P.'s original EtherTwist™ hub product. H.P.'s network systems expertise, coupled with AMD's mixed analog/digital CMOS semi-conductor strength, has produced a fully compliant and highly integrated product. This IMR™ has substantially reduced the cost and complexity of implementing a compliant 802.3 repeater. This has already resulted in an overall lowering of repeater pricing, an increase in offerings, and a more stable baseline of standard features. These factors will, in turn, increase user acceptance and broaden demand.

Since virtually all of the expertise to perform the repeater function is contained in the silicon itself, the technology entry barrier has been removed. In addition, integration of the repeater and 10BASE-T functionality, with the ability to provide management and modular port expansion, permits the implementation of applications, such as a "server-hub" (a repeater integrated onto a PC adapter card format), which were not previously possible with discrete solutions.

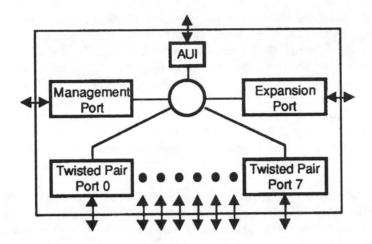

Figure 11.30   IMR™ block diagram.

The IMR™ provides raw information with respect to management, through its serial management port. The addition of external logic allows the requirements of the Repeater Management Draft to be accommodated. This allows product differentiation, as vendors can implement various levels of management features to compete in different market areas.

"Velcro™ Hubs"   The IMR™ provides a completely scalable solution to the repeater market. For low-end systems, the IMR™, combined with a power supply, crystal, and EMI/RFI filter/transformer modules, effectively produces a fully operational 10BASE-T repeater, with an AUI port to allow connection to an existing 10BASE2/5 coax backbone. See Figure 11.31.

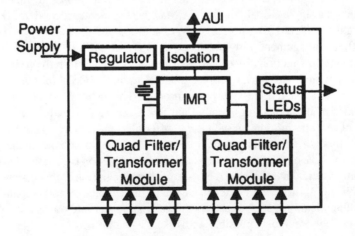

Figure 11.31   Simple "Velcro™ Hub" example.

Server-Hub/"ISA-HUB™"   An excellent example of a low-cost managed repeater is the ISA-HUB™ concept. In a client-server environment, the file server already acts as a hub from the point of concentration of shared resources. By implementing a repeater in a PC/AT™-compatible format, the power supply and case for the hub are provided by the server itself. In addition, the compute, graphics, and disk capabilities of the server can be used for local/remote management data processing, display, and storage, respectively. The port count can be increased by cascading multiple cards together using an intermodule expansion bus. This is precisely the type of solution that the Novell HMI specification is intended to address.

Fully Managed Hubs   High-end repeater/hub solutions typically require facilities such as modularity, fault tolerance, network management capabilities (MIB support), and remote management protocol software (such as SNMP). These applications typically break into two distinct categories:

1. Modular, rack-based systems. Typically based on a proprietary backplane, into which various multiport connection cards (such as 10BASE-T) can be plugged. The hubs typically support one or more separate backplanes for each major LAN technology (Ethernet, Token Ring, and FDDI) and also allow bridge modules to interconnect these backplanes. Since they are rack based, often with features such as a redundant power supply, the entry cost is high when only a small number of ports are required. However, future expansion of the network can be provided by simply plugging in additional modules, although that they must be purchased from the original vendor due to the proprietary backplane.
2. Non-modular, fixed port count systems. Almost always limited to a single LAN technology and media, largely Ethernet and 10BASE-T. These devices are frequently referred to as "workgroup concentrators," or "rack-and-stack" hubs, since they provide sufficient ports (12 to 48 typically) to support a workgroup cluster and also provide an AUI or 10BASE2 port to permit interconnection to other similar devices or an existing Ethernet backbone. Since the devices are fixed configuration, the entry cost barrier is typically lower for a small network than with a modular system, due to the simpler mechanical construction. However, some flexibility is sacrificed if multiple LAN technologies or multiple Ethernet media types need to be supported.

In both the above examples, external logic and intelligence can be added to the Physical Layer building blocks (such as the IMR) to provide all of these features in a cost-effective manner. In this way, low-end repeaters can be produced at optimum system cost, while the cost per port will increase accordingly as sophisticated management features are added. Once the Repeater Management specification becomes fixed, it can be assumed that silicon and system vendors will provide highly integrated solutions, which comply with the MIB requirements and further reduce the cost of network management.

CONCLUSION

Ethernet has been around more than ten years. It currently has the largest installed base and largest annual unit shipments of any LAN technology. Its success can be attributed to several key factors, including support from multiple vendors, proven interoperability, the availability of inexpensive semi-conductor implementations, and the fact that it provides adequate bandwidth for the vast majority of desktop applications.

The standardization of 10BASE-T, allowing the use of inexpensive telephone-grade UTP, has acted as a catalyst to revitalize the maturing Ethernet marketplace, and it is having a dramatic effect on the deployment of Ethernet in several key market sectors.

Semi-conductor vendors are continuing to drive the cost of connectivity for 10BASE-T networks down rapidly. The introduction of single-chip node and repeater solutions will guarantee inter-operability, compliance, and low-cost solutions and will allow significant board, power, and manu-facturing cost savings to be realized by manufacturers and passed on to system integrators and end users.

Three very significant changes will occur in the Ethernet marketplace during the early to mid 1990s.

1. PC vendors will rapidly move to embrace Ethernet connectivity on the motherboard for business-class machines, where LAN connectivity is mandated and the value that it brings to the user and PC manufacturer is compelling.
2. System integrators will enhance their offerings to maximize network management and fault tolerance attributes for products sold into the mission-critical corporate LAN arena, developed to a baseline of internationally endorsed standards.
3. Finally, a new breed of "plug-and-play" LANs will evolve as the connectivity cost per node and ease of use offered by 10BASE-T rivals that offered by less sophisticated peripheral sharing systems.

Simpler configuration and reconfiguration capabilities, combined with the ability to perform network management, mean that a 10BASE-T network is far more able to respond to personal and desktop computer movement than a coax-based Ethernet.

Current generation silicon is already allowing a reduction in pricing in 10BASE-T MAUs, add-in cards, and repeaters. Future integration of the 10BASE-T silicon is assured as the Repeater Manage-ment Standard solidifies, and security and fault-tolerance features are incorporated. These factors will ensure the continued dominance of Ethernet as the office network of choice throughout the 1990s.

GLOSSARY

AUI Attachment Unit Interface. IEEE specification for a node or repeater connection interface to an external medium attachment unit (MAU). The AUI cable between the DTE/repeater and the MAU may be up to 50 m in length. In systems where the MAU is embedded into the DTE or repeater (such as 10BASE-T or 10BASE2) a physical implementation of the AUI may not be present. Defined in Section 7 of ISO/IEC 8802-3: 1990 (ANSI/IEEE Std 802.3).

CI Control In. AUI differential pair circuit, operating at pseudo-ECL levels. The MAU drives a 10 MHz signal on the CI circuit to indicate to the DTE or repeater that a collision has been detected on the network and/or an SQE Test from the MAU to the DTE is in progress.

Concentrator A general term frequently used instead of repeater. Typically, a concentrator supports more than one network protocol, such as 802.3/Ethernet as well as 802.5/Token Ring. The terms "hub," "concentrator," and "intelligent hub" are frequently used interchangeably to reference a multiport, multiprotocol device, capable of statistics gathering, fault monitoring, and/or network management activities.

CRC Cyclic Redundancy Check.

CSMA/CD Carrier Sense Multiple Access/Collision Detect.

DI Data In. AUI differential pair circuit, operating at pseudo-ECL levels. Data received by the MAU from either the media or the DO circuit is driven onto the DI circuit for use by the DTE or repeater.

DO Data Out. AUI differential pair circuit, operating at pseudo-ECL levels. The DTE or repeater drives Manchester encoded data out on the DO circuit, which is transmitted by the MAU over the physical media and the DI circuit.

DTE Data Terminal Equipment. Communication station (or node) capable of reception and/or transmission of data. Generally includes the MAC and PLS sublayer functions, but may also include an embedded MAU.

ENDEC Encoder/Decoder.

FCS Frame Check Sequence.

FOIRL Fiber Optic Inter Repeater Link. IEEE specification for interrepeater communications for repeaters. Defined in Section 9.9 of ISO/IEC 8802-3: 1990 (ANSI/IEEE Std 802.3).

Hub A general term frequently used instead of repeater. See "concentrator."

ILACC Integrated Local Area Communication Controller (Am79C900)

IMR Integrated Multiport Repeater (Am79C980). Single-chip repeater incorporating eight 10BASE-T and one AUI–compatible ports, all 802.3 repeater requirements, management, diagnostics, and port expansion facilities.

IPG Inter Packet Gap. The minimum time permitted between back-to-back packets on the 802.3 network, specified as 96 bits (9.6 s) minimum. Note that a phenomenon known as IPG shrinkage can cause the IPG to be reduced below 96 bits.

LANCE Local Area Network Controller for Ethernet (Am7990).

MAC   Media Access Control.

MAU   Medium Attachment Unit. The physical and electrical interface between a DTE or repeater and the actual medium. The MAU is connected to the DTE by an AUI, although this may not be visible if the MAU is embedded within the DTE or repeater. A different MAU is required to support each different type of medium (cable type).

PLS   Physical Layer Signaling.

PMA   Physical Medium Attachment.

Repeater   An 802.3/Ethernet repeater in its most generic form is an "n" port device, which supports 802.3 protocol only. A repeater is used to extend the physical topology of the network, allowing two or more cable segments to be coupled together. No more than four repeaters are permitted between the path of two stations. When data is received on a single port, the repeater retransmits the incoming bit stream to all other ports, performing signal retiming and amplitude restoration. When data appears simultaneously on more than one port, the repeater transmits a collision to all ports, including the receiving ports. In addition, the repeater can isolate a port if it detects faults, such as excessive number or duration of collisions, to prevent disruption of the rest of the network. In a 10BASE-T network, the repeater provides a central point of connectivity, ideally suited to the incorporation of statistics gathering and network administration functions. Covered by Section 9 of ISO/IEC 8802-3: 1990 (ANSI/IEEE Std 802.3).

SIA   Serial Interface Adapter (Am7992). A Manchester Encoder/Decoder IC, which performs the Physical Layer Signaling (PLS) sublayer functions of the IEEE 802.3 Standard. The device encodes data and clock from the MAC for transmission over the network and drives the DO circuit of the AUI. It receives data from the network via the DI circuit of the AUI, extracts the data and clock into separate paths, and passes these back to the MAC.

SQE   Signal Quality Error. A 10 Mbps pulse train passed from the MAU (using the CI circuit) to a DTE or repeater to indicate an error condition on the network, such as collision or excessive transmit duration (jabber).

SQE Test   Signal Quality Error Test.

TPEX   Twisted Pair Ethernet Transceiver (Am79C98 or Am79C100). A transceiver IC that converts the electrical signals of the AUI to those of the 10BASE-T standard.

10BASE-FL   10 Mbps Baseband Fiber Optic Link. Covered by Section ?? (Draft) of IEEE 802.3. Uses 802.3 protocol, dual fiber point-to-point cabling, and repeaters to provide the network architecture. No defined maximum node count, maximum fiber distance 1–2 km, depending on system configuration.

10BASE-T 10 Mbps Baseband Twisted Pair. Covered by Section 14 of IEEE 802.3. Uses 802.3 protocol, point-to point twisted pair cabling, and repeaters to provide network services. No defined maximum node count, maximum cable distance 100 m. Defined in Section 13 and 14 of IEEE Std 802.3i-1990 (supplement to ISO/IEC 8802-3: 1990 [ANSI/IEEE Std 802.3]).

10BASE2 10 Mbps Baseband 200 m (Cheapernet). A low-cost version of 10BASE5 (frequently referred to as Cheapernet), eliminates the external AUI requirement, relaxes the network electrical interfaces, and allows use of thin 75 coaxial cable. Maximum 30 nodes (or mating connectors) on cable segment, 185 m per segment. Defined in Section 10 of ISO/IEC 8802-3: 1990 (ANSI/IEEE Std 802.3).

10BASE5 10 Mbps Baseband 500 m (Ethernet). Based on the original Ethernet specification proposed by DEC, Intel, and Xerox, for multidrop communication scheme using the CSMA/CD access protocol, over thick 75 coaxial cable. 802.3 is the corresponding IEEE standard, which varies in minor electrical and protocol specifications. Maximum 100 nodes on cable segment. Defined in Section 8 of ISO/IEC 8802-3: 1990 (ANSI/IEEE Std 802.3).

REFERENCES

1. Metcalfe, Robert M. and Boggs, David R. February 1980. "Ethernet: Distributed Packet Switching for Local Computer Networks." *The Ethernet Local Network: Three Reports.* Xerox Palo Alto Research Center, Xerox Corporation.

2. Metcalfe, Robert M. November 1991. "Let the Ethernet Chips Fall Where They May," *Network Computing.*

3. DEC/Intel/Xerox. September 30,1980. "The Ethernet, a Local Area Network, Data Link Layer, and Physical Layer Specification, Version 1.0."

4. ISO/IEC 8802-3: 1990 (E) ANSI/IEEE Std 802.3-1990 Edition, Section 3.2.3.1.

5. DEC/Intel/Xerox. November 1982. "The Ethernet, a Local Area Network Data Link Layer, and Physical Layer Specification, Version 2.0."

6. ISO/IEC 8802-3: 1990 (E) ANSI/IEEE Std 802.3-1990 Edition, Section 8.

7. ISO/IEC 8802-3: 1990 (E) ANSI/IEEE Std 802.3-1990 Edition, Section 7.2.4.2.

8. ISO/IEC 8802-3: 1990 (E) ANSI/IEEE Std 802.3-1990 Edition, Section 7.

9. ANSI/IEEE Std 802.3b, c, d, and e—1989 Edition (Supplement to ISO 8802-3: 1989/ANSI/IEE Std 802.3-1988), Section 12.

10. ANSI/IEEE Std 802.3b, c, d, and e—1989 Edition (Supplement to ISO 8802-3: 1989/ANSI/IEE Std 802.3-1988), Section 11.

11. ISO/IEC 8802-3 :1990 (E) ANSI/IEEE Std 802.3-1990 Edition, Section 8.

12. ISO/IEC 8802-3 :1990 (E) ANSI/IEEE Std 802.3-1990 Edition, Section 10.

13. ISO/IEC 8802-3 :1990 (E) ANSI/IEEE Std 802.3-1990 Edition, Section 13/14.

14. Crayford, Ian. "10BASE-T In The Office." Wescon/91, San Francisco.

15. Anderson, Rick and Woods, Kevin. November 21, 1990. "10BASE-T Ethernet : The Second Wave," *Data Communications.*

16. Draft Supplement to ANSI/IEEE Std 802.3-1990 Edition, Fiber Optic Medium Attachment Unit, Type 10BASE-FL, Section 18.

17. Draft Supplement to ANSI/IEEE Std 802.3-1990 Edition, Fiber Optic Medium Attachment Unit, Type 10BASE-FB, Section 17.

18. Draft Supplement to ANSI/IEEE Std 802.3-1990 Edition, Fiber Optic Passive Star and Medium Attachment Unit, Type 10BASE-FP, Section 16.

19. ISO/IEC 8802-3: 1990 (E) ANSI/IEEE Std 802.3-1990 Edition, Section 13.

20. ISO/IEC 8802-3: 1990 (E) ANSI/IEEE Std 802.3-1990 Edition, Section 9.

21. Draft Supplement to ANSI/IEEE Std 802.3-1990 Edition, Layer Management for 10 Mbps Baseband Repeaters, Section 19.

22. *Novell LAN Driver Developer's Guide.* Section 15: "Hub Management Interface for 10BASE-T Repeaters."

23. IDC, Analysis of PC LAN Operating System Market, August 91 (IDC #5756).

12

AN INTRODUCTION
TO THE IEEE 802.5
TOKEN RING STANDARD

Gary C. Kessler

INTRODUCTION

This chapter briefly describes the IEEE 802.5 standard for token-passing ring local area networks. This standard is the joint Institute of Electrical and Electronics Engineers (IEEE) and American National Standards Institute (ANSI) standard and has been adopted by the International Organization for Standardization (ISO) as ISO 8802-5. This standard is based upon proposals by IBM. In addition, IEEE 802.5 forms the basis for ANSI's Fiber Distributed Data Interface (FDDI).

This chapter also describes some of the physical aspects of the standard, token passing as a medium access control (MAC) scheme, the transmission format, token management issues, and source routing.

NETWORK TOPOLOGY

LANs are typically classified as broadcast networks. A ring network, in particular, is a **sequential broadcast network.** All stations hear the transmissions one bit at a time in some predetermined order.

The essence of token passing is that the token controls access to the transmission channel. The station that holds the token has momentary control of the transmission medium. When a station is finished using the medium, it must pass the token to the next station in sequence. On a token ring network, a station's successor is determined by how the stations are physically wired together. (See Figure 12.1.) Although typically drawn as a ring to reinforce this logical topology, most token ring LANs are, indeed, wired physically in a star topology. The central hub, or medium attachment unit (MAU), acts primarily as a wire concentrator for simplified network administration and management. (See Figure 12.2.)

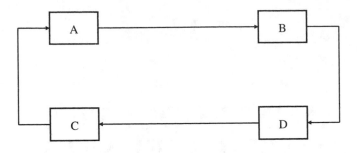

Figure 12.1   The token-passing sequence is defined by the physical topology of the ring. A ring is a geometrically closed set of point-to-point links.

The station holding the token is allowed to transmit one or more data frames for some period of time, called the **Token Holding Time.** It is the responsibility of the transmitting station to remove the frame(s) from the ring and to issue a new token.

PHYSICAL CONNECTION AND LINE CODING

A station on a token ring LAN connects to the medium with an active tap. The tap is, in effect, a bit repeater. The ring itself is not a single piece of cable; it is a geometrically closed set of point-to-point links. Therefore, any point-to-point medium may be used, including twisted pair, coaxial cable, and optical fiber. The current standard utilizes a shielded twisted pair medium at a data rate of either 4 or 16 million bits per second (Mbps).

The 802.5 standard specifies that Differential Manchester encoding will be used. (See Figure 12.3.) With Differential Manchester, every data bit is comprised of a half-bit time signal at a low or high polarity and another half-bit time signal at the opposite polarity. Unlike Manchester coding (Ethernet and IEEE 802.3), the mid-bit transition is for clocking only. The direction of the signal's voltage transition will change whenever a one is transmitted and will stay the same for a zero. Since each bit time comprises a half bit time at opposite polarities, the signaling scheme is said to be **dc balanced.**

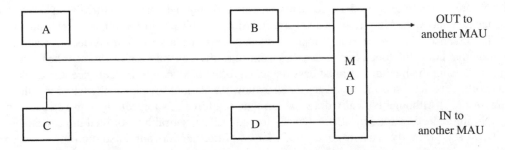

Figure 12.2   Most token rings are actually wired as a physical star, where the medium attachment unit (MAU) provides for central management and administration of the network.

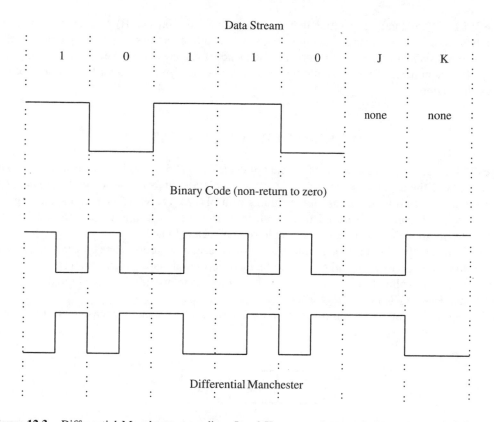

Figure 12.3   Differential Manchester encoding. J and K are non-data symbols, used for special signaling functions. The mid-bit signal transition is for timing and synchronization only.

Two non-data symbols, J and K, are also defined. These symbols are comprised of an entire bit time without a polarity change. The J symbol polarity is the same as that of the previous signal and the K symbol has the opposite polarity as the preceding J. The J and K symbols always appear in pairs to preserve dc balancing and, clearly, cannot be mistaken for either a zero or a one.

The token ring standard requires that an entire token sequence must be able to continuously circulate around the ring, even when all stations are in a repeat mode. Since a token is 24 bits in length (as will be discussed later), the medium must contain enough delay to accommodate those 24 bits. This would require an enormous amount of cable, however; a one kilometer cable operating at 4 Mbps can only hold 17 bits (assuming propagation at 0.77 times the speed of light).

To deal with this problem, a station called the Active Monitor contains a latency buffer that adds a 24-bit delay to the ring. This buffer also compensates for phase jitter in the transmissions. Source timing for all stations is also provided by the Active Monitor. The Active Monitor also has a major role in the management of tokens, which will be discussed later.

The IEEE 802.5 standard specifies that the most significant bit (MSB) of each octet is to be transmitted first. This is different from most other data communications standards, including other IEEE 802 LAN standards. This is of no great consequence if you are interconnecting token rings, but may be of great concern if you are building a gateway to other types of networks or multiprotocol bridges and routers.

IEEE 802.5 FRAME FORMAT

Figures 12.4a, 12.4b, and 12.4c show the format of the IEEE 802.5 transmission formats. The token (Figure 12.4a) is the means by which the right to transmit is passed from one station to another. The frame (Figure 12.4b) is used to transmit logical link control (LLC) or MAC data around the ring. An Abort Sequence (Figure 12.4c) is used to terminate the current transmission. An Abort Sequence may occur anywhere in the bit stream and does not have to be octet aligned.

To avoid an inactive line, the transmitting station will precede and follow each transmission (token, frame or abort sequence) with a fill pattern. Fill may be any combination of zeros and ones. The fill may be any length within the constraints of how long a station may control the medium (determined by the Token Holding Time).

In the descriptions and diagrams that follow, the MSB, or leftmost bit, of each octet is transmitted first.

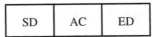

Figure 12.4a   Token: This is the means by which the right to transmit is passed from one station to another.

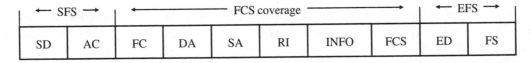

Figure 12.4b   Frame: Used to transmit LLC or MAC data around the ring. The Start Frame Sequence (SFS) is comprised of the SD, AC, and FC fields and the End Frame Sequence (EFS) is comprised of the ED and FS fields. The FCS protects the FC, DA, SA, RI, and INFO fields.

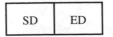

Figure 12.4c   Abort Sequence: Used to terminate the current transmission.

The **Start Delimiter (SD)** marks the actual beginning of the frame. It has the following format:

```
J K 0 J K 0 0 0
```

J and K represent the non-data symbols described earlier. Using non-data symbols in the SD guarantees that actual user data cannot be misinterpreted as framing information.

The **Access Control (AC)** field indicates whether this transmission is a token or a frame, and contains priority information. It has the following format:

```
P P P T M R R R
```

PPP are the priority bits. Every token has a priority between 0 (000) and 7 (111) associated with it (where 7 is high). In a multipriority system, the PPP bits will be set to indicate the priority of the transmitted data or the token.

T is the token bit. This bit is set to one in a token and zero in a frame. If a station is ready to transmit and it receives a token (T=1) with a priority (PPP) less than or equal to the priority of its transmission, it may change this bit to indicate a frame (T=0) and send its data. In this way, high-priority transmissions always take precedence over lower-priority transmissions.

M is the monitor bit and is set to zero by the transmitter of all frames and tokens. When this transmission is seen by the Active Monitor, it sets the M bit to one. If a frame or a high-priority token (i.e., a token with a non-zero priority) is received by the Active Monitor with the M bit already set to one, then the Active Monitor knows that this frame or token has been continuously circulating around the ring. In that case, the transmission is aborted and the Active Monitor issues a new zero-priority token. Only the Active Monitor examines and modifies this bit; all other stations merely transmit it as received. Continuous circulation of a frame or token can occur if a station fails to remove its transmission from the ring or if a high-priority station fails to seize a token. Only a zero-priority token is allowed to continuously circulate around the ring.

RRR are the reservation bits. These bits are initially set to zero by the transmitter. This reservation capability allows a station to place the priority of its intended transmission in the currently circulating frame. The RRR bits may be modified by a station only if its priority is higher than the current value of the RRR bits. When the frame's transmitter generates a new token, that token's priority (PPP) will be taken from the incoming reservation field.

The **Frame Control (FC)** field indicates the type of transmission and has the following format:

```
F F Z Z Z Z Z Z
```

Two different types of frames are supported, namely frames containing MAC data and those containing LLC data. FF are the frame-type bits, set as follows:

00 = MAC Frame
01 = LLC Frame
1x = (reserved)

MAC Frames are used for token and station management. The ZZZZZZ bits indicate the type of MAC control frame, which is described later.

LLC Frames contain LLC (or higher-layer user) data. The ZZZZZZ bits in this case are split among two subfields, designated rrrYYY. The rrr bits are reserved for future standardization and set to 000. The YYY bits indicate the priority (Pm) of the LLC data. The priority indicated in the AC field of the frame (PPP) must be less than or equal to Pm.

The **Destination Address (DA)** and **Source Address (SA)** fields may be either 16 or 48 bits in length.[1] The 16-bit addresses are of the form:

I/G	15-bit address

The 48-bit addresses are of the form:

I/G	U/L	46-bit address

The first bit transmitted is the Individual/Group (I/G) bit, used to distinguish between individual and group addresses. If I/G=0, this is an individual station's address. If I/G=1, this is a group address and the frame may be addressed to more than one station. An address of all 1 bits is the broadcast address.

The Universal/Local (U/L) bit distinguishes between locally and universally (globally) administered address plans. If U/L=1, the 46-bit address is assigned by a local administration. (This is the only option for the 16-bit address.) It is unique to this network only. If U/L=0, this station's address is assigned by a central administration (such as the IEEE) and is distinct from all other stations' addresses on all other networks.

The **Routing Information (RI)** field is an optional field that contains source routing information for interring communication. The RI field, if present, is 2–30 octets in length. Its use is described later in the section on source routing.

The source address in a frame must specify an individual station's address; therefore, the I/G-bit in the SA field must always be set to zero. Therefore, one can argue, the I/G-bit in the SA field is unnecessary. In those implementations supporting source routing, the first bit transmitted in the SA field will be a Routing Information Indicator (RII) bit. If RII=1, the RI field is present; if RII=0, the RI field is absent.

The **Information (INFO)** field contains an LLC protocol data unit or an MAC frame. The INFO field has no specified maximum length, but the time required to transmit the frame may be no greater

---

1 Although still a part of the IEEE 802 standards, the IEEE is withdrawing support for 16-bit address.

than the Token Holding Time. Typical maximum frame lengths are 4,472 octets for 4 Mbps rings and 17,800 octets for 16 Mbps rings. This field is octet aligned.

The **Frame Check Sequence (FCS)** field contains the 32-bit remainder from the bit error detection algorithm using a CRC-32 cyclic redundancy check polynomial.

The **End Delimiter (ED)** indicates the end of the frame and has the following format:

J	K	1	J	K	1	I	E

I is the Intermediate frame bit, indicating whether this frame is the last frame of a multiple-frame sequence (I=0) or whether there are more frames to be transmitted (I=1).

E is the Error-detected bit. The E bit is set to zero by the station transmitting a frame, token, or Abort Sequence. All stations on the ring check the transmission for errors (e.g., FCS error, inappropriate non-data symbols, illegal framing, etc.) and the first station detecting such an error sets the E bit to one. Except when detecting an error, a station will repeat the E bit as received. Stations keep track of the number of times that they set the E bit and, in this way, cable segments on which many errors occur can be localized.

The **Frame Status (FS)** field has the following format:

A	C	r	r	A	C	r	r

The r bits are reserved for future standardization and are set to zero. The A bit is the Address-recognized bit. It is set to zero by the transmitting station and set to one by any station recognizing the Destination Address as its own individual address or relevant group address (including the broadcast address).

C is the Frame-copied bit. This bit is set to zero by the transmitting station and set to one by a station that copies the frame. The frame will only be copied by the receiving station if it is good; i.e., the E bit is set to zero, the address is recognized by the station, and there is no FCS error.

Only three possible conditions (and AC bit values) may be signaled back to the transmitting station:

1. Station non-existent/non-active on ring; frame not copied (AC=00)
2. Station exists, but frame not copied (AC=10)
3. Frame copied (AC=11)

The A and C bits are duplicated in this field for redundancy since they are not protected by the FCS.
Is it possible for the E, A, and C bits to all be set to one? Remember that the frame will not be copied by the receiver unless the E bit is zero when the frame is received. If the A and C bits are both set to one, then the frame was copied by the station that recognized its address. Since the E bit is also set to one, it means that an error must have occurred after the frame was copied correctly by the intended receiver.

MAC FRAMES

The 802.5 standard defines six MAC control frames, which are used for various management functions on the ring.

As mentioned earlier, the ring has a station called the Active Monitor. This station is responsible for determining if the token has been lost, and monitors frames and high-priority tokens to determine if they are circulating endlessly (remember the M bit). One or more other stations may be Standby Monitors. The Active Monitor must take some sort of action on a regular basis to let the other stations know that it is still operational. If too much time elapses without an active monitor action, a Standby Monitor will take over the role of Active Monitor.

Note that the monitors are not special stations, per se. The rules and timers for the monitors are part of the 802.5 standard and may be implemented by any (or all) stations. The ring initialization procedures will automatically determine which station acts as the Active Monitor and the others will just act as Standby Monitors.

If no frames are circulating, the Active Monitor will periodically send an **Active Monitor Present (AMP)** MAC frame. Standby Monitors detect the AMP frame, thus they know that the Active Monitor is operational. Standby Monitors themselves send periodic **Standby Monitor Present (SMP)** MAC frames.

If a Standby Monitor determines that there is no Active Monitor on the ring, it starts to continually send **Claim Token (CL_TK)** MAC frames. The Standby Monitor will stop sending these frames if one of the following conditions occur:

1. A CL_TK frame is received and the sender's address is greater than this station's address
2. A Beacon (BCN) MAC frame is received (see below)
3. A Purge (PRG) MAC frame is received (see below)

In these cases, the Standby Monitor backs off and continues its standby function.

If a station receives a CL_TK frame that it generated, then it becomes the Active Monitor. At that point, it sends a **Purge** frame, inserts its 24-bit latency buffer onto the ring, and assumes Active Monitor functions. In this way, the station with the highest address that first detects the absence of the old Active Monitor becomes the new Active Monitor.

After ring initialization or claiming of the token, a Purge frame is sent by the Active Monitor. A token is then placed on the ring.

A **Beacon** frame is sent as the result of a major ring failure, such as a cable break, failed station or a jabbering station. The transmission of BCN frames is helpful in localizing ring faults since some station will find itself never being able to receive the frames.

The **Duplicate Address Test (DAT)** MAC frame is sent as part of a station's initialization procedure when joining the ring. The station sends the DAT frame with its own address in the Destination Address field. If the frame comes back with the Address-recognized bit set to one, then another station on the ring already has this address. In this case, the new station will notify its local human (i.e., the network manager) of the situation and does not join the network.

MAC frames are indicated when the FF bits in the Frame Control field are both zero; the ZZZZZZ-bit values specify the type of MAC frame:

MAC Frame	FF ZZZZZZ
CL_TK	00 000011
DAT	00 000000
AMP	00 000101
SMP	00 000110
BCN	00 000010
PRG	00 000100

LOST AND DUPLICATE TOKENS

The major potential token problems are when the token is accidently duplicated or lost. If two stations both believe that they hold the token, both may attempt to transmit a frame simultaneously. For this reason, when a station is transmitting frames, it will check that the SA field of the returning frame is the same as its own address; if different, then the station knows that there is another transmitter on the ring. The station will then abort the transmission and not issue a new token. Since both stations will follow these rules, the duplicate token problem collapses into the lost token problem.

The lost token problem has already been described. If the Active Monitor does not see a token or frame for more than some time-out period, it merely issues a new token.

EARLY TOKEN RELEASE

When a station transmits a frame, it has the responsibility of removing the frame from the ring (stripping) and then generating a new token. Typically, the station will wait until at least the SA field of the frame returns, so that the station can be sure that the frame, in fact, belongs to this transmitter. The rationale for this approach is that duplicate tokens are quickly detected should that condition occur.

The reality is that duplicate tokens rarely occur. Furthermore, as token ring LANs in the field become larger and operate at higher speeds, waiting for the returning SA field actually can cause delays. **Early Token Release (ETR)** was developed to alleviate this potential delay. With ETR, a transmitter is allowed to launch a new token immediately after transmitting the last bit of a frame.

SOURCE ROUTING

Source routing is a relatively new addition to token rings. It was proposed by IBM to support inter-LAN communication, particularly in the token ring environment. With source routing, a transmitting station must know how to route a frame to the intended receiver. The routing burden, then, is placed on the end user stations rather than on the network itself.

In a source routing environment, each station must determine the route that packets will take to get to any intended receiver(s). To determine the route, the station must send special **route discovery**

packets. These are typically broadcast packets that every station on the network hears, but to which only the specified receiver responds. The route discovery packet records its route as it propagates through the network. When the intended receiver responds to the transmitter, it merely has the response retrace the newly discovered route and now both stations know how to access each other.

On subsequent transmissions of frames, the route is placed in the RI field, which comprises a 2-octet Routing Control (RC) subfield and between one and fourteen 2-octet Route Designator (RD) subfields.

The RC subfield contains a variety of information, such as the length of the RI field, the maximum acceptable length of the INFO field, how the indicated route should be interpreted, and whether this frame should follow a specified route or is to be broadcast. Each RD subfield contains a ring number and bridge number, specifying the exact route to be followed.

Source routing is useful in the IBM environment because the Systems Network Architecture (SNA) uses virtual circuits. This suggests that most transmissions will be exchanged among relatively small sets of stations. While usually true in an SNA environment where terminals are connected to hosts and limited number of applications, it is not as true in the LAN environment with PC-class machines. Thus, there is a heavy processing burden for stations to determine all the routes that they might need to access all possible destinations.

Another potential problem with source routing is that once a station learns a route to another station, it has no easy way to find out about a better route, should one appear, nor can it learn about changes in the network topology due to reconfiguration or link/bridge failures. Thus, the stations have to periodically send out packets to ensure the integrity of their routing tables.

The IEEE did not adopt source routing for their MAC bridging standard, IEEE 802.1d. MAC bridging according to 802.1d is accomplished using the spanning tree algorithm, an approach that places the routing burden on the bridges themselves and makes the fact that the user is in a multinetwork environment totally transparent to the user. In addition, changes in network topology are also invisible to the user. This type of bridging is, for obvious reasons, called **transparent routing.**

A new concept, called source routing transparent (SRT), is an attempt to accommodate both approaches. An SRT bridge will examine the RII-bit in the SA field. If RII=0, then the bridge will transparently route the frame; if RII=1, the bridge will examine the RI field and route the frame accordingly.

CONCLUSION

This chapter has described some of the important features of the IEEE 802.5 token ring standard. Hopefully, some of the major points of this standard have been put more into focus and there is less magic left as to how all of this works.

REFERENCES

IEEE. *Token Ring Access Method and Physical Layer Specifications*. ANSI/IEEE Standard 802.5-1989 (also, ISO 8802-5). New York: IEEE, 1989.

IEEE. January 1987. Special issue on "Token Ring Networks." *Network*.

Kessler, G. C. and Train, D. A. *Metropolitan Area Networks: Concepts, Standards, and Services.* New York: McGraw-Hill, 1992.

Miller, M. A. *LAN Troubleshooting Handbook.* Redwood City, CA: M&T Publishing, 1989.

Stallings, W. *Local Networks: An Introduction*, 3rd ed. New York: Macmillan, 1990.

13

AN INTRODUCTION TO THE IEEE 802.4 TOKEN-PASSING BUS STANDARD

Gary C. Kessler

INTRODUCTION

This chapter briefly describes the IEEE 802.4 standard for token-passing bus local area networks. This standard is the joint Institute of Electrical and Electronics Engineers (IEEE) and American National Standards Institute (ANSI) standard and has been adopted by the International Organization for Standardization (ISO) as ISO 8802-4. This standard is based upon the Manufacturing Automation Protocol (MAP), first proposed by General Motors (GM).

PHYSICAL VS. LOGICAL NETWORK TOPOLOGY

Local area networks are usually classified as broadcast networks. More precisely, they can be categorized as **simultaneous broadcast** or **sequential broadcast**. In a simultaneous broadcast network, all stations hear all transmissions at about the same time. This is the case with stations on an LAN with a bus topology. In a sequential broadcast network, all stations hear the transmissions, but they hear the transmissions in some predetermined order. That is, one station hears the message first and passes it along to the next station in line.

An LAN with a ring topology (e.g., IBM Token Ring) is the most common example of a sequential broadcast LAN. The medium access control (MAC) scheme used in most rings is token passing.

The essence of token passing is that the token controls access to the transmission channel. The station that holds the token, then, has momentary control of the transmission medium. When a station is finished using the medium, it must pass the token to the next station in sequence. Note that token passing networks must have a ring structure.

A token ring network has both a physical and logical ring structure. Thus, the definition of a station's successor is determined by how the stations are physically wired together. (See Figure 13.1.)

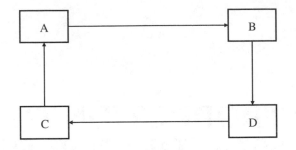

Figure 13.1   The token-passing sequence may be defined by the physical topology of the ring.

Stations on a bus, of course, have no such physical ordering. (See Figure 13.2.) In a token-passing bus, the sequence of the passing of the token is defined by a logical ordering of the stations on the bus. Each station must know the address of the station that precedes it and the one that follows it. Token-passing buses, then, have a physical bus topology and a logical ring topology.

The rules of token passing on a bus are different than that of the ring. A station on a token-passing bus sends a token addressed to the next station in sequence. (Recall that the bus has a simultaneous broadcast structure.) The new station with the token now has control of the medium for some period of time. The station may send one or more frames addressed to one or more other stations on the bus. When it is done transmitting or when the ownership time period expires, the station will send the token to the next station in logical sequence.

Token-passing buses have a relatively complex MAC scheme when compared to other LANs, such as Ethernet, IEEE 802.3, token rings, and IEEE 802.5. The complexity arises from the many physical layer options and the token management problems. The remainder of this chapter describes the physical options of the IEEE 802.4 standard, the frame format, and token management issues.

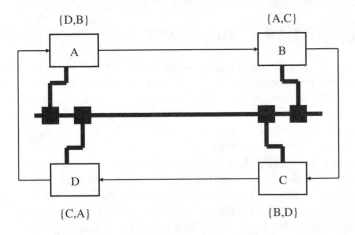

Figure 13.2   The token-passing sequence on a physical bus topology is defined by a logical ring structure, based on the station's addresses. Each station keeps track of the address of its logical predecessor and successor station.

PHYSICAL OPTIONS

The IEEE 802.4 standard specifies three different physical layer specifications, which differ in such characteristics as modulation scheme, bit rate, and connector type. All three specifications call for 75-ohm coaxial cable for the main trunk cable. Except where noted, the drop cables also use 75-ohm coaxial cable.

The first physical type is Phase-Continuous Frequency Shift Keying (FSK), a single-channel broadband system operating at 1 million bits per second (Mbps). This modulation scheme merely uses different frequencies for zeros and ones.

The phase-continuous FSK physical entity has an omnidirectional bus topology. LAN stations connect to the bus using a "T" connector and a short (<1.4 inches) drop cable. The drop cable is 35–50 ohm coax.

The second physical type is Phase-Coherent FSK, also a single-channel broadband scheme, operating at a rate of 5 or 10 Mbps. Phase-coherent FSK defines the signaling frequencies with respect to the data rate according to Table 13.1. A 0-bit is actually represented by two cycles of the higher frequency and a 1-bit is one cycle of the lower frequency. Thus, each bit time is constant.

Phase-coherent FSK also uses an omnidirectional bus topology. LAN stations connect to the bus using a passive tap and a short drop cable.

The final physical type is Multilevel Duobinary Amplitude Modulation/Phase Shift Keying (AM/PSK). This is an analog modulation scheme, intended for use over multiple broadband channels. This scheme uses a combination of phase and amplitude changes to encode the data. (This is a rather complex modulation scheme and is well beyond the scope of this paper. Interested readers are referred to the 802.4 standard, where the scheme is described in detail.)

Multilevel duobinary AM/PSK uses a directional bus with an active headend topology (i.e., a tree). LAN stations connect to the bus using a passive tap. This bus may operate on channels with a bandwidth of 1.5, 6 or 12 MHz, offering a data rate of 1, 5, or 10 Mbps, respectively. Standard community antenna television (CATV) channel assignments are utilized by this type of physical layer.

IEEE 802.4 FRAME FORMAT

Figure 13.3 shows the format of the IEEE 802.4 frame, specified as part of the MAC sublayer of the standard. A frame must contain an integral number of octets and can be no longer than 8,191 octets in length (exclusive of the Preamble, SD, and ED). The frame format is independent of the physical layer type that is used, although the actual coding of a field may be physical layer dependent.

Table 13.1   Token Bus

Bit rate	Frequency	
	1-bit	0-bit
5 Mbps	5 MHz	10 MHz
10 Mbps	10 MHz	20 MHz

Preamble	SD	FC	DA	SA	Data_Unit	FCS	ED

Figure 13.3 The IEEE 802.4 MAC frame format. The frame must be octet aligned and can be no longer than 8,191 octets (exclusive of the Preamble, SD, and ED fields).

The **Preamble** is a bit pattern sent to set the receiver's modem clock and signal level. The bit pattern is at least one octet with the pattern 10101010 in the phase-continuous FSK and multilevel duobinary AM/PSK cases, and at least one octet with the pattern 11111111 in the phase-coherent FSK case.

The preamble also serves to ensure a minimum amount of time between consecutive frames, required to allow a station sufficient time to process a previously received frame. The standard minimum interframe duration is at least 2 microseconds. Thus, the number of octets of preamble that are transmitted will be dependent upon the data rate. For example, one octet of preamble is required on a 1 Mbps bus, while three octets are required on a 10 Mbps bus.

The **Start Delimiter (SD)** marks the actual beginning of the frame. It has the following format (bit 1 is transmitted first):

bits: 1 2 3 4 5 6 7 8
              N N 0 N N 0 0 0

N is a non-data MAC symbol; that is, it is represented by a coding that is different than a zero or a one. As an example, consider phase-continuous FSK, which uses a Manchester-type encoding. In this scheme, a zero is comprised of a low-frequency tone for one-half of the bit time followed by a high-frequency tone for one-half of the bit time. A one bit is comprised of a high-frequency tone followed by a low-frequency tone. A non-data symbol in this coding scheme would be either a low- or high-frequency tone for an entire bit time.

The **Frame Control (FC)** field indicates the class and type of the frame. This field has one of the following formats:

bits: 1 2 3 4 5 6 7 8
             0 0 C C C C C
             F F M M M P P P

If bits 1 and 2 are 00, this is a MAC control frame. These types of frames are used for token and station management. The CCCCCC bits indicate the type of MAC control frame from the following list:

CCCCCC   Frame Type

000000   claim_token
000001   solicit_successor_1
000010   solicit_successor_2

000011	who_follows
000100	resolve_contention
001000	token
001100	set_successor

If the first two bits are not both zero, the FF bits indicate the class of the frame. If FF=01, this frame carries IEEE 802.2 Logical Link Control (LLC) data; FF=10 indicates a station management frame; and FF=11 is reserved for special-purpose frames.

The MMM bits indicate the expected MAC action. Frames may be requests that require no response (MMM=000), requests that do require a response (001), or frames that are themselves responses (010). The PPP bits indicate the priority of the frame, where 000 is the lowest priority and 111 is the highest priority.

The **Destination Address (DA)** and **Source Address (SA)** fields may be either 16 or 48 bits in length.[1] The 16-bit addresses are of the form:

bits: 1   2–16

| I/G | 15-bit address |

The 48-bit addresses are of the form:

bits: 1   2   3–48

| I/G | L/U | 46-bit address |

The first bit transmitted is the Individual/Group (I/G) bit, used to distinguish between individual and group addresses. If I/G=0, this is an individual station's address. If I/G=1, this is a group address and the frame may be addressed to more than one station. An address of all 1 bits is the broadcast address.

The Local/Universal (L/U) bit distinguishes between locally and universally (globally) administered address plans. If L/U=1, the 46-bit address is assigned by a local administration and is unique to this network only. If L/U=0, this station's address is assigned by a central administration (such as the IEEE) and is distinct from all other stations' addresses on all other networks.

The **Data_Unit field** contains an LLC protocol data unit, a MAC management data frame, or values specific to one of the MAC control fields. The FC field indicates the type of information to expect in this field. The length of this field will be dependent upon the type of information. The field must be octet aligned.

The **Frame Check Sequence (FCS) field** contains the 32-bit remainder from the bit error detection algorithm using a CRC-32 cyclic redundancy check polynomial.

---

1 Although still a part of the IEEE 802 standards, the IEEE is withdrawing support for 16-bit addresses.

The **End Delimiter (ED)** demarks the end of the frame. The format of the ED field is:

bits: 1 2 3 4 5 6 7 8
               N N 1 N N 1 I E

The N-bits are non-data MAC symbols, just as in the SD field.

I is the Intermediate-bit, indicating whether this frame is the last frame of a sequence of frames (I=0) or whether there are more frames to be transmitted that are associated with this one (I=1).

E is the Error bit, indicating whether a bit error was detected (E=1) in this frame or not (E=0). When the E-bit is set to one by a repeater, the repeater keeps track of the event. In this way, cable segments on which many bit errors occur may be localized.

TOKEN AND STATION MANAGEMENT

The complexity of token-passing buses is due mostly to the procedures for adding and deleting stations, initializing the bus, token fault management, and prioritizing transmissions.

Adding a Station to the Network

Successful token passing on a bus requires that the stations are properly ordered according to their addresses. Each station on the bus is required to periodically grant other stations not currently on the bus an opportunity to become part of the logical ring. This is accomplished through a controlled contention scheme using response windows. A **response window** is equivalent to the round-trip propagation delay of the bus.

While holding the token, the station transmits a solicit_successor_1 (or solicit_successor_2) frame, which contains this station's address (TS) in the SA field and the address of the next station (NS). This allows any station not currently on the ring that has an address between TS and NS to join the ring. The transmitting station waits for one (or two) response windows.

Four possible events may occur after a solicit_successor frame is transmitted:

1. No response. No new station wants to join the ring and the token is passed on to the next station as usual.
2. One response. One node sends a set_successor frame. The transmitting station resets its address pointers appropriately and sends a token to the new station.
3. Multiple responses. If more than one station sends a set_successor frame, the transmitting station hears a garbled message. The conflict is resolved when the transmitter sends a resolve_conflict frame and waits for four periods of time, called response windows. Each station that wants to be added to the ring can respond in one of the four response windows based upon the first two bits of its address. If a responding station hears any transmission prior to its response window, it refrains from responding. If a single set_successor frame is heard by the token holder, all is well. Otherwise, the token holder issues another resolve_contention frame. Only the stations that successfully transmitted during the previous round may access a response window during this round. The choice of the response window uses the next two

address bits. This process continues until only a single set_successor is received by the token holder. The current token holder then passes the token to its new successor.
4. Invalid response. If any frame other than a set_successor is received, the token holder assumes that another station thinks that it holds the token. To prevent a conflict, this station defers and goes into a listen state.

Deleting a Station

Deleting a station from the bus is easier than adding one. A station wishing to drop off of the ring merely waits until it has the token. It then sends a set_successor frame to its predecessor on the ring, carrying the address of its successor. It then sends the token on to its successor. During the next pass of the token, it will be skipped over.

Initializing the Ring

Ring initialization will occur when at least one station detects an absence of activity on the ring for some period of time. This loss of token may occur when the ring is first initialized or if the token-holding station fails.

After a node's lack-of-activity timer expires, the node sends a claim_token frame, followed by 0, 2, 4, or 6 response windows (the number will be based upon the first two bits of its address). After it is done transmitting, it listens to the bus. If it hears other transmissions, it will defer since another station is also trying to get the token. If silence is heard, it will send another claim_token frame, with the number of response windows based upon the next two address bits. Eventually, only one station will hear silence after sending claim_token frames based upon its entire address. That station now holds the token.

Token Fault Management

If a station holding the token hears a transmission that makes it believe that another station thinks that *it* holds the token, the first station will back off to listener mode. This method will ensure that the number of tokens on the bus drops back to zero or one, eliminating a multiple-token problem. If no tokens are left, the ring is reinitialized according to the rules.

Other type of token problems can also occur. When a station sends the token frame to its successor, the successor will immediately transmit either a token or data frame. Thus, a token issuer needs to listen for only one slot time to be sure that its successor is active. Problems occur if the token issuer believes that its successor has failed.

The following events may occur after a token is issued:

1. If the successor is active, the token issuer will hear a valid frame. All is well and the station becomes a listener on the bus.
2. If the token issuer hears a garbled transmission, it waits for four time slots. If it hears a valid frame, it assumes that the token got to its successor. Otherwise, it assumes that the token was lost and it will reissue the token.
3. If a valid frame is not heard, the token issuer sends another token to the same successor.

4. After two failures, the token issuer assumes that the successor station has failed and it sends a who_follows frame, asking for the identity of the node that follows the failed node (i.e., the successor's successor). The token issuer should receive a set_successor frame from the next station in the ring, and the failed station is dropped from the ring.
5. If there is no response to the who_follows frame, another who_follows frame is issued.
6. If there is still no response, the station sends a solicit_successor frame, where every station on the bus is invited to respond. If this succeeds, a two-node token-passing bus is established and transmission continues.
7. If there is still no response, the token issuer must assume that a major fault has occurred. Examples include failure of all other stations on the bus, a break in the medium, or failure of the receiver at this station. At this point, the station may transmit more data (if it has any) and try to pass to token again. It will then cease transmitting and will listen to the bus.

Prioritizing Transmissions

Token-passing bus systems have a class of service option, where data frames may have a priority associated with them. IEEE 802.4 defines four classes of service:

6—synchronous
4—asynchronous urgent
2—asynchronous normal
0—asynchronous time-available

The priority scheme is used to allocate bandwidth to higher-priority frames and to send lower-priority frames only if there is bandwidth available. In this context, synchronous service is time-dependent transmissions (e.g., digital voice samples must be sent at 125 microsecond intervals and delays cannot be tolerated). The asynchronous classes refer to transmissions that are not delay sensitive (e.g., most data transfer).

The 802.4 standard defines several variables that deal with the maximum amount of time that a station can hold the token for the transmission of the various classes of service. This ensures that each class of service gets the necessary bandwidth.

CONCLUSION

The IEEE 802.4 token bus specification is based upon work originally performed at GM for factory floor automation. Token passing is an attractive scheme in this application environment due to its characteristics of guaranteed access and a bounded maximum delay. A bus topology is attractive since stations use passive taps. Therefore, a single station failure does not cause network failure.

A disadvantage of the token-passing bus is the complexity of the MAC scheme. The complexity of the scheme yields more potential bugs in software and/or hardware design and more space required on interface boards for the chips.

REFERENCES

IEEE. *Token-Passing Bus Access Method and Physical Layer Specifications.* ANSI/IEEE Standard 802.4-1985 (also, ISO 8802/4). New York: IEEE, 1985.

Miller, M. A. *LAN Troubleshooting Handbook.* Redwood City, CA: M&T Publishing, 1989.

Stallings, W. *Local Networks: An Introduction.* 3rd ed. New York: Macmillan, 1990.

14

THE FDDI STANDARD

Emily Green

INTRODUCTION

As the first open networking standard to specify optical fiber, the fiber distributed data interface (FDDI) is ready to take its place as the data network transport protocol of tomorrow. What started in 1982 as a high-speed method to connect mainframes to storage systems has been transformed into a flexible next-generation local area network (LAN) standard. The FDDI products now offered by vendors promise to ease the congestion of Ethernet and Token Ring networks that have been pushed to the limit.

HISTORY OF FDDI

The American National Standards Institute in 1980 established the X3T9.5 committee to develop a high-speed interface for future high-performance storage systems. Two years later, three Sperry Corporation engineers presented the committee with a proposal for a 100 megabit per second (Mbps) token passing ring. Interest in FDDI as a "back-end" interface waned because storage system speeds outpaced the standards procedure, and proprietary interfaces were developed that offered speeds up to 800 Mbps and beyond. However, the explosion in LAN use in corporate computing environments prompted a new focus for the group, and the specification developed into an open standard for LANs.

By the beginning of 1992, FDDI was almost completely approved by the X3T9.5 committee. The committee had decided to break the specification into four areas to facilitate flexibility during its development—the Physical layer (PHY), the Physical Media Dependent (PMD), the Media Access Control (MAC) and Station Management (SMT). SMT is the final specification to be completed, and its approval is expected in mid-1992. Many vendors announced FDDI-compliant products in 1991, even before the SMT specification was complete. Because SMT is implemented in either software or firmware, those products announced before its completion can be updated by the vendor to accommodate changes in the standard.

FDDI OVERVIEW

The four basic specifications of FDDI designate a token-passing ring network with dual counter-rotating rings for fault tolerance. The dual counter-rotating rings are independent fiber-optic cables, with a primary link carrying data and the secondary link available for redundancy. If a node fails or a cable breaks, the data on the primary link is electronically wrapped around to the secondary link, maintaining ring integrity. FDDI specifies multimode fiber-optic cable (62.5 micron/125 micron core and cladding diameters) and a data transmission rate of 100 Mbps.

There are two types of FDDI networking devices. Class A devices feature dual attachments—one to each ring—to facilitate counter-rotating rings. Class A devices can be any network device, but are frequently hubs, routers, concentrators, servers, or other computing resources comprising the network backbone. The "failure wrapping" feature of FDDI is implemented through Class A devices. Each dual-attached station constantly receives "handshaking" information from its neighbor via the secondary link. If the station stops receiving that information, that device alerts the ring that its neighboring station is down. It may then wrap data from the primary ring to the secondary so that the disabled node is avoided and ring integrity is maintained.

Class B devices are workstations, printers, and other nodes that are attached only to the primary link. These class B, or single-attached, devices access the ring by plugging into a concentrator that is dual-attached to the ring or attached via a "B" link to another device that has a Class A interface. An FDDI network can operate with up to 500 dual-attached stations or 1,000 single-attached stations or an equivalent mix of the two types. Although data flows in a "logical ring," the typical structure of an FDDI network is a star configuration, with all workstations connected directly to a hub rather than the backbone itself.

Devices already connected to an existing Ethernet or Token Ring LAN can be linked to an FDDI network via an FDDI-capable bridge or router.

An FDDI ring can be as large as 100 kilometers with distances between nodes of up to 2 kilometers when multimode fiber is in use. The standard specifies a 1,300-nanometer light-emitting diode (LED) transmitter. This high-performance transmitter facilitates another of FDDI's fault-tolerance capabilities. The transmitter provides enough signal strength so that, with an optional optical bypass switch, a data packet can be switched past one or more FDDI nodes that have failed and have enough signal strength to be received by the next node without having been actively repeated by the intermediate node(s). See Figure 14.1.

FDDI is defined in the bottom two layers of the OSI Reference Model, the Physical Layer and the Data Link Layer. Both layers have been divided by the FDDI committee into two sublayers each to give the standard more flexibility. Thus, semiconductor manufacturers can begin designing a standard FDDI product using the coding definitions in the PHY specification, while new PMDs are added for different media types. See Figure 14.2.

FDDI: A FAMILY OF STANDARDS

FDDI was developed as a family of related standards beginning with four core specifications. The development of the four core specifications has taken more than ten years, much more time than it would have taken the standards bodies to develop one monolithic specification. In developing a family

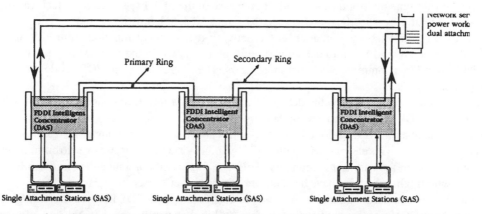

Data travels on the primary ring or link with the second ring available for failure wrapping. Dual-attach devices can access both primary and secondary rings and have the capability to facilitate failure wrapping. Single-attach stations access the ring through FDDI concentrators. Ethernet and token ring data can access the ring via a FDDI bridge.

Figure 14.1   FDDI network with dual- and single-attachment stations.

of standards, the standards committees have built into FDDI the flexibility to add more specifications as necessary.

By organizing like specifications, such as light wavelength and optical budgets, and separating them from unlike issues, such as packet organization and length, the committee has facilitated the development of early FDDI products.

This is similar to a concept in commercial architecture known as **fast-tracking,** in which a construction team can begin to build a skyscraper with fundamental plans in place, while the architects

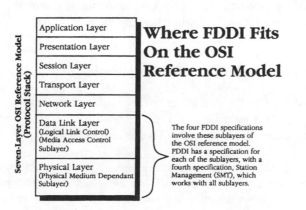

Figure 14.2   FDDI overlaid on the OSI stack.

continue to fine-tune interior design details. In the case of the FDDI specifications, fast-tracking has meant the FDDI core specifications associated with real LAN function could be completed and wrapped with a skeletal representation of the network management function. With this approach, FDDI developers could begin to design and build products, while the real SMT specification was refined in standards committees for two more years. The net result is that FDDI is delivered to the user sooner.

An example of this benefit is the design of the new media interface connector (MIC), which is specified for FDDI. Once the underlying standard for the MIC was approved, users were able to begin specifying and installing FDDI-compliant fiber-optic cable plants, even though FDDI equipment was still two years away. This early contact with FDDI by future-oriented users was key to building interest and support within the end user community. This also facilitated continued development by manufacturers who might otherwise have been unsure of the market's interest in the standard.

Similarly, by standardizing like issues, the effects of change on FDDI can be limited. Change is an inevitable fact of communications networks. An LAN protocol must be able to evolve as it is deployed in more user networks, each of which may be different.

Segmenting the standard has meant that efforts can be initiated to improve, for instance, the packet handling in the MAC specification, without having an impact on the approval process or features of the PMD or any other part of the standard.

The segmentation of the FDDI standard also makes it very appropriate for use in previously unanticipated applications. FDDI can be applied to other network types—for example, a metropolitan area network (MAN). With only a change in the Physical Layer specification, FDDI can be successfully adapted for use in the new environment.

Consequently, the development of a similar, but competing standard can sometimes be averted. Without the ability to add to the options for operating FDDI over media types other than optical fiber, FDDI might have given over in the marketplace to another competing standard that did accommodate the newer media choices. This could have resulted in an unfortunate drop-off in interest by manufacturers in developing FDDI products due to a perceived drop in potential market for their use.

Finally, the standards segmentation has broadened the number of people from both the user and manufacturer communities that can contribute to the standards development process; it means that the tasks, which are all accepted on a volunteer basis, can be smaller, and the members' involvement costs the participating organizations less, while keeping the benefit to the community as a whole at the same level.

Physical Media Dependent (PMD) Layer Specification

For the FDDI standard, the OSI Physical Layer has been broken into the Physical Media Dependent (PMD) and the Physical (PHY) sublayers. This division allows manufacturers to develop different PMD specifications to accommodate a variety of media, without affecting the data coding scheme in the PHY level.

The FDDI PMD specifies a transmission wavelength of 1,300 nanometers (nm) using an LED. The specification recommends 62.5/125 micron (core diameter/cladding diameter) multimode cable to ensure that light dispersion is small enough to meet a 10^{-9} bit specified error rate. While this cable is recommended, the PMD is written so that any multimode cable capable of 1,300 nm transmission can be used, including 50/125 micron, 85/125 micron, and 100/140 micron cable. (However, in practice, only the 50 and 62.5 micron diameters are actually used.) As a redundancy feature, the PMD also specifies an optional optical bypass switch that can bypass a failed Class A station. This can be used to maintain some ring integrity when multiple Class A failures threaten to segment a ring.

Efforts to develop additional alternative PMDs for various copper and low-cost fiber-optic cable are underway within the ANSI X3T9.5 committee. A discussion of the different PMD standards under consideration by the committee is included later in this chapter.

Physical (PHY) Sublayer Specification

The PHY level defines the encoding scheme for both data and control symbols; or how information is arranged for transmission onto the ring. The FDDI encoding scheme actually uses a transmission rate of 125 Mbps with the 4B/5B group-encoding scheme. Using this scheme, a five-bit code word is transmitted for each four-bit piece of data or control information. Thus, 100 Mbps of the bandwidth is actually used for data, and the remaining 25 Mbps goes to encoding overhead. The PHY sublayer also defines how to decode the 4B/5B signal from the network into symbols the station can recognize.

The 4B/5B scheme uses less bandwidth than encoding schemes for other protocols, but requires each FDDI station on the ring to regenerate the data to prevent **jitter,** a condition that occurs as data travels around the ring reducing the clarity of the optical signal. Each station has a phase-locked loop, which clocks the received data into a buffer, and a crystal-controlled frequency source, which clocks the data out of the buffer.

Media Access Control (MAC) Specification

The MAC specification defines the different fields of data that are present in an FDDI data packet (see Figure 14.2). The fields included in the data packet frame are headers, trailers, addresses, and cyclic redundancy checking (CRC) for a maximum size of 4,500 eight-bit units called octets.

The MAC sublayer is responsible for defining the FDDI information packet frame and for controlling the flow of data on the ring. Each station has an MAC sublayer that reviews every packet received by the station looking for its destination address. If it is destined for that station, the MAC copies the packet into the station's local memory before sending the packet on to the next station on the ring. The receiving station also turns on a bit, called a Copy or C bit, in the packet before it sends

The FDDI Data Packet

The Media Access Control (MAC) sublayer specifies the different frames of the FDDI data packet. Below is the layout of an FDDI data packet.

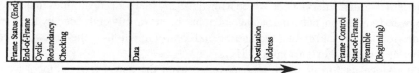

Figure 14.3   The FDDI data packet.

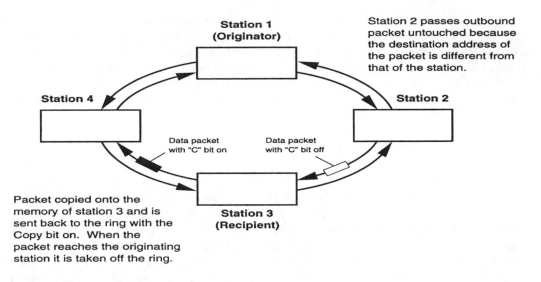

Figure 14.4   FDDI data transmission.

it out again. When the data packet returns to the original sending station, its own MAC sublayer deletes the packet from the ring. The originator can know the recipient got the packet by checking its C bit. If it is on, then the originator can generally conclude the recipient got the packet. (See Figure 14.4.)

As in the Token Ring standard (IEEE 802.5), data transmission from a station can only occur when it has the token. Each station observes a time limit for possessing the token and transmitting synchronous data called the target token-rotation time (TTRT). Every station also is required to measure the time that has passed since it last received the token under the timed token rotation (TTR) protocol. If the station receives the token before the previous station's time is up, it can transmit data asynchronously during the leftover time.

Station Management (SMT) Specification

SMT is the network management specification of FDDI and is responsible for configuring FDDI rings and reconfiguring rings in the event of failures. SMT is the final specification to be finalized by the X3T9.5 committee, with approval expected in mid-1992. It is generally agreed that the delays in SMT's completion have been due to the relative newness of incorporating network management into an LAN standard. Neither Ethernet nor Token Ring have any inherent capabilities that are equivalent to SMT's power. In addition, network management has been warmly embraced by the user communities. The desire for more and greater monitoring and control functions in their networks contributed to the number of functional extensions to SMT.

Fortunately, since its functionality was separated from the core FDDI protocol by a separate specification, developers and users alike have been able to move ahead with FDDI networks to which final implementations of SMT will be added as soon as it has been completed.

FDDI Data Wrapping Feature

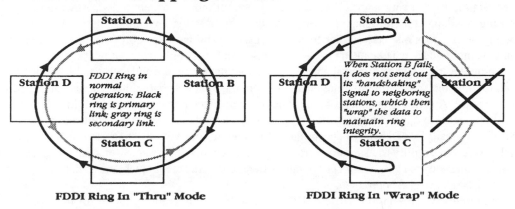

Figure 14.5   FDDI data wrapping feature.

Each station has an SMT agent that consists of a PHY layer management entity (LME), a MAC LME, and, for dual-attached stations, a station configuration switch. When the station is powered up, the PHY LME establishes a connection on the FDDI ring by broadcasting a "handshaking" signal to neighboring stations on the ring. While the PHY LME can only communicate with its neighboring nodes, the MAC LME can communicate with any other MAC LME on the ring. When communications to the PHY LME are disrupted, it assumes there has been a cable fault or other problem with the neighboring node and begins data wrapping procedures. The station configuration switch will wrap the data from the primary link to the secondary link if there is a single fault. If there are multiple faults, the optical bypass switch, which is optional in dual-attach stations, can forward the signal to the next station if it is in place. See Figure 14.5.

SMT also collects statistics on network traffic, but it differs from other network management protocols in that a statistics reporting function has not been specified. Where the simple network management protocol (SNMP) collects network statistics and specifies a standard way to report those statistics to a variety of network management systems, SMT collects the statistics. The reporting function can differ between vendors of different network management systems.

INTEROPERABILITY

The fact that FDDI products have been built before the standard is fully approved raises concerns about **interoperability.** Early products run the risk of not interoperating (either partially or fully) with similar products built by other vendors. In addition, products built today may not be in complete compliance with the final version of the SMT specification. This problem may be alleviated as SMT is implemented in software that can be upgraded when the standard is complete.

The X3T9.5 committee has acknowledged a bridging standard known as **transparent bridging.** The transparent bridge evaluates each data frame to determine on which side of the bridge its destination is located. The bridge puts the data on that ring, and it is then evaluated by the MAC in every station on that ring until it is forwarded by one (or more) of them to its destination. **Source routing** is a competing bridging approach developed by IBM for Token Ring networks. A source-routing bridge goes one step further than the transparent bridge to establish various internetwork routes using fields in a Token Ring packet to develop and record interring pathways.

A problem arises because transparent and source-routing bridges are not interoperable. Transparent bridging has the most hope for interoperability among vendors, but source routing offers better performance. An IEEE standards committee has developed a merged standard for bridging that uses both approaches as appropriate in a network. This new method is called **source routing/transparent (SRT).** Originally, FDDI bridges encapsulated Ethernet or Token Ring data packets in a proprietary FDDI packet to simplify transmission across the FDDI network. These encapsulation bridges are not interoperable between vendors or between the different bridging techniques, and limit the usefulness of FDDI as a native LAN protocol.

Two groups have been formed to test FDDI products for interoperability and certify those products. Both groups strive to test adapters, routers, bridges, and concentrators by different vendors in large networks under large traffic situations. The Advanced Networking Test Center (ANTC) is run by Advanced Micro Devices, a semiconductor manufacturer based in San Jose, California. The charter for the ANTC is to test the functionality and interoperability of components at each of the PMD, PHY, MAC, and SMT layers. The Interoperability Laboratory (IOL), run by the University of New Hampshire, focuses mainly on system-level testing. The IOL is populated with Ethernet subnets feeding into an FDDI ring on which it tests mainly for SMT interoperability.

ADDITIONAL FDDI SPECIFICATIONS

Because of the flexibility built in by FDDI's four-part specification, many changes and adaptations have been proposed for the standard. These new specifications allow FDDI transmission over new media and are attempting to lower the cost of installing FDDI.

FDDI Over Single Mode Fiber

Multimode fiber was chosen for FDDI because it could support the longer distance goals of FDDI and because it is the most common type of fiber found in intrabuilding applications. An ANSI subcommittee has now approved SMF-PMD, an extension to the PMD to allow single mode fiber, which has a much longer distance. The new PMD was adopted for long-distance data communication—such as between two buildings in one city—but can be used in any desired application.

Single mode fiber has a smaller inner core diameter (between 8–10 microns) and carries signals with less attenuation or signal deterioration. This allows the signal to be carried for up to 50 kilometers before it needs to be regenerated by an active transmitter. Single mode fiber is more expensive because a higher-cost laser diode transmitter must be used to direct the optical signal into the smaller aperture of the fiber. Telephone companies and alternate bypass carriers (including MCI, US Sprint, etc.) typically use single mode fiber for their land lines.

FDDI Over SONET

Synchronous Optical Network (SONET) is being promulgated by telephone companies as the next international standard for data and voice transmission over the public network. The X3T9.5 committee is developing a method to adapt FDDI packets to be transmitted on a SONET platform, so that internetworking over the public network is made easier.

A new PMD is being developed that will help match up the differences in speed between SONET and FDDI. SONET features different Optical Carrier (OC) levels that currently operate at speeds ranging from 51.84 Mbps to 2.488 gigabytes per second. The most appropriate level for FDDI is OC-3, which operates at roughly 155 Mbps. The new PMD would essentially add an extra 30 Mbps of frame stuffing—control information and other meaningless data to fill out the frame—to a regularly cycled 125 Mbps FDDI data frame. Typically, an FDDI over SONET bridge or repeater would be used to transmit and receive data over a SONET public network. The new PMD to allow these products is still being developed.

FDDI Over Copper

An alternative to FDDI is the Copper Distributed Data Interface (CDDI) or FDDI over copper wire. The ANSI FDDI committee is working on a new standard for a PMD interface that would allow data at FDDI speeds over shielded twisted pair (STP) copper wire for up to 100 meters. Under the specification, STP cable would be used to attach workstations to hubs that are attached to a fiber-optic ring. Several candidate FDDI-over-STP specifications have been advanced by allied groups of semiconductor and intelligent wiring hub manufacturers as open standards. These need to be studied by the committee before any are adopted as a base for a standard. Another CDDI standard for unshielded twisted pair (UTP) cable has also recently been considered by the X3T9.5 committee.

FDDI Over Low-cost Fiber Optics

An effort has been launched to reduce the cost of FDDI by making changes to some of the more expensive components specified in the PHY. The effort originally focused on replacing glass fiber-optic cable with less expensive plastic fiber-optic cable. The impurities in plastic fiber, however, meant signals might not reliably or consistently travel the 100 meters the committee felt is a uniform distance needed by users for the concentrator-to-device link. In addition, industry sources determined that connection costs for plastic fiber were just as expensive as for glass fiber, thus, not reducing the cost of installing new cable. This caused interest in this approach to wane and the effort was abandoned. Now, the focus is on changing the transmitter and the connector for the links between a concentrator and a workstation. These links typically do not go much farther than 100 meters. They do not need the optical power to travel two kilometers, as originally specified in the base PMD.

The high-powered 1,300 nanometer transmitter needed to provide the 11 decibels (dB) of optical gain specified for the two kilometers distance is being evaluated by a special subcommittee of the standards body. The subcommittee is reviewing a reduction in the optical gain to 7 or 8 dB, reducing the distance a signal can travel to a maximum of 100 meters. The subcommittee also is investigating alternatives to the MIC connector that was designed exclusively for FDDI. The connector is expensive to manufacture and is not specified for other uses that would lower the cost due to economies of scale. The low-cost fiber (LCF) subcommittee will review proposals in both of these areas during 1992.

FDDI-II

FDDI-II is being developed by the X3T9.5 committee as a high-speed standard that would accommodate circuit-switched traffic as well as packetized data. The basis for FDDI-II is the concept of **hybrid ring control (HRC),** a means of using an existing FDDI ring for two purposes at once: LAN packets and **circuit-switched,** or time-division-multiplexed data streams concurrently.

The HRC standard calls the new traffic that will be added to an FDDI ring **isochronous traffic;** the existing LAN traffic is called **packet traffic.** With the introduction of HRC, the relationship of FDDI and FDDI-II to each other will change. The current MAC standard will become the P-MAC, or packet-processing MAC layer, and will be augmented with a new MAC layer standard for processing isochronous traffic (I-MAC). A new entity, called the H-MUX, or hybrid multiplexer, is added to arbitrate between the PHY layer and the two MACs.

The H-MUX will build and dismantle the new fundamental data element of the HRC ring, called the **cycle.** Each cycle is composed of packets and a number of wideband channels, which are received from or passed to the I-MAC.

During network power-up, FDDI-II stations bid among themselves to become what is called the **cycle master.** The cycle master is responsible for controlling the timing and transmission of cycles on the ring. Stations on an FDDI ring that are equipped with HRC capability can operate either as FDDI-II stations, in which case they are said to be running in hybrid mode, or as FDDI stations, called **basic mode.** This ensures compatibility with existing FDDI rings; if a new station with HRC support is inserted into an existing FDDI ring, it will operate in basic mode as long as there are any stations on the ring that are not also equipped with HRC. If all stations on the ring have HRC, then the ring will operate in **hybrid mode.**

In the future, the PHY and MAC standards documents will be updated to support HRC. FDDI-II initially will be offered with a data rate of 100 Mbps, but may be enhanced to 400 Mbps in the future.

FDDI FOLLOW-ON LAN

Another subcommittee just getting underway is considering the future beyond both FDDI and FDDI-II. The standard they are developing is called FDDI Follow-on LAN (FFOL). It will consist of a set of standards replacing every current FDDI/HRC standard available or in development now. Proposals to form working groups for each FFOL standard component have just been drafted. They will be submitted to the ANSI review committee shortly. Target completion date for the standard set is December 1995, with some individual standards in the set becoming available up to two years earlier.

The purpose of an FFOL standard is to provide a backbone for multiple FDDI networks, with efficient connectivity to WANs and MACs with support for a wide variety of integrated services, including data, graphics, and video. FFOL would be available using a variety of physical media such as multimode and single mode private fiber and SONET.

REFERENCES

Burr, W. E. and Zuqiu, L. An Overview of FDDI. "National Bureau of Standards." Paper presented at EFOC/LAN 1988 Conference.

Greenfield, David and Keough, Lee. October 1991. "Smart Hub Vendors Move In on FDDI." *Data Communications.*

Reddy, Shyamala. December 1989. "FDDI Fever." *LAN Magazine.*

Tsao, David. September 21, 1991. "FDDI: Chapter Two." *Data Communications.*

Wallace, Scott and Levine, Judith. August 19, 1991. "Who Needs FDDI?" *Communications Week.*

15

NetBIOS AND ITS APPLICATIONS INTERFACE

Mike Kouri and William Nolde

INTRODUCTION

NetBIOS is a standardized software interface between application programs and a local area network (LAN). An application written to the NetBIOS interface will run unmodified on any network operating system that uses NetBIOS, regardless of the hardware or transport protocols used in the LAN.

Many network operating systems must have a NetBIOS interface to communicate with their own underlying transport protocols. For example, 3Com's 3+ and 3+Open, Microsoft's MS-Net and LAN Manager, and IBM's PC LAN and LAN Server all require a NetBIOS interface. Other network operating systems, such as Novell's NetWare and Banyan's VINES, provide a NetBIOS interface but do not require it.

Because NetBIOS is used so extensively in modern LANs, both for applications and for internal communication within the network operating system, it is vital for network administrators and technical support personnel to understand how NetBIOS works when tuning or troubleshooting a network. This article describes NetBIOS commands in detail and includes examples of the data structures used by applications to talk to NetBIOS, shown in both the C programming language and Intel 8086 assembly language. A sample NetBIOS program called NBCHAT, used to allow NetBIOS workstations to communicate interactively with each other, is available on request.

NetBIOS BASICS

NetBIOS (the Network Basic Input/Output System) is a programmatic interface between applications programs and the underlying network software and hardware. It was originally developed by Sytek Corporation as an interface to its intelligent broadband network interface. It gained popularity as a supported applications programming interface when IBM adopted it for its PC Network and PC LAN

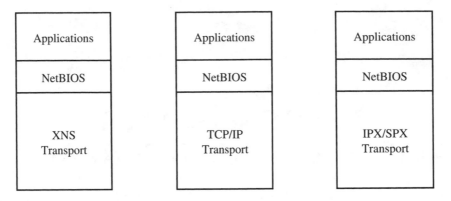

Figure 15.1   NetBIOS isolates applications from underlying transport protocols.

programs. Other vendors have implemented the NetBIOS interface for use with their own hardware and software to the point that it is a de facto standard used in PC local area networks. Using the NetBIOS interface isolates the application programs from the actual type of hardware used in the LAN and the transport protocols used to move data across that LAN, giving applications vendors a wider potential marketplace for their wares. (See Figure 15.1.)

NetBIOS NAMES

NetBIOS applications communicate with each other by using names. A name is an identifier for a logical entity, such as an application program or a process within an application. An application or a process may create one or more names to which it will respond. For each workstation, NetBIOS maintains a table of the names used by that computer. This table of local names has historically been fixed at sixteen entries long plus a special name called the permanent name. Names can be up to sixteen characters long. They should not contain an asterisk as the first (or only) character of the name.

The permanent name, also called the node number, is usually in ROM on the LAN adapter card. On some network adapters (but not 3Com's), the node number may be set by DIP switches on the LAN adapter card. The node number consists of ten characters of binary zeros followed by six more characters which must be unique on the network. Since all Ethernet adapters have unique addresses, the permanent name is usually the Ethernet address of the adapter, in byte-reversed order. This name is usually read by the transport protocol(s) and presented to the NetBIOS interface.

With Microsoft LAN Manager, the permanent name (burned into ROM) may be overridden by editing the PROTOCOL.INI file at that machine and adding a new statement to the appropriate adapter section that reads NETADDRESS= followed by twelve hexadecimal digits enclosed in double quotes (for example, NETADDRESS="02608C123456").

NetBIOS names are created locally by applications and processes within applications. NetBIOS names are used across the network to identify these logical entities. A table of locally defined names is maintained by the NetBIOS interface.

Most implementations of NetBIOS allow applications to add up to sixteen local names to the NetBIOS table. However, with the growing number of machines added to individual LANs, the limitation of sixteen names is becoming inadequate. Some recent implementations, such as 3Com's 3+Open XNS, NetBEUI, and NBP transport protocols, allow up to 254 local names to be defined.

Local NetBIOS names may be unique names or group names. A unique name is guaranteed by the NetBIOS to be unique across the LAN. A group name added at one computer may also be added, as a group name, at other computers.

Unique names are the more common of the two. Applications can be hard-coded for particular names. A common mistake when first beginning to program to the NetBIOS interface is to attempt to use group names to establish sessions to several stations. Only the first member of the group to respond will actually establish a session. Group names are useful both for sending datagrams, which will be described later, and when several machines provide the same service and the client doesn't care which of them provides the desired service.

NetBIOS SERVICES

The NetBIOS interface consists of five basic services:

- General Control
- Name Support
- Datagram Support
- Session Control
- Session Data Transfer

Some vendors may provide proprietary extensions to the basic services. Table 15.1 provides a summary of the commands available in each service.

General Control Services

The NetBIOS General Control Services include resetting the NetBIOS interface, canceling commands, and finding out the status of the network hardware adapter.

Name Support Services

The NetBIOS Name Support Services include adding unique and group names to the local name table and deleting local names from the table when they are no longer needed.

Datagram Support Services

The NetBIOS Datagram Support Services provide unreliable data transmission—meaning that there is no positive acknowledgment of data reception by the intended recipient's NetBIOS interface. Receipt of datagrams is not guaranteed. Datagram Support Services are also called "connectionless services." They are used to perform functions not possible with the Session Control Services such as

Table 15.1   NetBIOS Command Summary

Command Name	Wait Code	No-Wait Code	Command Description
General Control Services			
RESET	32	—	Reset NetBIOS
CANCEL	35	—	Cancel a pending command
ADAPTER STATUS	33	B3	Get status of a NetBIOS interface
UNLINK	70	—	Cancel boot redirection
Name Support Services			
ADD NAME	30	B0	Add unique name to name table
ADD GROUP NAME	36	B6	Add non-unique name to table
DELETE NAME	31	B1	Delete name from name table
Session Control Services			
CALL	10	90	Establish session with another
LISTEN	1	91	Wait for a CALL from another
HANG UP	12	92	Close session
SESSION STATUS	34	B4	Get status of sessions under name
Session Data Transfer Services			
SEND	14	94	Send session data
CHAIN SEND	17	97	Concatenate and send two buffers
RECEIVE	15	95	Receive session data
RECEIVE ANY	16	96	Receive data from any session under specified name
Datagram Control Services			
SEND DATAGRAM	20	A0	Send data, addressed by name
RECEIVE DATAGRAM	21	A1	Receive datagram to name
SEND BROADCAST	22	A2	Send data to all stations
RECEIVE BROADCAST	23	A3	Enable receive of next broadcast

sending and receiving broadcasts addressed to all machines. Datagram Support Services also include sending and receiving short messages addressed to specific NetBIOS unique names or group names. Datagrams are limited to 512 bytes or less of application data.

Session Control Services

The NetBIOS Session Control Services allow applications to establish sessions, to check their status, and to tear them down. **Sessions,** also called **virtual circuits,** are logical connections between two NetBIOS unique names established on a peer-to-peer basis. Data can only be transferred reliably between two nodes (in other words, guaranteed to arrive at one node, in the order it was sent from the other) after a session has been established.

Once a session is established on a node, it is assigned a unique number to differentiate it from all other sessions on that node. The two NetBIOS names connected by a session are usually on separate nodes, but they can be on the same node, or they can even be the same name on the same node. Also, the same two names can be used to establish multiple concurrent sessions.

The NetBIOS interface maintains error statistics and current parameter values on a session-by-session basis.

Session Data Transfer Services

The Session Data Transfer Services include sending and receiving data on already established sessions. The maximum application message size that can be sent in one command is 64 KB. If an error occurs while sending data, the session will be closed to maintain data integrity. The NetBIOS interface handles the details of network error detection and breaking larger messages into smaller messages to compensate for any physical limitations of the network.

A session-level data transfer sequence can be grouped into four steps. Each step on a system (application, process, or computer in the network) must have a complementary step performed on another system as shown in Figure 15.2.

1. Add a unique name to the NetBIOS local name table using the ADD NAME command (performed at both systems).
2. Initiate a session by using the CALL or LISTEN command. If using a CALL, then the other system should have already performed a LISTEN or the CALL will fail.
3. Transfer messages using the SEND and RECEIVE commands.
4. Terminate the session with the HANGUP command.

CALLING NetBIOS

NetBIOS commands are passed to the NetBIOS interface in the form of **Network Control Blocks (NCBs).** The application program is responsible for allocating space for and creating these NCBs. An NCB contains several fields, including a command code field and a command result field. Some fields are used to pass input values to NetBIOS; other fields are used by NetBIOS to return results from the command execution.

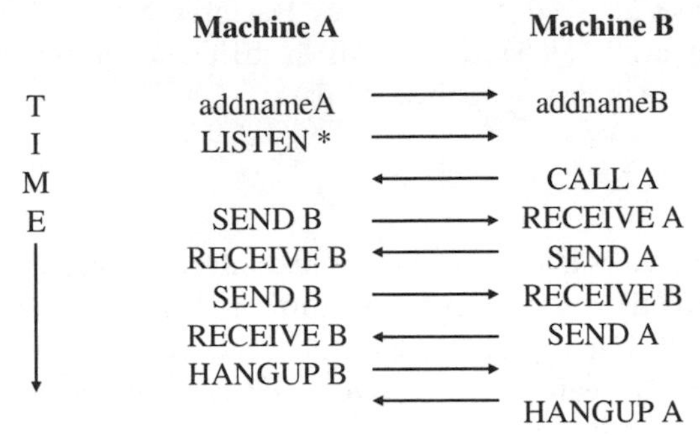

```
                 Machine A              Machine B

        T        addnameA  ——————→   addnameB
        I        LISTEN *  ——————→
        M                  ←——————     CALL A
        E        SEND B    ——————→   RECEIVE A
                 RECEIVE B ←——————     SEND A
                 SEND B    ——————→   RECEIVE B
                 RECEIVE B ←——————     SEND A
                 HANGUP B  ——————→
                           ←——————     HANGUP A
```

Figure 15.2   Data transfer sequence.

After creating an NCB, DOS machines pass it to the NetBIOS interface by loading the address (in the form of segment:offset) of the NCB into the ES:BX registers and then executing a software interrupt 5C hex. The NetBIOS interface will perform the operation specified by the command code field in the NCB.

NetBIOS COMMAND MODES

Three command modes are available to DOS machines when executing a NetBIOS command:

- Wait mode
- No-wait mode with completion post routine
- No-wait mode with polling

In wait mode, the NetBIOS interface will perform the command before returning to the calling program. The AL register will have the result of the operation.

The no-wait modes may queue the command for later execution and return program control to the application program immediately. The application can determine when the command has been completed by testing a flag in the NCB (i.e., polling) or by specifying the address of a POST subroutine to be executed when the command completes.

Under DOS, commands are issued to the NetBIOS interface by the following process:

1. Allocate and initialize an NCB.
2. Load the ES:BX registers with the address of the NCB.
3. Execute an INT 5C (hex) instruction.

The high-order bit of the COMMAND and POST fields of the NCB determine the resulting mode of operation. The COMMAND field is an 8-bit code that specifies the desired action. The POST field

MICROSOFT REDIRECTOR:
THE MOST POPULAR NetBIOS APPLICATION?

The Microsoft Redirector is very possibly the most popular NetBIOS application in use today. It is used in network operating systems such as MS-Net and its derivatives (3Com's 3+ and IBM's PC LAN) and Microsoft LAN Manager and its derivatives (like 3Com's 3+Open and IBM's LAN Server). The following describes some particulars of the Microsoft Redirector implementation.

SMB Names

The NetBios names used by the Microsoft Redirector are a subset of the allowable NetBIOS names.

When the Microsoft Redirector creates NetBIOS names, it uses the Server Message Block (SMB) naming convention that originated in MS-Net and the IBM PC-LAN programs. SMB names are up to fifteen characters long, padded with spaces (hex 20) if necessary, and terminated with a single-character suffix that identifies the purpose of this name.

Even though the NetBIOS interface allows names to be up to sixteen characters long, the SMB naming rules allow only fifteen characters in a name. The sixteenth character is reserved as the suffix. Valid characters that can be used in an SMB name are the uppercase alphabet characters, the numbers 0 through 9, and the following special characters: $%-_@{}~'!#(). Spaces are not allowed in SMB names except as pad characters.

The valid suffix characters for SMB names, in hexadecimal format, are:

00 Redirector Name. Also called a Machine Name. There are two major types: Unique and Group. A Unique Redirector Name is required for every LAN Manager machine.

03 Main or Additional Name. Also called User Names or Aliases. These names are used to send and receive messages. They are created by the Messenger service in LAN Manager.

05 Forwarded Name. A User Name or Alias forwarded from another machine, whose suffix has been changed to 05 hex. When users wish messages addressed to them to be received at another computer temporarily, they forward the User Name or Alias to another machine. The workstation software requests that the target computer add that name as a Forwarded name. The algorithm for sending messages across the network under LAN Manager is to first attempt to deliver this message to a Forwarded Name. If this fails because the target name has not been forwarded anywhere, then the sender directs the message to the User Name (ending with 03 hex).

20 Server Name. This is the name to which the Server service responds.

is either a double-word pointer to a user-supplied routine to be called when the command is completed, or it is set to 0:0, indicating that there is no user-supplied routine. The valid combinations of high-order bit in the COMMAND field and contents of the POST field are shown in Table 15.2.

The resulting modes of operation follow.

Table 15.2   COMMAND and POST Fields

High-order Bit of the COMMAND Field	Contents of the POST Field	Resulting Mode of Operation
0	(Any)	Wait
1	0:0	No-wait polling
1	Address of POST routine	No-wait post

WAIT Mode

When a wait mode command is issued, the NetBIOS interface will not return control to the user program until the command has been completed. Upon return, the AL register will contain 0 if no error occurred, or it will contain an error code value that matches the one contained in the NCB RETCODE field. The contents of the AH register are destroyed but other registers are not changed.

There is a risk when posting a NetBIOS LISTEN command in wait mode; it could hang the process or the machine until another process or machine completes a corresponding NetBIOS CALL command. Wait-mode NetBIOS commands are sometimes referred to as synchronous NetBIOS commands.

NO-WAIT Polling Mode

When a no-wait polling mode command is issued, the NetBIOS interface will, after minimal processing, return immediately to the user program—even before that command may not have been completed. On return, the AL register will contain either an immediate error code or 00 hex. If the AL register is 00 hex, the command has been successfully queued for processing.

When the command is queued successfully, the user program periodically polls the CMD_DONE field of the NCB. This field will contain 0FFh until the command completes, at which point it will contain the return value. Only when the command has completed will all other NCB fields be valid. The AH register contents are destroyed but other registers are not changed.

NO-WAIT Post Mode

Like the no-wait polling mode commands, the NetBIOS interface returns immediately after a no-wait post mode command, even though the command may not have been completed. On return, the AL register will contain either an immediate error code or 0.

If the command could not be queued, the POST routine will not be called. The AH register contents are destroyed; other registers are not changed.

If the command was successfully queued, then, when the command completes, the NetBIOS interface will call the user's POST routine with interrupts disabled, the stack will be set for an IRET, and ES:BX will contain the address of the completed NCB.

If another NetBIOS command is issued from the POST routine, it must also be a no-wait mode command.

The user POST routine should be as short as possible and no registers should be changed. Interrupts may be enabled in the POST routine.

In some cases, the user's POST routine will be called before control is returned from the INT 5Ch that started the command. This is most likely to occur when there is a great difference in speed between the two communicating machines. The faster machine may respond more quickly than the slower machine expects it to.

Both no-wait polling mode and no-wait post mode NetBIOS commands are sometimes referred to as asynchronous NetBIOS commands.

NETWORK CONTROL BLOCK FORMAT

NetBIOS commands must conform to an NCB format. Tables 15.3a and 15.3b show the NCB diagram and NCB fields. NCBs are 64 bytes long and consist of 14 different fields, from 1 to 16 bytes each. Each NetBIOS command uses a certain subset of the NCB fields.

All fields in an NCB should be initialized to zero. The fields used in a command should then be set. In DOS, ES:BX is set to point to the NCB and an INT 5C can then be used to pass this NCB to the NetBIOS application's interface. The results of the command are communicated back through the NCB.

The five most important fields for diagnosing network illnesses are, in order, the COMMAND, RETCODE, CALLNAME, NAME, and NUM fields. The following is a complete listing of NetBIOS fields:

COMMAND

A 1-byte field used for the NetBIOS command code. Set the high-order bit of this field to 1 to indicate no-wait mode or set it to 0 to indicate wait mode. The remaining seven bits are used for the command code. All NetBIOS commands except RESET and CANCEL have both wait and no-wait options. In wait mode, the NetBIOS interface waits for the command to complete before returning to the calling program. In no-wait mode, the NetBIOS interface queues the command for later execution and then immediately returns to the calling program, which may perform other processing or issue additional NetBIOS commands. In no-wait mode, the POST field must also be set.

RETCODE

A 1-byte field in which NetBIOS command results are returned. This field will contain an error code if an error was encountered or 0 if there was no error. (Refer to Table 15.4a for a full list of Return Codes. In addition, Table 15.4b shows Return Codes vs. Commands.)

CALLNAME

A 16-byte field used to indicate the name of the computer a user wants to communicate with for CALL, LISTEN, and datagrams. For a CHAIN SEND command, the CALLNAME field is used to specify the length and address of a second buffer. The first word specifies the length of the second buffer, and the next two words specify the address of that buffer. When used in the LISTEN command,

Table 15.3a   Network Control Block Diagram

00 - COMMAND	(1 byte)	01 - RETCODE	(1 byte)
02 - LSN	(1 byte)	03 - NUM	(1 byte)
04 - BUFFER@	(4 bytes)		
08 - LENGTH	(2 bytes)		
0A - CALLNAME	(16 bytes)		
1A - NAME	(16 bytes)		
2A - RTO	(1 byte)	2B - STO	(1 byte)
2C - POST@	(4 bytes)		
30 - LANA_NUM	(1 byte)	31 - CMD_CPLT	(1 byte)
32 - RESERVE	(14 bytes)		

usually only CALL commands issued by the name specified in this field will be answered. An asterisk (*) in this field indicates that any CALL made to the name in the next field (the NAME field) will be answered. The name making the CALL will be returned in place of the asterisk.

NAME

A 16-byte field used to specify a local name to add to the local name table for ADD NAME or ADD GROUP NAME commands. This field is also used in CALL commands to identify the caller. To establish a session, the name being called (i.e., the name in the CALLNAME field) must have issued a LISTEN command, either for this specific caller or for any caller (*).

Table 15.3b   Network Control Block Fields

NCB FIELDS	CALL	LISTEN	HANG UP	SEND	RECEIVE	RECEIVE ANY	CHAIN SEND	SEND DATAGRAM	RECEIVE DATAGRAM	SEND BROADCAST DATAGRAM	RECEIVE BROADCAST DATAGRAM	ADD NAME	DELETE NAME	RESET	ADAPTER STATUS	SESSION STATUS	CANCEL	ADD GROUP NAME
WAIT:	10H	11H	12H	14H	15H	16H	17H	20H	21H	22H	23H	30H	31H	32H	33H	34H	35H	36H
NO WAIT:	90H	91H	92H	94H	95H	96H	97H	A0H	A1H	A2H	A3H	B0H	B1H		B3H	B4H		B6H
NCB_COMMAND	>>	>>	>>	>>	>>	>>	>>	>>	>>	>>	>>	>>	>>	>>	>>	>>	>>	>>
NCB_RETCODE	<<	<<	<<	<<	<<	<<	<<	<<	<<	<<	<<	<<	<<		<<	<<	<<	<<
NCB_LSN	<<	<<	>>	>>	<<	>>	>>							1>>				
NCB_NUM						<>		>>	>>	>>	>>	<<		2>>				<<
NCB_BUFFER@				>>	>>	>>	>>	>>	>>	>>	>>				>>	>>	3>>	
NCB_LENGTH				>>	<>	<>	>>	>>	<>	>>	<>				<>	<>		
NCB_CALLNAME	>>	<>					4>>	>>	<<		<<				>>			
NCB_NAME	>>	>>										>>	>>					>>
NCB_RTO	>>	>>																
NCB_STO	>>	>>																
NCB_POST@ (Note 5)	>>	>>	>>	>>	>>	>>	>>	>>	>>	>>	>>	>>	>>		>>	>>		>>
NCB_LANA_NUM (Note 6)																		
NCB_CMD-CPLT (Note 7)	<<	<<	<<	<<	<<	<<	<<	<<	<<	<<	<<	<<	<<		<<	<<		<<

>> sent
<< received
<> both

Notes:

1. Number of sessions to be supported.
2. Number of commands to be supported.
3. Address of NCB to be cancelled.
4. Contains length and address of the second buffer in a 2-buffer chain.
5. Valid only for no-wait comands.
6. NCB_LANA_NUM is always set to 00H.
7. Contains status/return code for no-wait commands when NCB_POST@ is set to 00H.

NUM

A 1-byte field used for the name number associated with the name in the local name table. This number is returned by the ADD NAME command and must be supplied for RECEIVE ANY and datagram commands. The value of this number ranges from 1 to 255. The value of 1 is always assigned to the permanent node name. The value 255 is used with RECEIVE ANY and RECEIVE DATAGRAM functions instead of a specific name.

LSN

A 1-byte field containing the local session number (with a value between 1 and 254) that is assigned by the NetBIOS interface when a session is established. This field is returned by CALL and LISTEN and must be supplied for SEND and RECEIVE commands.

```
NCB struct
    ncb_command         db  ?    ;command code
    ncb_retcode         db  ?    ;err ret code
    ncb_lsn             db  ?    ;session number
    ncb_num             db  ?    ;name number
    ncb_buffer@         dd  ?    ;ptr to send/recv data
    ncb_length          dw  ?    ;length of data buffer
    ncb_callname db 16 dup (?)   ;remote name
    ncb_name     db 16 dup (?)   ;local name
    ncb_rto             db  ?    ;recv timeout
    ncb_sto             db  ?    ;send timeout
    ncb_post            dd  ?    ;async cmd complete post addr
    ncb_lana_num        db  ?    ;adapter number
    ncb_cmd_cplt        db  ?    ;0xFF until command completed
    ncb_reserve  db 14 dup (?)    ;reserved for use by NetBIOS
NCB ends
```

Figure 15.3 Assembly language NCB structure.

BUFFER@

A 4-byte field used for the address of data to be sent or received. When this field is used, it contains a pointer (segment:offset) to a buffer to be used by the issuing command. Only commands that send or receive data not contained in the NCB data structure use buffers. The exact contents of the buffer depend on the command and the application.

LENGTH

A 2-byte field containing the length in bytes of BUFFER@. For receive commands, this field is set to the maximum buffer size, and the actual length of the data received is returned in this field upon completion of the NetBIOS command.

```
struct ncb {
  byte command;         /* hex code for command to be executed  */
  byte retcode;         /* return code                */
  byte lsn;             /* local session number       */
  byte num;             /* number returned by the locator      */
  char far *buffer;     /* address of data buffer          */
  int length;           /* number of bytes to be sent or received */
  char callname[16];    /* name of the node to communicate with */
  char name[16];        /* name of your node       */
  byte rto;             /* receive timeout           */
  byte sto;             /* send timeout        */
  char far *post_routine;   /* pointer to post routine      */
  byte lana_num;        /* local adapter number    */
  byte cmd_cplt;        /* command complete        */
  byte reserve[14];     /* NetBIOS temporary variable storage   */
```

Figure 15.4 C language NCB structure.

Table 15.4a   List of NetBIOS Return Codes

Code	Description
00	No error.
01	Illegal buffer length. A SEND BROAD-CAST or SEND DATAGRAM command specified a length greater than 512 bytes, or a status command specified a buffer length smaller than the minimum allowed.
03	Invalid command.
05	Time-out. For SEND, RECEIVE, and HANG UP commands, the timeout specified when the session was established has elapsed. On a CALL or ADAPTER STATUS command, an internal timer has expired.
06	Message incomplete. The buffer size specified in the NCB was not large enough to hold the RECEIVE data. For RECEIVE or RECEIVE ANY commands, the next command will receive the rest of the data. For other commands, the remaining data will be lost.
07	NO-ACK command failed. One or more SEND NO-ACK and/or CHAINSEND NO-ACK commands failed. The session is still active. Resynchronize the data flow (if possible) and continue, or terminate the session and start over.
08	Invalid local session number (LSN).
09	Out of resources. The NetBIOS interface is out of some internal resource, such as buffers. Wait and reissue the command later.
0A	Session closed. For a SEND, RECEIVE, RECEIVE ANY, or HANG UP command, this indicates that the session was terminated by the remote computer.
0B	Command canceled. Command execution of the NCB was aborted by the CANCEL command.
0D	Duplicate local name. An ADD NAME command specified an existing name.
0E	Name table full.
0F	DELETE NAME completed, but the name has active sessions. The name will be deleted when all sessions have been closed. No new sessions will be allowed with the name.

Code	Description
11	Local session table full.
12	Remote computer not listening. On a CALL, the remote computer was found, but had no outstanding LISTEN for the CALL.
13	Invalid name number.
14	Name not found.
15	Either name not found or an asterisk (*) or 00H was in the first byte of the remote name field on a CALL.
16	Name already exists on network. The specified name is already in use as a unique name on another adapter.
17	Name was deleted.
18	Session terminated abnormally. Connection with the remote computer was lost.
19	Name conflict. Two computers were detected using the same name.
1A	Incompatible remote device.
21	Interface busy. The NetBIOS cannot execute because it was called from an interrupt handler, or because it is out of local resources.
22	Too many commands issued. The number of commands outstanding equals the maximum number allowed.
23	Invalid LAN adapter (LANA) number.
24	Command completed before it was canceled. This code is returned in CANCEL NCB when the target command completed normally.
25	Reserved name specified. An ADD NAME or ADD GROUP NAME command specified a reserved name. Use a different name.
26	Invalid cancel command. The target NCB could not be found.
30	Name defined by another process (specific to IBM OS/2 EE). The command referred to a locally defined NetBIOS name. Resources reserved for a given process within a workstation can only be used by that process and the specified local NetBIOS name is already reserved for another process. Use another name or remove the process that is using the required name.

(continued)

Table 15.4a (continued)   List of NetBIOS Return Codes

Code	Description	Code	Description
34	NetBIOS environment not defined (specific to IBM OS/2 EE). The RESET command must be the first command issued by a process. Issue the RESET command.		load time. NetBIOS is still available for the application, but with fewer resources than requested. The use of name number 01 can only be claimed by one process.
35	Required operating system resources exhausted (specific to IBM OS/2 EE). The NetBIOS interface cannot initiate the requested command because OS/2 EE resources are not available to support the command. Retry the command later.	40	System error.
		41	Hot carrier from remote adapter detected (PC network). Remove the offending adapter from the network and cycle power on your own machine before attempting to use the network again.
36	Maximum applications exceeded (specific to IBM OS/2 EE). This return code only applies to the RESET command. NetBIOS services requested in the RESET command are not available to this requesting process because the number of processes that the NetBIOS interface is currently serving is the maximum allowed by the NetBIOS load time parameters. Stop a process that is using NetBIOS services, or increase the value of the NetBIOS Application (APP) load time parameter and reboot.	42	Hot carrier from this adapter detected (PC network). You have a hardware malfunction. Replace your network adapter.
		43	No carrier detected (PC network).
		4E	Token ring status bits 12, 14, or 15 on longer than one minute.
		4F	Token ring status bits 8 through 11 set to "on."
		50-F6	Adapter malfunction or unknown error code.
		F7	Error initializing adapter.
		F8	Error opening adapter.
37	No SAPs available for NetBIOS (specific to IBM OS/2 EE). All allocated SAPs are already in use and none are left for NetBIOS. NetBIOS requires only one SAP to support all of its processes.	F9	IBM LAN Support Program internal error.
		FA	Adapter malfunction.
		FB	IBM LAN Support Program not loaded.
		FC	Error opening adapter or DLC.Open.SAP failed.
38	Requested resources not available (specific to IBM OS/2 EE). The requests for NetBIOS resources (names, commands, sessions, or the use of name number 01) exceed the number specified at NetBIOS	FD	Adapter closed unexpectedly.
		F7-FE	Adapter malfunction or unknown error code.
		FF	Indicates the command has not completed.

RTO

A 1-byte field used for RECEIVE time-outs in half-second increments. This field must be set for CALL and LISTEN commands. It indicates the maximum time that will be allowed to pass before an error condition will result on a RECEIVE command. Once a session is established, this value remains constant throughout the session.

Table 15.4b   Return Codes vs. Commands

Ret Code	NetBIOS Commands Return Code Meaning	CALL	LISTEN	HANG UP	SEND	RECEIVE	RECEIVE ANY	CHAIN SEND	SEND DATAGRAM	RECEIVE DATAGRAM	SEND BROADCAST DATAGRAM	RECEIVE BROADCAST DATAGRAM	ADD NAME	DELETE NAME	RESET	ADAPTER STATUS	SESSION STATUS	CANCEL	ADD GROUP NAME
WAIT:		10H	11H	12H	14H	15H	16H	17H	20H	21H	22H	23H	30H	31H	32H	33H	34H	35H	36H
NO WAIT:		90H	91H	94H	94H	95H	96H	97H	A0H	A1H	A2H	A3H	B0H	B1H		B3H	B4		B6H
00H	Command accepted/completed	■	■	■	■	■	■	■	■	■	■	■	■	■	■	■	■	■	■
01H	Illegal buffer length							■	■		■					■	■		
03H	Invalid command code	■	■	■	■	■	■		■	■	■	■	■	■		■	■	■	■
05H	Command timed-out	■			■	■	■	■								■	■		
06H	Message incomplete					■	■	■		■						■	■		
08H	Illegal local session number				■	■	■	■					■						
09H	No resource available	■	■																
0AH	Session closed				■	■	■	■	■										
0BH	Command cancelled	■	■	■	■	■	■	■				■				■			
0DH	Duplicate in local name table												■						■
0EH	Name table full												■						■
0FH	Name de-registered, but active													■					
11H	Local session table full	■	■																
12H	Session open rejected	■																	
13H	Illegal name number						■			■		■	■	■					
14H	Cannot find name/no answer	■																	
15H	Name not found, na or 00H	■	■										■	■			■		
16H	Name in use on remote adapter												■						■
17H	Name deleted		■					■			■		■						
18H	Session ended abnormally	■	■	■	■		■	■											
19H	Name conflict detected	■	■				■		■	■	■	■				■	■		
1AH	Incompatible remote device	■	■																
21H	Interface busy	■	■	■	■	■	■	■	■	■	■	■	■	■		■	■		■
22H	Too many commands outstanding	■	■	■	■	■	■	■	■	■	■	■	■	■		■	■		■
23H	Invalid number in NCB_LANA_NUM	■	■	■	■	■	■	■	■	■	■	■	■	■	■	■	■		■
24H	Command was not cancelled																	■	
25H	Reserved name specified																	■	■
26H	Command not valid to cancel																	■	
40H	Locator not responding	■						■							■				
4XH	Unusual network condition	■	■	■	■	■	■	■	■	■	■	■	■	■		■	■	■	■
50H-FEH	Adaptor malfunction	■	■	■	■	■	■	■	■	■	■	■	■	■		■	■	■	■
FFH	Command pending status*	*	*	*	*	*	*	*	*	*	*	*	*	*	*	*	*	*	*

* Value found in NCB_CMD_CPLT field — valid only for no-wait options

STO

A 1-byte field used for SEND time-outs in half-second increments. This field must be set for CALL and LISTEN commands. If the time expires before the SEND has completed, a time out error will result and the session will be terminated.

POST@

A 4-byte field containing the address of a user interrupt routine to be called when a no-wait mode command completes. If all four bytes are set to 0, then no interrupt will occur and the calling program must assume responsibility for control by polling the CMD_CPLT field to determine the status of the command's execution.

LANA_NUM

A 1-byte field that contains the number of the adapter card to be addressed by the command. If two adapter cards are installed on the same computer, a 0 in this field signifies that the command is addressing the first card and a 1 indicates that the command is addressing the second card. If there is only one adapter card in the computer, this field should contain a 0.

CMD_CPLT

A 1-byte field that is set by NetBIOS when a command is completed. A value of 0FFH indicates that the command has not completed. When the command has completed, this field is set to the same value as RETCODE.

RESERVED

A 14-byte field, used internally by NetBIOS, which should not be used for any other purpose. Different implementations of NetBIOS use this field differently, so applications should not make any assumptions about its contents.

NetBIOS UNDER OS/2

So far, we have focused exclusively on NetBIOS from the perspective of DOS. Now let's look at the differences in the NetBIOS interface between DOS and OS/2, and the differences between IBM's implementation of NetBIOS with IBM LAN Server and LAN Requestor in IBM OS/2 Extended Edition, and Microsoft's implementation of NetBIOS with OS/2 LAN Manager. 3Com's 3+Open OS/2 LAN Manager follows the rules for the Microsoft implementation.

In all instances, NetBIOS functions are available via OS/2 dynamic linking. Processes present requests to the NetBIOS interface using FAR CALL instructions rather than INT 5C or 2A interrupts. Also, instead of pointing ES:BX to an NCB and executing an INT 5C, OS/2 assembly language programs use the following sequence:

```
push NCB_Selector   ; "segment" to NCB
push NCB_Offset     ; "offset" to NCB
call NetBIOS_Submit ; NetBIOS dynamic link
```

The NCB structure for OS/2 is no different than for real-mode NetBIOS (NetBIOS for DOS). OS/2 uses the NetBIOS interface through Application Programming Interfaces (APIs). OS/2 NetBIOS is different from DOS NetBIOS in that, with asynchronous NCBs, the POST field contains a semaphore handle, not the address of a POST routine.

IBM OS/2 EE AND LAN SERVER

The RESET Command

In IBM OS/2 EE, each process operates independently. A process obtains NetBIOS resources by a RESET command, which must be the first NetBIOS command that process issues. Processes cannot share names, including the permanent node name. The right to use the permanent node name is obtained by issuing the RESET command.

Wait and No-wait Modes

When a command that specifies the wait mode is initiated, the requesting process thread is immediately blocked. When the command completes, execution returns to the requesting process's code. The effect is similar to the DOS commands that specify no-wait operation.

OS/2 EE handles no-wait commands by spawning child threads that are immediately blocked. Execution of the requesting process's thread continues without pause. If a POST routine was specified in the NCB, the NetBIOS interface will invoke it when the command completes. POST routines return by executing a FAR RETURN instruction rather than an IRET instruction.

Because commands specifying no-wait mode operation require more OS/2 EE resources than commands specifying wait operation, no-wait commands may fail (with a return code of 35H) where wait commands would succeed.

New Return Codes:

30H: Name defined by another process
34H: NetBIOS environment not defined
35H: Required operating system resources exhausted
36H: Maximum applications exceeded
37H: No SAPs available for NetBIOS
38H: Requested resources not available

MICROSOFT OS/2 LAN MANAGER

Microsoft OS/2 LAN Manager, unlike IBM LAN Server and DOS implementations of NetBIOS, allows multiple NetBIOS interfaces to be installed.

OS/2 uses the NetBIOS interface through APIs. OS/2 NetBIOS is different from DOS NetBIOS in that, with asynchronous NCBs, the POST field contains a semaphore handle, not the address of a POST routine.

The NCB structure itself has not changed from real-mode NetBIOS. Under real mode (in the DOS compatibility box), all NCBs (except no-wait mode POST commands) are supported. The application must instead poll for command completion. NCBs in the real mode are submitted using the same INT 5C as DOS, not by using the LAN Manager APIs.

Reserved Handle 0

An application should use the NetBiosOpen and NetBiosClose calls to obtain and release handles to the NetBIOS interface(s). These handles are intended to be used with NetBiosSubmit. An application can use the reserved handle 0 when submitting NCBs. Such NCBs will be submitted to the first NetBIOS interface, and implicit calls to NetBiosOpen and NetBiosClose will be performed. Since real-mode applications are restricted to using INT 5C to communicate with NetBIOS, they are restricted to the first NetBIOS interface.

Because more than one process may open the same NetBIOS interface, OS/2 LAN Manager allows the opener to specify how it is willing to share access to the NetBIOS interface with other processes. Three access modes are defined to accomplish this, as shown in Table 15.5.

NetBIOS APIS FOR OS/2 LAN MANAGER

Five NetBIOS APIs are documented for OS/2 LAN Manager to allow direct access to the NetBIOS interface(s): NetBiosEnum, NetBiosGetInfo, NetBiosOpen, NetBiosClose, and NetBiosSubmit. As mentioned earlier, use can be restricted to just NetBiosSubmit using handle 0. Figure 15.5 through 15.9 show these five NetBIOS APIs.

NetHandle is either a handle returned from a previous call to NetBiosOpen or 0. A handle of 0 always refers to the first installed NetBIOS interface. This interface will automatically be opened by NetBiosOpen (in regular access mode) the first time a NetBIOS call refers to it using the 0 handle.

NetNCB points to the NCB to be executed (unchained NCB) or to the link word preceding the NCB (chained NCB; see below). The caller need not fill in the ncb_lana_num field; this will be done based on the NetHandle used.

If the NCB is a no-wait NCB, the ncb_post field of the NCB should either be 0 or a system semaphore handle. If a handle is given, the semaphore will be cleared on completion of the NCB. The system semaphore must be public; that is, created without the "exclusive" option.

NetNCBOpt specifies NCB processing options. Allowable values are as follows:

0	single NCB being passed
1	single NCB with error retry
2	NCB chain with proceed-on-error
3	NCB chain with stop-on-error

Sequence of Data Transfer

Unlike real-mode NetBIOS (DOS NetBIOS), OS/2 LAN Manager allows multiple NetBIOS interfaces. Therefore, a session layer data transfer sequence using the OS/2 NetBIOS interface would still have the same four steps as DOS, but those steps would be enveloped by OS/2-specific steps to determine the correct NetBIOS interface and bind to it. Each step on a system (application, process, or computer in the network) must have a complementary step performed on another system. (See Figure 15.10.)

Table 15.5   NetBIOS access modes.

Access Mode	Permissions	Restrictions
NB_REGULAR	Any number of processes may open a NetBIOS interface in regular mode.	Does not allow RESET, RECEIVE BROADCAST DATAGRAM, RECEIVE ANY-TO-ANY NCBs, or the use of permanent names in any NCB.
NB_PRIVILEGED	One process may open the interface in privileged mode. This mode is compatible with NB_REGULAR; other processes may open the interface in regular mode, even while it is opened by a single process in privileged mode. A privileged open will fail if any other process has a current privileged or exclusive open handle to that interface.	Does not allow RESET or RECEIVE ANY-TO-ANY NCBs.
NB_EXCLUSIVE	One and only one process may open the interface, if the process opens it in exclusive mode. The open attempt will fail if any other process has an open handle to that interface.	All NCB operations are allowed.

1. List NetBIOS interfaces by using NetBiosEnum (performed at both systems).
2. Get a handle to the chosen NetBIOS interface with NetBiosOpen (performed at both systems).
3. Using the handle acquired in step 2, issue a sequence of NetBIOS commands using NetBiosSubmit (performed at both systems):
   * Add a unique name to the NetBIOS local name table using the ADD NAME command (performed at both systems).
   * Initiate a session by using the CALL or LISTEN command. If using a CALL, then the other system should have already performed a LISTEN or the CALL will fail.
   * Transfer messages using the SEND and RECEIVE commands.
   * Terminate the session with the HANGUP command.
4. Close the NetBIOS interface handle with NetBiosClose.

```
unsigned far pascal
NetBiosEnum(srvrname, level, buf, bufLen, entRead, totalEnts)
char far *    srvrname;          /* name of target PC (null if local) */
short         level;             /* level of info requested           */
char far *    buf;               /* pointer to info buffer            */
unsigned short bufLen;           /* length of info buffer in bytes    */
unsigned short far * entRead;    /* # of entries returned             */
unsigned short far * totalEnts;  /* total # of entries available      */
```

If level is set to 0 when this call is made, the information buffer returned will be filled with "struct netbios_info_0" containing only the names of the NetBIOS interfaces loaded. These names are defined in the [NETWORKS] section of the LANMAN.INI file, which is read by the portion of LAN Manager installed at boot time.

If level is set to 1 when this call is made, the following structures are returned in the information buffer:

```
struct netbios_info_1 {
      char            net_name[NETBIOS_NAME_LEN+1];
      char            driver_name[DEVLEN+1]; /* OS/2 device drive name   */
      unsigned char   lana_num;              /* LAN adapter of this net  */
      char            pad_1;
      unsigned short  driver_type;
      unsigned short  net_status;
      unsigned long   net_bandwidth;         /* Network bandwidth, bits/s  */
      unsigned short  max_sess;              /* Max. # of sessions         */
      unsigned short  max_ncbs;              /* Max. # of outstanding NCBs */
      unsigned short  max_names;             /* Max. # of names            */
}
```
Net_Status is a bitmapped field and is defined below:

```
Bit     Definition

0       Net managed by LAN Manager
1       Driver is a loopback driver
2-13    <Reserved>
14-15   Open status. The values of these two bits mean:
          0    net not opened
          1    opened in regular mode
          2    opened in privileged mode
          3    opened in exclusive mode
```

The open status bits of the net_status field will be set to 2 if any process has that NetBIOS interface opened in privileged mode, even though other processes may simultaneously have it open in regular mode.

Figure 15.5   NetBiosEnum (admin only). Purpose: enumerates NetBIOS interfaces.

```
unsigned far pascal
NetBiosGetInfo(srvrname, netBiosName, level, buf, bufLen)
char far *        srvrname;    /* name of target PC (null=local)  */
char far *        netBiosName; /* NetBIOS network name            */
short        level;            /* level of info requested         */
char far *        buf;         /* pointer to info buffer          */
unsigned short bufLen;         /* length of info buffer in bytes  */
```

Figure 15.6   NetBiosGetInfo (admin only). Purpose: gets information about a given NetBIOS interface.

```
unsigned far pascal
NetBiosOpen(netBiosName, netReserved, netOpenOpt, netHandle)
char far *            netBiosName;  /* name of network         */
char far *            netReserved;  /* MUST BE 0               */
unsigned short        netOpenOpt;   /* open options            */
unsigned short far *  netHandle;    /* word for returned handle */
```

The NetOpenOpt field is bitmapped as follows:

```
Bit      Definition
0-1      Access Mode
          0   <Reserved>
          1   NB-REGULAR
          2   NB_PRIVILEGED
          3   NB-EXCLUSIVE
2-15     <Reserved>
```

Note: Handles returned by NetBiosOpen are process-to-interface associations. Only the process that opened the handle may use it.

Figure 15.7   NetBiosOpen. Purpose: gets a handle to a NetBIOS interface.

```
unsigned far pascal
NetBiosClose (netHandle, netReserved)
unsigned short   netHandle;        /* handle to close    */
unsigned short   netReserved;      /* MUST BE 0          */
```

Figure 15.8   NetBiosClose. Purpose: closes a NetBIOS interface handle.

```
unsigned far pascal
NetBiosSubmit(netHandle, NetNCBOpt, netNCB)
unsigned short    netHandle;          /* handle to issue NCB against    */
unsigned short    netNCBOpt           /* option flags                   */
struct ncb far * netNCB;              /* address of NCB                 */
```

Figure 15.9   NetBiosSubmit. Purpose: passes one or more MCBs to the NetBios interface.

	Machine A	Machine B
T	NetBiosEnum	NetBiosEnum
I	NetBiosOpen	NetBiosOpen
M	NetBiosSubmit	NetBiosSubmit
E	addnameA	addnameB
	LISTEN *	
		CALL A →
	SEND B →	RECEIVE A
	RECEIVE B ←	SEND A
	SEND B →	RECEIVE B
	RECEIVE B ←	SEND A
	HANGUP B →	

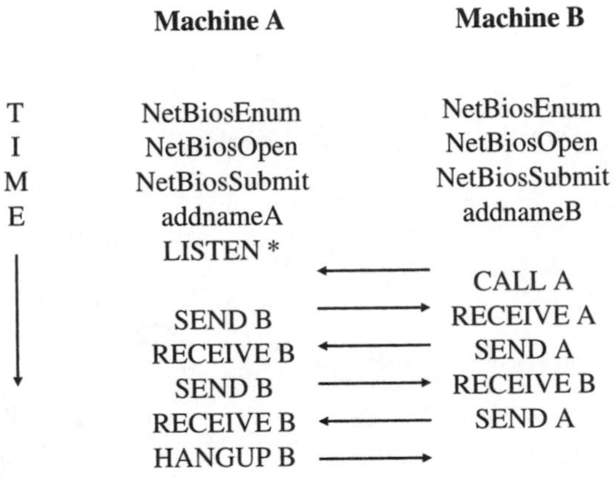

Figure 15.10   Sequence of data transfer for OS/2.

CONCLUSION

Microsoft has been quick to recommend that any other means of LAN Manager interprocess communication, such as Named Pipes, be used in place of NetBIOS. However, NetBIOS is available on all levels of LAN Manager workstations (OS/2, DOS Enhanced, and DOS Basic) where Named Pipes are only available at a penalty—support for them consumes valuable applications workspace. Applications written to the NetBIOS interface are transportable across a variety of network operating systems platforms including 3Com's 3+ and 3+Open, Microsoft's LAN Manager, Novell's NetWare, and Banyan's VINES. Named pipes applications are restricted to those network operating systems that support named pipes.

ACKNOWLEDGMENTS

The authors would like to acknowledge the invaluable assistance provided by the 3Com Technical Support team in reviewing this article, especially Cathy Anderson and Frank Burke.

REFERENCES

3Com Corporation. *3Com Network Architectures, Services, and Protocols.* Part no. 7310-00, revision A.

3Com Corporation. *NetBIOS Programmer's Reference.* Part no. 3260-00.

Microsoft Corporation. *Microsoft LAN Manager 1.0 API Summary.*

Ryan, Ralph. *The Microsoft LAN Manager, a Programmer's Guide.* Redmond, WA: Microsoft Press.

16

UNDERSTANDING TOKEN RING SOURCE ROUTING

Robert Perry and Paul Turner

INTRODUCTION

This chapter describes how source routing works with the IEEE 802.5 Token Ring Network, and explains basic concepts necessary to understand how source routing works in a generic Token Ring environment. It covers frame structure, route determination processes, and source-routing bridge operation.

The purpose of this chapter is to provide a solid understanding of Token Ring source routing. This document supplies critical conceptual information rather than extensive performance benchmarking data. This information will be most valuable to people who are designing, implementing, and administering complex Token Ring networks.

The information for this chapter came from various publications (listed in the References) and from interviews with engineers and consultants familiar with source routing in the Token Ring environment.

In this chapter, we use a combination of IBM, Novell, and industry terminology (unless otherwise noted).

Frame or packet—the basic unit of transmission on the network.

Bridge—a device using the ISO Data Link layer for frame-forwarding instructions (such as an IBM Token Ring Network bridge). There are two distinct types of bridges—transparent bridges and source-routing bridges. The term bridge as used in this chapter refers to a source-routing bridge.

Router—a dedicated device using the ISO Network layer for frame-forwarding instructions (such as a NetWare bridge, which is now called a router). A ring station that passes on source-routing packets (at the Data Link layer) is not considered a router in the same sense as a specialized router is.

Broadcast refers to two things: 1) An all-stations broadcast (common to all Token Ring networks) and 2) A route determination broadcast (specific to source routing). (We will define these two terms explicitly later. Since these are two distinct broadcast types, we'll use these labels to avoid confusion.)

Additional terms that IEEE, IBM, and Novell have come to use in different ways are listed and clarified in the "Use of Terms" section later in this chapter.

SOURCE ROUTING

IEEE has defined a method of routing that allows one node to communicate with another node up to thirteen rings away (fourteen rings total). This method of routing, called source routing, is necessary when at least two rings are interconnected by bridges.

Single-ring networks do not require source routing. The Token Ring architecture requires a frame on a single ring to automatically make a loop around the ring, so all stations can see the frame. Each station forwards the frame it receives from the station upstream, keeping a copy if necessary. When the transmission arrives back where it started, the originating station removes the frame from the ring. (See Figure 16.1.)

Multiple-ring networks, in which rings are linked by source-routing bridges, need an additional routing procedure to define how a frame originating on one ring crosses a bridge to another ring. This is where source routing comes in.

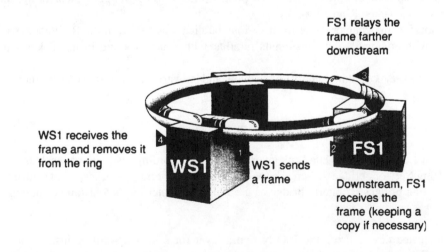

Figure 16.1 A single-ring network; source routing is not necessary for a frame to reach its destination.

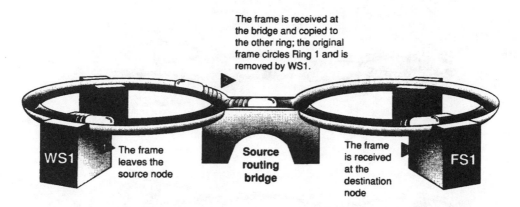

The frame is received at the bridge and copied to the other ring; the original frame circles Ring 1 and is removed by WS1.

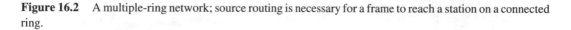

Figure 16.2   A multiple-ring network; source routing is necessary for a frame to reach a station on a connected ring.

A source-routing bridge will only pass certain types of frames from one ring to another ring. (These frame types are presented in detail later.) Source-routing bridges get their instructions for passing a frame between rings by reading source-routing information placed at the beginning of the frame. The source station (which originates the frame) is responsible for inserting these routing instructions in the frame before it is sent. Hence, the term source routing. Source routing defines the ring-bridge-ring routing information that is contained in the frame for bridges to read.

Source routing is illustrated in its simplest form in Figure 16.2, where WS1 sends a frame through a bridge to FS1.

Stated another way, source routing occurs when the source station determines the route that its data travels on the way to a destination station on another ring. After determining an appropriate route, the source station then includes routing information in subsequent frames sent to the destination station.

Because a station must know the route to another station before it can communicate with that station, source routing also defines how a station can determine if a route is available. Route determination is especially important where multiple routes exist between two stations, as shown in Figure 16.3.

In the IBM and Novell implementations, the source station chooses which route its data will follow to reach the destination station. The destination station begins using this route after it receives the first explicitly routed frame from the source station.

By design, source routing uses distributed routing tables rather than centralized routing tables. In source routing, bridges do not keep routing tables; instead, the tables are distributed over the network at each ring station. An individual station checks its own routing information table to find the route that frames must travel to reach the stations it communicates with.

This distributed method of routing contrasts with routing methods that use centralized routing tables (such as NetWare or TCP/IP) in two ways:

1. the location of the routing tables; and
2. the OSI layer used (source routing uses the Data Link layer and NetWare routing uses the Network layer).

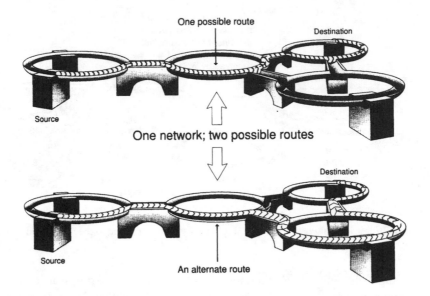

Figure 16.3 Two routes between the source and destination on a multiple-ring network; normally, the originating station chooses which path to use.

In centralized routing, a specialized router acts as an intelligent frame-forwarding device, maintaining a table of segments and the available routes to reach them.

WHY SOURCE ROUTING?

Without a way to connect separate network segments, each Token Ring network is limited to 72, 96, or 260 stations, depending on the type of cable used. Source routing is one method of linking network segments to create much larger networks.

Another reason source routing is useful is that it allows segmentation of network traffic to reduce the load on any one segment. Source routing also allows parallel bridging, a fault-tolerant technique which provides alternate routes for data in case bridges fail. The flexibility of source routing allows stations to adjust to network failures and discover alternate routes.

HOW SOURCE ROUTING WORKS

To understand how source routing works, you must first have a basic understanding of the following:

- the structure and types of Token Ring frames
- the operation of source-routing bridges
- the route determination process

The following sections summarize the most important aspects you need to understand. For more detailed explanations, refer to the publications referenced in the References.

Token Ring Frame Structure

As the basic unit of transmission on a Token Ring network, the frame is made up of several fields. These fields, each consisting of one or more bytes, define such things as addressing, error checking, and priority level of the frame. (The individual components of the frame are explained in detail in the "Token Ring Frame Structure" later in this chapter.)

Figure 16.4 shows the components of a simple 802.5/802.2 Token Ring frame—one that does not include source-routing fields.

This structure can hold sufficient information to get a frame from one station to another station on the same ring. However, it has no fields to hold information about the route between stations on different rings.

In order for a frame to hold the necessary information for travel between stations on different rings, the frame must be modified. A frame with routing information is shown in Figure 16.5.

Figure 16.5 highlights the three most important areas of the frame for source routing: the first bit of the Source Address Field, the Routing Control Field, and the Route Designator Fields.

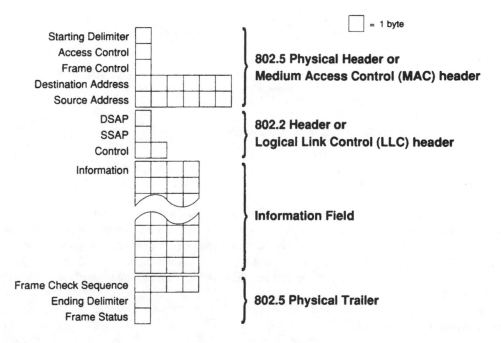

Figure 16.4   Structure of a simple Token Ring frame without source-routing fields.

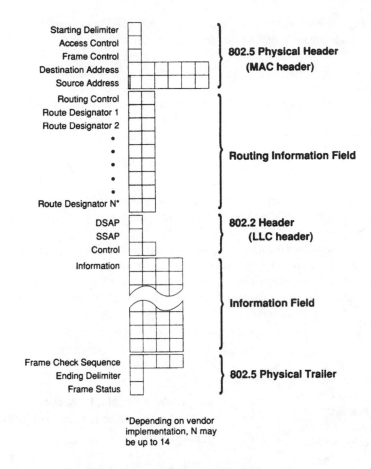

Figure 16.5   Structure of a Token Ring frame with source-routing fields.

The Source Address Field

A binary 0 in the first bit of the Source Address Field would indicate that the frame contains no source routing information. Whenever a station includes routing information in a frame, it sets this bit to 1. This signals a receiving station to account for the routing information when it parses the contents of the frame. When a bridge detects a 1 in the first bit of the Source Address Field, it examines the frame's Routing Information Field to see if it should pass the frame to the bridge's adjoining ring. See Figure 16.6.

The Routing Control Field

This field contains administrative information including the following:

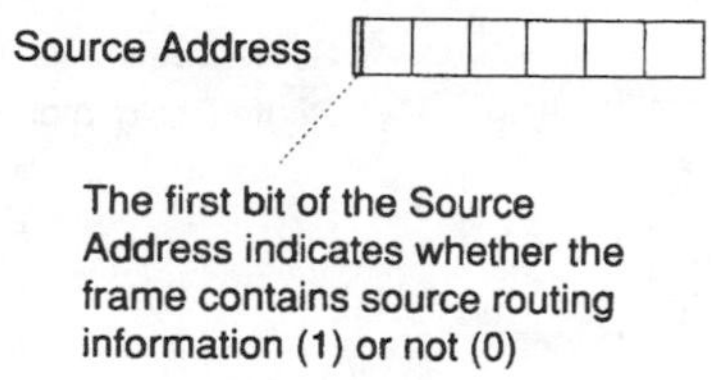

Source Address

The first bit of the Source
Address indicates whether the
frame contains source routing
information (1) or not (0)

Figure 16.6   The source address field.

- The frame type (single-route broadcast, all-routes broadcast, or specifically routed)
- The length of the entire Routing Information Field (the Routing Control Field plus the Route Designator Fields)
- The direction the Route Designator Fields should be read by the bridge (forward or backward)
- The largest size the Information Field can be as it is sent along the route

The meaning of the numbers in the field shown in Figure 16.7 is explained in detail later.

The Route Designator Fields

Under the IEEE definition, a frame can hold from two to fourteen Route Designators, allowing it to traverse up to fourteen rings across thirteen bridges in a given direction. (It is important to note that vendor implementations differ in this sense; IBM, for example, allows two to eight Route Designators, allowing frames to traverse up to eight rings across seven bridges in a given direction.) Because the information in the Routing Control Field gives the current length of the Routing Information Field, the number of Route Designators can vary without being parsed incorrectly by receiving stations. The Route Designator Fields in Figure 16.8 read "from Ring 001, across Bridge 1, to Ring 002."

Figure 16.8 shows empty Route Designators only to indicate that more than two may be used; in practice, only the needed number of Route Designators are added to the frame.

Although the Source Address Field and the Routing Information Field make source routing possible, a station on one ring must still obtain the route to a station on another ring before it can start

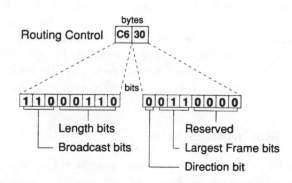

Figure 16.7   The routing control field.

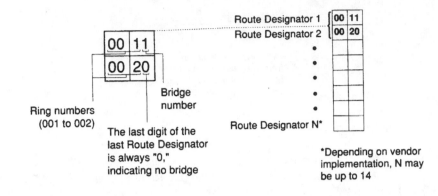

Figure 16.8 The route designator fields.

sending frames addressed specifically to that station. The process of obtaining this route is called **route determination.**

SOURCE-ROUTING BRIDGE OPERATION

One of the pillars of source routing is the source-routing bridge. An explanation of the basic function of this kind of bridge is vital to understanding route determination. Source-routing bridges come in a variety of platforms including 80286, 386, 486, and RISC machines. Although each kind may use different software, all of them have in common several functions that identify them as source-routing bridges. The basic function of a source-routing bridge is to provide a link between stations on different rings. When the bridge is started, several parameters are configured, including the bridge number, ring numbers, and the single-route broadcast selection mode.

Rules for Source-routing Bridges

Each source-routing bridge must be assigned a hexadecimal number (0–9, A–F). This number does not have to be unique unless bridges are used in parallel (attached to the same two rings). This bridge number is contained in the bridge portion of the Route Designators. (1 is the default bridge number.)

During bridge configuration, each ring, or segment, connected to a source-routing bridge is assigned a unique hexadecimal number (001–FFF). All bridges connected to the same ring must be configured to use the same ring number for that ring. When the Route Designator Fields are used, this unique ring number is placed in the ring portion of each Route Designator. The ring numbering feature of the bridge allows all stations on a ring to know the number of the ring they are connected to.

Ways to Configure a Source-routing Bridge

A bridge can be configured manually as a single-route broadcast bridge (the default setting) or as an all-routes broadcast bridge. Or, it can be allowed to configure itself automatically to all-routes or single-route mode by negotiating with other bridges on the network.

A source-routing bridge that is set up as a single-route broadcast bridge will forward frames that are:

- all-routes broadcast
- single-route broadcast
- specifically routed

A source-routing bridge that is set up as an all-routes broadcast bridge will forward frames that are:

- all-routes broadcast
- specifically routed

A bridge set up this way is also described as "single-route broadcast forwarding inactive" because it will not forward single-route broadcasts.

Two features of bridges prevent route determination frames from traveling endlessly around the network. The first is that a bridge will not forward a frame to its other ring if the Route Designator Fields indicate that the frame has already been on the bridge's other ring. The second feature is the Hop Count Limit, which restricts the number of bridges an all-routes broadcast frame may cross. The default setting for IBM's Token Ring bridge is 7, and the range is 1–7. Decreasing the value of this parameter does not affect single-route broadcasts or specifically routed frames, which in this case may cross up to seven bridges even if the Hop Count Limit on a given bridge is set to less than 7. When either an all-routes broadcast or a single-route broadcast frame has crossed seven IBM bridges and reaches the eighth, it is discarded.

ROUTE DETERMINATION

A ring station that requires the resources of a peer or server on a connected ring must first find a route to that station. Once a route is known, the two stations use it to exchange all frames. Ring stations may use either an all-routes or single-route broadcast frame to determine the route to another station.

Figure 16.9 illustrates how WS1 finds a route to FS1 using an all-routes broadcast frame. WS1 places a frame on Ring 1 that contains the node address of FS1 as its Destination Address and is labeled as an all-routes broadcast in the Routing Control Field. This frame is copied by all of the source-routing bridges onto their adjacent rings (unless the frame is marked in the Route Designator Fields as having been on the adjacent ring already).

Since there are two paths to Ring 4 from Ring 1, two copies of the frame will appear on Ring 4. (Two copies will also appear on Ring 3.) As each bridge copies the frame onto its adjoining ring, it adds Route Designators to indicate:

- the ring number the frame is copied from
- the number of the bridge passing the frame
- the ring number the frame is copied to

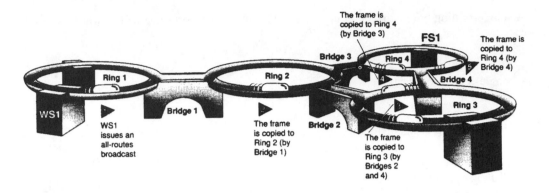

Figure 16.9 WS1 issues an all-routes broadcast in search of the route to FS1; FS1 receives one copy of the broadcast route between WS1 and FS1.

When FS1 receives the all-routes broadcast frames, it realizes that a station is trying to determine its location on the network. FS1 can respond to each of these frames either with a single-route or all-routes broadcast frame. Or, it can reverse the order of the routes that the bridges have placed in the Route Designator Fields of WS1's all-routes broadcast frames and return specifically routed frames addressed to WS1.

After receiving the response, WS1 can choose the shorter of the two routes (in this case, the route through Bridge 3) for all subsequent communication with FS1.

In contrast with this example, if WS1 were to use a single-route broadcast frame to locate FS1, only those bridges that are configured to pass single-route broadcasts will copy the frame to their adjacent rings. For example, if all of the bridges in Figure 16.9 (except Bridge 3) were configured to pass single-route broadcast frames, only one copy of the frame sent by WS1 will appear on Ring 4. (This frame would travel from Ring 1 through Bridge 1 to Ring 2, then through Bridge 2 to Ring 3, and finally through Bridge 4 to Ring 4.)

The example in the previous figure shows that FS1 can respond with several frame types. In fact, WS1 is not limited in the way it initiates the route determination to begin with. The options of the source and destination stations follow.

WS1	FS1
Send Options	Return Options
Single-route	Single-route
All-routes	All-routes
Include Data	Specifically routed

This combination of options is flexible enough to allow either the source station or the destination station to determine the best route. Which options are used in a network is an implementation issue, decided by each vendor whose software is used on the network stations (or by the user if the software is configurable).

The option for the sending station to include data in the route determination frame can conserve network bandwidth by reducing the total number of frames used in a particular communication. However, if multiple routes exist, using this option can degrade network performance because several copies of the larger frame (containing data) may circulate on the network.

A CLOSER LOOK AT ROUTE DETERMINATION

The preceding examples have shown the basics of route determination, but this is not enough for designers or administrators who may need to read network analyzer traces to examine what is happening on a network. To assist those who need this kind of information, the following example examines part of the source-routing frame at the binary level.

The Route Determination Process Begins

Figure 16.10 shows the broadcast frame sent by WS1 during the first three stages of the route determination process.

When WS1 originates the route determination frame (broadcast), it indicates in the first bit of the Source Address Field that the frame contains routing information. This signals the bridge that the frame should be examined and possibly passed on to the adjoining ring.

In the frame's Destination Address Field, WS1 inserts the unique node address of FS1. Higher-level protocols such as NetBIOS or NetWare Core Protocol (NCP) can obtain this unique address through a search for the name FS1 on the network.

Figure 16.11 shows the specific numbers placed in the Routing Information Field at the three stages shown.

Stage 1   As WS1 issues the frame, it places the Destination and Source Addresses in the MAC header.

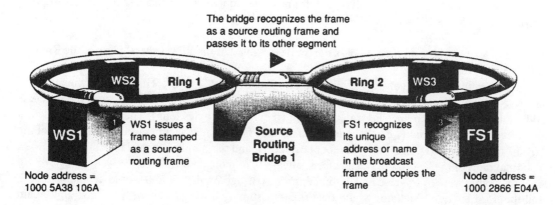

Figure 16.10   The first steps of route determination.

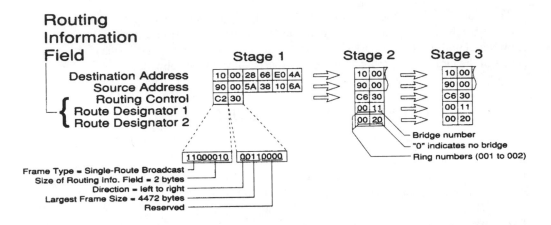

Figure 16.11 Number placement in the routing information field.

The first byte (C2) of the 2-byte Routing Control portion of the Routing Information Field contains the following information: the binary 110 at the beginning of the byte signifies a single-route broadcast; the remaining binary 00010 (or decimal 2) indicates that the Routing Information Field is 2 bytes long. The second byte (30) contains the following information: the binary 0 at the beginning of the byte indicates the Route Designator Fields (which don't exist yet) should be read from left to right; the next part, binary 011, designates the largest frame size (excluding headers) that WS1 can transmit, and is reduced by any bridge that cannot handle the current given size; the remaining binary 0000 is blank, reserved for future use.

The Destination Address and the Source Address remain the same through the first three stages. Note, however, that the hard-coded Source Address of the adapter in WS1 is actually 1000 5A38 106A; when WS1 changes the first bit of the Source Address set from 0 to 1 to designate a source-routing frame (before sending the frame), the equivalent hexadecimal Source Address becomes 9000 5A38 106A.

Stage 2   As the bridge prepares to pass the frame to Ring 2, it modifies several parts of the Routing Information Field.

It changes the first byte of the Routing Control Field from C2 to C6. This reflects changing the last five bits to indicate a new length of 6 for the Routing Information Field, because the bridge is adding 4 bytes to the Routing Information Field (previously 2 bytes long). These 4 bytes, added in the Route Designator Fields, can be interpreted directly in their hexadecimal form: the number of the "from" ring (Ring 001), the bridge number (Bridge 1), and the number of the "to" ring (Ring 002). The final digit of the last Route Designator is always 0, to indicate no bridge.

If the frame were to traverse an additional bridge (Bridge 2), that final 0 would be changed to 2, and the third Route Designator would read 0030 (assuming a Ring 003), with the last digit again indicating no bridge.

Stage 3   FS1 receives the frame exactly as it left the bridge.

To understand how all stations on each ring have access to all frames on the ring, it is important to note that the route determination frame originated by WS1 travels completely around Ring 1 before WS1 removes it from the ring. If FS1 were on the same ring, it would copy the frame as it moved around the ring and then issue a direct response. In this example, however, as the frame is traveling around Ring 1, Bridge 1 copies it. After Bridge 1 puts this copied frame on Ring 2, the frame travels completely around Ring 2 before Bridge 1 removes it. During the time this frame travels around Ring 2, FS1 copies it and formulates a response.

THE ROUTE DETERMINATION PROCESS ENDS

FS1 responds to WS1's broadcast because its unique address is in the Destination Address Field of the frame's MAC header. The other stations (WS2 and WS3) do not send response frames back to WS1 because they do not match the Destination Address of the frame. (See Figure 16.12.)

Figure 16.13 shows the specific numbers in the Routing Information Field at the three stages shown in Figure 16.12.

Stage 4   As FS1 issues the response frame, it includes 6 bytes in the Routing Information Field.

The first byte (06) contains the following information: the binary 000 at the beginning of the byte signifies a specifically routed frame; the remaining binary 00110 (or decimal 6) indicates that the Routing Information Field is 6 bytes long. The second byte (B0) contains the following information: the binary 1 at the beginning of the byte indicates the Route Designator Fields should be read backwards. (This feature allows all bridges to read the same Route Designator Fields for frame travel in either direction.) The next part, binary 011, designates the largest frame size (excluding headers) that can be transmitted between WS1 and FS1; the remaining binary 0000 is blank, reserved for future use.

The Destination Address now reflects the hard-coded unique adapter address of WS1 (1000 5A38 106A). The Source Address contains the unique adapter address of FS1 (1000 2866 E04A), slightly modified to 9000 2866 E04A to reflect the setting of the first bit of the Source Address Field from 0 to 1 to indicate a source-routing frame.

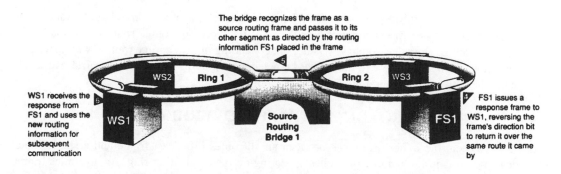

Figure 16.12   The final steps of route determination.

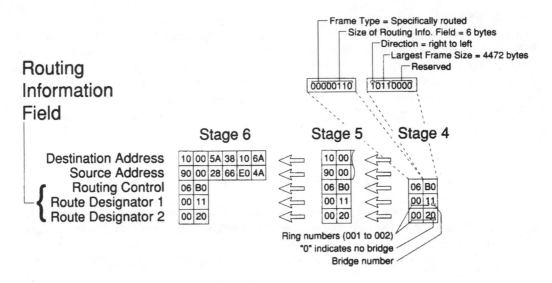

Figure 16.13 Specific numbers in the routing information field.

Stage 5 Because this frame is a specifically routed frame, the bridge does not change any of the information in the frame.

The Routing Information Field contains the routing information that directs the bridge to pass it from Ring 2 to Ring 1.

Stage 6 WS1 receives the frame exactly as it left the bridge (and FS1). WS1 and FS1 will continue to use this route until the route between them is altered.

Once route determination is complete, the stations on a network each maintain a table of the routes to other stations they communicate with. Figure 16.14 shows how three workstations (WS1, WS2, and WS3) maintain a table of individual routes to FS1, the file server they have a current session with. Conversely, FS1 maintains a table of the routes to WS1, WS2, and WS3. The same idea applies for peer-to-peer communication (for example, WS1 and WS3 could each keep track of the route to the other).

As you can see from the step-by-step examples in the last few pages, a thorough understanding of the route determination process requires knowledge of the pieces of source routing information in Token Ring frames. Now that you have a better understanding of how source routing works, we can look at a few examples of how to apply that knowledge in looking at broadcast traffic overhead, balancing the network load, and implementing parallel bridges.

BROADCAST TRAFFIC OVERHEAD

As we have seen, the major difference between an all-routes broadcast frame and a single-route broadcast frame is in the number of frames appearing on the destination ring. An all-routes frame will appear as many times on the destination ring as there are routes to that ring. See Figure 16.15.

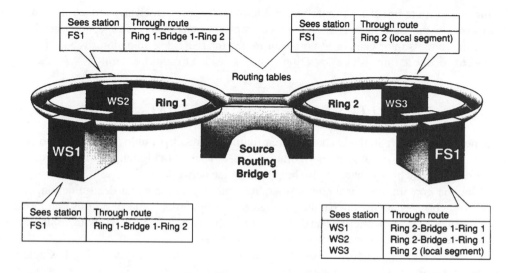

Sees station	Through route
FS1	Ring 1-Bridge 1-Ring 2

Sees station	Through route
FS1	Ring 2 (local segment)

Routing tables

Sees station	Through route
FS1	Ring 1-Bridge 1-Ring 2

Sees station	Through route
WS1	Ring 2-Bridge 1-Ring 1
WS2	Ring 2-Bridge 1-Ring 1
WS3	Ring 2 (local segment)

Figure 16.14   Routing tables are kept at each station that is communicating with any other station.

In contrast, a single-route frame will appear as many times on the destination ring as there are single-route broadcast routes to that ring. That is, if all the bridges on the network in Figure 16.15 were set up as single-route bridges, a single-route broadcast from WS1 would appear two times on Ring 4, just as with an all-routes broadcast. However, if only bridges 1, 2, and 3 were set up as single-route bridges, then only one copy of a single-route broadcast from WS1 would appear on Ring 4. Since the intent of having a single route over the network is to reduce traffic, creating more than one single route would defeat this purpose. It is important, therefore, to effectively place each bridge and know its broadcast mode.

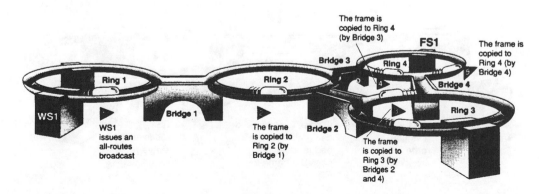

Figure 16.15   If WS1 issues an all-routes broadcast in search of the route to FS1, FS1 receives one copy of the broadcast for each route between WS1 and FS1.

Using single-route broadcast frames and single-route bridges can clearly reduce the amount of traffic caused by the route determination process. By placing single-route bridges strategically in the network, an administrator can create preferred routes for route determination, freeing from most broadcast traffic those rings whose operation is most sensitive to additional traffic.

PARALLEL BRIDGES AND LOAD BALANCING

As we mentioned earlier in the chapter, source routing makes it possible to connect two or more bridges to the same two rings. This configuration, called **parallel bridging,** not only guards against the failure of a single bridge, but can also help balance the network load.

This section contains two examples of parallel bridging during route determination. In both examples, two bridges are used in parallel: Bridge 1 is a single-route broadcast bridge and Bridge 2 is an all-routes broadcast bridge. The first example shows how they work with a single-route broadcast; the second shows an all-routes broadcast.

Figure 16.16 and Figure 16.17 show the operation of parallel bridges during a single-route broadcast. In Figure 16.16, WS1 sends a single-route broadcast to locate FS1 on the network. Since only the single-route bridge forwards the single-route broadcast from Ring 1 to Ring 2, FS1 receives just one copy of the broadcast frame.

In the second part of the example, FS1 responds to the single-route broadcast with a specifically routed frame. This response ensures that WS1 is able to choose from all available routes, ultimately balancing the load between Bridge 1 and Bridge 2.

WS1 chooses the route of the first response frame that it receives from FS1. It sends subsequent frames as specifically routed frames, containing the routing information (ring numbers and bridge

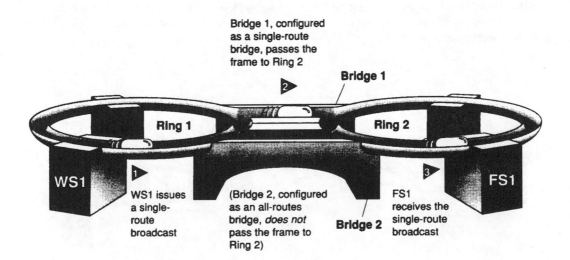

Figure 16.16   A single-route broadcast over parallel bridges.

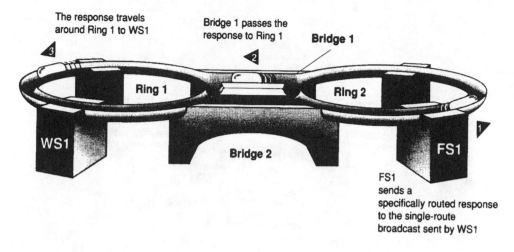

The response travels
around Ring 1 to WS1

Bridge 1 passes the
response to Ring 1

Bridge 1

Ring 1

Ring 2

WS1

Bridge 2

FS1

FS1
sends a
specifically routed response
to the single-route
broadcast sent by WS1

Figure 16.17   A response to a single-route broadcast over parallel bridges.

numbers) to route these frames to FS1. After FS1 receives the first specifically routed frame from WS1, it also uses the route selected by WS1.

In Figure 16.18, WS1 sends an all-routes broadcast frame in search of FS1. The frame is copied to Ring 2 by both bridges.

Remember that an all-routes broadcast route determination frame will appear as many times on the destination ring as there are routes to that ring. Although this increases network traffic compared to using single-route broadcast frames, all-routes broadcast frames have a unique advantage in balancing the load on the network.

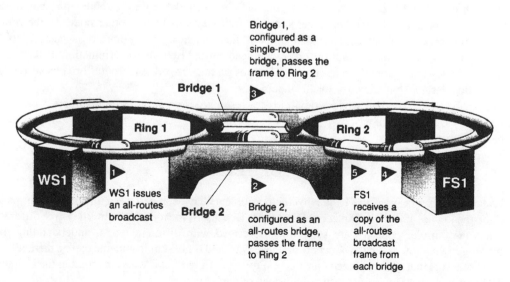

Bridge 1,
configured as a
single-route
bridge, passes the
frame to Ring 2

Bridge 1

Ring 1

Ring 2

WS1

WS1 issues
an all-routes
broadcast

Bridge 2

Bridge 2,
configured as an
all-routes bridge,
passes the frame
to Ring 2

FS1
receives a
copy of the
all-routes
broadcast
frame from
each bridge

FS1

Figure 16.18   An all-routes broadcast over parallel bridges.

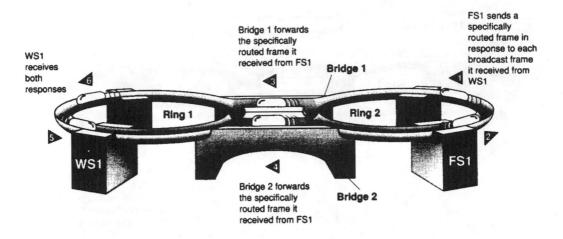

Figure 16.19 A response to an all-routes broadcast over parallel bridges.

In Figure 16.19, WS1 and FS1 have the option of selecting which of the bridges they will use to communicate with each other. If Bridge 1 is heavily loaded with traffic when WS1 issues the all-routes frame, WS1 and FS1 can route subsequent frames over Bridge 2 for better performance.

CONCLUSION

In this chapter we have outlined the fundamentals of source routing. In its simplest definition, source routing allows 802.5 Token Rings to be interconnected with source-routing bridges. Using special fields within the 802.5 packet, a node on the network can determine a route—through these source-routing bridges—to another node, and then route packets to that other node. In the route determination process, nodes can use either single-route broadcasts or all-routes broadcasts. Single-route broadcasts reduce the amount of traffic overhead caused by route determination packets and allow system administrators to create preferred routes on the network. All-routes broadcasts create more traffic overhead but allow for load balancing.

Ultimately, source routing provides flexibility for systems designers and administrators to customize networks to the needs of the environment, whether the priority is performance, reliability, or ease of management.

USE OF TERMS

Individuals who work in the IBM and Novell environments have come to use a mixed set of terms to describe the logical and physical pieces of networks. Because some identical terms describe different concepts and similar concepts are sometimes described with different terms, understanding the terminology when integrating products from these two (and other) environments can be difficult.

A list of terms that typically need clarification follows. Unless otherwise specified in the chapter, the IBM term is used (frame, for example, instead of packet).

Term	IBM Meaning	Novell Meaning

Broadcast	To send a frame to more than one station on a ring using FFFF FFFF FFFF in the Destination Address Field. (This is also called an all-stations broadcast.)
	
	  To send a route determination frame to determine the route to another station on the network. (This can be an all-routes or a single-route broadcast.)
		Same as an all-stations broadcast within the Token Ring environment. Also commonly used for Service Advertising Protocol (SAP) and Routing Information Protocol (RIP) broadcasts. SAP and RIP broadcasts are sent by NetWare routers and servers.
		
		  BROADCAST is also a NetWare command typed at the file server console to send a brief message to all users logged in to or attached to that file server or to a list of users or connection numbers.

Ring Number	A unique three-digit hexadecimal number (001–FFF) that differentiates bridged rings on a Token Ring network. The ring number is used at the ISO Data Link Layer (Medium Access Control sublayer). In a combined Novell/other-vendor environment, both ring number and network number are used. The term "LAN segment number" is synonymous with ring number.	Same definition as for IBM. Not the same as "network number."
Network Number	Not defined for the Token Ring network; should not be confused with ring number.	Synonymous with Novell's "network address." An eight-digit hexadecimal number (1 through FFFFFFFE) that uniquely identifies a network cabling segment. The network number used by NetWare is used at a higher OSI level than the ring number. The network number is set with NETGEN (v2.1x), INSTALL (v2.2), or with the BIND IPX command (v3.x).
Network Address	Not defined for the Token Ring network; should not be confused with ring number.	Synonymous with Novell's "network number."
Bridge Number	A one-digit hexadecimal number (0–9,A–F) given to a bridge in a multiple-ring network. This number is not necessarily unique on a network, but must be unique where parallel bridges are used.	Not defined. NetWare routers (traditionally called bridges) are not assigned an identifying number; instead, each network adapter in the bridge must use the network number, or address, of the segment to which it is attached.
Router	IBM does not define this as a specialized device in the Token Ring network. The function of routing in the Token Ring environment is handled by the source and destination nodes on the network. Source-routing bridges pass frames from ring to ring, but do not actually route the frames.	An internetwork device that keeps routing tables, answers queries, publishes routing information, and routes frames to their destination through the most efficient path. The function of routing in the NetWare environment is handled by what Novell has called bridges. (IEEE chose the term "router" some time after Novell began using "bridge.") New versions of NetWare refer to routers instead of bridges. This AppNote uses the term "router" to refer to what was previously called a Novell bridge, and "bridge" to refer to a source-routing bridge.

Term	IBM Meaning	Novell Meaning
Bridge	Source-routing bridge: a packet-forwarding device that gets its forwarding instructions from Route Designator Fields added to the MAC (Medium Access Control) header (currently used only in the Token Ring environment). Transparent bridge: a packet-forwarding device that gets its forwarding instructions from the Destination Address Field in the MAC header. Transparent bridges learn about the location of nodes on a network by examining the Source Address Field of packets sent on the network. Transparent bridges are currently used in both the Token Ring and Ethernet environments. End nodes need not be aware that transparent bridges exist on the network.	Same as IBM term for source-routing and transparent bridges. Novell has, in the past, referred to its routers as bridges. New versions of NetWare call a router a router. This AppNote uses the term "router" to refer to what was previously called a Novell bridge, and "bridge" to refer to a source-routing bridge.
Frame	The basic element of transmission in the Token Ring environment.	Same definition as for IBM. "Frame" and "packet" are synonymous. In this series of AppNotes we use "frame" except where "packet" makes sense (for example, Internetwork Packet Exchange, or IPX).
Packet	Synonymous with "frame." The *IBM Local Area Network Technical Reference,* for example, uses "packet" to describe data moving between stations (including Token Ring, PC-Net, and Ethernet); the *IBM Token Ring Network Architecture Reference,* however, uses "frame" to describe the same thing in the Token Ring environment.	The basic element of transmission in a NetWare network. "Packet" and "frame" are synonymous to Novell. In this series of AppNotes we use "frame" except where "packet" makes sense (for example, Internetwork Packet Exchange, or IPX).
SAP	Service Access Point. The logical point (made available by a network adapter) where information is received and transmitted. Similar to the "socket" used by IPX.	Service Advertising Protocol. Every 60 seconds, servers on a NetWare network advertise their services on the network using this protocol.

TOKEN RING FRAME STRUCTURE

This section provides additional information about the Token Ring frame structure, including the Routing Information Field used for source routing.

802.5 Physical Header

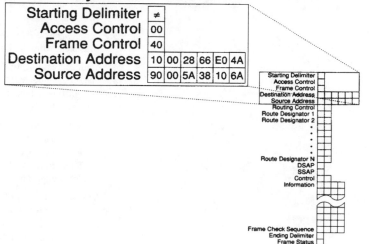

Starting Delimiter	≠					
Access Control	00					
Frame Control	40					
Destination Address	10	00	28	66	E0	4A
Source Address	90	00	5A	38	10	6A

Starting Delimiter
Access Control
Frame Control
Destination Address
Source Address
Routing Control
Route Designator 1
Route Designator 2
·
·
·
·
Route Designator N
DSAP
SSAP
Control
Information

Frame Check Sequence
Ending Delimiter
Frame Status

Figure 16.20   Physical header.

Field	Purpose	Explanation
Starting Delimiter	Synchronizes the receiving adapter with the frame (or token) to follow.	This one-byte preamble begins every frame and token. Be cause it is not distinguishable as a valid byte of data, this field is unique from the other fields in the frame. The starting delimiter is only a part of the frame while it is on the wire; intelligent components in the adapter never see it.
Access Control	Holds information that controls access to the ring.	This one-byte field is the second byte of every frame and token. It indicates the current priority of a frame (or token), distinguishes a frame from a token, prevents "homeless" tokens or frames from continuously circling the ring, and stores requests for priorities from ring stations.
Frame Control	Indicates the type of frame: Medium Access Control (MA) or Logical Link Control (LLC).	The example value of hexadecimal 40 (binary 0100 0000) indicates an LLC frame. Hexadecimal 00 (binary 0000 0000) indicates a MAC frame, which all stations with a matching individual or group destination address will copy.
Destination Address	Identifies the ring stations that should copy the frame.	This six-byte field contains a hexadecimal address, which contains one of the following:

Field	Purpose	Explanation
Destination Address (cont.)		• individual address (identifies a specific ring station)
		• group address (identifies a group of destination ring stations)
		• null address (identifies a frame that can be sent, but not received except by the originating station, for the purpose of clearing the ring)
		• all-stations broadcast address (identifies all ring stations on a given ring or interconnected rings, and is different from an all-routes broadcast, which is copied by all bridges)
		The first bit of byte 1 of the address identifies the address as an individual address (0) or a group address (1). The second bit of byte 1 identifies the address as universally administered (0) or locally administered (1).
		The first bit of byte 2 of the address indicates whether an address that is locally administered is a group address (1) or a functional address (0, used for LAN management functions).
Source Address	Identifies the originating ring station.	This six-byte field contains a unique hexadecimal address. Individual addresses may be assigned in one of two ways:
		• by universal administration (IEEE guarantees uniqueness)
		• by local administration (assigned by a local administrator; locally assigned addresses must still be unique in the Token Ring network where they are used)
		The first bit of byte 1 of the address is set to 1 when the frame contains a Routing Information Field; it is set to 0 when no routing information is present. By setting this bit to 0, a ring station that does not use source routing can use the same ring as source-routing stations do, but it cannot send or correctly receive frames that contain source-routing information.
		The second bit of byte 1 identifies the address as universally administered (0) or locally administered (1).

Routing Information Field

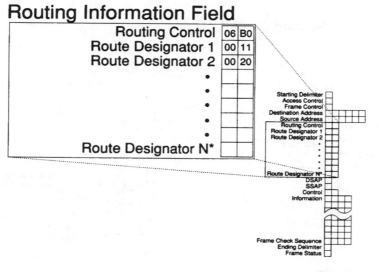

*Depending on vendc
implementation, N mε
be up to 14

Figure 16.21   Routing information field.

Field	Purpose	Explanation
Routing Control	Indicates several things about how the frame is to travel and how other stations are to parse the rest of the information in the frame.	This two-byte field is the first part of the Routing Information Field, which provides the vehicle for source routing. The Routing Information Field as a whole is optional when source routing is not needed. The two bytes of the Routing Control Field hold four distinctive pieces of information, as shown in Figure 16.21. They are as follows: • **Broadcast Indicators** (indicating the broadcast type of the frame) • **Length Bits** (indicating the binary length of the Routing Information Field, enabling stations to correctly parse the rest of the frame; in the example above, $00110 = 6$, which indicates a six-byte field, including the Route Designators) • **Direction Bits** (indicates whether bridges should read the Route Designators forward or backward, which allows the same Routing Information Field to be used for travel in either direction between two points)

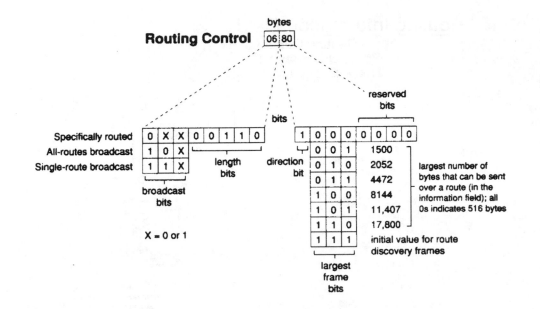

Figure 16.22   Routing control field.

Field	Purpose	Explanation
Routing Control (cont.)		• **Largest Frame Bits** (signifies the largest frame that can pass along a specific route between two stations) The fifth area in the Routing Control Field is reserved for future use. The first three bits (broadcast bits) of byte 1 indicate whether the route is: • Specifically routed (the Route Designator Fields already contain a specific route for the frame to travel; the source node determines what that route is) • All-routes broadcast (a frame that is to be copied to all routes on the network) • Single-route broadcast (a frame that is to be copied around the network in a manner that places only one copy on each ring)

Field	Purpose	Explanation
Route Designator	Indicates the route a frame has traveled or is to travel.	In a network with two rings joined by a single bridge, a frame passed from Ring 1 to Ring 2 will contain four bytes of Route Designators, 00 11 00 20, which is read "from Ring 001, across bridge 1, to Ring 002." If there were another bridge (Bridge 2) to pass the frame to another ring (Ring 003), the Route Designator Fields 1, 2, and 3 would read 0011, 0022, and 0030, respectively. The final digit of the last Route Designator is always 0, to indicate no bridge.
		Bridges examine the Route Designators in every source-routing frame to determine whether the frame has already been on the bridge's other ring (via another route). If the other ring number is in a Route Designator, the bridge doesn't pass the frame on.
		The frame may contain up to fourteen Route Designators (IEEE definition) or up to eight Route Designators (IBM definition). This limits the size of the network to fourteen rings/thirteen bridges (IEEE) or eight rings/seven bridges (IBM) in any one direction.
DSAP	Identifies the Destination Service Access Point the frame is sent to.	In Figure 16–23, E0 identifies NetWare as the DSAP. The DSAP is similar to a NetWare socket, which identifies a particular process within a station. The DSAP, SSAP, and Control fields constitute the Logical Link Control (LLC) portion of the frame. This AppNote does not deal with LLC in detail. For more information, refer to IEEE documents or the *IBM Token Ring Network: Architecture Reference,* listed in the References.
SSAP	Identifies the Source Service Access Point the frame is sent from.	In Figure 16–23, E0 identifies NetWare as the SSAP. The SSAP is similar to a NetWare socket, which identifies a particular process in the station, which originates a frame.

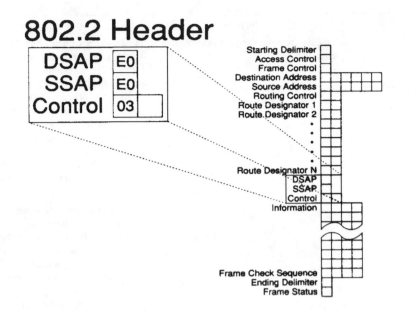

Figure 16.23 802.2 header.

Field	Purpose	Explanation
Control	Holds commands, responses, sequence numbers, and other information.	In Figure 16–23, 03 identifies the frame as an unnumbered information (UI) frame, commonly known as a datagram frame. Novell currently uses 03 as its default control type for source-routing frames. When a sequenced-type of frame is identified in the first byte, the second byte (which is otherwise optional) gives the frame's sequence number. Other control types are possible, but will not be covered here.
Information	Holds higher-level protocol information or actual data such as part of a file to be stored.	This field is variable in length. It holds information from protocols such as NetBIOS or IPX, layered around user data that is being sent in the frame. The Information Field provides a vehicle for network management protocols or other third-party protocols to travel across the network between the headers and trailers in the frame.

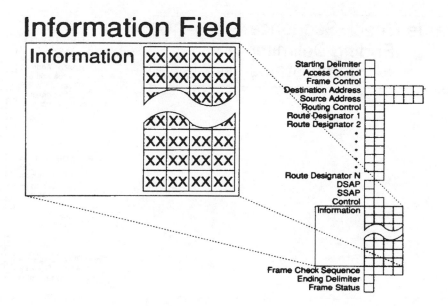

Information Field

Figure 16.24   Information field.

Field	Purpose	Explanation
Frame Check Sequence	Provides a four-byte cyclical redundancy check for parts of the frame.	The CRC covers everything from the Frame Control Field through the Frame Check Sequence itself, inclusive.
Ending Delimiter	Identifies the end of the frame.	This one-byte delimiter ends every frame and token. Because it is not distinguishable as a valid byte of data, this field is unique from the other fields in the frame. The ending delimiter is only a part of the frame while it is on the wire; intelligent components in the adapter never see it.
Frame Status	Provides status information to the source station about how the frame was received.	The information contained in this one-byte postscript allows the source station to know if the destination station: (1) copied the frame; (2) is inactive or does not exist; or (3) exists but did not copy the frame.

ACKNOWLEDGMENTS

Special thanks is given to Stephen Belisle and Bob Ross of Novell for their invaluable input in the creation of this chapter.

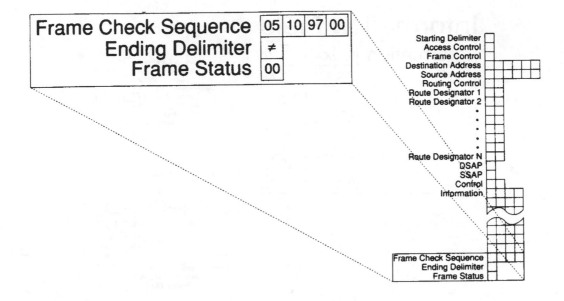

Figure 16.25   802.5 physical trailer.

REFERENCES

Administering Token Ring networks with source routing is a task that requires a thorough understanding of the subject. We recommend the following reference library as an information tool to assist you in designing, implementing, and administering Token Ring networks.

Books*

Bridge Program User's Guide. (This guide accompanies the IBM Token Ring Network Bridge Program, version 2.1.) IBM part no. 16F0493.

IBM Cabling System Planning and Installation Guide. IBM part no. GA27-3677.

IBM Local Area Network Administrator's Guide. IBM part no. GA27-3748.

IBM Local Area Network Technical Reference. IBM part no. SC30-3383.

IBM Token Ring Architecture Reference. IBM part no. SC30-3374-02.

IBM Token Ring Network Introduction and Planning Guide. IBM part no. GA27-3677.

Article

Taylor, Wayne and Belisle, Stephen. July 1990. "Token Ring Source Routing Made Easy." *NetWare Technical Journal*, pp. 64–76.

*Books are available from an IBM representative or IBM branch office

Note: Novell, Inc. makes no representations or warranties with respect to the contents or use of this chapter or of any of the third-party products discussed in the chapter. This chapter does not constitute an endorsement of the third-party product or products that were tested. Configuration(s) tested or described may or may not be the only available solution. Any test is not a determination of product quality or correctness, nor does it ensure compliance with any federal, state, or local requirements. Novell does not warranty products except as stated in applicable Novell product warranties or license agreements.

V

WIDE AREA NETWORKS

17

ISDN AND THE
GLOBAL NETWORK

Dale Gulick

INTRODUCTION

The emerging Integrated Services Digital Network (ISDN) is the logical next step in the evolution of the world telephone network. Essentially, ISDN is the conversion of the existing network from an analog to a digital infrastructure. The result is a network that combines the global interconnection capabilities of today's voice telephone network with universal, standardized, data transmission.

In this chapter we will investigate the ISDN from the standpoint of an environment for user applications, and not as the end applications themselves. We will look at the organization of the network; the function of the B, D, and H channels; the various types and classifications of hardware; the functions performed by software; and the structure of the required software.

THE GOAL OF ISDN

The compelling goal of the implementers of ISDN is the wholesale upgrade of the global telecommunications infrastructure utilizing the dramatic advances in electronic and computer technology of the past quarter century. As the name ISDN implies, the result is not only a network that is more efficient at doing the same tasks as the telephone network performs today, but one that enables new applications that were impractical in a network originally designed only for voice. Integrated services represent the combination of voice and data on a single, all-digital, network. This means more than voice and data communications sharing the same wire, it implies a synergistic relationship between voice and data information. Two examples of this synergy are: digitized voice stored on the hard disk drive of a personal computer, providing voice store-and-forward capability as well as voice-annotated e-mail; and providing an insurance agent with the ability to automatically call up a customer's policy data file whenever the customer calls. In the latter case, the agent's terminal is connected to the host computer via the same telephone line that is used for the voice call. The calling party's telephone number is automatically used to access the data file.

The key to ISDN is that it is totally digital from end to end. The present telephone network utilizes analog lines to transmit both voice and data (via a modem) between the user's site (customer's premises) and the telephone switching network. These analog lines have a restricted bandwidth of about 3 kHz. While it is true that the portion of the telephone network that connects one central office to another is primarily digital, the connection between the customer's premises and the central office is analog. This is called the **analog subscriber loop.** To oversimplify things, ISDN replaces this analog subscriber loop with a totally digital path, providing two 64 Kbps voice and/or data connections and a 16 Kbps signaling/data channel. This is referred to as the ISDN Basic Rate Interface (BRI). Obviously, there is more to ISDN than this, and we will go into detail later, but the totally digital nature of ISDN is the key.

REBUILDING THE NETWORK

ISDN as an Environment

From the user's standpoint, ISDN is the environment in which the system exists, as opposed to being part of the system. ISDN provides a worldwide, standardized, virtually seamless interconnection capability, but does not specify how this capability is to be used. The designer or manager of the computer network/system is free to take advantage of ISDN's global interconnectivity and voice/data synergy, without being hampered by incompatible protocol standards. The designer is not constrained by preconceived notions of how the network is to be used.

The universal nature of the network extends past the physical layer of voltage levels and connector pinouts, to data transmission protocols and software standards. ISDN is based on CCITT standards, conforming to the ISO-OSI seven-layer model. It is the fact that the international standards precede the existence of the network that leads to its seamlessness.

The ISDN Landscape

Channels The digital portions of the present telephone network are based on a 64 Kbps channel (voice is digitized as 8,000 eight-bit words per second). In general, ISDN retains this basic 64 Kbps rate, but allows it to be used for either voice or data.

ISDN service is divided into two classes, basic rate and primary rate. The **basic rate service** provides two 64 Kbps channels for either voice or data—referred to as bearer, or B channels, and a 16 Kbps signaling/data channel, labeled the D channel, for call control and low speed, up to 9,600 bps, packet data. This "2B plus D" capability is the standard service provided to the user; i.e., the telephone jack on the wall in a person's office provides the basic rate interface. **Primary rate service** provides a combination of 23 B channels and one 64 Kbps D channel. (In Europe, primary rate service is 30 B channels plus one D channel because the European inter-office trunk network is based on a 2.048 Mbps data rate instead of the 1.544 Mbps rate used in North America.) This "23B plus D" service is used primarily to connect central offices to PBXs, mainframe (or mini) computers, and network-based servers. The general idea is that the B channels from all of the basic rate interfaces are gathered by the switch, PBX, or central office (Centrex service), and routed within the switch to other local basic rate interfaces, or routed to distant basic rate interfaces via other switches and primary rate interswitch trunk lines, or concentrated and routed to a local or remote computing facility via primary rate lines. There are other options, such as providing primary rate service all the way to the user's desk, but these are the predominant configurations.

The bandwidth of the primary rate interface can be partitioned in ways other than 23B plus D. For instance, one D channel can support its associated 23 B channels, plus 24 B channels from each of an additional three primary rate interfaces. Alternately, the bandwidth of the primary rate channel can be partitioned into four 384 Kbps H0 channels, or one 1.536 Mbps H11 channel (1.92 Mbps H12 channel in Europe). H0 channels can be used in combination with 64 Kbps B channels on the same primary rate line.

Network Topography

Independent of whether basic or primary rate service is provided, the network topography from the desktop to the switch is the same. Figure 17.1 shows this topography, identifying reference points that make up the network. In addition, certain specific classes of equipment are defined. At each of the reference points the CCITT has established, or is in the process of establishing, standards for both hardware and software.

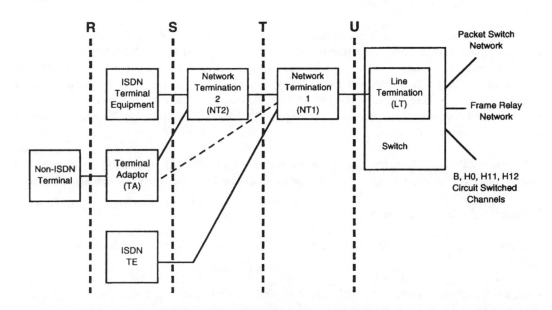

Figure 17.1   ISDN network topography. The physical connection between a piece of terminal equipment and the public network is divided into segments. These segments, shown here by vertical dashed lines, are call reference points (R, S, T, and U). The various international standards that define ISDN describe the operation of the network at each of these reference points. Separate standards (referred to officially as recommendations) exist for each of the appropriate layers of the ISO model at each reference point. For example, CCITT Recommendation I.430 defines the layer 1 operation of the basic rate S interface.

R Reference Point The R reference point establishes the boundary between non-ISDN compatible equipment and the network. Terminal adapters (TA) are used to convert the communication protocol used by the non-ISDN compatible terminal to the desired basic rate or primary rate protocol. It should be mentioned at this point that the network does not specify the data protocol used on either the B or H channels; all the network sees is a stream of bits. As a practical matter, however, standard protocols such as V.110, V.120, I.122, and X.25 are used.

S Reference Point The S reference point provides the connection between the NT2 equipment and the terminal equipment (TE) or terminal adapter (TA). If no NT2 is present, there is no S reference point. In this case, the TE or TA is connected directly to an NT1 device, and the interface is designated as a T reference point. Both primary rate and basic rate services can be provided at the S reference point. NT1 and NT2 devices will be discussed in some detail later.

It should be noted that it is common to refer to the four-wire basic rate service specified by CCITT recommendation I.430 as S interface service. While it is true that the S reference point is most often implemented this way, a two-wire basic rate interface or a primary rate interface can also be used at the S reference point. Additionally, the four-wire interface can be used to provide the U reference point. To keep the ISDN alphabet soup straight, it is important to remember that the various reference points identify the connection points between equipment classes, and not the specific implementation or protocol of the interconnection.

T Reference Point The T reference point connects NT1 devices to TAs or TEs. In addition, the T reference point provides the connection between an NT1 and an NT2. This NT1/NT2 connection is a bit of a canard since the user never sees the interface in practice, but it is useful to keep the network organization straight. In a PBX, for example, the line circuit that connects to the network in the upstream direction (U reference point) provides the NT1 function, and the line circuit that connects to the TE or TA equipment (S reference point) provides the NT2 function. The T reference point in this case is internal to the PBX.

U Reference Point The U reference point connects the LT to the NT1. Normally, a two-wire basic rate interface or a primary rate line is used, but the four-wire basic rate interface can also be used.

Equipment Classification

The equipment comprising the network is classified based on function and location within the network.

Line Termination Starting from the network and moving toward the user we have the Line Termination (LT), which is located in the telephone company's switch, often at the central office. The D channel is terminated at the LT, meaning that layers 2 and 3 of the OSI protocol are performed at this point. (The D channel is terminated at any point where switching of the B channels takes place.)

Network Termination Directly downstream of the LT is the Network Termination device (NT). There are two types of NTs—NT1 and NT2.

The NT1 performs such functions as line length extension (repeaters) and two-wire to four-wire conversion (U to S interface). A defining characteristic of NT1 devices is that they only deal with layer 1 of the OSI seven-layer model. Layer 1 involves electrical signal levels, the format of physical channels (such as the B and D channels), and sometimes network maintenance. One of the key issues for NT1 devices is power. At least in North America, the line termination does not feed power down the line toward the NT1. Thus, the NT1 must be powered locally.

NT2s are intelligent and actively participate in the call routing/control process. PBXs and line concentrators are examples of NT2 devices. (A PBX actually contains both an NT1 and an NT2, with the T reference point being contained internal to the switch.) Additionally, NT2 devices can be connected to multiple types of ISDN lines simultaneously.

Terminal Equipment   Further downstream is the Terminal Equipment (TE). TEs represent computers, telephones, data terminals, etc., which are directly compatible with the ISDN. The TE terminates the B (or H) and D channels.

Terminal Adapter   The last class of equipment is the Terminal Adapter (TA). TAs are the "box modems" of the ISDN world. They provide for the connection of non-ISDN compatible equipment to the network, i.e., existing equipment.

PROTOCOLS AND STANDARDS

ISDN is structured around the ISO-OSI seven-layer model. Layers 1, 2, and 3 provide the basic network infrastructure, while the higher layers provide services that are more specific to the user's system environment and application. For example, layers 3 and below are not dependent on the specific operating system, user interface, or application used in a TE, while layers 4 and above are. We will, for the most part, concern ourselves with the first three layers.

Layer 1

Layer 1 is the physical layer and is concerned with wire types, connector pinouts, encoding schemes, voltage levels, and the like. There are several layer 1 standards used in ISDN, including the I.430 four-wire basic rate interface, the 2B1Q (2 binary, 1 quaternary) and 4B3T (4 binary, 3 ternary) two-wire basic rate interface standards, and the G.703 primary rate standard. The four-wire basic rate interface is primarily, but not exclusively, used on the customer's premises to provide either the S or T connections.

One of the key characteristics of the I.430 interface is that it provides for multidropping of several terminals on a single line. This is referred to as a **passive bus configuration.** A typical office application would have a four-wire interface running to the desk where an ISDN telephone and an ISDN-equipped PC would share the same line. Recall that the basic rate interface provides two independent 64 Kbps channels that can be used for either voice or data.

The two-wire interfaces are primarily used for longer distance connections from the telephone company to the customer's premises (U reference point). The two-wire standards are designed to use the existing wire pairs currently providing the analog subscriber loop. While the two-wire schemes provide greater distance capabilities and use fewer wires, the electronics cost significantly more money and do not provide multidrop capability.

The primary rate interface is designed to use the existing T1 (CEPT in Europe) transmission facilities, and for the most part are compatible with T1 at layer 1.

Layer 2

Layer 2 is the link layer of the seven-layer OSI model and is responsible for the transmission of data from point to point. On the D channel, all data is sent as HDLC-like packets using the Link Access Protocol—D channel (LAPD). LAPD is an expansion of its LAPB predecessor used in X.25. The key new capability added to LAPD is the ability to support multiple logical connections on a single physical channel. On the B channel, there is no single protocol specified. It is a 64 Kbps clear channel. There are, however, several common layer 2 protocol standards, including LAPB and LAPD for X.25, LAPD (slightly modified) for V.120, SDLC for SNA, and a bit replication–based rate adaptation protocol for V.110. Of these, V.120 is perhaps of the most interest since it is the first real international standard for statistical multiplexing.

Layer 3

Layer 3 is the network layer of the seven-layer model. On the D channel, layer 3 provides the call control functions (call set-up/teardown) as well as packet data handling functions. CCITT Q.931 and Q.932 are used for call control. The X.25 packet layer protocol and layer 3 of V.120 are most often used for packet data.

SOFTWARE STRUCTURE

As mentioned before, ISDN is built along the lines of the ISO/OSI seven-layer model. This is of greater importance from a software standpoint than from a hardware point of view. Figure 17.2 shows the structure of the AmLink3™ ISDN code stack, supporting layer 3 and below. The AmLink3 software, which is a commercially available product from Advanced Micro Devices, is representative of practical ISDN software implementations.

Layer 1

Layer 1 of the code stack is responsible for interacting with and supporting the establishment of the physical channel. Tasks include the activation of the S, T, or U interface; support of network maintenance functions such as loopbacks; establishment and support of the R interface; and more. In general, the actual implementation of the layer 1 functions is hardware specific, meaning that this piece of code is not portable between hardware implementations using different ICs. As a consequence, the AmLink3 code partitions these functions into Low-level Driver (LLD) modules that are IC specific. This allows the higher-layer software to be completely hardware independent.

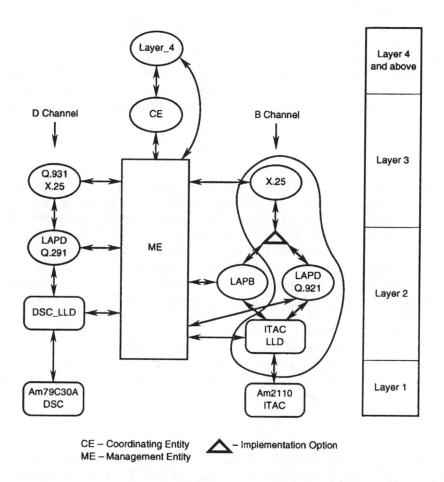

Figure 17.2   AmLink3™ ISDN software block diagram. ISDN software is divided into modules that perform specific B or D channel functions at each of the ISO layers. The arrows indicate the communications flow between the modules.

Layer 2–

There are a number of tasks that are hardware dependent, such as the movement of B and D channel data between the actual IC and memory-resident buffers, address recognition, and packet status reporting. These functions are a part of layer 2, but are not directly part of the LAPB or LAPD layer 2+ protocol. (LAPB and LAPD just assume that these functions are taken care of.) It is desirable to create a separation between these hardware-dependent tasks and the formal LAPB and LAPD software. Collectively, we will refer to these tasks as the layer 2 minus (or layer 2–) sublayer and the LAPB and LAPD functions as layer 2 plus (or layer 2+). In the AmLink3 software implementation, layer 2– is part of the LLD module. The layer 2– code sits directly on top of the hardware, communicating directly with the ICs' physical registers (and physical addresses). The interface between the layer 2– and LAPB or LAPD layer 2+ software is via command and event mailboxes, with **commands** coming from the higher layer to the lower layer and **events** being reported to the higher layer from the lower layer. The layer 2– software also communicates with the management entity via command and event mailboxes. (We will discuss the management entity in more detail later.)

Layer 2+

In ISDN, the only layer 2+ protocol allowed on the D channel is LAPD. This is not true of the B channel, which can use virtually any protocol. In practice, LAPB and LAPD are the most common protocols used on the B channel. Both LAPB and LAPD provide for guaranteed transmission of data packets across the layer 1 channel. LAPD supports multiple logical connections over a given physical channel. LAPB does not. In the AmLink3 software implementation there is a single LAPB module and a single LAPD module. The LAPB module supports simultaneous communication on both B channels. The LAPD module supports simultaneous communication on multiple logical connections on the D channel and on both B channels. The LAPB and LAPD modules each communicate with the management entity via their own mailboxes. Communication with layer 3 is via mailboxes associated with each of the various layer 3 modules.

The use of a single layer 2+ module for both B and D channels points out the benefit of the layered structure. In this case, not only can a single LAPD module support multiple logical connections on both B and D channels simultaneously, but the layer 3 X.25 module can be fed by either LAPB or LAPD from the B channel, and also from LAPD on the D channel.

Layer 3

The D channel supports both call control functions as well as packet data services, while the B channel need only be concerned with packet data. The D channel call control, or network signaling, functions are specified by the CCITT Q.931 and Q.932 standards. Virtually any packet based layer 3 protocol can be used for the data service. (The AmLink3 package provides an X.25 module for layer 3 data service.) The result is that layer 2 provides two types of data to layer 3, either signaling (D channel) or packet (B or D channel) data. This information, either signaling or packet data, is communicated between peer layer 3 entities, i.e., the layer 3 entity in an ISDN terminal communicates with the layer 3 entity in a mainframe computer. To do this, each end of the conversation utilizes the services of its respective layer 2 and layer 1 entities.

Each of the two layer 3 entities, signaling and packet data, have their own mailboxes to the management entity and to the LAPB and LAPD layer 2 entities. The interface with layer 4 is a bit more complex since layer 4 does not know about B and D channels. To solve this problem, a Coordinating Entity (CE) is used between the layer 3 and 4 entities.

Coordinating Entity (CE)

The software entity at layer 4 knows very little about ISDN. The details are hidden from it by the layered nature of the protocol—after all, this is the purpose of the seven-layer model. This creates a problem since layer 3 is made up of separate B and D channel entities (network signaling and user data) and layer 4 sees layer 3 as a single entity. A layer 4 to 3 conversation might go something like this: "Here is some data to send to so and so. I don't care how you send it, just tell me when he acknowledges receipt of the data." Something must exist at the layer 3 to 4 boundary that can understand this message and translate it into specific instructions to the layer 3 B and D channel entities. This something is called the Coordinating Entity (CE). The CE communicates with the management entity, network signaling entity, and the packet data entity via separate mailboxes.

The CE to layer 4 communication is also via command and event mailboxes. This is particularly important in applications such as a PC add-on board where two processors are often utilized. In the AmLink3 code, this is where the line is drawn between what is run on the communications processor (layers 1–3), and tasks left for the system processor (layers 4–7). The actual mailbox structure is usually constructed using a shared memory arrangement such as dual-port RAM.

Management Entity (ME)

Cleanly layered software is very nice in textbook applications, but the real world is rarely so accommodating. Such is the case with practical ISDN implementations. The problem is not any shortcoming of either the concept of layering in general, or of the ISDN model in specific. The problem is one of global services that are required by all layers. Examples of these services include timers, buffer allocation, and message exchange (mailbox support) mechanisms. These services are provided by the system and cannot be partitioned into any one of the layers. To get around this problem, a new entity is required, the Management Entity (ME). Each of the various layer entities passes requests for support to the ME via its mailbox mechanism. In return, the ME performs the required function, e.g., the allocation of a memory buffer to the layer 2– D channel handler, passing the response back through the mailbox.

One other note before we leave the discussion of software structure. ISDN software, by its nature, operates in a real-time multitasking environment. This implies the support of a real-time multitasking operating system kernel. The layers 1 through 3 code stack and the ME both sit on top of the real-time OS, relying on it for task scheduling functions.

OPEN STANDARDS ISSUES

With respect to the D channel, layer 2 (CCITT Q.921, LAPD) is essentially complete, while layer 3 is still being worked on. Q.931, which specifies the basic call set-up and teardown procedures, is stable. Q.932 (supplementary services such as placing a call on hold) is still being finalized. At present, each switch manufacturer has its own variation of layer 3 software that works only on its switch. As the standards are completed, more and more of the incompatibilities will be eliminated. However, it will be some time before there is a single layer 3 software package that works with all switches. Most commercially available software packages, such as the AmLink3 package, support the majority of ISDN switches via compile-time options. Having said this, it is important to keep in mind that compatibility is a fundamental goal of ISDN and in the United States the "National ISDN 1" goes a long way toward providing a single standard supported by all equipment manufacturers.

On the B channel, V.110 and DMI (AT&T's Digital Multiplexed Interface, which uses LAPD at layer 2 and X.25 at layer 3) are stable. Basic V.120 is essentially complete, but enhancements are still being worked on in the standards committees.

TERMINAL EQUIPMENT AND TERMINAL ADAPTERS

Having looked at the structure of the network and the organization of the software, it is time to take a look at ISDN terminal equipment. The variety of possible types of terminals and terminal adapters is unlimited. Some of these are of particular interest, specifically telephones, PC add-on boards, integrated voice/data terminals, adapters for async and SDLC video data terminals, D channel only terminals, and LAN gateways.

Telephones

From the user's perspective, an ISDN telephone is not much different from its analog or proprietary digital (PBX and key system) counterparts. The difference is that the ISDN telephone can take advantage of the global digital signaling environment provided by the ISDN D channel. While many of the ISDN features, such as displaying the number of an incoming call, are offered today by non-ISDN PBXs, the features only work at a local level. The features offered by an ISDN telephone are an evolutionary extension of those offered by modern PBXs. The revolutionary aspect of ISDN is that these features/services can now be standardized across the entire network, independent of the equipment vendor.

The ISDN telephone itself differs from its analog predecessors in that the voice signal is converted to digital form inside the telephone, as opposed to the central office. This eliminates any voice quality degradation caused by the analog connection between the telephone and the central office. The cost of this improved quality is complexity. Digital telephones require significantly more hardware than their analog counterparts. In return, additional features are possible, and the interface to those features can be made more friendly (displays, etc.). ISDN telephones are somewhat more complex even than proprietary digital telephones since they must conform to the ISDN software protocols—the benefits of standardization are not without cost.

PC/Workstation ISDN Boards

These boards provide ISDN connectivity to a personal computer or workstation, supporting either data or voice and data. This also allows PCs to be networked without the cost of additional cabling, since the existing telephone lines can be used for both voice and data. Figure 17.3 shows a block diagram of a typical implementation. There are three major issues concerning the incorporation of ISDN into a PC or workstation:

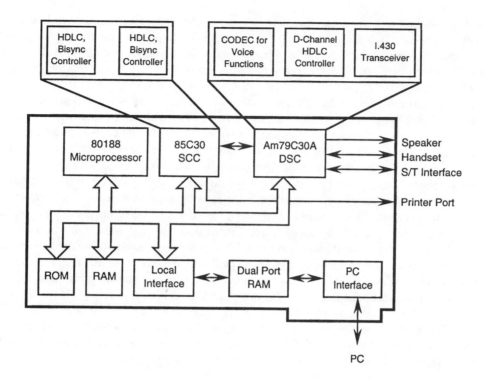

Figure 17.3   PC add-on board. In a PC or workstation environment it is common to use a dedicated microprocessor to handle the tasks at and below layer 3. The 85C30 dual serial communication controller provides protocol support for both B channels. The Am79C30A device provides the voice codec functions, the D channel LAPD hardware, and the layer 1 S/T interface transceiver. Communication between the ISDN board and the PC is via dual-port RAM.

1. Does the main microprocessor in the PC or workstation run the ISDN software below layer 4, or is there a dedicated processor on the add-on board?
2. What data protocols does the board support?
3. How are the voice telephone functions handled?

The question of one or two processors depends on how the ISDN services are to be used. In applications where data communication via the ISDN is infrequent, such as printing, the PC or workstation's microprocessor is sufficient. In applications that involve fairly heavy data traffic that must run in the background, an intelligent ISDN add-on board is required. The ISDN software protocol stack is fairly processor intensive, involving a fair amount of real-time processing. If the PC's or workstation's microprocessor is used to run this code, there is little extra processing power available for other tasks. If an intelligent add-on board is used, the PC's or workstation's microprocessor need only run the layers 4 through 7 functions, leaving it free to run other user applications.

The issue of protocol support is driven by the application. For the most part, X.25 and V.120 protocols will be used at the lower layers, but this is dictated by the protocol used by the computer/network that the PC/workstation is communicating with. The key point is that ISDN provides low error rate 64 Kbps data pipes (basic rate). These pipes are transparent and do not impose any specific protocol on the user.

A network that provides for the integration of voice and data creates the opportunity for many interesting applications, such as voice-annotated e-mail, PC/workstation–based voice mail with a clean graphical user interface, speech recognition/response, etc. (If you have ever used a voice mail system, I do not need to tell you that the telephone based user interface is less than optimum.)

The problem is how do you merge the PC/workstation with the telephone? One option is to build the telephone functions into the computer. Attempts to market such products in the past have met with little success for a number of reasons, but principally because such a combination restricts the user's freedom to choose his computer and telephone vendors, and it does not allow the computer to be placed on a table while the telephone is placed on the user's desk. A second option is to connect the telephone to the ISDN board in the computer. This allows the use of a separate telephone, while still providing a connection between the voice path and the ISDN board, enabling the voice information to be processed or stored in the computer. This is the approach most prevalent today. The only consideration with this approach is the nature of the interface to the telephone. If the ISDN board provides a traditional analog telephone interface, any existing standard telephone can be used, but the user will not have access to all of the interesting telephone services provided by the ISDN. If an ISDN S interface connection is provided, a standard ISDN telephone can be used, providing full ISDN capability. The restriction is that the existing analog telephone must be replaced.

Integrated Voice/Data Terminal

This is a native mode ISDN-based terminal that provides both voice and data capabilities. Terminals of this type are generally used in applications where data entry/retrieval occurs in combination with a phone call. For example, a client's insurance or medical file could be called up automatically whenever he calls his agent or doctor. This is possible since the terminal has access to the calling party's telephone number, which could be used to access his file. Figure 17.4 shows an example of an IV/D terminal.

Integrated voice/data terminals generally are based on a single processor architecture. This is practical since the processor overhead of the terminal functions is typically less than the overhead in a PC or workstation, and communications is a fundamental task for the terminal. This holds true even in a higher-end environment, such as an X-Windows terminal.

Adapters for Non-ISDN Terminals

These adapters are used to convert the serial communication channel of a non-ISDN terminal into an ISDN-compatible format. In effect, terminal adapters can be thought of as modem replacements.

The TA must perform several functions:

- Establish an end-to-end connection across the network
- Translate the data protocol/rate used by the terminal to a protocol/rate compatible with the network

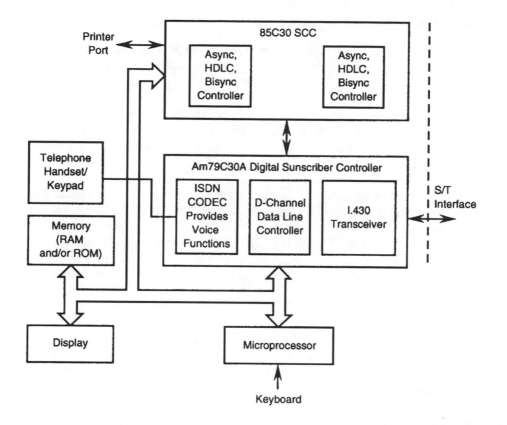

Figure 17.4   Integrated voice/data terminal. In a terminal designed to use ISDN as its serial communications link with the host computer, a single processor is usually sufficient for both communications and terminal operations tasks. The 85C30 dual serial communication controller provides protocol support for one channel and a printer port. The Am79C30A device provides the voice codec functions, the D channel LAPD hardware, and the layer 1 S/T interface transceiver.

- Transmit the data
- Reconvert the data to the original terminal protocol/rate
- Optionally, check for errors

The TA has two distinct interfaces, one to the host and one to the network. The host side interface is some serial protocol, such as RS-232, over which the user data and control information is passed. The network side is an ISDN S interface connection providing two B channels for user data, and one D channel for controlling the call.

The TA receives two types of information from the host (terminal or PC): user data to be transmitted to the terminal across the network and control information such as the address of the terminal to be called; and, in the case of stand-alone TAs, flow control commands (such as XON/XOFF).

Establishing the Connection

User data is conveyed from one S Reference Point to another via 64 Kbps channels. These B channels are circuit switched, meaning that an end-to-end connection is established for the duration of the call (as opposed to a connectionless network such as Ethernet). B channel connections are established by using the D channel.

The call set-up, maintenance, and teardown procedures are handled by software using the Q.921 LAPD protocol at layer 2 and the Q.931 protocol at layer 3. The problem, of course, is that terminals and PCs know nothing about D channels or Q.9xx protocols. In the case of a stand-alone TA, the control information is received from the terminal over the serial interface in the same format that would be used with a traditional modem.

The Q.921 and Q.931 protocol software is relatively complex. Depending on whether it is written in assembly language or in a higher-level language such as C, 32 Kbps–256 Kbps bytes of memory are required in the TA to store the program. From a processing power standpoint, an 8-bit microcontroller with external ROM, such as an 80C31, has sufficient power to handle the call control functions. If the TA uses a software-intensive protocol for handling the user data in addition to the Q.9xx call control functions, a 16-bit microprocessor, such as an 80C186, is required.

Sending the Data

Once a B channel connection is established between the two DTEs (Data Terminal Equipment), user data can be exchanged. The user data is received from the terminal via the serial interface at a rate that can be anything from 300 bps to 64 Kbps. The TA must then "rate adapt" the data up to 64 Kbps before it is transmitted.

Data Reception

On the surface, this seems straightforward enough: Simply receive the serial bit stream, perform the reverse of the protocol conversion process, and give the data to the DTE in the expected form. While the 64 Kbps data rate of the network is common to the TAs at both ends, the clock rates of the serial interfaces to the terminals is not. This mismatch can cause a buffer overflow problem. The problem is solved by a technique known as **rate adaptation** (often referred to as **rate adaption**). In a rate adaptation scheme, the receiving side transmits information back to the sender as to whether the sending side's clock leads or lags its own clock. The sending device can then make the necessary adjustments. If the sending clock leads the receiving clock, the sender must slow down. Since the TA does not normally have any control over the terminal's serial interface clock, the TA must either buffer the excess data and/or initiate flow control (XON/XOFF, etc.) to slow down the data coming from the terminal. If the sending clock lags the receiving clock, the receiver must make up the difference by increasing the idle time between characters sent to the receiving terminal. (Often this is done by stretching the stop bit by fractions of a bit time.)

Error Control

Some protocols provide a means of checking to make sure that the received data is correct. This is protocol specific. It is one of the fundamental influences on the choice of protocols.

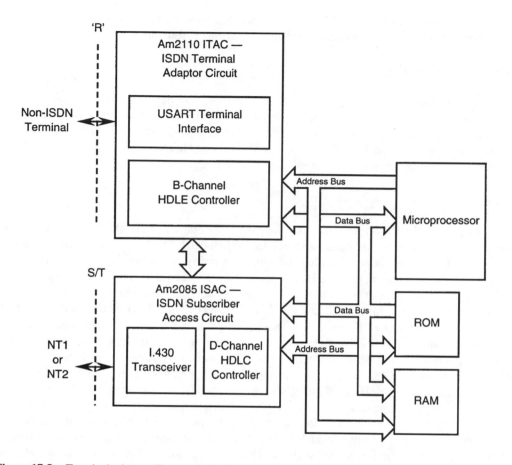

Figure 17.5   Terminal adapter. The terminal adapter performs a translation function, allowing the connection of non-ISDN compatible terminals to the network. The terminal connects to the Am2110 IC in the terminal adapter using the terminal's normal serial protocol. The Am2110, with the help of the microprocessor, converts the data rate to 64 Kbps and the data format to the protocol being used on the network. The Am2085 provides the D channel LAPD hardware and the layer 1 S/T interface transceiver.

Protocol Choices

As mentioned, the TA requires three different sets of protocols, one for interfacing to the terminal, one for interfacing with the network, and one for establishing the connection across the network. On the terminal side of a stand-alone TA, the vast majority of serial communication is asynchronous (approximately 75 percent), with the rest being packet-oriented protocols such as Bisync, SDLC, HDLC, LAPB, LAPD, etc. The choice of terminal interface protocol is dictated by existing interface on the terminal. The TA is chosen to match the protocol used by the terminal. The network protocol can theoretically be any 64 Kbps synchronous mechanism, but in practice is one of a small set of standards, such as V.110 or V.120. The network access protocol is the ISDN D-channel–based call

Q.921 (LAPD) and Q.931 layers 2 and 3 protocol stack. Since we have already discussed the network access protocol in detail, we will concentrate on the B channel protocol.

B Channel Protocols

On the ISDN network side, two basic protocols are used: bit padding and packet oriented (LAPB or LAPD primarily). These two usually take the form of V.110 and V.120 respectively. Each has advantages and disadvantages. V.110 requires less processing power and memory and is, therefore, less expensive to implement. V.120 makes more efficient use of the 64 Kbps bandwidth of the ISDN B channel and provides error detection/recovery at layer 2.

V.110

The V.110 protocol had its origin in Europe where it was first developed by the European Computer Manufacturers Association (the standard was called ECMA-102). ECMA-102 was combined with a similar CCITT protocol that only handled synchronous terminals to form the CCITT V.110 recommendation. V.110 is more prevalent in Europe than in North America or Asia.

Bit-padding protocols such as V.110 receive a serial bit stream from a terminal, convert it up to a 64 Kbps synchronous stream by replication of data bits, and transmit it across the ISDN over the B channel. At the receiving end, the padding is stripped, the data rate is adapted to the local terminal's clock, and the data is sent out in the same form as it was received from the originating terminal. The input from the terminal can be asynchronous (RS-232) at any of the standard baud rates up to 19.2 Kbps, or synchronous at 48, 56, or 64 Kbps. Asynchronous inputs are converted up to the closest intermediate speed, either 8, 16, or 32 Kbps. Multiple intermediate rate channels can be multiplexed together, or a single intermediate rate bit stream can be further padded up to the 64 Kbps B channel rate. For example, four separate 9.6 Kbps channels each convert to 16 Kbps bit streams that are multiplexed into a single 64 Kbps stream. While the V.110 protocol supports multiple channel subrate multiplexing, it is not common to find such capability in a stand-alone TA, since most stand-alone units are designed to connect directly to a single terminal.

V.110 does not provide any error detection/recovery capabilities. Error detection and recovery is left to the layers above layer 2, between the two terminals. This is a drawback when the TA is used with a "dumb" terminal, since most terminals have very limited error recovery capabilities.

V.120

V.120 is a packet-oriented protocol, based on a slight variant of HDLC-based LAPD protocol used on the ISDN D channel. Data is received from a terminal and placed in memory. When a sufficient number of bytes have been received, they are combined into a packet that includes an opening flag character, an address field, a control field, the user data, a CRC field for error control and a closing flag. This packet is then transmitted over the B channel. The packet protocol performs error detection (CRC) and automatic retransmission of packets received with errors.

V.120 allows statistical multiplexing via LAPD's inherent support of multiple logical channels. This is of significance for building statistical multiplexers as well as for supporting multiple logical pipes in a multiple window environment. The major drawback to V.120 is the current instability of

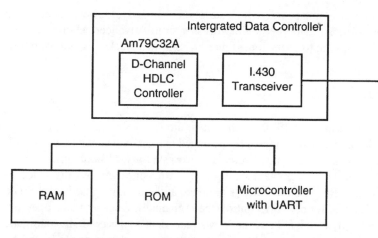

Figure 17.6   D channel only terminal. In some applications, only low-speed data, 9.6 Kbps, are required. A terminal that utilizes the ISDN D channel packet data capability can provide this function without using the B channels. The Am79C32A device provides the D channel LAPD hardware and the layer 1 S/T interface transceiver. Voice support can be added by using the Am79C30A device instead of the Am79C32A.

the standard itself. The standard has many options. It is likely that only a subset of the options will be supported by the majority of TA vendors. The question is what subset?

D Channel Only Terminals

There are many applications that require repeated low-speed transmission of data to one or more destinations. Packet data networks are ideal for this type of communication. Presently, devices such as credit card verification terminals, security systems, and remote telemetry (such as cash register–based inventory control) use dial-up modems for access to public or private packet networks. ISDN terminals that support only the D channel can be used as access points into these networks, since the D channel supports 9.6 Kbps LAPD packet data communications at layer 2 and can use X.25 at layer 3. Figure 17.6 shows a block diagram of a D channel only terminal adapter.

A variant on this theme is the addition of D channel packet data support to an ISDN telephone. Essentially this is a combination telephone/terminal adapter, where the terminal data is carried on the D channel. The telephone typically has an RS-232 connector for interfacing to the serial port of a terminal of PC. Data received from the RS-232 interface is packetized using the same hardware and layer 2 software that the telephone uses for call control over the D channel.

LAN Gateways

ISDN will not replace high-speed LANs. Instead, gateways between the LAN and the ISDN will provide global communications capabilities to the LAN environment. The trick is to make the new system as seamless as possible. As a rule, the more seamless an internetworking environment, the higher the required processing power in the gateway. Fortunately, the new generation of RISC-based processors, such as the Am29000™ microprocessor from Advanced Micro Devices, provides the level of processing required to do the job. Figure 17.7 shows a block diagram of an Ethernet-to-ISDN gateway.

New Capabilities

The most interesting aspect of ISDN is the integration of voice and data on the same network. Traditionally, voice and data functions have belonged in their own separate worlds. There have been numerous attempts to market integrated voice/data workstations, without much success. The problem was that there was no way to create a synergistic relationship between the voice and data. ISDN changes this equation. Because the voice is digitized at the terminal and because a common digital signaling channel is used for network control (the D channel), voice and data operations can now be linked. We have already discussed a scenario where a client's files could be automatically called up on a terminal whenever he called his doctor, insurance agent, stock broker, etc. This is but one example of the new services that are enabled by integrating voice and data on one network. Another example is PC/workstation–based voice store and forward. Since voice is digitized in the ISDN terminal, an ISDN-equipped computer can be used for this purpose, with the voice being stored on the PC's hard disk. The advantage of this is that the PC can be used to provide a user-friendly interface, for example, displaying on the screen the list of received messages, allowing random selection of messages. Voice-annotated e-mail is an extension of this concept, whereby digitized voice is stored along with

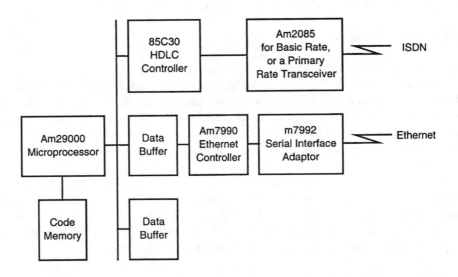

Figure 17.7 ISDN/Ethernet gateway. ISDN allows LANs in separate cities to be interconnected. The 85C30 dual serial communication controller provides protocol support for both B channels. The Am2085 provides the D channel LAPD hardware and the layer 1 S/T interface transceiver. The Am7990/7992 pair provide the Ethernet interface. An Am29000 RISC-embedded processor controls the gateway.

an e-mail message. It works like this: Person A sends person B the text of an upcoming press release via e-mail asking for comments. Person B reviews the text, inserting verbal comments much as he would make notes in the margin of a hard copy of the text. He then e-mails the press release with comments back to person A, who can listen to the comments and edit the press release as required.

18

CCITT RECOMMENDATION X.25: PACKET SWITCHING AND BEYOND

Fred M. Burg

INTRODUCTION

CCITT Recommendation X.25 is a simple phrase that is often taken to embody a wide range of networking concepts. Usually this range goes well beyond what was intended by CCITT. Recommendation X.25 (or X.25 for short) was never meant to provide a full networking solution. However, the bounds of X.25—what is included and what is excluded—has been a source of confusion to many for almost two decades.

This chapter will examine what Recommendation X.25 is and is not. This will not be a trivial task. One could focus on X.25 as an interface—the first word in its title—and miss the big picture of how it relates to the total communications puzzle. This puzzle involves standards (actually both CCITT Recommendations and ISO/IEC Standards) that both complement and supplement X.25. During its first decade of existence, many of the complementary standards were developed; others are still being developed today. In the early and mid 1980s, work began on supplementing X.25 to the point that what is meant by X.25 in data communications circles has expanded beyond the myopic view of just being an interface. In fact, the expanded meaning of X.25 has taken us to the point where it, along with its companion set of standards, does indeed provide for a full networking platform.

Nevertheless, Recommendation X.25 has been a major factor in the area of data communications for the past eighteen years. It has been the basis for wide area networking on a worldwide basis—most providers of data transport services have implemented it in their networks. Likewise, major computer vendors offer X.25 across their product lines for connecting to these networks. Many value-added environments, such as bulletin boards and news services, depend on it for transport and connectivity. Now as we move forward to new technologies, such as OSI, ISDN, Broadband ISDN, etc., it might appear that the role of X.25 may start to diminish. However, this is far from the truth. Not only is X.25 a viable service for the future in its own right, but X.25 has served as a basis for many of the concepts embodied in these emerging technologies. For example, some providers of X.25 services offer speeds in the megabit/second range; likewise, X.25 offers advanced features, like call forwarding, that are also available to ISDN users.

ORIGINS OF X.25

In 1972, CCITT had standardized Recommendation X.21 [1] as a method for connecting two data terminal equipments (DTEs) through a **circuit-switched public data network (CSPDN).** This work brought a combination of concepts to the standards table:

- the recognition of a **dedicated network** for data communications;
- the use of a **public network** for sharing networking equipment among customers to gain cost advantages; and
- the availability of the user's full communications bandwidth through the network (i.e., circuit mode of communication), whether it was actually used or not, for connecting its DTE to another DTE on a permanent (dedicated) or temporary (switched) basis; in the latter case, the bandwidth could be reused for communicating with another DTE once the connection to the first DTE was released.

While users were able to accept the first two aspects in the early 1970s, it was the third part that still caused concern. Given the relatively high costs of communications facilities at that time, the inefficiencies and wastefulness of allocating a fixed amount of resources, even if only for a temporary period, were unacceptable. Many instances of communications were of a bursty nature that did not justify large amounts of bandwidth on a continuous basis (for example, between a host computer and a terminal) while others (say between two host computers) required fixed resources for a longer duration. Moreover, some systems needed to communicate with many others simultaneously—for example, a database communicating with several hundred or thousand terminals at the same time. Such communication scenarios made it cumbersome, at best, to have to connect and then reconnect the circuit-switched connection to one destination and then another.

Furthermore, the benefits of packet switching were also starting to be recognized in the early 1970s. With the successes of the ARPAnet in the United States and the introduction of IBM's Systems Network Architecture (SNA) at about this time, the need for a companion standard for packet switching was quite apparent. Already several networking vendors were offering or planning a packet-switched mode of operation at that time (Telenet and Tymnet in the United States, DATAPAC in Canada, TRANSPAC in France, and DDX-P in Japan, as well as others). Technical work began in CCITT in 1974 on a new packet-switching standard and, two short years later, X.25 was adopted. [2]

Like X.21, X.25 was a "Recommendation." (The "X" denotes the series of Recommendations developed by CCITT's Study Group VII dealing specifically with public data networks.) The term "Recommendation" must be understood, however, in the context of the relationship between CCITT and its parent committee, the International Telecommunications Union (ITU). Most of CCITT's outputs are in the form of Recommendations to the ITU, the CCITT being a Consultative Committee created for recommending practices within the scope of its charter. Nevertheless, the Recommendations of CCITT are viewed as standards.

WHAT IS X.25?

Equally as important as knowing how X.25 works is understanding what X.25 is. While this has been discussed implicitly already, it is worthwhile examining more closely. For it is only by looking through a magnifying glass that one can start to understand what X.25 encompasses and what it excludes. The best way forward is to parse the title of Recommendation X.25 to see what it is all about.

The title, then, is:

Interface Between Data Terminal Equipment (DTE) and Data Circuit-Terminating Equipment (DCE) for Terminals Operating in the Packet Mode and Connected to Public Data Networks by Dedicated Circuit

From this above title, we see that X.25 addresses the following:

- first and foremost, X.25 describes an *interface;* as such, it specifies a set of services available at the interface and the allowed set of interactions by which these services are requested and received;
- the interface is between a DTE (user of service) and a DCE (provider of service); in the traditional meaning of telecommunications terms, the DCE can be viewed as the modem to which the DTE interfaces, where it is not important how the peer equipment (i.e., the X.25 packet switch) is connected to the modem; in a more contemporary view, the DTE side of the interface can be both the terminal and its modem while the DCE side is the X.25 packet switch plus its modem;
- although X.25 describes a single DTE/DCE interface, the goal, although perhaps only implicitly assumed, is to allow communications to take place between two users (i.e., DTEs) of the service without constraining the nature of that communication;
- the mode of operation of the terminal is the *packet mode,* as opposed to circuit mode (which X.21 describes), whereby messages are embedded in *packets* that have a distinct beginning and end; packets for one destination can be interleaved with packets for another;
- the terminal is to be connected to a network that is *public* (that is, open to all), as opposed to private;
- the network is dedicated to moving *data,* as opposed to voice or both voice and data; combined with the points above, the network is known as a *packet-switched public data network* (PSPDN);
- the connection between the DTE and DCE is to be by *dedicated circuit;* actually, this aspect was added in 1984 to distinguish connections whereby the network always knew who the customer was by virtue of the dedicated nature of the connection (and, therefore, was able to charge someone for its services), as opposed to cases where the connection was made dynamically (e.g., a *switched connection* via a dial-up line) whereby collection for services might not be possible.

Although it is not explicit in the title, X.25 only describes the behavior of a DCE as viewed at the DTE/DCE interface but it does not dictate how the DCE should operate internally. Figure 18.1 depicts the elements of X.25 described.

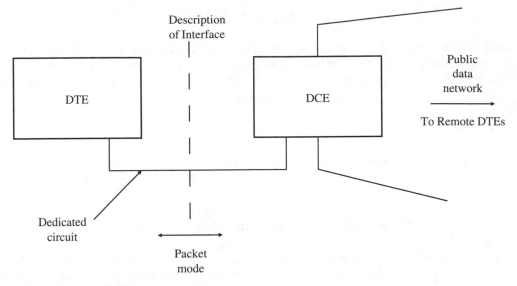

Figure 18.1 Elements of X.25.

From the description and Figure 18.1, it should now be clear, at least at a high level, what X.25 is. In contrast, we have also explicitly identified some aspects of communications that are outside the bounds of X.25 while inferring yet others. These items are equally important in gaining an understanding of what X.25 is not. Before delving into the details of how X.25 works, let us list these items.

X.25 does *not* address the following areas of communications:

- operations, administration, and maintenance (OA&M) procedures such as how a customer registers a DTE with the network to obtain service and specifies what services are desired;
- what services are required to be provided by the network and which ones are optional;
- how a DTE obtains service from the network when its interface to the network is via a switched connection instead of a dedicated line;
- how a DTE identifies the remote DTE with which it wishes to communicate; this aspect involves an addressing plan;
- how non-packet-mode terminals interface to the network and communicate with packet-mode terminals;
- how the network moves information from one DTE to another, once the remote DTE is identified; this involves not only routing strategies but a method for preserving the information conveyed by a user;
- how the network charges for its services;
- how the network interworks with other (public and/or private) data networks;
- what levels of performance need to be provided by the network;
- what management features/functions are available from the network;
- how X.25 relates to other technologies, such as **Open Systems Interconnection (OSI)** or **Integrated Services Digital Networks (ISDN).**

Although this list may appear lengthy, it was always understood in CCITT that X.25 by itself would not provide a complete networking solution. Rather, it was recognized that such issues should be addressed elsewhere. We have set the stage, however, for the discussion to follow later regarding how these "gaps" are filled in a complete X.25 networking environment. First, though, let us examine how X.25 works.

HOW DOES IT WORK?

X.25 specifies the allowed set of interactions to be used across the interface to a packet-switched public data network by which services are requested and received by a DTE. This set of interactions, including its method of encoding, is called a **protocol.** While one may speak of *the* X.25 protocol, Recommendation X.25 should actually be viewed as three protocols working together to facilitate communications. However, two of these three protocols actually were "borrowed" from elsewhere; only one of the three members of the X.25 protocol stack represented entirely new work in 1976.

Figure 18.2 shows the X.25 protocol stack. A critical element of this stack is the hierarchical relationship or **layering** of the protocols; that is, a higher-layer protocol makes use of the capabilities (**services**) provided by a lower-layer protocol. Furthermore, since this usage only depends on these capabilities being available in an abstract fashion without being tied to the actual protocol, then changes can be made to the lower-layer protocol or an entirely different lower-layer protocol providing the same capabilities can be used without any negative effects (**layer independence**). This is shown at each of Layers 1 and 2, where several protocols can be used interchangeably. While these concepts were somewhat new in the 1974 time frame, they provided the cornerstone for several key elements (layer, layer independence, layer service) to be embedded in work started just a few years later known as the OSI Reference Model.

Layer:

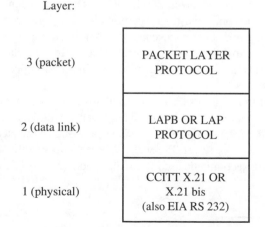

Layer	
3 (packet)	PACKET LAYER PROTOCOL
2 (data link)	LAPB OR LAP PROTOCOL
1 (physical)	CCITT X.21 OR X.21 bis (also EIA RS 232)

Figure 18.2　X.25 protocol stack.

From a functional point of view, the three layers of X.25 provide the following high-level capabilities:

- Layer 1, the Physical Layer, provides mechanical, electrical, functional, and procedural means for the transmission and reception of bits over a path between the DTE and DCE;
- Layer 2, the Data Link Layer, is responsible for detecting and correcting errors that may occur in the Physical Layer (i.e., across the DTE/DCE interface); and
- Layer 3, the Packet Layer, defines procedures that allow two DTEs to control the communication and exchange data between them.

Therefore, for a DTE to communicate with another DTE, it must first ensure that the Physical Layer is set up in order to be able to send bits into the network. Then Layer 2 must be initialized to ensure error-free communication between the DTE and DCE. Finally, the Packet Layer is used to convey information intended for the remote DTE.

Since the protocols of the X.25 Physical Layer are well known and were in use before the advent of X.25, we will not discuss them further here. Instead, we will focus on Layers 2 and 3. Table 18.1 compares the features of these layers in a general way. Although the table shows many features as being available in both layers, many of them operate somewhat differently depending on the layer.

Before getting into detailed discussion of the features of X.25 Layers 2 and 3, it is important to recognize the scope of these layers. As indicated in Table 18.1, Layer 2 is concerned with access to/from the network. This layer is viewed as providing the **logical** data link between the DTE and the DCE (i.e., the PSPDN). The data link is viewed as being logical since the connection between the DTE and DCE need not consist of a single physical connection but must maintain analogous properties. For example, the data link between the DTE and DCE may actually be carried over a permanent connection across a CSPDN.[1] Layer 3, on the other hand, provides the means by which a DTE makes known to the DCE the information to be communicated with the remote DTE. The information concerning the communication with each remote DTE is carried on a separate Layer 3 **logical channel**. Each logical channel at a DTE/DCE interface corresponds to one logical channel at a remote DTE/DCE interface once end-to-end communications have been established. This pair of logical channels and the network-internal mechanisms for tying them together form a **virtual circuit**. While X.25 provides for up to 4,095 Layer 3 logical channels to be multiplexed over a single Layer 2 logical data link, most DTEs use no more than several hundred logical channels. These concepts are depicted in Figure 18.3.

In general, a protocol that is part of a hierarchical structure carries **control information** to be consumed by itself as well as **data** for the next higher layer. Layer 2 carries control information and data in **frames** whereas Layer 3 carries these items in **packets**. In the case of Layer 2, the data for the next higher layer are always Layer 3 packets. Whereas the specification of Layer 2 data (i.e., Layer 3 packets) is part of Recommendation X.25, the specification of Layer 3 data is outside of the scope of X.25.

---

1 In this sense, the DTE and the DCE (i.e., the packet switch of the PSPDN) can both be viewed as DTEs of the CSPDN.

Table 18.1   Features in X.25

Feature	Layer 2	Layer 3
Layer Name	Data Link	Packet
Scope of Layer	Access to PSPDN	Communication across PSPDN[1]
Unit of Data	Frame	Packet
Layer Initialization	Yes	Yes
# Concurrent DTE/DCE Connections	1[2]	1 or More
Connection Types	Data Link	Logical Channel
Parameter Negotiation	No	Yes
Layer Termination	Yes	No[3]
Sequenced Delivery of "Normal" Data	Yes	Yes
Data Marking (Qualification)	No	Yes
Segmentation of Large Data Units	No	Yes
Transfer of "Expedited" Data	No	Yes
Request/Receive Acknowledgment	Yes	Yes
Flow Control	Yes	Yes
Error Detection	Yes	Yes
Retransmit Lost Data	Yes	Yes[4]
Reinitialize Data Transfer	Yes	Yes
Error Reporting	Yes	Yes

Notes:

1. Although X.25 only describes the DTE/DCE interface, most aspects of the Packet Layer are concerned with communications with a remote DTE.
2. The X.25 multilink capability, which is an optional feature, allows for more than one DTE/DCE connection at Layer 2. However, these connections appear as one to Layer 3.
3. Once Layer 3 is initialized, it does not terminate itself. Instead, termination is accomplished by terminating Layer 2 or Layer 1.
4. The Layer 3 retransmission capability is an optional feature that is rarely implemented.

The subsections to follow provide a detailed (but not exhaustive) description of the operation of the features of Layers 2 and 3 of X.25, starting with the lower layer first.

Data Link Layer Operation

As mentioned, the X.25 Data Link Layer is responsible for the movement of information across the communications line that connects the DTE and DCE. As such, it provides an error-free data link by

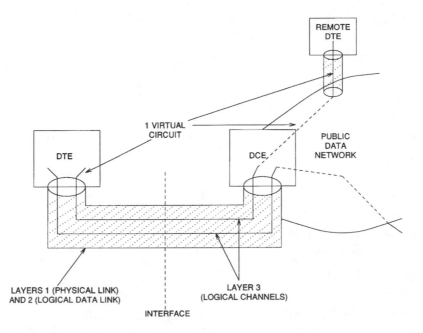

Figure 18.3   Layer 2 vs. Layer 3 at the DTE/DCE interface.

correcting any errors that occur in Layer 1 while providing a transparent data link connection for use by the Packet Layer. The procedures and encodings used at Layer 2 are derived from a subset of those defined by the High-level Data Link Control procedures [3] (HDLC), which were standardized by the International Organization for Standardization starting in the early 1970s. (HDLC is viewed as providing a toolkit from which tools are selected in order to develop a Data Link Layer protocol. This selection is then fleshed out by the developer to completely specify the operation of the protocol.)

There are two procedures specified in X.25 for use at the Data Link Layer—one is known as **LAP** (Link Access Procedure) while the other is known as **LAPB** (LAP-Balanced). From the perspective of the Packet Layer applying the concept of layer independence, it does not matter which one is used. LAP was part of the original specification of X.25 when it was adopted in 1976, but it was found to have problems [4] and was supplemented by LAPB in 1978. Almost all implementations today of X.25 Layer 2 use only LAPB. Although there are numerous similarities between LAP and LAPB, we will restrict our discussion to LAPB. It is conceivable that LAP will be deleted from Recommendation X.25 in the near future, since its description has been taken out of the 1992 version of X.25 and is contained only by backward reference to the 1988 version.

General Layer 2 Encoding Principles   Figure 18.4 depicts the general format of a **frame**, which is the unit of information transfer at the Data Link Layer. The basic mode of transmission available in all PSPDNs uses **synchronous framing,** where synchronization takes place at the bit level (i.e., no extra bits are added between octets for synchronization purposes). In addition, a **start-stop**

Octets:

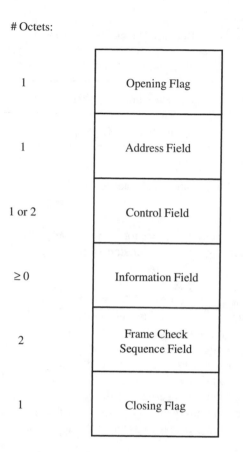

1	Opening Flag
1	Address Field
1 or 2	Control Field
≥ 0	Information Field
2	Frame Check Sequence Field
1	Closing Flag

Figure 18.4   Frame format at the Data Link Layer.

framing option[2] is available in some networks. X.25 Layer 2, as derived from HDLC, uses a unique bit pattern known as a **flag** to mark the beginning and end of a frame;[3] these flags are known as the **opening** and **closing flags** of the frame. Bits, if any, between flags constitute the remaining fields of the frame. While the Address, Control, and Frame Check Sequence (FCS) Fields must be present for a frame to be valid, consecutive flags in the bit stream indicate the absence of a frame. To allow the use of any bit pattern by the Packet Layer while still being able to detect a closing flag, the Data Link

---

2 The start-stop option was agreed to in 1991 for inclusion in the 1992 version of X.25. This allows DTEs that transmit in start-stop mode to use the X.25 procedures by surrounding each octet of the frame with start and stop bits to synchronize at the octet level.

3 Methods used in other environments for delimiting information include time synchronization of the bit stream or violation of the bit-encoding rules of the Physical Layer.

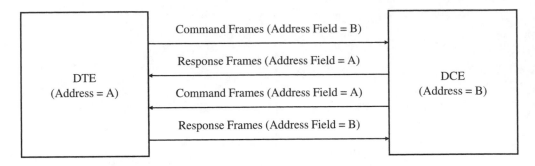

Figure 18.5   Exchange of frames with A and B addresses.

Layer employs a **transparency** procedure for the information between flags. This procedure inserts bits (for synchronous framing) or octets (for start-stop framing) before transmission while removing them upon reception.

Address Field   The one-octet Address Field, which is present in every X.25 frame, serves to distinguish between frames that are **commands** and those that are **responses**. This usage is a result of the X.25 Data Link Layer's heritage from HDLC.[4] Two values of the Address Field are used in X.25 for **single-link operation.** (Multilink operation is also allowed and is described later.) These are designated as A and B and have the values H'03'[5] and H'01', respectively. For operation on the DTE/DCE interface, the DTE is assigned the A address while the DCE is assigned the B address. This static assignment of addresses pertains to the X.25 case where a dedicated connection is used; when a switched connection is used, this assignment can change. Figure 18.5 illustrates the exchange of frames at the DTE/DCE interface with usage of the appropriate addresses.

Control Field   The Control Field is used to indicate the particular frame type as well as several other items depending on the frame type. The Control Field for all frame types contains one bit that serves as a **Poll bit** in command frames or a **Final bit** in response frames.

Table 18.2 identifies the different frame types used in LAPB and the function(s) each provides. These frames are classified into three groups of formats (not to be confused with the command/response classification): Information, Supervisory, and Unnumbered formats. **Information** and **Supervisory** format frames carry sequence numbers in the Control Field. The Control Field of these types of frames is two octets in length when **modulo 128** numbering is used. The Control Field of

---

4 In general, HDLC uses the Address Field to identify the destination station to receive a frame, where there can be more than two stations connected by the same Physical Layer. The scope of X.25, where the DTE and DCE are the only two stations, does not require the added functionality of this field. Of more importance is the actual frame type, which is determined by the Control Field augmented by the indication in the Address Field as to whether the frame is a command or a response.

5 The notation *H'nn'* is used to represent hexadecimal digits with value *nn*.

Table 18.2   LAPB Frames

Frame Format	Frame Types		Function	Frame Used As:[1]	Has Sequence Number(s)?[2]	Has Information Field?
Information	I	(information)	• carry packets for Packet Layer • acknowledge I frames received	C	Send and Receive	Yes
Supervisory	RR	(receive ready)	• ready to receive more I frames • acknowledge I frames received	C or R	Receive	No
	RNR	(receive not ready)	• not ready to receive more I frames • acknowledge I frames received	C or R	Receive	No
	REJ	(reject)	• request retransmission of I frames • acknowledge I frames received	C or R	Receive	No
Unnumbered	SABM	(set asynchronous balanced mode)	• request data link initialization with modulo 8 numbering • reset the data link	C	No	No
	SABME	(set asynchronous balanced mode extended)	• same as SABM except used with modulo 128 numbering	C	No	No
	DISC	(disconnect)	• request data link disconnection	C	No	No
	UA	(unnumbered acknowledgment)	• acknowledge SABM/SABME/DISC frames	R	No	No
	DM	(disconnect mode)	• indicate disconnected mode • request initialization	R	No	No
	FRMR	(frame reject)	• report certain error types and • request data link reinitialization	R	No[3]	Yes

Notes:

1.   "C" denotes a frame used as a Command while "R" denotes a frame used as a Response.

2.   The use of *Send Sequence Numbers* and *Receive Sequence Numbers* is described under Information Transfer.

3.   The FRMR frame does not carry a sequence number in its Control Field. However, its Information Field may carry sequence number information pertaining to the errored frame it is reporting on.

Unnumbered format frames, and Information and Supervisory format frames when **modulo 8** numbering is used, is one octet in length.

Information Field   In HDLC and LAPB, there are no explicit indications that an Information Field is present in a frame. Its existence is indicated by the presence of octets after the Control Field but before the FCS Field. In LAPB only two frames contain an Information Field: the I frame and the FRMR frame. Any other frame with octets between the Control and FCS Fields is considered to be in error. The Information Field of an I frame contains exactly one Layer 3 packet. In an FRMR frame, the Information Field contains information about the errored frame being reported on and is used for error analysis by Layer 2.

Frame Check Sequence Field   All frames carry the Frame Check Sequence (FCS) Field, which are the two octets preceding the closing flag. The FCS Field is used to ensure the integrity of frames transmitted across the DTE/DCE interface. The contents of this field are calculated based on the transmitted bits (not including any extra bits or octets inserted for transparency, start and stop bits, or flags) in the preceding fields of the frame. The receiver of a frame also generates an FCS as bits are received and then compares its FCS to that at the end of the frame. If they are equal, the receiver processes the frame further; otherwise, the frame is ignored.

LAPB Procedures   Rather than describing each frame in Table 18.2, the following discussion is focused on the various functions defined by LAPB. These functions, in turn, involve the exchange of frames across the data link to accomplish their objectives.

Note that a few procedural aspects have already been discussed under "General Layer 2 Encoding Principles" while describing the frame fields. These included frame delimiting by flags, transparency by bit/octet insertion and removal, and frame integrity by FCS generation and verification. These procedures, which are sometimes referred to collectively as **framing functions**, are considered as very basic functions; they apply to all frames in HDLC—including those not in the LAPB subset—as well as to many other protocols in common use (e.g., the SDLC of IBM's SNA). They are usually implemented in hardware on chips known as **framing chips**, which then can be used as a base for any protocol using the HDLC framing functions (even if not using the rest of HDLC). There are also chips that combine the framing functions with the X.25 LAPB procedures.

Data Link Initialization   Initialization of the logical data link at Layer 2 involves the exchange of an SABM or SABME frame and a UA frame. Either the DTE or the DCE can initiate link set-up by sending the SABM/SABME frame. The station receiving this frame indicates its willingness to accept link set-up by returning a UA frame; if the station is not willing to accept link set-up, then it returns a DM frame. In case of collision where both stations send an SABM (or both send an SABME) frame, then both stations also return a UA frame. The DCE may also invite the DTE to initiate link set-up by sending it an unsolicited DM frame.

The choice of which frame, SABM or SABME, to use for link set-up depends on the scheme to be used for numbering I (Information) frames during the information transfer phase. SABM is used for modulo 8 numbering whereas SABME is used for modulo 128. Modulo 8 numbering is available in all PSPDNs whereas modulo 128 numbering is an option that is available only in some networks. More detail on how these schemes operate will be given later.

Prior to setting up the link, there must have been agreement between the DTE and the DCE on the values of various parameters to use, since the Layer 2 initialization procedures do not allow for any negotiation. Such parameters include the modulo numbering scheme (thereby implying which link initialization frame to use—SABM or SABME), the maximum size of I frames, and several others.

Information Transfer   Once the data link has been initialized, information transfer using I frames may commence. In X.25, the sole purpose of transferring I frames is to carry Layer 3 packets—each I frame carries one packet. Each I frame is numbered using a **Send Sequence Number,** referred to as N(S). The receiver of I frames acknowledges their receipt by returning a **Receive Sequence Number,** referred to as N(R). Each direction of data transfer (DTE-to-DCE and DCE-to-DTE) is independent of the other; a separate N(S) and N(R) is used for each direction.

The counting for N(S) and N(R) starts at zero when link set-up has been completed. It continues up to the value of modulo − 1, as selected during the link set-up process with the SABM or SABME. For example, if an SABM frame was used for link set-up, then the counting for I frames goes from 0 through 7. The next I frame sent after 7 is again numbered 0, and the numbering continues to repeat.

Only a maximum number of I frames can be transmitted by a station before it must stop and wait for acknowledgment of at least the first I frame. This maximum number is referred to as a **window** and is a parameter (denoted by *k*) that must also be agreed to by the DTE and DCE. In X.25, the value of k must be the same for both directions of information transfer, although this restriction does not exist in HDLC. For example, if a value of 4 has been agreed for k, then after link set-up the DTE can send I frames with N(S) values of 0, 1, 2, and 3 (as can the DCE in the other direction) before stopping to wait for acknowledgment of at least I frame #0. The receiver of I frames returns an N(R) to indicate acknowledgment of I frames up through and including N(R) − 1 and that the next I frame expected is the one whose N(S) would equal N(R). However, this does not imply that the receiver must return an N(R) for each I frame it wishes to acknowledge; the receiver may send back an N(R) that acknowledges several I frames at the same time. Upon receipt of an N(R), the transmitter **rotates** its window so that the first N(S) in the window (sometimes referred to as the **Lower Window Edge** or **LWE**) is equal to N(R). The **Upper Window Edge** or **UWE** (that is, the N(S) of the last I frame that could be transmitted before being forced to stop) is just equal to LWE + k − 1. The concepts of numbering, window size, and window rotation are illustrated in Figure 18.6.

Under normal circumstances where I frames are not lost and the receiving station is able to keep pace with the transmitter, the process of transmitting I frames, receiving acknowledgments via N(R), rotating the window and updating the LWE, and transmitting new I frames can continue uninterrupted. However, unusual events can occur and the procedures of LAPB must be robust enough to recover in such cases.

Before going on to the discussion on error-recovery procedures, however, it is worth returning to the issue of selecting modulo 8 or 128 for numbering I frames. A goal of Layer 2 operation is to *not* become the bottleneck in allowing Layer 3 packets to be transmitted; at the same time, the bandwidth of Layer 1 (i.e., its throughput or the number of bits per second that can be sent) should not be wasted by having the circuit become idle. Since Layer 2 introduces numbering and windows, one must be careful not to choose too small a window lest it be forced to stop transmitting I frames while waiting for acknowledgment. In turn, the window is bounded by the modulo numbering scheme; because of the possibility of errors, the window size cannot be greater than the value of modulo − 1 (because of possible ambiguity as to which I frame an N(R) refers to). The selection of the smallest window size so that Layer 2 does not become the bottleneck depends on several factors. Among the primary factors are the throughput and round-trip delay of the Layer 1 circuit connecting the DTE and DCE. Another important parameter is the maximum I frame size used at Layer 2[6] (LAPB parameter N1). In addition, the processing time of a frame by a DTE and a DCE needs to be accounted for, but this is usually small compared to these factors.

Figure 18.7 [5] shows, as a function of throughput and delay, the dividing line between modulo 8 and modulo 128 usage for efficient Layer 2 operation (i.e., Layer 2 will not be the bottleneck). That

---

6   The actual distribution of sizes of transmitted I frames is more important but there is no way to know this at
    Layer 2 since it depends on the operation of Layer 3 and higher-layer protocols.

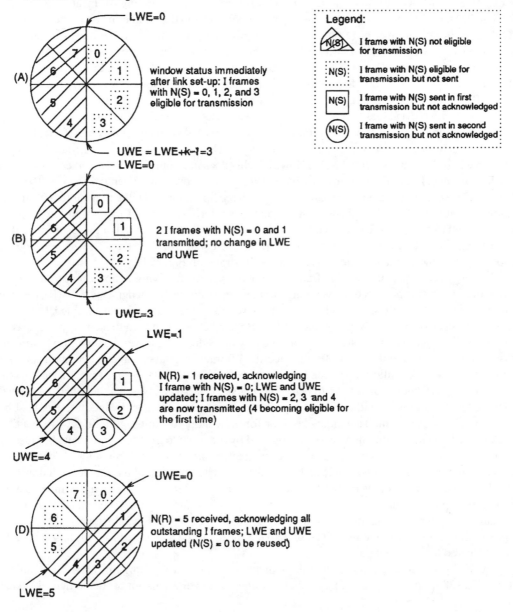

Figure 18.6   Numbering, window size, window rotation.

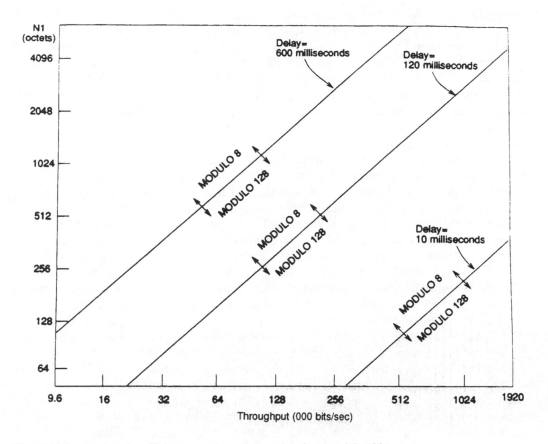

Figure 18.7   Regions for efficient operation using modulo 8 vs. modulo 128.

is, for a given throughput and round-trip delay at Layer 1, modulo 8 numbering will suffice if N1 is chosen large enough to be a point on or above the dividing line (recalling, however, that N1 is only the maximum frame size but it is the actual frame-size distribution that matters). In other words, if N1 lies on or above this line, then a window size (k) of 7 or less can be used and modulo 8 suffices. If N1 is chosen to be below the line, then modulo 128 numbering is needed so that a window size larger than 7 can be used. For most X.25 interfaces, the typical values for throughput (usually no more than about 10,000 bits per second), delay (usually no more than about 10 milliseconds), and frame size (usually at least 100 octets) are such that modulo 8 numbering suffices. However, if the X.25 interface is operating at a throughput and/or delay measured in the hundreds rather than the tens (bits per second of throughput or milliseconds of delay), then modulo 128 numbering is needed so that a larger window size can be used. For example, the round-trip delay when the Layer 1 circuit uses a satellite link is about 600 milliseconds; this is likely to require modulo 128 numbering for efficient operation, even at low throughput values if the value of N1 is small. Guidelines based on the above principles have been added to the 1992 version of X.25 to help implementors determine appropriate parameter values.

Receiving I Frames   As the transmitter numbers I frames consecutively, the receiver expects to receive I frames without any gaps in their numbering. The N(R) returned by the receiver indicates acknowledgment for all I frames up through and including N(R) − 1 and the fact that the receiver is next expecting the I frame with N(S) equal to N(R). If there are no unusual circumstances, then the N(R) is returned in either an I frame carrying data in the reverse direction[7] or an RR (receive ready) frame (as either a command or a response). The receipt of an N(R) different than the previous N(R) allows the transmitter to release the buffers associated with acknowledged I frames. It also allows the transmitter to update its LWE and to transmit *new* I frames whose N(S) is less than or equal to the revised UWE. (However, any I frames in the new LWE-UWE range that were previously transmitted are not sent again.) This was depicted in part (C) of Figure 18.6.

One cannot assume that I frames will always be received without errors. For example, a bit error at Layer 1 may have resulted in the receiver's calculated FCS being different than the FCS carried in the I frame. In this case the frame would have been discarded, but a gap in the N(S) values would be detected when the next I frame is correctly received. In this situation, the receiver asks for retransmission of the missing I frame by sending back an N(R) in an REJ (reject) command or response frame. This N(R) still carries the same meaning (vis-à-vis acknowledging I frames and indicating the next I frame to be received) but the use of an REJ frame is taken as a request for retransmission of *all* I frames starting with an N(S) equal to the N(R). Note that all such I frames are to be retransmitted, even though some of them may have been in transit and not yet received when the REJ frame was transmitted. In fact, these I frames may have been correctly received with respect to the FCS but their N(S) will also not be the next one expected. The I-frame receiver discards all I frames whose N(S) is not the next one it is expecting and awaits the retransmission of the I frame requested via the REJ frame and the subsequent I frames. This form of error recovery is known as **Go-Back-N (GBN)** since the transmitter goes back "N" frames and resumes transmission from there.

The GBN method of error recovery simplifies operations in the DTE or DCE as far as the receiving process is concerned—checking for the next expected I frame is straightforward and no reordering[8] is needed to maintain sequenced delivery as required by the Packet Layer. This comes about at the expense of retransmitting I frames that were received with a correct FCS but were not the next one expected—requiring extra processing at the transmitter while also wasting the bandwidth of the circuit connecting the DTE and DCE. While retransmission of a few extra I frames may not be significant when using small window sizes bounded by modulo 8 numbering, the above concerns become more significant when larger window sizes are used with modulo 128. To address this issue, it has been proposed that a selective retransmission capability, using the HDLC SREJ (selective reject) frame be

---

7 The ability to acknowledge data for one direction of information transfer at the same time as carrying information in the other direction is known as **piggybacking**.

8 In general, gaps in sequence numbers can be attributed to either loss or missequencing between a sending and receiving station. Both LAP and LAPB assume that I frames cannot get out of sequence between the DTE and DCE. That is, under normal operation without errors over a single link, I frame N(S)=3 will not arrive ahead of I frame N(S)=2. Recovery from lost I frames when it is assumed that they arrive in the same order as transmitted, if they arrive at all, uses simpler protocol mechanisms than if the sequentiality assumption cannot be made.

added to X.25. [6] The SREJ frame would be used to request retransmission of specific I frames, not necessarily consecutive, instead of all I frames starting at the N(R) in the REJ frame.

Another problem that may arise at the receiver is a temporary inability to accept more I frames. This may occur, even with a proper choice of window size, because of several reasons—for example, the receiving station's Layer 3 is not accepting packets from Layer 2. In these cases, a station may wish to acknowledge the I frames that it has received but indicate at the same time that the transmitter should stop sending I frames. To do so, the receiver can return an N(R) but in an RNR (receive not ready) command or response frame to indicate a **busy** condition. This allows the transmitter to update its LWE and UWE but requires it to stop sending new I frames. This is known as **flow controlling** the sender.[9] The status of any I frames that may have been in transit at the time of sending the RNR is indicated by the N(R) in subsequent I, RR, RNR, or REJ frames. When the receiver is ready to accept additional I frames, it sends back either an RR or an REJ frame to clear the busy condition. For example, if the receiver discarded I frames with a correct FCS after it had sent an RNR, then it could send back an REJ frame to indicate that it is now ready to accept I frames and the point at which retransmission is to begin.

Waiting Acknowledgment   It should be apparent from the preceding discussions that timely acknowledgments are crucial for proper LAPB operation. We have explicitly discussed the acknowledgment of I frames. Other frames may also require acknowledgment—the transmission of an REJ frame is acknowledged by the receipt of the requested I frame. Without acknowledgments, a station may be forced to stop transmitting while waiting for the other station to send a frame. If both the DTE and the DCE find themselves in this situation, then a situation known as **deadlock** has occurred. To ensure timely receipt of acknowledgments, a station starts a timer known as **T1** when it transmits a frame requiring acknowledgment. If this timer should expire before acknowledgment is received, the station invokes the proper recovery procedures as defined by LAPB.

We have seen that N(R) is used to acknowledge I frames up to N(R) − 1. However, if a gap in the N(S)s is detected by the receiver, then it sends back an REJ frame. But a gap can only be detected if subsequent I frames are received correctly. What if a lost I frame is the last frame to be transmitted? Clearly, in this case, no gap can be detected. What if it is the acknowledgment itself that is lost? In either case, the I-frame transmitter does not receive the required acknowledgment. One of the recovery procedures for unacknowledged I frames involves sending a Supervisory format command frame, such as an RR, with its Poll bit set to 1.[10] The other station responds by sending an RR or RNR response frame with its Final bit set to 1 and an N(R). If this N(R) corresponds to the N(S) of the last

---

9   An alternative method for flow control is to return N(R)'s that do *not* advance the sender's LWE, instead of using an RNR frame. However, this leaves previously transmitted I frames as unacknowledged, an undesirable effect as we shall see.

10 In the preceding discussions, it has not been particularly important as to whether the command or response version of a Supervisory format frame was used. Likewise, we have not paid attention to whether the Poll/Final bit was set to 0 or 1. However, for error recovery situations, these aspects become important. Transmission of any command frame with its Poll bit set to 1 requires acknowledgment by a proper response frame with its Final bit set to 1. If T1 should expire before receipt of such a frame, then the command frame is retransmitted up to a maximum number of times. After this, other procedures (including link disconnection) are invoked.

I frame transmitted, then it was lost and needs to be retransmitted. If, on the other hand, the N(R) acknowledges that the last transmitted I frame was received, then it was the acknowledgment that was lost and nothing more needs to be done.

Reinitialization   Certain error conditions are considered severe enough to require the logical data link to be reset. Some of these, such as receipt of a frame with an unrecognized Control Field, are reported using the FRMR frame. Upon receipt of a FRMR frame or recognition of a condition not reportable with an FRMR frame, the DTE or DCE reinitializes the link by sending an SABM/SABME frame. The remainder of the procedure, including setting N(S) and N(R) back to zero, is exactly the same as link initialization. In addition, any busy condition that may have existed as a result of sending an RNR frame prior to the link reinitialization is cleared.

Disconnect   After completing transmission of all I frames (as signaled by some process external to LAPB), the logical data link can be disconnected. The DISC frame is used to initiate the shutdown and needs to be confirmed by a UA frame from the other station. This exchange of frames can be viewed as an orderly disconnect. Of course, an abrupt shutdown (such as turning off the power) will have the same end result if there are no more I frames to transmit and all I frames have been acknowledged.

Multilink Operation   The preceding discussions have focused on the use of LAPB at Layer 2 operating over a single circuit at Layer 1. For a variety of reasons, it may be desirable to have multiple physical circuits at Layer 1. For example, multiple circuits can be used for reliability purposes or to increase the bandwidth capacity at the DTE/DCE interface.

X.25 Layer 2 also defines an optional multilink procedure (MLP). The MLP allows for data interchange over one or more **Single Link Procedures (SLPs)** between a DTE and a DCE. Each SLP operates according to the rules of LAPB, as described, or LAP except that different values are used in the Address Field. Figure 18.8 illustrates how the MLP relates to the other aspects of the DTE/DCE interface.

As Figure 18.8 shows, the MLP exists as an added upper sublayer of the Data Link Layer, operating between the Packet Layer and a multiplicity of SLPs in the Data Link Layer. The MLP accepts packets from the Packet Layer and distributes them across the available SLPs for transmission to the remote SLPs. Distribution of packets to SLPs can be done in any desired fashion (e.g., "round robin" for balancing traffic across links or to more than one SLP for redundancy). Depending on how packets are distributed, the receiving MLP may receive packets out of order or multiple copies of the same packet. Since the Packet Layer requires packets to be received in the same order as they were transmitted and without duplication (i.e., it depends on the Data Link Layer as a whole to provide this service), the MLP uses its own sequence number to enable it to resequence packets and to weed out duplicates across all links.

Packet Layer Operation

Sitting on top of the Data Link Layer is the Packet Layer. This section will discuss the operation of the X.25 Packet Layer Protocol (PLP), starting with encoding and then describing the procedures.

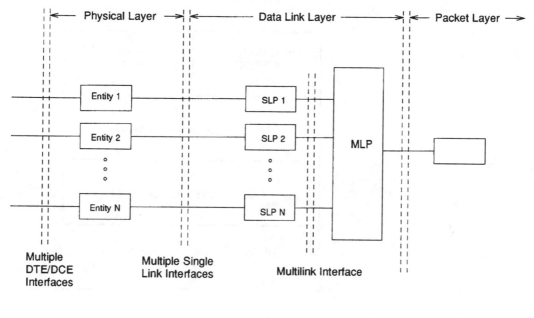

Legend:
    SLP: Single Link Procedure (LAPB or LAP)
    MLP: Multilink Procedure

Figure 18.8   Multilink functional organization.

Although X.25 strictly defines what goes on at the DTE/DCE interface, most Packet Layer interactions relate to virtual circuit communications between two DTEs. To fully appreciate Packet Layer operation, one must not lose sight of the end-to-end picture as well as the consequences of what is happening inside the PSPDN.

As was shown in Figure 18.3, communication at the Packet Layer is via a virtual circuit, which, in turn, is a binding of the logical channel used at each of the two DTE/DCE interfaces involved in an instance of communication. Although logical channels are numbered at each interface, the pair of logical channels associated with a particular virtual circuit need not have the same number; the assignment of logical channel numbers is local to each DTE/DCE interface. The properties of a virtual circuit are similar to those of the Layer 2 logical data link—perhaps the most fundamental one being the assumption of in-sequence delivery of data on the virtual circuit across the PSPDN(s).[11] X.25 specifies two types of virtual circuit services: a **Virtual Call (VC) service,** where a call set-up and

11 The 1980 version of X.25 defined a **datagram** service, where there was no guarantee of in-sequence delivery, in addition to the virtual circuit services. The datagram option was removed from X.25 in 1984 since no PSPDN operators showed any interest in developing it.

Octets:

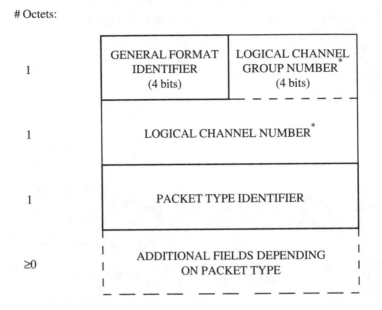

* These two fields can also be viewed as one 12-bit Logical Channel Identifier Field.

Figure 18.9   Packet format.

call clearing (i.e., release) phase precede and follow the data transfer phase, and a **Permanent Virtual Circuit (PVC) service** consisting only of the data transfer phase. For PVCs, some of the aspects of call set-up are accomplished in a static, *a priori* fashion through agreements between the two DTEs and the PSPDN. Although avoiding the call set-up phase would seem to be desirable, this phase offers unique functionality that applications may find beneficial. Furthermore, PVCs may not be available on an end-to-end basis when more than one PSPDN is needed to support the virtual circuit between DTEs.

General Layer 3 Encoding Principles   Figure 18.9 illustrates the general format of a packet. In contrast to a frame at the Data Link Layer, a packet does not have any explicit delimiters—instead, it is delimited by the boundaries of the Information Field of an I frame. The figure shows that all packets have four fields in common as well as some additional fields depending on the packet type. The common fields are discussed here; the additional fields are described below in the sections dealing with the procedures that use the specific packets.

General Format Identifier   Two bits of the General Format Identifier (GFI) are used to identify the format of the rest of the packet, distinguishing between the use of modulo 8 and modulo 128 numbering in packets that have sequence numbers.[12] The use of the other two bits depends on the type of packet.

Logical Channel Fields   As shown in Figure 18.9, there are two fields relating to the logical channel which, for all practical cases, can be regarded as one 12-bit field. When the combined fields contain a value between 1 and 4,095, inclusive, this value identifies the virtual circuit to which the packet belongs. Packets with a value of 0 in this field pertain to operation of the DTE/DCE interface as a whole rather than to an individual virtual circuit.

Packet Type Identifier   As its name indicates, this field identifies the type of packet in much the same way as the Control Field of Layer 2 identifies the frame type; however, the Layer 3 Packet Type Identifier does not have the equivalent of the Poll/Final bit in the Control Field. Table 18.3 shows the packets used at Layer 3 and their groupings.

Packet Layer Procedures   The procedures of the X.25 Packet Layer can be divided into two sets: those pertaining to a single virtual circuit (associated with the first three groups of packets in Table 18.3) and those pertaining to the DTE/DCE interface as a whole (associated with the last three groups in Table 18.3). These procedures are described below.

Call Set-up and Call Clearing   The call set-up and call clearing procedures, used to establish and terminate a VC, operate in a fashion analogous to a phone call in the voice world. In addition to the common fields shown in Figure 18.9, most of the packets in this group carry addresses (similar to phone numbers) to identify both the calling and called DTEs, **optional user facility** requests and/or indications to change the default mode of operation, and some amount of user data for the other DTE.

   To establish a VC, a DTE transmits a Call Request packet across its DTE/DCE interface specifying, among other items, the address of the remote DTE. If the PSPDN is able to support the call, it sends an Incoming Call packet to the remote DTE in which it identifies the calling DTE. Various other standards specify the addressing information that can be placed in the Address Fields. For some forms of address, the A-bit (which is part of the GFI) must be set to 1. If the call can be completed, then the called DTE returns a Call Accepted packet and the calling DTE receives a Call Connected packet. When the DTE sends a Call Request packet and when the DCE sends an Incoming Call packet, they each choose a non-zero logical channel number not in use to represent the virtual circuit at the DTE/DCE interface. These numbers are used to identify subsequent packets associated with the virtual circuit. As part of this process, the network also creates the internal binding that associates the logical channel numbers used with the virtual circuit.

   The clearing procedure is used for various reasons to terminate a call. A DTE sends a Clear Request packet across its DTE/DCE interface to indicate normal termination of an already-established VC or

---

12 Sequence numbers at the Packet Layer are separate from those at the Data Link Layer. Furthermore, while the selection of modulo 8 or modulo 128 numbering at one layer is independent from the selection at the other layer, there is little if any benefit to using modulo 128 numbering at the Packet Layer with modulo 8 numbering at the Data Link Layer.

390 THE HANDBOOK OF INTERNATIONAL CONNECTIVITY STANDARDS

Table 18.3 Packet Groupings, Functions and Types

Packet Group	Function	Packet Types	Service:* VC	PVC
Call Set-up and Call Clearing	Establish and terminate a Virtual Call for DTE/DCE communication; may convey data for higher layer protocol processing	CALL REQUEST	X	
		INCOMING CALL	X	
		CALL ACCEPTED	X	
		CALL CONNECTED	X	
		CLEAR REQUEST	X	
		CLEAR INDICATION	X	
		CLEAR CONFIRMATION	X	
Data and Interrupt	Convey data or interrupt information for higher-layer protocol processing	DATA	X	X
		INTERRUPT	X	X
		INTERRUPT CONFIRMATION	X	X
Flow Control and Reset	Control the flow of DATA packets across a DTE/DCE interface	RECEIVE READY	X	X
		RECEIVE NOT READY	X	X
		REJECT	X	X
		RESET REQUEST	X	X
		RESET INDICATION	X	X
		RESET CONFIRMATION	X	X
Restart	(Re)Initialize all communication between a DTE and a DCE	RESTART REQUEST	X	X
		RESTART INDICATION	X	X
		RESTART CONFIRMATION	X	X
Diagnostic	Pass error diagnostics to a DTE	DIAGNOSTIC	X	X
Registration	Perform registration procedure	REGISTRATION REQUEST	X	X
		REGISTRATION CONFIRMATION	X	X

*VC = Virtual Call
PVC = Permanent Virtual Circuit

to abort a call attempt. Likewise, this packet is used by a DTE to refuse an incoming call. A Clear Indication packet is used by a DCE

- at the calling DTE/DCE interface if it cannot support a new call (e.g., no available resources in the PSPDN or the remote DTE is not available);
- at a DTE/DCE interface to indicate clearing by the remote DTE; or
- at both DTE/DCE interfaces if the PSPDN must abruptly terminate a call.

Various error cases are also indicated by clearing the call. A station receiving a Clear Request or Clear Indication packet confirms it by transferring a Clear Confirmation packet across the interface to complete the process. Clear Request and Clear Indication packets have Cause and Diagnostic Fields to supply further information as to why the call was cleared. In some cases, further analysis of these fields by a DTE, especially when a new call attempt was cleared, can lead to the DTE retrying the call and possibly succeeding.

Figure 18.10 illustrates the call set-up and clearing procedures. Part (A) of the figure shows that the call set-up procedure is an end-to-end procedure; that is, this procedure involves an ordered,

(A) CALL SET-UP   **(B) CALL CLEARING BY DTE**

Packets:
- CR — Call Request
- IC — Incoming Call
- CA — Call Accepted
- CC — Call Connected

Packets:
- CLR — Clear Request
- CLI — Clear Indication
- CLC — Clear Confirmation

Figure 18.10   Call set-up and call clearing procedure.

four-packet exchange involving both DTEs and the PSPDN in the sequence shown. On the other hand, the VC clearing process can be end-to-end like call set-up or local as shown in part (B) of the figure. This is a design choice of the PSPDN. Some information in the call set-up and clearing packets, such as the user data in a Call Request packet, must be carried across the PSPDN(s) from one DTE/DCE interface to the other; X.25 does not specify how this is done. Other information in these packets pertains only to a single interface, in which case it is not carried across the network.

Data and Interrupt Transfer   Information transfer takes on several forms at the Packet Layer. For a VC, information transfer can take place only after successful establishment of a call; for a PVC, no call set-up is needed but the remote DTE must be operational. **Normal data** is transferred using Data packets whereas a limited amount of **expedited data** can also be exchanged using Interrupt packets. (Furthermore, a limited amount of data can also be transferred using the call set-up and clearing packets.)

Data packets are numbered with a **Packet Send Sequence Number**, referred to as **P(S),** that functions in the same fashion as N(S) at the Data Link Layer. These packets have a User Data Field for carrying information for the virtual-circuit user who, in turn, is defined by a standard other than X.25. There are also several other aspects of Data packets that are important.

- The User Data Field of a Data packet has a maximum size that is agreed to by the DTE and DCE. This value, usually referred to as the **packet size**, applies independently for each direction of data transfer at the DTE/DCE interface and to each interface of the virtual circuit. The default packet size is 128 octets; optional user facilities are available to change this value for both VCs and PVCs as well as to negotiate different sizes during VC set-up. Furthermore, if the two interfaces operate for a given direction of data transfer with different packet sizes (supported by some PSPDNs), then the PSPDN must also operate an internal segmentation and reassembly mechanism.
- While PSPDNs limit the packet size that can be used, there is no restriction on the size of the data unit (message) that the Packet Layer user can request to be transferred to its peer. To preserve the boundaries of the user's data, the Packet Layer provides a **segmentation** and

reassembly function, which uses the **More Data (M)** bit in a Data packet. When the M-bit is set to 1, the User Data Field of the current Data packet is to be logically concatenated with that of the next packet; a Data packet with its M-bit set to 0 marks the end of the sequence of User Data Fields that belong together. For example, if the Packet Layer user needs to have a 300-octet message sent, then at least three Data packets are needed (assuming 128-octet maximum User Data Fields): The first two packets could each carry 128 octets and have their M-bit set to 1; the last packet carries 44 octets and has its M-bit set to 0.

- Another capability is to mark Data packets as carrying **unqualified** or **qualified** data using the **Qualifier (Q)** bit (part of the GFI). This allows the user of the Packet Layer to transfer two streams of data—one for its own use and one for some other user. The decision to use the Q-bit and the meaning of unqualified (Q-bit=0) vs. qualified (Q-bit=1) data are controlled by the user of the Packet Layer. Data packets are numbered consecutively regardless of whether their Q-bits are set to 0 or 1.
- The Packet Layer also provides a **Delivery Confirmation** capability using the D-bit (also in the GFI). This capability is related to the flow-control functions of the Packet Layer and will be discussed later.

The features of maximum packet sizes and M-, Q-, and D-bit settings come together in a single Packet Layer concept called a **complete packet sequence (CPS).** A CPS consists of consecutive Data packets with the same setting of the Q-bit and

- zero or more Data packets with the exact maximum packet size and their M-bit set to 1 and D-bit to 0, followed by
- one Data packet different in any respect (packet size, M-bit, or D-bit setting) than the previous packets.

The PSPDN is responsible for maintaining the integrity of a CPS from one interface to the other. In cases where different packet sizes are used at each DTE/DCE interface for a given direction of data transfer on a virtual circuit, the PSPDN must manipulate the M- and D-bits to ensure the integrity of the CPS.

Interrupt packets, which are not numbered, are used to carry a small amount of data (up to 32 octets starting in 1984, one octet prior to that) from one DTE to the other. Although the routes traveled through the network by Data and Interrupt packets may be different, Interrupt packets are guaranteed to be delivered to the remote DTE prior to Data packets that were transmitted by the originating DTE subsequent to the Interrupt packet. An Interrupt packet may, in fact, get ahead of Data packets that were transmitted before it. When a DTE transmits an Interrupt packet, it must wait for an Interrupt Confirmation packet to be received from the remote DTE before transmitting another Interrupt (in effect, providing for a window of one).

Flow Control and Reset   Flow control and reset operate in much the same fashion at the Packet Layer as they do at the Data Link Layer with respect to the DTE/DCE interface. This section will also focus on some of the end-to-end consequences of these procedures as they relate to virtual circuit operation.

Packet Layer flow control makes use of the window,[13] window rotation, and LWE/UWE concepts introduced in the discussion on the Data Link Layer. Numbering of Data packets uses P(S), instead of N(S), and both modulo 8 and modulo 128 numbering are available, as already mentioned. The Packet Layer equivalent of N(R) is known as the **Packet Receive Sequence Number or P(R).** This value can be carried in RR, RNR, and Reject packets as well as piggybacked in Data packets. RR and RNR packets operate in an analogous fashion as their Layer 2 counterparts. However, the Reject packet, which is an optional Packet Layer feature that is rarely implemented, is used only by the DTE to request retransmission of Data packets by the DCE across the DTE/DCE interface (and not by the remote DTE across the virtual circuit). In addition to the interface-specific aspects, there are also some end-to-end items that pertain to Packet Layer flow control.

Although the window sizes at each DTE/DCE interface of a virtual circuit can be chosen independently, PSPDNs may force the two window sizes for a given direction of data transfer to be the same. Since PSPDNs cannot absorb an unlimited number of Data packets, they typically operate an internal window for the virtual circuit in conjunction with the interface-specific windows. Coupling of the two DTE/DCE windows simplifies matters. For example, advancing a window using P(R) is then related to what is taking place in the internal window and, perhaps, at the remote window. Likewise, use of RNR at one interface may be a result of a lack of window rotation of the internal window.

By setting the D-bit in a Data packet to 1, the DTE can force window rotation at its interface to be coupled with the rotation at the remote DTE/DCE interface. This can be used by a DTE as a method for end-to-end acknowledgments. When Data packet sizes for a given direction of transfer are the same at the two DTE/DCE interfaces, then the window rotations are coupled on a one-to-one basis; when they are not, then the rotation at the transmitting interface cannot be done until the rotation for all corresponding Data packets at the receiving interface has been done. Rotation of windows when the D-bit is set to 0 is local to the interface (or coupled with the network-internal rotation); however, window rotation for D-bit=0 packets cannot be done if there are any outstanding D-bit=1 packets for which rotation has not yet been done.

Just as one can talk about the throughput of the Layer 1 circuit between the DTE and DCE, the concept of a **throughput class** applies to each direction of data transfer of the Layer 3 virtual circuit. This can be regarded simply as the steady-state rate at which information could be transferred between the two DTEs across the PSPDN(s) under optimal conditions. The actual virtual-circuit throughput is affected by the statistical sharing of transmission and switching resources of the DTEs and the PSPDN. Included in these resources, for example, are the throughput of the Layer 1 DTE-DCE connection and the window sizes at each DTE/DCE interface of the virtual circuit. Because of the multiplexing of many logical channels onto a single physical link (unless MLP is used), it is possible for the sum of the throughput classes of all virtual circuits at the interface to exceed the Layer 1 throughput. The default throughput class for each direction of data transfer for all logical channels is chosen when the interface is established; it is either a value chosen by the DTE or bounded by the data rate of the Layer 1 circuit. The default throughput class serves as a maximum from which

---

13 A different window size can be chosen for each direction of data transfer at the Packet Layer of the DTE/DCE interface, unlike operation at the Data Link Layer. The default window size for each direction is two.

negotiation can take place at the time of setting up a VC. A value different than the default can be chosen for each PVC.

The reset procedure is used to report certain errors in Packet Layer operation, such as a gap in the P(S) numbers of received Data packets (unless the optional Reject packet can be used) or a Data packet size that is too long. Resetting a Layer 3 virtual circuit is similar to many concepts that have already been discussed: P(S) and P(R) are both set back to zero and any busy condition that existed is considered cleared. A DTE initiates the procedure by transmitting a Reset Request packet for the logical channel whereas a DCE initiates it by sending a Reset Indication packet; in either case, the corresponding logical channel at the remote DTE/DCE interface is also reset. Both of these packets carry Cause and Diagnostic Fields to aid in error analysis and are confirmed by the receiving station's sending a Reset Confirmation packet. Just like the VC clearing procedure, DTE-initiated resets can be either confirmed locally or as a result of the confirmation at the remote DTE/DCE interface. When a virtual circuit is reset, any Data and Interrupt packets in transit across the network may be lost.

Restart   The restart procedure is used to (re)initialize the entire Packet Layer operation at a DTE/DCE interface. As such, an exchange of Restart Request/Indication and Restart Confirmation packets must be completed before any VCs can be established or any data transferred on a PVC. While a restart procedure at one interface does not result in the same procedure at other interface(s), it does result in a clearing of any VCs and a resetting of any PVCs at all remote interfaces. The Restart Request and Indication packets also carry Cause and Diagnostic Fields.

Diagnostic   The diagnostic procedure, which uses a packet by the same name, is used only by a DCE to report errors where the usual methods of indication (using reset, clear, and restart with cause and diagnostic) are inappropriate. For example, after resending a Clear Indication packet for a specific logical channel and failing to receive a Clear Confirmation packet, a DCE may send a Diagnostic packet to report this. Another case where this procedure may be invoked is when the packet received by the DCE has an invalid GFI or when it does not appear to belong to a known logical channel. These indications are provided using additional fields after the Packet Type Identifier Field.

Registration   The optional registration procedure can be used by a DTE to ascertain what Packet Layer features are supported by a PSPDN as well as to change the set of features pertaining to its interface. The Registration Request packet is used by the DTE to initiate the process while the DCE uses the Registration Confirmation packet to respond. For example, the DTE can change the default values of the Data packet sizes or the Packet Layer window sizes. Some features can only be changed when there are no VCs existing at the interface; others can be changed at any time.

Optional User Facilities   The previous description has provided a glimpse of Packet Layer procedures. In many cases, default procedures have been explicitly mentioned—for example, the use of packet sizes of 128 octets and window sizes of 2, or non-use of Packet Layer Reject packets. Other aspects have been implicit, such as the DTE originating a VC pays for the call and the call can only be completed to the originally-called DTE (i.e., no "call-forwarding" actions take place). X.25 defines about 40 **optional user facilities (OUFs),** or facilities for short, that can be used to alter the default modes of operation. We have also mentioned some of the methods for accomplishing this—by negotiating changes at the time of setting up a VC or by use of the registration procedure (which itself is an OUF). A DTE is never required to use an OUF but agreement with the network to do so provides a useful alternative to the default approach if needed by an application. [7]

The OUFs available in PSPDNs can be categorized in the following groups:

- addressing related facilities;
- routing related facilities;
- charging related facilities;
- protection related facilities;
- data transfer related facilities;
- facilities to convey user data other than during the data transfer phase; and
- miscellaneous facilities.

Next, we will describe the use and application of some of the OUFs available in X.25. Further descriptions can be found in X.25 itself and in newly adopted Recommendation X.7. [8]

Call Redirection/Deflection and Related Facilities   **Call Redirection** and **Call Deflection** allow a VC to be completed to a DTE other than the originally called DTE. These OUFs, together with several others, provide complete control and feedback during the call set-up phase of how the call is completed.

Figure 18.11 illustrates the interaction among these OUFs. The figure shows DTE A calling DTE B but Call Redirection is used at DTE B's interface if, for example, it has been taken out of service for preventive maintenance. The PSPDN, using a database associated with DTE B, redirects the call to DTE C. DTE A need have no knowledge of DTE B being out of order. If DTE B had been operable, an Incoming Call packet would have been sent to it by the DCE. However, DTE B might then deflect the call to DTE C based on information in the packet such as the user data; such procedures could be used for security screening based on this data. From this point, redirection and deflection operate in the same fashion. A new call is made to DTE C, with the **Call Redirection or Call Deflection Notification facility** indicating that the call is a result of the corresponding action at another interface. Finally, the Call Connected packet sent to DTE A contains the **Called Line Address Modified Notification facility** to indicate that the call was completed to another DTE and the reason. DTE A may also have the ability to control the redirection/deflection action, since such actions could go from one network to another while incurring unexpected charges.

Alternative Addressing   A Call Request packet must identify the remote DTE to which a call is being made. By default, it is assumed that all addresses conform to Recommendation X.121 [9], which specifies the format of addresses used by PSPDNs. The set of **Alternative Addressing facilities,** which has been added to the 1992 version of X.25, allows the called DTE to be identified using an address belonging to some other standard[14] or by a mnemonic address.

---

14 X.121 also provides for escapes to other numbering plans for public networks under the control of CCITT. The standards recognized under the Alternative Addressing capabilities are not CCITT numbering plans. They include, for example, the OSI Network Layer address plan.

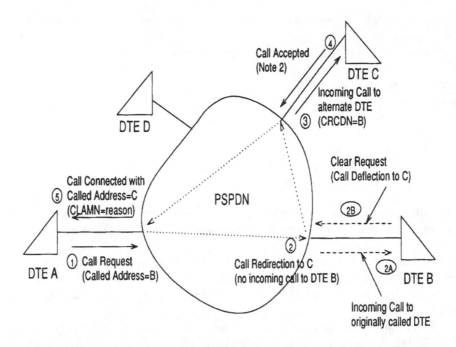

Figure 18.11   Use of call redirection/deflection and related OUFs.

The use of these facilities by DTEs requires registration with the PSPDN of a translation of alternative addresses to an X.121 address. Translations can be:

- of the form N-to-1 (i.e., N alternative addresses to one X.121 address) or 1-to-N (i.e., one alternative address to N different X.121 addresses, with translation of the alternative address to a single X.121 address being done by the PSPDN at the time of call set-up);
- dependent on time-of-day or call originator, etc. (as in the voice world); or
- dependent on other parameters in the Call Request packet (e.g., delay).

An example of 1-to-N mapping is illustrated in Figure 18.12. The example shows a multihomed host. Calls to this host use the alternative address "X" associated with it, which is translated by PSPDN1 into one of the N different X.121 addresses, including into an address on PSPDN2.

Closed User Group   The set of **Closed User Group (CUG)** facilities enables a DTE to form one or more groups with different combinations of restrictions for access from or to other DTEs. This provides for an extra level of protection from DTEs that do not belong to the group; the CUG identity can be viewed as an extra "password" needed to access another DTE. The administrative arrangements for operation of the CUG feature, including the assignment of the CUG identity itself, is specified in Recommendation X.180. [10] If a DTE belongs to more than one CUG, it also specifies a **preferential** CUG. Some PSPDNs allow a DTE to choose not to designate any CUG as being preferred (i.e., specification of a preferential CUG is always allowed).

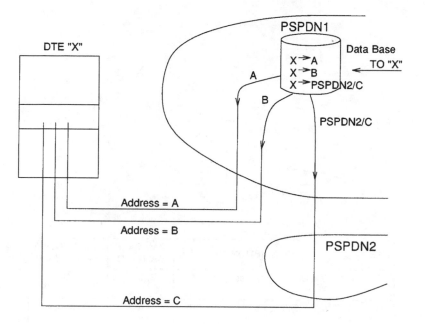

Figure 18.12   Use of alternative address calling in multihoming case.

The following CUG facilities are all optional user facilities that are agreed for period of time by the DTE and the PSPDN.

- Closed user group: This is the basic facility that enables a DTE to belong to one or more CUGs and to make/receive calls only to/from other DTEs in the same CUG.
- Closed user group with outgoing access: This is an extension of the basic CUG facility that also enables the DTE to make outgoing calls to the open part of the network (i.e., to DTEs not belonging to any CUG) and to DTEs in different CUGs that accept incoming access (calls from DTEs in other CUGs).
- Closed user group with incoming access: This is an extension of the basic CUG facility that also enables the DTE to receive incoming calls from the open part of the network and from DTEs in different CUGs that have outgoing access (they can make calls to DTEs in other CUGs).
- Incoming calls barred within the closed user group: This is a supplementary facility to the first three CUG facilities that, when used, applies per CUG and prohibits the DTE from receiving calls from other members of that CUG.
- Outgoing calls barred within the closed user group: This is a supplementary facility to the first three CUG facilities that, when used, applies per CUG and prohibits the DTE from making calls to other members of that CUG.

The indication of the relevant CUG pertaining to a call is specified at the time of setting it up. If a preferential CUG has been designated, then absence of a CUG when a call is set up is taken to implicitly select the preferred CUG as applying for the call.

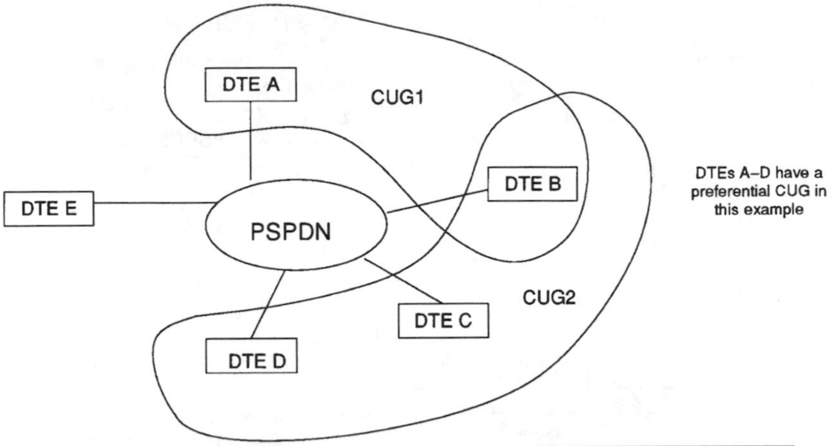

DTEs A–D have a
preferential CUG in
this example

DTE	SUBSCRIPTION	CAN MAKE CALLS TO	CAN RECEIVE CALLS FROM
A	CUG With Outgoing Access • CUG1	B, D, E	B
B	CUG With Incoming Access • CUG1 • CUG2 With Outgoing Calls Barred	A	A, C, D, E
C	CUG • CUG2	B	D
D	CUG With Incoming Access • CUG2 With Incoming Calls Barred	B, C	A, E
E	No CUG Subscription	B, D	A

Figure 18.13 Allowed access capabilities for hypothetical CUG environment.

Figure 18.13 illustrates some of the allowed combinations of access for a hypothetical set of CUG subscriptions of five DTEs.

Other Optional User Facilities   Following is a sampling of the other optional user facilities available in X.25.

- Modulo 8 is the default method for numbering Data packets at the Packet Layer. The **Extended Packet Sequence Numbering** OUF allows for modulo 128 numbering of packets. Whichever modulus is chosen applies to all logical channels on the DTE/DCE interface.
- The default use of window size of 2 and Data packet size of 128 can be changed using the **Non-standard Default Window/Packet Sizes** OUFs. The values chosen using these facilities pertain to all logical channels. For Virtual Calls, values different than the defaults can be negotiated at call set-up using the **Flow Control Parameter Negotiation** OUF. Alternative

window sizes that can be chosen range from 1 to modulo – 1; alternative packet sizes range from 16 to 4,096 octets in multiples of two.

- During the call set-up phase, only the Call Request packet may contain data to be carried from the calling DTE to the called DTE. The **Fast Select** facility expands the number of octets that can be carried from 16 to 128 and allows for all call set-up and clearing packets to carry this amount of data. The called DTE must also subscribe to the **Fast Select Acceptance** facility or else the network will not complete a Fast Select call to it (i.e., the DCE will clear the call with a cause of "Fast Select Acceptance Not Subscribed").
- When a Virtual Call is established, it is assumed that the calling DTE will be charged for the call. The **Reverse Charging** facility allows the calling DTE to request that the called DTE pay for the call. The network will only send an Incoming Call packet to the called DTE with a request for reverse charging if it subscribes to the **Reverse Charging Acceptance** facility.
- By default, each logical channel number associated with VC service can be selected by the DTE or the DCE when establishing a new call. This may result in no logical channel number being free when needed by the DTE or DCE. The **One-way Logical Channel Outgoing** OUF allows a set of logical channels to be reserved for the DTE's exclusive use when establishing new calls. The **One-way Logical Channel Incoming** OUF operates in a similar fashion for the PSPDN when it presents a new call to the DTE. Although VC establishment is uni-directional for logical channel numbers reserved with either OUF, data transfer is still bidirectional.

RELATED RECOMMENDATIONS AND STANDARDS

As mentioned in the Introduction of this chapter, there are many CCITT Recommendations and ISO Standards that both complement and supplement X.25. This section will provide a brief description of these Recommendations and Standards. Recommendation X.7 provides a more detailed overview of the CCITT Recommendations described below relating to the provision of packet-switched services.

Complementary Recommendations and Standards

As mentioned at the outset of this chapter, X.25 was never meant to stand alone. The Recommendations and Standards that follow fill in the "gaps" of X.25 in the PSPDN environment.

Actually one of the first Recommendations to do this was the 1980 version of X.25. The 1976 version, as discussed in [2], was necessary at that time to "put a stake in the ground" with respect to standardization of packet-mode operation. However, numerous items were not completely specified in the 1976 version, [11] such as values of allowed packet sizes or how to request a specific value. X.25-1980 closed many of the loopholes [12] described in reference [11] and provided the basis to allow manufacturers to implement it with confidence.

General PSPDN Access Arrangements.   Recommendation X.1 [13] describes the general access arrangements to public data networks. It describes the combinations of speeds and DTE modes of operation that can be used (user classes of service) as well as the allowed access scenarios to a public data network through other networks (categories of access).

Classification of Services and Facilities. Recommendation X.2 [14] indicates the level of support required of public data networks for services and optional user facilities. Items that must be supported are designated as Essential in X.2 whereas those that a network has the option of supporting are designated as Additional. For example, the Flow Control Parameter Negotiation facility is Essential whereas the Non-standard Default Packet Sizes facility is Additional.

DTE Specifications. While X.25 describes how a DCE operates, it does not pertain to DTE operation and leaves numerous options for DTEs to select. ISO/IEC International Standards 7776 [15] and 8208 [16] describe, respectively, Layer 2 and Layer 3 DTE operation.

Testing. Many PSPDNs require a DTE to undergo some type of testing before permitting it to connect. In many cases, a DTE may just need to show that it will not harm the network (basically, a Layer 1 test). In other cases, the DTE must also show that it is capable of correctly operating the Layer 2 and 3 protocols. The ISO/IEC 8882 set of International Standards [17] provides Layer 2 and 3 test definitions.

Addressing. As already noted above, Recommendation X.121 defines the numbering plan used in *public* data networks. This plan is a hierarchical scheme consisting of a maximum of 14 digits. Usually, the first four digits define a world zone, a country, and a network within the country. The remaining digits, up to ten, are assigned by the network to identify a particular DTE.

Call Progress Signals. Recommendation X.96 [18] defines the call progress signals that may be present in a Reset, Clear, or Restart Request or Indication packet and classifies them into several categories. For example, the call progress signal of "Fast Select Acceptance Not Subscribed" is classified as a permanent error for which retrying the call with the same Call Request packet will not succeed. However, a DTE may wish to retry a call if it fails for "Number Busy."

Arrangements for Providing Capabilities. As mentioned above, Recommendation X.180 describes the administrative arrangements for provision of the closed user group feature. X.181 [19] provides a parallel description for the X.25 PVC feature. Finally, X.301 [20] provides an abstract description of the flow of information, particularly for call set-up and clearing, within and across networks to support the features of public data networks.

Performance. Recommendations X.134 through X.140 [21] define various performance aspects, such as speed of service, availability, etc., of PSPDNs. Recommendation X.92 [22] provides a framework for the above Recommendations by splitting a virtual circuit in its component parts (e.g., DTE access links, internetwork links).

Interworking Between PSPDNs. Recommendation X.75 [23] defines the interface between two PSPDNs for supporting a virtual circuit that spans more than one network. Many of its procedures are similar or identical to those of X.25. Recommendation X.110 [24] describes the routing principles for the establishment of VCs across PSPDNs.

Charging.   While PSPDNs are free to specify their own tariffs for use on intranetwork virtual circuits, Recommendations D.10 through D.12 [25] specify the charging principles for virtual circuits that cross international boundaries. For example, D.11 indicates that a network may charge for a call attempt unless it fails due to network congestion or equipment problems.

Management.   Two ISO/IEC International Standards under development define **managed objects** that relate to X.25 resources to allow users to manage their operations. For example, the PVC object allows users to find out information such as the number of Data packets sent for accounting purposes. Likewise, information about the number of FCS errors at the Data Link Layer can also be obtained for fault-management purposes. ISO/IEC draft 10742 [26] is intended to define objects for the Data Link Layer while draft 10733 [27] is intended to define objects for the Packet Layer. The information is conveyed using general-purpose management protocols.

Higher-Layer Protocols.   A DTE may have several protocols capable of operating over the X.25 Packet Layer. ISO/IEC Technical Report (TR) 9577 [28] provides a mechanism for identifying these protocols so that the correct procedures can be used over each virtual circuit. This identifier can be carried in the User Data Field of a Call Request packet.

Supplementary Recommendations and Standards

In addition to filling in the gaps, CCITT and ISO have worked together to extend the use of X.25 (or X.25-like procedures) to environments beyond the packet-mode interface to a PSPDN. These Recommendations and Standards follow.

Switched Access to a PSPDN   As indicated in its title, X.25 assumes a dedicated circuit is used between the DTE and DCE. For backup or other purposes, it may be desirable that a switched connection be used between the DTE and DCE. Recommendation X.32 [29] specifies additional considerations for this mode of operation. For example, X.32 specifies authentication procedures to verify the identity of the DTE when it connects to the network. Furthermore, the assignment of the A and B Data Link Layer addresses may be reversed from the dedicated-connection X.25 case.

Figure 18.14 represents a more general view of the X.25 protocol stack depicted in Figure 18.2 that incorporates the aspects of X.32. In this case, a parallel set of Layer 2 and Layer 3 protocols exist for setting up the path between the DTE and DCE. The protocols on the left are used by the DTE to interact first with the switched network to establish a path to the DCE in the PSPDN.[15] Once this path is set up, the X.25 Layer 2 and Layer 3 protocols are used between the DTE and DCE.

Packet Assembly/Disassembly (PAD) Facilities   When X.25 was first adopted in 1976, it was recognized that there were many terminals that would not operate in the packet mode. Three Recommendations, X.3, X.28, and X.29 [30] (sometimes known as the Triple-X series of Recom-

---

15 This can be viewed as "dial-in" by the DTE to the DCE. "Dial-out" by the DCE to the DTE is also allowed by X.32.

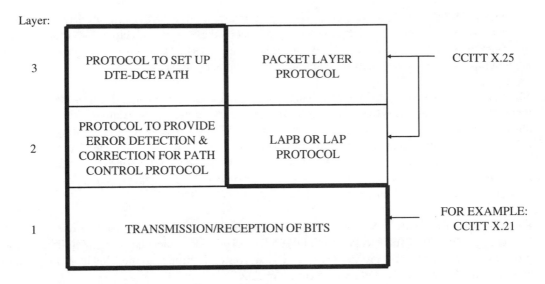

Figure 18.14 Generalized X.25 + X.32 protocol stack.

mendations), define how a start-stop terminal operating in character mode uses a PAD facility for communication. The PAD can be outside the PSPDN or inside of it as part of the service offered by the network. X.3 describes the operation of the PAD itself while X.28 describes the terminal's interface to the PAD. Functionally, many aspects of X.28 are similar to the X.25 Packet Layer. X.29 uses the X.25 Q-bit to separate control information meant for it, such as a break message sent by the PAD, from data intended for the application. More recently, three new Recommendations (X.5, X.38, and X.39 [31]) have been developed to specify how a Group 3 facsimile terminal connects to a PSPDN.

Multicast Operation Each logical channel at a DTE/DCE interface corresponds to one logical channel at a remote interface. With the adoption of Recommendation X.6 [32] in 1992, this would no longer be true. X.6 defines a general-purpose service definition for a multicast capability that could be made available in PSPDNs; however, this definition is not specific to X.25 nor PSPDNs. Under X.6, a logical channel at one DTE/DCE interface is associated with one or more logical channels at remote DTE/DCE interfaces. Data sent on one logical channel would be transmitted to all associated logical channels. Future work to specify multicast capabilities to be offered in PSPDNs would likely be documented in one or more new Recommendations.

DTE-to-DTE Operation DTEs using ISO/IEC 7776 and 8208 can also operate without an intervening PSPDN—in DTE-to-DTE mode. Issues that are prespecified in X.25 for a DTE/DCE environment are resolved for DTE-to-DTE operation in these standards. For example, the assignment of Layer 2 addresses, as described in Section 4.1, needs to be specified for DTE-to-DTE operation while remaining compatible with X.25 for the DTE/DCE environment. In the general case, these standards can be viewed as describing a DTE/DXE interface since, for the most part, it does not matter if the station at the other side of the interface is a DCE or a DTE (i.e., the other station is a "DXE").

Integrated Services Digital Networks (ISDNs)   ISDNs allow users to combine voice, data, and other information in one network. Recommendation X.31 [33] recognizes X.25 as the initial definition of packet-mode data services for an ISDN terminal. X.31 defines two scenarios for accessing X.25 services: **Case A,** where the X.25 services are provided by an existing PSPDN, and **Case B,** where they are provided by the ISDN itself (although, in fact, the X.25 packet handler may physically be located in the PSPDN). Depending on the specific details of the scenario, the resulting protocol stack may resemble Figure 18.2, where only Layer 1 is different, or Figure 18.14, with ISDN-specific protocols replacing X.21 on the left side of the protocol stack and at Layer 1. In one of the ISDN Case B scenarios, the Q.921 LAPD protocol, [34] which is quite similar to LAPB, is used below the X.25 PLP—again taking advantage of the layer-independence concepts. Recommendation X.75 is also used for interworking between a PSPDN and an ISDN providing packet-mode services (i.e., Case B operation). Recommendation X.122 [35] illustrates how numbers from the ISDN numbering plan in Recommendation E.164 [36] and from the PSPDN numbering plan in X.121 are carried from one network to the other.

Local Area Networks (LANs)   Many of the features of the X.25 Packet Layer, such as the ability to dynamically establish connections using the X.25 VC capability, are useful by stations on an LAN. ISO/IEC International Standard 8881 [37] provides additional considerations for operating ISO/IEC 8208 as the Layer 3 protocol in LANs. In this environment, ISO/IEC 8208 is usually used in the DTE-to-DTE mode and operates over a protocol other than LAPB, again invoking the layer-independence concept.

Public-to-Private X.25 Interworking   Many large organizations have their own private X.25 network to which only their systems can connect. It was decided in the early 1980s that X.25, rather than X.75, would be used as the interface between a PSPDN and a private X.25 network. Several enhancements have been made to X.25 over the years, such as extension of the Closed User Group capabilities, to facilitate this interworking. Recommendation X.327 [38] specifies a general framework for this interworking case. Furthermore, X.pvt [39] is being developed to provide more details, such as how addresses are carried between the two X.25 networks.

X.25/PLP-to-X.25/PLP Gateways   In line with X.327 and X.pvt, ISO TR 10029 [40] specifies the detailed procedures for a gateway between two networks for the special case when DTEs on both networks use the X.25 PLP as specified in ISO/IEC 8208. For example, TR 10029 could be used to connect an LAN where ISO/IEC 8881 is used to a PSPDN.

Open Systems Interconnection (OSI)   The work on OSI started a few years after X.25 was first adopted. Even in its initial drafts, the capabilities being defined for the OSI Network Layer closely resembled the X.25 PLP. A few enhancements have been added over the years to close this gap. Four sets of Recommendations and Standards have been adopted that relate the X.25 PLP to OSI.

- The mapping of X.25 PLP protocol elements to the abstract services provided by the OSI Network Layer to the Transport Layer is given in Recommendation X.223 and ISO/IEC International Standard 8878. [41] Note that not all elements of the X.25 PLP are needed in this mapping; some elements, such as the Q-bit, are outside of OSI.

- Special considerations when providing the OSI Network Layer service over specific network types are described in Recommendation X.612 and International Standard 9574 [42] for ISDNs, in Recommendation X.613 and International Standard 10588 [43] for CSPDNs, and in Recommendation X.614 and International Standard 10732 [44] for the telephone network.
- Generic operation of a "gateway" (referred to as an OSI **Intermediate System**) is specified in ISO/IEC International Standard 10177. [45] This standard is an abstraction of the approach of ISO/IEC TR 10029 previously mentioned.
- OSI routing in conjunction with Recommendation X.223 or International Standard 8878 is given in ISO/IEC International Standard 10030. [46]

The work on X.25 in conjunction with LANs, interworking and gateways, and OSI is of particular importance since many people in the early 1980s viewed X.25 as just a "PSPDN interface." It shows how X.25 (or at least the X.25 PLP) can be used in a general fashion across networks of different technologies to provide a uniform internet environment. Figure 18.15 illustrates how many of the Recommendations and International Standards described above fit into such a global internet environment.

CONCLUSION

X.25 has come a long way in its eighteen-year history—from a single protocol to one of a family of over fifty related ISO/IEC International Standards and CCITT Recommendations that together provide a complete networking platform. X.25 and packet-switched networks provide the foundation for much of the world's X.400 messaging and electronic-mail services, such as AT&T EasyLink. This application was not even standardized by CCITT until 1984.

Many enhancements have been made to X.25 over the years to keep it current. Features such as alternative addressing provide current users greater flexibility while start-stop framing, X.31, X.32, and ISO/IEC 8881 extend X.25 capabilities to new users. Today there are several PSPDNs and DTE manufacturers that provide or will soon provide access lines at megabit/second speeds, something unheard of just a few short years ago. The primary application for these high speeds is to connect LANs. In some arenas, frame relay technology is being pushed as a replacement of X.25 for LAN interconnect; however, it is unclear whether such replacement will actually occur. [47] Further work is planned over the next four years to extend X.25 to run at even higher speeds by making use of HDLC features such as selective retransmission and to use charge cards for billing purposes. Meanwhile, work continues in the areas of routing, management, security, and multicast operation.

At the same time, the features of X.25 have also found their way into other environments. For example, the X.25 Closed User Group feature is available as an ISDN supplementary service[16] (SS). As it turns out, there is a large amount of similarity between the X.25 OUFs and the ISDN SSs. [48] Likewise, X.25 has had a major influence on the evolution of the work on Open Systems Intercon-

---

16 ISDN supplementary services are similar in purpose to X.25 optional user facilities in that they augment a basic default mode of operation.

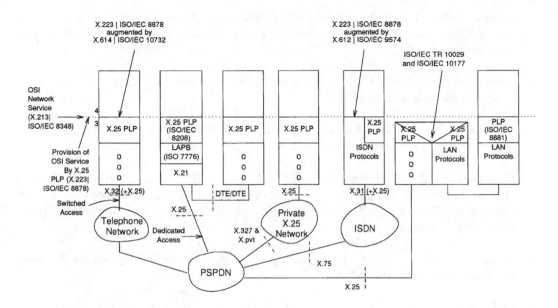

Figure 18.15   Global internet environment using the X.25 PLP.

nection. Although other technologies are starting to emerge, it is likely that X.25 will continue to play a dominant role in the data communications scene for quite some time.

REFERENCES

1.   CCITT Recommendation X.21, *Interface between data terminal equipment (DTE) and data circuit-terminating equipment (DCE) for synchronous operation on public data networks.*

2.   Sirbu, M. A. and Zwimpfer, L. E. March 1985. "Standards Setting for Computer Communication: The Case of X.25." *IEEE Network* 23, no. 3.

3.   ISO/IEC 3309 and Amendments, *Information technology—Telecommunications and information exchange between systems—High-level data link control (HDLC) procedures—Frame structure.*

ISO/IEC 4335 and Amendments, *Information technology—Telecommunications and information exchange between systems—High-level data link control (HDLC) procedures—Elements of procedures.*

ISO/IEC 7809 and Amendments, *Information technology—Telecommunications and information exchange between systems—High-level data link control (HDLC) procedures—Classes of procedures.*

4. Gostl, J. October 1977. "A Problem with the X.25 Link Access Procedure." *ACM Computer Communications Review* 7, no. 4.

5. Paper COM VII-217-E submitted to CCITT Study Group VII meeting of April 1992. "Modulos and Flow Control Parameters in X.2, X.25 and X.75." Source: Intelsat.

6. Paper COM VII-218-E submitted to CCITT Study Group VII meeting of April 1992. "Analysis of Multi-Selective Reject (SREJ) Throughput Performance for X.25 Link Access Procedures Across the DTE/DCE Interface and X.75 Link Layer Procedures Between Signalling Terminals." Source: Intelsat.

7. Burg, F. M. and Tewani, K. T. "Signalling for X.25: Meeting User Needs for Advanced Features." Paper submitted to ICCC '92.

8. CCITT Recommendation X.7, *Technical characteristics of data transmission services.*

9. CCITT Recommendation X.121, *International numbering plan for public data networks.*

10. CCITT Recommendation X.180, *Administrative arrangements for international closed user groups (CUGs).*

11. Hess, M. L. et al. June 1979. "A Comparison of Four X.25 Public Network Interfaces." *Proceedings of the International Conference on Communications* 3.

12. Rybczynski, A. M. and Palframan J. D. 1980. "A Common X.25 Interface to Public Data Networks." *Computer Networks* 4.

13. CCITT Recommendation X.1, *International user classes of service in and categories of access to public data networks and integrated services digital network (ISDNs).*

14. CCITT Recommendation X.2, *International data transmission services and optional user facilities in public data networks and ISDNs.*

15. ISO 7776, *Information processing systems—Data communication—High-level data link control procedures—Description of the X.25 LAPB-compatible DTE data link procedures.*

16. ISO/IEC 8208, *Information technology—Data communications—X.25 packet layer protocol for data terminal equipment.*

17. ISO/IEC 8882-1, *Information processing systems—X.25 DTE conformance testing—Part 1: General principles.*

ISO/IEC 8882-2, *Information technology—Telecommunications and information exchange between systems—X.25 DTE conformance testing, Part 2: Data link layer test suite.*

ISO/IEC 8882-3, *Information technology—Telecommunications and information exchange between systems—X.25 DTE conformance testing, Part 3: Packet level conformance test suite.*

18. CCITT Recommendation X.96, *Call progress signals in public data networks.*

19. CCITT Recommendation X.181, *Administrative arrangements for the provision of international permanent virtual circuits (PVCs).*

20. CCITT Recommendation X.301, *Description of general arrangements for call control within a subnetwork and between subnetworks for the provision of data transmission services.*

21. CCITT Recommendation X.134, *Portion boundaries and packet layer reference events; basis for defining packet-switched performance parameters.*

CCITT Recommendation X.135, *Speed of service (delay and throughput) performance values for public data networks when providing international packet-switched services.*

CCITT Recommendation X.136, *Accuracy and dependability performance values for public data networks when providing international packet-switched services.*

CCITT Recommendation X.137, *Availability performance values for public data networks when providing international packet-switched services.*

CCITT Recommendation X.138, *Measurement of performance values for public data networks when providing international packet-switched services.*

CCITT Recommendation X.139, *Echo, drop, generator and test DTEs for measurement performance values in public data networks when providing international packet-switched services.*

CCITT Recommendation X.140, *General quality of service parameters for communications via public data networks.*

22. CCITT Recommendation X.92, *Hypothetical reference connections for public synchronous data networks.*

23. CCITT Recommendation X.75, *Packet-switched signaling system between public networks providing data transmission services.*

24. CCITT Recommendation X.110, *International routing principles and routing plan for public data networks.*

25. CCITT Recommendation D.10, *General tariff principles for international public data communication services.*

    CCITT Recommendation D.11, *Special tariff principles for international packet-switched public data communication services by means of the virtual call facility.*

    CCITT Recommendation D.12, *Measurement unit for charging by volume in the international packet-switched data communication service.*

26. ISO/IEC 10742, *Information technology—Telecommunications and information exchange between systems—Elements of management information related to OSI data link layer standards.*

27. ISO/IEC 10733, *Information technology—Telecommunications and information exchange between systems—Elements of management information relating to OSI network layer standards.*

28. ISO/IEC TR 9577, *Information technology—Telecommunications and information exchange between systems—Protocol identification in the network layer.*

29. CCITT Recommendation X.32, *Interface between data terminal equipment (DTE) and data circuit-terminating equipment (DCE) for terminals operating in the packet mode and accessing a packet switched packet data network through a public switched telephone network or an integrated services digital network or a circuit switched public data network.*

30. CCITT Recommendation X.3, *Packet assembly/disassembly facility (PAD) in a public data network.*

    CCITT Recommendation X.28, *DTE/DCE interface for a start-stop mode data terminal equipment accessing the packet assembly/disassembly facility (PAD) in a public data network situated in the same country.*

    CCITT Recommendation X.29, *Procedures for the exchange of control information and user data between a packet assembly/disassembly (PAD) facility and a packet-mode DTE or another PAD.*

31. CCITT Recommendation X.5, *Facsimile packet assembly/disassembly facility (FPAD) in a public data network.*

    CCITT Recommendation X.38, *Facsimile equipment/DCE interface for G3 facsimile equipment accessing the facsimile packet assembly/disassembly facility (FPAD) in a public data network situated in the same country.*

CCITT Recommendation X.39, *Procedures for the exchange of control information and user data between a facsimile packet assembly/disassembly (FPAD) facility and a packet mode DTE or another FPAD.*

32. CCITT Recommendation X.6, *Multicast service definition.*

33. CCITT Recommendation X.31, *Support of packet mode terminal equipment by an ISDN.*

34. CCITT Recommendation Q.921, *ISDN user-network interface—Data link layer specification.*

35. CCITT Recommendation X.122/E.166, *Numbering plan interworking for the E.164 and X.121 numbering plans.*

36. CCITT Recommendation E.164, *Numbering plan for the ISDN era.*

37. ISO/IEC 8881, *Information processing systems—Data communications—Use of the X.25 packet level protocol in local area networks.*

38. CCITT Recommendation X.327, *General arrangements for interworking between packet switched public data networks (PSPDNs) and private data networks for the provision of data transmission services.*

39. CCITT Draft Recommendation X.pvt, *Interface between a PSPDN and a private PSDN which is based on modified X.25 procedures to define a gateway function that is provided in the PSPDN.*

40. ISO/IEC TR 10029, *Information technology—Telecommunications and information exchange between systems—Operation of an X.25 interworking unit.*

41. CCITT Recommendation X.223, *Use of X.25 to provide the OSI connection-mode network service for CCITT applications.*

    ISO 8878, *Information processing systems—Data communications—Use of X.25 to Provide the OSI connection-mode network service.*

42. CCITT Recommendation X.612, *Provision of the OSI connection-mode network service by packet mode terminal equipment connected to an integrated services digital network (ISDN) for CCITT applications.*

    ISO/IEC 9574 and Amendments, *Information technology—Telecommunications and information exchange between systems—Provision of the OSI connection-mode network service by packet mode terminal equipment connected to an integrated services digital network (ISDN).*

43. CCITT Recommendation X.613, *Information technology—Use of X.25 packet layer protocol in conjunction with X.21/X.21 bis to provide the OSI connection-mode network service.*

ISO/IEC 10588, *Information technology—Telecommunications and information exchange between systems—Use of X.25 packet layer protocol in conjunction with X.21/X.21 bis to provide the OSI connection-mode network service.*

44. CCITT Recommendation X.614, *Information technology—Use of X.25 packet layer protocol to provide the OSI connection-mode network service over the telephone network.*

ISO/IEC 10732, *Information technology—Telecommunications and information exchange between systems—Use of X.25 packet layer protocol to provide the OSI connection-mode network service over the telephone network.*

45. ISO/IEC 10177, *Information technology—Telecommunications and information exchange between systems—Intermediate-system support of OSI CONS using ISO/IEC 8208:1990 in accordance with ISO/IEC CD 10028.*

46. ISO/IEC 10030, *Information technology—Telecommunications and information exchange between systems—End system routing information exchange protocol for use in conjunction with ISO 8878.*

47. Duclos, D. February 1992. "X.25 or Frame Relay: Some Thoughts," presented at Telecom Network '92.

48. CCITT COM-VII-R 18, *Report of the November 1990 meeting of Study Group VII, Working Party VII/I*, Annex 2.

19

T1–T3 BASICS

Telecommunications Techniques Corporation

INTRODUCTION

When a technology gains rapid acceptance, it often reaches "buzzword" status before the details are commonly understood. So it is with T1: Although it is an important part of many communications networks, many of us are still trying to learn the fundamentals.

The objective of this chapter is to provide the reader with basic information about T1. It starts with a definition and brief history, evolves to describe how the technology actually works, and concludes with a summary of the benefits and techniques of testing T1 networks. T3 is also described.

OVERVIEW OF T1

T1 is a digital communications link that enables the transmission of voice, data, and video signals at the rate of 1.544 million bits per second (Mbps). Introduced in the 1960s, it was initially used by telephone companies who wished to reduce the number of telephone cables in large metropolitan areas.

In its early days, the expense of installing T1 made the technology cost-prohibitive for many end users. In fact, the primary user of T1 services outside of telephone companies was the federal government. But in the early 1980s, the service was retariffed so that substantial savings could be realized with the purchase of large amounts of bandwidth.

After retariffing, the demand for T1 pushed the waiting time for new installations to more than a year. What's more, T1 will continue to grow in the 1990s; analysts predict that the number of user-based T1 facilities will triple in the decade's first three years.

WHY IS T1 IN DEMAND?

The current demand for T1 services can be linked to a number of tangible benefits.

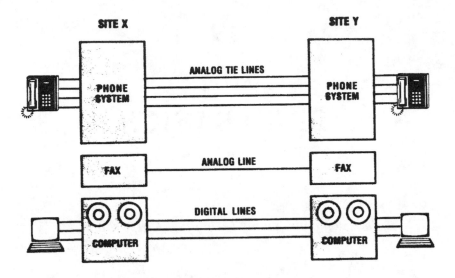

Figure 19.1a   A communications network without T1.

Simplification

T1 simplifies the task of networking different types of communications equipment. To illustrate, Figure 19.1a shows what a company's communications network might look like without T1.

Figure 19.1a shows that telephone, facsimile, and computer applications all require separate lines. Typically, voice and low-speed data applications are serviced by analog lines, while high-speed data applications are serviced by digital facilities.

Figure 19.1b depicts the same network with a T1 link installed. T1 links carry both voice and data on a single digital communications link. By reducing the number of lines needed to carry information, the task of managing many different networks is simplified. One example of equipment that merges these signals is the T1 multiplexer and is described in more detail later in the chapter.

Economy

T1 is extremely economical for organizations with high traffic volumes. As an example, Figure 19.2a depicts a multiline corporate network between Dallas and Denver (Flanagan, 1986). In 1985, the monthly operating costs of the network shown in Figure 19.2a were approximately $27,000.

Using a T1 link eliminated the expense of separate lines (Figure 19.2b). Monthly operating costs decreased by approximately $7,000 per month, or $85,000 per year. And since 1985, the tariffs have moved even more favorably toward T1 usage. The yearly savings on operating costs for this corporate network have since increased to over $150,000 (Flanagan, 1986).

In addition to cost savings, the T1 model shown in Figure 19.2b provides plenty of bandwidth for future expansion with no increased transmission costs.

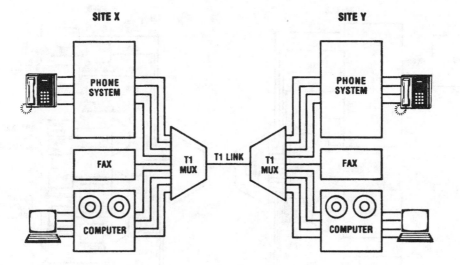

Figure 19.1b   A communications network with T1.

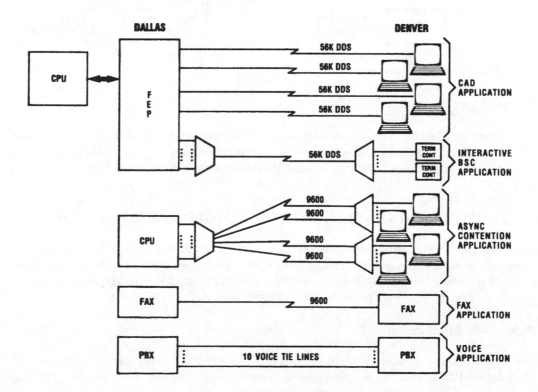

Figure 19.2a   A multiline corporate network.

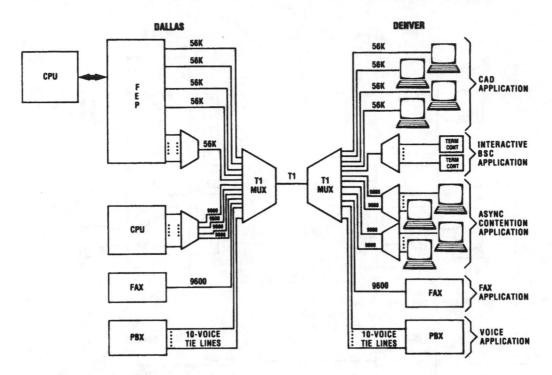

Figure 19.2b   A multiline corporate network with T1.

Signal Quality

T1 also provides a signal that is consistently superior in quality to that provided by analog facilities. Analog circuits amplify noise and distortion to levels that can impair voice and severely degrade data service. But T1 regenerates the original signal without the noise and distortion at various points along the link.

HOW T1 WORKS—MAKING VOICE AND DATA COMPATIBLE

Many benefits of T1 are attributable to the fact that voice and data are transmitted over a single digital communications link. Since computer data consists of 1s and 0s (the symbols of the binary system), it is already compatible with T1's digital format. However, because voice signals are actually complex analog wave forms, they must be digitized to achieve compatibility with T1.

Pulse Code Modulation

The most common method of digitizing analog voice signals a technique called **Pulse Code Modulation(PCM).** PCM is a sampling process that compresses a voice conversation into a 64 Kbps standard rate known as **digital signal-level zero (DS-0).**

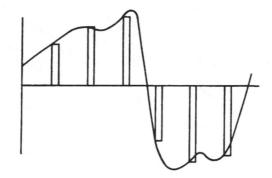

Figure 19.3   Pulse amplitude modulation.

PCM is actually a two-step technique. In the first step, the incoming analog signal is sampled 8,000 times per second, a rate sufficient to adequately represent voice information. These sample values are then converted to pulses using a process known as **pulse amplitude modulation (PAM).** (See Figure 19.3.)

In the second step, the height of each pulse is assigned an equivalent 8-bit binary value. (See Figure 19.4.) The resulting output is digital representation of the pulse and, by extension, the sample analog wave form.

Note that the 664 Kbps DS-0 rate is obtained by multiplying the number of samplings per second (8,000) by the number of bits in each sample (8).

Time Division Multiplexing

Once digitized, voice and/or data signals from many sources can be combined (i.e., multiplexed) and transmitted over a single T1 link. This process is made possible by a technique called **Time Division Multiplexing (TDM).**

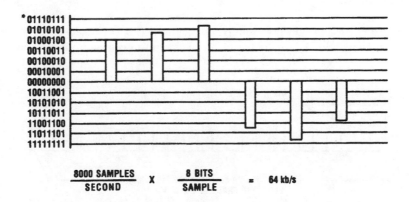

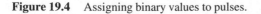

Figure 19.4   Assigning binary values to pulses.

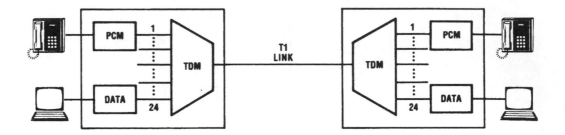

Figure 19.5 Time division multiplexing.

TDM divides the T1 link into 24 discrete 64 Kbps time slots. An identical number of DS-0 signals (representing 24 separate voice and/or data calls) is assigned to each time slot for transmission within the link. (See Figure 19.5.)

In addition to being critical operational techniques, PCM and TDM are also key to understanding the basic T1 rate of 1.544 Mbps.

1.544 Mbps Explained

In T1, the 8-bit digital samples created in the PCM step (for voice traffic only) are grouped into the 24 discrete DS-0 time slots created by TDM. Each group of 24 time slots is called a **T1 frame.** (See Figure 19.6a.) Additionally, a 193rd bit is added to mark the end of one frame and the beginning of the next. Appropriately enough, this added bit is called the **framing bit**.

Since the DS-0 signals are sampled 8,000 times per second, it means that 8,000 192-bit information frames are created during that period. The total is 1.536 Mbps. At 8,000 samples per second, framing bits are created at the rate of 8Kbps. The result is a single 1.544 Mbps signal known as **digital signal-level one (DS-1)** (see Figure 19.6).

Signal Regeneration

Any newly created DS-1 signal begins strongly, but degrades (i.e., attenuates) as it progresses along the T1 link. Such attenuation is usually the result of line noise caused by interference from other

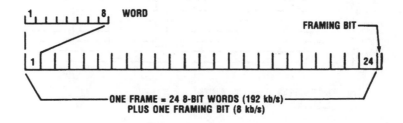

Figure 19.6a A T1 frame.

Step	What Happens	Calculation
1.	The 8-bit digital samples created by PCM (for voice signals only) are grouped into the 24 discrete time slots created by TDM. Each group of 24 time slots is called a *T1 frame*.	24 samples × 8 bits per sample 192 information bits per frame.
2.	A framing bit is added to mark the end of one frame and the beginning of the next.	192 information bits + 1 framing bit 193 total bits per frame.
3.	T1 frames are transmitted at the rate of 8,000 per second.	8,000 samples × 193 sample bits 1,544,000 bits per secod (1.544 Mbps).

Figure 19.6b   Calculating the 1.544 Mbps T1 rate.

electrical sources. To compensate for these negative effects, devices called **regenerative repeaters** sample and recreate the original signal at periodic intervals along the link. (See Figure 19.7.)

Since the digital signal consists of only two basic values (0 and 1), recreating it is not a complicated matter. In simple terms, a regenerative repeater samples the signal input, determines if the input represents a 0 or 1, and recreates each value accordingly. Since line noise deviates from the standard format of the DS-1 signal, it is discarded. In this way, a regenerative repeater produces a "clean" replica of the original signal.

The number of regenerative repeaters that may be required along the path of the T1 link varies with the type of transmission media used. For example, copper wire (a common short-haul metallic medium) is highly prone to signal attenuation; thus, repeaters are normally required at 6,000-foot intervals. In contrast, fiber-optic cable is a long-haul medium with low potential for attenuation; as such, repeaters are spaced at 30-mile intervals.

Table 19.1 describes the characteristics of a wide variety of T1 transmission media in detail.

THE DS-1 SIGNAL FORMAT

The DS-1 signal is transmitted on the T1 link in a binary format (1s and 0s). The ability to recognize the proper format if the DS-1 signal is why regenerative repeaters can distinguish valid input from

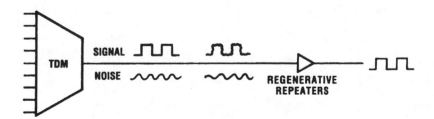

Figure 19.7   Signal regeneration.

Table 19.1   T1 transmission media

Media Type	Description	Often Used In	Prime Advantage	Prime Disadvantage
Twisted Pair Cable	Wood-pulp or plastic insulated wires twisted together into pairs. *Repeaters:* Normally required at 6,000-foot intervals.	Short-haul networks by loop and exchange carriers.	Low cost, easy installation.	Narrow bandwidth, prone to crosstalk.
Coaxial Cable	One or more center conductors surrounded by flexible braid or semirigid copper or aluminum tube. *Repeaters:* Normally required at 40-mile intervals.	Intercity routes in long-haul networks, areas of heavy traffic.	Large bandwidth for high-speed data or video, good noise immunity.	High installation costs, cable is expensive and must be placed carefully.
Microware Radio	Free-space transmission between ground stations. A line-of-sight transmission path is used, eliminating the need for a physical transmission medium. *Stations:* Typically placed at 20–30 mile intervals.	Medium-haul terrestrial transmission.	Inexpensive, bridges areas where right-of-way is expensive to obtain, very high capacity, low error rate.	Signals weaken when weather interferes with line of sight, problems with fading due to reflecting signals.
Fiber-optic Cable	Ribbon cable consisting of 1–12 flat ribbons, with each ribbon containing 12 glass fibers. *Repeaters:* Although practical at 30-mile intervals, some systems space repeaters at 100-mile intervals.	Medium- and large-capacity interoffice trunks, long-haul intercity routes, video hookups, transoceanic cable systems.	Very high capacity, low attenuation, very good noise immunity, small size, light weight, easy equipment connection.	Difficulty in obtaining right-of-way access, reliability affected by inability to predict cable cuts, high installation costs.
Satellite	Free-space transmission from ground station to a communications satellite and back to earth. *Repeaters:* One per satellite system.	Transmitting data at very long distances.	Transmission cost independent of distance, ability to send large amounts of data anywere.	Distance between earth and satellite produces long delays, which can impair voice and seriously damage data transmission.

Process	What Happens
Pulse Code Modulation (PCM)	1. Samples the incoming analog signals 8,000 times per second and converts the sampled values to pulses. 2. Assigns the height of each pulse an equivalent 8-bit digital value. 3. Creates a 64 Kbps DS-0 signal (8,000 samples per second multiplied by 8 bits).
Time Division Multiplexing (TDM)	Combines 24 DS-0 signals to create a single 1.544 Mbps signal (DS-1).
Signal Regeneration	Recreates the 1.544 Mbps signal at prescribed intervals along the transmission path.

Figure 19.8a   How T1 works.

line noise. As an example, Figure 19.8a depicts a format that is very commonly used over metallic transmission media (e.g., twisted pair cable, copper wire, etc.): **alternate mark inversion(AMI)** (Figure 19.8b).

In the AMI signaling format, the binary value of 1 is represented by a square wave (i.e., pulse); the binary value of 0 is represented by a straight line (i.e., the absence of a pulse). Note that each pulse alternates between positive and negative polarity, making the signal **bipolar** in format.

The primary advantage of the bipolar format is that it allows the DS-1 signal to travel twice as far on a pair of copper wires. Another advantage of the bipolar format is its ability to offer a built-in method of error detection. When consecutive pulses of the same polarity are detected, it constitutes a **bipolar violation (BPV)**. BPVs indicate that signal input has been disrupted due to defective equipment or poor environmental conditions (e.g., storms).

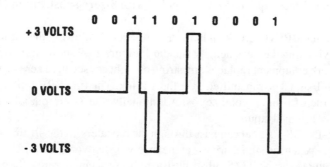

Figure 19.8b   Alternate mark inversion.

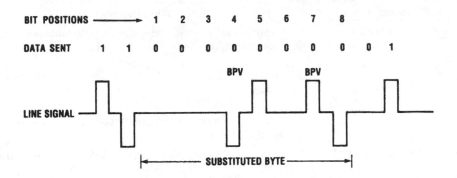

Figure 19.9 Bipolar with 8-zero substitution (B8ZS).

B8ZS, Signal Timing, and Ones Density

To correctly identify DS-1 input, the regenerative repeater must know when to sample the bipolar signal to determine whether a 0 or a 1 is being transmitted at any given time. To ensure proper sampling, the repeater relies on a timing method that uses the binary pulses (i.e., ones) to maintain synchronization with the network equipment that is transmitting the DS-1 signal.

Since pulses are critical to maintaining proper signal timing, all DS-1 signals are required to meet specific **ones density standards.** These standards require that at least one pulse be transmitted within any 8-bit sequence (i.e., 12.5 percent ones density). Further, since long strings of consecutive zeros between digital values can also hinder signal timing, ones density standards prohibit the transmission of more than fifteen zeros in succession.

Success in meeting ones density requirements can vary based on application. For example, since the size and content of the bit patterns that represent human speech are consistent, acceptable ones density in voice applications is a virtual certainty. But since computer data is highly variable in size and content, conformance to ones density standards cannot always be guaranteed. This technical problem is why a coding technique known as **bipolar with 8-zero substitution (B8ZS)** has gained in popularity.

B8ZS uses intentional BPVs to break up long strings of zeros, allowing their transmission through the T1 link without violating the ones density standard. Figure 19.9 shows how B8ZS works.

With B8ZS, network equipment replaces any string of eight consecutive zeros with two intentional BPVs before the DS-1 signal is transmitted over the T1 link: The first BPV replaces the fourth zero; the second replaces the fifth and seventh zeros. Additionally, the 8-zero bit, which normally would be coded as a zero, is assigned a pulse.

Using this format, the DS-1 signal can pass through the repeaters on the T1 link with an acceptable level of pulse density. When the signal arrives at the receiving network equipment, the pattern shown in Figure 19.9 is recognized as the B8ZS substitute for eight consecutive zeros; the equipment replaces the intentional BPVs with their zero values.

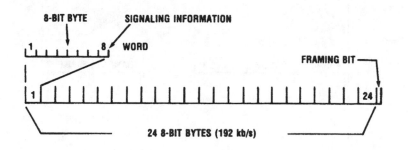

Figure 19.10   The D1 framing pattern.

DS-1 FRAMING

The bits in the 1.544 Mbps DS-1 signal are meaningless unless they are organized in an orderly, understandable way. **Framing** provides this organization.

A frame contains one sample (byte) from each of the DS-1's 24 time slots. Framing bits separate the frames and indicate the order of information arriving at the receiving equipment.

Although most standard T1 networks use framing, the pattern of the frame can vary depending on the sophistication of the equipment that is sending and receiving the DS-1 signal. The sections that follow describe typical DS-1 framing patterns starting with the most simple: the D1 frame.

The D1 Frame

Shown in Figure 19.10, D1 was the first framing pattern to be used in T1 transmission.

A D1 frame contains 24 time slots, each carrying an 8-bit word, with one bit serving as a framing boundary ($24 \times 8 + 1 = 193$). In the D1 framing pattern, bits 1–7 of each 8-bit word are reserved for customer information (e.g., digitized voice), bit eight of each word is reserved for signaling information (i.e., call set-up and routing), and bit 193 serves as the boundary between the end of one frame and the beginning of the next. (See Figure 19.11a.)

The D1 framing format can certainly simplify framing and signaling management for T1 networks with older, unsophisticated equipment. Unfortunately, D1 is also very inefficient: Reserving one bit every 8-bit word for signaling can degrade a voice signal to levels below toll quality.

Bit(s)	Contain(s)
1–7 of each 8-bit word	The customer's digitized voice or computer data.
8 of each 8-bit word	Signaling information that controls call set-up and routing.
193 of each frame	The boundary between the end of one frame and the beginning of the next.

Figure 19.11a   D1 framing organization.

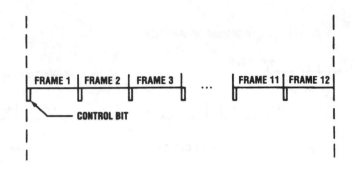

Figure 19.11b The superframe.

Fortunately, the sophistication level of the equipment in T1 networks has increased dramatically. As such, it is now possible for many frames to share the same framing and signaling information. Thus, the chance to free more bits for customer information (thereby improving signal quality) inspired the development of the **superframe.** (See Figure 19.11b.)

A superframe is made up of twelve individual frames, with the 193rd bit in each frame used as a control bit. When combined, these control bits form a twelve-digit word (100011011100) that provides frame and signal management.

D4 Framing

In today's public switched telephone network, the pattern commonly used to organize the superframe is the **D4 framing pattern.**

In D4 framing, the odd bits in the control word (called **terminal frame** or **ft** bits: 1X0X1X0X1X0X) mark frame and superframe boundaries so that the receiving equipment can correctly process the customer's voice or data information.

The even bits in the control word (called **signaling frame** or **fs** bits: X0X0X1X1X1X0) identify the frames that carry signaling information. Note that frames with signaling information are marked by changes in the bit pattern. For example, control bits 2 and 4 contain zeros; since control bit 6 is coded as a one, it means that the sixth frame contains signaling information. Further, control bits 8 and 10 contain ones; since control bit 12 is coded as a zero, it means that the twelfth frame also contains signaling information.

To enable the sharing of signaling bits by all frames in the superframe, D4 framing uses a process called **robbed bit signaling.** (See Figure 19.12.)

Using robbed bit signaling, the least significant (eighth) bit of the DS-0s in the sixth and twelfth frames is reserved for signaling information. The steady state of the bit, 0 or 1, indicates whether the called device is on-hook, off-hook, disconnected, busy, etc.

In summary, D4 framing improved signal quality by freeing more bits for customer information. But the continued emphasis on quality and the evolution of integrated circuit technology have farther enhanced the superframe.

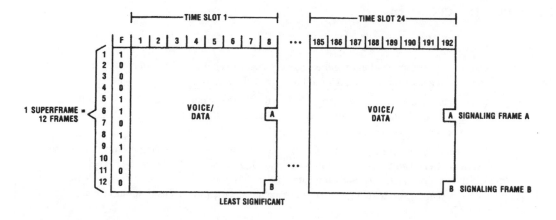

Figure 19.12   Robbed bit signaling.

Extended Superframe (ESF)

Since FCC tariffs require a specific standard of performance, providers of T1 circuits frequently test their links and equipment. But when a link is removed from service for test purposes, it is neither producing revenue nor serving the communications needs of the customer.

The need to obtain a true measure of system performance without disrupting service spurred the development of the **Extended Superframe Format (ESF).** ESF expands the superframe from twelve to twenty-four 193-bit frames. (See Figure 19.13.) Like the D4 format, the 193rd bit in each frame is always a control bit.

If ESF were merely D4 framing multiplied by two, then all of its twenty-four control bits (transmitted at 8 Kbps) would be used for frame and signal management. Instead, three-fourths are reserved for the evaluation of circuit performance.

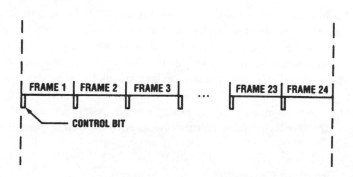

Figure 19.13   The extended superframe (ESF).

Table 19.2   How CRC-6 Works

Step	Activity
1.	The network equipment building the ESF performs a mathematical calculation on the signal to be transmitted across the T1 link. (Control bits are excluded from the calculation.)
2.	The signal is transmitted across the T1 link to the receiving equipment. The result of the mathematical calculation is a 6-bit word which is sent to the receiving equipment in the six CRC bit positions of the *next* ESF.
3.	The receiving network equipment performs the same mathematical calculation on the customer information, and compares the result with the 6-bit word which arrives in the next ESF. If the results match, it is likely that no bit errors have occurred; if the results do not match, it indicates that one or more logic errors have occurred, either in the customer information or in the CRC bits.

In ESF, six control bits are reserved for a **Cyclic Redundancy Check (CRC),** a method of detecting errors as information is transmitted along the T1 link (2 Kbps); twelve bits are reserved as a data link for communication between transmitting and receiving equipment at either side of the T1 link (4 Kbps); and six bits are used to manage signaling and framing (2Kbps).

The sections that follow briefly describe the ESF's CRC and data link capabilities.

CRC-6

CRC-6 is a 6-bit word that detects, with 98.4 percent accuracy, bit errors (i.e., zeros that should be ones and vice versa) in any block of live data. Table 19.2 depicts how CRC-6 works in very simple terms. Consult the References section at the conclusion of this chapter for a list of the publications that describe CRC-6 in greater detail.

The ESF Data Link

ESF reserves twelve bits (transmitted at 4 Kbps) as a data link for communication between the transmitting and receiving equipment on each side of the T1 link. Although it can be used for any purpose, one typical use is the transmission of trouble flags such as the **yellow alarm signal.**

The yellow alarm signal is sent by the receiving equipment when synchronization to a transmitting DS-1 signal cannot be achieved. The yellow alarm is a continuous 16-bit pattern of eight consecutive ones followed by eight consecutive zeros.

Note that the yellow alarm signal is only one example of how a data link can be used. Consult the References section at the conclusion of this chapter for a list of the publications that describe other uses for the data link.

ESF's Enhanced Signaling Capability

In addition to circuit management, ESF also provides enhanced signaling capability. By robbing the eighth bit from the sixth, twelfth, eighteenth and twenty-fourth frames (signaling bits A, B, C, and

D, respectively) in the superframe, more than sixteen signaling states can be represented. Enhanced signaling capability is essential for emerging services such as video, where signaling states beyond the few used in voice service may be required.

T1 EQUIPMENT—A SIMPLE T1 CIRCUIT

T1 networks are composed of different types of equipment, each with a unique role in making the technology work. The equipment that is required in any given T1 network is often based on what the network is designed to do. As an example, a simple private T1 circuit is shown in Figure 19.14a. Note that the circuit is specifically dedicated to connecting the corporate office in Dallas and Denver (previously shown in Figures 19.2a and b).

T1 circuits like the one shown in Figure 19.14a contain three general equipment types: termination equipment, user interface equipment, and transmission equipment.

Terminating equipment primarily serves to build the DS-1 signal from voice and data signals of various substrates. (Terminating equipment is where PCM and TDM are performed.) This type of equipment also "unbuilds" (i.e., demultiplexes) the DS-1 and returns voice and data signals to their original substrates at the receiving end. Examples of terminating equipment include **channel banks** and **T1 multipliers** (see Figure 19.14b).

User interface equipment connects terminating equipment with the T1 link, and ensures that both ends of the link send and receive a high-quality DS-1 signal. As such, user interface equipment checks for conformance to ones density standards, corrects BPVs, detects yellow alarms, determines AMI or B8ZS signal formatting, and performs CRC-6 calculations (ESF framing only). One common type of these functions is the **channel service unit (CSU).**

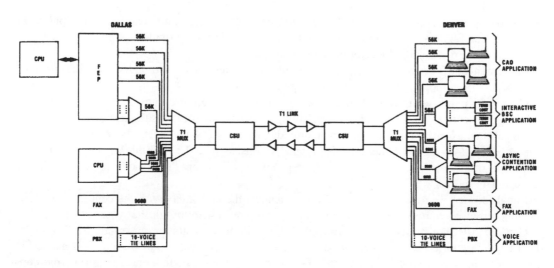

Figure 19.14a   A simple T1 circuit.

Equipment	Description
Channel Bank	A simple device typically used in T1 voice applications. Converts analog voice to digital code (i.e., PCM) and combines twenty-four such calls on a single DS-1 signal (i.e., TDM). "Unbuilds" (demultiplexes) the DS-1 signal and returns the voice signal to its original analog state at the receiving end.
T1 Multiplexer	Sophisticated termination equipment used in both voice and data applications. In addition to performing the functions associated with the channel bank, the T1 multiplexer also offers opportunities for network and bandwidth management. NETWORK MANAGEMENT: A company allocates more individual lines to its phone system during peak calling hours and later reassigns the capacity to its computer system for file transfers. BANDWIDTH MANAGEMENT: A company customizes T1 bandwidth to allocate a single 768 Kbps time slot for video conferencing. The remaining 768 Kbps is divided into twelve 64 Kbps time slots for standard voice and data transmission. Total: 1.544 Mbps (1.536 Kbps plus 8 Kbps for framing and signaling).

Figure 19.14b   T1 circuit equipment.

Transmission equipment is the physical media used to carry DS-1 information. Examples include **twisted pair**, **coaxial and fiber-optic cables**, and **satellite and microwave links**. Table 19.1 describes several types of transmission media in detail, including repeater requirements.

A Public T1 Network

Alternatively, the corporate offices in Dallas and Denver can also communicate through a public T1 network. (See Figures 19.15a and b.) Available from a variety of providers, a public T1 network differs from the dedicated T1 circuit in that it is shared by many users.

In the switched T1 network, equipment is divided into categories based on location: the customer premise, the local loop, and central office equipment.

Customer premise equipment is so named simply because the organization connected to the public T1 network (e.g., a hospital or corporation) is responsible for it. As the responsible party, the organization must ensure that its equipment provides a healthy DS-1 signal to the public T1 network. The equipment on the customer premise typically consists of a T1 multiplexer and a CSU (i.e., terminating and user interface equipment, respectively). Both operate exactly as they do in the dedicated T1 circuit.

Local loop equipment essentially serves to connect the customers with the central office. The local loop is also where the telephone company assumes responsibility for the switched T1 network.

Central office equipment connects the DS-1 signals of many customers and routes traffic through the T1 network based on final destinations. This type of equipment can also serve as a test access point for various DS-1 signal requirements. Examples of switching equipment are **digital cross-connect systems (DCS)** and **digital signal cross-connect patch panels (DSX).**

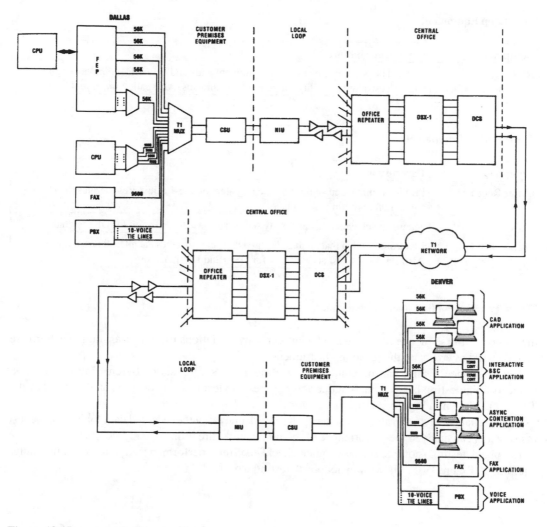

Figure 19.15a   A public T1 network.

T1 TESTING

Whether public or private, T1 circuits and network equipment must be properly tested and maintained to perform to maximum efficiency. Accordingly, all T1 testing falls under one of two prescribed categories: out-of-service testing and in-service monitoring.

Out-of-Service Testing

Out-of-service testing is so named because live traffic must be moved from the T1 link before testing can begin. In this place, a test instrument transmits a specific data pattern to a receiving test instrument

Local Loop Equipment

Equipment	Description
NIU (Network Interface Unit)	The point where customer equipment ends and network equipment begins. Test address facility for network technicians. Also called *smart jack*.

Central Office Equipment

Equipment	Description
Office Repeater	Provides simplex current for all the repeaters on the T1 link. Regenerates the DS-1 signal before routing takes place.
DSX	Manual patch panel that primarily serves as a test aceess point for DS-1 signals.
DCS	Electronic switch that "unbuilds" the DS-1 and reframes each DS-0 based on routing. Also serves as a test access point for DS-0 and DS-1 signals.

Figure 19.15b Public T1 network equipment.

that "knows" the sequence of the pattern being sent. Any deviations from the transmitted pattern are then counted as errors by the receiving instrument.

Out-of-service testing can be conducted on a point-to-point basis or by creating a loopback. Point-to-point testing is a general practice and requires two test instruments (one at either end of the T1 link, as shown in Figure 19.16).

By simultaneously generating a test data pattern and analyzing the received data for errors, the test instruments can analyze the performance of the link in both directions.

Loopback testing is often used as a "quick check" of circuit performance or when isolating faulty equipment. Figure 19.17 shows how loopback testing works.

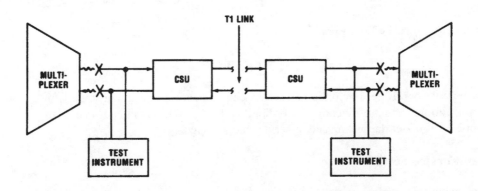

Figure 19.16 Point-to-point testing.

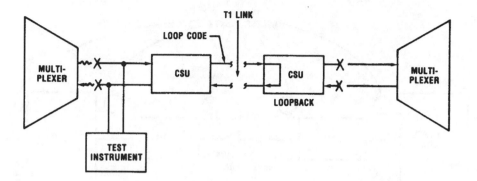

Figure 19.17   Loopback testing.

In loopback testing, a single instrument sends a loop-up code to the far-end CSU before data is actually transmitted. The loop-up code causes all transmitted data to be looped back toward the test instrument. By analyzing the received data for errors, the test instrument measures the performance of the link up to and including the far-end CSU.

Because loopback testing only requires a single test instrument (and, thus, only one operator), it is very convenient. However, loopback testing is limited in that it can only analyze the combined performance of both directions of the link, it is difficult to determine whether errors are originating on the transmit or the receive side of the T1 link at any given time.

As out-of-service methods, both point-to-point and loopback tests allow detailed measurement of any T1 link. However, since all out-of-service testing requires that live, revenue-generating traffic be interrupted, it is impractical for long-term testing. Thus, this type of testing is typically performed when a circuit is initially installed or when errors are discovered when monitoring live data.

In-service Monitoring of Live Data

The in-service method allows live data to be monitored at various access points without disturbing revenue-generating traffic. (See Figure 19.18.)

Since in-service monitoring does not disrupt the transmission of live traffic, it is more suitable for routine maintenance than out-of-service testing. Additionally, in-service monitoring indicates performance under actual operating conditions. But its primary disadvantage is that its measurements may not be as precise as those available in out-of-service testing. What's more, some network equipment may deter traditional in-service error measuring.

What Else Can Be Measured?

Choosing in-service monitoring or out-of-service testing at any given time often depends on knowing which measurements are available in each method. Table 19.3 offers a summary of the basic T1 test measurements and their associated limitations.

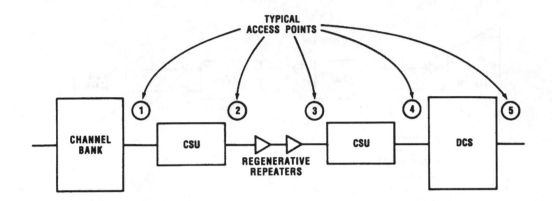

Figure 19.18   In-service monitoring.

Typical Test Scenarios

The measurements described in Table 19.3 can be performed in a variety of test scenarios. Here is a brief summary of the four scenarios where T1 is typically required.

Installing a T1 Link   When installing a T1 link, out-of-service testing is very useful for verifying equipment operation and point-to-point transmission quality. Start by testing the T1 link independent of other equipment. Then, after establishing the circuit point-to-point, loopback each CSU to ensure that they respond to both loop-up and loop-down codes. Finally, add terminating equipment to your test configuration.

Acceptance Testing   When completing installation testing, stress tests and long-term tests should be performed to ensure that the T1 link is operating within relevant specifications. Stress testing is performed by transmitting patterns that simulate minimum ones density and excess zero requirements through T1 equipment and monitoring the output for errors. Long-term testing detects time-related or intermittent errors using data patterns that simulate live data. (One such pattern, the Quasi-random Signal Source (QRSS) is designed specifically for this purpose.) It is recommended that long-term testing be performed over a 24- or 48-hour period.

Routine Preventive Maintenance   Once the T1 circuit is installed, routine maintenance can indicate degrading service before it disrupts normal operation. Preventive maintenance is usually performed in-service, and involves monitoring live data for BPVs, frame errors, and CRC errors. These tests should also be performed over a 24- or 48-hour period to detect time-specific or intermittent errors.

Fault Isolation   Fault isolation is required once excessive error rates have disrupted service. In-service monitoring is recommended to localize problems and minimize circuit downtime. By

Table 19.3   Basic Test Measurements

Measurement	Description	Available	Prime Advantage	Prime Disadvantage
Bit Errors	The basic performance evaluator, counts the number of logic errors in the bit stream (i.e., zeros that should be ones and vice versa). Provides specific error measurements.	Out-of-service only.	Truest measure of point-to-point circuit performance. Permits stress testing to ensure that T1 circuits and euipment are operating within applicable standards.	Live traffic must be removed to allow transmission of a known data pattern.
BPVs	A measure of the number of times pulses of the same consecutive polarity were transmitted across the T1 circuit, in violation of the bipolar signal format. Provides approximate bit error rate.	In-service or out-of-service.	Good indicator of circuit or repeater problem. Can be measured without disrupting live traffic.	Some network equipment corrects BPVs, making them useful only when testing metallic sections of a T1 circuit. Satellite, fiber optic, and microwave correct the bipolar format—only meaningful for metallic media.
Frame Errors	Measures the number of times an incorrect value appears in a bit position reserved from framing (i.e., 193rd bit). Provides approximate bit error rate.	In-service or out-of-service.	When monitored for a long period, can approximate actual bit error rate on an in-service basis.	Only evaluates overhead (not data) bits. Thus, analysis only takes place on every 193rd bit. Frame errors are often corrected by DCS and multiplexers; thus, frame errors are not good indicators of end-to-end performance in networks where this equipment is installed.
CRC Errors	Detects one or more bit errors in a block of data.	In-service or out-of-service.	Very accurate in-service error analysis. Detects bit errors at a 98.4 percent rate of accuracy.	Only available with ESF framing. DCS and other network equipment may recalculate the CRC.

monitoring the circuit at various points, you can analyze the results and discover where problems are originating. By performing standard out-of-service tests (i.e., loopback and point-to-point tests), technicians can identify the problem, isolate the faulty equipment, and verify proper operation once the problem is solved.

THE DS3 RATE

The nominal DS3 interface rate is 44.736 Mbps, which is about 1.5 Mbps greater than 28 times the DS1 bit rate of 1.544 Mbps. The "extra" bandwidth is used for bit stuffing and other overhead functions. T3 lines are based on the DS3 rate; consequently, T3 offers 28 times the bandwidth of T1.

The multiplexing involved in forming a DS3 signal is a two-step process. First, the twenty-eight DS1 signals are multiplexed into seven separate DS2 signals, where each DS2 signal contains four DS1 signals. Second, the seven DS2 signals are combined to form the DS3 signal.

Pulse Rate

The DS3 pulse shape must fall within a template that spreads over multiple pulse time slots. DS3 receivers are designed to tolerate the resulting "intersymbol interference" and still operate at very low error rates.

Line Code

DS3 signals use a line code called B3ZS or "bipolar with 3-zero substitution." In a B3ZS encoded signal, each DS3 time slot containing a pulse represents a logical one while each time slot without a pulse represents a logical zero. Normally, all pulses follow the bipolar rule—that is, alternate in polarity. However, to maintain a minimum pulse density of 33 percent, each block of three consecutive zeros is removed and replaced by "BOV" or "OOV" where B represents a pulse conforming with the bipolar rule and V represents a pulse violating the bipolar rule. The choice of BOV or OOV is made so that intentional bipolar violations ("V" pulses) alternate in polarity to maintain signal balance.

Because they contain an intentional bipolar violation and a particular bit sequence, the B3ZS codes can be identified and removed by DS3 receivers. The B3ZS encoding process is illustrated in Figure 19.19.

Overhead Bits

Every eighty-fifth bit in a DS3 bit sequence is called an overhead bit. All other bits are considered DS3 payload bits. Overhead bits are allocated to various functions including frame alignment, error detection, and terminal-to-terminal data communication.

Framing Formats

Three DS3 framing formats have been standardized by ANSI. They are

- M13,
- C-bit Parity, and
- SYNTRAN.

M13   The M13 framing format is technically known as **M23 Multiplex Application.** Almost all existing DS3 equipment is (more or less) M13 compatible. However, older equipment may not adhere

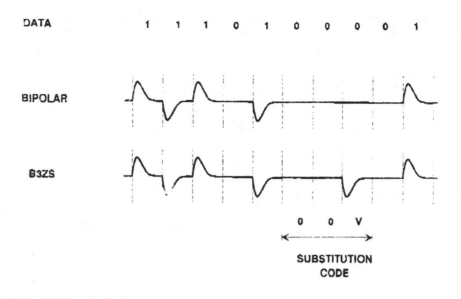

Figure 19.19   B3ZS example.

to the ANSI M13 specification in all aspects. For example, some designs use the "X-bit channel" for non-standard telemetry and alarm functions.

C-bit Parity   The C-bit parity format is technically known as the **Asynchronous DS3 C-bit Parity Application.** C-bit parity equipment is just becoming available. The C-bit parity format offers several maintenance and operations advantages over M13 including better error detection and an embedded operations channel for remote provisioning. Because of these advantages, it is expected that a significant fraction of DS3 equipment installed in the future will be C-bit parity compatible.

SYNTRAN   The SYNTRAN format is technically known as the **Synchronous DS3 M13 Multiplex Application.** Because it is designed to carry synchronous payloads, SYNTRAN offers the advantage of low-cost DS1 and DS (64 Kbps) drop and insert. However, rapid acceptance of SONET, the new synchronous optical hierarchy, is expected to minimize future demand for SYNTRAN.

THE FUTURE OF T-3

To meet the growing demands of voice and data communications, large organizations are exploring the high-speed worlds of optical fiber and DS3 circuits. As end users continue to demand more throughput, the move to DS3 circuits is often the best solution for DS1-based private networks. Today's DS3 tariff rates are designed to attract customers, even if customers can't immediately take advantage of the extra bandwidth. And, depending on location and distance, a DS3 circuit will cost about the same amount as four to ten DS1 circuits. Once the jump to the DS3 bandwidth is made, users have a cost-effective means to implement a host of new communication technologies including video conferencing, workstation-based graphics, distributed data processing, and more advanced facsimile transmission. As these benefits become more widely recognized, the role of T3 technology will increase.

REFERENCES

Bellamy, J. C. *Digital Telephony.* New York: John Wiley & Sons, 1982.

Flanagan, W. A. *The Teleconnect Guide to T1 Networking,* Telecom Library, 1986.

Gawdun, M. April 1987. "The T1 Transmission Media." *Telecommunications.*

Green, J. H. *The Dow Jones-Irwin Handbook of Telecommunications.* Homewood, IL: Dow Jones-Irwin, 1986.

Leben, J. and Martin, J. *Data Communications Technology.* Englewood Cliffs, NJ: Prentice Hall, 1988.

Minoli, D. *An Overview of T-Carrier Concepts.* Delran, NJ: Datapro Research Corporation, 1988.

VI

OTHER STANDARDS

20

Z39.50: AN APPLICATIONS SYSTEMS STANDARD FOR REMOTE QUERY AND RETRIEVAL

Michael Seadle

INTRODUCTION

Applications standards are very new to networks, and little real experience exists in their implementation. While the transportation and presentation standards provide the equivalent of operating systems services on stand-alone machines, applications standards handle business functions, where competition, not cooperation, has been the norm. Applications software also has an enormous diversity and complexity that has made standardization a real challenge.

Z39.50 and Z39.58 are interesting in part because they are among the first applications standards. They are National Information Standards Organization [NISO] protocols for remote query and retrieval of bibliographic, textual, or other information across an Open Systems Interface (OSI) network. Z39.50 provides the application-level interface, and Z39.58 is the standard query language for search requests. The two standards ideally function as a unit.

This chapter examines the business issues associated with Z39.50 as well as the protocol's technical specifications. The business-oriented questions follow.

- Why is a query and retrieval standard needed?
- Why is a common command language needed?
- Who wrote the standards?
- What are the hardware, software, and network requirements?
- What freedom of action must be given up?
- What accounting and security problems exist?
- What legal problems arise in maintaining data ownership?

The technical questions follow.

- How does Z39.50 query and retrieval work?
- How does the Z39.58 command language work?
- What applications have been written for them?

BUSINESS ISSUES

The Need for a Network Query and Retrieval Standard

Multiple, conflicting, and informal standards for remote query and retrieval operations have long existed because such operations are a normal part of modern business and predate the existence of national computer networks. One century-old example is the mail-order catalog business. The process a buyer follows in ordering goods fits easily into the stages of a Z39.50 operation. **Initialization** occurs when the buyer asks the store to send a catalog. **Searching** takes place when the buyer flips through the pages. A **result-set** of items that match the search criteria gets built with pencil and paper. A **retrieval request** goes to the company in the form of an order sheet. **Accounting** and **id-validation** take place when the company checks the buyer's credit card number. And the actual **retrieval** occurs when the packet of goods arrives a short time later. An **error message** in the form of a letter might go out when an item is sold out or out-of-stock. If the message is incomprehensible, the buyer might telephone for **help** in the hope that the clerk who answers can actually explain what to do next.

No one thinks much about the standardized procedures in an actual mail-order sale, because the protocols have become a customary part of the way business is done. But anyone who has attempted to place such an order without, for example, a required item number, knows what unforeseen consequences can arise when standards are ignored. The purpose of Z39.50 is merely to define and regularize these types of interactions for networked computers.

Z39.50 provides rules that are broad guidelines, not detailed instruction sets. They specify defaults and minimums and are less like the command sequences in a computer program than like the laws regulating commerce and trade. Critics have argued that Z39.50 is too broad and has too many undefined areas. The standard, for example, says nothing about the format of the data. But perhaps it should not. Formats that suit one industry might not serve the needs of another. Separate efforts can build on Z39.50 by defining standards on an industry-by-industry basis. Z39.50 represents a practical midpoint between pure communication protocols that carry any kind of message for any purpose, and vendor-specific requirements. To view it in any other context misinterprets its purpose and misunderstands its value.

The Need for a Common Command Language

Language is another critical element of any business operation. An English-language mail-order catalog requires that the buyer know some English, one in Japanese requires that the buyer know Japanese, and they are not readily interchangeable. Today's computers are even more inflexible about language. Most applications have few if any synonyms for their commands, and a single wrong letter can mean total incomprehension.

Z39.58 facilitates these interactions by providing a common command language of nineteen verbs. Six of them are basic control commands, such as START and STOP. Three more manage the search process to FIND particular results or SCAN indexes. Others move the display of the search results FORWARD and BACK, or SORT it in a particular order. A final set of five commands provides information about the system, the environment or the settings.

Z39.58 does not limit interactions to these nineteen verbs. All parties may agree on a larger and more complex vocabulary. The standard requires only that these nineteen verbs must be used, and they must have the same meaning at each site claiming to use the protocol. The nouns (parameters) used with these commands are not specified in the standard, because they depend on the contents of the database. A mail-order catalog buyer who tries to find shoes in a catalog devoted entirely to sweaters will get nothing, and should perhaps know better than to try.

Who Wrote the Standards?

The authors of these standards included computing professionals from a broad range of public and academic institutions, as well as some for-profit companies. The latter were poorly represented, in part because networking is relatively new to most firms and they still view the idea of operating in an open network environment with more trepidation than enthusiasm. Every story about network viruses makes corporate executives blanch at the prospect of exposing their critical data processing operations. Nonetheless, major companies like Sears, with its comarketing of Prodigy, have recognized the enormous market opportunities that networks represent. The authors of these standards have given less attention to problems like security and accounting than a more business-oriented group might have done, but they have addressed all the basic issues.

Z39.50 and Z39.58 officially come from NISO, which prepares standards for libraries, information sciences, and publishing, and submits them to the American National Standards Institute (ANSI). NISO is a very broad organization. Its members include associations such as the American Chemical Society, booksellers such as Waldenbooks, library organizations such as the Research Libraries Group, and major corporations such as IBM and Apple Computers. It is, in effect, the key standards organization for applications systems in the United States.

Network Requirements

Although the Z39.50 standard was written for OSI networks, it can also run on TCP/IP, SNA, and other networks, which have protocols that allow for independent application information. Network software limits Z39.50 applications less than the extent of the physical infrastructure over which it runs. For these applications to become practical and profitable, the network must reach enough customers directly and be able to carry enough data quickly.

The most numerous and most limited networks are company-only installations that preclude outside access for security reasons. In this environment, Z39.50 applications have no immediate attraction, since the company can and probably does enforce its own internal standards.

Proprietary networks that are open to the public for a regular subscription fee also have little immediate use for Z39.50 applications. This is partly because they are essentially closed networks that follow the company-only model and have a relatively small customer base as a result of their own exclusiveness. Z39.50 could be a valuable tool in standardizing access, but the owners would have to change their approach to networking and their software fundamentally.

The Internet connects thousands of universities, research companies, and military establishments. It is the second largest network in America and is the environment for which most Z39.50 applications are being written. The growth of the Internet is often compared to the development of the interstate highway system in the 1950s. Congress recently passed a bill authorizing funds for a major Internet upgrade and expansion. But like the highway system, there are no plans for it to reach into individual households.

The only network in the United States that currently does reach into individual households is the telephone system. Z39.50 products have enormous commercial potential for telephone users who connect to remote services via micro-computers and modems. Already numerous databases exist on the telephone network in the form of electronic bulletin boards. The more that customers can rely on standard query and retrieval methods, the more useful these databases will be. The growing commercial use of the Minitel system in France is an indication of what could develop.

Some practical hardware limits do exist on the amount of data that a Z39.50 query can retrieve. Even today's high-volume, high-speed networks such as the NSFNET backbone would reach saturation if, for example, it had to transmit large numbers of high-density graphic images. Such limitations will change as bandwidth expands. They should pose no real problem for the future.

Computer Hardware and Software Requirements

The basic hardware requirements for a Z39.50 remote query and retrieval operation are a set of network connected **server and client computers** running Z39.50-compliant applications software. The server can be any computer with a database that receives search requests. It can be as small as a personal computer, or as large as a mainframe with access to terabyte-size corporate databases. The same is true for the client machine. It is not size but function that determines the role. As database structures become more decentralized, the decision to house data on large mainframes or slower but cheaper workstations will depend mainly on the frequency of access. Large client machines will query small servers as often as the reverse.

Z39.50 is not dependent on any particular operating system software. The earliest servers ran UNIX, but MVS and other operating systems are being used today. All the operating system needs is networking capability and the right Z39.50-based applications software. Likewise, the server's database management system can be almost any product currently on the market, as long as the applications program translates standard commands into a form the database understands. At present, none of the major database vendors has built-in Z39.58 query language capabilities, but some specialized vendors do (such as NOTIS Inc.).

Other new types of software will help significantly by automating multiple database searching. One experimental type is **the knowbot,** an artificially intelligent program that spreads out across the network in search of specific information and stops once that information is found. Another option is a client-machine–based expert system that decides what databases to search and evaluates the results to decide whether to try again. Such a system could be as simple as a command list that runs through a set of databases and presents all results to a human operator, or it can have enough artificial intelligence to recognize partial, incomplete, or inadequate answers, and to reformulate queries based on related terms in the server's database. As Z39.50 systems become more common, such tools will liberate humans from repetitious search operations.

The Need for Cooperation

The growth of Z39.50-type query and retrieval systems will force the owners of data to face economic, security, and legal issues that do not exist in the current environment in which the ownership and use of data is controlled within a single corporation or institution. Cooperation between the owners of data is essential for creating agreements on common record structures, common error messages, and other incompletely defined features. A network environment in which the servers offer only minimal compliance leaves open such major issues as whether a server must run requests in real time, or can queue them for batch processing during off-peak hours.

Such cooperation can come in many forms. The ideal is perhaps for the owners of similar types of data to work together to propose additional data-specific standards. Such standards could be organized by industry. They should detail what information the records should contain, as well as the location of each data element. Software writers could then build applications programs that could use data from any Z39.50 server in that industry.

Another option is for a dominant software firm to set a de facto standard for each industry group or type of data. This works well enough when a majority of servers use the same software, though it builds a dependence on a particular vendor that many organizations prefer to avoid.

A third option is for an outside organization to set standards. This means some loss of independence for the individual institution, but is compensated for by the speed and flexibility such an organization has to meet changing needs. For-profit companies may find this option difficult to accept, because of the obvious external limit it places on their competitive freedom.

In all of these options, however, those who follow the standard are trading some individual freedom for the benefits of common access, much as a store in a shopping mall trades a private entrance for access to a broader public. It makes little sense to accept the open-network principles of the Z39.50 standard without cooperating to end the babel of record structures and processing assumptions that undermine it.

Chargeback and Theft

Cooperation on technical issues may be easier than on economic ones. Some public data are distributed free, but most organizations will want to charge for the use of their information resources. The Z39.50 standard includes an accounting facility that allows the server to charge clients as well as limit them, but the details of the implementation are undefined.

The implementation could take several forms. One is like a charge card. Clients could supply an external account number to which search costs are automatically charged. Another resembles a running tab where the server records costs and then bills the client at regular intervals. Or the client and server could set up a barter system that trades resources on one server for those on another. A host of other options are possible too. The nature of the mechanism itself matters less than having an agreement on how to implement it that is widely accepted across the network, otherwise a large number of servers will be as closed as if Z39.50 never existed.

Certain types of data pose greater economic issues than others. Libraries and retailers routinely provide information for free or at a nominal cost. Their goal is not to charge for the information itself, but to provide it as a way to get people to an end product.

The situation for a publisher is significantly different, because the publisher's business is the sale of information itself. If, for example, a book is available on a server in electronic form, the publisher may want to charge the full price to any client that retrieved it, even though in a bookstore the customer could normally glance through a book, and put it back on the shelf without being required to buy it. One way to emulate such browsing would be for the server to drop the charge for the book if the client machine indicated it did not intend to keep it, but the client would, in fact, have the book just as if a human had walked out of the store with it without paying. Another method would be for a server to allow the client to retrieve some percentage of the electronic book—the amount a person might read while browsing—and then charge for it only when a copy of the whole work was requested. In either case the problem exists that any large, coherent body of electronic data, such as a book, could be copied and resold more easily than by any existing means of photocopying.

Until these types of economic issues are more fully resolved, many information producers will be reluctant to make their data resources available on Z39.50-type servers.

Locks and Keys

Controlling access to the server is as critical as locking the shop door. Z39.50 includes a security facility, but does not specify its contents or implementation. A number of password-type security systems exist, or are well advanced in the planning stage, and any of these could be implemented. The problem is to get agreement on a common system and to work out the details of the implementation. Secure servers would, for example, have to agree on a common, unique form of identification, such as name, user-id, or social security number, and would have to agree on a common repository of identification information so that each server would not need to have a private identification database. A Kerberos style solution with a network-wide nameserver may provide the best option currently available.[1]

Local security schemes are also possible within the context of the Z39.50 standard, but such local schemes pose a limit that undermines the openness of the network. Local security is like requiring each customer to have an identification card from the store manager before being allowed in to look at any merchandise.

Ownership and the Law

Z39.50 raises a number of legal questions about the ownership of data. If, for example, a client machine retrieves and pays for data from half a dozen different servers, reorganizes that data, and then offers it on a server of its own, has it violated the original servers' ownership rights? A person can buy information in book or periodical form and legally reuse that information to make a new

---

1   Kerberos is a network security system proposed by the Massachusetts Institute of Technology. The name comes from the three-headed, dragon-tailed dog that guards the Underworld in ancient Greek mythology.

product, but the same person cannot (according to recent rulings) merely photocopy parts of the original and resell it. Is combining data from several servers creating a new product, or is it the computer equivalent of copying? The answer may depend not only on copyright law, but on the implicit and explicit contractual agreements that the operator of the client machine accepts when buying and retrieving the data.

The urgency of this issue varies with the type of data. Libraries encourage the creation of bibliographies that have records from multiple sources, but a similar compilation of product descriptions from one mail-order company for use in another would raise serious objections. Organizations of data owners and data consumers can either develop explicit contractual understandings for particular types of data as part of a network-wide Z39.50 implementation, or they can leave the issue for the law courts to decide. The former requires more effort and cooperation, but the latter may prove more troublesome in the end.

TECHNICAL ISSUES: Z39.50 SEARCH AND RETRIEVAL

The Parts of the Standard

This section gives a technical overview of Z39.50, and discusses some of its implications for network interactions. This is not intended to be a complete description of the standard. Those interested in the full details should obtain an official copy from NISO.

The Z39.50 standard consists of specifications in four basic stages of interaction:

1. initialization
2. searching
3. retrieval
4. resource control

Each stage has at least two **service elements** or records that are identified by a unique binary integer: one for the request and one for the response. The physical structure of these records consists of a header portion and variable length fields, each of which has a "tag value" to indicate the field type. Some fields are optional, others occur only under particular circumstances, and still others may occur more than once in a single record. These records may (and generally should) also contain a reference-id to facilitate communication between servers and clients that have multiple simultaneous search and retrieval processes underway. The formal name for these records is an **Application Protocol Data Unit** (APDU or sometimes simply PDU).

The outcome of a search process is called a result-set, and significant portions of the standard are devoted to creating, manipulating, retrieving, or deleting them. Z39.50 does not guarantee that a server will keep more than one result-set, or even that it will keep any result-sets longer than is necessary to make an immediate response to the initial request. But the standard does imply that clients can expect these facilities, and that servers should try to allocate enough resources to allow their use. Result-set manipulation is a key part of sophisticated search strategies, and can be important for using the network efficiently.

The next four sections describe each of the four basic stages of a Z39.50 interaction (see Figure 20.1).

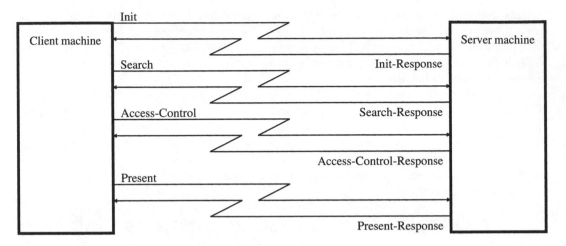

Figure 20.1   Four basic Z39.50 client-server interactions.

Initialization

The purpose of the initialization stage is to describe the server and client machines to each other. It uses two record types: Init-APDU (PDU-type 20) and Init-response-APDU (PDU-type 21). In the Init-APDU the client machine tells the server what options it wants, such as its preferred message size and the maximum record size. It may also include a **user-id,** information about what application and what version of that application it is running, a **reference-id**, and an unstructured extra field for any other information that the server might want or be able to use. The server responds with an Init-response-APDU that indicates whether it accepts or rejects the client's request for a connection, whether it supports the requested options, its preferred message size, and its maximum record size. The response may also include information about the server's applications software, a reference-id, and an extra field for any other useful information.

Initialization is a critical step for all connections, open or restricted, because it establishes whether and how the client and server applications can interact. The information about the type of software is particularly important. Machines running the same applications software can make assumptions about data structures and search algorithms, which are impossible in the absence of further agreements or extensions to the standard.

Searching

The purpose of the search stage is to find information in the server's database(s). It has two record types: search-APDU (PDU-type 22) and search-response-APDU (PDU-type 23). In the search-APDU the client machine specifies an upper and lower boundary for the number of records in the search result, an expected search-result size that is not smaller than the lower boundary, an indicator that says whether to replace a previous result-set, the name to use for the new result-set, the name or names of any databases to search, the format of the syntax for the query language (i.e., whether or not it uses the default reverse-polish notation), and the query itself. The client may also include an element-set name for saving the search command and a reference-id. The server responds with a search-response-PDU that includes an indication whether the client's search request succeeded or failed, the size of the whole search result, the number of records in the result-set (which could be fewer than in the whole search result because of size limitations), and the position of the next result-set (for future reference). If the search failed, the response indicates whether the contents of the result-set are valid but incomplete, invalid and incomplete, or whether the result-set is empty. If the search succeeded, the server indicates whether the expected number of records were retrieved, or gives the reason why not (an unavailable disk pack, for example). The server includes a reference-id if one was specified and may send back one or more diagnostic records.

This search process could take place several times before the client asks the server to return any result-sets. Or the client might never request the results. The search-and-retrieval processes are separate in the Z39.50 standard. This is possible because the search responses try to contain enough information for the client machine to determine whether the results seem plausible and useful without burdening the network by shipping all the records back. The value of the response does, however, depend on how well the client machine is able to evaluate the diagnostic records. When the client and server use the same applications software, the client can learn a great deal from the diagnostics. But Z39.50 searches are intentionally not limited to such cases. A search is still possible, with good results, in cases where the applications are significantly different and understand nothing of each other's diagnostics, but the consequence is likely to be a greater load on the network because clients will mistakenly request result-sets they do not actually want or need. Standardization of the diagnostic messages would enhance this part of the standard greatly.

Retrieval

The purpose of the retrieval stage is to transfer appropriate information to the client machine. It has four record types: present-APDU (PDU-type 24), present-response-APDU (PDU-type 25), delete-APDU (PDU-type 26), and delete-response-APDU (PDU-type 27). In the retrieval request, called a present-APDU, the client machine specifies the number of records it wants, the starting position of the result-set, and the result-set id. It may also specify the name of the original search request and a reference-id. The server's response specifies the current status of the result-set requested (i.e., whether it still exists), the number of records returned to the client, and the beginning position of the next result-set. It may also include a reference-id and diagnostic records. In the delete-APDU, the client specifies whether to get rid of a single result-set or to get rid of all the ones that client owns. When requesting a single deletion, it must include the id of the result-set. In either case it may include a reference-id. The server responds by indicating whether the deletion succeeded, or gives one of eight possible reasons why it failed. These reasons can include access control problems, resource constraints, or the fact that a result-set no longer exists. For a single-deletion request, the server's response includes the result-set id. If the client wanted all the result-sets deleted, and they could not be, the server returns a status of "8," tells the number of result-sets remaining, and gives individual reason codes for each failure. The server may also include a text message about the deletion and a reference-id.

It is important to note that the client does not have full control over result-sets. The resources used to manage the result-sets belong to the server. If the result-sets are too large or too numerous, a server could run out of storage space and have to delete them on its own. Security rules could also prevent the retrieval of a result-set, even though they did not interdict the search algorithm. For example, a search for information on jet engines in an engineering company's database could get both public information about safety features and private development data for a new engine design. At present such situations do not occur because public and private information is normally kept on separate databases. New security techniques and networked database structures could change that. The Z39.50 standard contains concepts that allow servers to protect secure data without having to close access entirely.

At the end of a search-and-retrieval session, the client should ask the server to delete all result-sets. The standard does not require this, however, and leaves final responsibility for clean-up with the server. This can lead to situations where the server believes the client is finished based on its own parameters for time-out or maximum session length, but the client still expects to find result-sets on the server. The difficulty becomes particularly troublesome during batch search processes. Nothing in Z39.50 requires immediate interactive processing, and in a batch process, result sets could be around for hours or even days. A server that is generous with its storage may also find some clients keeping long-term result-sets on the server because of their own space limitations. Such clients could be in for a surprise when the clean-up process finally runs.

Access and Resource Control

The purpose of the access and resource control stage is to protect the server. It has four record types: access-control-APDU (PDU-type 28), access-control-response-APDU (PDU-type 29), resource-control-APDU (PDU-type 30), and resource-control-response-APDU (PDU-type 31). One distinctive feature of access and resource control is that the server initiates the interactions. In the access-control-APDU the server sends a security challenge that can consist of any code or value, and can also include a reference-id. Such a challenge may refer only to certain types of searches or to particular retrieval requests, and more than one security challenge may occur during a Z39.50 session. The client should respond with the right authorization code or password. If the client is not prepared to respond to any security challenges, it can indicate that during initialization.

In the resource-control-APDU, the server indicates whether or not a process is suspended. It may include a text message. It should indicate whether partial or interim results are available. It can also include a reference-id. The client responds with a flag that indicates whether it wants the search or retrieval process to continue—which may imply a willingness to pay additional charges. If it does not want to continue, it must say whether to keep the result-set.

Access-control is the vaguest and most incomplete part of the Z39.50 standard. Its format can be arbitrarily different from server to server, even when security needs and access privileges are the same. This means that, until a network-wide security system is in place, a client machine must have a database with codes and formats for every security-conscious server it uses.

Resource-control is, in contrast, the most fully specified part of the standard. The only undefined portion is an optional text message that the server can send. But the meaning of the server's initial message can be ambiguous, because the flag merely indicates whether an operation has been suspended, and not whether that suspension is permanent or temporary. The latter is implied, but may not be possible if the server could save no intermediate results. The standard also misses an opportunity to indicate a preference for real-time or delayed-execution batch processing in the resource-control stage. Those searching large databases may prefer to delay expensive searches to get lower midnight rates.

To make up for some of these omissions, the Z39.50 Standard has an appendix that includes sample formats for resource-control records. The authors of the appendix suggest including information about the size of the results, the amount of processing time, and the cost of the operation. They also distinguish between current totals and final result projections. This information would allow the client to make a more informed judgment about continuing, but a server need not provide it. The appendices are only recommendations, not requirements for full Z39.50 compliance.

Diagnostic Records

Another appendix gives examples of a diagnostic record format and suggests codes that would indicate permanent or temporary system errors; incomplete, oversized, or incomprehensible commands; size problems for messages or result-sets; resource or security problems; errors in combining multiple databases for a single search; and errors for missing, in-use, or otherwise inaccessible result-sets. These codes are very general, and deal with only a small subset of the number of problems that can occur in any computing process. They are system-level messages only, and do not deal with application-specific problems such as bad data or ambiguous results. This needs to change. Unless the set of standard diagnostics expands, a client talking to a server running unrelated applications software cannot be entirely sure of the results.

Syntax

Syntax is a key part of unambiguous communication. Z39.50 specifies a default syntax called **reverse-polish notation** in which the command is evaluated from left to right and the verb is at the end. This order makes sense for computers, which need to know the inputs and outputs before performing an operation, though it may seem difficult for English-speaking humans. Z39.50 also allows use of any other syntax that the two parties agree on.

TECHNICAL ISSUES: THE Z39.58 COMMAND LANGUAGE

The purpose of the Z39.58 standard is to provide a common command language for on-line search-and-retrieval operations. It was designed to work in the context of an OSI network with Z39.50 servers, but could apply equally to any database search process. The names of the commands are all taken from English words, and punctuation is kept to an absolute minimum. Spaces are the only separator between most words, except in the FIND command, which requires commas to show where each qualifier ends, since a qualifier could be a phrase with a blank in the middle. Semicolons indicate

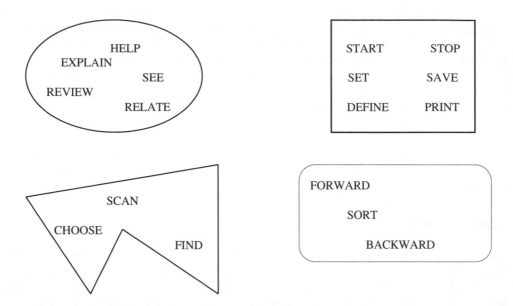

Figure 20.2   Z39.58 common command language verbs.

the end of a complete command, much as they do in some programming languages.[2] They may be used to stack several commands in a single data stream. Parentheses can also be used as separators when spaces and commas do not suffice. Z39.58 does not use periods, and it requires that servers ignore differences between upper- and lowercase input.

Z39.58 defines nineteen command words, the parameters each should take, and the defaults they should use. It tells which abbreviations are legal, and gives examples of how to use the command. Although the standard simply lists the commands alphabetically, they represent four different types of actions: search commands, system control commands, help commands, and display control commands (see Figure 20.2).

Search Commands

There are three search commands that help clients find information in a server's database.

CHOOSE (CHO) allows the client to specify which of the server's databases to search. The command needs a parameter, which means that the client must know the names of the databases, or must find them with the help commands. A server with multiple databases and no default may require clients to use the CHOOSE command. The standard also warns that some servers may purge previous search results each time CHOOSE is used.

---

2   SAS from SAS Institute and PLI from IBM are examples.

SCAN (SCA) displays index entries. If the command has no parameters, the display begins with the first entry in the default index. Or the client can specify a particular index, or a key word to begin from, or both the index and one or more key words. The index name is always the first parameter. It is distinguished only by the fact that it matches an index name in the database. This means that any search for a key word that is also an index name must specify both. The server must also display a line number (or other id) with the search results.

FIND (FIN) locates a specific record or set of records in the database and saves them (where permitted) in a result-set. FIND is a complex command that allows simultaneous use of multiple indexes, Boolean operators such as AND and OR, range operators such as "greater than" (>) or "less than" (<), wild-card substitutes for either a variable or a fixed number of characters ("?" and "#" respectively), and proximity operators that indicate the degree of adjacency between key words ("W1" for words that are next to each other, "W2" for words that may have one word between them, "W3" for words that are up to three words apart, etc.). Commas should separate multiple index names, and parentheses should enclose multiword searches with an embedded Boolean operator. Multiword searches with no Boolean operator do not need parentheses. Z39.58 assumes that all words between Boolean operators are part of a single search string, which means, of course, that no Boolean operator may be used in a search string.

FIND can also invoke a saved search command, if its first word matches the name of the previous search. Clients must therefore use some care in naming saved commands to avoid invoking them unintentionally. Z39.58 does not set aside any reserved words as index names, since the names and types of indexes can vary widely depending on the application. The client must either know what indexes the server has, or use the HELP commands to find them.

System Control Commands

There are six commands the client can use to perform critical system control functions.

START (STA) begins a new search and reinitializes any previously established variables. The server may also require new security information, and it may purge previous result-sets. The START command does not require the client or server to reestablish their OSI or Z39.50 connections, and it takes no parameters.

STOP (STO) ends a session and can close the OSI connection between the client and server machines. STOP may automatically purge any remaining result-sets from earlier searches. It, too, takes no parameters.

DEFINE (DEF) has two functions. It can temporarily rename a command on the server to some other legal character string. Or it can name a "command expression" that consists of one or more commands followed by their parameters, and separated from one another by semicolons. This enables the client to reduce repetitively used complex commands to a single verb. Some servers may retain these definitions permanently for a particular client. Others keep them for only a single session, or discard them at arbitrary times or after a period of disuse. Z39.58 sets no requirements for their duration.

SET controls the characteristics of a session. It can alter the number of records returned, the line-size, the type of scrolling, or any other feature the client is allowed to change. The first parameter should always be the name of the feature, and the second the new value. The SET command is particularly useful for interactive sessions where a human operator is expecting a well-formatted response. As with DEFINE, the permanence of the changes depends on individual servers.

SAVE (SAV) is like the DEFINE command in that it groups a set of commands under a single name. The difference is that it saves only previously used commands in execution order. SAVE followed by only a name will save all previously issued commands. SAVE followed by the letter "S" and an integer will save a particular statement that number of statements from the start of the session. The client can also save multiple statements (S1 S3 S5), or a range of statements (S1–5). Z39.58 allows servers to change the new command name to protect clients from accidentally selecting a reserved word. As with the commands above, the permanence of these changes depends on individual servers.

PRINT (PRI) asks the server to print search results off-line. PRINT with no parameters will print the results of the last command. To print other results, the client should refer by name or by number to previous searches or result-sets. The client can print part of a result-set by specifying the record numbers. A choice of print formats may be included with the command, but such formats or other specifications depend on the individual server. The standard leaves responsibility for picking up the printed output to human operators.

Help Commands

There are five help commands to provide information about the server and its information database.

HELP (HEL) provides context-sensitive information. This means, for example, that HELP will provide one kind of information when the client is using an index, and another kind of information when the client is reading a result. The information should be as specific as possible in showing the client's immediate range of choices. This might be a simple list of available commands, or a full tutorial about the commands and their capabilities. The standard provides no guideline for the amount or type of help. It specifies only that a client be able to enter the single word HELP at any point and receive some relevant response. The HELP command may take parameters, but it may not require them.

EXPLAIN (EXP) provides general information about the server, how it may be used, and what databases it has. The purpose is to provide an overview of the server and its resources. It is not context sensitive. When used without parameters, the EXPLAIN command should display a list of topics that can be used as parameters for getting more specific information. Both EXPLAIN and HELP may use some of the same information, but EXPLAIN is much broader and can be put to innovative uses such as providing floor plans or other diagrams that go beyond immediate system functions.

RELATE (REL) displays a list of terms that have some logical relationship to the client's search and will help retrieve more records. The command must specify a search term and can have other qualifiers, with commas separating them if there is more than one. This command functions essentially as a thesaurus. How large a list, or how closely the terms should be related, is left to the server.

REVIEW (REV) shows what commands have been executed. If REVIEW is used with no parameters, it will display the entire history of the session. The client can specify which commands to display by using the letter "S" followed by its relative position from the start (S3 for the third command, for example). A client can request a range of commands with a hyphen or can display a saved command sequence by specifying its name. The standard does not indicate how much information REVIEW should provide. The minimum is the actual command string, but the server may also give the size of the result-set, how much the command costs or other useful pieces of information.

SEE displays system-related information about the server or the current session. This includes the current values of any parameters used in the SET command, such as screen size or terminal type. Every SET parameter must have a corresponding SEE command display, but the server need not allow clients to SET every variable that SEE displays. SEE with no parameters should show a list of options. One special use of SEE displays a list of all saved searches (SEE SAVES).

Display Control Commands

There are three commands that control how interactive results are displayed.

FORWARD (FOR) scrolls forward through the data for a specific number of records. That number can either be a server default, which might be changed with the SET command, or it can be specified as a parameter. FORWARD can be used with any command that presents a list of data. The standard does not say whether the display should "wrap" by reshowing the first record after reaching the last.

BACK (BAC) scrolls backwards through the data for a specific number of records. As in FORWARD, that number can either be a system default or be specified as a parameter. BACK can be used with any command that presents a list of data and may wrap on some servers.

SORT (SOR) sorts the result-set into a specific order by one or more fields. The command requires at least one parameter to indicate the primary sort field. The client may include the name of a result-set or allow it to default to the results of the most recent search. The client may also specify a range of records to sort, or let it default to sorting the whole. The standard makes no provision for sorting by a range of bytes within a record, unless that range has a predefined field name. The standard also omits a parameter to control the sort order, though it may be controlled via the SET command. This SORT is very limited compared to its commercially available cousins, which can do ascending and descending sorts on fields of different types, and can merge multiple datasets. But the primary purpose of this SORT is to control the display order, not to manipulate result-sets, and should be judged in that context.

Is Z39.58 Useful?

The Z39.58 command language is by no means complete. It leaves out important kinds of commands for manipulating multiple result-sets (such as MERGE), commands for pruning data (such as EXCLUDE), and it has no IF... THEN... logic, which is critical for specifying complex search algorithms. It also leaves out explicit commands for controlling the retrieval capabilities of a Z39.50 server, except implicitly through the display commands. It is as if the authors of Z39.58 doubted the wisdom of Z39.50's clear separation of the search-and-retrieval processes and wanted to make them as transparent as possible to the client. Z39.58 is, in fact, fundamentally terminal-oriented and does little to exploit any underlying client-server architecture.

Despite these flaws, Z39.58 represents a significant achievement, because it defines a standard minimum vocabulary, which clients and servers should have in common. Without such a standard control vocabulary, a perfectly open network of Z39.50 servers would still remain a Tower of Babel.

ACTUAL APPLICATIONS

A number of product developers have put together a Z39.50 Implementers' Group. These include well-known organizations such as Sun Microsystems, Chemical Abstracts International, Software Kinetics Ltd., Mead Data Central, NeXT Inc., and the Library of Congress. The group also has observer-members, among which is the Central Intelligence Agency. These organizations believe that Z39.50 offers a real and practical basis for building the next generation of network applications.

The process of implementation is, however, never easy. The examples below show some of the standard's strengths and weaknesses.

Thinking Machines: Wide Area Information System

Thinking Machines' Wide Area Information System (WAIS) was the first Z39.50 product. It is a "prototype which gives flexible access to full-text documents."[3] Thinking Machines designed the product in cooperation with three other companies: Dow Jones, Apple Computer, and Peat Marwick. The goal was to provide a single, easily used interface to a wide range of corporate data by sending query results from remote Z39.50 servers to client machines, which would reformat the information for each user.

The developers faced questions about which databases to search, how to control the quantity of data returned, and how to protect the legal rights of the vendors and the privacy of the data users. The standard provided a flexible framework for resolving the technical problems, such as a presentation-set size that could vary with the capacity of the client machine. The legal and privacy issues appear to have been handled as an extension of existing information-service contracts in a closed environment where all clients are known to the vendor before network contact is established.

NOTIS Inc.: PACLINK

The second significant Z39.50 product to reach the market is NOTIS Inc.'s PACLINK, which joins together the public catalogs of multiple libraries. NOTIS provides automation software for about half of the major research libraries in the United States and has customers as far away as Venezuela and New Zealand. PACLINK is significant for two reasons. First, it allows direct comparisons between a Z39.50 product and existing alternatives. And, second, it uses standard IBM mainframe products like MVS and CICS that are at the core of most corporate data processing. This means that, even though NOTIS has mainly academic customers, its experience is applicable to business-related databases on existing mainframes.

The first stage of PACLINK allows on-line catalog users in one library access to the records in another, displayed exactly as if they belonged to the first. The second stage uses Z39.50 search results to build interlibrary loan request queues, which, currently, require human approval, but can eventually generate automatic loans. The third phase, which is still in development, will retrieve bibliographic

---

3 Brewster Kahle and Art Medlar. "An Information System for Corporate Users." PACS-L@UHUPVM1, April 8, 1991.

records from cooperating Z39.50 servers and incorporate them in the client's own database. These three phases are transforming tasks, which have, until now, required specialized networks and proprietary software into ones which any Z39.50/Z39.58–compliant system can use.

PACLINK encountered some technical problems that the standard did not readily solve, because of the enormous size of the databases involved and the fact that the product had tens of thousands of potential end users with little or no special training. Existing terminal-based NOTIS on-line catalogs provide a series of index screens to help end users navigate through big result-sets, but the Z39.50 standard had made no provision for such aids. One option was to let the client machine build them, but that would require a large-scale data transmission across the network, which would slow performance. Instead, NOTIS designed the PACLINK server to generate index-record result-sets and to transmit them initially. This solution lies completely outside the Z39.50 standard, but is not antithetical to it. Z39.50 discusses indexes only in the context of servers and says nothing about transmitting them or not transmitting them to clients. Nonetheless, a non-NOTIS Z39.50 client would not expect such search results, and might not be able to handle them correctly. To avoid excluding generic Z39.50 servers, NOTIS decided to give PACLINK two "implementation codes," one to signal a PACLINK client and one for other Z39.50 users. That way the product can have the benefits of both openness and high performance.

CONCLUSION

Critics of Z39.50, such as Martin Schoffstall, argue that the protocol is excessively vague in critical areas and "inadequate as the basis of an end user bibliographic retrieval service."[4] Such criticisms are true, but need to be considered in context. The current versions of both Z39.50 and Z39.58 are essentially first drafts. The Implementation Group already has a new and more complete version of Z39.50 to propose to NISO, and new versions of Z39.58 will follow. The process is slow and difficult because each draft must be patched together bit by bit through practical experience.

The real difference between these standards and the chaos of local protocols is a vision of consistency and predictability that makes open systems thinkable in the near future. Consistency matters. Today's computers are still essentially small minds, and until a new generation of highly intelligent processors comes into being, they will not be able to deal with more than a relatively small amount of variation.

Good, workable Z39.50 and Z39.58 standards are needed because information has become a capital good in the modern world, and a wide range of industries depend on open access to it as part of their daily operations. Credit card validation is one example of an existing remote query and retrieval process that would gain in accuracy and reliability if widespread use of Z39.50 servers allowed stores to query the issuing bank's database directly. Manufacturing firms also need data from remote sites where parts are made. And governmental services both use and provide data in large quantities. Today, much of this information is loaded onto tape and sent through the mail.

---

4 Martin Schoffstall. *Critique of Z39.50 Based on Implementation Experience.* NYSERNet Inc., 1990, p. 28.

Network access to such data can change the way businesses operate, but the query and retrieval functions must be as standard as the traffic signals on today's highways. Z39.50 and Z39.58 play an important role in bringing that about today.

21

ELECTRONIC DATA INTERCHANGE, X12[1]

Data Interchange Standards Association, Inc.

INTRODUCTION

The American National Standards Institute (ANSI) was founded in 1918 as the coordinator for national standards in the United States. The U.S. voluntary standards system consists of a large number of standards developers that write and maintain one or more national standards. Among them are professional societies, trade associations, and other organizations. Thousands of individuals and companies, labor, consumer, and industrial organizations, and government agencies voluntarily contribute their knowledge, talent, and effort to standards development.

ANSI is the U.S. member of non-treaty international standards organizations such as the International Organization for Standardization (ISO) and the International Electrotechnical Commission (IEC). As such, ANSI coordinates the activities involved in U.S. participation in these groups.

Many standards developers and participants support the American National Standards Institute (ANSI) as the central body responsible for the identification of a single consistent set of voluntary standards called American National Standards. ANSI provides an open forum for all concerned interests to identify standards needs, plan to meet those needs, and agree on standards. ANSI itself does not develop standards.

ANSI approval of standards indicates that the principles of openness and due process have been followed in the approval procedures and that a consensus of those directly and materially affected by the standards has been achieved. The *Procedures for the Development and Coordination of American National Standards*, published by ANSI, must be adhered to by standards committees accredited by ANSI for the development of American National Standards.

---

1 This chapter was printed by permission of the Data Interchange Standards Association, Inc.–DISA, 1800 Diagonal Road, Suite 355, Alexandria, VA 22314-2852.

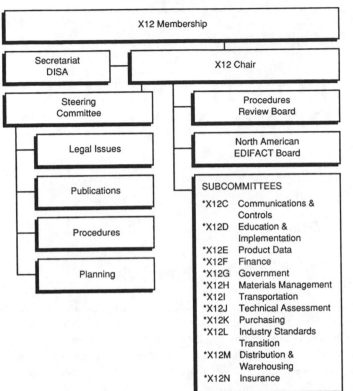

Figure 21.1 ASC X12 organization.

ACCREDITED STANDARDS COMMITTEE X12

In 1979 ANSI chartered a new committee, known as Accredited Standards Committee (ASC) X12, Electronic Data Interchange, to develop uniform standards for electronic interchange of business transactions. (See Figure 21.1.) The X12 Committee develops standards to facilitate electronic interchange relating to such business transactions as order placement and processing, shipping and receiving, invoicing, payment, and cash application data associated with the provision of products and services. (See Figure 21.2.)

The operations of ASC X12 are governed by the *Organization & Procedures Manual*, which provides a system of orderly administration, incorporating the procedures required by ANSI. The work of ASC X12 is conducted primarily by a series of subcommittees and task groups whose major function is the development of new and the maintenance of existing Electronic Data Interchange (EDI) standards. Their recommendations are presented to the full ASC X12 Committee for ratification.

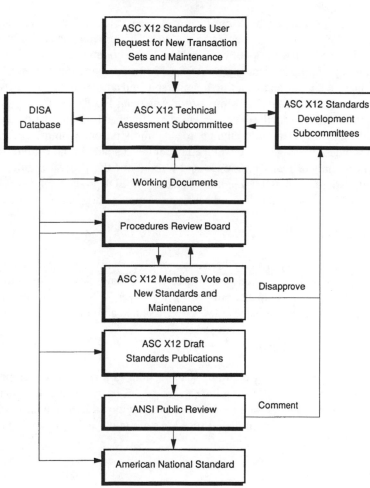

ASC X12 Standards Process

Figure 21.2   ASC X12 standards process.

Membership in ASC X12

Currently X12 has more than 500 members. Membership is open to virtually all organizations and individuals with a material interest in the standards. Benefits include an opportunity to vote on every issue before the X12 Committee, price discounts on standards publications and meeting and conference registration, and frequent information updates on committee activities and standards. Contact Data Interchange Standards Association, Inc. (DISA), the Secretariat of the X12 Committee, for information. Members of X12 are also members of DISA.

Secretariat, Data Interchange Standards Association (DISA)

The X12 Committee is supported by a not-for-profit organization, Data Interchange Standards Association, Inc. (DISA), which serves as its Secretariat. The principal activities of DISA include communicating with ANSI and the public on behalf of the committee; managing the standards database; publishing, planning, and managing ASC X12 meetings and the annual EDI Conference and Exhibit; conducting ballots; and handling membership and administrative matters.

DISA also serves as the Secretariat of the North American EDIFACT Board (NAEB), whose primary function is participation in the development and maintenance of international EDI standards. United Nations/Electronic Data Interchange for Administration, Commerce, and Transport (UN/EDIFACT) standard messages are developed under the auspices of the United Nations.

DISA sponsors an annual EDI Conference and Exhibit for the general public, featuring EDI information seminars and exhibits by vendors of numerous EDI products and services. Inquiries should be directed to DISA's Conference and Meetings Department.

ASC X12 Meeting Schedule

ASC X12 convenes for a five-day meeting three times yearly, usually in February, June, and October. These meetings are held in different sections of the country at major hotel facilities to accommodate attendance by members and participants numbering well over 750. X12 subcommittees and task groups may meet at other times and places to work on assigned activities.

Participation in Standards Setting

The family of ASC X12 standards is continually expanding as a result of development activities supported by the members of the X12 Committee and standards users. Businesses and industries new to ASC X12 are welcome to present their requirements for additional EDI standards, or maintenance to existing standards, to the X12 Committee. Procedures are in place for processing these requests; address inquiries to DISA, the Secretariat.

ASC X12 Ballots

After each X12 Committee meeting, a series of ballots incorporating subcommittee-approved documents is sent to X12 members for their approval. New draft standards approved by the members of ASC X12 are published individually as Draft Standards for Trial Use and immediately placed in maintenance status.

ASC X12 Publication Schedule

Once each year DISA publishes the entire set of X12 standards in a publication called a release. The release includes revisions of previously published Draft Standards for Trial Use and new draft standards approved by ASC X12 during that year. DISA also publishes separately other ASC X12–approved documents, such as ASC X12 Guidelines. To order the standards, call DISA and request a copy of the DISA Publications Catalog.

At approximately three-year intervals the latest release is reviewed by the ASC X12 subcommittees for selection of appropriate draft standards for submission to ANSI to begin the national public review process for their elevation to American National Standards. Those proposed standards surviving public review are published as American National Standards and assigned a new version number.

Publications and Copyright

ANSI published and owns the copyright for all Version 2 (1986–1987) ASC X12 American National Standards. DISA, as the publisher, holds the copyright on each new release and will publish future versions. Requests for permission to reproduce any part of a copyrighted document should be submitted in writing to DISA.

Publications and Version/Release Control

In 1983 the American National Standards Institute approved the publication of a series of standards developed by ASC X12 for electronic data interchange. These are referred to as Version 1 (1983) standards. Version 1 was superseded by the Version 2 family of standards published in 1986–1987. Version 2 includes revised Version 1 standards and a number of additional standards approved as American National Standards in 1986, including the Ship Notice/Manifest Transaction Set (856) and the X12.5 Interchange Control Structures published in 1987.

Since 1987, DISA has published a series of "releases." These documents (called Release 1, Release 2, etc.) represent ASC X12–approved revisions of those previously published American National Standards and new draft standards approved by ASC X12 during the previous year. As such, releases are not American National Standards, since their contents have not been subjected to the rigors of the public review process required by ANSI for such consideration. In the form provided in releases, all of the standards are considered to be Draft Standards for Trial Use. These standards are implementable, and users number in the thousands.

ASC X12's purpose in publishing these releases is to put current ASC X12–approved draft standards into the hands of users on a more frequent schedule, because the public review process resulting in American National Standards is lengthy. This technique is intended to speed implementation, reflect industry needs in the standards more quickly, and allow industry to gain experience with new draft standards before solidifying them as American National Standards. Draft Standards for Trial Use undergo the ANSI-required public review process approximately every three years.

A version/release represents a snapshot in time of the status of the development and maintenance efforts of ASC X12 as of a specified date. Releases are published generally once each year and are governed by version control numbers, reflected in the codes for Data Element 480 shown in parentheses.

Version 2 Release 0	ANSI	1986	(002000)
Version 2 Release 1	X12	08/87	(002001)
Version 2 Release 2	X12	08/88	(002002)
Version 2 Release 3	X12	04/89	(002003)
Version 2 Release 4	X12	12/89	(002040)

This code represents the standards' status at the time of the snapshot and is used to communicate implementation status to EDI trading partners, who must support the same version/release in order to effect interchange. It should not be assumed by implementors that different releases are upward or downward compatible. Transaction sets, segments, and data elements must all be used at the same version/release level.

For Release 4 the code structure was changed to permit the designation of subreleases. Draft Standards for Trial Use approved for publication in February or in June will be published as separate documents to permit implementation by interested users prior to the annual release publication in December. Thus, the fifth character of the code designates the release, and the sixth character the subrelease as shown below.

Version 2 Release 4 Subrelease 1	X12 02/90	(002041)
Version 2 Release 4 Subrelease 2	X12 06/90	(002042)

As required by ANSI, the standards included in Version 2, Release 4 (December 1989) were submitted for public review and comment in spring 1990. Those documents surviving public review and approved by ANSI will be published as American National Standards, Version 3, Release 0 (estimated 1992). Releases will continue to be published annually as well.

In February 1990, X12 approved the following version control numbers to support implementation of newer standards.

Version 3 Release 0	ANSI	1992	(003000)
Version 3 Release 1	X12	12/90	(003010)
Version 3 Release 1 Subrelease 1	X12	02/91	(003011)
Version 3 Release 1 Subrelease 2	X12	06/91	(003012)
Version 3 Release 2	X12	12/91	(003020)

Industry Conventions/Guidelines

Many industries have developed and published "subsets" of the ASC X12 draft standards as industry-recommended implementation guidelines. Industry conventions are designed to facilitate the implementation of selected standards between members of the industry and their trading partners. Most industries that publish guidelines periodically update them to reflect the enhancements and changes that appear in each new version/release of the standards. A list of industries with known EDI programs or publications is available from DISA.

ASC X12 Status Report

A detailed report on current X12 Committee activities is available from DISA on request. It gives the publication status of each draft standard, its purpose and scope, ballot status, approved project proposals, ASC X12 subcommittee activities, and other relevant information.

EDI STANDARDS

Electronic Data Interchange (EDI) is the exchange of routine business transactions in a computer-processable format, covering such traditional applications as inquiries, planning, purchasing, acknowledgments, pricing, order status, scheduling, test results, shipping and receiving, invoices, payments, and financial reporting. Additional standards cover interchange of data relating to security, administrative data, trading partner information, specifications, contracts, production data, and distribution and sales activities. Currently, standards are in development to support the EDI needs of the U.S. government and the insurance, education, entertainment, and mortgage banking industries. As other industries and businesses join ASC X12's development activities, additional types of transactions are included in the body of standards.

History of EDI

Organizations traditionally have conducted business on paper, often using preprinted business forms to exchange information with trading partners. With the explosive growth of these paper-based exchanges, and the amount of data associated with the manufacture and sale of new products and services, many organizations have been forced to seek a more expedient way to communicate and process business data.

The widespread use of computers for commercial business applications and the introduction of techniques for computer telecommunications enabled the solution. Early electronic interchanges used proprietary formats agreed upon between two trading partners for this purpose. However, the disadvantages of programming the widely varying formats required by different trading partners mitigated some of the benefits of this method of interchange.

In the 1960s some industry groups began a cooperative effort to develop industry EDI standards for purchasing, transportation, and financial applications. Many of these standards supported only intraindustry trading; but others, such as bills of lading and freight invoices, were applicable across industries. Eventually the idea of national standards for use across industries received substantial support from a number of different industries.

In the late 1970s, using the pioneering work of the Transportation Data Coordinating Committee and the National Association of Credit Management's Credit Research Foundation, ASC X12 began the development of its first standards for electronic data interchange. In 1983 ANSI published the first five American National Standards for EDI. In 1989, Release 4 contained 32 standards. The 1991 publication (Version 3, Release 2) will contain over 100 Draft Standards for Trial Use, including most of the transportation and retail industries' standards, and there are over 150 additional standards and guidelines now in development.

How EDI Works

In Figures 21.3a and b, a traditional paper invoice is "mapped" to an X12 invoice standard. Definitions of the terms used are provided in the pages following. The figures show how business information is formatted, according to the standard, prior to transmission to a trading partner.

An Introduction to Electronic Data Interchange

Notes	ASC X12 FORMAT	SAMPLE INVOICE CONTENT					
Interchange Control Header, ISA Segment, see X12.5	ISA*00*0000000000*01*PASSWORDME *01*123456789bbbbbb*987654321bbbbbb* 890714*2210*U*00204*000000008*0*P*:N/L	Outside Envelope					
Functional Group Header, GS Segment, see X12.22	GS*IN*012345678*087654321*900509 *2210*000001*X*002040N/L	Inside Envelope					
Transaction Set Header, ST Segment, see X12.22	ST*810*0001N/L	Invoice					
	BIG*900713*1001*900625*P989320N/L	DATE 7/13/90 ORDER DATE 6/25/90 INVOICE # 1001 CUSTOMER ORDER # P989320					
	N1*BT*ACME DISTRIBUTING CO.N/L N3*P.O. BOX 33327N/L N4*ANYTOWN*NJ*44509N/L	CHARGE TO Acme Distributing Co. P.O. Box 33327 Anytown, NJ 44509					
	N1*ST*THE CORNER STOREN/L N3*601 FIRST STREETN/L N4*CROSSROADS*MI*48106N/L	SHIP TO The Corner Store 601 First Street Crossroads, MI 48106					
	N1*SE*SMITH CORPORATIONN/L N3*900 EASY STREETN/L N4*BIG CITY*NJ*15455N/L	REMIT TO Smith Corporation (Selling Party) 900 Easy Street Big City, NJ 15455					
	PER*AD*C.D. JONES*TE*6185558230N/L	CORRESPONDENCE TO Accounting Dept. C.D. Jones (618) 555-8230					
	ITD*01*3*2**10N/L	TERMS OF SALE 2% 10 days from annual invoice					
		QUANTITY	UNIT	SUPPLIER BRAND CODE	DESCRIPTION		UNIT PRICE
	IT1**3*CA*12.75**VC*6900N/L	3	Cse	6900	Celluose Sponges		12.75
	IT1**12*EA*.475**VC*P450N/L	12	Ea	P450	Plastic Pails		.475
	IT1**4*EA*.94**VC*1640YN/L	4	Ea	1640Y	Yellow Dish Drainer		.94
	IT1**1*DZ*3.4**VC*1507N/L	1	Dz	1507	6" Plastic Flower Pots		3.40
	TDS*5111N/L	Invoice Total					
	CAD*M****CONSOLIDATED TRUCKN/L	Via Consolidated Truck					
Hash Totals	CTT*4*20N/L	(4 Line Items, Hash Total 20)					
Transaction Set Trailer	SE*21*000001N/L						
Function Group Trailer	GE*1*000001N/L						
Interchange Control Trailer	IEA*1*000000008N/L						

b = Space Character   * = Data Element Separator   N/L = Segment Terminator

Figure 21.3a A description of the ASC X12 format for a typical invoice.

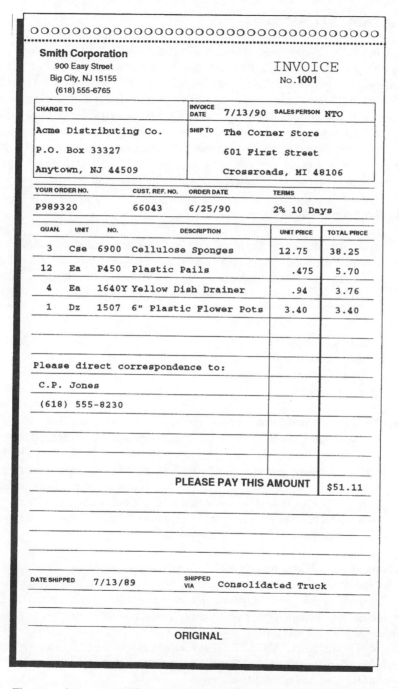

Figure 21.3b The same data on a traditional paper invoice. Note: In this example, not *all* data on the paper invoice has been mapped.

A Guide to the ASC X12 Standards

In developing the ASC X12 series of American National Standards, the X12 subcommittees seek to minimize the need for users to reprogram their internal data processing systems to effect interchange. For this reason, the standards are structured so that computer programs can translate data from internal to external formats and vice versa. In this way, either through internally or externally developed software and public-access communications vendors, all sizes of firms and institutions using intelligent computational devices may benefit from the use of the standard. Through the use of the standard, all institutions can enjoy the efficiencies of a common interchange language, rather than experience the difficulties of a proliferation of methods and procedures that could occur if each institution were to impose its own format on every institution with which it does business.

EDI Foundation Standards

The ASC X12 series of standards on electronic data interchange is based on interdependency. The "foundation standards" define the syntax of X12 EDI, as well as the data elements, data segments, and control structures. The following standards are required to interpret, understand, and use the ASC X12 series of transaction set standards, which in turn define the format and data contents of business transactions.

- X12.3 Data Element Dictionary
- X12.5 Interchange Control Structures
- X12.6 Application Control Structures
- X12.22 Segment Directory

X12.6 Application Control Structure   This is the syntax ("architecture") document which governs the other EDI standards. It contains the formal definitions of all terms related to electronic data interchange.

X12.6 is downward but not necessarily upward compatible with any version/release of the standards. Any edition of X12.6 Application Control Structure may be used in conjunction with a release so long as its publication date is the same as the release publication date or later.

Releases 1 through 3 do not contain X12.6. It is included in Version 2, Release 4 (and subsequent releases) and is also available as a stand-alone document in its most current form.

X12.5 Interchange Control Structures   X12.5 contains specifications for the control structures ("envelope") for the electronic interchange of one or more transaction sets (see Figure 21.4). This standard provides the interchange envelope of a header segment (ISA) and trailer segment (IEA) for the electronic interchange through a data transmission, and it provides a structure to acknowledge the receipt and processing of this envelope.

This document is available as ANSI X12.5-1987 Interchange Control Structures. Release 1-1987 does not include X12.5; however, Release 2-1988 and successive releases do contain X12.5, revised and issued as a Draft Standard for Trial Use.

This standard is self-contained and governed by version control independent of the transaction set standards (Data Element I11). X12.5 and transaction sets of any version/release can be implemented independently of each other.

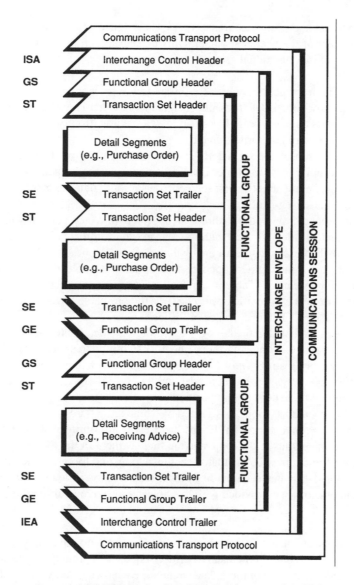

Figure 21.4   An extract from an ASC X12 release describing the structure of an EDI transmission.

X12.22 Segment Directory and X12.3 Data Element Dictionary   These define the segments and data elements, respectively, that are used to construct the transaction sets. They must be used at the same version/release level as transaction sets.

Standards Components

Functional Group   A functional group is a group of similar transaction sets (e.g., three purchase orders). A functional group, when transmitted, is bounded by a functional group header segment and a functional group trailer segment. Each transaction set is assigned a functional identifier code, which is the first data element of the header segment. Only those transaction sets with the same code are considered members of one functional group.

Transaction Set   The information included in a transaction set is the same as the information in a conventionally printed document. A transaction set is the data that is exchanged in order to convey meaning between parties engaged in EDI, consisting of a specific group of segments that represent a business document (e.g., purchase order, invoice).

The function of each transaction set is defined in a purpose and scope statement. Each transaction set is composed of one or more tables, which list the segments in a predefined position. Tables display a transaction set header segment as the first segment, one or more data segments in a specified order, and a transaction set trailer segment.

Many transaction sets are divided into three "areas" (tables), which generally relate to the format of a printed document. Table 1 is the heading area, in which information common to the entire transaction is placed. Table 2 is the detail area, which is usually one large loop, and Table 3 is the summary area. When the same segment appears in more than one table, the following semantic rule applies: A segment appearing in Table 1 applies to the entire transaction set, and this may be overridden for the duration of a specific occurrence of a loop in Table 2 when the same segment with a changed value is present in that occurrence of the loop.

Other specifications are listed in the tables. The requirement designator defines a segment's need to appear in the data stream of a transmission: mandatory (required to appear), optional (at the option of the sending party), or floating (only for the NTE segment that may appear anywhere in the transaction set between the transaction set header and trailer). Maximum use is the number of times the segment is permitted to be used in that position in the transaction set.

Segments may be repeated as loops, designated by a bracket; within each bracket a loop identifier and the maximum occurrence are given. Loops themselves are optional or mandatory. There is a specified sequence of segments in the loop, and the first segment in the loop may appear only once in each iteration. A segment may be mandatory within a loop, and loops may be nested within other loops. For nested loops, the same segment in an inner loop will override the data in an outer loop.

Notes and comments may be provided with the tables, to provide additional information to users (see Figure 21.5).

Data Segment   A data segment is an intermediate unit of information in a transaction set. A segment consists of logically related data elements in a defined sequence: a predetermined segment identifier (which is not a data element), one or more data elements, each preceded by a data element separator, and a segment terminator. Data segments are defined in the Segment Directory, which gives the segment identifier, name, purpose, and the data elements it contains in their specified order (see Figure 21.6).

Contiguous optional data elements that appear at the end of a segment that are not used are omitted; transmission of the segment terminator signifies this omission. The omission of data elements other than at the end of a segment is specified by successive data element separators.

Data Element   The data element is the smallest named unit of information in the standard. Data elements are defined in the Data Element Dictionary (see Figure 21.7). Each data element is identified

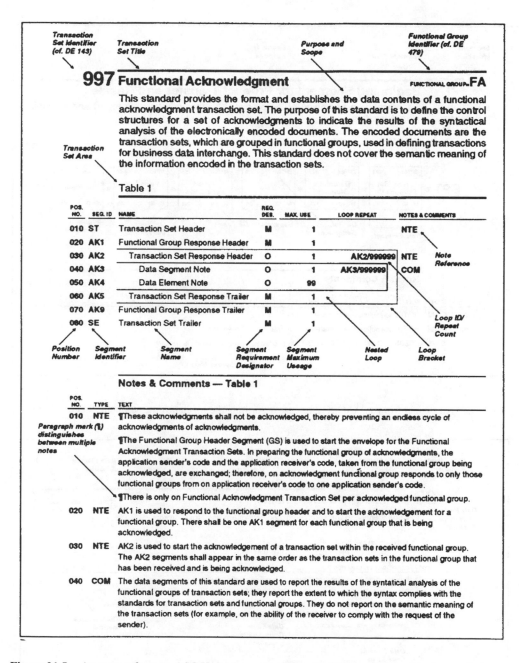

Figure 21.5   An extract from an ASC X12 release describing the format of the transaction set listings.

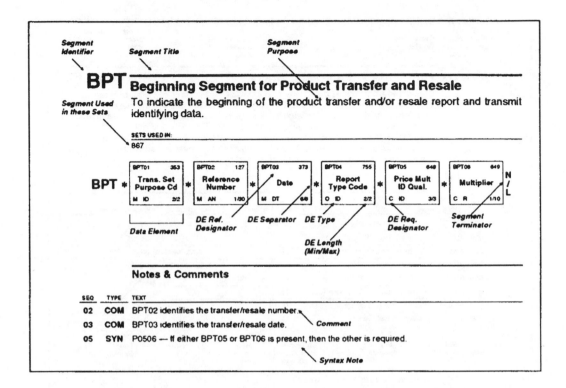

Figure 21.6 An extract from an ASC X12 release describing the format of the segment directory.

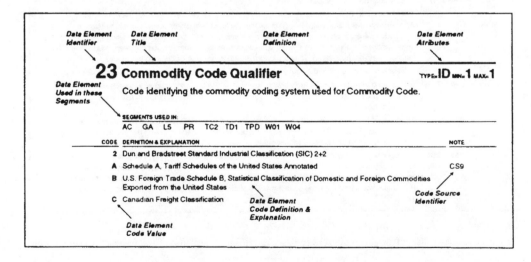

Figure 21.7 An extract from an ASC X12 release describing the format of the data element dictionary.

by a reference number. For each data element, the dictionary specifies the name, description, type, and minimum/maximum length. For ID-type data elements, the dictionary lists all code values and their definitions or indicates in an appendix where the valid code list can be obtained.

IMPLEMENTATION

EDI Benefits

It is estimated that 14,000 organizations use EDI standards and enjoy many of the following benefits of EDI.

- Reduction of paperwork and associated savings
  - One-time data entry
  - Reduced errors, improved error detection
  - On-line data storage
  - Faster management reporting
  - Automatic reconciliation
  - Reduced clerical workload and phone chatter
  - Higher productivity without increasing staff
- More timely communications
  - Rapid exchange of business data
  - Elimination of mail charges, courier services
  - Reduced inventory safety stocks
  - Improved production cycle
- Uniform communications with all trading partners
  - Customers
  - Suppliers
  - Carriers
  - Banks and financial institutions
- Better market position relative to non-EDI competitors

Transmitting Information

The X12 standards do not define how interchange partners shall establish the required communications link to exchange EDI data.

Considerations

Since the format of data in one company's computer is different from that in another, a common "language" is required for the interchange of data between the two computers. The conversion from paper documents to an electronic interchange will impose issues and considerations in three major areas.

Internal Considerations   These issues and considerations should be resolved within the organization planning to implement the standards.

- Determine the application to be used (purchase order, invoice, test results, etc.).
- Educate user personnel about why the company is implementing the standards and their impact on current procedures.
- Explain benefits of using a standard format for electronic data interchange.
- Explain why ASC X12 standards were chosen.
- Initiate an implementation schedule.
- Make certain the required data is available on existing systems.
- Review all documents to be interchanged and map each data element to the X12 format to ensure that all pertinent information can be included.
- Establish a liaison with all functional areas within your company that may be affected.
- Identify hardware requirements.
- Determine the method of achieving translation interface: internally develop software, purchase or lease software, or use a third-party service provider.
- Determine the method of transmission (direct, third party network, etc.).
- Determine the level of security required. Security precautions taken by EDI applications within a company's computer center should be at least as good as those for the most secure existing application with which EDI is to be used. Authentication and encryption may be added to completely secure contents of the message. The security functions may also be included as part of the company's existing data transport services.

External Considerations   These issues should be resolved with the trading partner prior to exchanging data electronically, using the standard.

- Identify potential business trading partners.
- Define terms of exchange and establish agreement between partners.
- Agree on the version/release of the standards that will be implemented with each trading partner.
- Verify that sufficient information is available for trading partners to correctly interpret the data.
- Ensure that partners have adequate translation interfaces.
- Agree on the method of transmission.
- Send sample data to trading partners for their evaluation (this does not need to be done on the same media in which interchanges will occur in actual operation).

Other Considerations   Contingency plans should be established to address the following situations.

- Backup procedures: establish a fall-back position (e.g., mail delivery, etc.) in the event of system failure.
- Error recovery: establish a maximum number of attempts to retransmit following a text transmission error, thus minimizing communications costs for bad connections.
- Security: agree on passwords. A general review of audit and legal issues may also be desirable.
- Network response time: establish a reasonable time frame for response (functional acknowledgment) to message receipt.

- Error reporting/contact support: names and telephone numbers of transmission partners and hardware and software vendors should be accessible. Some vendors provide diagnostic error routines to isolate failure prior to contact. If available, these routines should be attempted prior to contact to minimize service charges.

Start-up Checklist

After the partners agree on the operating environment, a schedule of implementation dates and checkpoints should be specified. The following should be considered during planning.

- Network availability
- Network communications (line type and speed)
- Line protocol, transmission mode
- Transmission initiation
- Hardware and translation software that will allow interface of ASC X12 formatted data with the present internal operating system
- Interface software testing under current environment, using internal data
- Internal edits and controls
- A plan for a "go-live" data while running parallel for "X" amount of time
- Troubleshooting procedures
- A date to drop the parallel system
- Upgrades to new versions of standards, hardware, etc.
- Other applications and standards users.

ABOUT THE AUTHORS

Mikael Edholm is the OSI Marketing Program Manager for Hewlett-Packard Corporation. As such, he defines and coordinates Hewlett-Packard's OSI marketing activities on a worldwide basis, and is a frequent speaker on open systems networking at major seminars and symposia around the world.

Mr. Edholm has published several articles on networking and related topics, including chapters in the *CIM Handbook* (Auersbach Publishers, 1990) and the *Open Systems Interconnect Handbook* (McGraw-Hill, 1991). He is a former member of the European MAP Users Group, has served on the Corporation for Open Systems Marketing Committee, and has been a member of the advisory board for the Euro-American Communications Newsletter, published in Palo Alto, California, and London, United Kingdom.

Prior to his current assignment, Mr. Edholm has held marketing positions with Hewlett-Packard in Europe, based in Grenoble, France; Allen-Bradley Europe, based in Amsterdam, the Netherlands; 3M Sweden, based in Stockholm, Sweden; and ABB Electronics, based in Västerås, Sweden.

Mr. Edholm is currently with the Hewlett-Packard Information Networks Division in Cupertino, California.

Anura Gurugé is a lead consultant in BBN Communications' (Cambridge, Massachusetts) Consulting Group. He is the author of "SNA Theory and Practice," the recently published "The New SNA," and the honorary conscience of SNA. Mr. Gurugé presents seminars and writes extensively on SNA, SAA, SystemView, and IBM, and has worked for IBM, ITT, Northern Telecom, and Wang.

Robyn Mosher is TCP/IP Product Marketing Manager at Digital Equipment Corporation. Digital Equipment Corporation, headquartered in Maynard, Massachusetts, is the leading worldwide supplier of networked computer systems, software, and services. Digital pioneered and leads the industry in interactive, distributed, and multivendor computing. Digital and its partners deliver the power to use the best integrated solutions—from desktop to data center—in open information environments.

Michael Smith is a Product Manager at 3Com Corporation, responsible for 3Com's Communications as their OEM Technical Services Manager. Early in his career, Michael worked for seven years as a systems analyst with NEC and Shell Oil Company.

While studying at De Anza College, Indiana University, and University of Houston, Michael received degrees in Computer Science, Journalism, and Business.

John Stidd is the Manager of Standards Development and Planning for Xerox Corporation. He represents Xerox in OSI-related consortia, including OSINET and the Corporation for Open Systems, and is a former chairman of the X.400 Special Interest Group at the National Institute of Standards and Technology OSI Implementors Workshop. Mr. Stidd has over 25 years of experience in the information processing industry as a software engineer and manager. Xerox Corporation, headquartered in Stamford, Connecticut, is a major manufacturer of electronic equipment, including copiers, electronic printers, and computer workstations and servers.

Kenneth M. Zemrowski, CDP, CCP, has over twenty years of experience in the information technology field, with management, development, and consulting experience in a wide range of technical and application areas. His current assignment for TRW is with the FAA System Engineering and Technical Assistance (SETA) project for Advanced Automation Program, where he evaluates interoperability issues and serves as a focal point for standardization and standards conformance issues. This program will result in the replacement of the existing Air Traffic Control system.

Previously, Mr. Zemrowski managed the development of operating system and network communications software for the Ocean Surveillance Information System (OSIS) Baseline Upgrade (OBU), a C3I system including message processing, automatic correlation, and report generation. He has managed and developed software to provide operating system support for Pascal compilers, developed communication emulators, tested communication hardware and software, and participated in several studies to evaluate problems in vendor and customer use of communication and transaction processing systems.

Kenneth Zemrowski is actively involved in ANSI and ISO standardization at technical and management levels. He represents the Association of the Institute for Certification of Computer Professionals (AICCP) on Accredited Standards Committee X3 (Information Processing Systems), which manages and approves the development of computer-related ANSI standards, and on the Technical Advisory Group to ANSI for ISO/IEC Joint Technical Committee 1, which develops the United States' positions on international standards issues in areas such as programming languages, OSI, microprocessors, applications portability, etc. He is Chair of Technical Committee X3T5, OSI Upper Layers. He also developed standards as Chair of the Joint Pascal Committee, and worked with other language committees to advance applications portability.

TRW's Systems Integration Group provides system development, systems engineering, and integration services, primarily in the civil, federal, and military marketplaces. The FAA SETA project is one of several major TRW projects involving OSI.

David Eng (editor) is Director of Marketing at Touch Communications, Inc., a privately held company based in Campbell, California, founded in March 1985 to develop end user communications solutions based on OSI standards. All of Touch's products are distributed worldwide, directly to large end users, systems integrators, and original equipment manufacturers.

Judy Cross is OSI Applications Product Manager at Digital Equipment Corporation. Digital Equipment Corporation, headquartered in Maynard, Massachusetts, is the leading worldwide supplier of networked computer systems, software, and services. Digital pioneered and leads the industry in interactive, distributed, and multivendor computing. Digital and its partners deliver the power to use the best integrated solutions—from desktop to data center—in open information environments.

Dale Gulick has extensive experience in defining and designing data communications, telecommunications, and computer products. He is currently Senior Member of the Technical Staff at Advanced Micro Devices, where he has been employed since 1985, and is involved in product planning for ISDN and digital cordless products. Prior to this, he was with Datapoint Corporation. Mr. Gulick is a 1978 graduate of Texas A & M University.

Bob D. Tausworthe graduated from the New Mexico Institute of Mining and Technology in 1980 with degrees in mathematics and computer science. He is currently employed by Hewlett-Packard as a software engineer in its Information Networks Division. He has been working as an OSI protocol specialist for the past five years and most recently architected the addressing and routing portions of HP's United States GOSIP-compliant OSI Transport Services (OTS/9000) product.

Ian Crayford is the manager of Systems Engineering and Network Development in the Network Products Division at Advanced Micro Devices Inc. He has been with the company for four years, during which time he has worked extensively on the definition and development of 802.3/Ethernet and 10BASE-T products. He served on the IEEE 10BASE-T Working Group and is currently involved in the IEEE Repeater Management Group. He has filed several architectural patents relating to VLSI network circuits, and has presented numerous papers on networking. Mr. Crayford has a BSc (Hons) in Electrical/Electronic Engineering from Kingston Polytechnic in London, England.

Gary C. Kessler provides course development, education, and consulting services in the area of data communications and computer networking for such companies as AT&T Bell Laboratories, Bell Atlantic, Contel, Digital Equipment Corporation (DEC), General Electric, International Computers Ltd. (ICL North America and ICL United Kingdom), and NASA.

Mr. Kessler has written several articles for technical journals, is a contributor to *LAN Magazine*, the author of *ISDN: Concepts, Facilities, and Services* (McGraw-Hill, 1990), and the coauthor of *Metropolitan Area Networks: Concepts, Standards, and Services* (McGraw-Hill, 1992). His primary areas of interest include ISDN, packet switching and X.25, frame relay, local and metropolitan area networks, FDDI, SMDS, and communications standards. He is an observer on the ANSI X3T9.5 (FDDI) and the X3S3.7 (Public Data Networks) Task Groups; a participant on the IEEE 802.6 (MANs), 802.9 (Integrated Voice/Data LANs), and 802.11 (Wireless LANs) subcommittees; and an observer on the SMDS Interest Group.

He received a B.A. in Mathematics (1975) from Humboldt State University in Arcata, California, and an M.S. in Computer Science (1980) from the University of Vermont in Burlington. Prior professional positions include Coordinator of Academic Computing at St. Michael's College in Colchester; Software Engineer at Lawrence Livermore National Laboratory in Livermore, California; and Member of the Technical Staff at Hill Associates in Winooski, Vermont.

Mr. Kessler can be contacted at 5 Creek Glen, Colchester, VT 05446-3641 or on 802-879-3375. Electronic mail can be addressed to KUMQUAT@SMCVAX.BITNET.

Emily Green is the Director of the Product Management group at Fibermux Corporation and has been with the company since 1987. During the past year she has been one of the company's representatives to the X3T9.5 FDDI committee and has been active in the industry's efforts to promote FDDI and assure interoperability. She holds an MSE in computer science from the University of Pennsylvania's Moore School of Electrical Engineering and was a cum laude graduate of Georgetown University with a B.S. in Theoretical Linguistics.

Mike Kouri has been working in 3Com's Technical Services Operation for about three years, specializing in Ethernet transmission system products. When 3Com began testing the initial release of 3+Open LAN Manager, he was transferred to that team and has been supporting 3+Open LAN Manager ever since. His main focus has been on the core LAN Manager product and 3Com's value-added transport protocols.

Bill Nolde is a member of the Engineering Group within 3Com's Technical Services Operation. He is in charge of third-party software development support and all 3Com APIs. Mr. Nolde has an M.A. in Mathematics and is a member of both the IEEE and ACM. He has been in the computing industry for 13 years and is the author of several outstanding PC software products.

Robert Perry is a Senior Technical Writer in Novell's Systems Research Department. He has written about various versions of NetWare for six years, and is currecntly researching the behavior of source routing nodes in a NetWare environment.

Paul Turner is a Corporate Integration Specialist in Novell's Systems Engineering Division. He supports Novell's large corporate customers with network design and system integration issues.

Novell, Inc., (NASDAQ:NOVL) is an operating system software company—the developer of network services and specialized and general-purpose operating system products including NetWare and DR DOS. Novell's NetWare network computing products manage and control the sharing of services, data, and applications among computer workgroups, departmental networks, and business-wide information systems.

Fred Burg is supervisor of Networking Standards Planning for AT&T Bell Laboratories. As such, he is responsible for coordination of AT&T's standards strategy, planning, and participation in areas dealing with data networking. He has participated in many of the activities described in this chapter for the past ten years, serving as author, editor, convenor, and Special Rapporteur in both ISO/IEC and CCITT. Within the United States, he serves as chair of ANSI task group X3S3.7, which is responsible for developing positions on X.25 and related matters for the international arena.

Mr. Burg is also involved in various areas concerning implementation of standards. He serves as chair of the Lower Layer Special Interest Group in the OSI Implementors' Workshop to reach agreements on features of the various OSI Layer 1–4 protocols among product developers. As a member of this group, he also participates in the international efforts at developing functional profiles for these protocols. In addition, he successfully led a demonstration of OSI/ISDN integration at Mather Air Force Base in 1989 as a prelude to inclusion of ISDN as a networking technology in U.S. GOSIP. He also participated in the work on GM's Manufacturing Automation Protocol (MAP) and was technically responsible for AT&T's involvement in this effort.

Beyond X.25 and data networking, Mr. Burg also participates in IEEE committee 802 on Local Area Networks, having served as chair of several subcommittees in the past. He was one of the initial proponents of the frame relay concepts, having participated in the initial phases of its standardization in ECMA and CCITT in the 1983–1985 time frame. He also served in CCITT's Study Group XVII, having been one of the primary developers of the V.42 error-correcting modem protocol.

Mr. Burg received his B.S. degree in Mathematics from the Polytechnic Institute of Brooklyn in 1972 and his M.S. degree in Operations Research from the same school in 1973 on a teaching fellowship. He has since taught classes at both the academic and professional levels. He has written many articles in various journals and served as guest editor for an issue of *IEEE Network* magazine dealing with OSI/ISDN integration. Mr. Burg was elected to Who's Who in America in the East in 1990.

The mission of **Telecommunications Techniques Corporation** (TTC) is to develop, market, manufacture, and sell the highest quality test products for worldwide communications markets. The communications test instrument market includes test and diagnostic products that are used in the development, installation, commissioning, and continuing maintenance of communications links and terminal equipment supporting voice, data, and image transmission.

The primary business development strategy used to accomplish TTC's mission is internally-funded, new-product development. TTC focuses on new products that feature both high functionality and ease of use. A secondary strategy is to search for and acquire or create new business units. A new business unit must meet high standards for growth, profitability, quality, and performance while substantially broadening TTC's product offerings and penetration of the communications test instrument market.

TTC has gained recognition as a leader in the markets for multifunction digital communications analyzers, protocol analyzers, T-Carrier test instruments, and fiber-optic test equipment with its FIREBIRD, INTERCEPTOR, T-BIRD, and fiber-optic product lines.

Michael Seadle began his data processing career in 1981 as an application programmer for Assembly Language Actuarial Systems in the insurance industry. Since then he has been an SQL database administrator, a VM systems programmer, a network applications programmer, and the head of user support services. Currently he works at Cornell University as manager of on-line operations for the University Library System. Michael received his Ph.D. in History from the University of Chicago. During the last decade he has lectured, written, and taught on computer-related subjects. He has also published numerous articles in *Mainframe Journal* and *Technical Support,* as well as a book, *Automating Mainframe Management: Using Expert Systems with Examples from VM and MVS* (McGraw-Hill, 1991).

INDEX